Items should be returned on or before the date shown below. Items not already requested by other borrowers may be renewed in person, in writing or by telephone. To renew, please quote the number on the barcode label. To renew online a PIN is required. This can be requested at your local library.
Renew online @ www.dublincitypubl‍
Fines charged for overdue items will ir‍
Damage to or loss of items will be chai‍

Le‍
Ch‍

J‍
i‍
t‍
r‍

Due Date	Due Date	Due Date

A Dictionary of Jews and Jewish Life

Dan Cohn-Sherbok

First published 2018
by Impress Books Ltd
Innovation Centre, Rennes Drive, University of Exeter Campus,
Exeter EX4 4RN 2018

British Library Cataloguing in Publication Data

A catalogue record for this book is available from the British Library

ISBN 978 19112932 17

Typeset in Plantin
by Swales and Willis Ltd, Exeter, Devon

Printed and bound in England by imprintdigital.net

All illustrations are the work of Dan Cohn-Sherbok

For Lavinia

Preface

For more than thirty years I have taught courses in Jewish studies at universities in the United Kingdom. During this time I have frequently directed students to such multi-volume encyclopedia of Judaism as the *Jewish Encyclopedia* and the *Encyclopaedia Judaica*. These vast repositories of material provide a wealth of information about all aspects of Jewish life and thought. I also directed them to use the web to find material related to their queries. Nonetheless, very often students – particularly those with more general interests – find such reference sources overwhelming.

Aware of this difficulty, I suggested they look at a number of single-volume encyclopedia and dictionaries of Judaism, but many of these works failed to meet their needs since they were highly selective in their choice of entires. Increasingly I came to see that what was needed was a single-volume comprehensive dictionary which contains basic information about Judaism and the Jewish people. Such a handy reference book would not take the place of standard multi-volume reference works or the Internet, but it could serve as a first point of entry into the Jewish world.

This volume, *A Dictionary of Jews and Jewish Life*, is designed to fill a gap in the types of reference books available to students, as well as to teachers and more general readers. The book is approximately 250,000 words in length and contains thousands of entries. Most are short since the dictionary aims to provider readers with a vast array of information in concise, clear and accessible form. Although all aspects of Jewish life and civilisation are covered, my main criterion for inclusion has been reference worthiness. My intention is that this volume should provide the type of information most commonly sought by students of Jewish life and thought.

A dictionary about Jews and Judaism would not be complete without Jewish humour. Through the centuries Jews have been making jokes about themselves, and it is a central dimension of Jewish life. For this reason, this volume also includes a range of Jewish jokes at the beginning of each letter. Without them the dictionary would not give a full picture of the Jewish world. In addition, scattered throughout the book are a number of cartoons which are designed to reflect the humorous dimensions of the faith.

Acknowledgements

I would like to acknowledge these sources from which I obtained information: Geoffrey Wigoder, *The New Standard Jewish Encyclopedia*, W.H. Allen, 1977; *Jewish Encyclopedia*, Funk and Wagnalls, 1901–1905; *Encyclopedia Judaica*, Keter, 1972; Yacov Newman and Gabriel Sivan, *Judaism A–Z: Lexicon of Terms and Concepts*, Department for Torah Education and Culture in the Diaspora of the World Zionist Organization, 1980; Raphael Judah Zwi Werblowsky and Geoffrey Wigoder, eds, *The Encyclopedia of the Jewish Religion*, Phoenix House, 1967; Glenda Abrahamson, *The Blackwell Companion to Jewish Culture*, Blackwell, 1989; Glenda Abrahamson, *Encyclopedia of Modern Jewish Culture*, Routledge, 2004; Geoffrey Wigoder, ed., *The Encyclopedia of Judaism*, Macmillan, 1989; David Bridget and Samuel Wolk, eds., *The New Jewish Encyclopedia*, Behrman House, 1976; *Encyclopedia Judaica*, Macmillan, 2006; Leo Rosen, *The Joys of Yiddish*, W.H. Allen, 1968; Michael Kransy, *Let There Be Laughter*, William Morrow, 2016; David Minkoff, *The Ultimate Book of Jewish Jokes*, Robson Books, 2004. I would also like to thank the publisher Richard Willis for his support, and the editor George Warburton for his help.

Jewish History

Jews in the Ancient World

The history of the Jewish people began in Mesopotamia where successive empires of the ancient world flourished and decayed before the Jews emerged as a separate people. The culture of these civilisations had a profound impact on the Jewish religion—ancient Near-Eastern myths were refashioned to serve the needs of the Hebrew people. It appears that the Jews emerged in this milieu as a nation between the 19th and 16th centuries BCE. According to the Bible, Abraham was the father of the Jewish people. Initially known as 'Abram', he came from Ur of the Chaldees. Together with his family he went to Haran and subsequently to Canaan, later settling in the plain near Hebron. Abraham was followed by Isaac and Jacob, whose son Joseph was sold into slavery in Egypt. There he prospered, becoming a vizier in the house of Pharaoh. Eventually the entire Hebrew clan moved to Egypt, where they remained and flourished for centuries until a new Pharaoh decreed that all male Hebrew babies should be put to death.

To persuade Pharaoh to let the Jewish people go, God sent a series of plagues upon the Egyptians. After this devastation, Moses, the leader of his people, led his kinsfolk out of Egypt. After wandering in the desert for 40 years, the Hebrews finally entered into the land that God had promised them. Under Joshua's leadership, the Hebrews conquered the existing inhabitants. After Joshua's death the people began to form two separate groups. At first there were 12 tribes named after the sons of Jacob: Joseph, Benjamin, Levi, Simeon, Reuben, Judah, Issachar, Zebulun, Dan, Naphtali, Gad and Asher. When Levi's tribe became a special priestly group excluded from this territorial division, the tribe of Joseph was divided into two and named after his sons, Ephraim and Manasseh. During this period the Hebrews were ruled over by

12 national heroes who served successively as judges. In Scripture the sagas of the major judges (Othniel, Ehud, Deborah, Gideon, Jephthah and Samson) are recounted at length.

Frequently the Covenant between God and his chosen people – first formulated by Moses – was proclaimed at gatherings in such national shrines as Shechem. Such an emphasis on covenantal obligation reinforced the belief that the Jews were the recipients of God's loving kindness. Now, in a more settled existence, the Covenant expanded to include additional legislation, including the provisions needed for an agricultural community. During this period it became increasingly clear to the Jewish nation that the God of the Covenant directed human history: the Exodus and the entry into the Promised Land were viewed as the unfolding of a divine plan.

Under the judges, God was conceived as the supreme monarch. When some tribes suggested to Gideon that he deserved a formal position of power, he declared that it was impossible for the nation to be ruled by both God and a human king. Nonetheless, Saul was subsequently elected as king despite the prophet Samuel's warnings against the dangers of usurping God's rule. In later years the Israelite nation divided into two kingdoms. The northern tribes, led by Ephraim, and the southern tribes led by Judah, had been united only by their allegiance to King David. But when his successor King Solomon, and his son Rehoboam, violated many of the ancient traditions, the northern tribes revolted. The reason they gave for this rebellion was the injustice of the monarchy, but in fact they sought to recapture the simple ways of the generation that had escaped from Egypt. Then there had been no monarch, and leadership was exercised on the basis of charisma. What the north looked for was allegiance and loyalty to the King of Kings, who had brought them from Egyptian bondage into the Promised Land. It is against this background that the pre-exilic prophets (Elijah, Elisha, Amos, Hosea, Micah and Isaiah) endeavoured to bring the nation back to the true worship of God. Righteousness, they declared, is the standard by which all people are to be judged, especially kings and rulers.

During the first millennium BCE the Jews watched their country emerge as a powerful state only to see it sink into spiritual and moral decay. Following the Babylonian Conquest in 586 BCE the Temple lay in ruins, Jerusalem was demolished and Jews despaired of their fate. This was God's punishment for their iniquity, which the prophets had predicted. Yet, despite defeat and exile, the nation rose phoenix-like from the ashes of the old kingdoms. In the centuries which followed, the Jewish people continued their religious traditions and communal life. Though they had lost their independence, their devotion to God and His law sustained them through suffering and hardship and inspired them to new heights of creativity. In Babylonia the exiles flourished keeping their religion alive in the synagogues. These institutions were founded so that Jews could meet together for worship and study; no sacrifices were offered since that was the prerogative of the Jerusalem Temple. When in 538 BCE King Cyrus of Persia permitted the Jews to return to their former home, the nation underwent a transformation. The Temple was rebuilt and religious reforms were enacted. This return to the land of their fathers led to national restoration and a renaissance of Jewish life which was to last until the first century CE.

The period following the death of King Herod in 4 BCE was a time of intense anti-Roman feeling among the Jewish population in Judea, as well as in the diaspora. Eventually such hostility led to war, only to be followed by defeat and the destruction, once again, of the Jerusalem Temple. In 70 CE, thousands of Jews were deported. Such devastation, however, did not quell the Jewish hope of ridding the Holy Land of its Roman oppressors. In the second century a messianic rebellion led by Simeon Bar Kokhba was crushed by Roman forces, who killed multitudes of Jews and decimated Judea. Yet despite this defeat, the Pharisees carried on the Jewish tradition through teaching and study at Javneh, near Jerusalem.

Rabbinic Judaism

From the first century BCE Palestinian rabbinic scholars engaged in the interpretation of Scripture. The most important scholar of the early rabbinic period was Judah ha-Nasi, the head of the Sanhedrin, whose main achievement was the redaction of the *Mishnah* (a compendium of the oral Torah) in the second century CE. This volume consisted of the discussions and rulings of sages whose teachings had been transmitted orally. According to the rabbis, the law recorded in the *Mishnah* was given orally to Moses along with the written law: 'Moses received the Torah from Sinai, and handed it down to Joshua, and Joshua to the elders, and elders to the prophets, and the prophets to the men of the Great Assembly'. This view recorded in the *Mishnah* implies that there was an infallible chain of transmission from Moses to the leaders of the nation, and eventually to the Pharisees.

The *Mishnah* is an almost entirely legal document, consisting of six sections. The first section ('Seeds') begins with a discussion of benedictions and required prayers, and continues with the other tractates dealing with various matters such as the tithes of the harvest to be given to the priests, Levites and the poor. The second section ('Set Feasts') contains 12 tractates dealing with the Sabbath, Passover, the Day of Atonement and other festivals, as well as shekel dues and the proclamation of the New Year. In the third section ('Women') seven tractates consider matters affecting women, such as betrothal, marriage contracts and divorce. The fourth section ('Damages') contains ten tractates concerning civil law: property rights, legal procedures, compensation for damage, ownership of lost objects, treatment of employees, sale and purchase of land, Jewish courts, punishments and criminal proceedings. In addition, a tractate of rabbinic moral maxims ('Sayings of the Fathers') is included in this section. In the fifth section ('Holy Things') there are 11 tractates on sacrificial offerings and other Temple matters. The final section ('Purifications') treats the various types of ritual uncleanliness and methods of legal purification. In addition to the *Mishnah*, the rabbis engaged in the composition of scriptural commentaries. The literature (known as *midrash*) was written over centuries and is divided into works connected directly with the books of the Bible and those dealing with readings for special festivals as well as other topics.

The Sanhedrin, which had been so fundamental in the compilation of the *Mishnah*, met in several cities in Galilee, but later settled in the Roman district of Tiberius. Simultaneously other scholars established their own schools in other parts of the country where they applied the *Mishnah* to everyday life, together with old rabbinic teachings which had not been incorporated in the *Mishnah*. During the third century the Roman Empire encountered numerous difficulties, including inflation, population decline and a lack of technological development to support the army. In addition, rival generals struggled against one another for power, and the Government became increasingly inefficient. Throughout this time of upheaval, the Jewish community underwent a similar decline as a result of famine, epidemics and plunder.

At the end of the third century the emperor Diocletian inaugurated reforms that strengthened the Empire. In addition, Diocletian introduced measures to repress the spread of Christianity which had become a serious challenge to the official religion of the Empire. But Diocletian's successor, Constantine the Great, reversed his predecessor's hostile stance and extended official toleration to Christians. By this stage Christianity had succeeded in gaining a substantial number of adherents among the urban population. Eventually Constantine became more involved in church affairs and just before his death he himself was baptised. The Christianisation of the Empire continued throughout the century and by the early 400s, Christianity was fully established as the State religion.

By the first half of the fourth century Jewish scholars in Israel had collected together the teachings of generations of rabbis in the academies of Tiberius, Caesarea and Sepphoris. These extended discussions of the *Mishnah* became the Palestinian *Talmud*. The text of this multi-volume work covered four sections of the *Mishnah* ('Seeds', 'Set Feasts', 'Women' and 'Damages'), but here and there various tractates were omitted. The views of these Palestinian teachers had an important influence on scholars in Babylonia, though this work never attained the same prominence as that of the Babylonian *Talmud*.

Paralleling the development of rabbinic Judaism in Palestine, Babylonian scholars founded centres of learning. The great third-century teacher Rav established an academy at Sura in central Mesopotamia. His contemporary, Samuel, was head of another Babylonian academy at Nehardea. After Nehardea was destroyed in an invasion in 259 CE, the school at Pumbedita also became a dominant Babylonian academy of Jewish learning. The Babylonian sages carried on and developed the Galilean tradition of disputation, and the fourth century produced two of the most distinguished scholars of the talmudic period, Abbaye and Rava, who both taught at Pumbedita. With the decline of Jewish institutions in Israel, Babylonia became the most important centre of Jewish scholarship.

By the sixth century Babylonian scholars completed the redaction of the Babylonian *Talmud* – an editorial task begun by Rav Ashi in the fourth to fifth century at Sura. This massive work parallels the Palestinian *Talmud* and is largely a summary of the rabbinic discussions that took place in the Babylonian academies. Both *Talmuds* are essentially elaborations of the *Mishnah*, though neither commentary contains material on every *Mishnah* passage. The text itself consists largely of summaries of rabbinic discussions: a phrase of the *Mishnah* is interpreted, discrepancies are discussed and redundancies are explained. In this compilation, conflicting opinions of the earlier scholars are contrasted, unusual words are explained and anonymous opinions are identified. Frequently individual teachers cite specific cases to support their views, and hypothetical eventualities are examined to reach a solution on the discussion. Debates between outstanding scholars in one generation are often cited, as are differences of opinion between contemporary members of an academy or a teacher and his students. The range of talmudic exploration is much broader than that of the *Mishnah* itself and includes a wide range of rabbinic teachings about such subjects as theology, philosophy and ethics.

Judaism in the Middle Ages

By the sixth century the Jews had become largely a diaspora people. Despite the loss of a homeland, they were unified by a common heritage: law, liturgy and shared traditions bound together the scattered communities stretching from Spain to Persia and Poland to Africa. Though subcultures did form during the Middle Ages which could have divided the Jewish world, Jews remained united in their hope for messianic redemption, the restoration of the Holy Land and the ingathering of the exiles. Living among Christians and Muslims, the Jewish community was reduced to a minority group and their marginal status resulted in repeated persecution. Though there were times of tolerance and creative activity, the threats of exile and death were always present in Jewish consciousness during this period.

Within the Islamic world, Jews along with Christians were recognised as 'Peoples of the Book' and were guaranteed religious toleration, judicial autonomy and exemption from the military. In turn, they were required to accept the supremacy of the Islamic State. Such an arrangement was formally codified by the Pact of Omar dating from about 800. According to this treaty, Jews were restricted in a number of spheres: they were not allowed to build new houses of worship, make converts, carry weapons or ride horses. In addition, they were required to wear distinctive clothing and pay a yearly poll tax. Jewish farmers were also obliged to pay a land tax consisting of a portion of their produce. Despite these conditions, Jewish life prospered. In various urban centres many Jews were employed in crafts such as tanning, dyeing, weaving, silk manufacture and metal work. Other Jews participated in interregional trade and established networks of agents and representatives.

During the first two centuries of Islamic rule under the Ummayad and Abbasid caliphates, Muslim leaders confirmed the authority of traditional Babylonian institutions. When the Arabs conquered Babylonia, they officially recognised the position of the exilarch, who for centuries had been the ruler of Babylonian Jewry. By the Abbasid period, the exilarch shared his power with the heads of the rabbinical academies which had been the major centres of rabbinic learning for hundreds of years. The head of each academy was known as the gaon, who delivered lectures as well as learned opinions on legal matters.

During the eighth century messianic movements appeared in the Persian Jewish community which led to armed uprisings against Muslim authorities. Such revolts were quickly crushed, but an even more serious threat to traditional Jewish life was posed later in the century by the emergence of an anti-rabbinic sect, the Karaites. This group was founded in Babylonia in the 760s by Anan ben David. The guiding interpretative principle formulated by Anan, 'Search thoroughly in Scipture and do not rely on my opinion', was intended to point to Scripture itself as the source of law. After the death of the founder new parties within the Karaite movement soon emerged, and by the tenth century Karaite communities were established in Israel, Iraq and Persia. The growth of Karaism provoked the rabbis to attack it as a heretical movement since these various groups rejected rabbinic law and formulated their own legislation.

By the eighth century the Muslim Empire began to undergo a process of disintegration. This process was accompanied by a decentralisation of rabbinic Judaism. The academies of Babylonia began to lose their hold on the Jewish scholarly world, and in many places rabbinic schools were established in which rabbinic sources were studied. The growth of these local centres of scholarship enabled individual teachers to exert their influence on Jewish learning independent of the academies of Sura and Pumbedita. In the Holy Land, Tiberias was the location of an important rabbinical academy, as well as the centre of the masoretic scholars who produced the standard text of the Bible. In Egypt Kairouan and Fez became centres of scholarship. But it was in Spain that the Jewish community attained the greatest level of achievement in literature, philosophy, theology and mysticism.

In their campaigns the Muslims did not manage to conquer all of Europe – many countries remained under Christian rule, as did much of the Byzantine Empire. In Christian Europe Jewish study took place in a number of important towns, such as Mainz and Worms in the Rhineland and Troyes and Sens in northern France. In such an environment the study of the *Talmud* reached great heights. In Germany and northern France scholars known as 'the tosafists' utilised new methods of talmudic interpretation. In addition, Ashkenazic Jews of this period composed religious poetry modelled on the liturgical compositions of fifth- and sixth-century Israel.

Despite such an efflorescence of Jewish life, the expulsion of the Jews from countries in which they lived became a dominant policy of Christian Europe. In 1182 the king of France expelled all Jews from the royal domains near Paris, cancelled nearly all Christian debts to Jewish moneylenders and confiscated Jewish property. Though the Jews were recalled in 1198 they were burdened with an additional royal tax, and in the next century they increasingly became the property of the king. In 13th-century England the Jews were continuously taxed and the entire Jewish population was expelled in 1290, as was that in France some years later. At the end of the 13th century the German Jewish community suffered violent attack. In the next century Jews were blamed for bringing about the Black Death by poisoning the wells of Europe, and in 1348–49 Jews in France, Switzerland, Germany and Belgium suffered at the hands of their Christian neighbours. In the following two centuries Jewish massacre and expulsion became a frequent occurrence. Prominent Spanish Jewish thinkers of this period were Solomon ibn Gabirol, Baḥya ibn Pakuda, Judah ha-Levi, Moses Maimonides, Ḥasdai Crescas and Joseph Albo. During this period the major mystical work of Spanish Jewry, the *Zohar*, was composed by Moses ben Shem Tov de Leon.

Jewry in the Early Modern Period

From the end of the fourteenth century political instability in Christian Europe led to the massacre of many Jewish communities in Castile and Aragon. Fearing for their lives, thousands of Jews converted to Christianity in 1391. Two decades later Spanish rulers introduced the Castilian laws which segregated Jews from their Christian neighbours. In the following year a public disputation was held in Tortosa about the doctrine of the Messiah. As a result increased pressure was applied to the Jewish population to convert. Those who became apostates (Marranos) found life much easier, but by the 15th century, anti-Jewish sentiment again became a serious problem. In 1480 King Ferdinand and Queen Isabella established the Inquisition to determine whether former Jews practised Judaism in secret. In the late 1480s inquisitors used torture to extract confessions, and in 1492 the entire Jewish community was expelled from Spain. In the next century the Inquisition was established in Portugal.

To escape such persecution many Spanish and Portuguese Marranos sought refuge in various parts of the Ottoman Empire. Some of these Sephardic immigrants prospered and became part of the Ottoman court, such as Gracia Nasi and her nephew Joseph Nasi. Prominent among the rabbinic scholars of this period was Joseph Caro who emigrated from Spain to the Balkans. In the 1520s he commenced a study of Jewish law, *The House of Joseph*, based on previous codes of Jewish law. In addition, he composed a shorter work, the *Shulḥan Arukh*, which became the authoritative code of law in the Jewish world.

While working on the *Shulḥan Arukh*, Caro emigrated to Safed in Israel which had become a major centre of Jewish religious life. In the 16th century this small community had grown to a population of over 10,000 Jews. Here talmudic academies were established and small groups engaged in the study of Kabbalistic literature as they piously awaited the coming of the Messiah. In this centre of Kabbalistic activity one of the greatest mystics of Safed, Moses Cordovero, collected, organised and interpreted the teachings of earlier mystical authors. Later in the 16th century Kabbalistic speculation was transformed by the greatest mystic of Safed, Isaac Luria.

By the beginning of the 17th century Lurianic mysticism had made an important impact on Sephardic Jewry, and messianic expectations had also became a central feature of Jewish life. In this milieu the arrival of self-proclaimed messianic King, Shabbetai Tzevi, brought about a transformation of Jewish life and thought. After living in various cities, he travelled to Gaza where he encountered Nathan of Gaza who believed he was the Messiah. In 1665 his messiahship was proclaimed and Nathan sent letters to Jews in the diaspora asking them to recognise Shabbetai Tzevi as their redeemer. In the following year Shabbetai journeyed to Constantinople, but on the order of the Grand Vizier he was arrested and put into prison. Eventually he was brought to court and given the choice between conversion and death. In the face of this alternative he converted to Islam. Such an act of apostasy scandalised most of his followers, but others continued to revere him as the Messiah. In the following century the most important Shabbetaian sect was led by Jacob Frank who believed himself to be the incarnation of Shabbetai.

During this period Poland had become a great centre of scholarship. In Polish academies scholars collected together the legal interpretation of previous authorities and composed commentaries on the *Shulḥan Arukh*. To regulate Jewish life in the country at large Polish Jews established regional federations that administered Jewish affairs. In the midst of this general prosperity, the Polish Jewish community was subject to a series of massacres carried out by the Cossacks of Ukraine, Crimean Tartars and Ukrainian peasants. In 1648 Bogdan Chmielnicki was elected hetman of the Cossacks and instigated an insurrection against the Polish gentry. As administrators of noblemen's estates, Jews were slaughtered in these revolts.

As the century progressed, Jewish life in Poland became increasingly more insecure due to political instability. Nonetheless the Jewish community increased in size considerably during the 18th century. In the 1730s and 1740s Cossacks known as Haidemaks invaded Ukraine, robbing and murdering Jewish inhabitants, and finally butchering the Jewish community of Uman in 1768. In Lithuania, on the other hand, Jewish life flourished and Vilna became an important centre of Jewish learning. Here Elijah ben Solomon Zalman, referred to as the Vilna Gaon, lectured to disciples on a wide range of subjects and composed commentaries on rabbinic sources.

Elsewhere in Europe this period witnessed Jewish persecution and oppression. Despite the positive contact between Italian humanists and Jews, Christian anti-Semitism frequently led to persecution and suffering. In the 16th century the Counter-Reformation Church attempted to isolate the Jewish community. The *Talmud* was burned in 1553, and two years later Pope Paul IV reinstated the segregationist edict of the Fourth Lateran Council, forcing Jews to live in ghettos and barring them from most areas of economic life. In addition, Marranos who took up the Jewish tradition were burned at the stake, and Jews were expelled from most church domains.

In Germany the growth of Protestantism frequently led to adverse conditions for the Jewish population. Though Martin Luther was initially well disposed to the Jews, he soon came to realise that the Jewish community was intent on remaining true to its faith. As a consequence, he composed a virulent attack on the Jews. Nonetheless some Jews, known as Court Jews, attained positions of great importance among the German nobility. A number of these favoured individuals were appointed by the rulers as chief elders of the Jewish community and acted as spokesmen and defenders of German Jewry.

In Holland some Jews had also attained an important influence on trade and finance. By the mid-17th century both Marranos and

Ashkenazi Jews came to Amsterdam and established themselves in various areas of economic activity. By the end of the century there were nearly 10,000 Jews in Amsterdam: there the Jewish community was employed on the stock exchange, in the sugar, tobacco and diamond trades, and in insurance, manufacturing, printing and banking. In this milieu Jewish cultural activity flourished: Jewish writers published works of drama, theology and mystical lore. Though Jews in Holland were not granted full rights as citizens, they nevertheless enjoyed religious freedom, personal protection and the liberty of participating in a wide range of economic affairs.

Jews in the Modern World

By the middle of the 18th century the Jewish community had suffered numerous waves of persecution and was deeply dispirited by the conversion of the 17th-century false messiah Shabbetai Tzevi. In this environment the Ḥasidic movement – grounded in Kabbalah – sought to revitalise Jewish life. The founder of this new sect was Israel ben Eleazer, known as the Baal Shem Tov (Besht). Born in southern Poland, he travelled to Medzibozh in Polodia, Russia, in the 1730s, where he performed various miracles and instructed his disciples in Kabbalistic lore. By the 1740s he attracted a considerable number of disciples who passed on his teaching. After his death, Dov Baer of Mezhirich became the leader of his sect and Ḥasidism spread to southern Poland, Ukraine and Lithuania. The growth of this movement engendered considerable hostility on the part of rabbinic authorities, and by the end of the century the Jewish religious establishment of Vilna denounced Ḥasidism to the Russian Government.

During the latter part of the century the treatment of Jews in Central Europe greatly improved due to the influence of Christian polemicists who argued that Jewish life should be ameliorated. The Holy Roman Emperor Joseph II embraced such views; he abolished the Jewish badge as well as taxes imposed on Jewish travellers, and proclaimed an edict of toleration which granted the Jews numerous rights. As in Germany, reformers in France during the 1770s and 1780s sought to advance the position of the Jewish population. In 1789 the National Assembly issued a declaration stating that all human beings were born and remained free and equal, and that no person should be persecuted for his opinions as long as they did not subvert civil law. In 1791 a resolution was passed which bestowed citizenship rights on all Jews. This

change in Jewish status occurred elsewhere in Europe as well. In 1796
the Dutch Jews of the Batvian Republic were granted full citizenship
rights, and in 1797 the ghettos of Padua and Rome were abolished.

In 1799 Napoleon became the First Consul of France and five years
later he was proclaimed Emperor. Napoleon's Code of Civil Law propounded in 1804 established the right of all individuals to follow any
trade and declared equality for all. After 1806 a number of German
principalities were united in the French kingdom of Westphallia, where
Jews were granted equal rights. In the same year Napoleon convened
an Assembly of Jewish notables to consider a series of religious issues.

After Napoleon's defeat and abdication, the map of Europe was
redrawn by the Congress of Vienna between 1814 and 1815, and
in addition the diplomats at the Congress issued a resolution that
instructed the German confederation to improve the status of the Jews.
Yet despite this decree the German government disowned the rights
of equality that had previously been granted to Jews by the French. In
1830, however, a more liberal attitude prevailed, and various nations
advocated a more tolerant approach. The French Revolution in 1848,
which led to outbreaks of unrest in Prussia, Austria, Hungary, Italy
and Bohemia, forced rulers to grant constitutions which guaranteed
freedom of speech, assembly and religion.

Within this environment Jewish emancipation gathered force. At the
end of the 18th century the Jewish philosopher Moses Mendelssohn
advocated the modernisation of Jewish life, and to further this advance
he translated the Torah into German so that Jews would be able to
speak the language of the country in which they lived. Following Mendelssohn's example a number of Prussian followers, known as maskilim,
fostered a Jewish Enlightenment – the Haskalah – which encouraged
Jews to abandon medieval forms of life and thought. By the 1820s the
centre of this movement shifted to the Austrian Empire, where journals
propounding the ideas of the Enlightenment were published. In the
1840s the Haskalah spread to Russia where writers made important
contributions to Hebrew literature and translated textbooks and European fiction into Hebrew.

Paralleling this development, reformers encouraged the modernisation of the Jewish liturgy and the reform of Jewish education. At the
beginning of the 19th century the Jewish financier and communal
leader Israel Jacobson initiated a programme of reform. In 1801 he
founded a boarding school for boys in Seesen, Westphalia, and later
created other schools throughout the kingdom. In this new foundation

general subjects were taught by Christian teachers, while a Jewish instructor gave lessons about Judaism. Subsequently, Jacobson built a Reform Temple next to the school and another in Hamburg. Although such changes were denounced by the Orthodox establishment, Reform Judaism spread throughout Europe. In 1844 the first Reform Synod took place in Brunswick; this consultation was followed by another conference in 1845 in Frankfurt. At this gathering one of the more conservative rabbis, Zacharias Frankel, expressed dissatisfaction with progressive reforms to Jewish worship and resigned from the Assembly, establishing a Jewish theological seminary in Breslau. In 1846 a third Synod took place in Breslau, but the Revolution and its aftermath brought about the cessation of these activities until 1868 when another Synod took place at Cassel.

In the United States, Reform Judaism had also become an important feature of Jewish life. The most prominent of the early reformers was Isaac Mayer Wise who had come from Bavaria to Albany, New York, in 1846. Later he went to Cincinnati, Ohio, where he published a new Reform prayer book as well as several Jewish newspapers. In addition he attempted to convene a Reform Synod. In 1869 the first conference of the Central Conference of American Rabbis was held in Philadelphia; this was followed in 1873 by the founding of the Union of American Hebrew Congregations. Two years later the Hebrew Union College was established to train rabbinical students for Reform Congregations. In 1885 a conference of Reform rabbis met in Pittsburgh, which produced a formal list of principles, the Pittsburgh Platform.

In Eastern Europe conditions were less conducive to emancipation. In 1804 Alexander I specified territory in western Poland as an area in which Jews would be allowed to reside (the Pale of Settlement). After several attempts to expel Jews from the countryside, the tsar in 1817 initiated a new policy of integrating the Jewish community into the population by founding a society of Israelite Christians which extended legal and financial concessions to baptised Jews. In 1824 the deportation of Jews from villages began. In the same year Alexander I died and was succeeded by Nicholas I who adopted a severe attitude to the Jewish community. In 1827 he initiated a policy of inducting Jewish boys into the Russian army for a 25-year period to increase the number of converts to Christianity. Nicholas I also deported Jews from villages in certain areas. In 1844 the tsar abolished the kehillot (Jewish communal bodies) and put Jewry under the authority of the police as well as municipal government. Between 1850 and 1851 the government attempted to forbid Jewish dress, men's side curls and the ritual shaving of women's hair. After the Crimean War of 1853–56 Alexander II emancipated the serfs, modernised the judiciary and established a system of local self-government. In addition he allowed certain groups to reside outside the Pale of Settlement. As a result Jewish communities appeared in St Petersburg and Moscow. Furthermore, a limited number of Jews were allowed to enter the legal profession and participate in local government.

Jews in the 20th and 21st Centuries

After the pogroms of 1881–82 many Jews emigrated to the United States, but a significant number were drawn to Palestine. By the later 1880s the idea of a Jewish homeland had spread throughout Europe. At the first Zionist Congress at Basle in 1887 Theodor Herzl called for a national home based on international law. After establishing the basic institutions of the Zionist movement, Herzl embarked on a range of diplomatic negotiations. At the beginning of the 20th century a sizeable number of Jews had emigrated to Palestine. After World War I Jews in Palestine organised a National Assembly and Executive Council. By 1929 the Jewish community numbered 160,000 with 110 agricultural settlements. In the next ten years the population increased to 500,000 with 223 agricultural communities. About a quarter of this population lived in cooperatives. Tel Aviv had 150,000 settlers, Jerusalem 90,000 and Haifa 60,000. Industrialisation was initiated by the Palestinian Electric Corporation and developed by the Histadrut. In 1925 the Hebrew University was opened. During this period Palestine was 160 miles long and 70 miles wide. Its population was composed of about one million Arabs consisting of peasants and a number of landowners, in addition to the Jewish population. In 1929 the Arab community rioted following a dispute concerning Jewish access to the Western Wall of the ancient Temple. This conflict caused the British to curtail Jewish immigration as well as the purchase of Arab land.

By the 1920s Labour Zionism had become the dominant force in Palestinian Jewish life; in 1930 various socialist and Labour groups joined together in the Israel Labour Party. Within the Zionist movement a right-wing segment criticised the President of the World Zionist Organisation, Chaim Weizmann, who was committed to cooperation with the British. Vladimir Jabotinsky, leader of the Union of Zionist Revisionists, stressed that the central aim of the Zionist movement was the establishment of an independent state in the whole of Palestine. At several Zionist Congresses, the Revisionists founded their own organisation and withdrew from the militia of the Haganah to form their own military force. In 1936 the Arabs, supported by Syria, Iraq and Egypt, launched an offensive against Jews, the British and moderate Arabs. In 1937 a British Royal Commission proposed that Palestine be partitioned into a Jewish and Arab state with a British zone. This recommendation was accepted by Zionists but rejected by the Arabs. Eventually the British Government published a White Paper in 1939 which rejected the concept of partition, limited Jewish immigration to 75,000 and decreed that Palestine would become independent in ten years.

As these events unfolded in the Middle East, Jews in Germany were confronted by increasing hostility, amounting to antipathy. Once the Nazis gained control of the government, they curtailed civil liberties. In 1935 the Nuremburg Laws made Jews into second-class citizens, and all intermarriage and sexual liaisons between Jews and non-Jews were described as crimes against the State. In 1938 Jewish community leaders were put under the control of the Gestapo, and Jews were forced to register their property. From 9 to 10 November of that year, the Nazi party organised an onslaught against the Jewish population in which Jews were killed and Jewish property destroyed. This event, known as Kristallnacht, was a prelude to the Holocaust and precipitated the next stage of hostility.

The first stage of Hitler's plan for European Jewry had already begun with the invasion of Poland. In September 1939 Hitler decided to incorporate much of Poland into Germany, and more than 600,000 Jews were gathered into a large area in Poland. When the Jewish population was ghettoised into what Hitler referred to as a huge Polish labour camp, a massive work programme was initiated. Jews worked all day, seven days a week, and were dressed in rags and fed on bread, soup and potatoes. Officially, these workers had no names, only numbers tattooed on their bodies. If one died, a replacement was sought without any inquest into the cause of death.

With the invasion of Russia in 1941 the Nazis used mobile killing battalions of 500–900 men to destroy Russian Jewry. Throughout the country these units moved into Russian towns, sought out the rabbi or Jewish court, and obtained a list of all Jewish inhabitants. The Jews were then rounded up in market places, crowded into trains, buses and trucks and taken to woods where graves had been dug. They were then machine-gunned to death. Other methods were also employed by the Nazis. Mobile gas units were supplied to these killing batallions. Meanwhile these mobile killing operations were being supplanted by the development of fixed centres – the death camps. The six major death camps comprised the major areas of killing. Over 2,000,000 died at Auschwitz; 1,380,000 at Majdanek; 800,000 at Treblinka; 600,000 at Belzec; 340,000 at Chelmno and 250,000 at Sobibor.

Despite acts of resistance against the Nazis, such as occurred in 1942 in Warsaw, six million Jews died in this onslaught. In Poland more than 90 per cent of Jews were killed. The same percentage of the Jewish population died in the Baltic states, Germany and Austria. More than 70 per cent were murdered in the Bohemian protectorate, Slovakia, Greece and the Netherlands. More than 45 per cent were killed in White Russia, Ukraine, Belgium, Yugoslavia and Norway.

During the war and afterwards, the British prevented illegal immigrants from entering the Holy Land. Campaigning against the policy, in 1946 the Haganah blew up the King David Hotel in Jerusalem, where part of the British Administration was housed. Later in the same year the British Foreign Secretary, Ernest Bevin, handed over the Palestinian problem to the United Nations.

On 29 November 1947 the General Assembly of the United Nations endorsed a plan of partition. Once this proposal was accepted, the Arabs attacked Jewish settlements. In March 1948 David Ben-Gurion read out the Scroll of Independence of the Jewish State. Immediately a government was formed, and the Arabs stepped up their assault. Following the War of Independence, armistice talks were held and later signed with Egypt, the Lebanon, Transjordan and Syria. Later President Gamal Abdel Nasser refused to allow Israeli ships to cross to the Gulf of Aqaba in 1956, seized the Suez Canal, and formed a pact with Saudi Arabia and various Arab states. In response Israel launched a strike conquering Sinai and opening the sea route to Aqaba. In 1967 Nasser began another offensive against Israel which resulted in the Six-Day War in which Israel emerged victorious. This was followed by another, the Yom Kippur War, in 1973 and, in the 1980s, by an Israeli offensive against the Palestinian Liberation Organisation (PLO) in Southern Lebanon in 1982.

In 1985 the Palestinian Intifada began in Israeli-occupied Gaza and the West Bank. Several years later Israel engaged with the PLO in dialogue, however, Prime Minister Yitzhak Rabin was assassinated in 1995. In the ensuing years Benjamin Netanyahu was elected Prime

Minister, followed by Ariel Sharon, and Palestinians engaged in suicide bombings of Israel despite Israel's determination to construct a wall to protect the country from attack. Despite attempts by the Obama Administration to resolve the conflict between Israel and the Palestinians, the struggle between these two peoples continues unabated.

A

A rabbi dies and is waiting in line to enter heaven. In front of him is a man dressed in a loud shirt, leather jacket, jeans and sunglasses. Gabriel says to the man, 'I need to know who you are so that I can determine whether or not to admit you to the kingdom of heaven.'

The man replies, 'I'm Moishe Levy, taxi driver.' Gabriel consults his list, smiles and says to the taxi driver, 'OK. Take this silken robe and golden staff and enter the kingdom of heaven.'

Now it's the rabbi's turn. He stands upright and says, 'I am Benjamin Himmelfarb and I have been a rabbi for 40 years.'

Gabriel looks at his list and says to the rabbi, 'OK. Take this cotton robe and wooden staff and enter the kingdom of heaven.'

'Hold on a minute,' says Rabbi Himmelfarb, 'that man before me was a taxi driver. Why did he get a silken robe and golden staff?'

'Up here, we only work by results,' says Gabriel. 'While you preached, people slept. But while he drove, people prayed.'

* * * * *

Rabbis are frequently targets of Jewish humour. There are literally hundreds of jokes pointing out their foibles and follies. Here Rabbi Himmelfarb is satirised for his self-satisfaction and ambition. Why, he asks, should a taxi driver receive a silken robe and golden staff rather than him? Surely rabbis deserve better treatment in heaven? In response he is told that his congregation slept through his sermons. But the taxi driver gets it too for being such a lousy driver.

Aaron (fl.? 13th cent. BCE) Israelite leader, elder brother of Moses. He and Moses freed the Jews from Egyptian bondage. He made the Golden Calf to placate the people when Moses did not descend Mount Sinai (Exodus 32). When the Tabernacle was established, he and his sons became priests. At the age of 123 Aaron died on Mount Hor, situated on the border of Edom. According to rabbinic sources, he is the personification of piety and peace.

Aaronides Hereditary priests. According to Numbers 18:7, the descendants of Aaron 'shall attend to your priesthood for all that concerns the altar and that which is in the veil.' In Scripture a distinction is made between the Aaronides and the Levites, even though it is sometimes implied that all the Levites were priests. Some scholars argue that the Aaronides were Egyptian in origin, since Egyptian names are found among their records.

Aaronson, Aaron (1849–1939) Palestinian leader. He studied agronomy in France. From 1895 he worked as an expert for Edmond de Rothschild. During World War I he organised an underground intelligence service (Nili) in Palestine. He promoted Zionist concerns at the Paris Peace Conference in 1919.

Abba [Ba] (fl. late 3rd–early 4th cent.) Babylonian amora. He was a disciple of Huna and Judah. In Tiberias he studied with Eleazar and Simeon ben Lakish. He often visited Babylonia and passed on Babylonian teachings in Israel.

Abbahu (279–320) Palestinian amora. He was the leader of the rabbis at Caesarea who engaged in the redaction of the juridical parts of the Jerusalem *Talmud*.

Abbaye [Naḥmani bar Kaylil] (278–338) Babylonian amora. He developed talmudic dialectic as head of the academy of Pumbedita. His arguments with Rava are recorded in the Babylonian *Talmud*. In his teaching he distinguished between the literal meaning of the biblical text ('peshat') and the figurative interpretation ('derash').

Abbreviations (Hebrew 'rashe tevot') Shortened word forms used in the *Talmud* and later rabbinic literature from as early as the 2nd century BCE. They also played an important role in rabbinic and mystical exegesis. The full form of the word is indicted by a dot, stroke or double stroke over the first, second or third letter. The other letters are eliminated. Abbreviating groups of words to form one word was also a frequent practice.

Abel Son of Adam and Eve. He was a shepherd. His elder brother Cain was a farmer. When God favoured Abel's sacrifice, Cain murdered him out of jealousy (Genesis 4:1–9).

Abigail (fl. 11th–10th cent.) Israelite woman, wife of David. After the death of her husband, Nabal, she became David's wife (I Samuel 25).

Abihu (fl.? 13th cent.) Israelite priest, second son of Aaron Together with his brother, Nadab, he ascended Mount Sinai to behold God's revelation (Exodus 24:1–11). Later they made a fire sacrifice on the altar against God's command and were struck dead by fire as a punishment (Leviticus 10:1–3).

Abijah (fl. 10th cent. BCE) King of Judah (914–912). He engaged in battle with Jeroboam, King of Israel (I Kings 15; II Chronicles 13).

Abimelech (fl.? 19th–16th cent. BCE) King of Gerar in Palestine. He had friendly relations with Abraham and Isaac (Genesis 20 and 26).

Abiram (fl.? 13th cent. BCE) Israelite rebel and leader. With Dathan and Koraḥ, he led an unsuccessful revolt against Moses in the wilderness (Numbers 16).

Abishag (fl. 11th–10th cent. BCE) Shulamite woman who ministered to David (I Kings 1:1–4).

Ablution In biblical and rabbinic usage, ritual washing. Women after menstruation or childbirth, and converts during the conversion process, completely immerse themselves in natural water or a ritual bath ('mikveh'). Priests wash their hands and feet during the Temple worship. Individuals wash their hands before eating or praying, after rising from sleep, touching a corpse, urinating or defecating.

Abner ben Ner (fl. 11th cent. BCE) Israelite general. He was commander of Saul's army. He supported Ishbosheth's claim to the throne when Saul died. Later he became a member of David's court. He was killed by Joab (I Samuel 3).

Abner of Burgos [Alfonso of Valladolid] (1270–1340) Spanish scholar. A convert to Christianity, he wrote anti-Jewish polemical tracts and engaged in disputes with Jewish scholars. He formulated an ideological justification for his conversion in *Epistle on Fate*.

Aboab, Isaac de Fonseca (1605–1693) Portuguese rabbi. He served as the first rabbi in the western hemisphere. Born a Marrano in Portugal, he emigrated to Holland. In 1641 he traveled to Recife, Brazil. Subsequently he went to Amsterdam, where he became ḥakham. He was a follower of Shabbetai Trevi, and a member of the tribunal with excommunicated Benedict Spinoza.

Aboab, Samuel (1610–1694) Italian rabbi. He was an opponent of the Sabbetaians. He was among the rabbis who interrogated Nathan of Gaza in Venice in 1668. He composed *Devar Shemuel*.

Abomination In Jewish law, any of three kinds of abhorrent thing grouped according to their severity. 'Toevah' is the worst. It consists of major sins such as idolatry and child-sacrifice. 'Shikkutz' is less serious. It applies to idolatrous usages and prohibited animals. 'Piggul' is the least serious. It refers to the flesh of a sacrifice which has become putrid.

Abortion Termination of a pregnancy. The Bible stipulates liability for monetary compensation (as opposed to capital punishment) in the case of an attack on a pregnant woman that results in the loss of the unborn child (Exodus 21:22–23). The rabbis interpreted this to mean that full human rights extend only to a child who is born. Thus the Mishnah rules in favour of destroying a foetus if its continued existence endangers the mother's life (as long as the head or a greater part of the child has not yet emerged from the birth canal).

Abraham [Abram] (fl.? 19th–16th cent. BCE) Israelite patriarch. He left Ur and travelled to Canaan. God appeared to him and promised that his offspring would inherit the earth. God made a covenant with Abraham and

tested his faith by asking him to sacrifice his son, Isaac (Genesis 11:26–25:10).

Abraham, Apocalypse of Pseudepigraphic book. It relates Abraham's conversion, destiny in heaven and the fate of all nations.

Abraham, Testament of Pseudepigraphic book. It depicts Abraham's initiation into the divine mysteries before his death and his ascent to heaven.

Abraham bar Ḥiyya [Abraham Judaeus; Abraham Savasorda] (fl. 12th cent.) Spanish scholar. He created the foundations of Hebrew scientific terminology and transmitted Greco-Arabic science to the Christian world. His *Meditation of the Sad Soul* is an ethical treatise influenced by Neoplatonism.

Abraham ben Alexander Katz of Kalisk [Kalisher, Abraham] (1741–1810) Polish Ḥasidic rabbi. He represented popular elements of the Ḥasidic movement. Yet the odd customs of his followers evoked criticism. With Menaḥem Mendel of Vitebsk, he led a group of Ḥasidim from Russia to Palestine in 1777.

Abraham ben David of Posquières [Ravad] (1125–1198) French talmudist. His strictures on the writings of Maimonides, Alfasi and Zerahiah ben Isaac Ha-Levi were widely read. He objected to Maimonides' *Mishneh Torah* because he believed such codes might take the place of talmudic study.

Abraham ben Moses ben Maimon [Maimon, Abraham ben Moses] (1186–1237) Egyptian rabbinic scholar. He succeeded his father Maimonides as nagid of the Egyptian Jewish community. His *Comprehensive Guide for the Servants of God* is an encyclopaedic work on the Jewish religion.

Abraham Joshua Heshel of [Apt (Opatav), Rabbi of] (1745–1825) Polish Ḥasidic leader. He opposed the maskilim for spreading heretical ideas among Russian Jewry. He recounted fantastic reminiscences about what he had witnessed in former incarnations as high priest, King of Israel, nasi and exilarch.

Abraham, Karl (1877–1925) German psychoanalyst. Born in Germany, he completed his medical studies in 1901. In 1905 he began to work as a psychiatrist at the Burgholzi Clinic in Zurich where he came into contact with C.G. Jung and Eugen Bleuler. In 1907 he met Sigmund Freud and became a member of his inner circle. He was the founder of the German Psychoanalytic School and Institute. He analysed many of the early analysts including Melanie Klein, Sandor Rado and Helene Deutsch.

Abrahams, Harold Maurice (1899–1978) British athlete. He studied law and became a senior civil servant. A brilliant athlete, he set a British long-jump record in 1924. At the Olympic Games in the same year he won the gold medal for the 100-metre sprint, a feat depicted in the 1981 film *Chariots of Fire.*

Abrahams, Israel (1858–1924) English scholar. He was reader in rabbinic at Cambridge University. With Claude Montefiore he founded and edited the *Jewish Quarterly Review.* His most important works were *Jewish Life in the Middle Ages, Studies in Pharisaism and the Gospels,* and *Hebrew Ethical Wills.*

Abramowitsch, Shalom Jacob [Sephordim, Mendel Mocher] (1836–1917) Russian Hebrew and Yiddish writer. He was born in Belorussia. With Ḥayyim Naḥman Bialik and Yehoshua Hana Ravnitzky he translated the Torah into Yiddish. He also wrote short stories. He is the father of prose literature in Hebrew and Yiddish.

Abrams, Lionel (1928–2004) South African artist. He was born in Johannesburg. He held his first exhibition in 1957. His interest in the Lubavitch

movement in the early 1970s led to a four-year period of work on Jewish themes. He produced a series of portraits of five generations of Lubavitcher rebbes and painted a number of traditional Jewish themes.

Abramsky, Chimen (1917–2010) British scholar of Russian origin. Born in Minsk, he emigrated to the United Kingdom where he was Professor of Hebrew and Jewish studies at University College, London. His publications include *Karl Marx and the English Labour Movement, First Illustrated Grace after Meals,* and *The Jews in Poland.*

Abravanel [Abrabanel], Isaac ben Judah (1437–1508) Portuguese biblical exegete and statesman. He was treasurer to Alfonso V of Portugal and served King Ferdinand and Queen Isabella of Castile. His writings include a commentary on the Bible, philosophical studies of an anti-rationalist nature, and theological treaties stressing the primacy of Judaism.

Absalom (fl. 10th cent. BCE) Israelite, son of David. He killed his brother Amnon who had raped his sister Tamar. He led an unsuccessful rebellion against David, in which his army was defeated and he was killed by Joab. (II Samuel 13–19).

Abse, Dannie (1923–2014) Welsh poet and playwright. He was born in Cardiff. He published his first volume of poetry while still a medical student. His *Collected Poems, 1948–1976* draw together his roles as Jew, Welshman, British poet, doctor, bourgeois family man, bohemian observer, pragmatist and mystic.

Abu Issa al-Isfahni [Isfahani] (fl. 8th cent.) Persian, self-proclaimed Messiah. He claimed to be the Messiah ben Joseph, the last of the five forerunners of the Messiah ben David. He prohibited divorce, eating meat and drinking wine. He recognised the prophecies of Jesus and Mohammed and decreed seven daily prayers. In a rebellion against the Abbasid rulers, he was killed in battle.

Abulafia, Abraham ben Samuel (1240–after 1291) Spanish Kabbalist and pseudo-Messiah. In 1280 he went to Rome to persuade Pope Nicholas III to help the Jews. He evoked hostility from Solomon ben Adret by prophesying his own messiahship and redemptive powers. He believed his Kabbalistic practices, based on letter manipulation, enabled one to receive prophetic gifts and commune with God.

Abulafia, Hayyim ben Jacob (1580–1668) Palestinian talmudist. In 1666 he was one of the delegation who went to Gaza to investigate the authenticity of Nathan of Gaza's prophecies about Shabbetai Tzevi.

Abulafia, Meir ben Todros ha-Levi (?1170–1244) Spanish talmudist and poet. He wrote about halakhah, masorah, and the controversy over Maimonides' opinion on the subject of resurrection. He also composed Hebrew poetry.

Abulafia, Todros ben Joseph (1220–1298) Spanish Kabbalist. He was the spiritual leader of the Jewish community in Castile. His *Ozar ha-Kavod* combines Kabbalistic doctrines of gnostic circles in Castile with those of the Gerona School.

Academy In Jewish usage a term applied specifically to a centre of rabbinic scholarship. After the fall of Jerusalem (70 CE), the first academy was founded at Jabneh. In Babylonia the major academies were located at Sura, Nehardea, and Pumbedita.

Academy on High The body of scholars in heaven. It is presided over by God and reserved for scholars after death.

Accents ('neginot') In liturgical texts a system of accents is used to aid cantilla-

tion. Accents are used in this context to indicate punctuation and stress, and to show the rise and fall of the chant.

Accident Biblical laws of liability for damage caused by an accident are found in Exodus 21:28–36 and 22:4–5. The rabbis categorised the cases cited into four standard types of accident: the ox (representing injury caused in the course of normal activity); the pit (injury caused by a stationary thing); the crop-devouring animal (standing for accidents caused not in public places but on the private property of the person injured); and fire (representing consequential damage).

Achan (fl. 13th cent. BCE) Israelite. He took some of the consecrated spoil when Jericho was captured, and because of this sacrilege the Israelites were unable to capture Ai. Achan and his family were put to death as a punishment for his sin (Joshua 7).

Achron, Joseph (1886–1943) American composer of Lithuanian origin. He was a founder of the Society for Hebrew Folk Music in St Petersburg. He composed *Hebrew Melody* (1911), as well as violin concertos and string quartets inspired by Jewish motifs.

Acosta, Uriel (1585–1640) Spanish heretic. He lived first in Spain and later in Amsterdam and Hamburg. He wrote against the Jewish faith and was excommunicated. Before his death he published a brief autobiography, *Exemplar humane vitae*.

Acrostic Literary device, in which successive verses of a text begin with the letters of the alphabet. Acrostics are found in the Bible (Psalm 34 and 37; Proverbs 31:10–31; Lamentations 1–4) and in many medieval liturgical compositions. They have mystical significance in Kabbalistic literature.

Acsady, Ignac (1845–1906) Hungarian historian and writer. He fought for equal rights for Hungarian Jews. In

1883 he published *Jewish and Non-Jewish Hungarians after the Emancipation.*

Adafina Foods eaten by Jews on the Sabbath in medieval Spain. The Inquisition regarded the eating of special foods on the Sabbath as a sign of loyalty to Judaism.

Adam First man. He was made in the image of God on the sixth day of creation. Eve was created out of one of his ribs. They were permitted to eat from all the trees in the Garden of Eden except the tree of the knowledge of good and evil. When they disobeyed God, they were expelled from the Garden. Adam was condemned to a life of work. Eve was to suffer the pain of childbirth (Genesis 1–3).

Adam and Eve, Book of the Life of Pseudepigraphic work. It relates the lives of Adam and Eve after their expulsion from the Garden of Eden, as well as their repentance, death and resurrection.

Adam Kadmon Primordial man. In Kabbalistic literature he is the spiritual prototype of man. According to the *Zohar*, he is a manifestation of the sephirot. In Lurianic Kabbalah he is the mediator between the En Soph and the sephirot.

Adar 12th month of the Jewish year.

Addir bi-melukhah ('Mighty in kingship') Opening words of an acrostic poem, based on Genesis Rabbah. It was introduced into the Passover Haggadah by Ashkenazic Jews in the Middle Ages.

Addir Hu ('Mighty is he') Opening words of an acrostic prayer for the rebuilding of the Temple. It was introduced into the Passover Haggadah by Ashkenazic Jews in the Middle Ages.

Additional Service Extra service for Sabbath and festivals. It is usually recited after the Torah and Haftarah readings. It corresponds to the additional sacrifices that were made in the Temple on Sabbaths and festivals.

Additional Soul Belief that an additional soul is given for the Sabbath. This notion is found in the *Talmud* and Kabbalistic sources. The use of spices in the Havdalah service is probably connected with the need to revive the original soul after the departure of the additional soul.

Adler, Alfred (1870–1937) Austrian psychiatrist. Born in Vienna, he studied medicine and opened a practice there. After meeting Sigmund Freud, he became a member of his inner circle. Later he disagreed with Freud about the role of sexual factors in neurosis and developed a psychology based on the role of the environment and society.

Adler, Cyrus (1863–1940) American scholar. He was president of the Jewish Theological Seminary and Dropsie College. He served as editor of the *Jewish Quarterly Review*. His publications include *Lectures, Selected Papers, Addresses* and *I have Considered the Days.*

Adler, Elkan Nathan (1861–1946) English bibliophile. His library contained some 4,500 Hebrew manuscripts. They are summarised in the *Catalogue of Hebrew Manuscripts in the Collection of E. N. Adler.*

Adler, Felix (1851–1933) American philosopher and educator. He founded the Society for Ethical Culture in 1867 and in 1902 was appointed Professor of Social Ethics at Columbia University. He viewed ethical culture as a way of applying morality to modern life. An elaboration of his philosophy is contained in *An Ethical Philosophy of Life.*

Adler, Hermann (1839–1911) English rabbi. He was principle of Jews College. In 1891 he was elected chief rabbi. A selection of his sermons were published in *Anglo-Jewish Memories.*

Adler, Jacob (1855–1926) American actor of Russian origin He began his acting career in Russia. In 1888 he went to the US where he became the most important actor on the Yiddish stage.

Adler, Nathan ben Simeon (1741–1800) German pietist. He founded a yeshivah in Frankfurt am Main. He conducted services in his home using Isaac Luria's prayer book. A ban was imposed on these prayer meetings under threat of excommunication.

Adler, Nathan Marcus (1803–1890) English rabbi. Appointed chief rabbi in 1844, he modernised the British rabbinate and paved the way for the establishment of Jews College in 1855 and the United Synagogue in 1870. He wrote a commentary on *Targum Onkelos.*

Adler, Samuel (1809–1891) American Reform rabbi of German origin. He was born in Worms and settled in the US in 1857. An early European reformer, he became rabbi of Temple Emanuel in New York in 1857.

Adler, Samuel H. (b.1928) American composer and educator of German origin. Born in Mannheim, he moved to the US in 1939. He was music director at Temple Immanuel in Dallas (1953–66), then became Professor of Composition at the Eastman School of Music in Rochester, New York. He composed cantatas dealing with Jewish themes, as well as synagogue services.

Adler, Victor (1852–1918) Austrian politician. He was born in Prague. Although he qualified as a physician he devoted his life to the cause of the working class. He was a member of the Austrian Parliament from 1905 to 1918. He converted to Christianity and opposed the idea of Jewish nationhood.

Adloyada Purim festival. It is derived from the saying in the *Talmud* that one should revel on Purim until one no longer knows ('ad de-lo yada') the difference between the phrases 'Blessed be Mordecai' and 'Cursed be Haman'.

Ad meah (ve-esrim) shanah ('[may you live] to a hundred (and twenty)') Expression of good wishes on a birthday, especially that of an elderly person.

Admor Title by which Ḥasidic rabbis are known. It is an abbreviation of 'Adonenu, morenu, ve-rabbenu' ('Our lord, teacher, and master').

Adonijah (fl. 10th cent. BCE) Son of David. When David was dying Adonijah attempted to prevent Solomon from becoming king. But under the influence of Nathan the prophet, David decreed that Solomon should reign after him. When Adonijah desired to marry David's concubine, Abishag, Solomon regarded this as an act of rebellion and had him executed (I Kings 1–2).

Adon Olam ('Lord of the world') Opening words of a liturgical hymn, extolling the unity of God and expressing trust in his providence. It has been attributed to Solomon ibn Gabirol.

Adonai Name of God. When the Tetragrammaton appears in Scripture, it is read out loud either as 'Adonai' or as 'Ha-Shem'.

Adoption The assumption of a parental relationship by one individual to another when the two are not natural parent and child. Although it is not a legal institution in Judaism, Jewish law provides for the child: a guardian is appointed with authority to care for a child's welfare and property.

Adorno, Theodor Wiesengrund (1903–1969) German philosopher and sociologist. He taught at the University of Frankfurt in 1931 and later lived in the US. In 1949 he returned to Germany, where he was Director of the Institute for Social Research in Frankfurt and Professor of Sociology and Philosophy at the university. In his later works he discussed the nature of modern antisemitism.

Adoshem   Name of God. Derived from 'Adonai' (Lord) and 'Ha-Shem' (the name). It is used in liturgical contexts to avoid the speaking of God's name.

Adret [Abraham], Solomon ben [Ibn Adret, Solomon ben Abraham; Rashba] (1235–1310)   Spanish scholar. He studied under Naḥmanides and was later the leader of Spanish Jewry. His legal decisions were viewed as authoritative because of his stature as a scholar; they constitute a primary source of information about Jews of the period. He defended Judaism from Christian and Muslim detractors. He also disputed the messianic claims of Abraham ben Samuel Abulafia.

Adultery   In Jewish law, sexual intercourse between a married woman and a man other than her husband. It is prohibited in the Decalogue (Exodus 20:14; Deuteronomy 5:18). It is punishable by death (Leviticus 20:10); Deuteronomy 22:22). A special ritual is prescribed to determine whether a woman suspected of adultery is guilty (Numbers 5:12–31).

Aelia Capitolina   Name given by the Romans to Jerusalem when they rebuilt it after the revolt led by Bar Kochba in 135.

Afikomen [aphikoman]   Part of the middle mazzah. During the Passover seder, the leader breaks the middle mazzah into two. The larger part is the afikomen which is a symbolic reminder of the destruction of the Temple.

Afterlife   The Jewish belief in the hereafter has undergone considerable development from biblical times. According to Scripture, the dead were thought to live in Sheol, a shadowy place under the earth. During the Second Temple period, the Pharisees taught that with the advent of the Messiah the dead would be resurrected and

there would be eternal reward for the righteous and everlasting punishment for the wicked. The medieval Jewish philosopher Maimonides maintained that the belief in the resurrection of the dead was a fundamental tenet of the Jewish faith. In modern times the notion of bodily resurrection remains a belief for the Orthodox, even though most now reject the idea of everlasting punishment.

Afternoon service [Minḥah]   A substitute for the Temple afternoon sacrifice. The service includes the Ashrei, Amidah and Taḥanun prayers and the Alenu. Traditionally, the service dates back to the time of the patriarchs. In modern times the maariv (evening service) is recited immediately afterwards.

Agam, Yaacov (b.1928)   Israeli painter and sculptor. He was born in Rishon le Zion. He was the first to introduce geometrical abstraction into Israeli art. From the early 1950s he produced experimental works involving techniques and concepts of his own invention, such as 'simultaneous writing' in which superimposed words suggest multiple ideas. In later works he used electrical motors to produce movement and change of composition, as well as light and sound effects. Some of his work contains traditional Jewish symbols.

Aggadah   Rabbinic teaching. It is an amplification of biblical narrative, history, ethics, and prophecy, and is found in midrashic literature and scattered throughout the Palestinian and Babylonian *Talmuds*. Unlike the halakhah, it is not authoritative. It contains parables, allegories, prayers, laments, polemics, stories, homilies, theology, ethics and letter symbolism.

Aggadat Bereshit   Midrash on Genesis, based on other midrashim, particularly the Tanḥuma. It dates from around the 12th century.

Aggadat Ester   Midrash on the Book of Esther. It is based on talmudic and midrashic sources. Its origin is probably Yemenite and originated not earlier than the 13th century.

Aggadat Mashiaḥ Collection of homilies describing the messianic era. Composed of early legends, it was edited by Tobiah ben Eliezer.

Agla Kabbalistic word made up of the initials of the Hebrew phrase 'Atta gibbor el-olam adonai' (Thou art mighty forever, O Lord).

Agnon, Shemuel Yosef (1888–1970) Galician Hebrew writer. He settled in Palestine and published novels and short stories dealing with life in Galicia and Palestine. Regarded as the greatest epic writer of modern Hebrew literature, he was awarded the Nobel Prize.

Agrarian laws A number of Biblical laws concerning agriculture are developed in the *Talmud*.

Agriculture After the destruction of the Second Temple, Jewish farmers lived in Palestine, Babylonia, Egypt, Arabia, Ethiopia and various European countries. Modern Jewish farming originated in Russia at the beginning of the 19th century. In Israel agricultural settlements began in 1855 and continued to develop throughout the 19th and 20th centuries.

Agron [Agronsky], Gershon (1894–1959) Jerusalem editor and mayor, of Ukrainian origin. His family went to the US when he was 13. He settled in Palestine during World War I. In 1932 he became the founder and editor of the *Palestine Post.* In 1949 he organised and directed the Israel Government Information Services, and later became mayor of Jerusalem.

Aguilar, Diego d' [Pereira, Moses Lopez] (1699–1759) Marrano financier. Born in Portugal, he settled in Vienna. He used his influence at court to assist Jews, preventing their expulsion from Moravia in 1742 and from

Prague in 1744. When the Spanish Inquisition asked for his extradition, he went to London where he was active in the Sephardic community.

Aguilar, Grace (1816–1847) English writer. She was born in London. In 1842 she published *The Spirit of Judaism: In Defence of her Faith and its Professors.* Her *Records of Israel: Two Tales* and *Women of Israel* presented idealised pictures of Jewish life in Spain and women in the Bible. Her own beliefs are contained in *The Jewish Faith, its Spiritual Consolation, Moral Guidance and Immortal Hope.* She also published novels dealing with Jewish life.

Agunah A woman who has been deserted by her husband or whose husband has disappeared. If a married woman has neither a certificate of divorce (get) nor proof of her husband's death, she cannot remarry for fear of contracting an adulterous relationship. Various solutions have been proposed to alleviate the problems of the agunah, but none has proved satisfactory.

Agus, Jacob (1911–1986) American rabbi and philosopher of Polish origin. He was a rabbi in Cambridge, Massachusetts, Chicago and Dayton, Ohio. Later he became Professor of Religion at Temple University and was a member of the faculty of the Reconstructionist Rabbinical Academy. He also served as rabbi of Beth El Synagogue in Baltimore.

Ahab (fl. 9th cent. BCE) King of Israel (874–852 BCE). He was reproved by Elijah for seizing Naboth's vineyard. When his wife, Jezebel, introduced the worship of Baal into Israel, a struggle took place between Elijah and the prophets of Baal. Ahab was victorious over Ben-Hadad of Damascus and later formed an alliance with him against the Assyrians (I Kings 16:29–22:40).

Aḥad ha-Am [Ginsburg, Asher] (1856–1927) Ukrainian Hebrew essayist. Born in Ukraine, he lived in Odessa and Tel Aviv. He advocated spiritual Zionism, which he believed would lead to the founding of a national spiritual centre. His writings include six volumes of collected essays.

Aḥa of Shabḥa (650–752) Babylonian scholar. When he failed to be appointed gaon of the academy at Pumbedita, he moved to Palestine. His *Book of Questions* contains lectures in Aramaic on weekly portions of the Torah.

Aḥaronim Later rabbinic authorities.

Ahavah rabbah ('Great love') Opening words of the prayer preceding the Shema in the morning service of the Ashkenazi ritual. In the Sephardi ritual the opening words of the prayer are 'Ahavat olam' ('Everlasting love'). This difference is based on a dispute between Rav and Samuel.

Ahaz (fl. 8th cent. BCE). King of Judah (743–727 BCE). When he introduced Assyrian cults into the Temple worship, he was criticised for doing evil in the eyes of the Lord (II Kings 16:3–4).

Ahaziah (i) (fl. 9th cent. BCE) King of Israel (853–852 BCE). He was influenced by his mother, Jezebel, who introduced the cult of Baal into Israel. He was injured in a fall from an upper chamber in his palace and asked for an oracle from Baal-Zebub. Elijah reproved him and prophesied his death (II Kings 1:2–17).

Ahaziah (ii) (fl. 9th cent. BCE) King of Judah (842–841 BCE). He and Jehoram, King of Israel, went to war against Hazael, King of Aram (II Kings 8:28–9; II Chronicles 22:5–60). When Jehoram was injured in battle, Ahaziah visited him in Jezreel. Both kings were assassinated by Jehu (II Kings 9:27–28; II Chronicles 22:9).

Aḥdut ha-Avodah Israel Socialist Party. It was formed in 1919. After a number of alliances contracted with other socialist groups, in 1968 it finally merged with Mapai and Rafi to form the Israel Labour Party.

Ahijah (fl. 11th cent. BCE) Chief priest at Shiloh during Saul's reign.

Ahimelech (fl. 11th cent. BCE) Israelite, priest of Nob. When David escaped from Saul, Ahimelech gave him bread and the sword of Goliath which was kept in the Temple. Saul put him to death (I Samuel 21–2).

Ahithopel (fl. 11th–10th cent. BCE) Adviser to David. He joined Absalom in his unsuccessful revolt against David (II Samuel 15–17).

Aizman, David (1869–1922) Russian writer. He wrote about the Jewish poor and about revolutionary-minded Jewish intellectuals. An eight-volume edition of his work appeared in Russian between 1911 and 1919

Akdamut Aramaic acrostic poem. It was written by Meir ben Isaac of Worms in the 11th century. It is recited by Ashkenazi Jews in the synagogue before the Torah reading on Shavuot.

Akedah ('binding') Word used of Abraham's binding and intended sacrifice of Isaac (Genesis 22:1–19). According to rabbinic literature, akedah is a symbol of self-sacrifice in obedience to God. This passage from Genesis is read in the synagogue on the first day of Rosh Ha-Shanah.

Akiva (50–135) Palestinian scholar, patriot, and martyr. He developed a method of biblical exegesis, systematised the Oral Law, and established an academy at Bene Berak. He believed that Simeon Bar Kochba was the Messiah. He was imprisoned by the Romans for teaching Torah and was tortured to death.

Akiva, Alphabet of Midrash attributed to Akiva. It is based on the letters of the Hebrew alphabet.

Akkum   Worshipper of stars and planets. The word was originally applied to Chaldean star worshippers, but was later used to refer to all idolators and forms of idolatry.

Alav ha-shalom ('Peace be on him')   Phrase uttered when mentioning a deceased person.

Albalag, Isaac (fl. 13th cent.)   Spanish translator and philosopher. He translated into Hebrew Al-Ghazzali's *Tendencies of the Philosophers*. He believed that there are two sources of knowledge: philosophical thought and prophetic intuition.

Albeck, Ḥanokh (1890–1972)   German talmudist. He lectured on *Talmud* in Germany and later became Professor of *Talmud* at the Hebrew University His work covers almost all areas of talmudic research.

Albo, Joseph (fl. 15th cent.)   Spanish philosopher. He was a pupil of Ḥasdai Crescas and participated in the Disputation of Tortosa (1413–14). His *Book of Dogmas* reduces the Jewish faith to three central principles: God's existence, divine revelation, and reward and punishment.

Alchemy   The practice of chemistry with the aim of transmuting metals into gold. It was ascribed to Jews in ancient times. The *Zohar* contains hints of it in its views on metals. Jewish mysticism contributed the use of numerical and letter combinations to alchemical studies.

Alenu ('It is our duty')   Opening words of a prayer proclaiming God's sovereignty and unity. It is ascribed to Rav. In the Middle Ages it was censored by Christians, who believed it contained an implied insult to Jesus. It is recited at the conclusion of the synagogue service.

Aleph   First letter of the Hebrew alphabet. Its numerical value is 1.

Aleph-baiz   The Hebrew alphabet.

Alexander (i) (80–49 BCE)   Son of Aristobulus II, King of Judea. He was taken captive with his father by the Romans in 63 BCE. He later organised unsuccessful resistance in Judea.

Alexander (ii) (35–7 BCE)   Son of Herod the Great. He and his brother Aristobulus were accused of plotting to kill their father. They were killed by strangulation.

Alexander, Haim (1915–2012)   Israeli composer and pianist. He was born in Berlin but emigrated to Palestine in 1936. He taught at the Academy of Music in Jerusalem. In addition to composing choral, chamber and orchestral work, he made a series of arrangements of traditional Jewish melodies.

Alexander Lysimachus (fl. 1st cent.)   Alexandrian official. He was the brother of Philo. He served in the Roman fiscal administration in Egypt. A man of great wealth, he made a gift to the Temple so that its gates could be plated with gold and silver.

Alexander Yannai (fl. 2nd–1st cent. BCE)   King of Judea and high priest (103–76 BCE). He added the coastal region to his kingdom. During his reign the Pharisees rebelled against him for violating Pharisaic law concerning Temple practice. A massacre took place and many leading Pharisees went into exile.

Alexandra (i) (fl. 1st cent. BCE)   Daughter of Aristobulus II, King of Judea. She married Philippion, son of Ptolemy of Chalcis. Ptolemy had his son killed and married her.

Alexandra (ii) (d.28 BCE)   Daughter of Hyrcanus II. When her son Aristobulus was drowned, she accused Herod of murder. Herod had her executed after she attempted to seize power.

Alfasi, David [David ben Abraham Alfasi] (fl. 10th cent.)   Karaite grammarian and commentator. Originally from Fez, he settled in Palestine. He composed a Hebrew–Arabic lexicon of the Bible.

Alfasi, Isaac ben Jacob (1013–1103) Talmudic scholar. Known as Rif, he lived and taught in Fez, North Africa. Late in his life, he became the victim of slander and was compelled to escape to Spain. In Africa, as well as in Spain, he attracted a wide circle of followers and composed important responsa.

Alfayyumi, Jacob (fl. 12th cent.) Leader of the Yemenite Jewish community to whom Maimonides addressed his *Letter to the Yemen* in 1172.

Alfonsi, Petrus [Sephardi, Moses] (1062–1110) Spanish writer and translator. He converted to Christianity and wrote a polemic against Judaism in the form of a dialogue. His collection of pious anecdotes for preachers introduced oriental tales to European readers.

Al ha-nissim ('For all the miracles') Opening words of a thanksgiving prayer recited in the Amidah and Grace after Meals during Ḥannukah and Purim.

Al-Ḥarizi, Judah [Taḥkemoni] (1170–1235) Spanish Hebrew poet and translator. He travelled widely through Mediterranean countries. His *Taḥkemoni* consists of 50 narratives in rhymed prose. It throws light on the culture of the period and describes the scholars and leaders he met on his travels. He translated Maimonides *Guide for the Perplexed* from Arabic and Hebrew.

Al ḥet ('For the sin') Opening words of a confession of sins, recited on the Day of Atonement.

Alimony Payment made to a divorced woman by her former husband. Although not a biblical ordinance, attempts were made in the rabbinic period to ensure the protection of

divorced women. The ketubbah (marriage settlement) served as the basis of this remedy by providing for payment of a fixed sum from the husband's estate in the case of divorce.

Aliyah (i) The calling up of a member of the congregation to read the Torah in the synagogue. Originally each person called up read a section of the weekly portion. Later a special reader was appointed for this purpose. Those who are called up read blessings instead.

Aliyah (ii) ('immigration') Term used specifically of the immigration of the Jews to Israel. Three main waves took place: the first from 1882 to 1903; the second from 1904 to 1914; and the third from 1918 to 1923.

Aljama (Arabic 'the gathering') Jewish community, specifically the self-governing Jewish communities in medieval Spain. It also denotes the Jewish quarter of a city or town.

Alkabetz, Solomon ben Moses (1505–1584) Palestinian Kabbalist and poet. Born in Salonica, he lived in Adrianople and Safed. He wrote on biblical and Kabbalistic subjects. His Sabbath hymn 'Lekhah dodi' ('Come, my beloved') is recited on Friday evenings.

Alkalai, Abraham ben Samuel (?1750–1811) Bulgarian codifier. He was the head of a yeshivah in Dupnitsa and later settled in Safed. His *Zekhor le-Avraham* contains the laws of the Shulḥan Arukh arranged alphabetically. He also wrote a collection of response, *Ḥesed le-Avraham.*

Alkalai, Isaac ben Abraham Alcalay (1881–1978) Yugoslav rabbi. He was chief rabbi of Yugoslavia, and the country's first Jewish senator. When the Germans invaded, he escaped to the US, where he became chief rabbi of the Sephardi congregations.

Alkalai, Judah ben Solomon Ḥai (1798–1878) Bosnian Zionist. He was born in Sarajevo. As rabbi to the Sephardi congregations in Semlin, near Belgrade, he encouraged Jewish settlement in Palestine. In 1874 he settled in Jerusalem. His writings supported a return to Israel on religious grounds.

Alkan, Charles Henri-Valentin (1813–88) French pianist and composer. Born in Paris, he studied at the Paris Conservatoire. A friend of Chopin, George Sand and Liszt, he became a recluse, devoting himself to religious studies and compositions. His works include: *Storm at Sea, The Dying Man* and *Grand Sonate.*

Alliance Israélite Universelle International Jewish organisation. It was founded in 1860 in Paris. Its aims were to defend Jewish civil and religious liberties, provide educational facilities and protect Jews from attack.

Allegory A narrative to be understood symbolically. Allegories are found in the Bible, biblical commentaries and rabbinic texts. Philo interpreted the Bible allegorically, as did many medieval philosophers such as Maimonides and Solomon ibn Gabirol. The kabbalists also employed allegorical interpretations of scripture.

Allen, Woody (b.1935) American film director and actor. He was born in Brooklyn. From the first his films used Jewish humour. Later he explored a range of American Jewish issues, including the role of the Jew in American life and Jewish paranoia and self-hatred.

Allon, Gedaliah (1902–50) Russian historian. Born in Kobin, he emigrated to Palestine in 1924. He taught *Talmud* and Jewish history at the Hebrew University. His writings include *History of the Jews in Palestine in the Period of the Mishnah and the Talmud.*

Allon, Yigal (1918–1980) Israeli statesman and soldier. He was born at Kefar Tavor in Lower Galilee. He served in the Haganah and was a founder and commander of the Palmaḥ. In 1954 he was elected to the Knesset and served as Minister of Labour, 1981–8. After 1969 he was appointed Deputy Prime Minister. His writings include *Curtain of Sand* and *Palmaḥ Campaigns.*

Allon-bachuth ('Oak of weeping') Sacred tree near Bethel. Rebekah's nurse Deborah was buried under it (Genesis 35:8).

Alman, Samuel (1877–1947) Russian liturgical composer. Born in Sobolevka, Podolia, he studied in Odessa and Kishinev, and later settled in London and served as the choirmaster of London synagogues and Jewish choral groups. He wrote musical works for cantor, choir, chorus and organ.

Almanazi, Joseph (1801–60) Italian Hebrew poet and bibliophile. He was born in Padua. He wrote poems of a moralistic character, and collected thousands of Hebrew manuscripts.

Almemar [bimah, tebah] Platform in the synagogue on which the reading desk stands. The Torah is read here. It is called 'bimah' in Ashkenazi congregations and 'tebah' in Sephardi congregations.

Almohades Muslim sectarians. They arose in north Africa in the 12th century and conquered southern Spain between 1149 and 1174. They attempted to convert non-Muslims. African Jews fled to Egypt and Palestine. Spanish Jews emigrated to Christian Spain and southern France.

Almosnino, Moses (1515–1580)   Greek scholar. He was born in Salonica. He was part of a delegation sent to Sultan Selim II to obtain the privileges and exemptions granted by Suleiman the Magnificent to the Salonican Jewish community. His writings include a description of Constantinople.

Al-Mukammas, David ben Merwan [David ibn Merwan al-Mukammas] (fl. c.900)   Iraqi philosopher. He translated Christian commentaries on Genesis and Ecclesiastes and wrote on different religions and sects. His *Twenty Treatises* contain most of his theological and philosophical work. He was the first to introduce the methods of Arabic philosophy into the Jewish world.

Alnakawa, Israel ben Joseph (d. 1391)   Spanish writer. He composed an ethical treatise, *Candlestick of Light.* When the Toledans attacked the Jewish community of the city, he was dragged through the streets. He subsequently killed himself.

Aloni, Nissim (1926–1998)   Israeli playwright and short-story writer. He was born in Tel Aviv. He was the first playwright to eschew the social realism characteristic of Israeli drama in the early 1950s. In 1963 he established his own theatre in Tel Aviv. His plays synthesise Israeli consciousness and European cultural sources. The Sephardi working-class quarter in Tel Aviv is the setting for his short stories.

Alphabet (Hebrew 'aleph-bet')   The Hebrew alphabet consists of 22 consonants, derived from the Canaanite alphabet. Until the first exile (6th cent. BCE), the alphabet was identical to that of the Phoenicians, but thereafter it was gradually replaced by letter forms based on an Eastern Aramaic script. The square script now used developed during the first two centuries CE. Originally vowel sounds were not indicated by Hebrew script, but in time certain letters came to serve as vowel indicators (yod, vav, he). In the 7th to 9th centuries various systems were developed for indicating all vowels by means of new signs placed above and below the consonants. However, no vowel signs are given in the Torah scroll. Each letter in the Hebrew alphabet has a corresponding numerical value and combinations of letters are used in the Hebrew numbering system.

Alroy, David [Ben Solomon, Menahem] (fl. 12th cent.)   Leader of the movement in Kurdistan. He was proclaimed Messiah among the Jews living in the mountains of the north-east Caucasus. He was subsequently murdered. He is the subject of *The Wonderous Tale of David Alroy* by Benjamin Disraeli.

Alshekh, Moses ben Hayyim (fl. 16th cent.)   Palestinian biblical commentator and talmudist. Born in Adrianople, he settled in Safed. He was a halkhic authority, a teacher in talmudic academies, a preacher and a member of the rabbinical court of Joseph Caro. He reworked his sermons into commentaries on most of the books of the Bible.

Altar   In Jewish practice, a place of sacrifice. In the desert a bronze altar for burnt offerings and a gold altar for incense were located in the Tabernacle. Later they stood in Solomon's Temple.

Alter, Abraham Mordecai, of Gur (1864–1948)   Polish leader of Augudat Israel. He urged his followers to participate in building Palestine, where he settled after World War II.

Alter, Isaac Meir, of Gur (1799–1866)   Founder of a dynasty of Hasidic rabbis in Gur near Warsaw. He published numerous halakhic works.

Alter, Robert (b.1935)   American scholar. Born in New York, he became Professor of Hebrew and Comparative Literature at the University of California, Berkeley. He has written on Hebrew and Jewish literature and the literary form and content of the Bible.

Alter kocker (Yiddish)   A crotchety, ineffectual old man.

Alterman, Nathan (1910–1970)   Israeli Hebrew poet. Born in Warsaw, he settled in Tel Aviv in 1925. Influenced by French and Russian symbolists, he became the leading imagist poet of his generation. He also wrote satirical poetry related to political events. His collected works are contained in four volumes, *Kol Shirei Alterman*.

Al tikre ('Do not read')   Talmudic exegetical device, written before a biblical verse, which alters its meaning.

Altman, Nathan (1889–1970)   Ukrainian painter, sculptor, and stage designer. He settled in St Petersburg and became head of the city's section of the Department of Fine Arts. From 1918 to 1922 he developed a constructionist style. After 1929 he lived in France, but later returned to the USSR. His work was influenced by Jewish themes and includes paintings, sculptures, graphic art, and stage designs.

Altmann, Alexander (1906–1988)   Rabbi and scholar of Hungarian origin. He served as rabbi in Berlin and taught philosophy at the Rabbinical Seminary there. In 1938 he settled in Manchester, England, where he founded the Institute of Jewish Studies. In 1959 he became Professor of Jewish philosophy at Brandeis University. He wrote studies on Jewish philosophy and mysticism.

Altschuler, David (fl. 18th cent.)   Galician biblical exegete. He planned a commentary on the Prophets and Hagiographa based on the work of earlier commentators. His son Jahiel Hillel Altschuler continued the work. His commentary on Psalms, Proverbs, and Job was published in 1753–1754.

Alvarez, Alfred (b.1929)   British author. Born in London, his writings include: *The Shaping Spirit, The School of Donne, Under Pressure, Beyond All This Fiddle, Beckett, The Savage God, Life after Marriage, The Biggest Game in Town, Offshore, Feeding the Rat, Rain Forest, Night, Lost, Apparition, Day of Atonement* and *The New Poetry*.

Amasa (fl. 11th–10th cent. BCE)   Israelite commander. He led Absalom's army in the unsuccessful rebellion against David. After the suppression of this uprising, David appointed Amasa his general. He was later killed by Joab (II Samuel 17–20).

Amatus Lusitanus (1511–1568)   Portuguese physician. Born in Portugal of Marrano parents, he went to Antwerp, where he published a book on medicinal botany, *Index dioscorides*. He later taught medicine at the University of Ferrara and treated Pope Julius III. His major work was *Centuriae curationum*.

Amaziah (fl. 8th cent. BCE)   King of Judah (796–780). He put to death the assassins who murdered his father Joash. He waged war against Edom and the Kingdom of Israel (II Kings 14; II Chronicles 25).

Amen ('true', 'truly')   Expression of affirmation made as part of blessings and prayers.

Am ha-aratz (sing. 'people of the land')   Term used in the Bible to refer to the masses of the Jewish people. In talmudic times it was applied to common people who did not observe rabbinic regulations and eventually came to mean an ignorant person.

Amichai, Yehuda (1924–2000)   Israeli poet and novelist. Born in Germany, he settled in Palestine in 1936. His poetry reflects the changes in the Hebrew language during World War II and the Israeli War of Independence. He introduced airplanes, tanks, fuel trucks, and administrative contracts into Hebrew poetry.

Amidah ('Standing')   The prayer is also known as the Eighteen Benedictions.

Amiel, Moses Avigdor (1893–1946)
Israeli rabbi and writer. After serving
as a rabbi in Poland and Antwerp, he
became chief rabbi of Tel Aviv in 1936.
He established the first modern high
school yeshivah in Tel Aviv.

Amittai (fl. c.800) Italian Hebrew
liturgical poet. Several piyyutim, signed
Amittai, are credited to him, including
the hymn 'Lord I remember thee and
am sore amazed'. This is included in the
concluding service for the Day of Atonement according to the Ashkenazi rite.

**Amittai ben Shephatiah (fl. 9th
cent.)** Italian Hebrew liturgical poet.
Several of his poems were incorporated
into the Italian and Ashkenazi liturgies.
His poems (more than 30 of which have
been published) contain references to
contemporary Jewish persecutions and
Jewish–Christian disputations.

**Ammi bar Nathan (fl. late 3rd
cent.)** Palestinian amora. He and
Assi headed the yeshivah in Tiberias.
Together with Ḥiyya bar Abba, he acted
as an education inspector in Palestine
with authority to introduce reforms.

Amnon (fl. 11th–10th cent. BCE) Israelite, eldest son of David. He raped his
half-sister Tamar. Her brother Absalom had him killed for this offence (II
Samuel 13).

Amnon of Mainz (fl. 10th cent.) German martyr. After attempts by the Bishop
of Mainz to convert him, he asked for
three days to consider the matter. When
he failed to appear, he was brought by
force; his arms and legs were amputated;
salt was poured into his wounds. On
Rosh Ha-Shanah he was carried to the
synagogue, where he recited *U-Netannah
Tokeph* ('Let us declare the mighty
importance') and died.

Am Olam ('Eternal people') Organisation founded by Russian Jewish
youth after the pogroms in 1881. They
desired to emigrate to Palestine and the
US. Members of the group founded the
New Odessa colony in Oregon and two
colonies in South Dakota.

Amon (fl. 7th cent. BCE) King of
Judah (642–640 BCE). His transgressions were greater than those of his
father Manasseh (II Chronicles 33:23).
He was assassinated by members of his
court (II Kings 21:23).

Amora ('scholar') Term used specifically of Jewish scholars in Palestine
and Babylonia in the 3rd–6th centuries. The amoraim expounded the
Mishnah and interpreted Scripture.
Some were known for their expertise
in the halakhah. Others were known
for their aggadah. The teachings are
recorded in the *Talmud* and various
midrashim.

Amos (i) (fl. 8th cent. BCE) Israelite
prophet. He prophesied during the
reign of Jeroboam II. He was disturbed
by the corruption in the country resulting from the exploitation of the poor.
At Bethel he foretold the destruction of
Israel. Amaziah, priest of Bethel, told
him to return to Judah, but he insisted
on fulfilling his mission.

Amram (fl. 13th cent. BCE) Israelite,
the father of Moses, Aaron and Miriam
(Exodus 6:18, 20; Numbers 26:58–59).

Amram bar Sheshna (d. c.875) Babylonian gaon. He was gaon of Sura.
He wrote numerous responsa and the
oldest surviving order of prayer. His
Seder Rav Amram contains the text of
the prayers for the entire year, as well as
the laws and customs pertaining to the
different prayers.

Amulet (Hebrew 'kamia') A charm
carried about the person. In Jewish
practice amulets are worn as protection
against evil. They usually bear sacred
letters or symbols, often the names of
angels or demons written in geometric
patterns. They were frequently worn
in the talmudic and gaonic periods. Under
the influence of later kabbalah they took
the form of kabbalistic diagrams, biblical

verses, and letter combinations, inscribed on paper, parchment or metal.

Anagram Literary device consisting of a word or phrase formed by the transposition of the letters of another word or phrase. It is found in medieval Hebrew and kabbalistic writings, and was frequently applied to divine and angelic names on amulets.

Anan ben David (fl. 8th cent.) Babylonian biblical scholar, founder of the Karaites. When his younger brother was appointed exilarch, he founded his own sect which opposed the talmudic tradition. In his *Sepher ha-Mitzvot* he argued that the Bible is the sole basis of Judaism. He was strict in his application of biblical law.

Ananias (fl. 1st cent.) Israelite, high priest. Appointed by Herod of Chalcis, he was involved in the prosecution of Paul (Acts 24). He was killed by Jewish extremists at the outset of the rebellion against Rome in the late 60s.

Anatoli, Jacob ben Abba Mari (fl. 13th cent.) French translator and philosopher. Originally from Provence, he settled in Naples, where he was physician to Emperor Frederick II. He translated Arabic philosophical and astronomical works into Hebrew. His *Malmad ha-Talmidim* consists of popular sermons.

Anatomy Anatomical facts, metaphors and expressions are found in the Bible. Talmudic anatomy contains explanations of the normal and pathological structure of the body.

Anav, Benjamin ben Abraham (c.1215–c.1295) Italian scholar and poet. His poetry is concerned with historical events. He also wrote treatises on Jewish law, notes on Rashi's biblical commentary and a satire on rich Jewish families in Rome.

Anav, Jehiel ben Jekuthiel (fl. c.1250–1300) Roman copyist and author. His *Maalot ha-Middot* deals with ethical

conduct and is based on midrashic and talmudic sources. The only complete extant manuscript of the Jerusalem *Talmud* was copied by him in 1289. He also wrote a liturgical poem about the burning of a Rome synagogue in 1268.

Anenu ('Answer us') Prayer inserted on fast days in the Shema Kolenu blessing during the repetition of the Amidah in the morning and afternoon services.

Angel Divine messenger. In Scripture angels are generally beneficent. They convey God's messages and carry out his will. In post-biblical literature they act as independent beings. In the *Talmud* and midrash they are depicted as participating in human affairs. Medieval philosophers often identified them with the higher intelligences of Aristotle. In the *Zohar* they occupy the seven heavenly halls. In Jewish liturgy their praise of God (based on Isaiah 6:1–3) is included in the kedushah, piyyutim and seliḥot.

Angel of Death [Malakh ha-Mavet] Divine being who takes the soul from the body. In the Bible the power of death is occasionally delegated to a messenger. In rabbinic sources the Angel of Death is depicted as a destroyer of human beings and is personified as Satan or represented as the Evil Inclination.

Ani Maamin [I believe] Prayer in most Ashkenazi prayer books based on Maimonides' Thirteen Principles of the Faith. It is of unknown authorship and dates back to around the 15th century.

Anilewicz, Mordecai (1919–1943) Polish Zionist. He was born in Wyszków. He became an active member of Ha-Shomer ha-Tzair and was arrested by the Soviet authorities in 1939 for organising the emigration of Jews to Palestine. As commander of the Jewish Fighting Organisation, he led the uprising in the Warsaw Ghetto in April, 1943.

Animals, treatment of   Cruelty to animals is forbidden in Scripture (Deuteronomy 22:4). Slaughter for food is permitted but must be humanely carried out. Rabbinic legislation applies the principle of care for animals to a wide range of circumstances.

Aninut ('Mourning')   Status of a bereaved person during the period between the death and burial of a relative. The mourner is exempt from daily prayer and should not eat meat or drink wine.

Annointing   Annointing with oil was practised in Ancient Israel to consecrate kings, priests and sacred vessels. It was also performed on joyous occasions and feast days, as well as for medical purposes. The descendant of David who will redeem Israel is called the 'Messiah' ('anointed one').

An-Ski, S. [Rapoport, Solomon Seinwil]   (1863–1920)   Russian author. He was born in Belorussia and settled in Paris in 1894. In 1905 he returned to Russia and joined the Social Revolutionary Party. He composed the party's hymn (*Di Shvue*) and wrote folk legends, Ḥasidic tales and stories about Jewish poverty. His play *The Dibbuk* was translated into Hebrew by Ḥayyim Naḥman Bialik. His Yiddish works were published in 15 volumes.

Anthropomorphism   The conception or representation of God as having human physical form or psychological characteristics. It is frequently found in the Bible. Rabbinic aggadah uses anthropomorphic imagery, as does the mystical tract *Shiur Komah*. Many medieval Jewish philosphers argued against conceiving of God anthropomorphically.

Anti-Defamation League   American civil rights organisation. Founded in 1913 as part of B'nai B'rith, it fights anti-Semitism, fosters interfaith relations and encourages civil rights reforms.

Antigonus II (fl. 1st cent. BCE)   Israelite, last king of the Hasmoneans. When Pompey captured Jerusalem in 63 BCE, Antigonus was taken to Rome. In 40 BCE he captured Jerusalem, put to death Herod the Great's brother Phasael, and cut off Hyrcanus II's ears so he would be disqualified from the high priesthood. He then ruled as king and high priest. From 39 to 37 BCE Herod besieged his army in Judea and was eventually victorious. Antigonus was executed by the Romans.

Antigonus of Sokho (fl. early 2nd cent. BCE)   Palestinian sage. Only one of his statements has been preserved: 'Be not like servants who minister to their master in order to receive a reward, but be like the servants who minister to their master not in order to receive a reward; and let the fear of Heaven be upon you.' His pupils Zadok and Boethus interpreted it as a denial of the afterlife and founded the Sadducees and Boethusians.

Antin, Mary (1881–1949)   American author of Belorussian origin. Her autobiographical work *The Promised Land* contrasts her early life with her experiences in the US.

Antinomianism   Opposition to law. It was found in early Christianity, among the Sabbetaians, and in the Frankist movement. It is also a characteristic of Reform Judaism.

Antiochus, Scroll of   Hebrew account of the revolt of the Hasmoneans. It was probably written in the 7th century. It is used in the Italian and Yemenite ritual for Ḥanukkah.

Antipater I (fl. 2nd cent. BCE)   Edomite administrator, governor of Idumea. He was a convert to Judaism. He served under Alexander Yannai and Salome Alexandra.

Antipater II (fl. 1st cent. BCE)   Edomite administrator, ruler of Judea (63–43 BCE). He supported Hyrcanus

II in his war against Aristobulus II. John Caesar made him financial administrator of Judea in 44 BCE. He appointed his sons to administrative positions.

Antipater III (1st cent.)   Son of Herod the Great. When Herod executed his other sons, Alexander and Aristobulus, Anipater was made Herod's heir. He was executed when his plan to murder Herod was revealed.

Anti-Semitism   Hatred of the Jewish people. The term was coined by Wilhelm Marr in 1879 to designate anti-Jewish campaigns in Europe. It became a general term to denote all forms of hostility towards Jews through the centuries.

Antokolski, Mark (1843–1902)   Russian sculptor. Born in Vilna, he created bas-reliefs dealing with Jewish subjects. Later he chose themes from Russian history. During waves of anti-Semitism prior to the pogroms of the 1880s, he was criticised by the Russian national press.

Anusim   Jews who were forced to convert to another faith. Instances of such forced conversion have occurred throughout Christian and Muslim history. Often the anusim attempted to preserve Jewish customs in secret and teach them to their children.

Apikoros (Greek 'Epicurean')   In Jewish usage, a heretic. The word is derived from the name of the Greek philosopher Epikouros (Epicurus), and refers to one who disobeys the commandments, derides the Torah and defames rabbis.

Apocalypse   Revelation of the end of days and final judgement – any book purporting to reveal the last things. Such revelation is found in Jewish writings from the 2nd century BCE to the 2nd century CE, represented by the Apocrypha and Pseudepigrapha. It deals with the mysteries of the heavens, secrets of world government, the function of angels and evil spirits, details of the end of the world, and the soul's existence in Heaven and Hell.

Apocrypha   Collection of non-canonical Jewish writings from the period of the Second Temple. It consists largely of historical and ethical works and contains I and II Esdras, Tobit, Judith, additions to Esther, the Wisdom of Solomon, Ecclesiasticus, Baruch with the Epistle of Jeremiah, The Song of the Three Holy Children, the History of Susanna, Bel and the Dragon, the Prayer of Manasseh, and I and II Maccabees.

Apologetics   Defensive argument or method of disputation. Judaic apologetics originated in response to pagan and Christian challenges Medieval apologetics defended the Jewish faith from external criticism, as well as from doubts arising from comparisons with other cultural traditions. It also attempted to demonstrate the virtues of the Jewish faith to gentiles.

Apostasy   The abandonment of one's religion or principles. In Jewish usage the term is applied to conversion from Judaism to another religion. Jewish law differentiates between forced and voluntary conversion. The apostate is referred to as 'mumar' (or 'meshummad'). He remains a Jew, and no ceremony is required if he returns to Judaism.

Appelfield, Aharon (b.1932)   Israeli writer. Born in Czernowitz, Bukovina, he settled in Palestine in 1947. His stories concern the Holocaust, which he often saw allegorically. They are collected in *Smoke, In the Fertile Valley, Frost upon the Land,* and *In the Wilderness.*

Aptowitzer, Avigdor (1871–1942) Galician rabbinical scholar. He taught *Talmud* at the Hebrew Teachers College in Vienna from 1919 until 1938, when he settled in Jerusalem. He published studies on various aspects of rabbinic literature and Jewish history.

Arakhin   Fifth tractate of the Mishnah. It deals with the valuations of persons, fields and objects vowed to the Sanctuary (Leviticus 27:2–29).

Arama, Isaac ben Moses [Isaac Arama] (1420–1494) Spanish rabbi, philosopher and preacher. As a rabbi of various Spanish communities, he delivered sermons on the principles of Judaism. He also engaged in public disputations with Christian scholars. After the Jews were expelled from Spain in 1492, he settled in Naples. His *Akedat Yitzḥak* is a philosophical commentary on the Pentateuch.

Aramaic Any of a group of Semitic languages, but specifically the northwestern branch of that family of languages. Aramaic is found in the Bible (Daniel 2:4–7:28; Ezra 4:8–6:18; 7:12–26; Jeremiah 10:11), the Palestinian and Babylonian *Talmud* and the *Zohar*. It became an international language from the period of the late Assyrian and Persian kingdoms (6th century BCE) and served as the vernacular language of Palestine for centuries. Biblical readings were translated into Aramaic in the synagogues.

Arazi, Yehuda (1907–54) Israeli Haganah leader. Born in Lódź, Poland, he emigrated to Palestine. In 1936 he organised the purchase of arms. After returning to Palestine, he worked with the Haganah. In 1947 he was sent to the United States to obtain arms for the yishuv.

Arba kosot The four cups of wine which are drunk at the Passover seder.

Arbaah Turim Code of Jewish law compiled by his Jacob ben Asher in the 14th century. The four-part structure of the work was adopted by the Shulḥan Arukh.

Arbitration The adjudication of a dispute by a third party. In biblical times arbitration was based on a system of courts. The *Talmud* provides for nominated arbitrators who choose a chairman. In the Middle Ages Jewish

tribunals acted as arbitrators. The Din Torah (decision by a rabbi or a group of rabbis) became the common method.

Archa (Latin 'chest') Chest in which financial documents are stored. The word was used for an official archive set up in England in 1194 for the recording of all transactions in which Jews were involved. The Exchequer of the Jews in Westminster coordinated these records.

Archisynagogos (Greek) Head of a synagogue in the Roman and Byzantine Empires. He arranged the service, administered the synagogue and supervised Jewish community affairs. Roman law exempted him from physical servitude to the state and state taxes.

Archives In the biblical period, laws, contracts and political documents were kept in the Temple. Groups of Jews in the diaspora often maintained records. and many medieval Jewish communities did so. After the Emancipation of the Jews in the 18th century few records were kept. In the 19th and 20th centuries Jewish organisations collected extensive documentation.

Archivolti, Samuel (1515–1611) Italian Hebrew grammarian and poet. From 1568 he lived in Padua, where he was secretary of the community, principal of a yeshivah and av bet din. His writings include a Hebrew grammar as well as poems and piyyutim. His poetry reflects the attitude of Jews to their Christian neighbours.

Ardon, Mordecai (1896–1992) Israeli painter. Born in Poland, he settled in Palestine in 1933 and became director of the Bezalel School of Arts and Crafts in 1940. From 1952 to 1962 he was artistic adviser to the Ministry of Education.

Arendt, Hannah (1906–1975) American political and social philosopher of German origin. Born in Hanover, she lived in Paris after Adolf Hitler came to power. In 1941 she escaped to the US. From 1963–1967 she taught at the New School for Social Research. Her writings include *The Origins of Totalitarianism, Rachel Varnhagen: the Life of a Jewess, Between Past and Future, On Revolution,* and *Eichmann in Jerusalem.*

Aristeas, Letter of Pseudepigraphic work. It was allegedly written by Aristeas to his brother Philocrates at the court of Ptolemy II Philadelphus. It describes the origin of the Septuagint and the virtues of the Jewish faith.

Aristobulus (c.35–7 BCE) Son of Herod the Great. He and his brother Alexander were accused of plotting to kill their faith. They were killed by strangulation.

Aristobulus I (fl. 2nd cent. BCE) King of Judah (104–103 BCE).Under the will of his father, John Hyrcanus I, he was to become high priest whereas his mother was to receive the throne. He put her in prison where she died, and also imprisoned his brothers except Antigonus, who he later put to death for treachery.

Aristobulus II (d.49 BCE) King of Judah (67–63 BCE). He usurped the throne of his brother Hyrcanus II in 67 BCE and civil war broke out. In 63 BCE both brothers urged their claims to the throne before Pompey. He ordered Aristobulus to surrender Jerusalem, but his supporters refused. Pompey besieged the city, captured the Temple and took him prisoner. When Julius Caesar came to power, Aristobulus was released and given troops to attack Pompey's men, but he was poisoned before he could embark on this campaign.

Aristobulus III (d.35 BCE) Hasmonean high priest. At the time he was due to become high priest, Herod the Great appointed Hananel in his place. Aristobulus' mother, Alexandra (a daughter of Hyrcanus II), asked Cleopatra to intercede for him with Herod. Hananel was subsequently dismissed and Aristobulus was appointed in his place. He was later drowned in the baths of Jericho by Herod's soldiers.

Ark   (Hebrew   'aron   kodesh,' 'heikhal')   Cabinet in the synagogue containing the Torah Scrolls. Among Ashkenazim it is called the 'aron' or 'aron kodesh'. The Sephardim refer to it as the 'heikhal'. In Israel it is placed on the wall of the synagogue that faces the Temple Mount. In other countries it faces Israel.

Ark of the Covenant   Chest in which the two Tablets of the Law were kept from the time of the Israelites' years in the wilderness. It is described in Exodus 25:10–22. Until the Temple was built, it was taken out from the Holy of Holies in times of national need. During the period of the first Temple it was never removed from the Holy of Holies. It is not mentioned among the vessels carried to Babylonia during the exile.

Arlosoroff, Ḥaim (1899–1933)   Ukrainian Zionist leader. He lived in Germany where he was active in the Ha-Poel ha-Tzair party. He emigrated to Palestine in 1924 and became an editor of the monthly journal of *Mapai*. In 1931 he was elected to the executive of the Jewish Agency for Israel and headed its political department in Jerusalem. In 1933 he aided the emigration of German Jews to Palestine. His writings were published in seven volumes.

Armilus   Enemy of the Messiah. He is mentioned in apocalyptic midrash from the 7th century onwards.

Arnshteyn, Mark (1879–1943)   Polish Yiddish playwright. He initially wrote Polish plays on Jewish themes for the Warsaw stage. From 1912 to 1924 he directed and wrote for the Yiddish theatre in Russia, Britain and North and South America. After returning to Poland, he translated and directed popular Yiddish plays. He founded and directed the New Chamber Theatre in the Warsaw Ghetto.

Arnstein, Fanny von (1757–1818) Viennese hostess. She was the daughter of the Berlin banker Daniel Itzig. She married Nathan Adam von Arnstein, court purveyor to Joseph II. During the Congress of Vienna, her balls and receptions attracted leading political figures.

Aron, Raymond (1905–83) French philosopher. Born into a Parisian family, he taught at various institutions before World War II. He wrote works on international relations, industrial society, Algerian independence and historical knowledge. His writings include *Peace and War, The Great Debate: Theories of Nuclear Strategy* and *Main Currents in Sociological Thought*.

Aronsohn, Zalman Yitzḥak [Anokhi, Z.I.; Onochi, Z.I] (1878–1947) Hebrew and Yiddish author of Russian origin. Born in Belorussia, he lived in Argentina and later settled in Palestine. His stories describe Jewish life in Eastern Europe. His collected works, *Between Heaven and Earth,* appeared in 1945.

Aronson, Solomon (1862–1935) Zionist leader and rabbi, of Ukrainian descent. He was chief rabbi of Kiev from 1906 to 1921. After the Russian Revolution, he sponsored the nationalist-religious Aḥdut Israeli movement. In 1921 he escaped to Berlin and later emigrated to Palestine, where he served as chief rabbi to the community in Tel Aviv and Jaffa. He took an active part in the Mizraḥi movement.

Arpachsad One of the sons of Shem (Genesis 10:22).

Arragel, Moses (fl. 15th cent.) Spanish scholar. Together with Arias de Enciena (of the Franciscan order in Toledo), he translated the Bible into Spanish (with a commentary) in 1433.

Arrow, Kenneth (1921–2017) US economist. Born in New York, he served as professor of economics at Stanford University and at Harvard. He was awarded the Nobel Prize in 1972.

Artapanus (fl. 2nd cent. BCE) Hellenistic Jewish writer. He wrote *On the Jews,* the purpose of which was to demonstrate that the foundations of Egyptian culture were laid by Abraham, Jacob, Joseph and Moses. Fragments of it are preserved in the writings of the Church Fathers.

Artificial insemination The principles regarding this practice are based on the *Talmud,* which discusses whether a high priest may marry a woman who, though a virgin, is pregnant; the marriage is permitted, the pregnancy having resulted accidentally from the woman's bathing in water carrying human semen. According to most responsa, regardless of the circumstances of the donor and recipient, adultery cannot be deemed to have taken place. The child is therefore legitimate. Nonetheless, Jewish religious authorities condemn the practice except in cases where the husband is the donor.

Artom, Isaac (1829–1900) Italian diplomat. Born into a distinguished Piedmontese family, he played an active role in the Risorgimento, the Italian struggle for independence from Austria. He was the first Jew to be elected to the Senate of the Italian kingdom.

Aryeh Leib Sarahs (c.1730–1791) Russian Ḥasidic tzaddik. He was the subject of various legends.

Asa (fl. 10th–9th cent. BCE) King of Judah (908–867 BCE). He restored the worship of the Lord in Jerusalem and built fortified cities in Judah (II Chronicles 14:5–6). There was warfare between the kingdoms of Israel and Judah during his reign.

Asaph ben Berechiah (fl. 11th–10th cent. BCE) Israelite musician. He was one of the Levites appointed by David to supervise music in the Sanctuary. Psalms 50 and 73–83 are attributed to him. The sons of Asaph were singers in the Temple during the reign of the kings of Judah (10th–6th centuries BCE) and at the time of Ezra and Nehemiah.

Asaph the Physician (fl. 6th cent.) Syrian physician. He is allegedly the author of a Hebrew book on medicine, *Sepher ha-Rophe*. This work is a source of information about Jewish medical ethics, and ancient Jewish remedies and medical terminology.

Asceticism Mortification of the flesh in pursuit of the spiritual. Apart from fasting for festivals, the practices of the Nazirites and Rechabites, and Ezekiel's abstinence, asceticism is not encouraged in the Bible. The rabbis considered it a sin. Nevertheless, it was occasionally adopted by Jewish individuals and groups, such as the Essenes and the Therapeutae.

Asch, Sholem (1880–1957) Polish Yiddish author. He lived in the US, France and Israel. In short stories, novels, and plays he depicted shtetl life in Eastern Euorpe, as well as the American Jewish experience. His later novels deal with the Jewish–Christian idea of messianic redemption.

Ascher, Saul (1767–1822) German philosopher. In his early writings he encouraged Jews to abandon their traditional lifestyle in order to obtain civic emancipation. In *Leviathan, oder Ueber Religion in Ruecksicht des Judentums* he argued that the uniqueness of Judaism arises from its philosophical world-view rather than the revelation of divine law.

Asenath (fl.? 19th–16th cent. BCE) Israelite woman, wife of Joseph. She was the mother of Manasseh and Ephraim (Genesis 41:50; 46:20).

Ashamnu ('We have trespassed') Opening word of the acrostic alphabetical confession of sin recited on the Day of Atonement.

Asher (fl.? 19th–16th cent. BCE) Israelite, son of Jacob. His mother was Zilpah, Leah's handmaid (Genesis 30:12). One of the tribes of Israel was named after him.

Asher ben Jehiel [Rosh] (1250–1327) German talmudist. He was a pupil of Meir of Rothenberg and became the spiritual leader of German Jewry. In 1303 he settled in Toledo. His responsa reflect the cultural life of Spanish and German Jews. In *Piske ha-Rosh* he recorded the decisions of earlier codifiers and commentators.

Ashi (335–427) Babylonian amora. He was head of the academy at Sura. With the help of other sages, he assembled and arranged in appropriate tractates the sayings of earlier amoraim. He is credited with the redaction of the Babylonian *Talmud*.

Ashkenazi, Bezalel (c.1520–1591) Palestinian talmudist. Born in Israel, he settled in Egypt, where he became chief of the Egyptian rabbis. After he excommunicated the nagid of Egyptian rabbis, this office was abolished. He later lived in Jerusalem, where he was chief rabbi. He travelled extensively to collect money for the community and encourage immigration. His *Shittah Mekubbetzet* is a collection of medieval talmudic commentaries.

Ashkenazi, Tzevi [Ḥakham Tzevi] (1660–1718) Moravian talmudist. He travelled widely and became head of the rabbinic academy in Altona, then in 1710 he settled in Amsterdam, where he was head of the Ashkenazim. After a controversy concerning Nehemiah Ḥayyon, a follower of Shabbetai Tzevi, he resigned his position in 1714. He later settled in Lwów. His *Ḥakham Tzevi*, after which he was known, is a collection of responsa.

Ashkenazim One of the two main divisions of Jewry in the diaspora. The word comes from the Hebrew 'Ashkenaz' (people of the north). Originally it was used of German Jewry, but later came to designate the Jews of northern France, Poland, Russia and Scandinavia. Most American Jews are Ashkenazim. The Ashkenazim are distinguished from the Sephardim, the Jews of Spain, Portugal and the Mediterranean countries. Aspects of liturgical practice and the pronunciation of Hebrew differ in the two groups. Until the 20th century Yiddish was widely spoken by the Ashkenazim.

Ashre ('Happy are those') Opening words of verse 5 of Psalm 84. With Psalm 144:15, this verse is prefixed to Psalm 145 and recited in the morning and afternoon services.

Ashmakta   (Aramaic: 'support', 'reliance') Talmudic term denoting a biblical text used to support a halakhah. It is also applied to a contract in which one of the parties binds himself to an unreasonable penalty

Asmodeus Evil spirit. His name is derived from Aeshma Daeva, the Persian god of anger. He first appears in the Book of Tobit. In the *Talmud* he described as king of the demons. His name is involved in spells and incantations in the Kabbalah.

Assaf Simḥah (1889–1953) Israeli historian and rabbinic scholar. From 1915 to 1919 he taught *Talmud* and was director of a yeshiva in Odessa. In 1921 he settled in Jerusalem. He later became a professor and rector at the Hebrew University and a member of the Israeli Supreme Court. He wrote many studies of the gaonic period, the history of Jewish law, medieval Jewish culture and the history of the Jewish community in Palestine.

Asser, Tobias Michael Carel (1838–1911) Dutch statesman. He came from a distinguished family of Dutch jurists, and served as Professor of International Law at the University of Amsterdam. He

was a member of the Council of State in the Netherlands from 1893, and chairman of the Royal Commission on Private International Law in 1898. He was awarded the Nobel Prize in 1911.

Assi (fl. late 3rd–early 4th cent.) Palestinian amora. Born in Babylonia, he settled in Tiberias. He and Ammi bar Nathan were the most distinguished scholars of their generation.

Assi, Rav (fl. early 3rd cent.) Babylonian amora. He was a contemporary of Rav and Samuel.

Assimilation Word used specifically of the integration of Jews into another culture after the diaspora. In Hellenistic times many Jews were influenced by the civilisation of the Greeks and Romans. In Muslim countries, Jews were frequently attracted to various aspects of Islamic life and thought. During the Middle Ages anti-Jewish persecution and Jewish cohesiveness deterred Jews from assimilating, but since the 19th century assimilation has become a dominant feature of Jewish life.

Astrology Study of the influence of the stars on human events. It was condemned by the prophets (Isaiah 47:13; Jeremiah 10:2). During the talmudic period Jews believed that the stars influenced human destiny, and in the Middle Ages many rabbis and philosophers engaged in astrological studies, some serving as court astrologers. Kabbalistic literature shows familiarity with the discipline. A number of Jewish customs have an astrological basis.

Astronomy Study of the heavenly bodies. It is not specifically referred to in the Bible. Apocryphal literature discusses astrological questions such as the length days, months and years, and in the *Talmud* there are astronomical calculations for determining the new moon and the dates of festivals. In Islamic lands many Jews engaged in the science, and translated astronomical works from Arabic into Latin and Spanish. During the Renaissance Abraham Zacuto prepared astronomical tables, which were used by Spanish and Portuguese explorers.

Astruc, Levi (fl. late 14th-early 15th cent.) Spanish rabbi. He participated in the Disputation of Tortosa in 1413–14.

Atarah ('crown') Term applied since the Middle Ages to the symbol used as one of the Torah ornaments.

Athaliah (fl. 9th cent. BCE) Queen of Judah (842–836 BCE). When her son Ahaziah was murdered by Jehu she seized power and murdered all her rivals except Joash. Six years later she was killed when Joash was crowned king in the Temple (II Kings 11:4–16; II Chronicles 23:1–5).

Athias, Joseph (fl. 17th cent.) Dutch publisher and printer. He founded a publishing house in Amsterdam. His first publication was a Sephardic prayerbook (1658). In 1659 he produced a commentary on the Pentateuch and in 1661 a Bible. In 1689 he announced that he had printed more than a million Bibles for England and Scotland.

A-Tiflisi, Abu Imran [Abu Imran of Tiflis] (fl. 9th cent.) Russian religious leader, founder of a dissident Karaite sect. He was born near Baghdad, and was taught by Ishmael al-Ukbari, who greatly influenced him. His followers were known as 'Abu-Imranists' or 'Tiflisists'. The sect persisted until the 12th century.

Atlan, Jean-Michel (1913–60) French–Algerian painter and poet. Born in Constantine, Algeria, he went to Paris and studied at the Sorbonne. He published collections of poems, but from 1946 worked as a painter.

Atonement Reconciliation with God following repentance for sin. In the Bible it is connected with sacrifice (Leviticus 5:14). The rabbis emphasised the centrality of prayer, repentance and charity. For sins committed against God, repentance is sufficient to earn atonement. If the sin involves injury to another person, resitution and forgiveness are necessary.

Attar, Ḥayyim ben Moses ben (1696–1743) North African Kabbalist. Born in Morocco, he lived in Livorno and later settled in Jerusalem, where he founded the Midrash Keneset Israel Yeshivah. His *Or ha-Ḥayyim* is a commentary on the Pentateuch.

Auer, Leopold (1845–1930) Russian violinist and teacher, of Hungarian origin. Born in Veszprem, Hungary, he studied at the Vienna Conservatory. He served as concert-master at Dusseldorf, and then at Hamburg. In 1868 he became Professor of Violin at the Imperial Conservatory, St Petersburg. In 1894 he was knighted by Nicholas II. After the Revolution, he went to New York where he taught violin.

Auerbach, Berthold (1812–1882) German author. Born at Nordstetein in Würtemberg, he was an active supporter of Jewish emancipation. He wrote short stories and novels, and translated Benedict Spinoza's works.

Auto-da-fé Public ceremony at which the sentences of the Inquisiton were announced in Spain and Portugal. After a procession through the streets, the condemned heretics were brought to the city square. A sermon was preached and the sentences were announced and carried out. The most servere penalty was public burning.

Av [Ab] Fifth month of the Jewish year.

Avadim Minor tractate of the *Talmud*. It discusses laws concerning slavery.

Av bet din [Father of the law court] Title conferred on the president of an ecclesiastical court. During the period of the Second Temple the title was given to the vice-president of the Supreme Court in Jerusalem. In gaonic times it designated the assistant to the gaon of the academies in Babylonia and Israel. From the 14th century a local rabbi, the head of a yeshivah or the district rabbi of a large community used the title. In the modern period the head of a rabbinical court is called av bet din or rosh bet din.

Avele Zion ('Mourners for Zion')   Jews who mourned the destruction of the Temple and prayed for the redemption of Zion. In the *Talmud* they are known as 'perushim' (abstainers) because they refused meat and wine. After the rise of Karaism they became important in Jewish life.

Avenger of blood (Hebrew 'Goel ha-dam')   Next of kin of a murdered person who is responsible for avenging the murder. (Dueteronomy 19:6).

Averah ('transgression')   Word used specifically of the trangression of Jewish law.

Averroes (1126–1198)   Spanish Muslim philosopher. He was born in Córdoba. His writings on Aristotle were translated into Hebrew. Some Jewish philosophers sought to harmonise his teaching with Judaism. Others attempted to reconcile his views with those of Maimonides.

Av ha-raḥamim ('Father of mercy')   Opening words of a medieval dirge in memory of martyrs. It is recited among the Ashkenazim during Sabbath prayers.

Avidan, David (1934–1995)   Israeli poet. He was born in Tel Aviv. From the start his work was highly experimental, using composite words, loan words and neologisms in Hebrew. He played an important role in the development of Hebrew poetry.

Avidom, Menaḥem (1908–1995)   Israeli composer. Born in Poland, he settled in Palestine in 1925 where he taught music. From 1945 to 1952 he was General Secretary of the Israel Philharmonic

Orchestra, and then became Adviser on the Arts to the Ministry of Tourism. He was appointed Director-General of the Israeli Performing Rights Society in 1955, and was also Chairman of the Israel Composer's League.

Avinoam, Reuben (1905–1974)   Israeli poet and translator. Born in Chicago, he settled in Palestine in 1929, where he taught English at the Herzliah High School in Tel Aviv. In 1950 he became Supervisor of English Studies at the Israeli Ministry of Education and Culture. He published poetry, translations and a collection of literary writings of those who died in the Israeli War of Independence.

Avinu malkenu ('Our father, our king')   Opening words of a prayer of supplication recited during the Ten Days of Penitence and on public fast days.

Aviv [Abib] [('spring')   The word is also used to mean 'period of the ripening of corn'.

Avi-Yonah, Michael (1904–1974)   Israeli archaeologist and art historian. Born in Galicia, he emigrated to Palestine in 1919. He was Professor of Classical and Byzantine Architecture at the Hebrew University. His writings concern the late Hellenistic, Roman and Byzantine periods and the topography of Palestine.

Avni, Ahron (1906–1951)   Israeli painter. Born in Ukraine, he emigrated to Palestine in 1925. In 1936 he founded the Histadrut Seminary for Painting and Sculpture in Tel Aviv, of which he was director until his death. He painted members of the Haganah and later soldiers on the battlefield during the Israeli War of Independence.

Avodah ('service,' 'prayer')   Temple sacrificial service and ritual of the high priests on the Day of Atonement. It also refers to the Musaph service in the synagogue on the Day of Atonement.

Avodah Zarah Eighth tractate of Nezikin in the Mishnah. It deals with idolatry.

Avot [Pirke Avot] ('Ethics of the Fathers') Ninth tractate of Nezikin in the Mishnah. It contains the teachings of sages from the 3rd century BCE to the 3rd century. CE. It is part of the liturgy of the Ashkenazim and is studied on Sabbath afternoons in the summer. It is recited at home by the Sephardim on Sabbath days between Passover and Shavuot.

Avot de-Rabbi Nathan ('Fathers according to Rabbi Nathan') Extra-canonical minor tractate of the *Talmud* attributed to Nathan the Babylonian. It is a commentary on Avot.

Avtalyon (fl. 1st cent. BCE) Palestinian scholar. He and Shemaiah constituted the fourth of the zugot in Palestine. He served as av bet din of the Sanhedrin.

Axelrod, Julius (1912–83) US biochemist. Born in New York City, he was awarded the Nobel Prize in Medicine in 1970 for research on nerve impulses and the treatment of nervous disorders.

Axenfeld, Israel (1787–1866) Russian Yiddish writer. He was born in Nemirov. He was originally a follower of Naḥman of Bratzlav, but after contact with the maskilim, he became anti-Ḥasidic. He wrote 30 novels and plays which satirise Ḥasidic life.

Aydem Son-in-law.

Ayin 16th letter of the Hebrew alphabet. Its numerical value is 70.

Ayllon, Solomon ben Jacob (1655–1728) Greek rabbi and Kabbalist. He was born in Salonica. He became a follower of Shabbetai Tzevi. In 1689 he was appointed Ḥakham in London. He later served as rabbi to the Portuguese Jews in Amsterdam, where he came into conflict with Tzevi Ashkenazi.

Azazel Name of the place or power to which the scapegoat was consigned on the Day of Atonement. On that day two of the goats in the Temple service were designated as sin offerings. The high priest cast lots and prescribed one for the Lord and the other for Azazel. The latter was sent into the wilderness and cast over a cliff.

Azei ḥayyim Staves which hold the Torah scrolls.

Azharot ('exhortations') Liturgical poems for Shavuot, in which the 613 commandments are enumerated. They were composed by many authors, including Saadyah Gaon and Solomon ibn Gabirol.

Azleff, Yevno (1869–1918) Russian revolutionary. He was born in Lyskovo, and moved to Rostov with his family. He served as a reporter for a local newspaper, and later as a clerk. His activities in the revolutionary movement were observed by the authorities, and he fled to Germany. Later he returned to Russia and became a member of the Union of Social Revolutionaries underground. Appointed to the party's first triumvirate, he became a leader of the Battle Organisation.

Azriel of Gerona (fl. early 13th cent.) Spanish Kabbalist. His work reflects the process whereby Neoplatonism permeated the Kabbalistic tradition. He wrote a commentary on the ten sephirot, the Sepher Yetzirah, talmudic aggadot and the liturgy, as well as several treatises on mysticism.

Azulai, Ḥayyim Joseph David (1724–1806) Palestinian emissary and writer. He was born in Jerusalem. He came to be regarded as the leading scholar of his generation, and also travelled abroad as an emissary of the Jewish community in Israel. His *Maagal Tov* is a literary diary covering the years 1753–78. His *Shem ha-Gedolim* contains 1,300 brief biographies.

B

A young Jewish man tells his mother he plans on marrying and invites her to meet his chosen bride-to-be. He asks the bride-to-be and two other attractive women friends of hers to stand in a row, and after his mother arrives, he asks her if she can pick out the woman he plans on marrying. Without hesitation, his mother goes right to the bride-to-be and says, 'Her!' The son is dumbfounded and wants to know how his mother could possibly have selected the right woman so quickly and unerringly. His mother answers: 'She's the one I didn't like.'

* * * * *

Jewish mothers are also the frequent target of Jewish jokes. They are portrayed as demanding and difficult, unwilling to let go of their sons. Here a Jewish mother is given scope to pick out her future daughter-in-law from three attractive women. She immediately chooses the right person. But it is the woman she dislikes most. It is her aim to make her future daughter-in-law miserable. She cannot let her son grow up and is determined to make him suffer.

Baal ha-bayit ('Head of the household') The term is used in its literal sense, and also to denote a rich person or a married taxpaying member of a congregation. The feminie form, 'baalat bayit', refers to an efficient housewife.

Baal Kore ('Master of a reading') Title used by the Ashkenazim for the reader of the Torah portion in the synagogue.

Baal Nes ('Master of a miracle') Miracle worker. The title was accorded to various individuals including Meir.

Baal Shem ('Master of the divine name') Title accorded to one who works miracles by using divine names. In the medieval German Ḥasidic tradition it was given to liturgical poets. Spanish Kabbalists used the title from the mid-

dle of the 13th century, and during this period it also applied to writers of texts for amulets based on holy names. In the 17th and 18th centuries it referred to miracle workers who healed the sick.

Baal Shem Tov, Israel ben Eliezer [Besht; Israel ben Eliezer] (1700–1760) Polish spiritual leader, founder of Ḥasidism. He was born in Podolia and lived in the Carpathian mountains. He emerged as a healer and spiritual leader and travelled about curing the sick and expelling demons and evil spirits; in the course of these journeys his influence grew. Prayer rather than study was his major approach to God. He attracted many followers and has remained the inspiration for Ḥasidim to the present day.

Baal Tekiyah ['Master of blowing'] Title accorded to the person who blows the shophar during synagogue services on Rosh ha-Shanah and Yom Kippur.

Baasha (fl. 10th-9th cent. BCE) King of Israel (906-883 BCE). He assassinated Nadab (son of Jeroboam I), proclaimed himself king, and killed all the members of the royal family. He lived at Tirzah. Throughout his reign he was at war with King Asa (I Kings 15:16, 32).

Babel, Isaac (1894-?1939) Ukrainian writer. He was born in Odessa. He served on the Romanian front after the Russian Revolution. From 1923 he devoted himself to literature and many of his stories contain Jewish themes. He was arrested and disappeared in 1939.

Babel Tower built by Noah's descendants in Shinar, intended to be high enough to reach Heaven. God frustrated this project and confused their tongues. As a result, there are diverse languages throughout the world (Genesis 11:1-9). Modern scholars note the similarlity between this building and the Sumerian Ziggurat.

Bacharach, Jair Hayyim (1638-1702) German talmudist. He served as rabbi in Koblenz and Worms. Thirteen scholars met under his leadership to study and prepare themselves for redemption. He collected writings connected with Shabbetai Tzevi. His *Havvot Yair* consists of responsa demonstrating an extensive knowledge of secular subjects.

Bacher, Simon (1823-1891) Hungarian poet and translator. He lived in Budapest, where he was the treasurer of the Jewish community. He wrote poems in the florid style of the Haskalah and translated German and Hungarian poetry into Hebrew. His *Zemirot ha-Aretz* (Songs of the Land) is an anthology of translations of Hungarian poetry. His translations of Gotthold Ephraim Lessing's *Nathan the Wise* appeared in Vienna in 1865.

Bacher, Wilhelm (1850-1913) Hungarian Semitic scholar. He was professor and head of the rabbinical seminary in Budapest, where he taught biblical exegesis, midrash, homiletics and Hebrew poetry and grammar. He published on various aspects of Judaism. His works include studies of talmudic aggadah, Hebrew grammarians, medieval biblical exegesis, and Judeo-Persian literature.

Bader, Gershom (1868-1953) Polish Hebrew and Yiddish author. Born in Kraków, he lived in Lemberg from 1893 until 1912. He founded the first Yiddish daily in Galicia, the *Tagblat,* in 1904. In 1896 he established the *Yidisher folks-kalender,* which he edited until 1912; in that year he settled in New York. His writings include a life of Jesus, a lexicon of Galician Jewish cultural figures and a dictionary of talmudic abbreviations.

Badge, Jewish Distinctive emblem or mark which Jews were forced to wear. It usually took the form of a cloth badge. From the 7th century Muslim rulers decreed that Jews should wear special clothing. The Fourth Lateran Council of 1215 laid down a similar order so that Jews could be distinguished from Christians. The badge was usually yellow. In medieval England it represented the two Tablets of the Law. In France and Germany it was a circular patch. In Germany it was a large yellow circle. Under the Nazi regime it was a yellow Star of David with the letter 'J' or the word '*Jude*' inside.

Badhan Merrymaker or entertainer. Medieval rabbinic literature refers to Jewish itinerant singers who entertained at weddings and at Hanukkah and Purim celebrations. They sang folk songs, told comic stories and made jests based on scriptural verses and talmudic passages. In Eastern Europe they acted as the professional wedding jesters and musicians.

Baeck, Leo (1873-1956) German rabbi and religious leader. He served as rabbi in Berlin, where he lectured on midrashic literature and homiletics at the

Hochschule für Wissenschaft des Judentums. From 1933 he was President of the Richsvertretung or representative body of German Jews. He was deported to Theresienstadt in 1943. After the war he settled in London, where he served as Chairman of the World Union for Progressive Judaism. He was visiting professor at the Hebrew Union College. His writings include *The Essence of Judaism*.

Baer, Seligmann (1825–1897) German masorah scholar and linguist. He taught in the Jewish community school in Biebrich. Together with Franz Delitzsch he published the Psalms and other books of the Bible with masorah texts. His *Avodat Yisrael* (Service of Israel) became the standard prayer-book text for most subsequent editions of the siddur.

Baer, Werner (1914–92) German composer. He studied piano composition and conducting at the Hochschule für Musik Berlin. Before the First World War, he was the organist at the Church of St Thomas, Leipzig and served as choirmaster and organist for the Liberal synagogue group in Berlin. In 1938 he left Germany and settled in Singapore. He subsequently emigrated to Australia. His compositions include *Test of Strength, Life of the Insects, Harvester's Song* and *Psalm 8*.

Baer, Yitzhak (1888–1980) German historian. He was born in Halberstadt. He became Professor of Medieval History and head of the history department at the Hebrew University. His writings include studies of the Jews in Christian Spain and the period of the Second Temple. He was one of the founders and editors of the Jewish historical review *Zion*.

Baerwald, Paul (1871–1961) American banker and communal leader. Born in Frankfurt, he went to the United States in 1896. In 1908 he became a partner in Lazard Frères. After he retired, he served as treasurer of the

American Joint Distribution Committee (JDC). In 1938 he joined President Roosevelt's Advisory Committee on Political Refugees, was active in the JDC rescue work during World War II, and arranged for funds for the War Refugee Board. After the war, the JDC helped more than half a million refugees to reach Israel.

Baginsky, Adolf Aron (1843–1918) German founder of modern paediatrics. Born in Ratibor, Silesia, he studied medicine at the University of Berlin. In 1881 he joined the faculty of paediatrics and later became professor.

Bahir Kabbalistic work. According to tradition it was composed by Nehunyah ben ha-Kanah in the 1st century. Modern scholarship believes it to have been compiled in Provence in the 12th century, though it incorporates ancient texts. It deals with letter mysticism and hints at the doctrine of the sephirot. Much of the terminology used in the book became part of the vocabulary of the kabbalah. It also contains a reference to the doctrine of the Transmigration of Souls.

Bahur ('young man') In the Bible it designates a fighting man. In rabbinic literature it refers to one who is unmarried. In the Middle Ages it was used of an advanced yeshivah student.

Bahya ben Asher ibn Halawa (fl. 13th cent.) Spanish exegete and Kabbalist. He lived in Zaragoza where he was dayyan and preacher. In his commentary on the Torah he used literal, philosophical, homiletical and mystical interpretation.

Bahya ben Joseph ibn Pakuda [Ibn Bakuda; Ibn Pakuda, Bahya] (fl. 11th cent.) Spanish moral philosopher. He lived in Zaragoza. In *Duties of the Heart* he examined the obligations of a person's inner life, which he regarded as having equal importance with ritual and ethical observances.

This work draws on Islamic mysticism and Neoplatonism.

Bailment   The making over of movable property by the owner to someone else on the understanding that he will return it. Rabbinic law concerning bailment is based on Exodus 22:6–14 and sets out the duty of the bailee to restore the property in good condition. The Mishnah specifies four types of recipient: the unpaid guardian, the paid guardian, the hirer and the borrower.

Bakkashah ('supplication')   A type of liturgical composition. It includes a wide range of prayers in prose or verse. Petitionary and abstract in content, they are used throughout the year. A number in the Sephardic prayer-book are to be recited before dawn as a prelude to the regular service.

Bakst, Leon [Rosenberg, Lev Samuilovich] (1867–1924)   Russian artist. Born in St Petersburg, he was baptised and later returned to Judaism. He was employed by Sergei Diaghilev as chief designer of costumes for ballets. He had a deep influence on Marc Chagall.

Balaban, Meir (1877–1942)   Polish historian. He was born in Lemberg. He became director of the Taḥkemoni rabbinical seminary in Warsaw and lectured in Jewish history at the University of Warsaw. He was the founder of the historiography of Polish Jewry. His writings deal with the history of the Jews in Poland and Russia.

Balmes, Abraham ben Meir de (1440–1523)   Italian physician and grammarian. He was born in Lecce. He became court physician to King Ferdinand I of Naples. He translated a number of medieval Arabic works from the Hebrew versions into Latin. His *Mikneh Avraham* is a standard work of Hebrew grammar.

Bal tashḥit ('do not destroy')   Biblical prohibition against destroying fruit-bearing trees when laying siege to a city (Deuteronomy 20:19–20). The *Talmud* extends the concept to cover any senseless destruction or waste.

Bamberger, Fritz (1902–1984).   German philosopher. He was born in Frankfurt am Main. He was Professor of Philosophy at the College of Jewish Studies in Chicago from 1937 to 1942, then until 1961 was Professor of Intellectual History at the Hebrew Union College-Jewish Institute of Religion in New York. His writings include studies of Moses Mendelssohn and Benedict Spinoza.

Bambus, Willi (1863–1904)   German Zionist. He was a leading member of the Ezra Society in Berlin, which supported agricultural settlements in Palestine. He was opposed to political Zionism. In 1901 he was a co-founder of the Hilfsverein der deutschen Juden.

Ba-meh, madlikin ('With what may one kindle?')   Opening words of the second chapter of the Mishnah tractate Shabbat, which deals with the oils and wicks to be used for Sabbath lights, and with what may be done on Fridays before the commencement of the Sabbath. The chapter is recited during the Friday evening service before or at the end of the Arvit prayer. The reading of the chapter was instituted during the gaonic period as a reminder of the duty of kindling the Sabbath lights, as a warning against unintentional desecration of the Sabbath by adjusting the lamp, and as a safeguard for latecomers to the synagogue so that they could catch up with the service.

Ban (excommunication)   In Jewish usage, the sentencing of an individual to exclusion or severance from the Jewish community. A short-term ban ('niddui') is used to cut off an individual from social and business contacts. A more severe ban ('ḥerem') involves a complete boycott of the indivdual (the cessation of personal, social, religious and business contact) for an indefinite period. In the rabbinic period it was frequently employed against those Jews whose views were considered dangerous to the community, such as heretics or followers of sects not approved by the Jewish authorities. In the Middle Ages and afterwards it played an important role in Jewish life. Among those to whom the punishment was applied were Uriel Acosta, Benedict Spinoza, the followers of Shabbetai Tzevi and Jacob Frank. In the modern period, the practice of inflicting bans has largely fallen into disuse.

Band, Arnold (b.1930) American literary scholar. He was born in Boston. He served on the faculty of the University of California at Los Angeles from 1959, becoming Professor of Hebrew Literature and Chairman of the Department of Comparative Literature. His publications include a study of Shemuel Yosef Agnon.

Bandes [Miller], Louis E. (1866–1927) American Yiddish journalist. Born in Russia, he settled in the US, where he became a leader of the socialist movement. In 1890 he founded the Yiddish Marxist weekly *Die Arbeiter-Zeitung*, and in 1897 helped to establish the labour daily newspaper *Forverts*. In 1905 he founded *Die Wahrheit*, which later altered its ideology from socialism to Zionism.

Baneth, David Tzevi Harwig (1893–1973) Israeli Arabist, son of Eduard Baneth. He was born in Krotoszyn, Poland. He settled in Palestine, where he became Professor of Arabic Language and Literature at the Hebrew University. His writings concern the influence of Arabic thought on medieval Jewish philosophy.

Baneth, Eduard (1855–1930) Prussian talmudist. He was born in Liptó-Szent-Miklós, Hungary. He served as rabbi at Krotoszyn and lectured on *Talmud* at the Lehranstalt für die Wissenschaft

des Judentums in Berlin. His work was concerned primarily with talmudic and rabbinic literature, the development of halakhah and the Jewish calendar.

Baneth, Ezekiel (1773–1854) Hungarian rabbi. He was born in Alt-Ofen. He served as rabbi of Paks, Balassagyarmat and Nyitra, and his yeshivah was attended by students from all over the country. He was a halakhic authority and an eloquent preacher.

Banishment Exclusion from one's native soil. It was the punishment decreed by God for Adam (Genesis 3:23–24) and Cain (Genesis 4:14–16). In biblical times, those who killed by accident were banished to cities of refuge, where they were given asylum. During the period of the Second Temple, banishment was imposed for misdeeds or political reasons. In the Middle Ages Jewish courts expelled individuals to protect the community.

Banking During the 11th–13th centuries in Europe Jewish finance and credit were based on the resources of individuals and small groups. The growth of world currency markets in the 18th century gave rise to the private banks of Jewish families (Rothschild, Worms, Stern, Bischoffsheim), who financed international trade and industry. The revolutions of 1848 led to their decline. In the US in the early 19th century a number of banks were founded by Jewish merchants (Lazard, Erlanger, Guggenheim). In the 20th century, however, such Jewish banking firms lost their former signifinance owing to the rise of larger, more impersonal corporations.

Banu Kainuka [Kainuka] One of the Jewish tribes in Medina, Arabia, in the 7th century. They engaged in commerce and worked as goldsmiths. When Mohammed failed to gain Jewish converts to Islam, they were attacked. They left Medina and migrated to Jewish centres in Wadi-i-Kura and Adhirat.

Banu Kuraiza [Kuraiza] One of the three Jewish tribes in Medina, Arabia, in the 7th century. They engaged in agriculture. One of the women in the tribe, Raihana, was married to Mohammed; when he accused them of treason, the men were executed and the women and children sold into slavery.

Banu Nadir [Nadir Banu] One of three Jewish tribes in Medina, Arabia, in the 7th century. They cultivated the soil, engaged in moneylending, and traded in weapons and jewels. They were besieged in their strongholds by Mohammed and surrendered. Their property was confiscated, and they founded settlements in Khaybar and Syria.

Baptism Ablutionary rite symbolising purification or consecration. In the Bible it was practised by priests and laymen. Later it played an important role in the rites of the Essenes, Hemerobaptists and Christians. Baptism by total immersion is a necessary rite for a convert to Judaism, but it is also practised by men and women as a means of purification.

Baptism, forced Subjection to the Christian ritual of baptism. When Christianity became the religion of the Roman Empire, large numbers of Jews were forcibly baptised. From the time of Pope Gregory I (590–604), this practice was condemned. Nevertheless baptism was frequently imposed on Jews through the centuries.

Bar (Aramaic 'son') It occurs as a particle in many male personal names.

Baraita (Aramaic 'external') Any halakhah, halakhic midrash, historical or aggadic tradition not included in the Mishnah. The term is employed in the Babylonian *Talmud* to emphasise a view opposed to that in the Mishnah. A baraita is introduced by the formulae 'Teno rabbanan' (The rabbis taught) and 'Tanya, tena' (It was taught). The

largest collection of extra-Mishnaic halakhot is the Tosephta.

Barash, Asher (1889–1952) Hebrew author of Galician origin. Born in eastern Galicia, he emigrated in 1914 to Palestine, where he taught high school in Tel Aviv and Haifa. He wrote novels, short stories, poems, essays and translations. His fictional works depict life among Galician Jewry and the pioneering efforts in Palestine.

Barekhi naphshi ('Bless [the Lord], o my soul') Opening works of Pslam 104, and the title by which it is known. The psalm glorifies God as creator and sustainer of nature. It is recited on Rosh Ḥodesh, and in some rites also on Sabbath afternoons between Sukkot and Passover.

Barekhu ('Bless') The opening word of the synagogue formula of invitation to prayer. The entire phrase, 'Barekhu et Adonai ha-mevorakh' (Bless ye the Lord who is [to be] blessed), is based on the biblical expression 'Bless ye the Lord'. It serves as the opening of both the morning and evening prayers in the synagogue and also functions as the introduction to the public reading of the Torah. It was also used for the zimmun (invitation to Grace), but was later replaced by the formula 'Nevarekh' (Let us bless). When the reader chants 'Barekhu', the congregation silently reads a prayer beginning 'Yitbarakh'. When the reader concludes the invitation, the congregation responds: 'Blessed is the Lord who is (to be) blessed forever and ever'.

Bar Giora, Simon [Simeon] (fl. 1st cent.) Palestinian military leader in the war against Rome in 66–70. He fought in the battle at Beth-Horon in 66, in which the Jews defeated the Romans. He gathered together a band of patriots who attacked opponents of the revolt and Roman sympathisers. He opposed the moderate Jewish government in Jerusalem, which wished to come to terms with Rome. When Titus' forces reached Jerusalem in 70, he fought with the rebels against him. He eventually surrendered, was taken prisoner to Rome and executed.

Bar-Hanina (fl. 4th cent.) Palestinian scholar. He lived in Bethlehem and was a teacher of Jerome. He introduced the Church Fathers to rabbinic exegesis and influenced the translation of the Hebew Scriptures into Latin.

Bar-Ilan [Berlin], Meir (1880–1949) Zionist leader of Russian origin. He was born in Volozhin. He represented the Mizraḥi movement at the Seventh Zionist Congress in 1905. In 1926 he settled in Jerusalem, where he became President of the World Mizraḥi Centre. Opposed to the Palestinian partition plan and the British White Paper of 1939, he advocated civil disobedience. After the establishment of the State of Israel he organised a group of scholars to examine the legal problems of the state in the light of Jewish law. He was editor of the *Mizraḥi* daily newspaper and organised the publication of the *Talmudic Encyclopedia*.

Bar Kappara (fl. 3rd cent.) Palestinian scholar. A disciple of Judah Ha-Nasi, he was the author of compilations of Jewish law. This collection explains obscure passages in the Mishnah and transmits traditions that differ from it. He valued natural science and encouraged the use of Greek, but was opposed to metaphysical speculation. He founded an academy in the south of Israel.

Bar Kokhba, Simeon [Bar Kosiba, Simeon, Ben Koziba] (d.135) Palestinian military leader in the war against Rome in 132–35. At the outbreak of the war Akiva proclaimed him Messiah. The appelation Bar Kokhba ('son of the star') was given to him because of his messianic role. His forces captured Jerusalem, but in 133 the Romans counter-attacked with an army of 35,000 under Hadrian and the commander Julius Severus. In

134–35 they besieged Bar Kokhba's stronghold Betar, and he was killed.

Bar-Lev, Haim (b.1924) Israeli military commander. Born in Vienna, he settled in Palestine in 1939. In 1946 he was in charge of blowing up the Allenby Bridge during the struggle with the British. In the War of Independence and the Sinai Campaign of 1956, he served as military commander of various units. In 1964 he was appointed head of the General Staff Branch at GHQ. From 1968 to 1971 he was chief of staff of the Israeli Defence Forces. In 1972 he became Minister of Commerce and Industry.

Barminan ('Far from us') Exclamation used by Sephardim to ward off misfortune. It is equivalent to the Ashkenazi phrase 'Lo alenu' (not on us), which is sometimes used among Ashkenazim to refer to a corpse.

Bar mitzvah ('Son of the commandment') Term applied to the attainment of legal and religious maturity, also the occasion on which this status is assumed. At 13 a boy is obligated to fulfil all the commandments, and in the synagogue he may be called up to read the Torah and the Haphtarah. A special service is held at which he reads for the first time and the rabbi may deliver a sermon stressing his new obligations. After the service a festive kiddush frequently takes place. Reform congregations initially instituted a ceremony of confirmation as a substitute, but it is now adopted as an additional ceremony.

Baron, Devorah (1887–1956) Hebrew author of Russian origin. She was born in Belorussia and settled in Palestine in 1911. Childhood reminiscences and Jewish life in Eastern Europe are major themes of her fiction.

Baron, Salo Wittmayer (1896–1989) Galician Jewish historian. He taught history at the Jewish Teacher's

College in Vienna, at the Jewish Institute of Religion in New York and at Columbia University. He served as President of the American Academy for Jewish Research and as a member of other academic bodies. His writings include the multi-volume *Social and Religious History of the Jews*.

Barrenness The inability of a woman to conceive and bear children. In rabbinic Judaism it is considered a misfortune since the procreation of children is the principal purpose of marriage. Talmudic law stipulates that a man is compelled to divorce his wife if his marriage is without issue after ten years. However, from the Middle Ages no compulsion has been exercised in such cases.

Barros Basto, Arturo Carlos de (1887–1961) Portuguese leader of the Marrano revival. He was born at Amarante near Oporto. He entered the military, and in the revolution of 1910 it was he who hoisted the Republican flag on the town hall of Oporto. After World War I he embraced Judaism and was active in the regeneration of the Marrano community. His periodical *Ha-Lappid* spread Jewish ideas among the Marranos. He also edited handbooks of religious guidance and wrote a history of Jewry in Oporto.

Barsimon, Jacob (fl. 17th cent.) Dutch emigrant, the first Jewish resident of New Amsterdam (New York). He arrived in the New World in July 1654, aboard the Dutch ship *Peartree*. In 1655 he joined Asser Levy in petitioning for the right to stand guard instead of paying a special tax. The Dutch West India Company overruled Governor Peter Stuyvesant who had rejected the petition.

Bartov, Hanokh (1926–2016) Israeli novelist. Born in Petah Tikvah, he served in the Jewish Brigade during World War II and in the Israeli army during the War of Independence. He was cultural attaché at the Israeli embassy in London. His writings include stories, novels, plays and journalism.

Baruch (i) (fl. 7th cent. BCE) Israelite scribe of the Book of Jeremiah. He set down in writing all Jeremiah's prophecies and may have composed the biographical narrative about him. (Jeremiah 36:4).

Baruch (ii) Apocryphal book. The prose section relates how Baruch wrote the work in Babylon and read it to Jehoiachin and the exiles. They confessed their sins and sent money to Jerusalem to purchase sacrifices. The lyrical part consists of a hymn to the wisdom of the law, lamentations and consolations.

Baruch, Apocalypse of Apocalyptic work ascribed to Jeremiah's scribe Baruch. The Syriac version contains Baruch's visions on the eve of the destruction of Jerusalem and in its aftermath. The Greek version describes Baruch's journey through the heavens. The Ethiopic version contains stories of Baruch and Jeremiah at the period of the destruction of Jerusalem.

Baruch of Medzibozh [Baruch of Tulchin] (1757–1810) Ukrainian Hasidic tzaddik. He was the grandson of the Baal Shem Tov, and regarded himself as the heir to his leadership. He held court in Medzibozh in a luxurious fashion and aroused the opposition of other Hasidic leaders. He believed the tzaddik could save the whole world. He was the first to institute payments to the tzaddik from the Hasidim.

Baruch, Bernard (1870–1965) American statesman. He served as chairman of the War Industries Board, and as an adviser to President Wilson and later to President Roosevelt. In 1944 he was a member of a committee that studied post-war adjustment issues. His writings include *American Industry in the War*, *My Own Story* and *Public Years*.

Barukh ('blessed') Opening word of a benediction, also of phrases and salutations deriving from benedictions. According to the *Talmud*, many benedictions beginning with the formula 'Blessed art thou, O Lord our God, king of the universe' derive from the Men of the Great Synagogue, a group of around 100 sages who constituted a spiritual and legislative body in the period after the Prophets.

Barukh dayyan (ha-)emet ('Blessed be the true judge') Benediction pronounced on hearing evil tidings. On hearing the report of a death, relatives are to recite the full formula: 'Blessed art thou, O Lord our God, king of the universe, the true judge'.

Barukh ha-ba ('Blessed is he who comes') Greeting to a visitor or new acquaintance.

Barukh ha-shem ('Blessed be the name [of God]') Expression of thanksgiving pronounced on hearing good tidings.

Barukh hu u-varukh shemo ('Blessed be he, and blessed be his name') Response by the congregation to the mention of God's name in the first half of a benediction. The response to the second half is 'Amen.'

Barukh she-amar ('Blessed be he who spoke') Benediction pronounced at the beginning of the section of the morning service called Pesuke de-Zimra (passages of song). In the Ashkenazi rite it is said at the beginning of the whole section. In the Sephardi rite verses and psalms are recited before it.

Barukh shem kevod malkhuto le-olam va-ed ('Blessed be his name whose glorious kingdom is eternal') Benediction recited after the first verse of the Shema. It is spoken in an undertone, except on the Day of Atonement when it is recited aloud. According to the *Talmud*, when Jacob was dying he asked his sons if they believed in the one God. In reply they spoke the Shema, to which Jacob responded with this phrase.

Barukh she-petaroni ('Blessed be he who has relieved me') Benediction pronounced by the father at his son's bar mitzvah. It refers to the father being relieved of responsibility for his son's conduct. In Yiddish it became a familiar expression on getting rid of an annoying thing or person.

Bar-Yehuda, Yisrael [Idelson, Yisrael] (1895–1965) Israeli political leader. Born in Russia, he settled in Palestine in 1926. From 1949 he was a member of the Knesset. After the split in Mapam in 1954, he became a member of the Ahdut ha-Avodah-Poale Zion party. From 1955 to 1959 he was Minister of the Interior, and from 1962 to 1965 Minister of Communications.

Basch, Victor (1863–1944) French philosopher. Born in Budapest, he was professor at the universities of Nancy, Rennes and Paris. He championed Alfred Dreyfus. In 1926 he served as President of the League for the Rights of Man. During World War II he was a member of the central committee of the French Resistance. His writings concern literature, philosophy and political issues.

Baskin, Leonard (1922–2000) American artist. He was born in New Jersey. He taught printmaking and sculpture at Smith College from 1953. He was influenced in his early years by Ben Shahn and many of his drawings and prints concern Jewish subjects.

Bass, Shabbetai ben Joseph (1641–1718) Polish cantor and publisher. He became the first Jewish bibliographer. When his parents were killed in a pogrom, he fled to Prague, where he served as an assistant cantor. From 1674 until 1679 he visited libraries in Poland, Germany and Holland. His *Siftei Yeshenim* is a list in Hebrew of some 2,200 items of Hebraica and Judaica.

Bassani, Giorgio (1916–2000) Italian writer. Born in Bologna, he lived in

Ferrara until 1943, when he moved to Rome. He edited *Bolteghe oscure,* an international literary review. His *Garden of the Finzi-Continis* depicts an aristocratic Italian Jew unable to come to terms with Fascism.

Bassevi [von Treuenberg], Jacob (1570–1634) Court Jew. He engaged in large-scale trading and business transactions. In 1622 Friedrich II granted him a coat of arms. As head of the Jewish community in Prague he took an active role in Jewish communal life and defended the Jews from persecution.

Bathing In Jewish practice, specifically a means of ritual purification. It was a daily requirement for those who participated in Temple services. Groups such as the Essenes made it a cult. In post-biblical times it was of less significance. The Kabbalists and several Ḥasidic sects revived the practice.

Bathsheba (fl. 11th–10th cent. BCE) Israelite woman, wife of Uriah then of David. When David from his rooftop saw her bathing, he had Uriah her husband killed in battle by placing him in the front lines. Bathsheba was the mother of Solomon (II Samuel 11–12; I Kings 1–2).

Bat kol ('daughter of a voice') Rabbinic expression referring to a divine voice, sometimes heard to give heavenly approval to halakhic decisions.

Batlan ('ban of leisure') Talmudic term referring to a man who has spare time for communal business such as synagogue attendance. In Yiddish usage it denotes a man who is lazy and shiftless and cannot make his way in the world.

Bat mitzvah ('Daughter of a commandment') Ceremony for girls corresponding to a boy's bar mitzvah. A girl reaches her religious majority at the age of 12 years and one day. The ceremony celebrating this occasion differs widely. In some congregations girls read from the Torah. In others, they recite the Haphtarah and conduct certain prayers.

Bava ('gate') Word used to denote a section of a book. The first tractate of the Mishnah order of Nezikin was divided into three such sections: Bava Kamma, Bava Metzia and Bava Batra.

Bava Batra ('the last gate') Third section of the first tractate of the Mishnah order of Nezikin. It deals with property, usurpations, hereditary succession and legal documents.

Bava-buch [Bava buch] Yiddish adaption made at the beginning of the 16th century by Elijah Levita of the Anglo-French romance *Sir Bevis of Hampton.* The Yiddish phrase 'bobe-meise' (grandmother's tale) is probably derived from this.

Bava Kamma ('The first gate') First section of the first tractate of the Mishnah order of Nezikin. It deals with the four principal types of damage to property and personal injury (Exodus 21:33; 22:5ff).

Bava Metzia ('The middle gate') Second section of the first tractate of the Mishnah order of Nezikin. It deals with found property, the laws of chattels, bailment, sales, interest, fraud, hiring and partnership.

Beard The Bible explicitly forbids cutting the corners of the beard (Leviticus 19:27). The *Talmud* regards the beard as the ornament of the face, and mystics ascribed esoteric significance to it. In Europe the emphasis shifted from the obligations to wear a beard to the prohibition of shaving. However, it is permitted to clip it using scissors or an electric shaver with two cutting edges.

Bedersi, Abraham ben Isaac (c. 1230–c.1300) French Hebrew poet. He lived most of his life in Perpignan. His poems and satires contain numerous historical details and provide an insight into the contemporary cultural scene. His *Ḥotam Tokhnit* was the first dictionary of Hebrew synonyms in the Bible.

Bedersi, Jedaiah [Jedaiah ha-Penini] (c.1270–c.1340) French philosopher and poet. He lived in Perpignan and Barcelona. His *Examination of the World* is an ethical work stressing the worthlessness of the world and indicating the way to attain eternal happiness. Among his poems is the prayer *Eleph Alaphim,* each word of which begins with the letter aleph. His *Apologetic Letter* addressed to Solomon ben Adret vindicates philosophical studies.

Bedikah ('examination') Word used in connection with various kinds of inspection. It is applied especially to the examination of a slaughtered animal to ensure that it is not suffering from a serious disease.

Beer-Hofmann, Richard (1866–1945) Austrian poet and playwright. Born in Vienna, he emigrated to New York in 1939 after the Nazi occupation of Austria. Much of his work deals with Jewish themes. In a trilogy of biblical plays he sought to restate in modern terms the Hebraic position on fundamental questions of human existence.

Be-ezrat ha-shem ('With the help of the name [of God]') Expression of pious hope or trust, uttered or written at the beginning of letters.

Begin, Menaḥem (1913–1992) Israeli statesman. He was the leader of Betâr in Poland. In 1942 he emigrated to Palestine and became Commander of the Irgun Tzevai Leumi. From 1944 to 1948 he led the Irgun's underground war against the British. In 1948 he founded the Ḥerut Party. He led the Likud Party to victory in the general election of 1977 and became Prime Minister.

Behemoth Creature depicted in Job 40:15–24. It ate grass, lived in a shady marsh, and could swallow the waters of the Jordan river.

Beilis, Menaḥem Mendel (1874–1934) He was the victim of a blood libel charge in Russia in 1911, having been accused of the ritual murder of a 12-year old boy. In 1913 a trial was held and he was acquitted.

Bekhorot ('Firstlings') Fourth tractate of the Mishnah order of Kodashim. It deals with laws relating to first-born animals and men.

Bekhor Shor, Joseph ben Isaac [Joseph Bekhor Shor] (fl. 12 cent.) French scholar. He lived at Orléans. His commentary on the Torah was based on a literal and rationalistic understanding of the text. He opposed the allegorisation of the commandments, and the Christological interpretation of Scripture.

Bel and the Dragon Apocryphal book. It contains two stories about Daniel's exposure of the falsity of pagan cults. In *Bel* he reveals the footprints of the priests who secretly remove the sacrifices placed before the idol. In *The Dragon* he causes the death of a dragon worshipped by the Babylonians by feeding it a mixture of pitch, fat and hair.

Belial   Term denoting subversive individuals. In rabbinic and apocryphal literature it is often synonymous with Satan.

Beli en ha-ra ('without the evil eye') Expression used to ward off the supposed ills resulting from praise or from the admission of good fortune. In Yiddish it is 'kinanhora'.

Belkin, Samuel (1911–1976)   American rabbi and educator of Polish origin. He settled in the US in 1929. In 1943 he became President of the Elchanan Theological Seminary and Yeshiva College. At Yeshiva he launched an extensive programme of academic and physical expansion. In 1945 the college became Yeshiva University. He published studies on Philo, rabbinic literature and traditional Jewish thought.

Belkind, Israel (1861–1929)   Zionist leader of Belorussian origin. He was a leader of the first Bilu group to go to Palestine in 1882. He founded the first Hebrew school in Jaffa in 1889 and an agricultural school for orphans of the 1903 Kishinev pogroms. After World War I he established another agricultural school for orphans of the Ukrainian pogroms. He was the author of Hebrew, Yiddish and Russian textbooks on Jewish subjects.

Bellow, Saul (1915–2005)   American novelist. Born in Quebec, he lived in Montreal and Chicago. Many of his novels deal with Jewish life. *The Victim* is a treatment of antisemitism. *The Adventures of Augie March* deals with the experience of a Jewish boy from Chicago during the depression of the 1930s. And *Herzog* portrays a Jewish professor who attempts to relate humanistic values to the modern world.

Ben-Ammi [Rabinowicz, Mordecai] (1854–1932)   Russian author. He became a maskil and organised Jewish defence in Odessa. He emigrated to Geneva and later settled in Palestine. His stories portray traditional Jewish life.

Ben Asher, Aaron ben Moses (fl. first half of the 10th cent.)   Palestinian masoretic scholar. He lived in Tiberias. He produced a biblical manuscript incorporating vocalisation and accentuation, which formed the basis for the accepted Hebrew text of the Bible. He also wrote grammatical works in the traditions of the scholars of Tiberias.

Ben Avigdor [Shalkovitz, Leib; Shelkowitz, Abraham Leib] (1867–1921)   Polish Hebrew writer and publisher. He lived in Warsaw, where he founded the series of small booklets called 'Penny Books', which contained Hebrew belles-lettres. These introduced European literary trends into Hebrew literature. In 1893 he established the Ahiasaph publishing company, and later the Tushiyyah company which published hundreds of Hebrew books. He founded the children's weekly *Olam Katan* in 1901, and the Ahisepher publications in 1913.

Ben Azzai, Simeon (fl. early 2nd cent.)   Palestinian rabbinic scholar. He lived in Tiberias. He was one of four sages who engaged in esoteric speculation (thereby entering Pardes). According to the tradition, he was one of the ten martyrs who died during the Hadrianic persecutions.

Benediction [blessing] (Hebrew 'berakhah')   Formula of blessing or thanksgiving used in public and private services. Benedictions constitute a central part of synagogue and individual prayer. The phrase 'Blessed art thou, O Lord' is incorporated into every benediction. The rabbis taught that a man should recite a hundred benedictions daily.

Bene Israel ('Sons of Israel')   Jewish community in India. Its members claim that their ancestors left Galileee because of the persecution under Antiochus IV Epiphanes in the 2nd century BCE. They retained many aspects of the Jewish tradition. Despite emigration to Israel, a small community of Jews still survives in India.

Bene Mosheh ('Sons of Moses') An exclusive group of Ḥovevei Zion. It was founded in 1859 by Ahad ha-Am and Joshua Barzilai because of dissatisfaction with the Zionist leadership. It established Hebrew schools and a publishing house in Warsaw. Its aim was to bring about a spiritual renaissance among the Jewish people and the return to Israel.

Ben-Gurion, David (1886–1973) Israeli statesman and prime minister. Born in Poland, he joined the Zionist movement and settled in Palestine in 1906. He was among the labour leaders who founded the Aḥdut ha-Avodah Party in 1919 and Mapai in 1930. From 1921 to 1935 he was General Secretary of the Histadrut. He was Chairman of the Zionist executive and the Jewish Agency executive from 1935 to 1948. In April 1948 he became head of the provisional government in which he served as Prime Minister and Minister of Defence. In 1956 he was responsible for the Sinai Operation. His writings include speeches, articles and memoirs.

Ben-Haim, Paul (1897–1984) Israeli composer. Born in Munich, he settled in Tel Aviv in 1933. He helped to create the eastern Mediterranean school of composition. His compositions evoke the pastoral atmosphere of the Israeli countryside and the youthful spirit of the people.

Benjamin (i) (fl.? 19th–16th cent. BCE) Israelite, youngest son of Jacob. The tribe of Benjamin occupied territory between Ephraim and Judah, which included Jerusalem.

Benjamin, Judah Philip (1811–1884) American lawyer and statesman. He was born in the Virgin Islands. He was elected to the US Senate in 1852. In 1861 he became Attorney-General of the Confederate Government and he later served as Secretary of State until the collapse of the Confederacy. After the Civil War he settled in England, where he had a distinguished career as a barrister.

Benjamin ben Moses Nahavendi [Nahavendi, Benjamin] (fl. 19th cent.) Persian Karaite scholar. He lived in Nahavend in Persia, where he established a community that observed Karaite principles and methods of biblical study. He was the first Karaite author to write in Hebrew, and was responsible for the use of the name 'Karaites' to designate the members of the sect.

Benjamin of Tudela (fl. second half of the 12th cent.) Spanish traveller. A resident of Tudela, he set out on his travels in about 1167 and returned in 1172 or 1173. He visited France, Italy, Greece, Syria, Palestine, Iraq, the Persian Gulf, Egypt and Sicily. His *Book of Travels* is an important source of Jewish history of the period.

Benjamin, Walter (1892–1940) German philosopher. Born in Berlin, he worked as a critic, translator and reviewer. At the outbreak of World War II he was interned as a German citizen, but released in November 1939. He fled to the south of France, and then crossed the Spanish border. When threatened with deportation, he committed suicide. His writings include a study of the origin of German drama.

Ben Kalba Sabbua (fl. 1st cent.) Israelite, citizen of Jerusalem. He was active during the Roman conquest in 70. According to the *Talmud*, he possessed sufficient grain to feed Jerusalem for several years, but this was destroyed by the Zealots.

Bensh (Yiddish: 'Bless') Expression used in saying grace after meals or blessing children. It is also used in connection with the prayer for the new moon, the benediction recited by a person who has had a perilous escape, and the kindling of Sabbath and festival lights.

Ben Sira [Jesus ben Sira] (fl. 2nd cent. BCE) Palestinian sage. He lived in Jerusalem. He was the author of the apocryphal book known as Ecclesiasticus or The Wisdom of Ben Sira.

Ben Sira, Alphabet of Medieval work containing folklore, proverbs and aphorisms arranged alphabetically. It recounts the story of the life, adventures and teachings of Ben Sira.

Benveniste, Abraham (1406–1454) Spanish rabbi. He was rabbi to the court in Castile and financial agent to John II of Aragon. In 1432 he was appointed Chief Justice and Tax Superintendent of Castilian Jewry. In the same year he convened a synod at Valladolid which encouraged Jewish education, the correct administration of Jewish courts and equitable tax apportionment.

Benveniste, Hayyim ben Israel (1603–1673) Turkish rabbinic codifier. He was born in Constantinople and served as a rabbi in Smyrna. He was opposed to the Sabbetaian movement. His *Keneset ha-Gedolah* is a guide to the halakhah embodying decisions made after the completion of the Shulhan Arukh.

Ben-Yehudah [Perelmann], Eliezer (1858–1922) Hebrew writer and lexicographer of Lithuanian origin. He went to Paris in 1878 to study medicine and in 1879 he published articles encouraging Jewish settlement in Palestine. In 1881 he emigrated to Jerusalem, where he edited Hebrew journals. He advocated the acceptance of Hebrew as a spoken language and in 1890 founded the Hebrew Language Council of which he was chairman. He wrote a comprehensive dictionary of ancient and modern Hebrew.

Ben-Zion, Simhah [Gutmann, Simhah Alter] (1870–1932) Hebrew author. He was born in Bessarabia and settled in Palestine in 1905. He wrote short stories as well as novels, and translated German classics into Hebrew.

Ben Zoma, Simeon (fl. 2nd cent.) Palestinian sage. He was a contemporary of Akiva. It appears that he studied under Joshua ben Hananiah. The Mishnah declares that that he was the last of the authoritative biblical expository. Many of his sayings became proverbs.

Ben-Zvi [Ben-Tzevi], Yitzhak [Shimshelevitz, Yitzhak] (1884–1963) Israeli statesman. Born in Ukraine, he was one of the pioneers of the Poale Zion movement in Russia. In 1907 he settled in Palestine, where he was active in the Jewish defence movement. He was a founder of the Ahdut ha-Avodah party in 1919, of Histadrut in 1921, and of Mapai in 1930. He succeeded Chaim Weizmann as president of the state in 1952. His wife, Rachel Yanait (1886–1979), was involved with the Palestinian labour movement, Jewish self-defence, and agricultural training for women.

Berab, Jacob (1474–1546) Talmudist of Spanish origin. He lived in north Africa before settling in Safed. He initiated a plan to reintroduce ordination (semikhah) in order to establish an authoritative leadership and reconstitute the Sanhedrin. This project was opposed by Levi ibn Haviv. A controversy ensued and the plan failed.

Berakhah Aharonah ('Last blessing') The shorter form of Grace after Meals. It is recited after eating food other than bread prepared from the five primary grains, after drinking wine and after eating food characteristic of Israel (Deuteronomy 8:8).

Berakhot ('Blessings')   First tractate of the Mishnah order of Zeraim ('Seeds'). It consists of nine chapters dealing with blessings and prayer in general.

Berdichevsky [Bin-Gorion], Micah Joseph (1885–1921)   Ukrainian Hebrew writer. He lived in Breslau and Berlin. In his writings he attacked the limited scope of Hebrew literature, the inadequacy of Haskalah, the ideology of Aḥad ha-Am, and Ḥibbat Zion. Influenced by Nietzsche, he called for a re-evaluation of Judaism and Jewish history and the expansion of the canons of Hebrew literary taste. His fiction depicts Jewish towns of Eastern Europe at the end of the 19th century and the life of Eastern-European Jewish students in the cities of central and western Europe.

Berechiah (fl. 4th cent.)   Palestinian amora. His aggadic sayings are found mostly in the midrashim and the Jerusalem *Talmud*. In his homilies he stressed the virtues of charity and the uniqueness of the Jewish people.

Berenice (b. 28)   Judean woman, eldest daughter of Herod Agrippa I. She married her uncle Herod of Chalcis. After his death in 48 she was suspected of incest with her brother Herod Agrippa II and was induced to marry Polemon II of Cilicia. In 60 she rejoined Herod Agrippa and supported his efforts to suppress the revolt against Rome. She fled with him to the protection of the Romans and became the mistress of Titus. Because of the adverse reaction of the Roman populace, she was forced to part from Titus.

Bererah ('choosing')   In rabbinic law a term used of a situation in which the facts or legal implications of a case will become known only at a future time. According to the *Talmud*, there are two types of bererah: in the first, the condition of doubt is due to an individual but the situation is certain; in the second, the situation itself is uncertain. In the first category the outcome may depend either on the individual or on the intention or action of others.

Bereshit Rabbati   Midrash on Genesis. Composed by Moses ha-Darshan of Narbonne in the 11th century, it was quoted by Raymund Martini as *Midrash Bereshit Rabbah Major* in the 13th century.

Bergmann, Samuel Hugo (1883–1975)   Czech philosopher. He was born in Prague. He was active in the Czech Zionist movement and in 1920 he settled in Palestine. He directed the National and University Library in Jerusalem and from 1928 taught philosophy at the Hebrew University, where he was Rector from 1936 to 1938.

Bergner, Yosl (1920–2017)   Israeli painter. Born in Vienna, he grew up in Warsaw. In 1937 he emigrated to Australia and in 1951 settled in Israel. His paintings depict the emotional world of early Russian settlers in Palestine.

Bergson, Henri (1859–1941)   French philosopher. Born in Paris, he taught philosophy at the Angers Lycée and later at Claremont-Ferrard. In 1889 he returned to Paris and in 1900 became Professor at the Collège de France. In 1928 he received the Nobel Prize for Literature.

Berit Shalom ('Peace Covenant')   Society founded in 1926 to promote peace between Arabs and Jews in Palestine. It was founded by Arthur Ruppin and recommended an Arab-Jewish state based on equal rights. It was replaced by Iḥud in 1940.

Berkovits, Eliezer (1908–1992)   American rabbi of Transylvanian origin. He served as a rabbi in Berlin, Leeds and Sydney. He later settled in the US, where he was Chairman of the department of Jewish philosophy at the Hebrew Theological College in Chicago. His writings include studies of religious faith after the Holocaust.

Berkovitz, Yitzhak Dov (1885–1967)
Hebrew and Yiddish author and trans-
lator of Belorussian origin. He lived in
the US and settled in Palestine in 1928.
His early writing deals with Jewish life in
Eastern Europe and Jewish immigrants
in the US. His later work includes
Menakhem Mendel beretz Yisrael and
Yemot Hamashiah. He translated from
Yiddish into Hebrew the writings of
Sholem Aleichem.

**Berlin, Irving [Balin, Israel] (1888–
1989)** American songwriter. Born in
Tumen, Siberia, he was the son of a
cantor. His family went to the US, and
he founded his own music publishing
company. He composed more than
1,000 songs and wrote songs for numerous films and Broadway shows.

Berlin, Sir Isaiah (1909–1997) English philosopher of Latvian origin. From
1957 he was Professor of Social and
Political Theory at Oxford University
and wrote widely on philosophical and
political subjects. He supported Israel
and Zionism. He also served as a governor of the Hebrew University.

**Berlin, Naphtali Tzevi Judah [Ha-
Natziv] (1817–1893)** Lithuanian talmudist. He was born in Mir and was
head of the yeshivah at Volozhin for 40
years. He was one of the first rabbis to
support Zionism.

Berliner, Abraham (1833–1915) German literary historian. Born in Posen,
he taught Jewish history and literature
at the Berlin Rabbinical Seminary.
His publications include an edition of
Rashi's commentary on the Pentateuch,
studies of medieval Bible commentators, an edition of the *Targum Onkelos*,
studies of Jewish life in the Middle Ages,
and a history of the Jewish community
of Rome.

Berman, Hannah (1883–1955) English novelist and translator of Lithuanian origin. She translated novels by
Shalom Aleichem and I.A. Lisky as well

as Yiddish short stories. She also wrote
two novels in English which describe
Jewish life in Lithuania under the rule
of Nicholas I.

Bermant, Chaim (1929–1998) British
writer of Polish origin. After settling in
the US, he worked as a school teacher,
economic television writer, and journalist. His writings include *Jericho Sleep
Alone, Diary of an Old Man, Israel, Trou-
bled Eden: An Anatomy of British Jewry,
The Cousinhood: The Anglo-Jewish Gentry, Point of Arrival: A Study of London's
East End, Coming Home* and *The Jews*.

Bernays, Isaac (1792–1849) German
rabbi. He was born in Mainz and served
as rabbi in Hamburg from 1821. In his
struggle against Reform Judaism, he
denounced the Reform prayer book.
His modern approach to Orthodoxy
influenced his disciple, Samson Raphael Hirsch.

Bernstein, Leonard (1918–1990)
American composer and conductor. He
was born in Lawrence, Massachusetts.
He became director and conductor of
the New York Philharmonic. His many
works on Jewish subjects include the
symphonies *Jeremiah* and *Kaddish*.

**Ber of Bolechov [Birkenthav, Ber]
(1723–1805)** Galician writer. As one
of the first maskilim, he took part in
a debate with the Frankists at Lvov in
1759. He wrote a polemic against the
Sabbetaians and the Frankists. His
memoirs are a major source for the
study of the economic and cultural conditions of Galician Jews in this period.

Bershadski, Isaiah (1817–1908) Russian Hebrew novelist. He was born
in Belorussia and lived in Russia. His
novel *To No Purpose* depicts Jewish life
in the Pale of Settlement, and *Against
the Stream* describes the collapse of traditional Russian Jewish life.

Bertinoro, Obadiah of (c.1450–1510)
Italian scholar. In 1485 he went to
Palestine and settled in Jerusalem,

where he founded a yeshivah. He was recognised as the chief halakhic authority in Palestine and Egypt. His writings include a commentary on the Mishnah, in which he incorporated the explanations of the *Talmud* as well as medieval commentators.

Beruryah (fl. 2nd cent.) Palestinian scholar. She was the wife of Meir. She is the only woman in Talmudic literature whose views on legal matters were recognised by contemporary scholars.

Besamim ('spices') They are used in the Havdalah ceremony at the end of the Sabbath.

Be-siman tov ('in good omen'). Expression of congratulation. It is the Sephardic equivalent of 'mazzal tov'.

Bet Second letter of the Hebrew alphabet. Its numerical value is 2.

Betar Youth organisation of the Zionist Revisionist Party, formed in Latvia in 1923 and spread to other countries. It played an important role in Zionist education, teaching Hebrew language and culture, and self-defence. Its members set up the National Workers Organisation in Palestine, founded settlements, and held prominent positions in the Irgun Tzevai Leumi. It was led by Vladimir Jabotinsky until 1940 when Menaḥem Begin became its leader.

Bet din ('house of judgement') Rabbinic law court. In the Temple period the Sanhedrin, which was made up of 70 or 71 scholars, decided on questions of religious law and approved judges. After the destruction of the Temple, the Sanhedrin became the central religious authority for all Jews. With the decline of Palestinian Jewry, the Sanhedrin was abolished and every Jewish community had a local court, which exercised authority over community matters. After Jewish Emancipation in the 19th century the authority of the bet din was limited to voluntary arbitration and ritual matters.

Bet ḥayyim ('house of the living') Term used of a cemetery.

Bet Hillel and Bet Shammai Two schools of sages during the 1st century. They differed in their decisions concerning more than 300 legal issues. Bet Shammai generally adopted a stricter interpretation. Rabbinic scholars subsequently accepted the majority of opinions of Bet Hillel.

Bet midrash [bet ha-midrash] ('house of study') Rabbinic school, where Jews gather for study, discussion and prayer. In the Second Temple period the Great Bet Midrash stood in the Temple hall. In the *Talmud* the term is used of an academy presided over by a legal scholar. Later, most synagogues had a bet midrash.

Betrothal (engagement) In Jewish law betrothal creates no matrimonial relationship, and either party may retract the promise of marriage. However, an aggrieved party can claim reimbursement for loss suffered and demand compensation. It is customary to draw up the terms of a betrothal in a document called the 'tenaim', which specifies the penalties payable by the defaulting party.

Bettelheim, Bruno (1903–1990) American psychologist and educator. He was born in Vienna. In 1938 he was transported to the Dachau concentration camp and then to Buchenwald. In 1939 he was released and settled in the US. He was Principal of the University of Chicago's Orthogenic School for children with severe psychological problems and Professor of Educational Psychology at the University. His psychological theories were based on his experiences in the concentration camps.

Betzah ('Egg') Seventh tractate of the Mishnah order of Moed. It deals with laws relating to festivals, and contains a list of differences of opinion between Hillel and Bet Shammai.

Bezalel (fl.?13th cent. BCE) Israelite craftsman, who constructed and decorated the Ark of the Covenant (Exodus 36:2).

Bezem, Naftali (b.1924) Israeli artist. He was born in Essen, Germany and went to Palestine in 1939. In 1947 he was a teacher of painting in the detention camps of Cyprus. A number of his works deal with biblical and Jewish themes. After the death of his son (caused by a booby trap) in Jeruslaem, he worked in Paris where he painted a series of pessimistic paintings.

Bialik, Ḥayyim Naḥman (1873–1934) Russian Hebrew poet, essayist, storywriter and translator. He was born in Zhitomir and lived in Volozhin, Odessa, Korostyshev, Sosnowiec and Warsaw. In 1924 he settled in Palestine. His poetry is infused with Jewish hopes, memories and national aspirations; written in a simple lyric style, it uses Hebrew metrics and biblical parallelism. His essays trace the course of Jewish culture, the state of Hebrew literature, and the development of language and style. Together with Yehoshua Ḥana Ravnitzky he published *Sepher ha-Aggadah*, which classified midrashic material according to subject matter.

Bibago, Abraham ben Shemtov (fl. 15th cent.) Spanish philosopher and writer. He was born in Aragon and became head of the yeshivah in Zaragoza. He engaged in disputations with Christian scholars at the court of Juan II, King of Aragon. His *The Path of Faith* examines the principal tenets of Judaism. He also wrote commentaries on Aristotle's works.

Bible [Old Testament; Scripture] The Hebrew Bible consists of 24 books divided into three sections: Torah (Pentateuch), Neviim (Prophets) and Ketuvim (Hagiographa). The Torah contains Genesis, Exodus, Leviticus, Numbers and Deuteronomy. The Prophetic books are subdivided into the Former Prophets (Joshua, Judges, I and II Samuel and I and II Kings) and the Latter Prophets, which are further subdivided into the Major Prophets (Isaiah, Jeremiah and Ezekiel), and the 12 Minor Prophets (Hosea, Joel, Amos, Obadiah, Jonah, Micah, Naḥum, Habakkuk, Zephaniah, Haggai, Zechariah and Malachi). The Hagiographa consists of Psalms, Proverbs, Job, The Song of Songs, Ruth, Lamentations, Ecclesiastes, Esther, Daniel, Ezra, Nehemiah, and I and II Chronicles. Early translations of the Bible are the Targum (Aramaic), Peshitta (Syriac), Septuagint (Greek) and Vulgate (Latin).

Bible, lost books of the Works cited in the Bible which have not survived. The principal lost books are the *Book of the Wars of the Lord;* the *Chronicles of the Kings of Israel* and the *Chronicles of the Kings of Judah;* the *Book of the Words of Solomon;* and the *Words of Iddo the Seer.*

Bible, translation of the The Aramaic Targum was the earliest translation of the Hebrew Scriptures, followed by the Greek Septuagint in the 3rd century BCE. The Syriac translation, the Peshitta, was made in the 2nd century CE and St Jerome created the first Latin version, the Vulgate, in the 4th century. Saadyah Gaon translated the Bible into Arabic in the 10th century, and Spanish and Yiddish editions were produced from the 15th century onwards.

Bible commentaries There are two basic types of commentary on the Bible: peshat (literal) and derash (homiletical). Biblical interpretation is regarded as falling into three periods: (1) before the age of the geonim (until the 6th century); (2) from the gaonic period to the Haskalah (6th–18th centuries); and (3) from the Haskalah to modern times. In the earliest period principles of exegesis were formulated by Hillel and later expanded by Ishmael. Commentators of the second period include Saadyah Gaon, Abraham ibn Ezra, Rashi, David Kimḥhi and Naḥmanides. Prominent among the commentators of the third period are Moses Mendelssohn, Samuel David Luzzatto and Abraham Kahana.

Biblical criticism   Critical study of the Hebrew Bible. Higher or literary criticism deals with questions of authorship, date of composition, style and the literary aspects of Scripture. Lower or textual criticism is concerned with textual matters and attempts to establish the true wording of the Bible.

Bibliography   The study, listing and description of books. Jewish bibliography makes two principal categories of works: Hebraica (works written or printed in Hebrew) and Judaica (works by or about Jews in other languages).

Bickerman, Elias J. (1897–1981) American historian. He was born in Kishinev in Ukraine. He taught at the University of Berlin from 1929 to 1932, when he emigrated to France. He later settled in the US, where he taught at the New School for Social Research, the Jewish Theological Seminary, the University of Judaism in Los Angeles, and Columbia University. His published writings cover ancient history, law, religion, epigraphy, chronology, and the political history of the Hellenistic world.

Bikkure ha-Ittim ('First fruits of the times')   Title of a Hebrew literary and scientific annual, published in Vienna from 1821 to 1832. It served as a forum for Haskalah literature.

Bikkurim ('first fruits')   11th and last tractate of the Mishnah order of Zeraim. It deals with the offering of the first fruits in the Temple (Exodus 23:19; Deuteronomy 26:1–11), and contains a description of the ceremony associated with it.

Bilah (fl.?19th–16th cent. BCE)   Israelite woman, concubine of Jacob. She was the mother of Dan and Naphtali. Rachel, whose servant she was, gave

Bilah to Jacob when she herself proved to be baren (Genesis 30:18; 32:25–26).

Bilu (Hebrew initials of Isaiah 2:5 'House of Jacob, come ye and let us go')   Russian Zionist youth group. It was formed in Khar'hov in 1882 in response to the pogroms of 1881 in southern Russia, and pioneered the return to Israel. A small group of men and women from its ranks reached Jaffa in the summer of 1882. Its name is made up of the initial letters of the phrase 'Bet Yaakov lekhu ve-nelkhah'.

Bimah ('elevated place')   Platform in the synagogue on which the reading desk stands. The Torah is read here. Alternative names are 'almemar', or among Sephardi Jews 'tebah'.

Binder, A.W. (1895–1966) American composer. He was born in New York. He became an instructor in Jewish music at the Jewish Institute of Religion in 1921 and Music Director at the Stephen Wise Free Synagogue the following year. In 1948 he was appointed Professor of Jewish Liturgical Music at the Hebrew Union College-Jewish Institute of Religion. He wrote synagogue services and songs, Hebrew and Yiddish songs, cantatas and oratorios, as well as chamber and orchestral music.

Biographies   The Book of Nehemiah, Josephus' apologetic *Vita*, and hagiographic works are the only works of biography and autobiography produced in ancient times. The first true Jewish biography is of Saadyah Gaon by his two sons at the request of Ḥasdai ibn Shaptrut. Biographical writing was almost unknown in medieval Hebrew literature, but after the Enlightenment biographical works began to make their appearance. In modern times biography has become a common genre of Jewish literature.

Birkat ha-Minim   Twelfth benediction recited before studying the law, and before and after being called to the public reading of the Torah. Special blessings are also recited before and after the reading of the Scroll of Esther on Purim.

Birnbaum, Nathan [Acher, Mattathias] (1864–1937) Austrian political philosopher. He was born in Vienna. An advocate of Jewish nationalism, he cooperated with Theodor Herzl and served as general secretary of the World Zionist Organisation. However, after the Third Zionist Congress in 1899, he became an opponent of the Zionist movement. He regarded cultural and political autonomy in the diaspora as the means of attaining Jewish national existence. He was a convenor of the conference at Czernowitz in 1908, which proclaimed Yiddish as a national language. Later he embraced Orthodoxy.

Birnbaum, Solomon (1891–1990) British palaeographer and Yiddish philologist of Austrian origin. He was born in Vienna. He lectured in Yiddish at Hamburg University from 1922 to 1933, when he emigrated to England. He taught Yiddish and Hebrew palaeography at the London School of Oriental Studies and the School of Slavonic and East European Studies. He wrote for Yiddish newspapers and journals and published works on Yiddish grammar. His major work is in the field of palaeography.

Birth control According to the midrash, this practice goes back to the wicked generations before the Flood. In Genesis birth control is referred to in connection with Onan who spilled his seed on the ground (Genesis 38:9–10). The *Talmud* and responsa deal with the subject in detail. Birth control methods may be used only by the wife; the highest preference is for oral contraceptives.

Birthright In ancient Jewish law the privilege of the first-born son to lead the family and receive a double share of the inheritance. It was an ancient prac-

tice reflected in the Bible. Talmudic law provides for the disposal of property in accordance with parental preference, so that the biblical inheritance laws should not be applied.

Biur Hametz ('Elimination of leaven') Household ceremony at which all leaven is burnt on the morning before Passover begins. It follows the search for leaven the previous evening.

Black Death Plague which killed a large portion of the population of Europe in the 14th century. Jews were accused of causing the disease by poisoning wells, and were attacked throughout Europe.

Black Jews A number of black Jewish congregations exist in New York. Claiming descent from the Falashas, the main group was organised in 1930 by Wentworth A. Matthew.

Blankfort, Michael (1907–1982) American novelist, playwright and screen-writer. He was born in New York. He taught psychology at Bowdoin College and Princeton, and worked as a clinical psychologist. Subsequently, he was a freelance novelist, dramatist and screenwriter. His novel *The Juggler* portrays the disturbance and eventual recovery of a Holocaust survivor in Israel. *Behold the Fire* deals with the Nili, a secret group of Palestinian Jews who served as spies for the British.

Blaser, Issac ben Moses Solomon (1837–1907) Lithuanian rabbi and educator. He was born in Vilnius. A disciple of Israel Salanter, he served as rabbi in St Petersburg and later settled in Kovno, Lithuania, where he headed the advanced talmudic academy. He helped to found the yeshivah of Slobodka. In 1904 he emigrated to Palestine and settled in Jerusalem. He made an important contribution to the Musar movement in his emphasis on acquiring piety by emotional meditation on works of musar.

Blasphemy Insult directed against religious belief or sacred things. Speaking contemptuously of God is forbidden in the Bible and was punishable by death (Leviticus 24:10–23). This punishment was later replaced by excommunication. The Mishnah restricts the definition of blasphemy to cases in which the name of God is pronounced.

Blau, Amram (1894–1974) Palestinian religious leader. He was born in Jerusalem. He was a founder of the anti-Zionist Ḥevrat Ḥayyim and refused to recognise the State of Israel when it was established in 1948. When Ḥevrat Ḥayyim was reconstituted as the ultra-Orthodox sect Neturei Karta he became its leader. After his first wife's death he married a proselyte, Ruth Ben-David.

Blemish In Jewish law a physical or moral defect that disqualifies a person for the Temple service or an animal for sacrifice. Any of the 12 physical defects debars a priest from performing his duties (Leviticus 21:16–23). Rabbinic law extends this list to 142. Moral blemishes also render a priest unfit. Biblical law lists defects that make an animal unsuitable for sacrifice (Leviticus 22:20–25), and rabbinic law lists 73. An animal set aside for idolatrous worship is also forbidden.

Blessing of children In the Bible importance is attached to parental blessing; however, the custom of blessing children on the Sabbath eve is a later innovation. The formulae used are 'God make thee as Ephraim and Manasseh' for boys, and 'God make thee as Sarah, Rebekah, Rachel and Leah' for girls. This is followed by the Priestly Blessing. Both hands are placed on the head of the child while saying the blessing. Among the Sephardim the blessing is also given after the father or child has performed a religious duty in the synagogue. There are special formulae for specific occasions (such as the eve of the Day of Atonement).

Bloch, Ernest (1830–1959) American composer of Swiss origin. He was Pro-fessor of Composition at the Geneva Conservatory. In 1917 he settled in the US, where he served as Director of the San Francisco Conservatory of Music. His works include *Trois poèmes juifs*, *Israel Symphony*, the rhapsody *Shelomoh*, and *Avodat ha-kodesh*.

Blondes, David (fl. late 19th–early 20th century) Lithuanian barber. He was accused of wounding a girl in order to use her blood for ritual purposes. He was convicted of injurious intent and sentenced to prison. On appeal in 1902 he was acquitted of all charges.

Blood In the Bible blood is spoken of as life itself. (Leviticus 17:11, 14; Deuteronomy 12:23). The prohibition against consuming it is one of the seven laws given to Noah (Genesis 9:4). Jewish law prescribes that blood must be drained from a slaughtered animal before it is eaten. Blood was sprinkled on the altar during the Temple sacrifice as a symbol of atonement.

Blood avenger One who takes revenge for the murder of a relative by killing the murderer. In the Bible, blood vengeance is permitted without punishment only in cases of accidental manslaughter. The slayer could seek asylum in any of the six Cities of Refuge (Deuteronomy 19:1–10). Intentional murder was to be punished by the regular processes of law (Exodus 21:12–14; Deuteronomy 19:11–13). The *Talmud* outlines varous rules on the subject.

Blood libel (ritual murder libel) Allegation that Jews murder non-Jews to obtain blood for Passover or other rituals. In Christian countries Jews were accused of murdering children at Easter to use their blood in the preparation of matzot or in the seder rites. This led to trials and massacres of Jews in the Middle Ages and the early modern period.

Bloom, Harold (b.1930) American literary critic and editor. He was born in New York and taught at Yale. In his literary work he has been influenced by the kabbalah and by Martin Buber.

Bloom, Hyman (1913–2009) American painter. He was born in Bounoviski, Lithuania, and emigrated to the US in 1920. Following the Depression he was employed in the Federal Arts Project in Boston. Early in his career he painted works dealing with European Jewry and he later returned to themes of the synagogue and Jewish observance.

Blum, Léon (1872–1950) French statesman. He first worked as a literary critic and author. He was premier in the Popular Front government of 1936–37, vice-premier from 1937–38, and premier in 1938. In 1943 he was handed over to the Germans, who deported him to Buchenwald, but he survived the war and was liberated in 1945. In 1946–47 he was head of an interim government and he became vice-premier in 1948. He was active in Jewish affairs and served on the council of the Jewish Agency.

Boaz Israelite landowner, husband of Ruth. When Ruth came to glean in his fields, Boaz saw and admired her devotion to her widowed mother-in-law Naomi. As a kinsman of Elimelech (Ruth's father-in-law), Boaz undertook to marry her (Ruth 2-4).

Bobemeise (Yiddish: 'grandmother's tale', 'incredible story') The word is derived from the title of the chivalric romance that Elijah Levita adapted from *Buovo d'Antona* (the Italian version of *Sir Bevis of Hampton)*. Levita's work appeared as *Bovo d'Antona* and was later printed as *Bove-bukh*. In later editions it was titled *Bove-mayse*. The Yiddish word for grandmother ('bobe') led to the substitution of *Bobe-mayse* for *Bove-mayse*.

Bodek ('examiner') Official who inspects a slaughtered animal to ensure that it is ritually acceptable. A licensed ritual slaughterer is refered to as 'shohet u-vodek'.

Bodo (fl. 9th cent.) French churchman, who converted to Judaism. Originally a deacon of the palace of Louis the Pious, he went to Spain in 838 and adopted Judaism under the name Eleazar. He engaged in religious debate with Paolo Alvarez of Córdoba, a Christian layman.

Body The belief in the duality of the body and soul is not found in Scripture. In rabbinic literature, however, the body is regarded as the seat of passion and the cause of sin, though both body and soul are accountable for misdeeds. The human body is viewed as the possession of God, of which human beings are simply custodians. At death the body must be kept inviolable; hence Orthodox Jews are opposed to creation, dissection, embalming or any other violaton of the body's integrity. The doctrine of the resurrection of the body is a central aspect of rabbinic eschatology.

Boethusians Jewish religious and political sect, active in the 1st century BCE. It was named after Boethus, a disciple of Antigonus of Sokho (or possibly after the high priest Simeon ben Boethus). Its adherents denied the belief in the resurrection and an afterlife.

Bohr, Niels (1855–1962) Danish physicist. Born in Copenhagen, he was the son of a non-Jewish father. He became Professor of Chemical Physics at the University of Copenhagen, and in 1920 Head of the Institute of Theoretical Physics. In 1922 he was awarded the Nobel Prize.

Bomberg, Daniel (d. between 1533–1549) Hebrew printer. He was born in Antwerp. He founded a Hebrew publishing firm in Venice in 1516, which published about 200 books, including the first complete editions of the Palestinian and Babylonian Talmuds, the Tosephta and the Rabbinic Bible. His pagination of the *Talmud* has become standard.

Bomberg, David (1890–1957) English painter. He was born in Birmingham and lived in the East End of London. A number of his paintings were influenced by scenes in the Whitechapel area. From 1923 to 1927 he lived in Palestine and later travelled widely. He returned to England and taught at the Borough Polytechnic in London from 1945 to 1953.

Bonfils, Joseph ben Samuel [Tov Elem; Tuv Elem] (fl. 11th cent.) French talmudist. He was born in Narbonne and lived at Limoges and Anjou. He wrote religious poems, biblical and talmudic commentaries, and codifications of Jewish law.

Book of Life A book kept in Heaven, in which the names of the righteous are inscribed. The belief in the existence of heavenly ledgers is alluded to several times in the Bible. In the Mishnah, Akiva describes the heavenly book in which all human actions will be written down until the Day of Judgment. The same belief is expressed in the liturgy of the high holy days.

Bookplate Label pasted into a book indicating its owner. Bookplates made by Christian Hebraists are known from the early 16th century. The earliest known bookplate made for a Jew was that of Isaac Mendes of London engraved by Benjamin Levi in 1746. In the 19th and 20th centuries Jewish bookplates often used Jewish symbols and motifs.

Books Books were originally written in the form of a scroll, but under Roman influence the volume with leaves was adopted. Older Hebrew books were small, but in many cases larger volumes were created by binding a number together. In the Middle Ages illumination was common in Hebrew books such as the Passover Haggadah. In the early modern period Amsterdam and cities in Italy and Eastern Europe became important centres for the production of Hebrew books.

Books, burning of The attack on Jewish literature in the Middle Ages began with the Disputation of Paris in 1240; the *Talmud* was condemned and cartloads of Hebrew books were burned. Similar incidents took place in other cities. In 1553 thousands of volumes of Jewish literature were burned in Rome. This example was followed throughout Italy. In 1757 copies of the *Talmud* were burned in Poland after a disputation with the Frankists. On 10 May 1933, Nazis burned vast numbers of Jewish books throughout Germany.

Books, prohibited The proscription of Jewish literature by the Roman Catholic Church began in the 13th century at the time of the Disputation of Barcelona. In 1564 the Council of Trent published the *Index librorum prohibitorum*, which listed, among other things, the *Talmud* and its glosses, annotations, interpretations and expositions. In the Jewish community itself attempts were made to ban the writings of Maimonides (13th century), Immanuel ben Solomon of Rome (16th century) and Azariah dei Rossi (16th century).

Borochov, Dov Ber (1881–1917) Ukrainian Socialist Zionist leader and writer. He was a founder of Poale Zion in 1906 and served as Secretary of the World Confederation of Poale Zion. Having left Russia, from 1914 he was a spokesman for the American Poale Zion and for the World and American Jewish Congress movements. He later returned to the USSR. He analysed the economic and social situation of the Jewish people along Marxist lines, and argued for their settlement in Palestine.

Borowitz, Eugene (1924–2016) American theologian. He was born in New York. He became Professor of Education and Jewish Religious Thought at the Hebrew Union College-Jewish Institute of Religion in 1962. He is the author of numerous books about contemporary Jewish thought and has served as visiting professor at various universities including Princeton, Columbia and Harvard.

Boscovitch, Alexander Uriah (1907–1964) Israeli composer. He was born in Cluj, Transylvania, and conducted the Jewish Goldmark Orchestra there. In 1938 he settled in Palestine, and later became a music critic for the daily paper *Ha-Aretz*. He advocated the development of a nationalist school of composition in which the composer would reperesent the new reality of life in Palestine.

Bostanai, ben Ḥanina (fl. 7th cent.) Babylonian exilarch. He was the first exilarch after the Arab conquest and his office was confirmed by the caliph Omar. He was appointed a member of the Council of State, and married a daughter of Chosroes, the former Persian king.

Botany The study of plants. The Bible mentions about 100 types of plant. The Mishnah refers to 180 species in connection with various aspects of Jewish law. Maimonides presented a systematic classification of plants in his *Mishneh Torah*. In the Middle Ages Jewish scholars translated Greek studies of botany. The earliest scientific description of plants by a Jewish scholar is in the *Colloquies* by the 16th-century Marrano physician Garcia d'Orta.

Brafman, Jacob (c.1825–1879) Russian scholar. He was born in Kletsk. He converted to Christianity, joining the Greek Orthodox Church, and served as teacher of Hebrew at the government theological seminary in Minsk. Later he was Censor of Hebrew and Yiddish books in Vilnius and St Petersburg. His *The Book of the Kahal* is a translation into Russian of the minutes of the kehillah of Minsk; it describes how Jews acquire power over gentiles and it was used to justify anti-Semitic acts.

Brainin, Reuben (1862–1939) American Hebrew and Yiddish author of Russian origin. He was born in Belorussia and lived for a time in Vienna and Berlin. At the beginning of the 20th century he encouraged the infusion of humanistic themes and new literary forms into Hebrew literature. From 1909 he lived in the US and Canada. During his later years he devoted himself to journalism, through which he supported Jewish settlement in the Russian province of Birobidjan. He edited a number of Hebrew and Yiddish periodicals.

Brandeis, Louis Dembitz (1856–1941) American lawyer and Zionist leader. He served as a justice in the Supreme Court from 1916 to 1939, its first Jewish member. He was active in American Zionism and the World Zionist Organisation. Brandeis University was named after him.

Brandstätter, Mordecai David (1844–1928) Galician Hebrew novelist. He was a successful manufacturer and owing to the circles in which he moved became interested in Haskalah. He contributed stories about Ḥasidic life in Galicia to the Hebrew journal *Ha-Shaḥar*. In his writing he ridiculed the Ḥasidim and the materialism of Galician Jewry. He later joined the Ḥibbat Zion movement and extolled Zionism in his stories.

Braudes, Reuben Asher (1851–1902) Lithuanian Hebrew novelist and reformer. He was born in Vilnius and lived in Odessa, Warsaw and Lemberg, where he edited the monthly journal *Ha-Boker Or*. He later lived in Romania and Vienna. His novel *Two Extremes* depicts the limitations of Haskalah and Orthodoxy, and endorses Jewish nationalism. His writings, which advocate social and religious reform, reflect the intellectual changes taking place in Eastern-European Jewish society at the end of the 19th century.

Brauer, Erich (b.1929) Austrian painter. He was born in Vienna. From

1938 to 1945 he was interned in a concentration camp. After the liberation he traveled extensively, and lived in Austria and Israel. His paintings depict crimes against the Jews, such as pogroms and the Holocaust.

Breach of trust   Biblical laws dealing with this topic relate to bailment. A bailee suspected of misappropriating the property entrusted to him must taken an oath that he has not 'put his hand on his neighbour's goods' (Exodus 22:10). By analogy, others suspected of wrongdoing are obligated to take a similar oath. If a bailee falsely denies possession of the bailment and his deception is proved, he is rendered untrustworthy and is debarred thereafter from taking an oath or acting as a witness.

Bread   In the Bible and hence in Jewish life bread is regarded as the most important element of a meal. The blessing of bread takes precedence over that of any other solid food. The full Grace after Meals is recited only when bread has formed part of the meal.

Breaking of the Vessels   Kabbalistic term used to describe the primordial catastrophe that took place during Creation. According to Isaac Luria, divine light emanated from Adam Kadmon into Creation. It burst the vessels which were to contain it and many divine sparks fell and were captured by the realm of darkness. As a result, the cosmos is in need of repair ('tikkun') and restoration.

Breastplate   Sacred object worn by the high priest (Exodus 28:15ff). It consisted of a square gold frame in which were set 12 gems of different colours representing the tribes of Israel. It also held the Urim and Thummim. The term is now applied to the silver ornament placed in front of the cover of the Torah scroll in Ashkenazi congregations.

Brenner, Yoseph Ḥayyim (1881–1921)   Hebrew author and editor of Ukrainian origin. He edited the *Bund* newspaper in Homel in 1898. His sketches of Jewish poverty in Russia appeared in 1900 and were followed by his novels *In Winter* and *Around the Point.* From 1904 to 1907 he lived in London, where he published the journal *Ha-Meorer,* which criticised Jewish political life. Later he lived in Lemberg, where he edited *Revivim.* In 1909 he settled in Palestine and became a leader of the workers' movement. His stories of this period describe contemporary Palestinian life. In 1919 he became the editor of the journal *Ha-Adamah.* He was murdered by Arabs.

Breuer, Isaac (1883–1946)   Leader of Orthodox Jewry, of Hungarian origin, son of Solomon Breuer. He lived in Frankfurt am Main where he was active in Jewish organisations. When Agudat Israel was founded in 1912 he became one of its ideologists. He settled in Jerusalem in 1936 and he served as president of Poale Agudat Israel. He published works on Judaism and Jewish problems.

Bribery   Bribery is condemned in the Bible and *Talmud*, where it is considered particularly in relation to judges. A judge is disqualified form adjudicating in a case if he receives a favour. When judges were given a salary, they were paid a year in advance to discourage the accepting of bribes. However, the *Talmud* regards the bribery of non-Jewish rulers, officials and judges as legitimate in view of their prejudice against Jews.

Brill, Jehiel (1836–1886)   Hebrew journalist of Russian origin. He settled in Palestine, where he edited the journal *Ha-Levanon* in 1863–64. The periodical reappeared under his editorship in Paris in 1865, and later in Mainz from 1872 to 1882. It supported Jewish law and the Jerusalem rabbis, and attacked the Haskalah and religious reform. After the Russian pogroms of 1881, Brill returned to Palestine and helped to found the colony of Ekron. As a result of a dispute he left the country and settled in London, where he founded the Yiddish newspaper *Ha-Shulamit*. He also published editions of several medieval texts.

Broche (Yiddish: 'blessing') A prayer of thanksgiving or praise.

Brod, Max (1884–1968) Austrian author and composer. He was born in Prague. He was a founder of the National Council of Jews of Czechoslovakia and became active in the Zionist movement. In 1939 he settled in Tel Aviv, where he worked as a music critic and drama adviser to the Ha-Bimah Theatre. His writings include a trilogy of historical novels, a story of the Israeli War of Independence and studies of Judaism. He was the discoverer and biographer of Franz Kafka, whose works he edited.

Broderson, Moses (1890–1956) Russian Yiddish poet and theatre director. He was born in Moscow and lived in Lódź from 1918 to 1938. He was a journalist, poet and writer of songs for children. He founded a number of small theatres and wrote modest plays and librettos for operas. He was confined to a Siberian labour camp from 1948 to 1955. His wife, Sheyne Miriam Broderson, described their years of misery in *My Tragic Road with Moshe Broderson.*

Brodie, Sir Israel (1895–1979) English rabbi. He was born in Newcastle upon Tyne. He served as senior minister in Melbourne, Australia, from 1923 to 1937. After several years as a senior chaplain in the British Army he was appointed Chief Rabbi of the British Commonwealth.

Brodski, Iosif [Joseph] Aleksandrovich (1940–1996) Russian poet. After having been arrested several times, he left the USSR in 1972, and settled in the US. His publications include the poem *Isaak i Avraam*, which deals with the sacrifice of Isaac. He also wrote a poem about the Jewish cemetery near Leningrad.

Brody, Heinrich (1868–1942) Hebrew scholar of Hungarian origin. He was appointed Chief Rabbi in Prague in 1912. He settled in Palestine in 1933 and was apponted head of the Schocken Institute for Hebrew Poetry. He was co-founder and editor of the *Zeitschrift für hebraïsche Bibliographie* and edited poems of Judah Ha-Levi, Moses ibn Ezra and Immanuel of Rome.

Bródy, Sándor (1863–1924) Hungarian novelist and playwright. He prepared the ground for the development of Hungarian prose in the 20th century. A number of his stories and plays introduce Jewish characters. His collection of short stories, *Misery*, was the first work of Hungarian literature to describe the Jewish worker, and his play *Timár Liza* portrayed the decadence of assimilated Jews in Hungary.

Brokerage The function of an intermediary acting for another in a legal transaction. According to Jewish law, the broker acts as an agent. Since he is paid for his services, he is liable for the loss or theft of the property of the person retaining him, and for personal negligence. In cases of dispute, the broker may clear himself by taking an oath if there are no witnesses and he insists that he was authorised to accept the terms realised. The marriage broker ('shadḥan') acts as a go-between in arranging marriages.

Bronfman, Samuel (1891–1971) Canadian liquor and oil magnate. Born in Brandon, Manitoba, he left school at the age of 15. He later joined his brothers in the hotel business, and in his early twenties took charge of a hotel in Winnipeg. The Bronfman family subsequently entered the liquor trade. With the end of prohibition, Bronfman expanded his business; later he took the firm into the petroleum business.

Brooks, Mel (b.1926) American film director, writer and actor. He was born in New York, and first worked as a comedian in the Borscht Belt of New York's Catskill Mountain resorts. Later he was one of a team of comedy writers for *The Sid Caesar Show* and *Your Show of Shows*. He also wrote, directed, produced and acted in a number of films. He is one of those comic writers and performers who see humour as a traditional Jewish response to adversity and a way of effacing anger.

Bubbe (Yiddish) Term of endearment.

Buber, Martin (1878–1965) Austrian theologian, grandson of Solomon Buber. He was born in Vienna. He joined the Zionist movement and became editor of *Die Welt* in 1901. He founded the Jewish National Council in Berlin during World War I and in 1916 established the monthly journal *Der Jude*. With Franz Rosenzweig he translated the Bible into German. From 1924 to 1933 he taught at the University of Frankfurt. He settled in Palestine in 1938 and became Professor of Social Philosophy at the Hebrew University. His writings include *I and Thou, For the Sake of Heaven, Between Man and Man, Tales of the Ḥasidim, The Prophetic Faith,* and *Two Types of Faith.*

Buber, Solomon (1827–1906) Galician rabbinic scholar. He was born in Lemberg and was a governor of the Austro-Hungarian Bank and the Galician Savings Bank. He published scholarly editions of midrashim, edited works by medieval scholars and wrote on the history of the Jews of Poland.

Bubkes (Yiddish) Something trivial, worthless, absurd or foolish.

Bublick, Gedaliah (1875–1948) American Yiddish journalist and Zionist leader. He was born in Russia. In 1900 he helped to lead a group of 50 Jewish families to Argentina. He settled in New York in 1904, where he became editor of the Yiddish *Jewish Daily News*. He was a founder of the American Jewish Congress and served as President of the

Mizraḥi Organisation of America from 1928 to 1932.

Budko, Yoseph (1888–1940) Polish painter and graphic artist. He was born in Plonsk then lived in Berlin from 1910 to 1933, when he settled in Jerusalem. He served as Director of the Bezalel School of Arts from 1935. His work was influenced by Eastern-European Jewish life and scenes in Jerusalem.

Bulan (fl. 8th cent.) King of the Khazars. After a religious debate in Khazaria on the merits of Christianity, Islam and Judaism, he and his servants converted to Judaism.

Burglary In Scripture house-breaking by night is regarded as a more serious offence than ordinary theft since danger to life is assumed to be involved (Exodus 22:1). The house owner is exonerated if he kills a thief who breaks in at night, but not if the burglary takes place during the day. The *Talmud* states that the burglar must restore the stolen article or its equivalent without an additional fine.

Burial In ancient times the dead were buried in earthen graves or caves cut in rock. Whenever possible burial took place on the day of death. Bodies were sometimes dressed in costly garments, but later it became standard practice to bury the dead in a plain linen garment. Coffins consisted of a simple wooden casket. Eventually, the Ḥevra kaddisha ('holy brotherhood') was organised in every Jewish community to provide for the rites of burial; its members helped to read the deathbed confession ('viddui'), wash and dress the corpse, carry out the burial service and actual burial and provide the special meal for the mourners.

Burla, Yehudah (1886–1969) Israeli novelist. He was born in Jerusalem. He became head of the Arab Department of the Histadrut, an envoy of Karen Hayesod to Latin American countries, and Director of Arab affairs in the Israeli Ministry of Minorities He wrote stories and novels depicting the life of the Middle-Eastern Sephardim.

Burning Bush The desert shrub from which God appeared to Moses at the foot of Mount Horeb. The bush was aflame but was not consumed (Exodus 3:2–4).

Buxtorf, Johannes (1564–1629) Swiss Hebraist. He was Professor of Hebrew at the University of Basle. He edited *Biblia Hebraica Rabbinica* (the Hebrew Bible with rabbinic commentaries) and compiled the *Bibliotheca Rabbinica* (a rabbinic bibliography). He also wrote a Hebrew grammar and a Hebrew and Aramaic lexicon.

Byzantine rite Liturgical rite of the Jews of the eastern Roman Empire. It was contained in the *Maḥzor Romania*, which was printed in the 16th and 17th centuries. Eventually it was superseded in Turkey and the Balkans by the Sephardi rite.

C

A poignant scene. A man is on his deathbed with his loving daughter by his side. It is clear he is fading fast and his death is drawing nigh. With his voice weak and barely audible, he suddenly tells his daughter he smells kugel (noodle pudding). 'Yes,' she says, 'Mom is making kugel.' Could she, he asks his daughter, get him a piece so, before he dies, he could have a final taste of his wife's kugel? 'Of course, Daddy,' she says as she bounds over to the kitchen to fulfil her father's dying wish. In the meantime, her father is barely hanging on, and when she returns she sits down at his bedside and folds her hands but says nothing. Barely able to utter the words, he asks: 'Where's the kugel?' His daughter answers, 'Mom says it's for after.'

* * * * *

Jewish wives are frequently portrayed in Jewish jokes as heartless. Not only do they dominate their sons and daughters, they are callous about their husbands. Here the father is terminally ill. He is on his deathbed. In his last moments he craves a kugel. His daughter is by his side and goes to ask her mother for a piece to give him. She refuses and the daughter comes back empty-handed. Apologetically she explains that her mother was saving it to give to guests after his death. Jews laugh at this tale because it is so terrible. But there is tragedy under the surface.

Caceres, Abraham (fl. 18th cent.) Dutch composer of Portuguese origin. He was the leading musician of the Portuguese community of Amsterdam. In 1726 he provided music for the consecration of the Ḥonen Dal synagogue in The Hague.

Caceres, Francisco [Joseph] de (b. c.1580) Spanish Marrano writer. After leaving Spain he lived in France and Amsterdam. His writings include *Nuevos fieros españoles*, *Dialogos satýricos*, and *Visión deleytable y sumario de todas las sciencias*.

Caceres, Simon [Jacob] de (d. 1704) English merchant. He was born in Amsterdam and settled in London before 1656. He lived openly as a Jew and urged Marranos in London to practise Judaism. He advised Cromwell during the Conquest of Jamaica. He was one of the signatories of a petition organised by the Jews of London requesting freedom of worship, and he helped with the acquisition of the first congregation cemetery in 1657.

Cahan, Abraham (1860–1951) American Yiddish journalist and author. He was born in Lithuania and settled in the US in 1882. He organised the first Yiddish periodicals to propagate his theories of socialism and Americanisation. From 1897 he was editor-in-chief of the Yiddish newspaper the *Forverts*. His novel *The Rise of David Levinsky* portrays the urban immigrant experience in America.

Cahan [Cohen], Yaakov (1881–1961) Hebrew author of Russian origin. He taught at the Institute for Jewish Studies in Warsaw from 1927 to 1933. The following year he settled in Palestine. He wrote lyrics, ballads, epic poems, folk stories, and novels. Many of his poems and ballads were influenced by Jewish folklore.

Caiaphas, Joseph (fl. 1st cent.) High priest. Appointed by the procurator Valerius Gratus, he also served under Pontius Pilate. The New Testament portrays him as largely responsible for the prosecution of Jesus (Matthew 26).

Cain Eldest son of Adam and Eve. When God accepted the animal sacrifice of Abel his brother but rejected his offering, Cain killed Abel (Genesis 4).

Caleb (fl.? 19th–16th cent. BCE) Israelite, one of the 12 spies sent to explore Canaan. He and Joshua were the only two spies to bring back a favourable report. As a result Caleb was allowed to enter the Promised Land. He captured Hebron and expelled its inhabitants, the Anakim (Numbers 13–14; Joshua 14–15).

Calendar (Hebrew 'luaḥ') The Jewish calendar consists of 12 months, calculated according to the lunar cycle. The months are Nisan, Iyyar, Sivan, Tammuz, Av, Elul, Tishri, Marheshvan (Ḥeshvan), Kislev, Tevet, Shevat and Adar. In a leap year there are two months of Adar. The numbering of years in the Jewish calendar is calculated from the creation of the world, which coincides with 3760 BCE. The year 5000 began on 1 September 1239. To calculate the Jewish year since 1240, 1240 should be deducted from the year of the Common Era (CE) and 5000 added. For dates in September–December another year is added.

Calendar, reform of the The irregularity of the Gregorian calendar has led to a movement to reform it: a year of 364 days would be kept; a 'blank' day every year (two 'blank' days in a leap year) would not be reckoned part of any week. This change would cause the Sabbath to fall on different days of the week every year. The American League for Safe-guarding the Fixity of the Sabbath is a Jewish organisation which has taken action opposing this change.

Calf worship Calves or young bulls were regarded as symbols of strength and fertility by ancient Semitic peoples. Traces of calf worship are found in the account of the Golden Calf (Exodus 32) and the golden calves set up at Dan and Bethel by Jeroboam (I Kings 12:28–30).

Candles In Jewish practice the lighting of candles characterises both joyful and sorrowful occasions. As a symbol of joy it is a feature of the Sabbath and of feast days. This custom was instituted by the Pharisees during the period of the Second Temple. The lighting of candles on these occasions (accompanied by the appropriate blessing) is the prerogative of the principal woman in the household. Candles are also placed by the head of a deceased person, and are used during the week of mourning for the dead, on the anniversary of a death, and on the eve of the Day of Atonement.

Canetti, Elias (1905–1994) Austrian novelist, essayist and dramatist. He was born in Ruse in Bulgaria. He was a freelance writer and translator and in 1938 he went to London, where he settled. In 1981 he received the Nobel Prize for Literature.

Cantarini, Issac Cohen (1644–1723) Italian rabbi and physician. He lived in Padua and his *Paḥad Yitzḥak* describes the anti-Jewish outbreaks in the city in 1684. His *Vindex Sanguinis* is a refutation of the blood libel charge.

Cantillation Musical or semi-musical chanting of a liturgical text in the Jewish synagogue tradition.

Cantonists Name given to conscripts between the ages of 12 and 18 in tsarist Russia. The system of conscription was in force from 1805 to 1856 and Jews beame subject to it from 1827. Many Jewish boys were conscripted with the intention of converting them to Christianity. From the age of 18 military service for Jewish males lasted for 25 years. Jewish communal leaders who were responsible for selecting recruits frequently filled their quota with children from poor homes. They were trained outside the Pale of Settlement and sent to distant lands.

Cantor (Hebrew 'ḥazzan') In Jewish worship the synagogue official who leads the worshippers in prayer and is in charge of the music. In the ancient Temple the liturgy was intoned by priests and Levites. In the synagogue service a prominent member of the community conducted the prayers. During the Middle Ages more complex music, known as 'cantorial' music ('ḥazzanut'), came into fashion, and the office of cantor was established. Further musical developments in the 18th century had an impact on cantors who studied musical composition and instrumental playing. In the 19th and 20th centuries outstanding cantors included Joseph Rosenblatt, Zavel Kwartin, Mordecai Hershman, David Roitman, Aryeh Leib Rutman, Mosheh Kusevitsky and Leib Glanz.

Capital punishment The death penalty was decreed by biblical law for murder, sexual crimes (such as adultery and incest), blasphemy, idolatry, desecration of the Sabbath, witchcraft, kidnapping and dishonour of parents. According to talmudic law, it may not be carried out unless two eyewitnesses testify to the crime. In addition, the perpetrator must have previously been warned concerning the crime and its punishment. The Bible specifies three types of capital punishment: stoning, burning and hanging. Rabbinic law also specifies slaying by the sword and strangulation. Capital punishment was rarely imposed under Jewish law and many rabbis advocated its abolition. In the diaspora Jews were subject to the laws and punishments of the lands in which they lived, and particular forms of execution were inflicted on them because of their race and faith. In the Middle Ages they were frequently executed by being hung by the heels. It was also common practice to exacerbate the punishment by stringing up dogs on either side of the condemned person.

Capsali, Elijah (1483–1555) Cretan rabbi and historian. He was head of the Jewish community in Crete. His *Seder Eliyahu Zuta* contains a survey of the history of Jewry in the Ottoman Empire down to his day, as well as an account of Spanish Jewish history, His *Divrei ha-Yahmim le-Malkhut Venezia* depicts the condition of the Jews in Venice and the Venetian dominions. It is a central source for the social, cultural and political history of north-Italian Jewry in the early 16th century.

Cardozo, Abraham (1626–1706) Spanish Marrano physician and mystic. He was born in Rio Seco. He became an adherent of Shabbetai Tzevi, supporting him even after his apostasy. He expounded Sabbetaian doctrines in a number of published works. His theology was based on gnostic dualism. He disparaged the value of the hidden First Cause and placed supreme importance on the God of Israel.

Cardozo, Benjamin (1870–1918) American Supreme Court Justice. Born in New York, he practised law until he was elected to the Supreme Court of New York. Eventually he became Chief Judge of the Court of Appeals, and in 1932 was appointed to the United States Supreme Court.

Cardozo, Isaac (1604–1681) Portuguese Marrano physician and philosopher. He was physician at the Royal Court of Madrid. Persecuted by the Inquistion, he fled to Venice where he embraced Judaism. He later settled in Verona. In his *Philosophia Libera* he opposed the teachings of the kabbalah and Shabbetai Tzevi. His *Las excelencias y calumnias de los Hebreos* describes ten virtues of the Jewish people and refutes ten calumnies.

Caricatures The earliest caricatures of Jews are Roman terracotta figures. An early example in modern times is found in an English Exchequer Roll of 1233. At the close of the Middle Ages caricatures were common in Germany and with the invention of printing they circulated in engraved form. In England the readmission controversy (1655–56) and the 'Jew Bill' gave rise to a new wave of popularity and a similar effect was produced in France by the Dreyfus case. Anti-Jewish caricatures were widely circulated throughout the 19th century in Germany and reached a climax during the Nazi period.

Carlebach, Azriel (1908–1956) Israeli journalist. He was born in Leipzig. He was secretary of the International Sabbath League. After serving as a foreign correspondent for several newspapers, he founded and edited *Maariv,* the most important Hebrew newspaper in Israel.

Carlebach, Joseph (1882–1942) German rabbi and educator. After teaching in Jerusalem, he founded a Hebrew high school in Kovno, Lithuania. He then succeeded his father, Solomon Carlebach, as rabbi of Lübeck. He became Chief Rabbi of Altona and later of Hamburg. He published commentaries on the Song of Songs, the Prophets and Ecclesiastes, as well as a study of Levi ben Gershon.

Carmi, Tcharney (1925–1994) Israeli poet and literary historian. He was born in New York, but in 1946 he left the US for France, where he worked with Jewish war orphans. In 1947 he emigrated to Palestine. His publications include *There are No Black Flowers, Snow in Jerusalem,* and *At the Stone of Losses.* He edited the *Penguin Book of Hebrew Verse,* and was one of the editors of *The Modern Hebrew Poem Itself.* In addition he translated numerous classic works into Hebrew.

Carmoly, Eliakim (1802–1875) German rabbi, writer, and editor. He was born in Alsace. He served as a rabbi in Brussels in 1832 and later settled in Frankfurt am Main, where he published articles about ancient manuscripts and books. His other publications include a work on the Ten Lost Tribes, descriptions of his travels in Palestine, a genealogy of the Rapoport family and a coronation poem in praise of Louis-Philippe of France. He was a pioneer in the study of Jewish medicine and Jewish physicians.

Caro [Karo], Joseph (1488–1575) Spanish talmudic codifier. He was born in Toledo, then settled in Turkey after the expulsion of the Jews from Spain in 1492. In 1536 he left Turkey for Safed, where he was the head of a large yeshivah. His *Bet Yoseph* (House of Joseph) is a commentary on Jacob ben Asher's *Arbaah Turim.* He also compiled its classical abbreviation, Shulḥan Arukh (The Prepared Table). His codes were criticised by Ashkenazi scholars, who claimed that they ignored French and German traditions. Nevertheless,the Shulḥan Arukh (printed with Moses Isserles' strictures) became the authoritative code for Orthodox Jewry.

Carrière des Juifs (French: 'Jewish area')   Term applied in Avignon and the Comtat Venaissin to the ghetto. Local Jews referred to it by the Hebrew term 'mesillah'.

Carrion, Santob de (fl. 14th cent.) Spanish poet. His *Proverbios morales* is a collection of aphorisms dedicated to King Pedro of Castile. It is the principal work by a medieval Jew in secular Spanish literature. Santob de Carrion has been identified with the Hebrew poet Shem Tov ibn Ardutial.

Cartography   The science of map making. Cartograhy flourished in the Middle Ages in Majorca, where Abraham Cresques was 'Master of Maps and Compasses' to the Infant Juan of Aragon. The work of Abraham Cresques and his son Judah included the Catalan Atlas. About 1500 Judah Abenzara of Alexandria and Safed produced important maps. The first Jewish map of Palestine with Hebrew lettering appeared in Amsterdam in the 17th century.

Carvajal, Antonio Fernandez (c. 1590–1659) Portuguese merchant. He settled first in the Canary Islands and later in Rouen. He eventually lived in London, where he engaged in trade with the East and West Indies. He organised a foreign information service for Oliver Cromwell. He was head of the crypto-Jewish community at the time that Manasseh ben Israel requested the readmission of the Jews to England (1655–56).

Caspi, Joseph ben Abba Mari (1280–c.1340)   French commentator, philosopher, and grammarian. He was born in L'Argentière and lived in Tarascon in southern France. He wrote commentaries on Maimonides' *Guide for the Perplexed*. As a follower of Aristotle and Averroes, he equated their teaching with Judaism. He evoked the oppositon of many rabbis who regarded his views as heretical.

Cassel, David (1818–1893) German scholar. He was born in Silesia. He lectured at the Hochschule für die Wissenschaft des Judentums in Berlin. His publications include a history of Jewish literature, German translations of the Apocrypha and Judah ha-Levi's *Kuzari* and critical editions of classical texts.

Cassin, René (1887–1976) French statesman. He was born in Bayonne. He was Professor of Law at the universities of Lille and Paris, and French delegate to the League of Nations from 1924 to 1938. He served as National Commissoner for Justice and Education under De Gaulle (1941–3), head of the Conseil d'État (from 1944), and French delegate to the UN General Assembly (1946–51). He was awarded the Nobel Peace Prize in 1968. He also served as President of the Alliance Israélite Universelle.

Cassirer, Ernst (1874–1945) Philosopher of Polish origin. Born in Breslau, he studied under Hermann Cohen at the University of Marburg. In 1903 he began teaching at the University of Berlin. He published studies of Leibniz, as well as a fourteen-volume treatment of the problem of knowledge. Later he was offered chairs at the universities of Frankfurt and Hamburg, where he developed theories of symbolic form and myth. In 1929 he was elected Rector of the University of Hamburg. With Hitler's rise to power, he left Germany and subsequently settled in the US.

Cassuto, Moses David [Umberto] (1883–1951) Italian biblical scholar. He was born in Florence and became Chief Rabbi there and Director of the Collegio Rabbinico Italiano. He was Professor of Hebrew at the University of Rome, and from 1939 Professor of Bible at the Hebrew University. He was editor-in-chief of the *Biblical Encyclopedia* and prepared the *Jerusalem Bible* for publication. His other publications include studies of Italian Jewish history and Immanuel of Rome, and catalogues of the Hebrew manuscripts in Florentine libraries.

Castel, Moshe (1909–1991) Israeli painter. He was born in Jerusalem. He was a member of the New Horizons group of Israeli painters. Judaism and Israel were dominant themes in his art. He produced a stained-glass window for the synagogue of the SS *Shalom* in 1956. His later paintings are reminiscent of ancient steles, in which writing is incorporated into the subject matter.

Castelnuovo-Tedesco, Mario (1895–1965) American composer of Italian origin. He was a member of an old Florentine family. He settled in Hollywood, where he wrote film music. In 1925 he found a notebook of Jewish melodies in his grandfather's house, which encouraged him to write Jewish compositions.

Castration According to Scripture, castrated animals were unfit to be used as sacrifices on the altar (Leviticus 22:24). Any man who was crushed or maimed in his private parts was not allowed to enter into the assembly of the Lord or to marry within the Jewish congregation (Deuteronomy 23:2). In the *Talmud* and the codes the prohibitions were extended to cover any man, domestic animal, beast or bird whose reproductive organs were impaired, as well as any man who had been impotent and was then castrated.

Castro, Abraham de (fl. 16th cent.) Egyptian financial administrator. He was Director of the Mint in Cairo and Supervisor of Economic Affairs in Egypt. When the Egyptian pasha (in revolt against Sultan Suleiman I) ordered Castro to issue a new coinage bearing his name, he refused. He escaped to Constantinople and informed the sultan of the pasha's rebellion. As a result the pasha was put to death. Egyptian Jews commemorate the date of the pasha's execution (28 Adar) as a feast day (Purim of Egypt).

Castro, Jacob de (1758–1824) English comedian. He was born in London. He acted in traditional Purim plays and in 1786 joined Philip Astley's troupe known as 'Astley's Jews'. In 1803 he was appointed manager of the Royal Theatre, London. His *Memoirs* cast light on English Jewish life.

Castro Tartas, Isaac de (c.1625–1647) Portuguese Marrano martyr. He was the son of Portuguese New Christians (i.e. Jews converted to Christianity), who settled in Tartas in southern France. He lived in Amsterdam and Brazil before moving to Bahia. There he lived outwardly as a Catholic, but his pretence was detected and he was arrested. He was condemned and burned alive in Lisbon in 1647. He recited the Shema before he died, and his memory inspired many Marranos in the diaspora.

Catacombs Subterranean tunnels with side recesses for tombs. The practice of burying the dead in catacombs originated with the Palestinian Jews. Catacombs are found in Rome, elsewhere in Italy, and in north Africa. They were also used by the early Christians in Rome.

Catechism Instruction in religious doctrine by question and answer; a book containing such instruction. The first published Jewish catechism was Abraham Jagel's *Lekaḥ Tov*. During the period of Emancipation, many catechisms were published and occasioned religious controversy.

Catechumens, House of Hostel in Rome for Jewish converts to Christianity. It was established in 1548 with the support of the Roman Jewish community. Similar institutions were founded in other Italian cities. The potential convert received instruction for 40 days. If he then refused baptism, he was allowed to return to the ghetto.

Cattaui, Joseph Aslan (1861–1942) Egyptian politician, nephew of Moses Cattaui. He was an official in the ministry of public works, directed a sugar factory, and set up other industrial plants. In 1915 he became a member of the Egyptian delegation to London to negotiate the independence of Egypt. In 1924 he was appointed Minister of Finance, and in the following year Minister of Communications. He served as a senator (1927–36) and as President of the Jewish community.

Celan, Paul (1920–1970) German poet. He was born in Czernowitz and after the war lived in Bucharest, where he worked as a translator. In 1947 he escaped and went to Vienna and Paris, continuing to translate and also teach languages. Several of his poems commemorate the victims of the Holocaust.

Cemetery In ancient times cemeteries consisted of a series of caves cut in rock. Later the dead were buried in graves. According to Jewish law, cemeteries are to be located far from human habitation. A special benediction is recited on entering a cemetery, and no priest may enter one. Buildings for discharging burial rites are usually attached. Graves are visited on anniversaries, fast days and during the month preceding Rosh Ha-Shanah.

Censorship Censorship of Jewish literature began in the Middle Ages. After the Disputation of Paris in 1240 the *Talmud* was condemned and burned. As a result of the Disputation of Barcelona in 1263 Jews were ordered to delete references to Jesus from Maimonides' *Code*. A papal bull of 1554 specified that works other than the *Talmud* could be owned by Jews only if they contained no blasphemies against Christianity. Subsequently in most of Italy Hebrew books could not be kept unless they had been approved by a Christian censor. The Jewish Synod of Ferrara instituted a form of pre-censorship in 1554 to ensure that nothing obejctionable was published. Similar censorship existed in the Austrian dominions in the 17th and 18th centuries, and in Russia after 1790.

Census The Bible discourages the counting of the population. Nonetheless the first census of the Jewish people took place at Mount Sinai following the Exodus from Egypt (Exodus 38). Another census was conducted at Shittim in Moab before the Israelites entered the Promised Land (Numbers 26). The last census mentioned in the Bible took place at the close of David's reign (II Samuel 24). Estimates of the Jewish population since biblical times have generally been speculative, but they have become more reliable in recent years.

Ceremonial laws Observances prescribed by Jewish law, such as rites connected with the Sabbath and festivals, dietary laws, circumcision, marriage, death etc. Jewish sources emphasise the practical importance of such observances, and the laws concerning them were codified by such Jewish scholars as Maimonides, Jacob ben Asher and Joseph Caro. Today, while Conservative Judaism encourages modifications of the legal system where relevant, Reform Judaism regards many ceremonial laws as outmoded.

Ceremonial objects They are used in the synagogue and at home on the Sabbath and festivals, as well as during ceremonies marking life-cycle events. They include Torah scrolls, Torah cases and covers, Torah crowns, Torah breastplates, pointers, Arks, curtains for the Ark, lamps, spice boxes, Sabbath candlesticks, kiddush cups, Sabbath tablecloths, Hannukah menorahs, Esther scroll cases, seder plates, etrog containers, chairs of Elijah, wedding rings, wedding canopies and mezuzahs.

Cerfberr, Herz (1726–1794) Alsatian Jewish leader. He worked as an army contractor and employed many Jews in his factories. In 1780 he asked Moses Mendelssohn to help him in his efforts to improve the condition of Jews in Alsace. He commissioned a translation into French of Christian Wilhelm von Dohm's book encouraging Jewish emancipation. This resulted in the appointment of a commission to report to the king concerning the legal position of the Jews. As a consequence the poll tax for Jewry was abolished.

Chagall, Marc (1887–1985) French artist of Russian origin. He was born in Vitebsk and studied in St Petersburg and Paris. In May 1914 he had a one-man show in Berlin. In 1917 he was appointed Commissar for Fine Arts in Vitebsk and Director of the Free Academy of Art. Later he became Designer for the Chamber State Jewish Theatre. He settled in France in 1923, and emigrated to New York in 1941. Later he returned to France. Eastern-European Jewish life is a dominant theme in his work.

Chair of Elijah Symbolic chair set aside for the prophet Elijah at the circumcision ceremony. It is positioned to the right of the sandak and the child is placed for a moment in the chair before being moved to the sandak's lap for the circumcision to be carried out.

Chajes, Tzevi Hirsch (1805–1855) Galician rabbi and scholar. He was a rabbi at Zolkiev and Kalisz. He was influenced by Naḥman Krochmal and corresponded with leading maskilim of Galicia and Italy (such as Solomon Judah Rapoport, Samuel David Luzzatto, and Isaac Samuel Reggio). Although he introduced modern critical methods into talmudic and cognate studies, he was a defender of Orthodoxy. He wrote on the principles of the Written and Oral Law, the Targums and midrash, and the *Talmud*.

Chajes, Tzevi Peretz (1876–1927) Galicial rabbi and scholar, grandson of Tzevi Hirsch Chajes. He taught at the Collegio Rabbinico Italiano in Florence and at the University of Florence. In 1912 he was appointed Chief Rabbi at Trieste. From 1918 until his death he was Chief Rabbi of Vienna. He served as Chairman of the Zionist Actions Committee from 1921 to 1925. He published studies of biblical exegesis, archaeology, the *Talmud* and Hebrew poetry.

Chao Ting Ch'eng (d.1657) Chinese civil servant. He was born in Kaifeng. He entered public service as a mandarin and served at Fukien, and in Hukwang. He was largely responsible for rebuilding the Kaifeng synagogue. Although he was regarded as a Confucian mandarin when in Fukien, he lived as a religious Jew when in Honan, his home province.

Chapbook A small, cheap book of popular ballads, stories etc. Chapbooks were a regular feature of Eastern-European Jewish life in the 19th and 20th centuries. Vast numbers of poorly printed works of popular appeal were sold in markets and streets by itinerant pedlars. They included miraculous tales about Ḥasidic rabbis, ethical treaties, religious works and instructions on divination. With the development of Yiddish literature, cheap novels were distributed in the same fashion.

Chaplain A priest or clergyman attached to an institution or ministering to a military group or professional body. The first known Jewish military chaplains are those apointed in the US Army curing the Civil War. In World War I American chaplains served full-time, and during World War II a chaplaincy committee of the National Jewish Welfare Board was organised. Military chaplaincy services also exist in other countries. In Israel the chaplaincy plays an active role in army life. A Jewish chaplaincy system for hospitals and prisons is organised in most Western countries.

Charity (Hebrew 'tzedakah') The giving of money or material goods to help the poor and needy. In the Bible it is spoken of as an obligation, and involves offering succour to the widow, the orphan, the stranger, and the aged. The Mishnah assumes a well-defined system of organised relief. The rabbis stipulated that the highest form of charity is that in which the donor and recipient are unknown to one another. Maimonides believed that the best kind of charity involved helping the needy person to support himself in some occupation. By the Middle Ages philanthropic institutions were firmly established in the Jewish community. In the 19th and 20th centuries Jews took an active part in a wide range of Jewish charitable work. In modern times the development of state welfare activities has significantly altered the nature of Jewish philanthropy, the state having assumed some of the traditional functions of charity, such as care of the aged and destitute.

Charney, Daniel (1888–1956) Belorussian Yiddish poet and journalist. He was born in Minsk. He suffered from illness from early childhood and when he attempted to emigrate to the US in 1925 he was refused entry because of ill-health, and was forced to return to Europe. He finally settled in New York after the rise of Nazism. His stories, fables and articles (including a series on the conditions of Jews in Lithuania, Latvia and Poland) were printed in newspapers in Russia, Poland and the US.

Chasanowitsch, Leon [Schub, Kasriel] (1882–1925) Labour Zionist leader, of Lithuanian origin. He was born near Vilnius. He became active in Labour Zionism in 1905 and in 1908 was forced to flee from the Russian police to Galicia. He served as secretary of the world Poale Zion movement from 1913 to 1919. He published studies on the Polish and Ukrainian pogroms and

represented Labour Zionism at international socialist congresses.

Chastity Abstinence from sexual commerce. The biblical emphasis on sexual purity is linked with the condemnation of idolatry. Four of the 12 curses in Deuteronomy 27 are directed against those guilty of sexual sins which must not be committed under pain of death. Sexual commerce outside marriage is forbidden by Jewish law. Early marriage was seen as the best safeguard against sexual impurity.

Chayefsky, Paddy (1923–1981) American playwright. He was born in New York. His work draws on Jewish life and tradition. His *The Tenth Man* is based on the legend of the dybbuk and *Gideon* was inspired by the biblical account of the Hebrew judge's victory over the Midianites.

Chazanovitz, Joseph (1844–1919) Lithuanian Zionist. He practised medicine in Grodno, Bialystock, and Yekaterinoslav. He was one of the first members of Ḥovevei Zion. He helped to establish a central Jewish library in Jerusalem, which became the basis of the Jewish National Library.

Chernaikov [Tcherniakov; Tchernikhovski], Adam (1881–1942) Polish labour leader. He was head of the organisation of Jewish craftsmen in Poland after World War I. Under Nazi occupation, he was chairman of the council of the Warsaw Ghetto. In 1942, when confronted by a demand to supply the names of Jews for deportation, he committed suicide. His diary is an important historical source about the Warsaw Ghetto.

Cherub Supernatural being, or image of such a being, depicted variously in the Bible as a winged figure with human, animal or bird's head and body. The cherubim gurarded the gates to the Garden of Eden (Genesis 3:24). In the Tabernacle images of cherubim were placed on either side of the Ark, forming the throne of God (Exodus 25:18–20; 37:7–9). Later such images were located in the Holy of Holies in the Temple. Ezekiel describes four cherubim carrying the divine throne (Ezekiel 1). In post-biblical literature they are identified with angels.

Chief rabbi Principal rabbinical authority of a national or provincial Jewish community. Chief rabbis were appointed in various countries in the Middle Ages. In modern times Napoleon desired to set up consistories presided over by a grand rabbi. In Germany before unification the chief rabbinate existed in various provinces. In England the chief rabbi represents British Jewry. In Israel there are two chief rabbis from the Ashkenazi and Sephardi communities. Not all countries, however, have a chief rabbi. The US is a notable example.

Childbirth In biblical literature birth pangs are viewed as the legacy of Eve's disobedience. Rabbinic literature contains discussion of problems connected with birth. Superstitious practices connected with birth, including the wearing of amulets, were known in talmudic times and the Middle Ages and are condemned in rabbinic literature. A special prayer of thanks is recited in the synagogue after childbirth.

Child sacrifice It was practised as a religious act in Moab and Canaan. The account of the binding of Isaac (Genesis 22) illustrates that child sacrifice was not required of the ancient Israelites. The Mosaic code specifically prohibits such a practice, laying down in its place symbolic and vicarious redemption or consecration to the service of God.

Choir A choir of Levites participated in the services of the First Temple. After the destruction of the Temple, the rabbis prohibited all music as a sign of mourning. In Babylonia the ceremony for the installation of the exilarch included singing by a choir. In the Renaissance synagogue choirs were introduced and by the 19th century choirs were accepted in many Western synagogues. Also in the 19th century Ḥasidic groups introduced unaccompanied congregational singing. Reform congregatons have used mixed choirs and an organ in the synagogue service.

Cholent Dish made of beans, eaten by the Ashkenazim for the Sabbath midday meal. Prepared on Friday afternoon, it is placed in the local baker's oven to cook overnight; it is taken home to be eaten after the Sabbath service. The Sephardim prepare a similar hot dish for the Sabbath called 'hamin'.

Chomsky, Noam (b.1928) American linguist. He studied at the University of Pennsylvania and was Professor of Linguistics at Massachusetts Institute of Technology. In addition to studies of linguistics, he wrote works critical of American foreign policy and Israeli politics.

Chosen people The belief that the Jews were the chosen people of God is based on the covenant between God and Abraham (Genesis 15). The covenant was renewed on Mount Sinai, but the Jews' election was now made conditional on their observance of the Torah (Deuteronomy 7:6). Israel is spoken of in Exodus as a kingdom of priests and a holy nation (Exodus 19:6). The prophets taught that election is based on righteousness. In the Mishnah and *Talmud* the role of Israel as the teacher of all nations is emphasised. The Jewish idea of chosenness does not imply superiority, but rather the obligation to fulfil religious and moral duties.

Chouraqui, Nathan André (1917–2007) Israeli author and politician. He was born in Algeria. From 1959 to 1963 he was an adviser to David Ben-Gurion on the immigration to Israel of ethnic minorities. He was later deputy mayor of Jerusalem (1965–69). His publications include *Between East and West: a History of the Jews of North Africa.*

Christiani, Pablo (fl. 13th century) French Dominican monk. He was born in Montpellier. He converted to Christianity and joined the Dominican order. In 1263 a public disputation took place in Barcelona between him and Naḥmanides in the presence of King James I of Aragon. In 1269 he persuaded Louis IX of France to compel Jews to listen to his sermons and to wear the Jewish badge.

Christianity A Jewish sect of followers of Jesus Christ emerged in Palestine in the 1st century. They believed that Jesus was the Messiah and had brought about the Kingdom of God. The New Testament preserves traditions about Jesus' life and teaching, and the epistles of Paul and others addressed to scattered Jewish Christian communities. The Early Church accepted Jesus as God incarnate, regarded the Hebrew Scriptures as authoritative and developed its own traditions. Christianity quickly spread from the Jewish to the gentile community and over the centuries became a world religion with its own theology, liturgy moral code and way of life. Because of their failure to recognise Jesus as Messiah and their role in his death, Jews have frequently been persecuted by Christians, however there has been a remarkable reconciliation with Judaism over the last couple of generations.

Chronicles (Hebrew 'Divre ha-Yamim') The name of two biblical books in the Hagiographa. They contain geneaological lists of the Israelite tribes from Adam to the time of David (I Chronicles 1–9); an acount of David's rule (I Chronicles 10–29); an account of Solomon's reign (II Chronicles 1–9); and a history of the Kingdom of Judah to its destruction by the Babylonians (II Chronicles 10–36).

Chronology The establishing of the proper sequence of past events. The Bible uses events such as the Flood, the reigns of kings, and the Babylonian exile to establish dates. Subsequently Jewish dates were fixed according to the number of years that have traditionally lapsed since Creation. In Western countries Jews use the abbreviations BCE (before the Christian or Common Era), and CE (Christian or Common Era) instead of BC and AD.

Chuetas Name given to the Marranos of Majorca, who were descended from the victims of forced baptism in 1391 and 1435. They were subjected to inquisitional persecutions in the 17th century.

Church councils Ecclesiastical assemblies. During the history of the church such assemblies have been much concerned with Jewish matters. It was the task of regional councils to enforce local anti-Jewish regulations, whereas general councils were concerned with an overall policy toward the Jewish community. The Council of Nicaea in 325 widened the breach between Christianity and Judaism. The Third Lateran Council in 1179 enacted restrictive measures against the Jews, and the Fourth Lateran Council of 1215 decreed that Jews must wear a Jewish badge. In the 15th century the Council of Basle condemned the *Talmud* and recommended conversionist sermons. The Second Vatican Council (1962–65) declared that the Jewish people cannot be blamed for the death of Jesus.

Churgin, Pinkhos M. (1894–1957) Scholar of Belorrusian origin. He emigrated to Palestine in 1907 and later settled in the US. He was Professor of Jewish History and Literature at Yeshiva University and dean of its teachers' institute. In 1955 he emigrated to Israel and became head of Bar-Ilan University. He published studies of the Targumim and the history of the Second Temple period.

Chwolson, Daniel (1819–1911) Russian orientalist of Lithuanian origin.

He was born in Vilnius. He converted to Christianity in 1855. He was Professor of Hebrew, Syriac, and Chaldaic Philology at the University of St Petersburg and the the Russian Orthodox and Roman Catholic theological academies in the same city.

Circumcision (Hebrew 'bris', 'brit milah')   The removal of the foreskin of the penis. In Jewish practice circumcision is carried out at a ceremony which also includes the naming of the child and is held when he is eight days old. It is a sign of the covenant between God and the Jewish people and is performed according to instructions given to Abraham (Genesis 17:11–12). The child to be circumcised is first placed in the Chair of Elijah. Then the sandak holds the child in his lap and the mohel carries out the circumcision. Blessings over a cup of wine follow the operation while the child is given his name. Male converts must also undergo circumcision.

Cities of refuge   Moses assigned six cities as places for those who accidentally committed manslaughter (Numbers 35:13; Deuteronomy 19:9). There the person was free from persecution by an avenger.

City of David   Title used generally as a synonym for Jerusalem. More precisely it means that area which constituted the city in David's time.

Civil courts   According to Jewish law, Jews are prohibited from having recourse to non-Jewish courts of justice. In the 2nd century Tarphon applied such a prohibition even in cases where the dispensation of justice was identical with that of Jewish courts. Medieval Jewish authorities insisted that Jews bring their disputes only before their own courts. Such a prohibition has been largely abandoned in the modern period. The only occasion on which systematic attempts are made to avoid recourse to civil courts is when the dispute affects the internal regulations of the community.

Civil rights   The personal rights of the individual citizen, usually upheld by law. In Ancient Israel civil rights were enjoyed only by those belonging to a tribe. Later some Jews became citizens of Greek cities or obtained Roman citizenship and enjoyed the rights that accompanied such a status. The Edict of Caracalla in 212 gave citizenship to all free members of the Roman Empire excpt those recently conquered. Subsequently Jews were excluded from full citizenship in Christian lands. During the Middle Ages they were royal dependants. In the Western world the acquisition of full civil rights by the Jews began in the 18th century.

Classical literature, Jews in   Hellenistic writers regarded Judaism as a barbarous religion and interpreted the Jewish rejection of the Greek deities as atheism. They mocked circumcision, the dietary laws, and the Sabbath. A number of Roman writers such as Cicero, Juvenal, and Tacitus also criticised Judaism and the Jewish people.

Clean animals   Animals which, according to Jewish law, may be eaten and whose milk may be drunk. Detailed descriptions of clean and unclean animals are given in Leviticus 11:1–47 and Deuteronomy 14:3–20.

Coat of arms   The heraldic bearings of a family or person. The midrash describes the flags of the 12 tribes of Israel, some of which became family badges in the Middle Ages. Priestly families used the symbol of hands spread in blessings on tombstones. From the 16th century many Italian Jewish families had distinctive badges. Coats of arms are found among Jews only from the 17th century.

Coffin   In the Bible there is a reference to the use of a coffin for the body of Joseph (Genesis 50:26). During the Hasmonean period Jews collected the bones of the dead in sarcophagi. The use of coffins dates only from the Second Temple period.

Cohen, Abraham (1887–1957) English scholar. He was born in Reading. He served as minister to the Birmingham Hebrew Congregation and was the first minister to preside over the Board of Deputies of British Jews. He edited the Soncino Books of the Bible.

Cohen, Ḥayyim (1911–2002) Israeli lawyer. He was born in Lübeck and settled in Palestine in 1930. From 1953 to 1960 he was Attorney General and contributed to the founding of the Israeli legal and judicial system. He was Minister of Justice in 1952–53 and in 1960 was appointed a justice of the Israeli Supreme Court. His publications include *Foreign Laws of Marriage and Divorce* and *The Trial and Death of Jesus*.

Cohen, Hermann (1842–1918) German philosopher. He was born in Coswig. He was Professor of Philosophy at the University of Marburg until 1912 and later taught at the Hochschule für Wissenschaft des Judentums. In 1880 he began to resume his hitherto lapsed links with Judaism and to defend the Jewish people and tradition.

Cohen, Israel (1879–1961) English writer. He was born in Manchester. From 1922 he was secretary of the Zionist Organisation in London, on whose behalf he visited Jewish communities in Egypt, Australia, China, Manchuria, Japan, Java, and India. His writings include *Jewish Life in Modern Times*, *The Zionist Movement*, *A Short History of Zionism*, and *Theodor Herzl: Founder of Political Zionism*.

Cohen, Naphtali ben Isaac (1649–1719) German rabbi and Kabbalist. He served as rabbi at Ostrog, Posen, and Frankfurt am Main, where he was known as a practical Kabbalist. He resigned his post when it was alleged that his Kabbalistic experiments were responsible for the destruction of the Frankfurt Ghetto by fire. He died at Constantinople on his way to Palestine. He was an opponent of the Sabbetaians.

Cohen, Sir Robert Waley [Waley Cohen] (1877–1952) English Jewish communal leader. He was Managing Director of the Shell Transport and Trading Company and Chairman of the Palestine Corporation. He served as President of the United Synagogue and Vice-President of the Board of Deputies of British Jews.

Cohen, Shalom ben Jacob [Ha-Cohen, Shalom] (1772–1845) German Hebrew poet of Polish origin. He joined the circle of maskilim in Berlin. In 1809 he revived the journal *Hameasseph*, then in 1821, after settling in Vienna, he founded the annual *Bikkure ha-Ittim*. He later lived in Hamburg. He wrote poems on biblical themes and Jewish textbooks.

Cohen, Tobias [Tobias the Doctor] (1652–1729) Turkish physician and author, of German origin. He was born in Metz. He served as court physician in Turkey until he was 62. He then went to Jerusalem to concentrate on the study of Torah. His *Maaseh Tovyah* is an encyclopedia dealing with theology, astronomy, cosmography, geography, botany and medicine. It also contains references to Shabbetai Tzevi.

Cohon, Samuel Solomon (1888–1959) American theologian. He was born in Minsk. He became Professor of Theology at the Hebrew Union College in 1923. He was active in the Central Conference of American Rabbis and served as the principal draftsman of the Columbus Platform, the statement of principles of Reform Judaism. He was an editor of the *Union Haggadah* and the *Rabbi's Manual*, and his writings include *What We Jews Believe*.

Coins The basic unit of weight and therefore the basic coin in the Bible was the shekel. Hasmonean coins (135–37 BCE) carry Hebrew inscriptions and certain symbolic images (lulav, etrog, chalice, palm). In the war against Rome (66–70) Jewish patriots issued silver shekels bearing Hasmonean symbols. Many of the coins circulated by Simeon Bar Kokhba (132–35) were defaced Roman issues, altered to show the rebuilt Temple. Subsequently Jews used the coinage of the countries in which they lived, until the establishment of a Jewish homeland in the 20th century.

Colon, Joseph (c.1420–1480) Italian rabbinic scholar. He was born in France. He served as rabbi in various Italian communities, including Pavia, which he made the centre of Italian talmudic learning. After his death his responsa were collected and published. His decisions had considerable influence on later Italian halakah.

Columbus, Christopher (1451–1500) Explorer of Italian origin, discoverer of America. He was possibly of Marrano extraction. He boasted about his connections with King David and was interested in Jewish and Marrano society. His name was not unknown among Italian Jews of the late medieval period. On his journeys he used nautical instruments perfected by Jews such as Joseph Vecinho, and nautical tables drawn up by Abraham Zacuto.

Commerce In biblical times Solomon encouraged international commerce. After his reign, it did not flourish again until the Maccabean period. With the rise of Islam, Jews served as middlemen in trade between the Islamic world and countries in Christian Europe. In the Middle Ages Jews were excluded from merchant guilds. Later, Marranos developed trade between Europe, America and the Levant. With the Industrial Revolution and the rise of capitalism, Jews became widely involved in banking, foreign trade, and railway construction. In the 19th and 20th centuries Jews have engaged in the whole spectrum of commercial activities.

Communal affairs In Ancient Israel the Jews were able to control communal affairs in their own country. After the Babylonian exile, the synagogue became the focus of religious life. The patterns of institutional development which evolved during the exile served as the foundation of Jewish communal structures in many other countries. In the Hellenistic world nearly all Jewish communities modelled their organisation on that of Greek cities. In the Roman Empire the Jews, like all other subjects, were permitted to establish and maintain religious organisations and municipal corporations. In Babylonian, the Jewish community was headed by a dynasty of exilarchs. In other countries the head of the community was often a nagid. In the Middle Ages Jewish communities had authority over their own internal affairs. After the Emancipation Jews were granted full citizenship rights and no longer exercised jurisdiction over their own civil life.

Communism Political movement which aims to achieve through revolution the proletarian control of society and public ownership of the means of production. It is based on the writings of Karl Marx. At the time of the Russian Revolution, nearly all Jewish socialist parties opposed communism, whereas the communist movement regarded Zionism as a tool of imperialism. Nevertheless some leaders of the Russian Communist Party were of Jewish origin and in several countries Jews took an active role in promoting communism.

Community council Local body elected by the Jewish community to govern some aspects of its life. Community councils are an adaption of the European kehillah to the requirements of Jewish life in the US. They represent the variety of views in the community, and their activities include philanthropy, community relations, education, and internal Jewish affairs.

Compassion   In the Bible God is frequently described as compassionate. Human beings must imitate this divine attribute in their dealings with one another and their treatment of animals. Rabbinic Judaism enlarged this biblical concept, regarding compassion as of primary importance.

Comtino, Mordecai ben Eliezer (1420– before 1487)   Turkish rabbinic scholar and scientist. He was born in Constantinople and became one of the leaders of the Hebrew cultural movement there. Two of his hymns were incorporated into the Karaite liturgy.

Concentration camps   The term is applied specifically to the prison camps established after the accession to power of the National Socialists in Germany in 1933. Initially they were intended for the detention of opponents of the new regime, then individuals were sent there on orders of the Gestapo. Later entire groups (particularly those racial groups condemned under the Nazis' Aryan policies) were arrested and committed to the camps, which grew to about 1,000 in number. In six major camps (Auschwitz, Treblinka, Belzec, Maidanek, Sobibor and Chelmo) the mass extermination of millions of victims was carried out in specifically constructed gas chambers.

Confession of sin   The Bible mentions the efficacy of public and individual confession of sin. Sin offerings accompanied by prayer played an important role in the Temple sacrifice service. In the synagogue the confession of sins was part of the liturgy for daily services and the Day of Atonement. At death a special confession ('viddui') is prescribed.

Conforte, David (1618–c.1690)   Greek rabbi and literary historian. He was born in Salonica. He founded a bet midrash in Jerusalem and served as rabbi in Cairo. His *Kore ha-Dorot* is a chronicle of authors and works from post-talmudic times until the 17th century.

Congratulations   The most common expressions of congratulations among the Ashkenazim are 'mazzal tov' (good luck) and 'mazzal u-verakhah' (luck and blessing). Among the Sephardim, the expression 'be-siman tov' (in good omen) is used. On performing a religious duty, the form of congratulation among the Ashkenazim is 'yeyasher koaḥ' (may he increase your strength). Among the Sephardim it is 'ḥazak u-varukh' (be strong and blessed). As a toast the expression 'le-ḥayyim' (to life) is used. A birthday greeting is 'ad meah (ve-eserim) shanah' [may you live] to a hundred (and twenty).

Conscription   Compulsory military service. During the tribal period in Ancient Israel, all able-bodied men were to serve in the military from the age of ten (Numbers 1:3). The kings retained the power of conscription (II Kings 15:19). In the 4th century Jews were legally excluded from the forces of the Roman Empire and in the Middle Ages they were forbidden to bear arms.

Consecration   The making holy of someone or something, thus the dedication of a person or thing for a special use or function. Ceremonies of consecration, involving anointing with oil, are mentioned in the Bible in connection with kingship and priesthood. Vessels used in the Tabernacle were similarly anointed. The rededication of the altar by the Maccabees is commemorated by Ḥanukkah. In post-biblical times consecration ceremonies took place when synagogues were established. The bar mitzvah marks the consecration of a boy to the observance of the commandments.

Conservative Judaism   Religious movement which arose in the middle of the 19th century in Europe and the US. Reacting against Orthodox and Reform Judaism, its founders believed that the traditional forms and precepts of Judaism were valid but permitted some modifications of the halakhah. In the

US it has its own rabbinical seminary (Jewish Theological Seminary of America). It has become a major force both there and in other countries.

Consistory Official organisation of Jewish congregations in France. The system was introduced by Napoleon in 1808. Each local consistory represented Jews of a particular area and sent delegates to Paris to the Central Consistory, which was responsible for the maintenance of the chief rabbinate and the rabbinical seminary.

Contract A formal agreement between two or more parties. In Jewish law a contract cannot be enforced by a bet din unless there has been a symbolic acquistion of rights before two proper witnesses, and through a process known as 'kabbalat kinyan' (acquiring possession). In this act obligation is effected by one of the parties taking up or pulling at a garment or another object (such as a handkerchief) belonging to the other person. Contracts between Jews which violate Jewish law are invalid. There is no standard form of contract except in the cases of marriage and divorce.

Controversies, religious The oldest post-biblical controversy concerned the Samaritans' adherence to the Pentateuch. In Hellenistic times Pharisees and Sadducees differed about the status of the Oral Law and belief in the afterlife. The Karaite movement, in the 8th century, rejected the Oral Law and the rabbinic tradition. In the 17th and 18th centuries traditionalists engaged in controversy with the Sabbetaians and the Frankists, and in the 18th century there was a schism between the Ḥasidim and Mitnaggedim. In modern society there is a wide gulf between Orthodox and non-Orthodox Judaism (the Reform, Conservative and Reconstructionist movements).

Conversion, forced Compulsory submission to the practice of a religon other than one's own. The forcible conver-

sion of Jews was common after the rise of Christianity and Islam. During the 4th–6th centuries conversion to Christianity took place throughout the Roman Empire and it later became state policy in the Byzantine Empire. In the 14th and 15th centuries it was carried out in the Iberian Peninsula. This resulted in the emergence of a class of crypto-Jews (Marranos). Forced conversion to Islam occurred in the Arabian peninsula during Mohammed's lifetime, and in the 12th century it was imposed by the Almohades in North Africa and Spain. In the 17th–19th centuries forced conversion to Islam in Persia gave rise to another group of crypto-Jews (Jedid Al-Islam).

Conversos (Spanish and Portuguese: 'the converted') Term used to designate Jewish converts to Christianity in Christian Spain and Portugal. It was also applied to their descendants.

Cooperatives The cooperative movement began among Jews in Palestine at the end of the 19th century. Its pioneers were the vintners' association and the Pardes society, which exported citrus. Later, credit cooperatives were established and the movement spread to other fields of economic activity, including transport, agriculture and industry. At the beginning of the 20th century Jewish cooperatives were formed in eastern and central Europe. They provided financial credit to merchants, shopkeepers, craftsmen, and farmers. This movement was destroyed during World War II.

Copland, Aaron (1900–1991) American composer. He was born in Brooklyn. He served as head of the composition department of the Berkshire Music Centre in Tanglewood from 1940 to 1965. His compositions include symphonies, ballets, film scores, orchestral works, and operas. His chamber work Vitebsk is based on a Jewish melody.

Copper Scroll One of the Dead Sea Scrolls; it is made of copper and was discovered in 1952. Its contents include an inventory of the Qumran community's treasures and the places where they were hidden when its headquarters were abandoned in the 1st century.

Cordovero, Moses ben Jacob [Ramak; Remak] (1522–1570) Palestinian kabbalist, of Spanish origin. He was the most important Kabbalist in Safed before Isaac Luria. His first systematic work, *Pardes Rimmonim*, covers a wide range of Kabbalistic problems. He also wrote a second systematic work, *Elimah Rabbati*, and a commentary on the *Zohar*.

Corporeal punishment Physical punishment is one of the oldest forms of punishment in Jewish law. According to the Bible 40 lashes were the maximum that could be inflicted for any single offence. Three judges were to be present at the time of punishment. One ordered it, another counted the lashes, and a third read the relevant passage from Deuteronomy (28: 58–59). The rabbis decreed that corporal punishment should be administered only in Palestine, except for the offence of disobedience. Maimonides enumerated 207 cases for which corporal punishment was specified.

Corpse According to biblical law a dead body renders all persons and things which come into contact with it ritually unclean. Special purification by the ashes of the Red Heifer (Numbers 19) was required before a person contaminated in this way was rendered fit again to enter the Sanctuary, or unsanctified food. In rabbinic law the restrictions concerning contact with a corpse applied only to a priest.

Costa, Isaac de (1798–1860) Dutch writer and poet. The son of a distinguished Sephardi family in Amsterdam, he converted to Christianity in 1822. He published studies of Jews in Spain, Portugal, and the Netherlands. His *Israel and the Gentiles* is a history of the

Jewish people written from a Christian point of view. Many of his poems have biblical themes.

Costa, Uriel da (1585–1640) Portuguese rationalist. He was born in Oporto into a Marrano family. After moving to Amsterdam in c.1614 he returned to Judaism, but he was later excommunicated because of his heretical views about rabbinic doctrine and practice. His subsequent attack on the Bible led to a second ban.

Council of Four Lands (Hebrew 'Vaad Arba Aratzot') Autonomous institution for the self-government of Polish-Lithuanian Jewry. It was established in the middle of the 16th century and functioned until 1764. It represented Jewish communities in four provinces (Major Poland, Minor Poland, Red Russia and Lithuania).

Court Jews Individuals who served as financial or other agents of European rulers. Court Jews were a feature of the absolutist state, especially in central Europe, from the end of the 16th century. They enjoyed special privileges, were exempt from wearing the Jewish badge, and were allowed to live anywhere. Many became extremely wealthy. Because of their position, they were often influential in obtaining rights for their fellow Jews.

Covenant Binding agreement among persons, nations or parties. In the Bible a covenant was effected by a ceremony such as passing between the two halves of a sacrificed animal (Genesis 15:9–11). The covenant made between God and individuals or nations was always accompanied by an external sign. The covenant made with Noah was symbolised by a rainbow (Genesis 9:13); the covenant with Abraham by the act of circumcision (Genesis 17:10); and the covenant with the children of Israel by the institution of the Sabbath (Exodus 31:13). God made a covenant with the house of Aaron to ensure them the priesthood (Numbers 15:12–13). He also made a covenant with David to establish that the monarchy would continue through his descendants (II Samuel 23:5).

Covering of the head   According to Jewish law, married women must cover their hair. Head-coverings for men were originally required only when special respect was to be shown. Babylonian Jewry, however, placed emphasis on the covering of the head by men and this practice was later adopted in other countries. Islamic influence contributed to its adoption in Spain. In France and Germany as late as the 12th century men could be called up to read the Torah bareheaded. In the 17th century David ha-Levi of Ostrog found a religious basis for this practice in the proscription of gentile customs among the Jews. In the modern period Orthodox Jewish men cover thier heads at all times as a sign of humility before God. The covering takes the form of a skullcap known as 'kipah' or 'yarmulke'. Conservative Jews, as well as Reform Jews, cover their heads during prayer.

Covetousness   The envious desire to possess what belongs to another person. It is forbidden by the tenth commandment (Exodus 20:17). According to the rabbis, the violation of the tenth commandment is a transgression of the entire Decalogue.

Cowen, Joseph (1868–1932)   English Zionist. He was the founder and leader of the Zionist movement in England. He encouraged the creation of the British Zionist Federation in 1899. In 1902 he accompanied Theodor Herzl during his audience with the Turkish sultan. He served as director of the Jewish Colonial Trust.

Cowen, Philip (1853–1943)   American journalist and author. He was born in New York. In 1879 he founded the weekly *American Hebrew*, which he edited and published for 27 years. From 1905 he served as an official of the US Immigration Service at Ellis Island, and in 1906 he went to Russia on a special mission to report on the causes of immigration from Eastern Europe.

Crafts   Craftsmen are referred to in the Bible in connection with the construction of the Tabernacle and the Temple. They included workers in brass, iron, gold, silver, linen and wood; refiners, smiths, potters, masons and stone-cutters. In the Talmudic period craftsmanship was regarded highly. In the Middle Ages, Jews engaged in wood and silk weaving, dyeing, goldsmithery, and glass manufacture. In modern times Jews have been active in such crafts as tailoring, diamond cutting, shoe-making and working with furs.

Creation   According to biblical and rabbinic Judaism, God created the cosmos. The biblical depiction of the Creation resembles creation myths in the Babylonian religion. The rabbis of the *Talmud* accepted gnostic ideas of Creation, whereas many rabbinic scholars believed in *creatio ex nihilo*. Speculations about the nature of the visible universe ('maaseh bereshit') and the transcendental world ('maaseh merkavah') are found in Jewish mysticism. Medieval Jewish philosophy was influenced by the Ptolemaic conception of the cosmos. The *Zohar* propounds various theories about the nature of Creation, which were later modified by Isaac Luria.

Creed   Authoritative statement of religious belief. Judaism does not contain a crededal formulation, but a number of Jewish thinkers have drawn up articles of faith. Philo set out five essential beliefs, and Maimonides listed 13 Principles of Faith. Other scholars such as Ḥasdai ben Abraham Crescas and Joseph Albo proposed different formulations. Some scholars believed it to be impossible to separate out the essential beliefs of Judaism.

Creizenach, Michael (1789–1842)
German educator and proponent of
Reform. He was born in Mainz and
founded a Jewish boy's school there
based on the principles of Reform Judaism. In 1825 he was appointed teacher
and preacher at the Philanthropin high
school in Frankfurt am Main. With
Isaac Marcus Jost he edited the Hebrew
periodical *Zion*. In his writings he
attempted to show that since talmudic
Judaism represented a reform of biblical
Judaism, Reform Judaism is a legitimate
approach to the Jewish tradition.

Cremation   Disposal of a dead body by
burning. It is forbidden by Orthodox
Judaism, though some modern Orthodox authorities permit the ashes of a
person who has been cremated to be
interred in a Jewish cemetery. Reform
Judaism permits cremation and its rabbis officiate at cremation ceremonies.

Crémieux, Isaac-Adophe (1796–1880)
French lawyer and statesman. He
fought for the abolition of the oath
more judaico. In 1843 he was elected
President of the Central Consistory of
French Jews. On several occasions he
intervened with the government in an
attempt to gain protection of Jewish
rights in other countries. From 1864 to
1880 he served as President of the Alliance Israélite Universelle.

**Crescas, Hasdai ben Abraham (c.
1340–1412)**   Spanish rabbi and theologian. He was born in Barcelona and
was active as a merchant and communal leader there. In 1367 he was imprisoned on a charge of desecrating the
Host, but was later released. With the
accession of John I in 1387 he became
associated with the royal household
of the Court of Aragon. He later settled in Zaragoza, where he served as
rabbi. In 1391 his son was killed in
anti-Jewish riots in Barcelona, which
he described in a Hebrew account.
His *Light of the Lord* is a refutation of
Maimonides.

Cresques, Abraham (fl. 14th cent.).
Majorcan catrographer. He was Master of Maps and Compasses to the king
of Aragon. In 1375–77 he and his son
Judah made the *Catalan Atlas*, which
was sent as a gift to the king of France.
In 1381 they were granted royal protection and exemption from wearing the
Jewish badge.

**Cresques, Judah [Ribes, Jaime]
(fl. 14th–15th cent.)**   Majorcan car-
tographer, son of Abraham Cresques.
He made maps for John I and Martin
of Aragon. During the anti-Jewish outbreaks in Spain in 1391, he converted
to Christianity and changed his name
to Jaime Ribes. He settled in Barcelona in 1394. From 1309 he is referred
to in documents as 'magister cartarum
navegandi'.

**Cresson, Warder [Israel, Michael
Boaz] (1798–1860)**   American religious zealot and Zionist. He was born
in Philadelphia and emigrated to Palestine, where he converted to Judaism. On his return to the US he was
declared insane by a court, but successfully appealed against the decision.
He returned to Jerusalem as Michael
Boaz Israel and undertook propaganda
campaigns against Christian missionary
groups and on behalf of the agricultural
colonisation by Jews of Palestine. Many
of his writings were published in the
journal *The Occident*.

Crime   In Jewish law no distinction
is made between ritual and secular
offences in respect of procedure and
punishment. However, various degrees
of seriousness of offence are recognised.
In rabbinic law a distinction is made
between civil law and criminal law.

Crown [official] rabbi   Rabbi appointed by the secular authority to represent
the Jewish community in dealings with
the state. In medieval England he was
called the 'Presbyter Judaeroum'; in
Spain 'Rab de la Corte'; in Portugal
'Arrabi-Mor'; and Sicily 'Dienchelele'.

In 19th century Russia the Crown Rabbi was appointed to carry out the government's requirements regarding registration and various regulations. He functioned alongside local rabbis.

Crucifixion Execution by fastening the condemned to a wooden cross, usually by binding or nailing the hands and feet. The position of the body resulted in death by suffocation. It was common among the Greeks and Romans but unknown in Jewish law. The practice was introduced into Palestine by the Romans, and many Jews were punished in this way.

Crusade Any of the military expeditions undertaken by the Christian powers of Europe in the Middle Ages to win back the Holy Land from the Muslims. The crusades provoked religious passion and anti-Jewish sentiment and resulted in the massacre of many Jewish communities. During the preparations for the First Crusade (1096–9) Jews in northern France and the Rhineland were killed. Similar attacks took place in Prague and later in Salonica. When Jerusalem was captured in 1099 Jews and Karaites were slaughtered. During the Second Crusade (1147–49) outbreaks of violence again occurred in France and the Rhineland, and in the course of the Third Crusade (1189–92) Jews in England were attacked.

Crypto-Jews Jews who, while remaining covertly faithful to Judaism, outwardly practised another religion, which they were forced to accept. The phenomenon arose frequently after the forced conversion under the Visigoths in Spain in the 7th century, and under the Alhomades in North Africa and Spain in the 12th century. Other groups of crypto-Jews were the Neofiti in southern Italy from the end of the 13th century to the 16th, and the Conversos (or Marranos) in Spain after the persecutions of 1391 and the expulsion

of 1492, and in Portugal after 1497. In Majorca such Jews were known as the Chuetas. In Persia in the 19th century forcible conversion to Islam gave rise to a group known as the Jedid Al-Islam.

Cukerman, Yitzḥak [Antek] (1915–1981) Polish communal leader in the Warsaw Ghetto. He was one of the four commanders of the Jewish Fighting Organisation set up in Warsaw on July 22 1942. During the ghetto uprising in April 1943 he took part in the battle against the Germans. He helped to organise the Jewish National Council, a Jewish underground resistance movement among Jews hiding on the Aryan side of the ghetto boundary. He emigrated to Israel in 1946 and served as a prosecution witness at the Eichmann trial in 1961.

Cuneiform Script employed in the writing of several ancient languages of Mesopotamia and Persia, including Sumerian and Akkadian. The wedge-shaped characters were incised on tablets with a stylus.

Cup of Elijah Cup of wine placed on the table at the Passover seder which is not drunk. It is prepared to welcome the prophet, who visits every Jewish home on the Passover night.

Cups In the Jewish tradition the drinking of wine plays an important role. The cup of benediction is an essential element of all joyous occasions (such as circumcisions, weddings, and the kiddush). At the Passover seder four cups of wine are drunk.

Curse An appeal to a supernatural power to bring harm on a person or group; also a profane expression of anger. The Bible prohibits cursing God, one's parents, authorities, and the deaf. The *Talmud* expresses belief in the efficacy of curses. The uttering of a curse is permitted in some cases if it is done for religious reasons. Any curse involving God's name is forbidden.

Custom   Many Jewish regulations are not based on the written or oral law but are binding because they are customarily observed. Different customs developed among Jews in the diaspora, which accounts for variant practices in the Jewish communities of different countries. These variations have been noted by codifiers. Joseph Caro, for example, cited the custom of Spanish Jewry in the Shulḥan Arukh, whereas Moses Isserles in his glosses to this work refers to the customs among the Ashkenazim.

Czacki, Tadeusz (1795–1813)   Polish statesman and historian. From 1786 to 1792 he served in the Polish Treasury and was responsible for supervising Jewish affairs in the country. He sought to ameliorate the position of the Jewish population. He wrote a comprehensive history of Polish Jewry.

D

A young Jewish woman goes to see a rabbinic sage. She tells him that both Stanley and Sherman are in love with her. Then she asks the rabbi, 'Who will be the lucky man? Who will marry me?' The rabbi strokes his beard and ponders, then answers: 'Sherman will marry you. Stanley will be the lucky man.'

* * * * *

It is not only Jewish wives who are satirised. Jewish young women (referred to as Jewish princesses) are often depicted as selfish and spoiled. The joke is intended to make fun of this young Jewess' conceit and self-centredness. Jewish princess jokes abound in the community and serve as a warning about how not to behave.

Da Costa, Isaac (1721–1783) American merchant and shipping agent. He was born in London and emigrated to Charleston, South Carolina, in the late 1740s. He was a founder in 1749 of Congregation Beth Elohim, where he served as cantor. Later he settled in Philadelphia, where he helped establish Congregation Mikveh Israel.

Dagesh Diacritical mark in Hebrew, taking the form of a dot in a consant. It indicates one of two things: that the consonant (e.g. bet, gimel, dalet, kaph, pe, tav) is to be pronounced with a hard sound; or that the consonant, which is written once, is to be pronounced as though it were doubled (this does not apply to aleph, he, ḥet, ayin, resh.) In every case the dagesh is written inside the letter form.

Dahlberg, Edward (1900–1977) Amercian novelist. Born in Boston, he lived a vagabond existence and eventually settled in Europe. His novels *Bottom Dogs* and *From Flushing to Calvary* reflect his early childhood experiences. His *Those who Perish* deals with the impact of Nazism on a small American Jewish community.

Daiches, David (1912–2005) English literary critic, nephew of Samuel Daiches. He was born in Sunderland. He taught at the universities of Chicago, Cornell, Cambridge and Sussex. His *Two Worlds: An Edinburgh Jewish Childhood* depicts his rebellion against Orthodox Judaism personified by his father. His interest in Hebrew matters is reflected in *The King James Version of the English Bible.*

Daiches, Israel Ḥayyim (1850–1937) British Orthodox rabbi and scholar. He was born in Darshunishek, Lithuania, and eventually settled in England, where he served as a rabbi in Leeds. He founded the Union of Orthodox Rabbis of England. His writing includes annotations on the Jerusalem *Talmud*, responsa and sermons.

Daiches, Samuel (1878–1949) British rabbi and scholar, son of Israel Ḥayyim Daiches. He was born in Vilnius. He served as rabbi in Sunderland, England, and later became a lecturer in the Bible,

Talmud and midrash at Jews College. He took an active part in the work of B'nai B'rith, the Anglo-Jewish Association, the Board of Deputies of British Jews, the Jewish Agency, and Jewish relief organisations. His published works include studies of Babylonian antiquity and its influence on Judaism, the Psalms, the *Talmud* in Spain, and Jewish divorce law.

Dainow, Tzevi Hirsch [Maggid of Slutsk] (1832–1877) Russian preacher. He was born in Slutsk. He advocated combining Torah with the Haskalah, and upheld the efficacy of manual labour and the need for educational reform. He was active on behalf of the Society for the Promotion of Culture among the Jews of Russia. Due to opposition to his views, he emigrated to England and settled in London, where he preached to Russian and Polish immigrants.

Dalet Fourth letter of the Hebrew alphabet. Its numerical value is 4.

Dan Israelite, fifth son of Jacob and the firstborn of Bilhah, Rachel's maid (Genesis 30:1–6). One of the 12 tribes of Israel took his name.

Dan, Joseph (b.1935) Israeli scholar. He was born in Bratislava, Czechoslovakia, and went to Palestine in 1938. He taught at the Hebrew University, where in 1983 he was appointed the Gershom Scholem Professor of Kabbalah. His publications include *Ideological Movements and Conflicts in Jewish History.*

Dance In Ancient Israel meals, wine festivals, weddings, funerals and ceremonials were accompanied by dancing. In the Maccabean period the Jews adopted Greek and Roman dances. During the Middle Ages almost every Jewish community in France, Germany and Poland had a wedding house, where dancing took place. With the rise of Ḥasidism in the 18th century, dance assumed great religious importance for the Jewish masses. Many folk dances have evolved in modern Israel.

Danger The biblical verses 'Only take heed to yourself and keep your soul diligently' and 'Take good heed to your souls' (Deuteronomy 4:9,15) were interpreted in rabbinic sources as constituting a commandment prescribing the duty of personal safety and the avoidance of danger to life. The *Talmud* contains a long list of prohibitions for the purpose of preventing danger to life. The duty of preserving life takes precedence over and annuls all commandments, with the exception of the sins of idolatry, immorality, and the shedding of innocent blood.

Daniel (fl. 7th–6th century BCE) He was a Judean exile in Babylon. Several miraculous experiences occurred to him and his friends at the courts of Nebuchadnezzar, Darius the Mede and Belshazzar.

Daniel [Belteshazzar] Biblical book in the Hagiographa. It relates the story of Daniel, a Judaean exile in Babylon (where he was known as Belteshazzar) and the miraculous experiences that occurred to him and his friends at the courts of Nebuchadnezzar, Darius the Mede and Belshazzar. The second half of the book contains visions of the rise and fall of empires from Babylon to Macedon and beyond. Daniel is also the hero of the story of Susanna and the Elders and two other tales in the book of *Bel and the Dragon.*

Daniel ben Moses al-Kumisi [Al-Damagani] (fl. 9th–10th cent.) Karaite scholar and leader of the Avele Zion (Mourners of Zion). He was born in Damghan in northern Persia, and was the first eminent Karaite scholar to settle in Jerusalem. His *Pitron Sheneim-Asar* is a commentary on the Minor Prophets, which contains criticism of the rabbinate.

Danziger, Itzchak (1916–1978) Israeli sculptor. He was born in Berlin and settled in Palestine in 1923. He later taught at the Haifa Technion. His early sculptures achieved a balance between Near-Eastern sculpture and a modern concept of human form. He was awarded the Israeli Prize for Sculpture in 1968.

Darmesteter, Arsène (1846–1888) French philologist, brother of James Darmesteter. He was born at Château-Salins. He was appointed Lecturer in French Language and Literature at the Sorbonne in 1877 and also taught at the École Rabbinique. He was a founder of the Société de Études Juives and the *Revue des Études Juives*. His writings include a dictionary of 11th-century French, based on medieval Jewish commentators, and a dictionary of Rashi's French glosses in his commentaries on the Bible and the *Talmud*.

Darmesteter, James (1849–1894) French orientalist, brother of Arsène Darmesteter. He was born at Château-Salins. He became Professor at the Collège de France. He translated the sacred books of the Zoroastrian religion into French and English, and published material concerning the relationship between Zoroastrianism and Judaism.

Darmstadt Haggadah Illuminated codex of the Passover evening service, produced in western Germany in about 1430. It is one of the most beautiful Jewish illuminated manuscripts of the Middle Ages.

Darshan ('Expounder [of Scripture]') Title conferred on a preacher. Originally one given this title expounded both halakhically and aggadically on the biblical text. In the Middle Ages the term was used for a professional preacher. In some Eastern-European communities a person was appointed to be the official darshan of the community. An alternative title, given to both the official and the itinerant preacher was 'maggid'.

Daube, David (1909–1989) British jurist and biblical scholar. He was born in Freiburg, Germany. He taught at the universities of Cambridge, Aberdeen and Oxford, and at the University of California at Berkeley. He wrote studies of biblical and rabbinic law, the New Testament and rabbinic Judaism, and various themes in Scripture.

Daughter(s) of Zion Biblical phrase referring to Jerusalem or the Jewish people.

Daven Term used among the Ashkenazim, meaning to pray.

David (fl. 11th–10th cent. BCE) King of Israel (c.1001–986 BCE). David's life is divided into three main phases: the first when Saul was alive; the second when he was king in Judah (c.1008–1001 BCE); the third when he was king over all Israel. A warrior king, he succeeded in uniting the tribes of Israel and created a kingdom that dominated surrounding peoples and attained power and riches. The Psalms were supposed to have been written by him. The account of his life appears in I Samuel 16ff, II Samuel, I Kings 1–2, and I Chronicles 10ff.

David ben Samuel ha-Levi (1586–1667) Polish rabbi and halakhic authority. He was born in Ukraine. He established his own bet midrash in Kraków, and later served as a rabbi in Posen and Ostrog, where he maintained a yeshivah. During the Chmielnicki pogroms (1648–49), he escaped to a fortress in Ulick. In 1654 he was appointed rabbi of Lwów. His *Ture Zahav (Taz)* is a commentary on the Shulḥan Arukh.

David ben Zakkai I (fl. 10th cent.) Babylonian exilarch (917–40). He appointed Saadyah ben Joseph gaon of Sura, but later quarrelled with him and had him deposed. The supporters of Saadyah attempted to appoint a new exilarch, Josiah-Hasan. After a bitter dispute the two parties reached a compromise.

Davidson, Israel (1870–1939) American Hebrew scholar. He was born in Lithuania and emigrated to the US in 1888. He became Professor of Medieval Hebrew literature at the Jewish Theological Seminary. His *Thesaurus of Medieval Hebrew Poetry* lists in alphabetical order the initial words of more than 35,000 poems and prayers from post-biblical times to the Haskalah period.

Davin [David] de Caderousse (fl. 15th cent.) French dyer. He was the first Jew to attempt the printing of Hebrew. He lived in Avignon, where he met a Christian goldsmith (Pocop Waldvogel) from Prague. He promised to teach Waldvogel the art of dyeing, in return for which Waldvogel was to give him 27 iron letters of the Hebrew alphabet, as well as instruments for printing. This arrangement broke down, and no specimen of the earliest Hebrew printing press has survived.

Davka ('exactly') Hebrew and Yiddish term used to emphasise the accuracy of a fact or to draw attention to something unexpected. It also indicates obstinacy.

Dayan, Moshe (1915–1981) Israeli military commander and politician, son of Shemuel Dayan. He was born in Deganyah Alef. During the War of Independence in 1948, he commanded the defence of Jewish settlements in the Jordan Valley. In 1952 he was appointed chief of operations at GHQ and later became commander-in-chief. In 1959 he was elected to the Knesset as a member of the Mapai party. Later he was elected to the Sixth Knesset representing Rafi. He conducted the Six-Day War in 1967 and the Yom Kippur War in 1973 as Minister of Defence.

Dayan, Shemuel (1891–1968) Israeli pioneer and politician. He was born in Ukraine and settled in Palestine in 1908. He was a founder of Deganyah and Nahalal and a leader of the moshavim cooperative settlement organisation. He represented Mapai in the Knesset from 1949 to 1959.

Day of Judgement The occasion of the last judgement by God at the end of the world, when he will decide the final fate of all individuals. The Bible refers to an eschatological Day of Judgement. The Mishnah states the the judgement of the world is continuing and takes place at four different periods during the year. In the Jewish liturgy the New Year (on 1 Tishri) is considered an annual day of judgement for all people. Decrees are finally sealed on the Day of Atonement.

Day of the Lord The time when God will punish the wicked and justice will triumph. The term is found in various prophetic passages, the prevailing feature of which is a dramatic sense of doom. The usual message is that the Day of the Lord is near.

Dayyan Title conferred on the judge in a rabbinical court. The title is confined to the members of the bet din (other than its head, who is referred to as 'av bet din' or 'rosh bet din'). Sometimes elders of the community or guild functionaries were given the title. In England the title is accorded to members of the official religious law courts, particularly that of the chief rabbi.

Dayyenu ('It would have satisfied us') Refrain of a song of thanksgiving in the Passover Haggadah. The song enumerates 15 stages of the redemption of the Jews from Egyptian bondage.

Dead Sea Scrolls Collection of ancient manuscripts found between 1947 and 1956 in caves in various areas west of the Dead Sea. They are written in Hebrew and Aramaic and date mainly from c.150 BCE to 68 CE, when the monastic community at Qumran, which owned them, was destroyed by the Romans. They contain fragments of nearly every book of the Bible, as well as copies of the book of Isaiah. Fragments have also been found of the Apocrypha and Pseudepigrapha. In addition, they contain the plan of a struggle between the Sons of Light and the Sons of Darkness, religious hymns, the rule by which the sect was governed, details of a hidden treasure and minute descriptions of the Temple. Many scholars believe they were written by the Essenes. They are housed in the Shrine of the Book in Israel.

Deaf, imbeciles, and minors Individuals who fall into any of these three categories are deprived of legal rights in Jewish law, since they are viewed as lacking understanding and being incapable of exercising responsibility. The *Talmud* decrees that they cannot claim property, their business transactions are invalid, and they are debarred from acting as witnesses.

Death The last act of a dying Jew is to recite a special confession of sin ('viddui') and the Shema. After death the body is washed and watched until it is buried. According to the Bible, the dead continue to exist in Sheol. The concept of resurrection and reward and punishment in the afterlife became a central tenet of Pharisaic Judaism.

Deborah (fl. 12th cent. BCE) Israelite woman, judge and prophetess. She promoted the war of liberation from the oppression of Jabin, King of Canaan (Judges 4). She was the author of the Song of Deborah (Judges 5), which describes the battle and victory of the Israelites over the Canaanites.

Debt Biblical law contains many ordinances to ease the burden of debt: a creditor may not charge interest; debts are automatically cancelled every seven years; and chattels may not be taken in lieu of payment of a debt. Eventu-

ally these provisions were modified to facilitate credit. Hillel introduced the prosbul to overcome the cancellation of debts in the Sabbatical year, and the rabbis decreed that chattels could become security.

Dedication In Jewish religious practice a liturgical ceremony is performed to dedicate a building for a sacred purpose or a plot of land for a cemetery. The dedication of a sanctuary dates from the biblical period. In post-biblical times the Temple was rededicated by Judah Maccabee and this occasion is celebrated by the festival of Ḥanukkah. Ceremonies for the dedication of other sacred buildings are of later origin. The order of service for the dedication of a cemetery includes the recitation of penitential prayers at the morning service on the day of dedication.

Deed (Hebrew 'shetar', 'sepher') In Jewish law a document witnessed by two individuals which confirms the conveyance of property, marriage contract, and bill of divorce on the occasion of a marriage. In the Bible it is known as a 'sepher', but in rabbinic sources it is referred to as a 'shetar' or 'get'. The 'shetar ḥov' is a sealed bond acknowledged by two witnesses. It makes liable for seizure all property held by the giver of the bond at the time of its signature.

De Haan, Jacob Meijer (1852–1895) Dutch painter. He was born in Amsterdam, where he ran a biscuit factory with his brothers. They also formed a string quartet which gained a reputation throughout the Netherlands. A disciple of Gauguin, he was a popular painter of Jewish subjects.

De Lange, Nicholas (b.1944) English scholar. He was born in Nottingham. He became lecturer and later Professor of Rabbinics at Cambridge University. His publications include *Jewish Literature of the Hellenistic Age*.

Delilah (fl. 12–11th cent. BCE) Philistine woman, mistress of Samson. She persuaded Samson to tell her the secret of his strength, which lay in his hair (as a Nazirite he abstained from cutting his hair). While Samson was asleep she cut his hair so that he could be taken captive by the Philistines, who blinded and enslaved him (Judges 16).

Delitzsch, Franz (1813–1890) German theologian and Judaist. He was born in Leipzig and taught at the universities of Leipzig, Rostock and Erlangen. He translated the New Testament into Hebrew and in 1880 established the Institutum Judaicum in Leipzig for the training of missionary workers among Jews. His writings include a history of Jewish poetry and commentaries on several books of the Bible. He defended the Jewish community against anti-Semitic attacks.

Delitzsch, Friedrich (1850–1922) German orientalist. He was a professor of Semitic languages and Assyriology in Leipzig, Breslau and Berlin. He published studies of Babylonian culture and the world of the Bible, and a critical account of Judaism and the Jews.

Della Torre, Lelio (1805–1871) Italian rabbi and scholar. He was born in Cuneo in Piedmont. He became Professor of *Talmud* at the Padua Rabbinical College. He published volumes of Hebrew poetry, sermons and a commentary on the Pentateuch; he also translated and annotated the Psalms, and rendered the prayers according to Ashkenazi custom into Italian.

Delmedigo, Elijah ben Moses Abba (c.1460–1497) Greco-Italian philosopher and talmudist. He was born in Crete and emigrated to Italy, where he served as head of the yeshivah in Padua. He engaged in a bitter controversy on a halakhic question with Judah Mintz, the rabbi of Padua. Subsequently he left Italy and returned to Crete, where he completed his major work, *The Examination of Religion*.

Delmedigo, Joseph Solomon ben Elijah [Medigo, Joseph Solomon ben Elijah del] (1591–1655) Cretan rabbi, philosopher, mathematician and astronomer. He studied astronomy and mathematics under Galileo at the University of Padua, then travelled widely, visiting Egypt, Turkey, Poland, Germany, Holland and Bohemia. He wrote studies of religious, metaphysical, and scientific topics.

Demai Third tractate in the Mishnah order of Zeraim. It deals with the requirements for tithing produce in cases where there is doubt whether propert tithes have been given.

Dembitzer, Ḥayyim Nathan (1820–1892) Polish talmudist and historian. He was born in Kraków and became a dayyan there. He was active in financial support of the old yishuv in Palestine. He published works on responsa literature, the tosaphists, and talmudic and rabbinic literature. He also wrote biographies of the rabbis of Lwów/Lemberg and neighbouring communities.

Demonology The study of demons or demonic beliefs. The Bible and rabbinic literature refer to various demonic beings. In the kabbalah there is a dichotomy between the demonic and the divine spheres. Demons also play a role in Jewish folklore and legend. Amulets and magic formulae were used to protect Jews from evil influence.

Denunciation In Jewish law it is a serious offence for one Jew to denounce another Jew to gentile authorities, except where a criminal act has been committed. A prayer for condemnation of such slanderers was included in the daily Amidah prayer from the 1st century.

Derekh eretz ('way of the land') Desirable behaviour, in keeping with accepted social and moral standards. It includes rules of etiquette and polite behaviour. In rabbinic sources it refers to normal human behaviour, worldly occupation, and correct conduct.

Derekh Eretz Rabbah Minor tractate appended to the Babylonian *Talmud* at the end of Nezikin. It includes laws relating to forbidden marriages, moral sayings, rules of conduct, and a list of practices that are dangerous to life.

Derekh Eretz Zuta Minor tractate appended to the Babylonian *Talmud* at the end of Nezikin. It consists of exhortations to self-examination and modesty and extols temperance, resignation gentleness, patience, respect for the elderly, and forgiveness.

Derenbourg, Hartwig (1844–1908) French orientalist, son of Joseph Derenbourg. He lectured in Arabic at the École des Langues Orientales Vivants in Paris, and on oriental languages at the École Rabbinique. In 1885 he became Professor of Arabic at the École des Hautes Études. He wrote studies of Arabic grammar, literature, and religion, and of Semitic manuscripts and inscriptions.

Derenbourg, Joseph (1811–1895) French orientalist. He worked as a domestic tutor in Amsterdam in 1835–38, and then settled in Paris. In 1852 he became Corrector at the Imprimerie Nationale, and also catalogued the Hebrew manuscripts at the Bibliothèque Nationale. In 1877 he was appointed to a chair for rabbinic Hebrew language and literature at the École Pratique des Hautes Études. He published studies of oriental languages and inscriptions as well as works on various subjects.

Derrida, Jacques (1930–2004) French philosopher. Born in Algiers, he taught at the École Normale Superieure and later at the École de Hautes Études en Sciences Sociales. His works include *Speech and Phenomena, Writing and Difference, Margins of Philosophy, Dissemination, Glas, Trust in a Painting, The Post Card, Shibboleth, Feu la Cendre,* and *Ulysses Gramophone.*

Dershowitz, Alan (b.1938) is the Felix Frankfurter Professor of Law at Harvard Law School. A graduate of Brooklyn College and Yale Law School, he joined the Harvard Law School faculty at age 25 after clerking for Judge David Bazelon and Justice Arthur Goldberg. He has published more than 1,000 articles in magazines, newspapers, journals and blogs such as *The New York Times Magazine, The Washington Post, The Wall Street Journal, The Harvard Law Review, The Yale Law Journal, Huffington Post, Newsmax, Jerusalem Post* and *Ha'aretz.* He is the author of 30 fiction and non-fiction works with a worldwide audience.

Derush Homiletic or aggadic interpretation.

Desecration of the host The defilement of the consecrated bread or wafer used in the Christian sacrament of the Eucharist. After the recognition by the Fourth Lateran Council in 1215 of the doctrine of transubstantiation (according to which the bread becomes the body of Christ), the accusation that Jews defiled the host became common in Europe. It was the pretext for a number of Jewish massacres, the first of which took place in Belitz in 1243. Other outbreaks occurred in Paris in 1290, in Brussels in 1370 and in Segovia in 1410.

Detention camps They were set up in the 1940s by the British Administration for Jewish immigrants who entered Palestine in contravention of the Mandatory regulations. They were also used for those accused of political offences. From January 1940 immigrants were confined to Athlit. From August 1946 most were sent to Cyprus. Alleged members of Jewish terrorist organisations were sent to camps at Latrun and in Kenya and Eritrea.

Determinism The philosophical doctrine that all acts, choices and events are determined by causal necessity or by God's decree. Judaism combines a belief in free will with a belief in divine foreknowledge. In the Middle Ages a number of Jewish theologians discussed how these concepts could be compatible.

Deuteronomy (Hebrew: 'Devarim') Biblical book, the fifth book of the Torah. It contains Moses' review of events after the giving of the law on Mount Sinai; his ethical exhortation and a summary of divine legislation; his final speeches, his farewell song and blessing; and an account of his death.

Deuteronomy Rabbah (Hebrew: 'Devarim Rabbah') Aggadic midrash on the book of Deuteronomy. It is part of Midrash Rabbah. It consists of 27 expositions each beginning with a halakhic statement. It draws upon tannaitic literature, the Palestinian *Talmud*, Genesis Rabbah, and Leviticus Rabbah.

Deutsch, Moritz (1818–1892) German cantor and teacher of Moravian origin. He became second cantor of the Liberal Temple in Vienna. He later served as Chief Cantor of the Reform synagogue in Breslau. He taught cantorial music at the Breslau Theological Seminary for 30 years and composed original arrangements of liturgical music.

Deutscher, Isaac (1907–1967) British historian and political scientist. He was born in Kraków. He was a member of the Communist Party in Poland, but was expelled, and in 1939 went to London, where he was on the editorial staff of the *Economist* and the *Observer*. Later he devoted himself to historical research. He wrote political biographies

of Stalin and Trotsky, and published works on Stalin, Soviet Russia and Communism.

Devekut ('cleaving [to God]') Spiritual state of communion with God, achieved during prayer and meditation. The term is based on the phrase 'love the Lord your God ... and cleave unto him' (Deuteronomy 11:22). Usually devekut is described as the highest step on a spiritual ladder. It plays an important role in the kabbalah.

Devotion (Hebrew 'kavvanah') The Bible and rabbinic literature stress that observances and prayer must be conducted with inner devotion and steadfast intent ('kavvanah'). The concept of devotion is of particular importance in the kabbalah, since prayer can influence the upper realms ('sephirot'). Kabbalists maintain that devotion in prayer can be attained by the mystical action of combining the letters of God's name.

Devotional literature In Jewish religious practice devotional literature consists of the traditional Jewish liturgy; services for prayer meetings (such as Joseph Jedidiah Carmi's hymn collection); private meditations for various occasions (such as those collected by Nathan Hannover in *Shaare Zion);* and pious writings such as Solomon ibn Gabirol's *Keter Malkhut*. In addition, many devotional handbooks have been published, such as *Prayers and Meditations* by Hester de Rothschild.

Dhimma (Arabic) Legal term used in Muslim lands to denote the relationship between protector and protected. It fixed the legal status of Jews and Christians and involved mutual obligations. The Muslim government agreed to protect the life and property of non-Muslims, exempted them from military service, and guaranteed them religious freedom. Those who were protected were under the obligation to pay the poll tax, not to insult Islam, not to convert Muslims, and not to betray the Muslim government.

Dialects Jewish dialects fall into two groups. The first consists of local dialects of the language of the country in which the speakers live (Judeo-Aramaic, Judeo-Arabic, Judeo-Persian, Judeo-German, Judeo-Italian, Judeo-Provencal). These differ from the vernacular by preserving old forms of speech or the addition of Hebrew words. The second group consists of languages of the Jews of particular regions, which continue to be spoken when they migrate to another country (Yiddish, Ladino).

Diaries As a source of information on Jewish history, diaries are a comparatively recent phenomenon. The first significant diary is *Maagal Tov* (1753–78) by Hayyim Azulai, which records details of his travels in the Holy Land. Other important diaries include the record of his travels by Sir Moses Montefiore, the diaries of Theodor Herzl, which describe his Zionist activities, and the numerous diaries of Holocaust victims.

Diaspora The dispersion and settlement of the Jews outside of Palestine after the Babylonian captivity. When the Temple was destroyed in the 6th century BCE, large numbers of Jews settled in Babylonia. From the Hellenistic period onward Jews lived in many lands, including Islamic and Christian countries. In the Middle Ages Jews in northern and western Europe were much persecuted and often expelled from the countries in which they lived. Eventually they gravitated to eastern Europe, then to the US. Many also sought to return to Palestine. The establishment of the State of Israel and the emigration there of many Jews have profoundly affected Jewish life in the diaspora.

Dibbuk [dybbuk] Evil spirit, which enters into a person. It cleaves to the soul, causes mental illness, talks through his mouth, and represents an alien personality. It can be exorcised by conjuring the divine name. Such exorcism was practised in the circle of Isaac Luria and later by wonderwokers and Hasidic tzaddikim. A play entitled *The Dybbuk* was written by S. An-Ski.

Dick, Isaac Meir (1814–1893) Polish Yiddish author. He was born in Vilnius. As an exponent of the Haskalah, he advocated reforms in Jewish life. He was the first popular writer of Yiddish fiction, producing more than 300 stories and short novels, which introduced sentimental and realistic storytelling into Yiddish literature. He also popularised knowledge of the Bible, wrote on the Passover Haggadah, and composed a popular version of the Shulhan Arukh.

Dictionaries, Bible [concordances] The first dictionary of the Hebrew Scriptures was Blasius Ugonlini's *Thesaurus antiquitatum sacrarum* (1744–69). This was followed by *Dictionnaire historique et critique, chronologique, géographique et littéraire de la Bible* by Auguste Calmet, which was published in 1772. The development of oriental archaeology led to the publication of the *Encyclolpaedia biblica* (1899–1903); *Dictionary of the Bible* (1898–1904); and *Dictionnaire de la Bible* (1891–1912). The first Jewish Bible dictionary was the *Entziklopedia Mikrait* (1950–68). The *Encyclopaedia Judaica* 1972–), a comprehensive work in many volumes, also contains numerous entries on biblical subjects.

Dictionaries, Hebrew The first Hebrew dictionary was written in 912 by Saadyah ben Joseph. Others followed in the 10th–11th centuries. In the 13th century Tanhum Yerushalmi composed a dictionary of mishnaic Hebrew. Non-Jewish Hebrew lexicography began with Johannes Buxtorf's *Lexicon Hebraicum* (1607) and *Lexicon Chaldaicum, Talmudicum et Rabbinicum* (1639). Biblical lexicography was placed on a new basis by Wilhelm Gesenius' *Handwörterbuch*

(1810–12). The first dictionary to
include Hebrew of all perios was Eliezer
Ben-Yehudah's *Thesaurus totius Hebrai-
tatis* (1910–52).

Dietary laws (Hebrew 'kashrut') The
Bible and rabbinic legislation permit
certain foods for consumption; they are
referred to as 'kosher' (fit). They prohibit other foods, including meat from
birds and animals which are 'unclean'
or not ritually slaughtered; certain parts
of animals (such as the sinew of the hip);
meat and milk products eaten together;
any kind of fish that does not have both
fins and scales. They also deal with
the preparation of food: for example,
since Jews may not consume blood in
any form all meat must be soaked and
salted before it is eaten. Although no
reason is given in Scripture or rabbinic
literature for these prohibitions, various
explanations have been advanced: that
dietary restrictions in themselves regulate holiness in everyday life, encourage
self-discipline and keep Jews separate
from gentiles, and that abstention from
the particular foods named prevents
disease.

Dillon, Abraham Moshe (1883–1934)
American Yiddish poet. He was born
in Russia and emigrated to the US in
1909. As a poet he was affiliated with
the New York impressionistic movement of Yunge. HIs writings include
Gele bleter and *Lider fun A.M. Dillon.*

Din ('judgement') The words is used
in the context of secular or religious law
to refer to a legal decision or lawsuit.

**Dina de-malkhuta dina (Aramaic:
'the law of the country is law')** The
halakhic rule that the law of the country is binding; in certain cases the law
of the country is to be preferred to
Jewish law. It was laid down in the
3rd century by the sage Samuel, who
imbued Babylonian Jewry with the
consciousness that they must be reconciled with the government of the Sas-
sanid kingdom.

Dinah (fl.? 19th–16th cent. BCE) Israelite woman, daughter of Jacob and
Leah (Genesis 30:21). She was raped
by Shechem. Jacob's sons Simeon and
Levi avenged their sister by slaughtering the male population of the town of
Shechem, carrying off their women and
children, and taking their goods and
livestock as spoil (Genesis 34).

Dinesohn, Jacob (1856–1919) Russian Yiddish novelist. He was born in
the district of Kovno. His first Yiddish
novel, *For the Parents' Sins*, was banned
by the Russian censor. His second, *The
Beloved and the Pleasant, or The Black
Youth*, sold more than 200,000 copies.
In 1885 he settled in Warsaw. He was
the pioneer of the Yiddish sentimental
novel and also helped to modernise elementary Jewish education by founding
secular schools.

Din Torah ('judgement of the law') A
judicial hearing conducted in accordance with Jewish law.

**Dinur, Benzion [Dinaburg, Ben Zion]
(1884–1973)** Israeli historian and educator of Ukrainian origin. He emigrated
to Palestine in 1921. From 1923 to
1948 he taught at the Jewish Teachers'
Training College in Jerusalem, of which
he later became head. In 1948 he was
appointed Professor of Modern Jewish
History at the Hebrew University. He
was elected to the first Knesset (1949–
51) as a Mapai delegate and from 1951
to 1955 was Minister of Education and
Culture. He edited the Jewish historical
quarterly *Zion* and wrote on Jewish and
Zionist history.

Disabilities In Jewish usage the civil
and social disadvantages suffered by
Jews as a result of restrictive laws and
customs. Before the 18th century rights
accorded to Jews were limited. In most
parts of Europe Jewish disabilities
ranged from extreme severity to minimal deprivation. After the Enlightenment Jews aspired to rights which they
had previously been denied. As an indi-

rect result of the French Revolution they gained full legal equality. In modern times Jews have been given full civil rights under the law.

Discipline Scroll [Manual of Discipline]   One of the Dead Sea Scrolls. It describes the organisation and some of the beliefs of the Dead Sea sect that originally owned the scrolls.

Discrimination   The singling out of an individual or group for special treatment on the basis of race, religion, colour, or national origin. Before the modern period anti-Jewish legislation was enacted by civil and religious authorities. Modern anti-Semitism is generally not enshrined in law but finds expression in non-legislative discriminatory patterns.

Diskin, Yehoshua Leib (1817–1898)   Russian rabbi and halakhist. He was born in Grodno and served as a rabbi in various Russian cities. He opposed the religious authorities, was imprisoned, and in 1887 emigrated to Palestine. He settled in Jerusalem, where he served as a rabbi and was in the vanguard of Orthodox activism. He founded an orphanage and directed the Ohel Moshe yeshivah.

Dispensation   Permission to dispense with or modify rules to relieve hardship. In rabbinic practice it is referred to as 'giving a heter' (permission). It is generally limited to laws having only rabbinic validity or arising from custom.

Displaced persons   Individuals forced or deported from their homes, especially as a result of war. The term is applied particularly in Jewish parlance to those deported to other lands by the Nazi regime in World War II. After the war the United Nations specialised agency, the Relief and Rehabilitation Administration, assisted the repatriation of displaced persons. In 1947 this body was replaced by the International Refugee Organisation. Between 1948 and 1950 the majority of the 450,000 Jews in camps for displaced persons emigrated from Europe to Israel, the US, and elsewhere.

Disputation   Formal debate between the adherents of different philosophies or religious faiths. Disputations took place between Jews and philosophers during the Hellenistic period. With the growth of Christianity, Jews engaged in debate with Christian theologians about such subjects as the Virgin birth, the nature of messianic prophecies, and the divinity of Jesus. In the Middle Ages disputations between Jewish and Christian scholars (such as the Disputation of Paris in 1240 and the Disputation of Barcelona in 1263) commonly resulted in the formal condemnation and burning of the *Talmud*.

Disraeli, Benjamin, Earl of Beaconsfield (1804–1881)   English statesman and novelist. His father Isaac d'Israeli, quarrelled with the London Sephardi community and had his children baptised. Disraeli was already an established novelist when he was elected to parliament in 1837 as a Tory. In 1868 he became Prime Minister. Although he was defeated in the next general election, he became Prime Minister again in 1874. In 1876 he was created Earl of Beaconsfield. Jewish figures and themes appear in several of his novels.

Divination   The art or practice of discerning future events of unknown things. All forms of pagan divination, including augury, soothsaying, charming and conjuring the spirits of the dead, are prohibited in the Bible. Yet despite the denunciation they were occasionally used. Prophecy and prophetic dreams were approved by God, as was the use of the divinatory purposes of the Urim and Thummim and the ephod. In the rabbinic period the belief in omens and oracles flourished despite official disapproval.

Divorce (Hebrew 'get') The dissolution of a marriage. It is effected in Jewish law by a bill of divorce termed 'sepher keritut' in Scripture (Deuteronomy 24:3), or 'get' in the *Talmud*. This bill is written by the husband and handed to his wife in the presence of witnesses. Biblical law stipulates that divorce is permitted if the husband finds an 'unseemly thing' in his wife (Deuteronomy 24:1). This phrase was diversely interpreted by rabbinic authorities. Although the power of divorce is vested in the husband, Jewish divorce laws have developed in the direction of establishing greater equality between husband and wife.

Dizengoff, Meir (1861–1937) Politician of Russian origin. He was born in Bessarabia. He became active in Russian revolutionary circles and later in the Hovevei Zion movement. In 1892 he was sent by Baron Edmond de Rothschild to establish a bottle factory in Palestine. He returned to Russia, but in 1905 went back to Palestine and settled in Jaffa. He was a founder of Tel Aviv and became its first mayor in 1921. He published his memoirs, *With Tel Aviv in Exile*, in 1931.

Doctorow, Edgar Lawrence (1931–2015) American writer. Born in New York, he began his career as an editor, but later taught at the University of California, Sarah Lawrence College, Yale and New York University. His works include *Welcome to Hard Times, Big as Life, The Book of Daniel, Loon Lake, World's Fair* and *Billy Bathgate.*

Dogma A religious doctrine or system of doctrines proclaimed as true by the religious authority. Abstract dogmas are not found in the Bible, but when Judaism came into contact with the Greek world, such formulations began to be proposed. Philo was the first to lay down articles of faith. Karaism and the rise of Islam brought about further attempts to establish the essential beliefs of Judaism. Maimonides' 13 principles of the Jewish faith became influential in the Middle Ages. Other scholars such as Hasdai ben Abraham Crescas and Joseph Albo also proposed formulations of the doctrines of Judaism.

Dolitzki, Menaḥem Mendel (1865–1931) American Hebrew and Yiddish writer of Russian origin. He was born in Bialystok. He was Hebrew secretary to Kalonymos Ze'ev Wissotzky in Berlin from 1882 to 1892, when he emigrated to the US and settled in New York. In his early works he described the sufferings of Jewish people in Russia; later he wrote poems of yearning for Zion. He also published a biography of Wissotzky. In the US his descriptions of Jewish persecution in Russia appeared in the journal *Ha-Ivri.*

Domain Ownership and control of the use of land; the land thus owned and controlled. In rabbinic literature a distinction is made between public and private domain. For purposes of the rules of Sabbath observance, there are four types: private, where carrying is permitted; public, such as streets, where carrying is forbidden; semi-private, such as fields, where carrying is forbidden; and semi-public. In cases of ritual uncleanliness, a private domain is one where there are fewer than three persons; where there are three or more the domain is public. In cases of claims for damages, a public domain is any place or road where there is public access; in such cases the person who causes injury is liable to pay compensation.

Donin, Nicholas (fl. 13th cent.) French Franciscan monk. He was a pupil of Jehiel ben Joseph of Paris, who excommunicated him for his heretical ideas. He joined the Franciscan order and compiled a list of 35 accusations against the *Talmud*. He was the main instigator of the Disputation of Paris in 1240, as a consequence of which 24 cartloads of copies of the *Talmud* were burned in 1242.

Dönmeh   Judeo-Muslim sect formed in the 17th century by a group of Shabbetai Tzevi's followers. Like Shabbetai Tzevi, they converted to Islam, but they retained many Jewish observances as well as their belief in him as the Messiah. Eventually the sect divided into several groups based largely in Salonica.

Donnolo, Shabbetai (913–c.982)   Italian physician. He was born in Oria. He travelled widely and served as physician to the Byzantine governor in Calabria and to church officials. He wrote a commentary on the Sepher Yetzirah. His *Book of Remedies* was the first Hebrew treatise on medicine written in Christian Europe.

D'Orta, Garcia (c.1500–1568)   Portuguese Marrano scientist and physician. He was born in Castelo de Vide, and taught at Lisbon University. In 1534 he left Portugal for India, where he served in Goa as a physician to Portuguese vicroys, Christian dignitaries, and the Muslim ruler. His *Coloquios dos simples e drogas he cousas medicinais da India* laid the foundation for the study of tropical diseases. He was posthumously condemned by the Inquisition.

Dosa ben Saadyah (930–1017)   Babylonian communal leader and head of the academy of Sura. Seventy-one years after the death of his father, Saadyah ben Joseph, he became gaon of Sura. He wrote a biography of his father, responsa, commentaries on the *Talmud* and philosophical works.

Doubt   In Jewish law a state of doubt exists in cases where the law is undecided or where the facts are uncertain. A code of procedures and criteria has

been evolved, according to which each instance is to be resolved. The basic guide to be followed is the general rule that doubts affecting biblical law are to be decided in conformity with the stricter view, whereas those involving rabbinic law are to be resolved according to the more lenient position. Exceptions to this rule concern doubts in monetary matters (decided according to the lenient view) and cases involving danger to life (decided according to whatever policy will most effectively remove the danger).

Dov Ber of Mezhirich [Ber [Maggid] of Mezhirich] (c.1710–1772)   Russian Hasidic teacher. Originally a folk preacher (maggid), he became a disciple of the Baal Shem Tov, after whose death he became the leader of the Hasidim. He transferred the movement from Medzhibozh to Mezhirich and under his leadership it spread into Ukraine, Lithuania and central Poland. Many of his homilies are included in works written by his disciples. He provided Hasidism with a speculative-mystical system based on the kabbalah.

Dowry   Property a wife brings to her husband at marriage. The Bible mentions gifts brought by the husband to the bride and also by the wife to the husband. In talmudic times, the practice of giving a dowry was well established. The dowry is recorded in the marriage contract. It reverts to the wife upon divorce or the death of her husband.

Dream   In the Bible dreams are frequently regarded as divine communications. Joseph and Daniel were noted for their ability to interpret dreams. In the *Talmud* various views are presented about the significance of dreams. Interest in dreams continued through the Middle Ages to modern times, especially among the Kabbalists and Hasidim.

Dreck (Yiddish)   Excrement, rubbish, cheap things, works of art of any kind that are of inferior quality.

Dreidel [trendel] (Yiddish). Spinning top. The word is applied specifically to a traditional Jewish toy which bears the initial letters of the Hebrew words: 'A great miracle happened there'. It is spun in a game played at Ḥanukkah.

Dress In biblical times the dress of the Jews was similar to that of neighbouring peoples, and during the Hasmonean period Greek and Roman costumes became prevalent among the Jewish upper classes. Later the wearing of fringes (tzitzit) on four corners of a garment differentiated Jews from gentiles. From the Middle Ages Jews were often forced to wear the Jewish Badge or other distinctive clothing. In North Africa the prohibition of bright colours in Jewish dress resulted in the evolution of the black robe and skullcap. But in Eastern Europe the wearing of a fur-trimmed hat (streimel) and a long kaftan reflected local customs. In certain Mediterranean areas, Jews wore Spanish fashions introduced by Sephardi exiles in 1492.

Dreyfus, Alfred (1859–1935) French soldier. He was born in Alsace. He became a captain on the general staff of the French army in 1892. In 1894 he was accused of treason, found guilty and sentenced to life imprisonment. He protested his innocence and was eventually exonerated, but the case plunged France into a state of virulent anti-Semitism for a decade. The so-called Dreyfus Affair deeply influenced Theodor Herzl and contributed to the development of Zionism. Dreyfus' *The Letters of Captain Dreyfus to his Wife and Five Years of my Life* depict his ordeal.

Drink offering Offering of wine added to all sacrifices in the Temple. The quantities varied from a fourth part of a hin of wine for a lamb, a third part of a hin for a ram, and half a hin for a bullock (Numbers 15:5–9).

Drunkenness According to the *Talmud* a person under the influence of alcohol is legally responsible for his actions unless he has reached the state of oblivion attributed to Lot. A drunken person is not allowed to conduct a religious service. However, on Purim a person is permitted to become so intoxicated that he is unable to distinguish between the expressions 'Blessed be Mordecai' and 'Cursed be Haman'.

Druyanow, Alter (1870–1938) Polish Hebrew writer and Zionist leader. He was born in Druya in the district of Vilnius. He was a member of the Ḥibbat Zion movement and secretary of its Odessa committee from 1890 to 1905. He lived in Palestine from 1906 to 1909 and from 1923. He edited the Zionist organ *Ha-Olam* and wrote a history of Ḥibbat Zion. He also published a collection of Jewish folk humour, *The Book of Jokes and Witticisms*.

Dualism Religious or philosophical doctrine. The term is used of two different beliefs: (1) The belief in a cosmic struggle between the powers of good and evil. This doctrine was taught in the ancient religion of Persia and later by gnostics. The rabbis condemned those who recognised two divine powers. Dualistic trends affected some Jewish theologians and is found in Jewish mysticism. (2) The belief in a radical opposition of matter and spirit. Stemming from Greek thought, this belief influenced Philo as well as medieval Jewish philosophy.

Dubinsky, David (1892–1982) American labour leader. He was born in Belorussia, and emigrated to the US in 1910. He became President of the International Ladies Garment Workers' Union in 1932, and Vice-President of the American Federation of Labour in 1934. After World War II he was a founder of the International Confederation of Free Trade Unions. He was a supporter of Israel, and in particular the Histadrut.

Dubno, Solomon (1738–1813) Dutch Bible scholar and Hebrew poet of

Ukrainian origin. He lived in Amsterdam and Berlin, where he served as a tutor for Moses Mendelssohn's son. He helped with Mendelssohn's German translation of the Bible and commentary. He eventually returned to Amsterdam, where he published a commentary on the Torah as well as Hebrew poetry.

Dubnow, Simon (1860–1941) Russian historian. Born in Belorussia, he lived in St Petersburg, Odessa, Vilnius, Berlin and Riga. He wrote a ten-volume history of the Jewish people, a history of the Jews in Russia and Poland and a history of Ḥasidism. In his writings he propounded the doctrine of national autonomy. He believed that the Jews are a nation, spiritually and should aspire to social and cultural, rather than political, independence.

Dujovne, Leon (1899–1984) Argentine philosopher and communal leader. He was born in Russia and went to Argentina as a child. He taught at the University of Buenos Aires and published studies of Benedict Spinoza and Martin Buber. He also translated the writings of a number of medieval Jewish philosophers into Spanish. He served as president of the Sociedad Hebraica Argentina and the Instituto de Intercambio Culural Argentina-Israel.

Duker, Abraham Gordon (1907–1987) American educator and historian. He was born in Poland and went to the US in 1923. From 1956 to 1962 he was president of the Chicago Spertus College of Judaica. In 1963 he became Director of Libraries and Professor of History and Social Institutions at Yeshiva University. He wrote studies of Polish-Jewish relations and American Jewish sociology.

Dukes, Leopold (1810–1891) Hungarian historian. He was born in Pressburg. He visited libraries in Europe and uncovered many unknown medieval works. His research covered aggadic literature, Bible exegesis, medieval

Jewish literature, Hebrew grammar and masoretic texts, as well as talmudic maxims and truisms. He translated Rashi's Torah commentary into German and published studies of the poetry of Solomon ibn Gabirol and Moses ibn Ezra.

Dukhan Platform. According to talmudic literature, it refers variously to the place in the Temple where the Levites sang while the sacrifice was being offered; the place where the priests stood while reciting the Priestly Blessing; the place where the Priestly Blessing was recited in the synagogue after the destruction of the Temple; or the platform where teachers sat while teaching children.

Dunash ben Labrat [Ibn Labrat, Dunash] (c.920–990) Iraqi Hebrew poet and grammarian. He was born in Baghdad, studied at Fez, and later settled in Córdoba. He applied Arabic forms of Hebrew to poetry and laid the foundation for medieval Hebrew poetry. He wrote 200 criticisms of Menaḥem ben Saruk's dictionary, the *Maḥberet*. This led to a controversy which influenced the development of Hebrew philology and grammar.

Dunash ben Tamim (c.860–after 955/6) North African scholar. He wrote studies of philology, mathematics, astronomy and medicine, as well as a commentary on the Sepher Yetzirah.

Dünner, Joseph Hirsch (1833–1911) Dutch rabbi and talmudist. He was born in Kraków. He was appointed director of the rabbinical seminary in Amsterdam in 1862. In 1874 he became Chief Rabbi of the Ashkenazi community in the city, and later a leader of the Mizraḥi party. He published glosses to 19 tractates of the *Talmud* as well as an enquiry into the origin of the Tosephta.

Duran, Profiat [Ephodi] (fl. 13th–14th century) Spanish scholar and polemicist He was born in Perpignan.

He was forcibly converted to Christianity in 1391 but later reverted to Judaism. He wrote two polemical tracts against Christianity, a Hebrew grammar, a commentarhy on Maimonides' *Guide for the Perplexed*, and a history of the persecutions and expulsions of the Jews from the destruction of the Second Temple until his own time.

Duran, Simeon ben Tzemaḥ [Rashbatz] (1361–1944) North African rabbinic scholar, philosopher and surgeon in Palma. After the massacre there in 1391, he settled in Algiers where he served as Chief Rabbi. His writings include an encyclopedic philosophical work, *Magen Avot*. His responsa deal with religious and legal problems as well as grammar, philology, exegesis, literary history, philosophy, kabbalah, mathematics, and astronomy.

Duran, Solomon ben Simeon [Rashbash]. (c.1400–1447) North African scholar, son of Simeon ben Tzemaḥ Duran. He was born in Algiers. He joined his father's bet din at an early age and became the head of the yeshivah. His *Milḥemet Mitzvah* is a defence of the *Talmud* against the accusations made by the apostate Joshua Lorki (Geronimo de Santa Fe).

Duress According to Jewish law, a person is responsible for his actions only if they are initiated and performed by his own free will. However, compulsion may be used as an extenuating circumstance only where it takes the form of physical violence or threat to the life of the individual concerned. The compulsion to commit idolatry, murder or engage in an adulterous or incestuous act is to be resisted even if it involves the loss of one's life. A divorce granted under duress is invalid, and a woman who is forced to agree to marriage is considered unwed by law. Oaths or vows made under duress are invalid. Similarly a gift given under duress may be rescinded. But a sale or purchase

made under duress remains valid, and notwithstanding the circumstances an injury caused by duress to someone else must be compensated.

Durkheim, Émile (1858–1917) French sociologist. He was born in Épinal. He became Professor of Sociology at the University of Bordeaux in 1887, and in 1902 he was appointed Professor at the Sorbonne. He founded and edited *L'année sociologique* and wrote numerous sociological works including *The Elementary Forms of the Religious Life*. Although he did not work directly on Jewish topics, his work reflects his Jewish background.

Duschak, Moritz (1815–1890) Moravian rabbi, teacher and writer. He served as a rabbi in Aussee and Gaya. From 1877 he occupied the post of preacher and teacher in Kraków. He published studies on talmudic topics and Jewish scholarship.

Dushkin, Alexander (1890–1976) American educator. He was born in Poland and was taken to the US in 1901. He was Director of Chicago's Board of Jewish Education (1923–34) and Executive Director of the Jewish Education Committee in New York (1939–49). From 1962 he headed the Department of Jewish Education in the Diaspora at the Hebrew University Institute of Contemporary Jewry. He published numerous studies of Jewish education.

Duty An action that a person is obliged to perform for God or another person. Jewish law recognises different kinds of duty. 'Ḥovah' (an obligation) is distinct from 'mitzvah', which can signify both duty and a commendable action ('reshut'). According to Baḥ ya ibn Pakuda a distinction should be made between the duties of the limbs (involving ceremonial and practical obligations), and the duties of the heart (involving the spiritual life).

Dyeing The dyeing of cloth is mentioned in the Bible. The craft developed considerably during mishnaic and talmudic times and in the Middle Ages the Jewish trade in dyestuffs also expanded greatly. In the modern period Jews continued to practise this profession in the Near East.

Dymov, Ossip [Perelmann, Joseph] (1878–1959) Russian Yiddish author and playwright. He was born in Bialystok. He first wrote fiction in Russian, blending symbolism, irony and wit. His plays deal with Jewish suffering and experience. After he emigrated to the US in 1913, he wrote for the Yiddish theatre.

E

An older Jewish woman on an airplane is in first class. She is seated next to an attractive younger woman. The younger woman looks at the ring on the older Jewish woman's hand and cannot help but tell her how extraordinary and beautiful it is. 'I've never seen a larger or more beautiful diamond!' she exclaims. 'Yes,' the older Jewish woman says. She then confides, 'It is worth nearly as much and is almost as big as the famous Hope Diamond. But just like the Hope Diamond, it carries a curse.'

'A curse?' says the young woman fearfully. 'What kind of curse?'

'It goes back many years. It is called the Goldberg curse.'

'Who or what is Goldberg?'

'Goldberg. He's my husband.'

* * * * *

The message of this joke is clear. Money isn't everything. Numerous jokes convey how difficult it is for Jewish wives to abide their overly rich husbands. There is an important lesson here: don't marry a rich man for his money.

Eban, Abba (1915–2002) Israeli statesman and diplomat. He was born in Cape Town. He lectured in Arabic at Cambridge University from 1938 to 1940. After World War II he settled in Israel. He was a member of the Jewish Agency delegation to the UN (1947–48) and then represented Israel at the UN (1948–49) before serving as Israeli Ambassador to the US (1950–59). He was President of the Weizmann Institute from 1958 to 1966. Elected to the Knesset as a Mapai delegate, he was successively Minister of Education and Culture (1960–63), deputy Prime Minister (1963–66), and Foreign Minister (1966–74).

Ecclesiastes (Hebrew 'Kohelet) Biblical book, one of the five scrolls in the Hagiographa. The name Ecclesiastes is Greek, meaning 'convoker', and is a rendering of the Hebrew word 'Kohelet', by which the author is referred to. The book discusses the meaning of life: the central theme is that all is futile, but the last verses are optimistic and pious. The work is read in the synagogue during Sukkot.

Ecclesiastes Rabbah (Hebrew 'Kohelet Rabbah') Post-talmudic midrash on the book of Ecclesiastes. It is an exegetical midrash which gives a chapter-by-chapter and verse-by-verse exposition of Ecclesiastes. It is based on various older midrashic works.

Ecclesiasticus [Wisdom of Ben Sira] Apocryphal book. It was written by Ben Sira and translated into Greek by his grandson in 132 BCE. It contains moral maxims, as well as liturgical poems and psalms.

**Edels, Samuel Eliezer [Maharsha]
(1555–1631).** Polish talmudist. He was
born in Kraków and settled in Posen,
where he married the daughter of Moses
Ashkenazi Heilpern. His mother-in-law
Edel (by whose name he became known)
supported him and his disciples for 20
years. He was later a rabbi in Chelm,
Lublin and Ostrog, where he founded a
yeshivah. His *Ḥiddushe Halakhot* is a talmudic commentary which is included
in most editions of the *Talmud*.

Eden, Garden of   The abode of Adam
and Eve (Genesis 2–3). They were
excluded from the garden because they
disobeyed God and ate the forbidden
fruit. In rabbinic literature the Garden
of Eden is the place where the righteous
dwell after death.

Eder, Montagu David (1865–1936)
English psychoanalyst and physician.
He was born in London. He was a
founder of the Psychoanalytical Association in England. He also established
a children's clinic and edited the journal
School Hygiene. He was active in Zionist
affairs and served on the Zionist commission in Palestine from 1918 to 1921.
He later served on the World Executive
Committee of the Zionist Organisation
in Jerusalem and London.

Education   The Bible stipulates that
divine precepts must be taught to
the people, especially children. The
religious revival under Ezra in the
5th century BCE centred on the regular reading of and instruction in the
Torah (Ezra 7:1–10:44). In the rabbinic period there was a comprehensive educational system for Jewish
boys. Synagogues had a bet sepher for
elementary study and a bet midrash for
advanced learning. In the Babylonian
academies Jewish scholarship reached
great heights. Subsequently yeshivot
were established throughout the Jewish world which carried on the tradition of Jewish learning. In the modern period traditional Jewish religious
educational institutions have been
established, as well as neo-Orthodox
religious schools and day schools. All
these institutions are, in their different
ways, committed to perpetuating Jewish learning.

Eduyyot   Seventh tractate in the
Mishnah order of Nezikin containing a
great variety of laws. Its purpose is to
put on record the testimonies of later
sages on the legal pronouncements and
controversies of earlier authorities.

Efros,   Israel   (1891–1981)   American Hebrew scholar. He was born in
Ukraine and emigrated to the US in
1905. He was Professor at John's Hop-
kins University, Buffalo University,
Hunter College, and Dropsie College.
In 1955 he settled in Israel and served
as Rector and later Honorary President
of Tel Aviv University. He published
studies of medieval Jewish philosophy, translated *Hamlet* into Hebrew
and Ḥayyim Naḥman Bialik's poetry
into English, co-authored an English-
Hebrew dictionary, and wrote volumes
of poetry.

Eger, Akiva ben Moses (1761–1837)
German rabbi. He was born in Eisenstadt and served as a rabbi at Markisch-
Friedland in 1791, and from 1814 at
Posen, where he established a yeshivah.
As one of the foremost rabbinic authorities in Europe, he opposed the Reform
movement. He published glosses on
the Mishnah and the *Talmud*, as well as
numerous responsa.

**Eger,   Akiva   ben   Simḥa   Bunem
(c.1720–1758)**   German rabbi and
author. He was born in Halberstadt
and served as rabbi of Zuelz in Upper
Silesia. In 1756 he became head of the
yeshivah of Pressburg. He was one of
the foremost talmudic scholars of his
generation. He published novellae on
the *Talmud* and responsa.

Eger, Judah Leib (1816–1888)   Polish
Ḥasidic leader. He was born in Warsaw and led a Ḥasidic congregation in

Lublin. After the death of Menaḥem Mendel of Kotsk in 1859, he assumed the role of tzaddik and propounded his own teaching. He spent much time in prayer, devoting himself to it with fervour accompanied by weeping and loud cries. His teachings on the law and festivals were arranged by his son Abraham in *Torat Emet* and *Imrei Emet*.

Eger, Samuel Levin ben Judah Leib (1769–1842) German talmudist. He was born in Halberstadt and served as rabbi of Braunschweig. An opponent of the Reform movement, he insisted on the retention of Hebrew in prayer. He wrote talmudic novellae, homiletic discourses, and responsa.

Eger, Solomon ben Akiva (1786–1852) Polish rabbi and communal leader. He was born in Lissa and served as rabbi of Kalisz and Posen. He encouraged Jews to move away from commerce into farming, solicited contributions for Palestine, and campaigned for the emancipation of the Jews in his own country. He was an opponent of the Reform movement. He published notes on the *Talmud* and Isaac ben Jacob Alfasi's code.

Eglah arupah Heifer sacrificed on the occasion of an unsolved murder (Deuteronomy 21:1–9). The elders of the community nearest to the place where the corpse is discovered must break the heifer's neck, wash their hands over it, and profess their innocence.

Eḥad mi yodea ('Who knows one?') Opening words of a medieval Hebrew riddle of numbers, appended to the Passover Haggadah in certain rites.

Ehrenburg, Ilya Grigoryevich (1891–1967) Russian author and journalist. He was born in Kiev. He was exiled from 1908 to 1917 for revolutionary activities. On his return to Russia in 1917 he opposed the Bolsheviks and he again left the country in 1921. He returned once more in 1941 and became a spokesman for Stalin. He wrote against Nazi anti-Semitism and Zionism. He was awarded the Stalin Prize in 1942 for his novel *The Fall of Paris* and in 1948 for *The Storm*. His autobiography appeared in six volumes.

Ehrenkranz, Benjamin Wolf [Zbahrz, Velvel of] (1819–1883) Galician Yiddish and Hebrew poet. He travelled to various European cities as a singing bard. His poems were concerned with nature and man, poverty and wealth, and the struggle of light and darkness (symbolising the opposition of the maskilim and the Ḥasidim). Much of his poetry employs parody and satire. His collected poems appeared between 1865 and 1878.

Ehrenpreis, Marcus (1869–1951) Swedish rabbi and author. He was born in Lemberg, and served as rabbi in Djakovo, Croatia, from 1896 to 1900. He later became Chief Rabbi of Sofia, and from 1914 of Stockholm. At the request of Theodor Herzl he translated the invitation to the First Zionist Congress into Hebrew. He acted as consultant on cultural matters at Zionist congresses. He translated modern Hebrew literature into Swedish, founded a Jewish-Swedish journal and edited a Jewish encyclopedia in Swedish.

Ehrenstein, Albert (1886–1950) Austrian poet and author. He was born in Vienna. He lived in Berlin, travelled widely in Europe, and eventually settled in New York in 1941. His poetry was pessimistic in character and occasionally bears witness to a yearning for the oriental world. He published several volumes of Chinese poetry in his own free adaptions, as well as narrative works and essays.

Ehrlich, Arnold Bogumil (1848–1919) American biblical exegete of Polish origin. He was born in Wlodawa near Lublin. He worked as a librarian in the Semitics department of the Berlin Royal Library. At the age of 30 he settled in the US. He helped Franz

Delitzsch to translate the New Testament into Hebrew and later published Hebrew and German commentaries on the Bible.

Ehrlich, Joseph (1842–1899) Austrian writer. He was born in Brody, Galicia. He worked as a poet and journalist in Vienna. His autobiography, *My Life's Way,* describes the life of the Jewish community in Brody in the 1840s and 1850s.

Ehud (fl. 12 century BCE) Judge of the tribe of Benjamin. He delivered Israel from Eglon, King of Moab. Under the pretext of having a secret message for the king, he drew a dagger and killed him. This ended Moabite rule over Israel for several generations (Judges 3).

Eibeschütz, Jonathan (c. 1690–1764) Bohemian talmudist and Kabbalist. He was head of a yeshivah in Prague and became the rabbi at Metz in 1741. From 1750 he officiated in turn at Altona, Hamburg and Wandsbeck. He was accused of being a follower of Shabbetai Tzevi but denied the charge. He was one of the greatest talmudic scholars of his time.

Eichelbaum, Samuel (1894–1967) Argentine playwright and short story writer. He was born in Domínguez, Entre Ríos. His play *El Judío Aarón* is based on a Jewish theme, and his short story *Una buena cosecha* is set in Rosh Pinna, Israel.

Eichenbaum, Jacob (1796–1861) Polish Haskalah poet, educator, and mathematician. He was born in Krystianopol, Galicia. He was married at 11, but divorced when his father-in-law suspected him of secular leanings. He married again in 1815, lived again in Zamość, and later settled in Odessa, where he established a Jewish school. In 1844 he was appointed Director of the Kishinev Jewish school, and in 1850 Inspector of the Zhitomir Rabbinical Seminary. A collection of poems by him was one of the first books of poetry published in the Haskalah period.

Eighteen Benedictions (Hebrew 'Shemoneh Esreh) [Amidah; Tephillah] The principal prayer in the Jewish liturgy. It consists of blessings and prayers on the following subjects: (1) the commemoration of the patriarchs; (2) the mightiness of God in natural phenomena; (3) the sanctification of God; (4) understanding; (5) penitence; (6) forgiveness; (7) redemption; (8) healing; (9) the harvest; (10) the ingathering of the exiles; (11) the restoration of the judges; (12) the destruction of the heretics; (13) the rewarding of the righteous; (14) the rebuilding of Jerusalem; (15) the restoration of the Kingdom of David; (16) the acceptance of prayer; (17) the restoration of Temple service; and (18) thanksgiving. It ends with the blessing of priests and a prayer for peace. The benedictions were written at various times between 100 BCE and 100 CE and were gathered together in their final form by Rabban Gamaliel II. The first three and the last three benedictions are recited at every service. The intermediate ones are used only on weekdays.

Einhorn, David (1809–1879) American reform rabbi of German origin. He was born in Bavaria and succeeded Samuel Holdheim as Chief Rabbi of Mecklenburg-Schwerin. In 1855 he became rabbi of the Har Sinai Congregation of Baltimore, and he later served as rabbi of Kenesseth Israel in Philadelphia and Congregation Adath Israel in New York. He was the leader of the extreme reform wing of American Jewry.

Einhorn, Ignaz [Horn, Éduard] (1825–1875) Hungarian Reform rabbi and economist. He was born in Nove Mesto. He organised the Society for the Reform of Judaism in Pest in 1847. Later he served as rabbi of the society's first Reform Temple. He also helped to found the Society for the Propagation of Hungarian Language and Culture, and edited the first Jewish-Hungarian yearbook. After the suppression of the Hungarian uprising in 1849 he settled in Paris, where he published works on economic problems. In 1867 he returned to Budapest and was elected to the Hungarian parliament.

Einhorn, Moses (1896–1966) American physician and editor. He was born in Russia, and was taken to Palestine in 1908. He was forced to emigrate by the Turkish authorities in 1916, and later settled in the US. He was head of the gastroenterological department of the Bronx Hospital in New York. In 1926 he founded (with Asher Goldstein) the Hebrew medical journal *Ha-Rophe ha-Ivri*.

Einstein, Albert (1879–1955) German physicist. He was born in Ulm. He worked in the patent office at Berne and later was Professor at the University of Prague and at the Prussian Academy of Science in Berlin. In 1921 he received the Nobel Prize for Physics, in recogniton of his work on relativity quantum physics and Brownian motion. In 1933 he settled in the US and became Professor of Theoretical Physics at the Princeton Institute for Advanced Studies. He was an active supporter of Zionism and served as a trustee of the Hebrew University.

Eisendrath, Maurice Nathan (1902–1973) American Reform rabbi. He was born in Chicago, and served as rabbi in Charleston, South Carolina, and Toronto. In 1943 he became Presi-

dent of the Union of American Hebrew Congregations. He was active in interfaith activities and social action.

Eisenmenger, Johann Andreas (1654–1704) German writer. He was born in Mannheim. He studied midrash and *Talmud* with Jewish scholars for 19 years. In 1700 he published *Entdecktes Judentum*, which maligned the Jews and collected rabbinic quotations critical of Christianity. After its publication the intervention of the Jewish community resulted in its withdrawal, but a second edition was published in 1711.

Eisenstadt, Benzion (1873–1951) American rabbi and Hebrew writer of Belorussian origin. He settled in the US in 1903. He published lexicographic and biographical works on contemporary rabbis and writers.

Eisenstadt, Meir ben Isaac [Maḥaram Ash] (c.1670–1744) Polish rabbinic authority. He served as rabbi in Szydlowiec, Poland, and later settled in Worms, where he became head of a yeshivah. When the French occupied Worms in 1701 he went to Prossnitz, Moravia, where he served as rabbi. In 1714 he was appointed rabbi of Eisenstadt and its seven communities, where he established a yeshivah. His *Panim Meirot* contains responsa and novellae on the *Talmud*.

Eisenstein, Ira (1906–2001) American rabbi. He was born in New York. He led the Society for the Advancement of Judaism, and subsequently served as rabbi to Anshe Emet synagogue in Chicago. Later he became President of the Reconstructionist Foundation and editor of the *Reconstructionist*. In 1968 he was appointed President of the Reconstructionist Rabbinical College. His writings include *Creative Judaism, What We Mean by Religion,* and *Judaism Under Freedom.*

Eisenstein, Judah David (1854–1956) American Hebrew writer and editor of Polish origin. He emigrated to the US in 1872, where he became a coal manufacturer. He was a founder in 1880 of Shoḥarei Sefat Ever, the first Hebrew society in the US. He published in Hebrew a Jewish encyclopedia in ten volumes (*Otzar Yisrael*), as well as several anthologies of Jewish literature.

Eisenstein, Sergei Mikhailovich (1898–1948) Russian film director. Born in Riga, Latvia, he studied architecture at the Petrograd Institute of Civil Engineering. Later he joined the Red Army. In 1920 he became a set director of the Moscow Proletkult Theatre. His films include *Strike, Battleship Potemkin, October, The General Line, Alexander Nevsky* and *Ivan the Terrible.*

Eisler, Moritz (1823–1902). Moravian educator and historian of Jewish philosophy. He founded and served as President of an organisation for the support of disabled Jewish teachers and their widows and children. His *Lectures on Jewish Philosophy in the Middle Ages* were one of the first attempts to summarise and present the main systems of medieval Jewish philosophy.

Elah (fl. 9th cent. BCE) King of Israel (883–882 BCE), son of Baasha. He was murdered, while in a state of intoxication, by Zimri, the captain of his chariots. His murder arose from the army's dissatisfaction with his indifference to the campaign against the Philistines near Gibberthon.

El Al. Israeli airline It was established in 1948, initially to facilitate the transporting of Jewish immigrants. It eventually became a major world airline

Elath [Epstein], Eliahyu (1903–1990) Israeli diplomat. He was born in Russia and settled in Palestine in 1924. From 1934 to 1945 he was Director of the Middle East section in the Jewish Agency's Political Department, and from 1945 to 1948 head of its Political Office in Washington. In 1949 he served as ambassador in Washington, and was then ambassador in London (1950–59). He was President of the Hebrew University from 1962 to 1968. His writings include *Israel and its Neighbours.*

Elazari-Volcani [Volkani; Wilkanski; Wilkansky] Yitzḥak Avigdor (1880–1955) Israeli agronomist. He was born in Lithuania and settled in Palestine in 1908, where he became one of the leaders of the Ha-Poel ha-Tzair Party. He founded and directed workers' farms at Ben Shemen and Ḥulda from 1909 to 1918, and in 1921 he established the Agricultural Experiment Station at Ben Shemen. He was appointed Professor of Agricultural Economics at the Hebrew University in 1938.

Elbogen, Ismar (1874–1943) American scholar. He was born in Schildberg, in the Posen district. He began teaching Jewish history and biblical exegesis at the Collegio Rabbinico Italiano in Florence in 1899. In 1903 he joined the faculty of the Hochschule für die Wissenschaft des Judentums in Berlin. In 1938 he emigrated to New York, where he was appointed research professor at the Jewish Theological Seminary, Hebrew Union College, Jewish Institute of Religion, and Dropsie College. He published studies in Jewish history and the history of Jewish liturgy.

Eldad (fl. 13th cent. BCE) Elder of Israel. He was one of the 70 Israelite elders appointed by Moses to aid him in governing the people (Numbers 11:16ff). He and Medad aroused the suspicion of Joshua by prophesying within the camp, but their conduct was approved by Moses (Numbers 11:26–29).

Eldad ha-Dani (fl. 9th cent.) Traveller. His origins are obscure. He claimed to belong to the tribe of Dan and asserted that the tribes of Dan, Naphtali Gad, and Asher formed an independent kingdom in Africa. He visited Jewish communities in north Africa and Spain. The Kairouan community sought the opinion of the gaon Tzemaḥ about the halakhic practices described by him.

Elder In Jewish usage, one of the members of the governing body of the nation or community. In biblical times the elders helped to rule the Israelites. Moses appointed 70 elders to aid him in this task (Numbers 11:16ff). The elders served as judges and representatives of the people until the Second Temple period. In the Middle Ages the title 'zaken' (elder) was given to communal councillors in some areas.

Elders of Zion, Protocols of the Forged document, purporting to prove the existence of international Jewish aspirations to attain world power. It has been widely used to inspire anti-Semitic feeling. It was first published in Russia at the beginning of the 20th century. After the Russian Civil War, the work was introduced into Western Europe by Russian émigrés. It describes a plan supposed to have been made by a conference of leaders of world Jewry to attain global domination and overthrow of Christian society The *Protocols* circulated in many countries, played a part in Nazi propaganda, and continues to be reprinted particularly in Arab lands.

Eleazar (i) (fl. 13th cent. BCE) Israelite, third son of Aaron (Exodus 6:23). After his father's death, he was appointed high priest (Exodus 20:28; Deuteronomy 10:6). The priestly family of Zadok traced its descent from him.

Eleazar (ii) [Auran] (fl. 2nd cent. BCE) Hasmonean warrior and brother of Judah Maccabee. At the battle of Bet Zechariah, he stabbed an elephant of the enemy's army, believing that its rider was Antiochus Eupator, the Syrian ruler. He was killed when the animal fell on him.

Eleazar ben Arakh (fl. 1st cent.). Palestinian tanna. He was the most outstanding of the inner circle of the five disciples of Johanan ben Zakkai. He engaged in mystical speculation concerning the divine chariot ('merkavah'). He later settled in Emmaus.

Eleazar ben Azariah (fl. 1st–2nd cent.) Palestinian tanna. He traced his ancestry back ten generations to Ezra. When Rabban Gamaliel II was temporarily deposed as nasi, Eleazar ben Azariah was chosen to succeed him. The school of Jabneh, the centre of rabbinic learning, was opened to all who wished to study, and no longer restricted (as it had been under Gamaliel) to those considered worthy. According to tradition, Eleazar ben Azariah went on a mission to Rome with Rabban Gamaliel II. He was both a halakhist and an aggadist.

Eleazar ben Dinai (fl. 1st cent) Palestinian Zealot leader. He ravaged Judea for 20 years until he was captured by the procurator Felix and sent to Rome.

Eleazar ben Hananiah (fl. 1st cent.) Palestinian scholar. He was a leader of the school of Shammai.

Eleazar ben Jair (fl. 1st cent.) Palestinian Zealot leader. After the assassination of Menaḥem ben Judah in 66, he led Jewish forces to the fortress of Masada and held it for seven years. When it was surrounded by the Romans, he persuaded the Jews to kill one another in order to avoid capture.

Eleazar ben Judah of Worms [Eleazar Rokeaḥ] (c. 1165–1230) German talmudist, Kabbalist, and liturgical poet. Born in Mainz, he spent most of his life in Worms. He witnessed the murder by crusaders of his wife and children. He published works on halakhah, liturgical poetry, theology, ethics and exegesis. His *Sepher ha-Rokeaḥ* was intended to educate the common reader in the details of halakhic law. He was the last major scholar of the Ḥasidei Ashkenaz movement.

Eleazar ben Parta (fl. 2nd cent.) Palestinian tanna. He was one of the sages arrested by the Romans for contravening Hadrian's decree forbidding the public teaching of the Torah and observance of the commandments. Although the offence carried the death penalty he was miraculously delivered from execution.

Eleazar ben Pedat (fl. 3rd cent.) Palestinian amora. He was born in Babylonia and settled in Palestine. After the death of Johanan in 279, he was appointed head of the council in Tiberius. He was a major exponent of the Oral Law and a prolific aggadist.

Eleazar ben Shammua (fl. 2nd cent.) Palestinian tanna. He was one of the last pupils of Akiva. After Simeon Bar Kokhba's revolt (132–35), he was ordained by Judah ben Bava. Several of his teachings were incorporated into the Mishnah by his pupil Judah ha-Nasi. He is included among the Ten Martyrs of the Hadrianic persecutions.

Eleazar ben Simeon (i) (fl. 1st cent.) Palestinian Zealot leader. He played an important role in the war against Cestius Gallus. He was responsible for the entry of the Idumeans to Jerusalem and the subsequent massacre of the opponents of the Zealots. He fought against John of Giscala until the beginning of the siege of the city by Titus.

Eleazar ben Simeon (ii) (fl. 2nd cent.) Palestinian tanna. He was the son of Simeon ben Yohai, with whom he escaped from the Romans by hiding in a cave for 13 years. He engaged in halakhic controversy with Judah ha-Nasi as well as in halakhic and aggadic discussions with other scholars. He eventually accepted a position in the Roman administration as an official responsible for the apprehension of thieves and robbers.

El Elyon ('Most high God') Name of God, used only in Genesis 14:18; it occurs in the description of Melchizedek a priest in the time of Abraham.

El erekh appayim ('O God, slow to anger') Opening words of the selihah prayer recited in the synagogue during the morning service on Mondays and Thursdays before the reading of the law. It is omitted on the New Moon, the eve of Passover, the Ninth of Av, Hanukkah and Purim.

Elhanan (i) (fl. 10th cent. BCE) Israelite warrior. According to II Samuel 21:19 he killed Goliath. In I Chronicles 20:5 it is stated that he killed Lahmi, the brother of Goliath.

Elhanan (ii) [Andreas] (? 10th century) Legendary Jewish pope. According to tradition he was the son of Simeon the Great of Mainz. Kidnapped by monks, he was baptised, educated in a monastery, and became a priest. Eventually he was elected pope. When he discovered his Jewish origins, he threw himself from a tower. Another tradition relates that he reverted to Judaism.

Eli (fl. 11th cent. BCE) Israelite, head priest in the Sanctuary at Shiloh during the period of the Judges. When Elkanah made an annual pilgrimage to Shiloh, his wife, Hannah, made a vow in the presence of Eli and received the assurance that her prayer for a son would be answered (I Samuel 1:11ff). After her son, Samuel, was weaned Hannah brought him to Eli to serve in the Sanctuary. Eli's family was subsequently depirived of the priesthood (I Kings 2:26–7) because of the immoral conduct of Eli's sons, Hophni and Phinehas (I Samuel 2:11–36; 3:11–14).

Eliashib (fl. 5th cent. BCE) Israelite, high priest in the time of Ezra and Nehemiah. He and his priestly colleagues were responsible for rebuilding the wall guarding the north-western approach to the Temple Mount. Their portion was the Tower of Hananel, the

Tower of the Hundred, and the Sheep Gate (Nehemiah 3:1).

Eliezer (i) (fl.? 19th–16th cent. BCE) Israelite, steward of Abraham's household (Genesis 15:2). He was to have been Abraham's heir in the absence of any offspring. But when Abraham complained to God that material goods were of little use to him since he had no children to whom to bequeath them, God responded with the promise of a son (Genesis 15:4ff). Eliezer was identified by the rabbis with the servant sent by Abraham to find a wife for Isaac.

Eliezer (ii) (fl. 13th cent. BCE) Israelite second son of Moses (Exodus 18:4).

Eliezer (iii) (fl. 9th cent. BCE) Israelite, prophet of Mareshah. He denounced Jehoshaphat's alliance with Ahaziah (II Chronicles 20:37).

Eliezer ben Hyrcanus (fl. 1st–2nd cent.) Palestinian tanna. He was a pupil of Johnan ben Zakkai and teacher of Akiva. After the destruction of the Temple in 70 he was among the important scholars of the great bet din of Jabneh. Later he established an academy at Lydda. He was a member of a delegation to Rome led by the nasi to obtain concessions for the Jews. He also travelled to Antioch on behalf of the scholars.

Eliezer ben Joel ha-Levi [Rabiyah] (1140–1225) German scholar. He wandered from place to place, visiting Bonn, Worms, Würzburg, Mainz, Metz, Cologne and Regensburg. He refused to accept rabbinic office in order not to derive material benefit from his learning. Eventually he accepted the rabbinate of Cologne in 1200. His *Sepher ha-Rabiyah* contains halakhot and legal decisions according to the order of the tractates in the *Talmud* and also responsa.

Eliezer ben Nathan of Mainz [Raben] (c.1090–c.1170) German scholar. He

lived in Slavic countries, then settled in Mainz. His *Sepher ha-Raban* (also called *Even ha-Ezer*) is the first complete book emanating from the German Jewish community to have survived. It contains responsa, and various extracts and halakhic rulings following the order of the talmudic tractates. He was also the first commentator on liturgical poetry in Germany. Some of his own piyyutim were influenced by the terrors of the First Crusade.

Eliezer ben Yose ha-Galili (fl. 2nd cent.) Palestinian tanna. He was one of the last pupils of Akiva and was among those who re-established the academy in Jabneh, and then in Usha after the Hadrianic persecutions. He wrote the *Baraita of the Thirty-Two Rules*, which enables the aggadah to be expounded, like the halakhah, by fixed hermeneutical rules. He was one of the greatest aggadists of his time.

Elijah [Elijah the Tishbite; the Tishbite] (fl. 9th cent. BCE) Israelite prophet. He prophesied during the reigns of Ahab and Ahaziah. He attempted to restore the purity of the worship of the God of Israel when Ahab's wife, Jezebel, introduced the cult of Baal into the country. In a contest with the prophets of Baal, he emerged victorious (I Kings 18). According to II Kings 2:1–11, Elijah did not die but was carried to heaven in a chariot of horses and fire. In the rabbinic tradition he is viewed as the harbinger of the Messiah. At the Passover seder a glass of wine is traditionally poured for him.

Elijah, Apocalypse of Apocryphal work. It describes the archangel Michael's account to Elijah of the end of Rome, the destruction of the wicked, the last judgement, and the heavenly Jerusalem.

Elijah Be'er ben Shabbetai [Elijah Sabot] (fl. 14th–15th cent.) Italian physician. He taught at the University of Padua, and was in the service of several popes (Innocent VII, Martin V and Eugene IV), as well as Italian rulers. He was summoned to England in 1410 to attend on Henry IV.

Elijah ben Judah of Chelm [Baal Shem, Elijah of Chelm] (1514–1583) Polish rabbi and Kabbalist. He was known for his miracle cures by means of charms and amulets According to legend, he created a golem.

Elijah ben Solomon Zalman [Vilna Gaon] (1700–1797) Lithuanian talmudist. After travelling throughout Poland and Germany he eventually settled in Vilnius. He encouraged the translation of works on natural science but was opposed to philosophy and the Haskalah. He also led the opposition to the Hasidic movement and was regarded as the spiritual leader of the Mitnaggedim. He wrote commentaries on the Bible, annotations on the *Talmud*, midrash and *Zohar*, and works on mathematics, the geography of Palestine, and Hebrew grammar. In his studies of halakhah he sought to establish critical texts of rabbinic sources. He avoided pilpul and based his rulings on the plain meaning of the text.

Elimelech (fl. 12th–11th cent. BCE) Israelite, husband of Naomi and father of Mahlon and Chilion. Owing to the famine during the time of the Judges, he crossed over from Judah to Moab, where he and his sons died. Following their deaths, his wife Naomi returned to Judah with her dauther-in-law Ruth (Ruth 1:1–3; 2:1, 3; 4: 3, 9).

Elimelch of Lizensk (1717–1787) Galician rabbi. He was one of the founders of Hasidism in Galicia. A disciple of Dov Ber of Mezhirich, he is regarded as the theoretician and creator of practical tzaddikism. His *Noam Elimelkh* describes the role of the tzaddik in the Hasidic movement; it stresses the holiness and perfection of the tzaddik and his influence in the earthly and spiritual realms.

Elisha (fl. 9th cent. BCE) Israelite prophet. He prophesied during and after the reign of Jehoram. He was the disciple and successor of Elijah. He foretold Hazael's accession to the Syrian throne, and anointed Jehu king over Israel.

Elisha ben Avuyah [Aher] (fl. 2nd cent.) Palestinian tanna. He was born in Jerusalem. He came to doubt the unity of God, divine providence, and reward and punishment, and ultimately renounced Judaism. Although befriended by Meir, the rabbis disassociated themselves from him and referred to him as Aher (the other). He was the subject of several historical novels including *As a Driven Leaf* by Milton Steinberg.

Elisheva [Zhirkhova, Yelizaveta] (1888–1949) Russian Hebrew poet. She was attracted by the movement for Jewish national renaissance and her poems are full of yearing for the beautiful and nobel qualities of Judaism. She also wrote literary criticism of Hebrew literature. She settled in Palestine in 1925.

Eliya, Joseph (1901–1931) Greek poet and scholar. He was born in Janina and taught French at the Alliance Israélite Universelle school there. He wrote poetic love songs dedicated to Rebekah and also produced Greek translations of Isaiah, Job, the Song of Songs, Ruth and Jonah, as well as the works of medieval and modern Jewish writers.

Eli Zion Acrostic elegy for the fast day of the Ninth of Av. Written in the Middle Ages, it consists of 12 stanzas, each closing with the refrain: 'Wail, Zion and its cities, as a woman in labour pains, and like a maiden that dons sackcloth to mourn for the husband of her youth'. It is sung by the congregation standing.

Elkan, Benno (1877–1960) German sculptor. He was born in Dortmund, went to Paris in 1905, and returned to Germany in 1911. In 1933 he settled in

England. His seven-branched candelabrum embellished with biblical scenes was presented by members of the British Parliament to the Israeli Knesset.

Elkus, Abram Isaac (1867–1947) American lawyer. He was born in New York. He served as special US attorney to prosecute bankruptcy in 1908. In 1911 he was Counsel for the New York State Factory Investigating Commission. He was ambassador in Turkey from 1916 to 1919, and then President of the New York Free Synagogue until 1927.

El male raḥamim ('O God, full of compassion') Opening words of the prayer for the dead. It is recited at a funeral service, on the anniversary of a death, on visiting the grave of a relative, and after being called up for the reading of the law. In some Ashkenazi rites it is also part of the memorial service on festivals and the Day of Atonement. It originated in Jewish communities of Western and Eastern Europe, where it was recited for the martyrs of the crusades and the Chmielnicki massacres.

Elman, Mischa (1891–1967) American violinist. He was accepted at the Odessa music academy at the age of six, and made his debut in St Petersburg. In 1908 he went to the US where he was known for his purity of tone and technique. He also composed light opera.

El melekh ne'eman ('O God, faithful, king') Phrase interposed between the Ahavah benediction and the recitation of the Shema. Its initial letters form the word 'Amen'. It was introduced either in order to preface the Shema with the idea of divine kingship, or to bring the total number of words in the Shema to 248 (to correspond with the 248 members of the human body according to the rabbis). It is recited only when the Shema is said in private.

Elon, Amos (1926–2009) Israeli journalist and writer. He was born in Vienna and emigrated to Palestine as a child. He was a journalist, editorial writer, and columnist for *Ha-Aretz*. His books include *Journey through a Haunted Land, the Israelis: Founders and Sons,* and *A Certain Panic.* He also wrote a biography of Theodor Herzl and a play entitled *Herzl.*

Elul Sixth month of the Jewish year. It immediately precedes the High Holiday season and has become the traditional month of penitence and spiritual preparation. The shophar is sounded after the morning service on weekdays throughout the month.

Elyashar, Jacob Saul ben Eliezer Jehoram (1817–1906). Palestinian Sephardi rabbi. He was born in Safed. He was appointed dayyan in Jerusalem in 1853 and became head of the bet din in 1869. In 1893 he became Sephardi Chief Rabbi of Palestine. He wrote thousands of responsa to questions from Ashkenazim and Sephardim throughout the world.

Elyashev, Isidor [Baal Mekhshoves] (1873–1924) Russian Yiddish and Hebrew critic. He devoted himself to Yiddish journalism in Russia and Poland and later in Berlin. He was the founder of modern aesthetic criticism in Yiddish.

Emanation Philosophical theory explaining the origin of the universe as a flowing out from a primary source. It was taken over from Neoplatonists by Arab philosophers, and passed into medieval Jewish philosphy and kabbalah. In Kabbalistic literature it is an essential part of the concept of sephirot.

Emancipation In Jewish usage the word is applied to the removal, particularly in the Western world in the 18th–20th centuries, of restrictions imposed on Jews. From the 4th century the Holy Roman Empire imposed a system of discrimination against Jews, which was intensified in medieval Europe. Jewish emancipation stemmed from utopian political and social thought in the 18th century. In the 19th and 20th centuries Jews have been granted full civil equality in nearlly all countries where they live.

Embezzlement The fraudulent conversion to one's own use of money or property in one's care. It differs from theft in that the possession of the property by the embezzler is lawful. According to Jewish law if the embezzler denies his fraud on oath, and it is later proven, he must restore the property plus one fifth of its value. In addition he is required to offer the sacrifice of a guilt offering.

Emden, Jacob Israel [Yavetz] (1697–1776) Danish halakhic authority. He was born in Altona. He served as rabbi at Emden from 1728 to 1733, when he returned to Altona and set up a printing press. He regarded Sabbetaianism as a danger to Judaism and engaged in a prolongued dispute about this movement with Jonathan Eibeschütz. He wrote studies on halakhic subjects as well as polemical pamphlets.

Emet ('truth') In biblical and rabbinic Hebrew the word signifies honesty, loyalty, truthfulness and right action. God is often described as the God of truth in the Bible (Psalm 31:6), the *Talmud*, and later Jewish philosphical writings. Traditionally truth is understood as one of the 13 attributes of God. In medieval philosophical literature 'emet' is used as a logical term.

Emet ve-emunah ('True and trustworthy') Opening words of the blessing immediately following the Shema in the evening service.

Emet ve-yatziv ('True and valid') Opening words of the prayer immediately following the Shema in the morning service.

Encyclopedias General surveys of knowledge were written by Jewish scholars in the Middle Ages. In the 18th century Isaac ben Samuel Lampronti produced a talmudic encyclopedia, *Paḥad Yitzḥak*. In 1870–84 Jacob Hamburger published the *Real-Encyklopädie für Bibel und Talmud*. The first comprehensive Jewish encyclopedia was the American *Jewish Encyclopedia* published between 1901 and 1906. This was followed by encyclopedic works in Russian, Hebrew, and German. From 1939 to 1943 the *Universal Jewish Encyclopedia* appeared, which served as the basis for a Spanish work, *Enciclopedia Judaica Castellana*. The *Encyclopaedia Hebraica* appeared in 1949, and the *Encyclopaedia Judaica* began publication in 1972, and a second edition was published in 2001.

Endeks Polish anti-Semitic political party. Its members played a leading role in the elimination of Jews from Polish economic and intellectual life in the 1930s.

Enelow, Hyman Gerson (1877–1934) American rabbi and scholar. He was born in Lithuania and went to the US as a youth. He served as a rabbi in Kentucky and at Temple Emanuel in New York from 1912 to 1934. He was President of the Central Conference of American Rabbis from 1927 to 1929. His writings include *The Synagogue in Modern Life, The Faith of Israel,* and *A Jewish View of Jesus.* He also edited Israel Alnakawa's *Menorat ha-Maor,* as well as the *Midrash of 32 Hermeneutic Rules* ascribed to Eliezer ben Hyrcanus.

Engel, Yoel (1868–1927) Russian composer. He was music critic of the journal *Russkiye Vedomosti* for 20 years. In 1900 he began to adapt Jewish folk songs. In 1912 he took part with S. An-Ski in an expedition to southern Russia to collect folk songs among the Jewish population. He later contributed the music to An-Ski's play *The Dybbuk.* He settled in Tel Aviv in 1924, where he composed Hebrew songs.

En [ayin] ha-ra ('evil eye') A look or glance believed to have the power of inflicting harm or injury. Although a belief in the evil eye is not found in the Bible, it occurs in rabbinic literature and Kabbalistic lore. Many practices developed for averting its power, including reading the Scriptures, wearing amulets and reciting incantations.

En k-Elohenu ('There is none like our God') Opening words of an ancient hymn, which is sung during the Sabbath additional service. In its original form it was an acrostic constituting the word 'Amen.'

Enoch (i) Son of Cain and father of Irad. The world's first city was named after him (Genesis 4:17ff).

Enoch (ii) Father of Methuselah (Genesis 5:18–24). According to Genesis he 'walked with God; then he was no more for God took him' (Genesis 5:23). This verse was traditionally interpreted to mean that he did not die naturally but was transported to heaven on account of his righteousness. Several apocalyptic books are centred on his decease. Early Christians utilised this interpretation to expound Jesus' immortality. In later Jewish legend he was identified with the angel Metatron.

Enoch (iii) Apocryphal work, translated in the 10th or 11th century from Greek into Slavonic. It describes Enoch's ascent, his journey through the seven heavens, his return to earth, his address to his son, and his second ascent.

Enoch (iv) Apocalyptic work of Ethiopic origin one of the most important of the apocalyptic works. Dating from the period of the Second Temple, it contains accounts of visions, messianic yearnings, and moral discourses.

En Soph ('Infinite') The name given to the divine infinite in Kabbalistic thought. Early Kabbalists conceived of the En Soph as the absolute perfection in which there is no distinction or plurality. It does not reveal itself and is beyond all thought. In Kabbalistic teaching creation is bound up with the manifestation of the hidden God as En Soph.

En Yaakov ('fountain of Jacob') Popular compilation of aggadic passages from the Babylonian and Palestinian Talmuds. It was compiled by Jacob ibn Ḥaviv, and first published in 1513–16.

Ephah Ancient Hebrew dry measure. It is equivalent to a tenth of a homer, and is itself ten times as large as an omer. The size of the ephah differed in biblical and mishnaic times.

Ephod Upper garment worn during sacred rites in Ancient Israel. In the Bible the word is usually used of the ornamented vestment which the high priest wore over the blue robe. To this he bound the breastplate with the Urim and Thummim. Although soothsaying and divination were prohibited, the ephod and the Urim and Thummim were to be used as a means of seeking God's counsel. By the beginning of the Second Temple period, consultation of the ephod no longer took place.

Ephraim (fl. 19th–16th cent. BCE) Israelite, younger son of Joseph. His name became that of one of the tribes of Israel and of the more northern of the two Israelite kingdoms. During the period of the Judges, the tribe of Ephraim claimed priority. When the northern tribes seceded after Solomon's death, the first king of the northern kingdom of Israel (Jeroboam I) belonged to this tribe. The prophets later referred to the House of Judah and the House of Ephraim.

Ephraim ben Isaac of Regensburg (1110–1175) German tosaphist and liturgical poet. As a youth he lived in France, where he was among the first pupils of Jacob ben Meir Tam. He wrote piyyutim which reflect the hardships suffered by the Jews of Germany in the Regensburg massacre of 1137 and during the Second Crusade (1146–7).

Ephraim ben Jacob of Bonn (1132–c.1175). German liturgical poet and commentator. When Joel ben Isaac ha-Levi left Bonn, Ephraim ben Jacob succeeded him as av bet din. He also taught in Mainz and Speyer. He wrote the *Book of Remembrance* and dirges on the sufferings of Jews during the Second Crusade. He also composed liturgical poems for the festivals, responsa, tosaphot, and commentaries on benedictions and various customs.

Ephraim ben Shemariah (c.980–1060) Egyptian rabbi. He was leader of the Palestinian community in Fostat (Old Cairo). Although he was engaged in commerce, he became the community's rabbi in about 1020. He corresponded with the gaon Solomon ben Judah for many years.

Ephraim Veitel Heine (1703–1775) German court jeweller and community leader. In 1745 he was appointed court jeweller to the King of Prussia. Three years later he was elected head of the Berlin Jewish community. He built a school for the children employed in his factories and set up an educational foundation.

Ephron, Elia (1847–1915) Russian publisher. With P. Brockhaus he founded the Brockhaus-Ephron publishing house, which published a general Russian encyclopedia in 86 volumes. It also participated in the publication of the 16 volume Russian-Jewish encyclopedia, *Yevreyskaya Entziklopedia.*

Epitaph Inscription on a tomb. Commemorative inscriptions marking places of Jewish burial are known from the First Temple period. In the Second Temple period sarcophagi and ossuaries generally bore the names of the deceased. From the period of Roman and Byzan-tine domination in Palestine many epitaphs have been preserved, usually bearing the name of the dead in Hebrew. In the 16th century elaborate rhymed epitaphs were frequently used. By the next century Spanish and Portuguese communities in Venice, Amsterdam, London and New York had introduced the use of Spanish in epitaphs, and eventually the use of the vernacular became a common practice.

Epstein, Isidore (1894–1962) English rabbi and scholar. He was born in Lithuania and emigrated first to France and then, in 1911, to England. He served as rabbi in Middlesbrough from 1921 to 1928. In 1928 he began teacing Semitics at Jews College, and he became principal there in 1948. His publications include: *Studies in the Communal Life of the Jews of Spain, as Reflected in the Responsa of Rabbi Solomon ben Adreth and Rabbi Simeon ben Zemah Duran; Faith of Judaism;* and *Judaism.* He also supervised the English translation of the Babylonian *Talmud.*

Epstein, Sir Jacob (1880–1959) British sculptor. He was born in New York and settled in England in 1905. His works include a number of sculptures on Jewish themes.

Epstein, Jacob Naḥum (1878–1952) Israeli talmudist. He was born in Brest-Litovsk. He became a lecturer at the Hochschule für die Wissenschaft des Judentums in Berlin in 1923, and in 1925 he was appointed Professor of Talmudic Philology at the Hebrew University. He published studies on the Mishnah and *Talmud* and edited the journal *Tarbitz* from 1930 to 1952.

Epstein, Louis M. (1887–1949) American Conservative rabbi. He was born in Lithuania and emigrated to the US in 1904. He was appointed rabbi of Kehilath Israel in Brookline, Massachusetts in 1925. He served as President of the Rabbinical Assembly and Chairman of its committee on Jewish law. His writings include *The Jewish Marriage Contract, Marriage Laws in the Bible and Talmud,* and *Sex Laws and Customs in Judaism.*

Epstein, Yitzḥak (1862–1943) Writer and teacher of Belorussian origin. He settled in Palestine in 1886. From 1908 to 1915 he directed the Alliance Israél-ite Universelle school in Salonica. After World War I, he returned to Palestine and engaged in educational activities. He was a pioneer in teaching Hebrew by the direct method. He wrote studies on the Hebrew language problems and Arab-Jewish relations, and a Hebrew textbook *Ivrit be-Ivrit.*

Epstein, Zalman (1860–1936) Russian Hebrew essayist and critic. He was born in Belorussia and moved to Odessa in 1876, where he lived for 30 years. Later he lived in St Petersburg, Warsaw and Moscow; he eventually settled in Palestine in 1925. He published studies on Zionism and the settlement of Palestine, as well as Hebrew and general literature. He also wrote a number of poetic sketches.

Erev ('evening') The word is used specifically to refer to the evening of the Sabbath and festivals.

Erhlanger, Joseph (1874–1965) American physiologist. He was a professor of physiology at Washington University in St Louis. He received the 1944 Nobel Prize for Medicine and Physiology.

Erikson, Erik Homberger (1902–1994) American psychoanalyst. He was born in Frankfurt am Main and emigrated to the US in 1933. He taught at Harvard, Yale, and the University of California. In 1960 he was appointed Professor of Human Development and Psychiatry at Harvard. His publications include *Childhood and Society,* in which he discusses anti-Semitism and the role of Jews in society.

Erter, Isaac (1791–1851) Galician Hebrew satirist. He was born in Kon-iuszek and lived in various cities before settling in Brody in 1831. In addition to his literary work, he was active in Haskalah circles. *The Watchman of the House of Israel* consists of five satires on Jewish society in Galicia and Poland in the first half of the 19th century.

Eruv (lit. 'mixing') Term applied to various symbolical acts which facilitate the accomplishment of otherwise for-bidden acts on the Sabbath and festi-vals. They include carrying burdens on the Sabbath (permitted through Eruv Ḥatzerot – amalgamating individual holdings), walking further than the per-mitted 2,000 cubits beyond the inhab-ited area of the town (through Eruv Teḥumim – amalgamating boundaries), and cooking for the Sabbath on a festi-val day falling on Friday (through Eruv Tavshilin – amalgamating meals).

Eruvin Second tractate in the Mishnah order of Moed. It deals with the laws of Eruv. The last chapter is a collection of laws concerning the Sabbath.

Esau Israelite, firstborn son of Isaac and Rebekah and twin brother of Jacob. After Jacob obtained Esau's birth-right and the firstborn's blessing, Esau became Jacob's enemy and Jacob fled to Haran. When he returned 20 years later, his brother greeted him affection-ately (Genesis 35ff). The Bible identi-fies him with Edom (Genesis 36:1). In the *Talmud* he was associated with wickedness and violence.

Eschatology Theology, biblical exe-gesis, or doctrine concerning the end of days. All eschatology supposes a fundamental alternation of the present world by divine intervention. Initially Jewish eschatology was an expression of faith in a glorious future for the nation after a period of suffering. Later it was introduced by the Hebrew prophets into their teaching. They added moral content and threatened catastrophe in the absence of repentance. Such expec-tations were subsequently transformed into apocalyptic beliefs, which regarded the end as a sign of the coming of the

Messiah, who would bring about the ingathering of exiles, the Kingdom of God, and the Day of Judgement, when the righteous will receive eternal reward and the wicked will be punished.

Esdras The name of two apocryphal books ascribed to Ezra; they are known as III Esdras and IV Esdras (the books of Ezra and Nehemiah are regarded as I Esdras and II Esdras). III Esdras describes the history of Israel from the time of Josiah to the reading of the law by Ezra. IV Esdras (also known as the Apocalypse of Ezra) discusses the problem of human suffering, the fate of Israel, and the advent of the Messiah.

Eshet ḥayil ('a woman of valour') The phrase occurs in Proverbs 31:10. This verse and succeeding verses are recited in the Jewish home on Friday evenings before the Kiddush by the head of the house.

Eshkol, Levi (1895–1969) Israeli politician. He was born in Oratov, in Ukraine, and settled in Palestine in 1914. After World War I he became Director-General of the Ministry of Defence. He represented Mapai in the Knesset from 1949. In 1951 he joined David Ben-Gurion's government as Minister of Agriculture and Development and the following year he became minister of finance. In 1963 he succeeded Ben-Gurion as prime minister, remaining in office until his death.

Esnoga Term for 'synagogue' among the Sephardim.

Espinoza, Enrique (1898–1987) Argentine writer, editor and journalist. He was born in Kishinev and was taken to Argentina as a child. He edited monthly literary reviews in the 1920s. In 1928 he helped to found the Argentine Writer's Association. From 1935 he lived in Chile.

Essenes Monastic Jewish sect in Palestine at the close of the Second Temple period. Their main group was located on the north-western shore of the Dead Sea. Their religious outlook was closer to that of the Pharisees than the Sadducees, but they had their own specific beliefs and observances. They withdrew from everyday life to their own communities, where emphasis was placed on meticulous ritual purity. The Dead Sea Scrolls illuminate their beliefs and practices.

Esther (i) [Hadassah] Israelite woman, wife of Ahasuerus, King of Persia, and niece of Mordecai. Through her intervention, the plan of Haman (the prime minister) to annihilate the Jewish community was thwarted.

Esther (ii) Biblical book relating the story of the deliverance of the Jews from Persia. It is part of the Hagiographa and was composed around 350 BCE. The scroll ('megillah') of Esther is read in its entirety on the festival of Purim.

Esther (iii) Apocryphal book containing additions to the biblical Book of Esther. It consists of six passages found in the Septuagint but not in the Hebrew text.

Esther (iv) [Lifshitz, Malkah] (1880–1943) Russian writer and communist leader. She was born in Minsk. She edited Bundist periodicals after the revolution of 1905. She was one of the main promoters in the Bund of Jewish education in Yiddish. After the Russian Revolution in February 1917 she became a member of the central committee of the Bund. From 1921 to 1930 she was a leader of the Yevsektzia. She published a Yiddish edition of Lenin's writings, and edited the Moscow Yiddish daily *Emes*.

Esther, Fast of Fast on 13 Adar, the day before Purim. If the fast falls on a Sabbath, it is observed the preceding Thursday.

Esther Rabbah Midrash on the Book of Esther. Initially it was divided into six sections. Later editions have ten sections, the last being subdivided into five smaller ones. The work consists of two different midrashim: Esther Rabbah I (sections 1–6) and Esther Rabbah II (sections 7–10).

Estimate   In Jewish usage a term found in connection with a special type of vow regarding a money-offering in the Temple. One could vow to give a sum equivalent either to one's own or another's 'value'. A vow involving 'value' is called 'arakhin'. Such value is estimated on a scale depending on the age of the person (Leviticus 25).

Ethical will   Verbal or written testament expressing the ethical instructions of a deceased person to his family. Such wills are described in the Bible, Apocrypha, and *Talmud*. During and after the Middle Ages, they became a common feature of Jewish life.

Ethics   A code of moral behaviour; also the philosophical study of the values governing human conduct. It is a fundamental aspect of biblical teaching that Jews have the free choice to live moral lives in accordance with God's law. The first systematic presentation of Jewish ethics was made by Philo. Ethics also pervade rabbinic literature, and theoretical and practical ethics were developed by medieval Jewish philosophers. Kabbalistic thought also influenced the evolution of Jewish ethics. In the 19th century the Musar movement particularly encouraged moral reflection.

Ethnarch   The ruler of a people. The title 'ethnarch' was given to Hyrcanus II and his sons by Julius Caesar in 47 BCE. It was also used to designate the head of the Jewish community at Alexandria.

Ethronges [Athrongaios] (fl. 1st cent. BCE–1st cent. CE)   Palestinian rebel and pretender to the Judaean throne. After the death of Herod the Great in 4 BCE he claimed the Judean throne. Supported by his four brothers, he began a campaign of guerilla warfare against Romans and royalists. He was defeated after an attack near Emmaus.

Etrog [citron]   Citrus fruit eaten on Sukkot. It was a popular Jewish symbol used on coins and graves, and in the decoration of synagogues during the Second Temple period. Silver boxes for the etrog were a common object of Jewish ritual art.

Ettinger, Akiva Yaakov (1872–1945)   Zionist leader of Belorussian origin. He went to London as an adviser on settlement matters during the negotiations over the Balfour Declaration. He settled in Palestine in 1918 and served as Director of the agricultural settlement department of the Jewish National Fund until 1924. From 1924 to 1932 he played a prominent role in the purchase of land and the drafting and implementation of Jewish settlement plans. He wrote many articles on agriculture and settlement in Palestine.

Ettinger, Solomon (1803–1856)   Polish Yiddish poet and dramatist. He was born in Warsaw and settled in Zhdanov near Zamość. He wrote parables, satirical ballads, epigrams, poems and dramas. His *Serkele* portrays an ambitious woman who pursues power and wealth.

Ettlinger, Jacob (1798–1871)   German rabbi and champion of neo-Orthodoxy. In 1826 he was appointed district rabbi for the districts of Ladenburg and Ingolstadt and settled in Mannheim, where he founded a yeshivah. He was appointed Chief Rabbi of Altona in 1836. He wrote numerous studies of Jewish law.

Etz ḥayyim ('tree of life')   Expression found in Proverbs 3:18. It is applied to the wooden staves on which the Torah scroll is rolled.

Euchel, Isaac (1756–1804)   German Hebrew author and Bible commentator of Danish origin. He became a leader of the Haskalah in Germany. He was born in Copenhagen and in 1787 settled in Berlin, where he managed the printing press of the Jüdische Freischule. His writings include a comedy satirising Orthodoxy, a study of Moses Mendelssohn, a translation of and commentary on the Book of Proverbs, and a German translation of the prayer book.

Eulogy, funeral Funeral or memorial oration. From ancient times it was a custom to praise and lament the dead. Talmudic literature also contains funeral orations. In later times a eulogy ('hesped') was recited at the funeral. Among the Sephardim the eulogy consists of a talmudic discourse after the expiration of the 30-day mourning period ('sheloshim').

Euphemism An inoffensive word substituted for one which is indelicate, blasphemous, or taboo. Euphemisms are found in the Bible and in rabbinic literature. Typical examples include 'house of the living' to mean a cemetery and the use of the verb 'to know' to indicate sexual commerce.

Eve First woman. She was created out of Adam's rib, and lived with him in the Garden of Eden. Seduced by the snake into eating the forbidden fruit of the tree of knowledge of good and evil, she persuaded Adam to eat as well. This act of disobedience was punished by their expulsion from Eden. Eve was condemned to suffer in childbirth and to be subservient to her husband. She was the mother of Cain, Abel and Seth (Genesis 2–4).

Evel Rabbati [Semahot] Minor tractate included in the Babylonian *Talmud*. It deals with death and mourning. It was written in Palestine during the tannaitic period with later accretions from the amoraic and gaonic eras.

Evel Zutrati [Semahot of Rabbi Hiyya] Minor tractate included in

the Babylonian *Talmud*. It contains discourses on mourning customs.

Even-Shoshan, Avraham (1906–1984) Hebrew educator of Russian origin. He emigrated to Palestine in 1925. From 1954 to 1968 he was Director of the Bet ha-Kerem Teacher's Institute in Jerusalem. He published stories, poems and plays for children, translated children's books into Hebrew and compiled a Hebrew dictionary.

Ever min ha-hai ('a limb from the living') Prohibition based on Deuteronomy 12:23 against eating a limb taken from a living animal, beast or bird. It is one of the seven Noachian Laws.

Evidence Data on which to base proof or establish the truth. Biblical law calls for the testimony of at least two witnesses in criminal cases (Deuteronomy 19:15; 17:6). Rabbinic law limits suitable witnesses by disqualifying usurers, gamblers, individuals of improper character, non-Jews, slaves, women and minors. In civil cases documents are acceptable where witnesses are not available.

Evil According to the Bible, evil entered the world when Adam ate the forbidden fruit in the Garden of Eden. Human beings, whose behaviour is guided by both good and evil inclinations according to rabbinic sources, are granted free will to choose which they will follow. In the *Talmud* and in medieval Jewish philosophy the existence of evil posed numerous theological dilemmas. Medieval Jewish mysticism viewed evil as grounded in the manifestations of the divine essence in the form of ten sephirot. Modern Jewish theologians have grappled with the religious perplexities caused by the death of six million Jews at the hands of the Nazis.

Evolution Theory formulated by Charles Darwin that plant and animal species evolve through successive generations, and that lower forms of life thereby become the ancestors of higher forms. Initially traditional Judaism rejected this view, but some Orthodox writers have attempted to reconcile the biblical account of creation with the theory of evolution by interpreting the six days of creation figuratively.

Ewald, Georg Heinrich August (1803–1875)   German theologian and biblical scholar. He was Professor at Göttingen and Tübingen. He wrote about Hebrew and Arabic grammar, biblical texts, and the history of the Jews.

Exchequer of the Jews   Medieval English government department for Jewish affairs. The Exchequer controlled the system of chests ('archae') in which all moneylending transactions were registered. In addition most legal cases in which Jews were concerned were heard by the Exchequer. It also handled revenues from the Jewish community.

Exilarch (Aramaic 'resh galuta')   Head of the Jewish community in Babylonia during the 1st–13th centuries. The office was hereditary and its holder was traditionally a member of the House of David. He was recognised by the royal court, served as chief tax collector among the Jews, appointed judges, and exercised criminal jurisdiction in the Jewish community. There were close ties as well as frequent conflicts between the exilarchs and the geonim.

Exile, Babylonian   Exile of the Jews in Babylonia in the 6th century BCE. The period of exile began with the destruction around 585 BCE of the Kingdom of Judah by Nebuchadnezzar and ended with the return of the Jews from captivity in c.538 BCE. Encouraged by the prophecies of Jeremiah and Ezekiel, the Jewish exiles maintained their Jewish identity, worshipped in the synagogue and generally prospered under foreign rule.

Exiles, ingathering of the   During the Babylonian Exile, Ezekiel prophesied the return of the exiles to their native land. He addressed himself first to Judean exiles and then extended his prophecy to include the exiles of the northern kingdom. The belief that the exiles would be restored became a central aspect of rabbinic belief and was an important theme of the liturgy. In modern times the concept of the ingathering of the exiles ('kibbutz galuyyot') is often used to designate the immigration of Jews in the diaspora to the State of Israel.

Exodus (i)   The flight of the Israelites from Egypt. It is a central event in the history of the Jewish people. With the accession of a new king who did not know Joseph (Exodus 1:8), the Jews in Egypt were reduced to slavery. Under the leadership of Moses, they were delivered from their bondage and escaped their pursuers on dry land when the Red Sea miraculously parted. The Exodus was the prelude to the years in the wilderness during which the Jews sought the Promised Land.

Exodus (ii) (Hebrew 'Shemot')   Biblical book, second book of the Pentateuch. It consists of 40 chapters. Chapters 1–17 describe the oppression of the Israelites by the Egyptians, the rise of Moses, the ten plagues, and the Exodus from Egypt. Chapters 18–24 give details of the divine revelation and legislation, and the covenant between God and Israel. The episode of the Golden Calf and subsequent events are contained in Chapters 25–40.

Exodus 1947   Name of the ship that attempted to carry more than 4,000 Jewish refugees to Palestine under the auspices of the Haganah in 1947. It was seized by the British in the Mediterranean, and the refugees were forcibly returned to Hamburg.

Exodus Rabbah (Hebrew 'Shemot Rabbah')   Midrash on the Book of Exodus. It consists of two different midrashim: Exodus Rabbah I (sections 1–14), and Exodus Rabbah II (sections 15–32).

Exorcism   The driving out of an evil spirit. The practice is mentioned in the Apocrypha, New Testament and the *Talmud*. Magical formulae were used to bring about the expulsion of evil spirits, and amulets were employed to ward off their influence. Exorcism was commonly performed by Kabbalists and Ḥasidim, who were anxious to rid individuals of the souls of the dead who possessed them.

Exploration   In the early biblical period the Jewish world comprehended Egypt, Chaldea, and Babylon. This was extended by Solomon's traditional expeditions. In the diaspora Jews came into contact with Greece, western Asia and the lands of the Roman Empire. Under the rule of Byzantium and Islam Jews traded with India and China. Later they pioneered routes from north Africa to the Niger. The major contribution of Jews to voyages of exploration at the close of the Middle Ages was the production of maps and nautical instruments. Some sources suggest that Christopher Columbus was of Jewish descent.

Explusions   Throughout their history in the diaspora the Jewish people have been subjected to expulsion from the places in which they settled, as part of a general pattern of persecution. As early as 139 BCE Jews were driven out of Rome. In the Middle Ages Jews who refused to convert to Christianity were expelled from England (1290), France (1306, 1322, 1394), and Germany (1348–50). Professing Jews were excluded from Andalusia in 1484, and expelled from Spain and Spanish dominions in 1492. This was followed by the expulsion from Portugal (1497), Navarre (1498), Provence (1512) and Naples (1541). In 1569 they were expelled from the smaller centres of the papal dominions in Italy and France. In the 18th century Jews were expelled from Little Russia (1727, 1739, 1742), and in the 19th

century from areas outside the Pale of Settlement.

Ezekiel (i) (fl. 6th cent. BCE)   Israelite prophet. He prophesied among the Babylonian exiles from 592 to 570 BCE. After the destruction of Jerusalem, he consoled and encouraged those in captivity.

Ezekiel (ii)   Biblical book, the third of the books of the Latter Prophets. The first chapter contains a description of the divine chariot ('merkavah'), which served as the basis of later mystical speculation. Chapters 1–24 of the book contain prophecies of destruction before the fall of Jerusalem; chapters 25–32 prophesy catastrophes that will befall the gentiles; chapters 33–39 contain words of consolation for Israel; and chapters 40–48 record visions of the restored Temple and kingdom.

Ezekiel, Jacob (1812–1899)   American communal leader. He was born in Philadelphia and moved to Baltimore and then to Richmond, Virginia, where he was active in Jewish affairs. He fought against legislation which discriminated against Jews. Later he moved to Cincinnati, where he served as secretary to the board of governors of the Hebrew Union College.

Ezekiel, Moses Jacob (1844–1917)   American sculptor. He served in the Civil War, only later becoming a sculptor. His *Religious Liberty* is a large marble group commissioned by the B'nai B'rith for the Centennial Exposition of 1876.

Ezra (i) (fl. 5th cent. BCE)   Israelite prophet. He served as a scribe in the Persian Government. Later he received permission from Artaxerxes I to lead the Jewish exiles back to Jerusalem. Together with Nehemiah, he persuaded the people to return to the Torah, observe the Sabbath and sabbatical year, pay Temple dues, and refrain from intermarriage. The story of Ezra is contained in the books of Ezra and Nehemiah.

Ezra (ii) Biblical book, part of the Hagiographa. It relates the story of the Jews' return from exile in Babylon, from the return of Zerubbabel to Judah in the 6th century BCE, until after the return of Ezra.

Ezrat Nashim ('women's court') Court in the Temple beyond which women were not permitted to pass. Later the term was applied to the section of the synagogue where the women sit during the service.

F

A Jewish man, sitting in a delicatessen, notices a Jewish funeral. Two hearses go by with a man behind them walking a dog on a leash. A line of hundreds of men is walking behind him. Curious, the man walks toward the person walking the dog. When he reaches him, he tells him he has never seen a Jewish funeral with two hearses. The man with the dog tells him that one hearse is for his wife, who yelled at him and was attacked and killed by the dog he is walking. The second hearse, he explains, is for his mother-in-law, who was attempting to help his wife, and was also attacked and killed by the dog. The man from the deli offers his condolences, and the two share a moment of male connectedness until the man from the deli asks if he can borrow the dog. The mourner replies: 'Get in line.'

* * * * *

This joke is a satire of nagging wives and mothers-in-law. It suggests that there are many married Jewish men who would like to rid themselves of them. The wife yells at her husband. She is then joined by her mother. A cruel fate awaits them. The joke is a humorous warning.

Fable (Hebrew 'mashal') Short moral tale in which the characters are usually animals. Fables are frequently found in the midrash and the *Talmud*. In the Middle Ages popular collections of fables were produced by Jewish authors, who based their writing on Arab sources.

Fackenheim, Emil (1916–2013) Canadian theologian. He was born in Halle, Germany. He emigrated to Canada in 1940, where he became Professor of Philosophy at the University of Toronto. His major work concerns the religious response to the Holocaust. His writings include *God's Presence in History, The Jewish Return into History* and *To Mend the World.*

Fair A gathering held regularly for the sale of goods. The gathering of large numbers of Jews at the annual fair held in Lublin and at the early summer fair at Jaroslaw was responsible for the development of the Council of the Four Lands in the 16th century. In Western Europe fairs were frequently held in Jewish quarters on Purim.

Faitlovitch, Jacques (1881–1955) Polish researcher and activist on behalf of the Falashas. He went to Ethiopia in 1904 and spent 18 months among the Falashas. He published *Notes of a Voyage among the Falashas* and organised committees in Italy and Germany to raise money for their education. Later he continued with his activities on the Falashas' behalf in the US and Israel, and published books on their literature.

Falaquera, Shemtov ben Joseph [Ibn Falaquera] (c. 1225–1295) Philosophical author. Born in Spain, he lived there and in the border provinces of

Spain and France. His writings include a defence of Maimonides' *Guide for the Perplexed*, a compilation of ethical aphorisms, an introduction to the study of the sciences, an encyclopedia of the sciences, and translations of sections of Solomon ibn Gabirol's *Fountain of Life*.

Falashas Black ethnic group of Ethiopia, which claims to be of Jewish origin. They follow a form of the Jewish religion based on the Bible, the Apocrypha and other post-biblical Scripture. They claim to have originated from the notables of Jerusalem who accompanied Menelik, the son of King Solomon and the Queen of Sheba, when he returned to his country. In the mid-1980s there was a secret airlift of about 20,000 Falashas to Israel, and a further large airlift took place in 1991.

Falk, Ḥayyim Samuel Jacob (c. 1708–1782) English mystic. He was born in Podolia and settled in England in about 1742. He was reputed to be a miracleworker and became known as the Baal Shem of London.

Falk, Jacob Joshua ben Tzevi Hirsch (1680–1756) Polish rabbi and halakhic authority. He was born in Kraków and lived and worked in Lwów before serving as rabbi in the communities of Tarnów, Kurów and Lesko. In 1717 he became rabbi of Lwów; from 1730 to 1734 he was rabbi of Berlin, and he later became rabbi of Metz and Frankfurt am Main. His *Penei Yehoshua* is an outstanding work of novellae on the *Talmud*.

Falk, Joshua ben Alexander ha-Cohen [Walk, Joshua] (1555–1614) Polish educationalist and communal leader. He was born in Lublin. He devoted his life to teaching and took an active part in the Council of the Four Lands. His *Bet Yisrael* is a commentary on Jacob ben Asher's *Turim*. In *Sepher Meirat Enayim,* he amended and interpreted part of the text of the Shulḥan Arukh. He also wrote responsa as well as commentaries on the Pentateuch and *Talmud*.

Fall of man Adam's state of disobedience and the state of innate sinfulness into which all mankind is born as a consequence of his sin. According to rabbinic teaching, death, labour and pain were brought into the world when Adam ate the forbidden fruit in the Garden of Eden, and his sin doomed all human beings to death. The acceptance of the Torah on Mount Sinai restored man's original state, but this was again lost by the worship of the Golden Calf. Christian theology maintains that human beings suffer from original sin because of Adam's disobedience.

False witness The biblical injunction against bearing false witness (Exodus 20:13) embraces all types of slander, defamation and misrepresentation. In Jewish law evidence must be presented by at least two witnesses if a case is to be proved. If a second pair of witnesses states in court that the first pair was with them at the time of the criminal act and not at the scene of the crime, the testimony of the second pair of witnesses incriminates that of the first pair. This is referred to as 'hazammah'.

Family In biblical times Jewish families were based on polygamy and included all male descendants and dependants. Talmudic literature reflects a monogamous society and the idealisation of family life. It was the duty of the father to educate his sons and prepare them for a useful trade. Monogamy became firmly established in northern Europe as a result of the takkanah of Gershom in the 11th century. Family solidarity and loyalty are regarded as central virtues and strengths of the Jewish tradition.

Fano, Jacob (fl. 16th cent.) Italian scholar and poet. He lived in Cento, Ferrara and Bologna. His elegy on the Marrano martyrs of Ancona of 1555 provoked church authorities. He was punished and his book was burned.

Fano, Joseph (c.1550–1630) Italian communal leader. He was on familiar terms with the dukes of Mantua and Ferrara and occasionally acted as their intermediary. Some time before 1628 he was raised to the rank of Marquis of Villimpenta. He was the first Jew to be ennobled in Europe.

Fano, Menaḥem Azariah (1548–1620) Italian rabbi and Kabbalist. He was active in Ferrara, Venice, Reggio Emilia, and Mantua. He published a collection of 130 responsa and also wrote works on the kabbalah, prayer and the transmigration of the soul.

Farabi, Abu Nasr Muhammad Al- (c.870–c.950) Babylonian Muslim philosopher. He spent most of his life in Baghdad and played a major role in the dissemination of ancient philosophy in the Islamic world. He influenced medieval Jewish philosophers, including Maimonides.

Farbstein, David Tzevi (1868–1953) Swiss lawyer and Zionist. He was born in Warsaw and settled in Zurich in 1894. He served as a member of the Swiss parliament after World War I until 1939. He was the first president (from 1920) of the Karen ha-Yesod in Switzerland. When the State of Israel was founded, he suggested that its legislation be based on the model of the Swiss Republic. He wrote studies of Judaism, Zionism and law.

Farbstein, Joshua Heschel (1870–1948) Polish communal leader. He was born in Warsaw. He was president of the Zionist Organisation in Poland from 1915 to 1918. A founder of Mizraḥi in Poland he was its president from 1918 to 1931. He was also President of the Keren ha-Yesod in Poland and of the Warsaw Jewish community from 1926 to 1931. He moved to Jerusalem, where he led the Community Council from 1938 to 1945.

Farḥi [Parḥi], Estori [Estori ha-Parḥi] (1280–?1355) Palestinian topographer. Born in Provence, he lived in various cities in Spain, and later settled in Palestine. His *Kaphtor va-Pheraḥ* presents the results of his travels throughout Palestine: it establishes the names of Palestinian towns and villages, describes the geography and natural history of the country and identifies ancient sites.

Farḥi, Ḥayyim Mu'Allim (c.1760–1820) Palestinian statesman. He entered the service of Aḥmad al-Jazzar Pasha in Damascus and was responsible for Palestine's treasury affairs. He participated in the city of Acre's stand against Napoleon in 1799. Later he was imprisoned, but was restored under Al-Jazzar's successor, Suleiman Pasha (ruled 1805–18). He acted as the protector of the Jews of Palestine.

Farrisol, Abraham (c.1451–c.1525) Italian biblical scholar, geographer, and polemicist. He was born in Avignon and lived in Ferrara and Mantua, working as a cantor and copyist. He represented Judaism before the Duke of Ferrara in a religious dispute with two Dominican monks. He wrote a commentary on the Torah, Ecclesiastes and Job, a defence of Judaism, and the first modern Hebrew work on geography.

Fast Abstention from eating all or certain foods. Fasting may be undertaken individually as a sign of mourning or in expiation of sin; the community as a whole observes a number of traditional fast days: 3 Tishri, the Fast of Gedaliah commemorating the assassination of Gedaliah; 10 Tishri, the Day of Atonement; 10 Tevet, commemorating the siege of Jerusalem begun by Nebuchadnezzar; 13 Adar, the Fast of Esther; 14 Nissan, the Fast of the Firstborn, commemorating the last of the ten plagues of Egypt; 17 Tammuz, commemorating the breaching of the walls of Jerusalem by Nebuchadnezzar and by Titus; and 9 Av, commemorating the destruction of the First and Second Temples. The major fast days, the Day of Atonement and the Ninth of Av, last from sunset to sunset and involve abstention from eating, drinking, sexual intercourse, and the wearing of footgear. Other fasts last from sunrise to sunset and involve abstinence only from food and drink.

Fast, Howard (1914–2003) American author. He was born in New York. He wrote novels about American history, injustice and oppression. He also published books on Jewish themes.

Father According to the Jewish faith, the father has legal obligations toward his children. Conversely children are obligated to honour and respect their father (and mother). A father's legal responsibility generally ends when his children attain their majority.

Fear of God It is regarded as the basis of religious awareness. Thus Proverbs states that fear of God is the beginning of knowledge (Proverbs 1:7), and of wisdom (Proverbs 10:10).

Fefer, Itzik (1900–1952) Ukrainian Yiddish poet. He was born in Shpola. He made his debut as a Yiddish poet in 1920 and became prominent in Soviet Yiddish literature. The majority of his poems are propaganda for the Communist Party. He also wrote poetry about Birobidjan, the Jewish autonomous region in eastern Siberia. He was arrested in 1948 in the Stalinist anti-Jewish purges.

Feierberg, Mordecai Ze'ev (1874–1899) Russian Hebrew author. He wrote essays and lyrical novels. In his novels he expressed the plight of Eastern-European youth at the end of the 19th century, who were disillusioned with the Haskalah movement but were unable to accept traditional Judaism.

Feiffer, Jules (b.1929) American playwright and cartoonist. He grew up in New York and contributed cartoons to the *Village Voice* in the 1950s. Much of his satire is based on Jewish sensibility. His characters are often victims at the mercy of a hostile world. He also wrote a number of plays dealing with Jewish themes.

Feigenbaum, Benjamin (1860–1932) American Yiddish writer and activist. He was born in Warsaw. He became a militant atheist and agitator for socialism. He settled in London in 1887, where he published pamphlets on socialism, then in 1891 he emigrated to the US. He attempted to win support for socialism and atheism among Jewish workers and in 1900 became General Secretary of the Workmen's Circle.

Feinberg, Avshalom (1889–1917) Palestinian writer and leader of the Nili. He was born in Gedera. He founded the Nili movement with Aaron Aaronsohn. He was shot and killed by Bedouin on a journey to Egypt. His writings depict the world of the first generation born in Jewish settlements in Palestine.

Feiwel, Berthold (1875–1937) German Zionist leader. He was born in Moravia. He was a close associate of Theodor Herzl and helped to organise the first Zionist Congress in 1897. In 1901 he became editor-in-chief of the central organ of the Zionist Organisation, *Die Welt*. He translated Hebrew and Yiddish works into German and was a founder of the Judischer Verlag in Berlin. In 1933 he settled in Palestine.

Feldman, Louis (1896–1975) South African Yiddish writer. He was born in Lithuania and went to South Africa in 1910, where he worked as a businessman. His publications include *Jews in South Africa, Oudtshoorn: the Jerusalem of Africa, Jews in Johannesburg*, and *Israel as I see it*.

Feminism In all areas of Jewish life feminism has brought marked changes in Jewish consciousness. Outside the Orthodox world, women have been ordained as rabbis, trained as cantors, and have taken a leading role in Jewish communal life. Within Orthodoxy a number of women wish to see changes in the status of women in the Jewish community.

Fence around the law (from Hebrew 'seyag': fence) Preventive rabbinic ordinance enacted to safeguard traditional practices. In the Mishnah one of the three precepts of the Men of the Great Synagogue is the prescription to make fences around the law. The practice consisted of producing stringent regulations to safeguard the original commandments.

Ferber, Edna (1887–1968) American novelist. Born in Kalamazoo, Michigan, she worked first as a journalist. Her works include *Show Boat, Giant, So Big, Dawn O'Hara, The Girls, Cimarron, Come and Get It* and *Saratoga Trunk*.

Ferenczi, Sandor [Fraenkel, Sandor] (1873–1933) Hungarian psychiatrist. He met Sigmund Freud in 1908, and went with him to the US the next year. In 1913 he joined the Hungarian Psychoanalytic Society. He was the first to stress the importance of loving, physical contact with the mother.

Ferrer, Vicente (c.1350–1419) Spanish Dominican monk. He advocated conversion to Christianity and his preaching provoked mass demonstrations and anti-Jewish outbursts at the beginning of the 15th century. In 1412 he helped to formulate the laws of Valladolid, which were directed against the Jews. He wrote over 6,000 sermons.

Festival prayers An extra prayer (Musaph) is added to the festivals to the regular morning prayer. It corresponds to and describes the additional sacrifice offered on these days in the Temple. Appropriate verses are read from the Torah and the Prophets. Special commandments such as blowing the shophar have given rise to special festival prayers, and it has become customary to recite piyyutim in honour of the festival. The festival prayer book is referred to as the Maḥzor.

Feuchtwanger, Lion (1884–1958) German historical novelist. He was born in Munich. He wrote plays as a young man and in 1926 his novel *Jud Süss* was published. Eventually he settled in the US. His novel *The Oppermanns* deals with a German Jewish family during the rise of Nazism. He also wrote a historical novel on the life of Josephus.

Feuerberg, Mordecai Ze'ev (1874–1899) Ukrainian Hebrew writer. He was born in Novograd Volynskiy. His literary career began in 1896, when he went to Warsaw. He broke with his Hasidic background and wrote short stories about the conflict between traditional Judaism and modern secular culture.

Feynman, Richard (1918–88) American physicist. Born in New York City, he worked on the atom bomb project. In 1965 he shared the Nobel Prize for Physics. From 1950 he was professor at the California Institute of Technology.

Fichman, Yaakov (1881–1958) Palestinian Hebrew poet, critic and literary editor. He was born in Bessarabia and lived in various cities in Russia and Western Europe before settling in Palestine in 1912. He edited literary periodicals, anthologies and textbooks, and wrote poetry.

Fiedler, Leslie A. (1917–2003) American writer and critic. He was born in Newark, New Jersey. He taught at the University of Montana and the State University of New York at Buffalo. Jewish themes have played an increasing role in his later work. His writings include *Image of the Jew in American Fiction* and *The Jew in the American Novel*.

Fifteenth of Av (Hebrew 'Tu b'Av) Day of rejoicing marking the beginning of the vintage. It was observed during the period of the Second Temple. Girls dressed in white danced and sang in the vineyards and wood offerings were brought to the Temple.

Fifteenth of Shevat (Hebrew 'Tu bi-Shevat') The date on which the new year begins for the purposes of tithing fruit. It is celebated as Hamishah Asah bi-Shevat ('New year for trees'). A different system of tithing is applied to fruit harvested before and after this date. It is elebrated by eating special fruits particularly oranges and lemons, which have a special place in Israel's horticulture. In modern Israel, the day is celebrated by tree-planting.

Filipowski, Herschell Philips (1816–1872) British Hebraist, editor and actuary. He was born in Lithuania and emigrated to London in 1839, where he taught at a Jewish school. He was the editor of the Hebrew annual *Ha-Asif* from 1847 to 1849. In 1851 he founded a Jewish antiquarian society for the purpose of publishing medieval Hebrew texts on which he wrote various studies. In 1862 he printed a pocket edition of the prayer book. His *Biblical Prophecies* discusses the Jewish view of prophecy and messianism.

Finding of property The Bible stipulates that lost property must be returned to its owner (Exodus 23:4; Deuteronomy 22:3). The person who finds lost property must make a public announcement. In Ancient Israel announcements were made over a period covering the festival celebrations. Later they were made in the synagogue. Proper identification should be made by the owner of lost property. No reward should be claimed for its return, but the finder is entitled to reimbursement for expenses in caring for it. If the owner does not claim the property the finder is regarded as the owner. The subject is discussed in the talmudic tractate Bava Metzia.

Fines The Bible imposes a fine payable to the injured party as the punishment for wrongdoing in four cases: (1) 50 shekels for ravishing a virgin; (2) 50 shekels for seducing a virgin; (3) 100 shekels for falsely accusing one's wife of prenuptial unchastity; (4) 30 shekels for the killing of a slave by an ox. Later the rabbinical courts imposed fines payable to the community fund for a number of public

offences. In addition, Jewish communities stipulated fines as punishment for refusing communal office or synagogue honours, and for absence from religious services or communal meetings.

Finkelstein, Louis (1895–1991) American conservative rabbi, scholar and educator. He was born in Cincinnati. He began teaching at the Jewish Theological Seminary in 1920 and later became provost, president and chancellor there. He served as President of the Rabbinical Assembly from 1928 to 1930. He wrote and edited books and articles on general problems in religion, sociology, culture and ethics. His publications include *Pharisees, Jews: their History, Culture, and Religion*, and *Jewish Self-Government in the Middle Ages*.

Finta (Spanish: 'fine') The assessment of dues payable to the Sephardi congregation by its members.

Finzi, Angelo Mordecai (d.1476) Italian banker and scientist. He lived in Bologna and Mantua. He wrote studies on mathematics and astronomy, translated various works on mathematics, geometry, and astronomy into Hebrew, explained recently invented astronomical instruments, and published treatises on grammar and mnemonics.

Finzi, Isaac Raphael (1728–1812) Italian preacher. He served as a rabbi in Padua and was widely acclaimed as a preacher. He was a member of the French Sanhedrin in 1806 and served as its vice-president.

Finzi, Solomon (fl. 16th century) Italian rabbinical scholar. He served as a rabbi in Forli and Bologna. His methodological work *Mafteah ha-Gemara* was reprinted in 1697 in Helmstedt with a Latin translation and notes, and again reprinted in the 18th century in *Clavis Talmudica maxima*.

Firkovich, Abraham (1786–1874) Palestinian Karaite leader of Polish birth. He engaged in bitter disputes with rabbinic authorities. In 1830 he accompanied Simḥah Bobowich to Palestine, where he collected numerous manuscripts. When in 1839, the governor general of the Crimea addressed a series of questions dealing with Karaite origins to Bobowich, he recommended Firkovich, who initiated archeological expeditions to the Crimea and the Caucasus to uncover ancient tombstones and manuscripts. Firkovich's travels and his discoveries are described in his *Avnei Zikkaron.*

Firstborn   In biblical times special privileges and a double-share of the father's inheritance belonged to the firstborn (Deuteronomy 21:17).

Firstborn, Fast of the   Fast observed by firstborn sons on the day before Passover. It stems from the desire to express gratitude for the saving of the firstborn Israelites during the tenth plague of Egypt (Exodus 13:1ff). Eventually it became a custom to finish the study of a *Talmud* tractate on the morning before Passover, when a festive banquet was arranged in the synagogue. Since firstborn sons were allowed to partake of this meal, they were not obliged to fast.

Firstborn, redemption of the (Hebrew 'Pidyon ha-Ben')   The Bible stipulates that every firstborn son belongs to God (Exodus 13:11–16). Redemption is achieved by the payment to the priests of 5 shekels, or its equivalent in goods, on the 31st day after the birth of a son. Redemption does not apply to the firstborn of priests or Levites. The ceremony of the redemption of the firstborn takes place on the 31st day after birth; a sum is paid to a cohen and this act is accompanied by the recital of special prayers.

First fruits   The Bible decrees that the first choice fruits of the harvest should be brought to the Temple and the declaration in Deuteronomy 26:5–10 be recited. The third chapter of the Mishnah tractate Bikkurim deals with this custom.

Fischer, Bobby (1943–2008)   American chess master. He won the US chess championship seven times, and in 1972 defeated the Russian Boris Spassky, becoming the world chess champion.

Fiscus judaicus   Fund of the Roman Empire into which was paid the money from the tax levied on the Jews by Vespasian after the destruction of the Second Temple. During the reign of Domitian its exaction was especially harsh. The tax continued to be collected until the 4th century.

Fish   The Bible decrees that man is to exercise dominion over the fish as well as over other living things (Genesis 1:28). Fish are divided into clean and unclean creatures: 'These you may eat, of all that are in the waters that has fins and scales … you may eat. But anything in the seas or the rivers that has not fins and scales … is an abomination to you' (Leviticus 11:9–11).

Fishman, Jacob (1878–1946)   American Yiddish editor and Zionist leader of Polish origin. After he emigrated to the US he was active in Zionist societies that pre-dated those founded under the influence of Theodor Herzl. He was a founder of the Zionist Organisation of America. He co-edited the New York Yiddish dailies *Tageblat* (1893–1914) and *Varhayt* (1914–16). Later he served as managing editor of the *Jewish Morning Journal.*

Five Scrolls   Name given to five books of the Hagiographa, which are read on particular festivals: the Song of Songs on Passover; Ruth on Shavuot; Lamentations on the Ninth of Av; Ecclesiastes on Sukkot; and Esther on Purim.

Flag   According to the Bible each of the 12 tribes of Israel had its own banner (Numbers 2). The midrash describes them as having the colours of the 12 stones in the high priest's breastplate.

The Maccabees are said to have carried a banner on which were inscribed the intial letters of the words 'Who is like you among the gods, O Lord?' The flag adopted by the Zionist movement (and later by the State of Israel) consisted of a Shield of David with two broad blue horizontal stripes on a white background.

Flayshig (Yiddish: 'made of meat') Meats, poultry or foods prepared with animal fats. They may not be eaten with dairy foods.

Fleckeles, Eleazar ben David (1754–1826) Bohemian rabbi and author. He was born in Prague and served as a rabbi there. He was also head of a large yeshivah and president of a three-man rabbinate council. When the Frankists made their appearance in the city in 1800, he led the opposition to them. He published a collection of sermons on halakhic and aggadic themes, as well as a volume of responsa.

Fleg, Edmond (1874–1963) French poet, playwright and essayist. He lived in Paris, where he worked as a theatre critic and playwright. Jewish themes are found throughout his work. His writings include *Écoute Israel, Pourquoi je suis Juif, Ma Palestine, L'anthologie juive,* and *Jésus, raconté par le Juif Errant.*

Fleisher, Ezra (1928–2006) Israeli poet and scholar. He was born in Translylvania and emigrated to Israel in 1960. He became a lecturer on medieval Hebrew literature at Bar Ilan University, and then at the Hebrew University. His writings include *Merhsalim* and *Be-Ḥehalek Laylah.*

Flesh In the Bible the term refers variously to the body as a whole; humanity; the impressionable side of human nature; and an item of food. Initially flesh was forbidden as food (Genesis 1:29–30), but it was later permitted as long as it was not torn from a living creature. According to Jewish law only certain kinds of animals may be eaten,

and they must be slaughtered and prepared in specific ways. Rabbinic teaching does not encourage mortification of the flesh or the view that flesh is inherently sinful.

Flogging Harsh beating, especially with a whip. Punishment by inflicting stripes is prescribed in Deuteronomy 25:1–3. Although the Bible decrees a maximum of 40 stripes, the rabbis interpreted this as a maximum of 39. Two-thirds were administered on the back, and one-third on the chest. It was the normal punishment for actively transgressing the negative commandments; it was also viewed as sufficient punishment for severe violations of laws, for which the traditional punishment was 'karet' (cutting off). There is no physical punishment for failure to observe the positive commandments. Nonetheless the rabbis were empowered to administer such punishment for the good of the community when they saw fit.

Flood The Flood was brought about by God to destroy human beings because of their wickedness (Genesis 6–9). Noah was commanded to make an ark in which to place his family as well as males and females of all living creatures. Eventually the waters abated, and God promised not to destroy mankind again.

Foa, Eleazar Naḥman (d. after 1641) Italian rabbi and Kabbalist. He lived at Reggio Emilia and became chief rabbi of the duchy of Modena. He was head of Ḥevrat ha-Aluvim, which sponsored the printing of a commentary on the Haggadah. He also wrote a philosophic and Kabbalistic commentary on the Torah.

Foa, Moses Benjamin (1729–1822) Italian bibliophile and bookseller. Living in Reggio Emilia, he supplied books to the ducal library at Modena and become one of the most important booksellers of his day. He wrote a Hebrew grammar and copied several Hebrew manuscripts.

Folklore   The traditions of a people as expressed in popular beliefs, customs, stories, songs and practices. The Bible records folklore reflecting the civilisation of the ancient Near East. Rabbinic literature contains Jewish folklore, influenced by the cultural environment in which the Jews lived. The scientific study of Jewish folklore began at the close of the 19th century.

Fonseca, Daniel de (1672–c.1740)   Turkish physician and diplomat. He was born in Portugal. Although he was brought up as a Christian and even became a priest, he adhered to Judaism in secret. He was pursued by the Inquisition and fled to France. In 1702 he arrived in Constantinople, where he embraced Judaism. He later became medical attendant to Prince Mavrocordato at Bucharest. After returning to Constantinople, he became physician to the sultan, and eventually settled in Paris.

Ford, Aleksander (1908–80)   Polish film director. Born in Lódź, he studied at Warsaw University. His first feature film, *Mascot*, was made in 1930. At this time he became a co-founder of the society of the Devotees of the Artistic film. His 1932 film, *The Secret Legion* was set in Warsaw. The next year he made *Sabra in Palestine*. In 1937 he founded the Co-operative of Film Authors in Poland. From 1939 he was in the Soviet Union where he produced films for the Red Army. Later he became head of the Lódź film school, and in 1970 emigrated to Israel.

Forgery   The false making or altering of a document in an attempt to defraud. To aid the detection of alterations to legal documents, rabbinic legislation established the type of paper and ink which could be used. When it was suspected that an entire document was a forgery it could be submitted for certification by a court. Forgery is viewed as a sin, but there is no prescribed punishment for it. At worst the person involved is not allowed to serve as a witness in other cases.

Forgiveness   According to the Bible, it is one of God's attributes (Exodus 34:6). To be forgiven by God human beings must repent of their sins and resolve to improve their ways. Forgiveness for sins committed agaisnt others cannot be obtained until the wrong is righted and pardon sought from the injured party. The final sections of the tractate Yoma in the *Talmud* deal with repentance and the ritual of the Day of Atonement.

Formstecher, Solomon (1808–1889)   German philosopher and rabbi. He was born in Offenbach and served as rabbi there from 1842. He was active in the Reform movement and edited *Der Freitagabend* and *Die Israelitische Wochenschrift*. His *Die Religion des Geistes* presents a basis for the aims of the Emancipation and Reform movements in Judaism.

Four species   Term applied to the four plants used during Sukkot, as stipulated in Leviticus 23–40: 'And you shall take on the first day [of Sukkot] the fruit of goodly trees, branches of palm trees, and boughs of thick trees, and willows of the brook.' The four species are the etrog, palm, myrtle, and willow, which are held or waved during the festival.

Fram, David (1903–1988)   South African Yiddish poet. He was born in Lithuania and became a member of the Yung Vilne school of poets. In 1927 he settled in South Africa, where he published poems about Jewish life in Lithuania. His later poetry deals with South Africa, but is rooted in the tradition of Lithuanian Jewry. He served as editor of the Johannesburg Yiddish periodical, *Der yidisher ekspres*.

Frances, Immanuel ben David (1618–c.1710)   Italian Hebrew poet. He was born in Livorno. He led an unsettled life, wandering from town to town and suffering many misfortunes, including the death of his family. He later served as a rabbi in Florence. He wrote love poems, satirical epigrams, polemics against the Shabbetaians, and religious poetry.

Franck, Adolphe (1809–1893)   French philosopher and writer. He was born in Liocourt. He taught philosophy at several lycées and lectured at the Sorbonne. He was later appointed to the Collège de France as Professor of Ancient Philosophy and then Professor of Natural and International Law. He served as President of the Alliance Israélite Universelle. His writings include *The Kabbalah, or The Religious Philosophy of the Hebrews.*

Franck, Henri (1888–1912)   French poet. He was born in Paris. He wrote philosophical essays literary criticism, and poetry. His poem *La danse devant l'Arche* seeks to harmonise biblical inspiration with the French Cartesian tradition. In this work he saw himself as a new David dancing before the Ark of the Covenant.

Franco-Mendes, David (1713–1792)   Dutch Hebrew writer. He was born in Amsterdam and became a leading Hebrew poet there. He engaged in trade and served as honorary secretary of the Amsterdam Spanish and Portuguese community. Besides poetry, he wrote plays, articles, biographies of famous Sephardi Jews and responsa.

Frank, Anne (1929–1945)   Dutch diarist. Her family fled from Germany to Amsterdam in 1933. When deportations of Jews from Holland began in 1942, she and her family went into hiding. In December 1944 she was deported to Bergen-Belsen, where she died. Her diary about her experiences while hiding from the Nazis was published in 1947.

Frank, Jacob (1726–1791)   Polish communal leader, founder of the Frankist movement. He was born in Podolia. He was regarded as the successor to Shabbetai Tzevi. His mystical festivities were alleged to be accompanied by sexual orgies. He and his followers were excommunicated in 1756. The Frankists later renounced the *Talmud,* and debates were held between Frankists and rabbis, which concluded with the baptism of members of the Frankist sect. When the Polish authorities discovered that the Frankists revered Frank as their lord, he was tried and secluded in a monastery. He was released by the Russians in 1772 and settled at Offenbach, which became the centre of his movement.

Frankel, Zacharias (1801–1875)   German rabbi and scholar. He was born in Prague. He served as rabbi at Litomerice and Teplice and became Chief Rabbi of Dresden in 1836. In 1854 he became Director of the Breslau Rabbinical Seminary. He founded the positivist-historical school which later influenced Conservative Judaism in the US. At the second Reform rabbinical conference at Frankfurt am Main in 1845 he protested against the gradual abolition of Hebrew in the liturgy and withdrew from the conference.

Frankfurter, Felix (1882–1965)   American jurist. He was born in Vienna and was taken to New York at the age of 12. He served as professor at Harvard Law School (1914–39), and Associate Justice of the US Supreme Court (1939–62). In 1919 he was the legal adviser to the Zionist delegation at the Paris Peace Conference, and later maintained an interest in the establishment of a Jewish national home in Palestine.

Frankl, Ludwig August, Ritter von Hochwart   (1810–1894)   Austrian poet. He was born in Bohemia. He was appointed secretary and archivist of the Vienna Jewish community in 1838 and in 1842 he started to edit the literary periodical *Sonntagsblätter.* Half a million copies of his revolutionary poem *Die Universität* were circulated, and it was set to music 28 times. In 1856 he founded the Lamel school in Palestine, which offered a secular as well as a religious education for children. In 1876 he founded the Vienna Jewish Institute for the Blind and was ennobled.

Frankl, Victor E. (1905–1997) Austrian psychiatrist. He was a prisoner at Auschwitz and other concentration camps. His experiences led to the formulation of his existential psychotherapeutic approach (known as logotherapy), which he described in *Man's Search for Meaning*.

Franklin, Jacob Abraham (1809–1877) English editor and communal leader. He founded and edited the journal *Voice of Jacob* as a forum for anti-Reform opinion. He was active in communal organisations and left most of his fortune to endow educational projects, including the publication of Jewish textbooks.

Franks, Jacob (1688–1769) American merchant. He was born in London and settled in New York in 1708. In 1712 he married Abigail Bilhah Levy, the daughter of one of New York's richest Jews. He was active in the congregational affairs of Shearith Israel in New York. He served as President of the congregation in 1729, and was a founder of the congregation's Mill Street synagogue.

Franzos, Karl Emil (1848–1904) Austrian novelist and journalist. He was born in Czortkow. He worked as a journalist for several newspapers and in 1873 he began publishing in the *Neue Freie Presse* tales about the life of Eastern-European Jewry.

Fraternal [friendly] societies Mutual aid organisaitons, particularly active in the US. Jewish societies, whose aim was to foster fellowship, relieve distress, and provide life insurance and sickness and death benefits, originated in the 19th century. Initially many were composed of immigrants from the same areas. The largest and oldest is B'nai B'rith.

Fraud Deliberate deception or cheating in order to gain an advantage. In Jewish law fraud annuls a contract, and the injured party is entitled to damages. The Bible contains numerous laws against the use of weights and measures. A purchaser must be informed of any blemish in an object before it is sold or the transaction is fraudulent. If a false description is given, the buyer has the right to have the contract annulled and his money refunded.

Freed, Isadore (1900–1960) American composer, organist, pianist, and educator. He was born in Brest-Litovsk, Belorussia, and went to the US as a child. He taught at music schools in Philadelphia and New York, and at the Hartt School of Music in Hartford, Connecticut. He also served as an organist and choir director in several temples. His work includes the book *Harmonizing the Jewish Modes*.

Freedom Although slavery existed in biblical times, the freedom of the individual and nation was of supreme value to the Jews. Biblical law provides for the release of even the gentile slave in the Jubilee year. During the Passover seder freedom is the central theme. The political and social concept of freedom was spiritualised in later theological writings.

Freehof, Solomon (1892–1990) American Reform rabbi and scholar. He was born in London and was taken to the US in 1903. He served as Professor of Liturgy at the Hebrew Union College, and was later a rabbi in Chicago and at Congregation Rodeph Shalom in Pittsburgh. In 1955 he was appointed head of the Responsa Committee of the Central Conference of American Rabbis. He published numerous volumes of responsa.

Freemasonry Widespread secret order, founded in London in 1717 to promote brotherliness and mutual aid. Some of the words and phrases used in its rituals are derived from Hebrew terms, and Solomon's Temple plays a role in its symbolism. In the 18th century Jews became members in Holland, England,

France, Germany and the US. Free-masonry was established in Palestine before World War I.

Free will   The human ability to make choices that are not predetermined. The Bible stresses the ability of each individual to choose between good and evil. The concept of punishment and reward is based on this principle. According to the *Talmud*, God is omniscient but human beings have the power to choose their own way of living. Although rabbinic sources do not discuss the apparent contradiction between free will and divine omniscience, it was examined by medieval Jewish philosophers.

Free-will offering   An offering made spontaneously rather than as the result of an obligation or a vow. Jews often made such gifts to the Temple. According to Leviticus, a free-will offering might be a burnt offering or a peace offering (Leviticus 22:18,21).

Freidus, Abraham Solomon (1867–1923)   American librarian and bibliographer. He was born in Riga, Latvia, and lived in Paris, Palestine and London before settling in New York in 1889. In 1897 he was appointed first chief of the Jewish Division of the New York Public Library. He developed a classification scheme used for Judaica.

Freier, Recha (1892–1984)   German youth leader. She was born in Norderney. In 1932 in Berlin she founded the Youth Aliyah movement to aid Jewish young people to prepare for agricultural life. After 1933 she organised agricultural training outside Germany and directed pupils to Palestine, where she settled in 1941.

Freimann, Aron (1871–?)   German scholar, son of Israel Meir Freimann. He was born in Filehne, in the province of Posen. He worked at the municipal library in Frankfurt am Main, where he assembled a large collection of Judaica and Hebraica. After the Nazis came to power, he emigrated to the US. Between 1939 and 1945 he served as consultant to the New York Public Library. He was the author and editor of books and articles about Jewish history, culture and bibliography.

Freimann, Avraham Ḥayyim (1889–1948)   Jurist and rabbinic scholar of Moravian origin. He served as a magistrate in Königsberg and county judge at Braunsberg. In 1944 he began lecturing on Jewish law at the Hebrew University in Jerusalem. In 1947 he was appointed head of an advisory committee for Jewish law on personal status in the proposed Jewish state. He published studies of medieval rabbinics and Jewish law in modern Israel, and also wrote a work which deals with changes in Jewish marriage laws after the talmudic period.

Freimann, Jacob (1866–1937)   German rabbi, scholar and editor. He was born in Kraków. He served as a rabbi at Kanitz in Moravia and Holleschau (1890–1913). In 1913 he became Chief Rabbi of Posen. In 1928 he joined the rabbinate of the Berlin Jewish community and he later lectured on rabbinics and Jewish history at the Berlin Rabbinical Seminary. He published studies in medieval rabbinic literature.

Frenk, Azriel Nathan (1863–1924)   Polish journalist and historian. He was born in Wodzislaw. He began to write for the Jewish press in Warsaw in 1884, publishing articles about current events, stories about Ḥasidic life, and studies of Jewry in Poland.

Fress (Yiddish)   To eat gluttonously.

Freud, Anna (1985–1982)   Psychoanalyst of Austrian origin, the daughter of Sigmund Freud. She was an elementary school teacher and later gravitated to the Vienna Psychoanalytic Society. She founded and edited the journal, *The Psychoanalytic Study of the Child*. Her most noted work was *The Ego and the Mechanism of Defence*. In 1943 she founded the Hampstead Clinics in Great Britain.

Freud, Sigmund (1856–1939) Austrian psychologist, founder of psychoanalysis. He was born in Freiberg. He worked as a neuropathologist and clinical neurologist in Vienna and, as a result of his work and research, formulated a new approach to understanding the human mind. In addition to numerous psychoanalytical studies, he published *Moses and Monotheism*. He was a member of the Jewish community in Vienna and was a loyal member of B'nai B'rith.

Friedberg, Abraham Shalom [Har-Shalom] (1838–1902) Polish Hebrew writer, editor and translator. He was born in Grodno, Belorussia, and after wandering from town to town in southern Russia returned to his native city in 1858. After the pogroms of 1881 he joined the Hibbat Zion movement. In 1886 he went to Warsaw, where he was an editor of the first Hebrew encyclopedia, *Ha-Eshkol*. His *Memoirs of the House of David* is a series of stories embracing Jewish history from the destruction of the Temple to the beginning of the Haskalah period in Germany.

Friedberg, Bernhard (1876–1961) Israeli scholar and bibliographer. He was born in Kraków and moved to Frankfurt am Main in 1900. In 1904 he set up his own publishing firm. He later entered the diamond trade and moved to Antwerp. In 1946 he settled in Tel Aviv. He published Jewish biographies, family histories and a series of works on the history of Hebrew printing. His *Beit Eked Sepharim* is a bibliographical lexicon.

Friedenwald, Harry (1864–1950) American ophthalmologist, son of Aaron Friedenwald. He was born in Baltimore and taught at the Baltimore College of Physicians and Surgeons. He was president of the Federation of American Zionists from 1904 to 1918. In 1911 and 1914 he went to Palestine, where he was a consultant for eye diseases in several hospitals. His writings include *The Jews and Medicine* and *Jewish Luminaries in Medical History*.

Friedlaender, Israel (1876–1920) American scholar and communal leader. He was born in Kovel, Poland, and grew up in Warsaw. He became lecturer in Semitics at the University of Strasbourg, then in 1904 was appointed professor of Bible at the Jewish Theological Seminary of America. He also taught at Dropsie College in Philadelphia and was active in Jewish communal life. He published studies of Islamic sects, Judeo-Arabic literature, and Jewish influences on Arabic folklore, and translated Simon Dubnow's *History of the Jews in Russia and Poland*.

Friedländer, David (1750–1834) German communal leader and author. He was born in Köningsberg and settled in Berlin in 1770, where he established a silk factory. He was a founder and director of the Jewish Free School in Berlin and led the fight for equal rights for Prussian Jewry. After the death of Moses Mendelssohn he was the leader of the German Jewish Enlightenment movement. He championed extreme religious reform.

Friedländer, Michael (1833–1910) British educator and writer. He was born in Jutrosin in the province of Posen. He served as the head of the *Talmud* Torah school in Berlin from 1862, and was Principal of Jews College in London from 1865 to 1910. He took an active part in the communal and cultural life of Anglo-Jewry. His writings include *Jewish Religion*, *Textbook of the Jewish Religion*, and *Jewish Family Bible*.

Friedländer, Moritz (1844–1919) Hungarian educator and writer. He became secretary of the Israelitische Allianz and worked in Galicia assisting the emigration of Russian Jews to the US. With the help of Baron Maurice de Hirsch and his wife, he established and supervised more than 50 schools for boys and girls in Galicia. He wrote studies of the relationship of Hellenism and Christianity to Judaism.

Friedländer, Saul (b.1932) Israeli historian. He was born in Prague, lived in France from 1939 to 1948, and then emigrated to Israel. He later taught at the Institut des Hautes Études Internationales in Geneva, and he was appointed Professor of History and International Relations at the Hebrew University in 1969. His writings include *Hitler et les États-Unis, 1939–41, Prelude to Downfall: Hitler and the United States,* and *Pius XII and the Third Reich.*

Freidman, Bruce Jay (b.1930) American novelist. He was born in the Bronx and in his novels satirised middle-class American Jewish life. His works include *Stern, A Mother's Kisses,* and *The Dick.*

Friedman, Elisha Michael (1889–1951) American economist. He acted as economic consultant to several US governmental agencies. He was an active Zionist and a supporter of the Hebrew University. His *Survival or Extinction* is a discussion of the Jewish problem.

Friedman, Lee Max (1871–1957) American lawyer and historian. He was born in Memphis, Tennessee. He was Professor of Law at Portia Law School in Boston and Vice-President of the school. He served as President and later Honorary President of the American Jewish Historical Society. He published studies on various aspects of Jewish history.

Friedmann, David Aryeh (1889–1957) Israeli critic and editor. After studying medicine at Moscow University, he emigrated to Palestine in 1925, where he practised ophthalmology. He published studies on Hebrew and world literature, art criticism and the history of Jewish medicine.

Friedmann, David ben Samuel [David of Karlin] (1828–1917) Lithuanian rabbi and halakhic authority. He was born in Biala, and served as rabbi of Karlino near Pinsk from 1868. His *Piskei Halakhot* is an exposition and summary of matrimonial law. In his *Emek Berakhah* he discussed the conditions under which a religious ban should be imposed. Although he initially was active in the Ḥibbat Zion movement, he later became an opponent of Zionism.

Frigeis, Lazaro de (fl. 16th cent.) Italian physician. He was a friend of the anatomist Andrea Vesalius in Padua and supplied the Hebrew names for some of the anatomical strucutres described in Vesalius' work, *De humani corporis fabrica.* The terms were taken from the Hebrew translation of the *Canon* of Avicenna and from the *Talmud.*

Frischmann, David (1859–1922) Polish Hebrew and Yiddish writer. He was born in Zgierz, near Lódź. His first works were written in the spirit of the Haskalah; later writings include satires, stories, critical essays and poems. He also published translations of European literature and worked in journalism. He served as editor of several periodicals and anthologies and contributed to the Hebrew press.

Fromm (Yiddish) Strict in religious observance.

Fromm, Erich (1900–1980) American psychoanalyst and social philosopher. He was born in Frankfurt am Main and worked at the Institute for Social Research there from 1929 to 1932. After the Nazis came to power, he emigrated to the US and taught at Bennington College, the National University of Mexico, Michigan State University and New York University. Much of his writing was influenced by Jewish sources. His publications include *The Art of Loving* and *You shall be as Gods.*

Frug, Simon Samuel (1860–1916) Ukrainian Yiddish poet. He was born in Kherson province. He published three volumes of Russian poetry and was the first poet to treat Jewish themes in Russian verse. Later he published Yiddish songs and ballads. In his Zionist lyrics he pleaded for a return of the Jews to productive labour in their ancestral homeland.

Frumkin, Aryeh Leib (1845–1916) Palestinian rabbinic scholar and writer, of Lithuanian origin. He visited Palestine in 1867 and 1871, and began research for a history of the rabbis and scholars of Jerusalem. He returned to Europe and served as a rabbi at Ilukste in Latvia. Later he became a farmer-scholar in Petaḥ Tikvah, Palestine, where he established a yeshivah. In 1894 he settled in London, but he eventually emigrated to Palestine. His *Seder Rav Amran* is a siddur with notes and a commentary.

Frumkin, Israel Dov (1850–1914) Palestinian journalist. He was born in Belorussia and was taken to Jerusalem when he was nine. He edited the Jerusalem periodical *Ḥavatzelet* from 1870 to 1910. From the mid 1880s his journalistic writings attacked the Ḥibbat Zion movement.

Fuchs, Daniel (1909–1993) American novelist, short-story writer and screenwriter. He was born in New York. He taught elementary school in Brooklyn and wrote several novels during summer vacations. His *Summer in Williamsburg* depicts the lives and fantasies of several poor Jewish families.

Fuchs, Ernst (1930–2015) Austrian painter. He was born in Vienna and became a member of the Viennese school of Fantastic Realism. Some of his paintings include allusions to the kabbalah, Hebrew script and biblical themes.

Fulvia (fl. 1st cent.) Roman proselyte. She sent presents of purple and gold to the Temple which were never delivered. When her husband reported the matter to the emperor, Tiberius expelled all the Jews from Rome in the year 19. Thousands of young Jews were drafted into military service and sent to fight the brigands in Sardinia.

Fünn, Samuel Joseph (1818–90) Lithuanian Hebrew writer. He was born in Vilnius and was a founder of the first Jewish school in the city. He taught the Bible and Hebrew there, and later taught at the local rabbinical school. In 1856 he was appointed Inspector of the government Jewish schools in the Vilnius district. In 1863 he opened a printing press in Vilnius, which enabled him to publish *Ha-Karmel,* a journal which he edited and to which he contributed studies of Russian Jewry. He wrote a biographical lexicon of notable Jews and a Hebrew dictionary.

Fürst, Julius (1805–1873) Polish Hebraist, bibliographer and historian. He settled in Leipzig, where he taught at the university. His publications include a bibliography of Jewish books and books on Judaism, a history of Karaism, a Bible concordance, a Hebrew and Aramaic lexicon, and a history of Jewish literature.

Fürstenthal, Raphael Jacob (1781–1855) German author and translator. He wrote poetry and translated Maimonides' *Guide for the Perplexed,* Baḥya ibn Pakuda's *Hovot ha-Levavot,* and Isaac Aboab I's *Menorat ha-Maor* from Hebrew into German. He also translated Jewish liturgical works.

Furtado, Abraham (1756–1817) French politician and communal leader. Of Portuguese descent, he lived in Bordeaux. He was elected President of the Assembly of Jewish Notables convened by Napoleon, and acted as Secretary of the Paris Sanhedrin. He published *Mémoire d'Abraham Furtado sur l'état des Juifs en France jusqu'à la Revolution.*

G

Morris and his wife Shelia were having dinner at an expensive restaurant in the upper East Side of New York when an attractive redhead walks by. She smiles and says: 'Hello, Morris.'

Agitated, Shelia asks: 'And just who was that girl who spoke to you?'

Morris replies: 'Oh her? That's my mistress.'

'You have a mistress? How long has this been going on?'

'About five years, on and off,' Morris sighs.

'Five years? You bastard. I'm going to see a solicitor tomorrow and start divorce proceedings. I'll ruin you...'

'Hold on Shelia,' Morris says. 'Think about it for a minute. If we get a divorce, you will only get half. You won't have our big house in Queens. You won't have a new Jaguar for your birthday present each year. You won't be able to play cards at the country club. You won't...'

But before Morris can continue, a blond walks past and says to him: 'Hi Morris. Nice to see you here.'

Incensed, Shelia asks: 'And just who was that, another of your mistresses?'

'No that's Max's mistress.'

'You mean Max also has a mistress?' Shelia asks.

'Of course,' Morris replies. 'She's been with him for ten years.'

'Ours is better,' Shelia proudly declares.

* * * * *

This is a terrible tale of deception, money and pride. The husband cheats on his wife. When she finds out, he points out how her life will be materially and socially diminished if she divorces him. And when she sees a rival to her husband's mistress, she brags that her husband's mistress is better than someone else's. This is an amusingly pointed satire of corrosive attitudes and values.

Gabbai ('collector') Communal official. In biblical times the title was used for one who collected dues and charitable contributions, but from the Middle Ages it applied to any communal official.

Gabriel, Archangel With Michael, he is the only angel mentioned by name in the Bible (Daniel 8–10). In rabbinic literature he is referred to as a leader of the angelic host and one of the highest angels in the celestial hierarchy.

Gad (i) (fl. 19th–16th cent. BCE) Israelite, son of Jacob and Zilpah (Genesis 30:10–11). His tribal territory lay to the east of the Jordan. The tribe of Gad flourished during the rule of Saul and David.

Gad (ii) (fl. 11th–10th cent. BCE) Israelite prophet. He was one of the three prophets during the days of King David. He joined David when he fled from Saul to Abdullam, and persuaded him to return to Judah (I Samuel 22:5). He remained at the court of David in Jerusalem (II Samuel 24:11–14; I Chronicles 21:9–30), and was one of the organisers of the Levitical service in the Temple (II Chronicles 29:25).

Galante, Abraham (1873–1961) Turkish scholar. He was born in Bodrum. He was first a teacher and inspector in the Jewish and Turkish schools of Rhodes and Smyrna. Later he lived in Egypt, where he edited the Ladino newspaper *La vara*. He encouraged the acculturation of Turkish Jewry to its homeland, and fought for Jewish rights. Eventually he returned to Istanbul where he became a professor at the university. He wrote studies of Jewish history in Turkey.

Galante, Moses ben Jonathan (1620–1689) Palestinian rabbi. He studied in Safed and later moved to Jerusalem, where he was a leading rabbi and head of a yeshivah. Influenced by the Sabbetaians, he and other rabbis went to Gaza to seek purification of the soul from Nathan of Gaza. He accompanied Shabbetai Tzevi to Smyrna and Constantinople. He wrote responsa and commentaries on the Torah.

Galante, Moses ben Mordecai (fl. 16th cent.) Palestinian talmudist and Kabbalist. He was born in Rome. He became a disciple of Joseph Caro and his teacher in the field of kabbalah was Moses ben Jacob Cordovero. From 1580 he served as av bet din in Safed. He wrote responsa, an index of biblical passages interpreted in the *Zohar*, and a homiletic and Kabbalistic commentary on Ecclesiastes.

Galili, Israel (1910–1986) Israeli Labour and Haganah leader. He was born in Ukraine and was taken to Palestine at the age of four. In 1924 he was among the founders of the youth wing of the Histadrut. He joined the central command of the Haganah in 1941 and from 1945 to 1947 he was one of the principal organisers of underground armed activities in Palestine. In 1947 he was appointed head of Haganah's territorial command. He served as Deputy Minister of Defence in the provisional government in 1948. From 1966 to 1970 he was Minister without Portfolio in the Israeli government, responsible for the information services.

Gallico, Abraham Jagel ben Hananiah [Jagel, Abraham] (fl. 16th cent.) Italian writer on ethics. He served as mint-master to the Prince of Correggio. His *Valley of Vision* is an imitation of Dante's *Divine Comedy*. He also wrote *Lekaḥ Tov*, the first Jewish catechism.

Galut ('exile') The word is used to refer to the condition of the Jewish people in the diaspora, and has connotations of alienation, degradation and persecution.

Gamaliel the Elder (fl. 1st cent.) Palestinian elder, grandson of Hillel. He was President of the Sanhedrin and, according to Acts, Paul was one of his pupils. He maintained close contact with Jews in Palestine and the diaspora. He was responsible for many takkanot.

Gamaliel II (fl. 1st–2nd cent.) Palestinian elder. He was President of the Sanhedrin at Jabneh and strengthened the new centre there. He consolidated Jewish law and sought to unite the Jewish people around the Torah. He provoked a revolt against his authority and Elezar ben Azariah was appointed nasi in his place. Later he was reinstated.

Gambling Judaism is traditionally opposed to gambling. Although the tendency of rabbinic law is to forbid all forms of gambling, a distinction is made between those who indulge in it as a pastime and those who are professional gamblers. Professional gamblers are viewed as untrustworthy and may not act as witnesses.

Gamoran, Emanuel (1895–1962) American educator. He was born in Russia and was taken to the US in 1907. In 1923 he became the education director of the Commission of Jewish Education of the Union of American Hebrew Congregations. He also served as President of the National Council for Jewish Education (1927–8). His writings include *Changing Conceptions in Jewish Education.*

Gam zo le-tovah ('This is also for the good') Expression of resignation to divine providence. It was frequently uttered by Naḥum of Gimzo.

Ganef [gonif] (Yiddish) Word used variously to mean thief, clever person, dishonest businessman, shady character, prankster.

Gans, David ben Solomon (1541–1613) Bohemian chronicler, astronomer and mathematician. He was born in Lippstadt, Westphalia. He studied with Moses Isserles in Kraków and later settled in Prague, where he was in contact with Johann Kepler and Tycho Brahe. He wrote works on astronomical and mathematical problems, Jewish and general history, the calendar and the geography of Israel.

Gans, Eduard (1798–1839) German jurist and historian. Together with Leopold Zunz and Moses Mosher, he founded in 1819 the Society for Jewish Culture and Learning, of which he became president. In 1820 he was appointed a lecturer at the University of Berlin. He converted to Christianity in 1825 and became professor at the university. He wrote studies of law, edited Hegel's lectures on the philosophy of history and founded the journal *Jahrbücher für Wissenschaftliche Kritik.*

Ganzfried, Solomon (1804–1886) Hungarian rabbi and author. He was born in Ungvar. He served as rabbi of Brezewicz and later head of the bet din of Ungvar. His *Kitzur Shulḥan Arukh* is an abridgement of the Shulḥan Arukh.

Gaon Religious leader of the Babylonian Jewish community in the post-Talmudic period (6th–11th centuries). The geonim were the heads of the leading academies at Sura and Pumbedita. The title 'gaon' (literally 'eminence,' 'pride') derives from their position as 'rosh yeshivat gaon Yaakov' (head of the academy which is the pride of Jacob). In the 12th–13th centuries the title was also used by the heads of academies in Baghdad, Damascus and Egypt. It eventually became an honorific title for any rabbi who had a great knowledge of Torah.

Gardner, Herb (1934–2003). American playwright He was born in Brooklyn. His plays deal with Jewish characters and include *The Goodbye People, I'm Not Rappaport,* and *Who is Harry Kellerman and Why is he Saying Those Terrible Things about me?*

Gardosh, Kariel [Dosh] (1921–2000) Israeli cartoonist. He was born in Budapest. He emigrated to Israel in 1948, and joined the staff of the paper *Maariv* as editorial cartoonist. Signing himself 'Dosh', he created the figure of Little Israel, a young boy who became the popular symbol of the State and its people. He also illustrated books and wrote short stories and plays. He exhibited in Israel and other countries.

Gary, Romain (1914–1980) French novelist. He was born in Vilnius, moved to Poland when he was seven, and in 1926 settled in Nice. He served in the French diplomatic service and was Consul-General in Los Angeles from 1956 to 1960. His *A European Education* includes elements of Jewish interest. In *The Dance of Genghis Cohn,* he tells the story of a Jewish comedian shot by the Nazis who haunts his executioner. Jewish characters frequently appear in his novels.

Gaster, Moses (1856–1939) British rabbi and scholar. He was born in Bucharest and taught Romanian language and literature in the university there from 1881 to 1885. Later he settled in England, where he taught Slavonic literature at Oxford University. In 1887 he was appointed Ḥaham of the English Sephardi community. From 1891 to 1896 he was Principal of Judith Montefiore College in Ramsgate. He was active in Ḥibbat Zion and later in the Zionist movement. He published studies of Romanian literature, comparative and Jewish folklore, Samaritan history and literature, rabbinic scholarship, liturgy, Anglo-Jewish history and biblical studies.

Gaster, Theodor Herzl (1906–92) American educator and scholar, son of Moses Gaster. He was born in London. He taught comparative religion at Dropsie College in Philadelphia and at other universities in the US. His writings include *Passover: Its History and Traditions; Purim and Hanukkah in Custom and Tradition; Thespis: Ritual Myth, and Drama in the Ancient Near East; Festivals of the Jewish Year; Holy and Profane;* and *New Year: Its History, Customs and Superstition.*

Gebirtig, Mordecai (1877–1942) Polish Yiddish poet. He was born in Kraków and worked as a carpenter. Regarded as a Yiddish bard, he composed the words and melodies for his songs, which were collected in 1936 in a volume edited by Menachem Kipnis. His most famous song, *Our Town is Burning,* was written in 1938 under the impact of the pogrom in Przytyk.

Gedaliah (fl. 6th cent. BCE) Babylonian governor of Judah. He was murdered by Ishmael ben Nethaniah, who hoped to overthrow Babylonian rule. Gedaliah's supporters fled to Egypt, taking Jeremiah with them (II Kings 25:25–26); Jeremiah 41:1ff).

Gedaliah, Fast of Fast kept on 3 Tishri (after Rosh ha-Shanah) to commemorate the assassination of Gedaliah.

Gefilte fish (Yiddish) Fish cakes or fish loaf made of various types of fish.

Gehazi (fl. 9th cent. BCE) Israelite, servant of Elisha. In the story of the wealthy Shunammite woman (II Kings 4:8–37), he acted as Elisha's faithful messenger and loyal protector. However, he is depicted as greedy and cunning in the story of Naaman; after trying to deceive Elisha he was cursed with the leprosy of which Naaman was cured (II Kings 5). In the story of the woman from Shunem and the King of Israel (II Kings 8:1–6) he told the king about the great deeds which Elisha had performed.

Geiger, Abraham (1810–1874) German Reform leader and scholar. In 1832 he became rabbi in Wiesbaden, where he reformed the synagoguge services and published the *Wissenschaftliche Zeitschrift für jüdische Theologie.* In 1837 he convened the first meeting of Reform rabbis. He later became rabbi in Breslau, where he established a school for religious studies and led a group that worked on Hebrew philology. He participated in subsequent Reform synods and from 1863 served as rabbi in Frankfurt am Main. In 1870 he became rabbi of the Berlin congregation, and he helped to establish the Hochschule für Wissenschaft des Judentums in the city. His works include studies of the Bible, the Sadduccees and Pharisees, Jewish history, mishnaic Hebrew, and Maimonides.

Gelber, Natan Mikhael (1891–1966) Austrian historian and Zionist leader. He was born in Lemberg. He was general secretary of the eastern Galician delegation of the Vaad Leumi in Vienna (1918–21), and later became secretary of the Austrian Zionist Organisation. In 1934 he emigrated to Palestine where he worked in the head office of Keren ha-Yesod in Jerusalem. He published books and articles on Jewish history and contemporary Jewish life.

Gelilah The rolling up of the Torah scroll after its reading in the synagogue.

Gélleri, Andor Endre (1907–1945) Hungarian novelist. He was born in Budapest and worked as a dyer and locksmith. His writings include *The Laundry, Thirsty Apprentices, Hold Street, The Harbour,* and *Lighting and Evening Fire.* Jewish figures appear in many of his works.

Gelman, Aryeh Leon (1887–1973) American journalist and Zionist leader. He was born in Russia and went to the US at the age of 23. He was the principal of various Hebrew schools in St Louis, and later served as editor and publisher of the Yiddish *St Louis Jewish Record.* He was President of the American Mizraḥi movement from 1935 to 1939 and subsequently was editor of various Mizraḥi publications in New York.

Gelt (Yiddish) Money.

Gemara Commentary on the Mishnah; together, the Mishnah and the Gemara make up the *Talmud.* Traditionally the Mishnah is printed in the centre of the page with the Gemara surrounding it.

Gemar ḥatimah tovah ('A final good sealing') Traditional greeting during the period between Rosh ha-Shanah and the Day of Atonement. It is sometimes used until Hoshana Rabbah. It alludes to the belief that on the New Year a person's fate is inscribed in the Book of Life and on the Day of Atonement the decree is sealed.

Gematria (from Greek 'geometria'; geometry) Method of biblical exegesis based on the numerical value of Hebrew words. It appeared among tannaim in the 2nd century. Later it was used in midrashic sources and in Kabbalistic writings from the 12th century onward.

Gemilut ḥasadim ('doing kindness') Charity in the broadest sense. It encompasses the various duties of sympathetic consideration toward others.

Genealogy The study of the relationship and descent of an individual, family or group. Genealogical material is found in the Pentateuch and the Book of Chronicles, which demonstrates the descent of the Jewish people from the patriarchs. The priests claimed descent from Aaron. Although genealogies were maintained during the period of the Second Temple, the practice declined in talmudic times. Nonetheless the patriarchs in Palestine and the exilarchs in Babylonia were believed to have descended from David. In the medieval period and later descent from distinguished scholars was valued in the Jewish community.

Genesis (Hebrew 'Bereshit') First book of the Bible. It describes the creation of the world and the beginning of humanity (1:1–6:8); gives an account of the ten generations to Abraham including the episode of the Flood (6:9–11:32); and tells the stories of Abraham (12–20), Abraham and Isaac (21:1–25:18), Esau and Jacob (25:19–36:43), Jacob and his sons (37:1–47:27), and Jacob and Joseph (47:28–50:26).

Genesis Rabbah (Hebrew 'Bereshit Rabbah') Midrash on the Book of Genesis. It is the first work in the Midrash Rabbah, comprising 101 sections. Each is headed by a quotation from Genesis, followed by interpretative aggadot. It was produced by Palestinian amoraim.

Genizah (lit. 'hiding') Repository, usually associated with a synagogue, for books or ritual objects which have become unusable. Ritual objects and books containing the name of God cannot be destroyed and were therefore buried when they wore out. The genizah might be a cave or plot of land, or part of a house. The practice fell into disuse after the Middle Ages.

Genocide   The deliberate killing of a nationality, race or ethnic group. The word was first used by Raphael Lemkin in a report to the Fifth International Conference for the Unification of Penal Law held in 1933 in Madrid. In the UN convention on the Prevention and Punishment of the Crime of Genocide, it signifies a coordinated set of acts intended to destroy a national, ethnic, racial or religious group. It is frequently applied to the Holocaust.

Gentile [heathen]   Any person (especially a Christian) who is not a Jew. According to Jewish law, a person whose mother is not Jewish is considered a non-Jew, regardless of whether the father is Jewish. American Reform Judaism, however, has decreed that if a person is born of either a Jewish mother or father, that individual is Jewish provided the person has observed Jewish timely acts. The seven Noachian laws are binding on a gentile. A righteous gentile is entitled to enter into the afterlife.

Gentili, Gershom ben Moses (1683–1700)   Italian rabbinic scholar, son of Moses ben Gershom Gentili. He was the author of *Yad Ḥaruzim*, a Hebrew rhyme lexicon. It contains an introduction, 12 rules for Hebrew usage in poetry, and an appendix containing a poetical formulation of the 613 commandments.

Gentili, Moses ben Gershom (1663–1711)   Italian scholar. He was born in Trieste. He served as rabbi in Venice and was the author of *Melekhet Maḥashevet*, a philsophical commentary on the Torah. His *Ḥanukkat ha-Bayit* deals with the construction of the Second Temple.

George, Manfred (1893–1965)   American journalist and editor. He was born in Berlin. He worked as a newspaper editor and writer in Germany until the Nazis came to power. He then moved to Prague and later emigrated to the US. In New York he took over the news letter (*Aufbau*) of the German-Jewish New World Club.

Gerchunoff, Alberto (1884–1950)   Argentine journalist and writer. He was born in Russia and was taken to Argentina as a child. In 1908 he joined the staff of the daily *La nación* with which he was associated for over 40 years. His *The Jewish Gauchos of the Pampas* contains a collection of articles describing the life of Jewish colonists in Entre Ríos at the beginning of the 20th century. Following the rise of Hitler, he became an ardent Zionist.

Gerim ('Proselytes')   Minor tractate appended to the *Talmud*. It contains halakhic statements concerning the conversion and the acceptance of proselytes.

Gerondi, Isaac ben Zerachiah (fl. 13th cent.)   Spanish Hebrew poet. About 20 of his liturgical poems survive.

Gerondi, Jacob ben Sheshet (fl. 13th cent.)   Spanish Kabbalist. He lived in Gerona. He wrote *Meshiv Devarim Nekhoḥim*, in which he formulated Kabbalistic meanings of the essence of the Torah, the creation of the world, divine providence and retribution.

Gerondi, Jonah ben Abraham (fl. 13th cent.)   Spanish talmudist. While living in Montpellier, he signed the ban that led to the burning of the works of Moses Maimonides. He subsequently vowed to go on a pilgrimage to Palestine to seek forgiveness, but was induced to remain in Toledo to direct a yeshivah. He wrote novellae on talmudic tractates as well as ethical treatises.

Gerondi, Nissim ben Reuben [Nissim, Rabbenu Gerondi; Ran] (fl. 14th cent.)   Spanish talmudist, physician and astronomer. He lived in Barcelona, where he played an important role in communal life. He wrote commentaries on the writings of Isaac ben Jacob Alfasi and on numerous talmudic tractates.

Gerondi, Zerachiah ben Isaac (fl. 12th cent.) Italian rabbinic scholar and poet. He was born in Gerona and settled in Lunel. His *Sepher ha-Maor* is a critical examination of the writings of Isaac ben Jacob Alfasi. In *Sepher ha-Tzava* he provided an introduction to talmudic methodology. He also composed liturgical poems.

Gershom ben Judah (c.960–1028) German talmudic scholar and spiritual leader. He was born in Metz and lived in Mainz, where he conducted a yeshivah. He issued legal decisions and takkanot, laid the foundations for a commentary on the *Talmud*, transcribed and corrected the Mishnah and the *Masorah Gedolah* of the Bible, and composed selihot and piyyutim.

Gershom ben Solomon (fl. 13th cent.) Provençal scholar. He lived in Béziers. His *Shalman* gives the halakhic rulings of the *Talmud* according to the order of the halakhot of Isaac ben Jacob Alfasi, and approximating the codes of Maimonides in his *Mishneh Torah*.

Gershwin, George (1898–1973) American composer. Born in Brooklyn, he was responsible for forming the jazz style into acceptable concert music. Her wrote successful musical comedies and film scores as well as the opera, *Porgy and Bess.*

Gertler, Mark (1891–1939) Born in Spitalfields, his family returned to Austria but settled in England in 1896. He was a member of the Whitechapel School in painting. He was part of the intellectual, social and artistic elite in London. He was the inspiration for Loerke in D H. Lawrence's novel, *Women in Love.*

Gerushin ('driving out') In Jewish law, a term denoting divorce. Among the kabbalists in the 16th century it also designated peregrinations undertaken in order to share the exile of the Shekinah and gain mystical illumination.

Gerusia (Greek: 'old people') Council of elders. According to Josephus, the earliest Jewish gerusia dates back to biblical times. During the Hellenistic period, the Jewish gerusia served as a legislative, judicial and representative body. It eventually evolved into the Sanhedrin of Jerusalem. A similar body existed in Alexandria.

Geullah ('Redemption') The name of several benedictions in the liturgy. It designates one of the petitions in the weekday Amidah; the benediction giving thanks for the redemption from Egypt, with which the central part of the Passover Haggadah is concluded; and the benediction following the Shema in the Shaharit and Maariv prayers.

Gevalt (Yiddish) Cry of fear, amazement, astonishment, or protest, or a cry for help.

Gezerah ('decree') In Jewish law a technical term for a rabbinic prohibition. It is distinct from a positive enactment (takkanah). In a non-legal context it came to denote an evil or anti-Jewish decree; by extension it also referred to anti-Jewish persecutions and pogroms.

Ghetto Area of a city in which Jews were required to live. The term derives from the foundry ('ghetto') in Venice where Jews were segregated in 1517. The institution was established in cities and towns throughout Europe. The ghetto enjoyed a degree of autonomy and had its own spiritual and intellectual life, but the segregation of the Jews in their own quarter was frequently accompanied by forced baptism, the wearing of the Jewish badge, occupational restrictions, and conversionist activities. Ghettos largely disappeared after the Emancipation of the Jews in the 19th century, but the system was re-imposed in some cities (notably Warsaw) under Nazi rule.

Giants The Bible refers to races of giants, the Nephilim, Anakim, and Gibborim (Genesis 6:4; Numbers 13:28).

Other giants mentioned in the Bible include Goliath (I Samuel 17) and Ishbi-benob (II Samuel 21:16).

Gideon [Jerubaal] (fl. 12th cent. BCE) Judge of the tribe of Manasseh. He defeated the Midianites near En Harod. When offered the kingship of Israel he refused, out of loyalty to the principle that God is the King of Israel (Judges 6–8). In Judges 6:32 he is referred to by the name Jerubaal.

Gideon, Miriam (1906–1996) American composer and eucator. She was born in Greeley, Colorado, and grew up in Boston. She taught at Brooklyn College, City College of New York, the Cantors Institute of the Jewish Theological Seminary and the Manhattan School. Her works on Jewish themes include *Friday Evening Service, Sabbath Morning Service, Adon Olam, Psalm 84; Biblical Masks,* and *Aetet Hashahar.*

Gikatilla, Isaac (fl. 10th cent.) Spanish Hebrew poet and grammarian. A student of Menaḥem ben Saruq, he took part in the controversy on grammar between his teacher and Dunash ben Labrat. He lived at Lucena.

Gikatilla, Joseph ben Abraham (1248–c.1325) Spanish Kabbalist. He was born in Medinaceli, Castile, and lived in Segovia. His *Ginnat Egoz* is an introduction to the mystic symbolism of the alphabet, vowel points and the divine names. In his *Shaare Orah* he explained Kabbalistic symbolism and the designations of the ten sephirot.

Gikatilla [Ibn Gikatilla], Moses ben Samuel (fl. 11th cent.) Spanish liturgical poet and grammarian. He was born in Córdoba and lived in Zaragoza. He wrote poetry as well as studies of Hebrew grammar and Bible exegesis.

Gilbert, Martin (1936–2015) English historian. He was born in London. He was a fellow of Merton College, Oxford, and visiting Professor at the Hebrew University and Tel Aviv University. His

publications include *Exile and Return: a Study in the Emergence of Jewish Statehood, The Holocaust, Auschwitz and the Allies, The Jews of Hope, The Plight of Soviet Jewry Today,* and *Jerusalem: Rebirth of a City.*

Gilboa, Amir (1917–1984) Israeli poet. He was born in Radzywilow, Volhynia, and went to Palestine in 1937, where he worked initially as a labourer. He began to publish poetry while serving in the Jewish Brigade during World War II.

Ginsburg, Christian David (1831–1914) British biblical scholar. He was born in Warsaw. He converted to Christianity in 1846 and settled in England, where he wrote studies of the masoretic text of the Bible; his *The Massorah* contains the original text of the masorah as well as additional notes. He also published standard editions of the Hebrew Bible, contributed to a new critical Hebrew Bible text, wrote commentaries on several books of the Bible, and produced studies of the Karaites and Kabbalistic literature.

Ginsburg [Günzburg], Jekuthiel (1889–1957) American mathematician and Hebrew writer. He was born in Russia and emigrated to the US in 1912. In 1930 he was appointed professor and head of the department of mathematics at Yeshiva College. His publications include studies of the Jewish contribution to mathematics.

Ginsburg, Ruth (b.1933) American lawyer. Born in Brooklyn, she studied at Cornell, Harvard and Columbia Universities. She taught at Rutgers and Columbia Law Schools and became a circuit judge in 1980. She was appointed to a Justice of the Supreme Court in 1993.

Ginzburg, Natalia (1916–1991) Italian novelist and playwright. She was born in Palermo and studied in Turin. The characters in her novels include many Jews. Her works include *Family Sayings,* a psychological novel based on the author's recollections of her own family and the events of her youth.

Ginsburg, Saul (1866–1940) Russian author and historian. He was born in Minsk. In 1903 he established the first Yiddish daily in Russia. Later he devoted himself to the study of the cultural history of the Jews in Russia. He left the USSR in 1930 and settled in Paris, later moving to New York. Together with Peretz Marek he published *Jewish Folk Songs*. His *Historical Works* contains material on 19th-century Russian Jewry.

Gittelsohn, Roland (1910–1995) American rabbi. He was born in Cleveland. He was rabbi at the Central Synagogue of Nassau County in Long Island from 1936 to 1953, then served as rabbi of Temple Israel in Boston. In 1968 he became President of the Central Conference of American Rabbis. His writings include *Modern Jewish Problems, Little Lower than the Angels, Man's Best Hope, My Beloved is Mine,* and *Fire in my Bones.*

Gittin Sixth tractate of the order Nashim in the Mishnah. It deals with the laws of divorce (Deuteronomy 24:1–4).

Glanz, Leib (1898–1964) American cantor and composer. He was born in Kiev and held cantorial positions at Kishinev and in Romania before emigrating to the US in 1926. He served as cantor of the Ohev Shalom Synagogue in Brooklyn and of Heikhal Sinai Synagogue and the Shaarei Tefillah Synagogue in Los Angeles. In 1954 he settled in Israel and became chief cantor of the Tiferet Zevi Synagogue in Tel Aviv. He founded the Tel Aviv Institute of Religious Jewish Music.

Glaser, Eduard (1853–1908) Bohemian explorer and Arabist. He was born in Deutsch-Rust. He made four journeys to Arabia between 1883 and 1894, discovering many geographical locations, numerous inscriptions, archaeological remains, and Arabic manuscripts.

Glatstein, Jacob (1896–1971) American Yiddish poet, novelist and critic. He was born in Lublin and emigrated to the US in 1914. He helped to inaugurate Inzikhist, an introspective school of American Yiddish poetry. He later became one of the most important elegists of Eastern-European Jewish life. He was also a columnist for the New York Yiddish daily, and contributed to various periodicals.

Glatzer, Nahum Norbert (1903–1990) American scholar, teacher and editor. He was born in Lemberg. He became Professor of Jewish Philosophy and Ethics at the University of Frankfurt am Main in 1932. In the next year he left Germany and settled in Palestine, where he taught at Bet Sepher Reali in Haifa. From 1938 he lived in the US, and became Professor of Near Eastern and Judaic Studies at Brandeis University in 1956. He was also a director of the Leo Baeck Institute. His writings include studies of talmudic history the history of 19th-century Jewry, and the life and thought of Franz Rosenzweig.

Gleanings (Hebrew 'leket') Useful remanants of the crop left in the field after harvesting. In biblical times the gleanings were left for the poor (Leviticus 19:9–10; 23:22; Deuteronomy 24:19–21) in the corners of the field. The regulations for gleaning are found in the tractate Peah in the *Talmud.*

Glicenstein,   Enrico   (1870–1942) American sculptor, painter and printmaker. He was born in Poland, lived in Munich, settled in Italy in 1897, and finally emigrated to New York in 1928. He produced 60 plates to illustrate an edition of the Book of Samuel. A Glicenstein Museum containing his library was established in Safed, Israel.

Glick, Hirsch (1922–1944) Lithuanian Yiddish poet. He was born in Vilnius and was influenced in his writing by the Yiddish poets of the Yung Vilne group.

He edited and published four issues of the poetry review *Yungvald*. His *Lider un poems* were published posthumously in 1953. His poem *Mir zaynen do* became the battle song of the Vilnius partisan fighters in World War II.

Glick, Srul Irving (1934–2002) Canadian composer, conductor and music producer. He was born in Toronto. He taught theory and composition at the Royal Conservatory of Music in Toronto and at York University. From 1962 to 1986 he was a music producer for the Canadian Broadcasting Corporation. In 1969 he became the choir director of Beth Tickvah Synagogue in Toronto. His works include *Hashirim Asher l'Yisrael, Kedusha, Sing unto the Lord a New Song, Deborah, Music for Passover, Yiddish Suite, Suite Hebraïque, Sonate Hebraïque, Psalm for Orchestra*, and *Sonata for Orchestra 'Devequt'*.

Glickson, Mosheh (1878–1939) Palestinian author and Zionist leader of Lithuanian origin. He edited the weekly *Ha-Am* in Moscow, as well as the micellanies *Olamenu* and *Massuot* published in Odessa during World War I. In 1919 he settled in Palestine and was the chief editor of *Ha-Aretz* from 1922 to 1937. He wrote studies of Aḥad ha-Am and Maimonides.

Gloss A short explanation or interpretation of a word or phrase added to a text or manuscript. Commentators on the Bible and *Talmud* frequently explain words by giving equivalents in the vernacular language (written using Hebrew script). Such glosses are an important source for knowledge of French, Italian, German and Greek.

Glückel of Hamelin (1646–1724) German Yiddish writer. She lived mainly in Hamburg. After her husband's death, she wrote her memoirs in Yiddish. They are an important source of information about German Jewish life, court Jews, the impact of Shabbetai Tzevi and the history of Yiddish.

Glueck, Nelson (1900–1971) American archaeologist. He was born in Cincinnati. He was Director of the American School of Oriental Research at Jerusalem and at Baghdad. In 1947 he was elected President of the Hebrew Union College. His writings include *Explorations in Eastern Palestine, The Other Side of the Jordan, The River Jordan, Rivers in the Desert*, and *Deities and Dolphins: The Story of the Nabateans*.

Gnessin, Uri Nisan (1881–1913) Ukrainian Hebrew author. He was born in Starodub, but lived an unsettled life, wandering from city to city and often enduring hardship. He published poems, literary criticism, stories, translations and sketches. He was among the first Hebrew writers to explore the alienation and uprootedness of Jews in modern society.

Gniessin, Michael Fabianovich (1883–1957) Russian composer. He was born in Rostov-na-Donu. He was Professor of Composition at the Moscow Conservatory, taught composition at the Leningrad Conservatory, and later headed the composition department at the music school in Leningrad which bore his and his sister's name. He published books on composition, aesthetics and Jewish music, and a study of Rimsky-Korsakov. In addition, he pioneered the new Russian symphonic style in his music, and the use of the folk music of the peoples of the USSR. Many of his works have Jewish titles.

Gnosticism Religious movement characterised by a belief that through intuitive knowledge of spiritual truth the spiritual element of man could be released from its bondage in matter. It flourished in the Hellenistic period and later. Gnostics believed that the material world is the result of a primeval fall and was created by an intermediary fallen from the divine realm. Gnosticism contained oriental mythological elements combined with Greek philosophy. Gnostic dualism was regarded by the rabbis as a heresy and condemnation of such heretics ('minim') is contained in rabbinic sources. Gnosticism influenced later Jewish mysticism.

God Divine creator and ruler of the universe. The belief in God is the foundation of the Jewish faith and the basis of the legal system. The Bible depicts creation and God's activity in ancient Israelite history. Medieval Jewish philosophers attempted to prove the existence of God and investigated the nature of the divine attributes. Kabbalists explored the hidden depths of the Godhead, and God's activity in the world.

God, attributes of The Bible ascribes certain traits to God, such as mercy, justice and benevolence. In addition he is described as possessing human physical characteristics. Medieval Jewish philosophers debated whether these should be understood literally or figuratively. Some philosophers, such as Maimonides, decreed that only negative attributes (e.g. incorporeality) are permissible. Others, such as Ḥasdai Crescas, disagreed. In rabbinic sources God is described as omnipotent, omniscient, incorporeal and all good.

God, names of Because it was forbidden to pronounce the Tetragrammaton, substitutions and circumlocutions were adopted to refer to God. Various Hebrew terms are used in the Bible. Other names arose as a result of rabbinic, philosophical and Kabbalistic usage. Such names include El (God), El Elyon (most high), El Olam (eternal God), El Shaddai (God almighty), El Brit (God of the covenant), Elohim (God), Adonai (Lord), YHWH (God of Israel), Yahweh Zeva'aot (Lord of Hosts), Ha-Shem (the name), Shem ha-Mephorash (the ineffable one), Kedosh Yisrael (the holy one of Israel), Ha-Makom (the place), Shekinah (divine presence), Ha-Kadosh Baruch Hu (the holy one, blessed be he), Ha-Gevurah (the strength), Ha-Raḥaman

(the merciful) and Attik Yomin (Aramaic: Ancient of Days).

Gog and Magog Apocalyptic figures. They are mentioned in Ezekiel 38–39 in the vision of the end of days. Ezekiel describes the war of the Lord against Gog of the land of Magog. According to rabbinic sources the wars of Gog and Magog will precede the coming of the Messiah.

Goido, Isaac (1868–1925) American Hebrew and Yiddish author. He published a number of popular Yiddish editions in Vilnius. In 1894 he settled in New York, where he was active as a theatre critic and dramatist; among his works is a history of Yiddish drama.

Goitein [Koitein], Shelomoh Dov (b.1900) Israeli orientalist. He was born in Burgkunstadt, Germany, and emigrated to Palestine in 1923. In 1928 he became a member of the faculty of the Institute of Oriental Studies at the Hebrew University, where from 1947 he was professor. From 1957 to 1970 he was Professor of Arabic at the University of Pennsylvania. He published works on the religious institutions of Islam, the culture of the Jews of Yemen, and texts from the Cairo Genizah.

Golah ('exile') The word is used to refer to the conditions of the Jewish people in the diaspora.

Gold, Herbert (b.1924) American novelist. He was born in Cleveland. He taught at the University of California at Berkeley. His novels deal with the search for love between men and women and children and parents. A number of his novels deal with American Jewish life.

Gold, Michael (1893–1967) American communist author and journalist. He was born in New York. He worked as a copy editor on the socialist *Call* and contributed articles and poetry to *Masses*. He also worked with the left-wing New Playwrights' Theatre. His novel *Jews Without Money* is an account of Jewish immigrant life in New York.

Gold, Ze'ev (1889–1956) American rabbi and leader of religious Zionism. He was born in Poland and became rabbi in Juteka. In 1907 he emigrated to the US where he served several congregations and was in the forefront of Zionist workers. He was President of the American Mizraḥi from 1932 to 1935, when he settled in Palestine. He later became head of the country's Department for Torah Education and Culture.

Goldberg, Abraham (1883–1942) American journalist and Zionist leader. He was born in Russia and settled in New York in 1901. He was co-founder of Poale Zion in the US, and editor of its newspaper, *Freie shtimme*. He became editor of the New York Zionist journal *Dos yiddishe folk* in 1909. In 1920 he was appointed editor of the Hebrew monthly *Ha-Toren.*

Goldberg, Dov Ber (1801–1884) French scholar of Polish origin. He devoted himself to the publication of editions of Jewish manuscripts housed in European libraries. He travelled widely, visiting libraries in Europe and England, and from 1852 lived in Paris. He wrote numerous articles in Hebrew periodicals.

Goldberg, Isaac Leib (1860–1935) Lithuanian Zionist leader and philanthropist. After studying at the Kovno yeshivah, he settled in Vilnius. He was one of the first members of the Ḥibbat Zion movement, and founded the Ohavei Zion society in Vilnius. In 1908 he established a farm at Hartuv and purchased the first plot of land on Mount Scopus for the future Hebrew University. In 1919 he settled in Palestine.

Goldberg, Leah (1911–1970) Israeli Hebrew poet and critic. She was born in Königsberg and lived in Russia until after the Revolution, when she settled in Kovno, Lithuania. In 1935 she emigrated to Tel Aviv. In 1952 she was invited to organise the Department of Comparative Literature at the Hebrew University, where she became a professor. She published poetry, literary criticism, translations, children's works, a novel and a play.

Golden, Harry Lewis (1902–1981) American author, editor and publisher. He was born in New York. He was sentenced to five years' imprisonment for running a Wall Street gambling house. Later he became the editor of the *Carolina Israelite*. His publications include *Only in America, For 2 Cents Plain,* and *Enjoy.*

Goldenberg, Eliezer (1846–1916) Russian socialist. He was arrested while a student in St Petersburg, but escaped to London. Together with Aaron Samuel Liebermann he was a founder of the Society of Hebrew Socialists.

Golden Book Zionist role of honour, instituted in 1902. It is kept at the headquarters of the Jewish National Fund in Jerusalem.

Golden Calf Idol constructed by Aaron at the behest of the Israelites when Moses was absent on Mount Sinai. Moses later burnt it and ground it to dust (Exodus 32).

Golden rule Term applied to the exhortation to treat others as one would wish to be treated oneself. The injunction of Jesus in the gospels 'Do unto others as you would have them do unto you' (Matthew 7:12) is a positive formulation of a principle laid down earlier by the sage Hillel.

Goldenthal, Jacob (1815–1868) Austrian orientalist. He was born in Brody. He was principal of the Jewish school in Kishinev. Then in 1846 he settled in Vienna and taught oriental languages, rabbinics and literature at the University of Vienna. He published studies of medieval Jewish literature and philosophy, as well as the first Hebrew textbook for the study of Arabic.

Goldfaden, Abraham (1840–1908) Ukrainian Yiddish poet. He established the first modern Yiddish theatrical company in Romania in 1876. By 1880 his troupe was giving performances throughout Russia. When in 1883 the Russian government banned performances in Yiddish, Yiddish theatres were established in Paris, London and New York. In 1887 Goldfaden moved to New York, but he returned to Europe to produce and direct performances. He wrote 60 plays, many of which are in the form of operas or operettas.

Goldhar, Pinchas (1901–1947) Australian Yiddish writer. He was born in Lódź and in 1928 settled in Melbourne, where he operated a dye-shop. He edited the first Yiddish weekly in Australia. His stories describe the integration of Polish-Jewish immigrants into Australian life.

Golding, Louis (1895–1958) English novelist. He was born in Manchester. He joined an ambulance unit during World War I and served in Macedonia and France. During the 1920s he travelled widely and his novels reflect his experiences. His *Magnolia Street* is the first of a cycle of novels about Anglo-Jewish life. In *The Glory of Elsie Silver* he depicted his response to Nazism and his sympathy for Zionism. He also wrote *The Jewish Problem* and *Hitler through the Ages*.

Goldman, Emma (1869–1940) American anarchist. She was born in Kovno, Lithuania, and emigrated to the US in 1885. Her lectures and journal (*Mother Earth*) aimed to illustrate the injustice of American society. In 1919 she was deported to the USSR. She eventually fled Russia, disillusioned with the suppression of the individual. Her writings include *Anarchism and Other Essays, My Disillusionment in Russia, My Further Disillusionment in Russia* and *Living my Life*.

Goldman, Solomon (1893–1953) American Conservative rabbi. He was born in Volhynia and was taken to the US as a child. He was rabbi of the Anshe Emet Synagogue of Chicago from 1929. He was known as an orator, scholar, communal leader and Zionist. His publications include *A Rabbi Takes Stock, The Jew and the Universe, Crisis and Decision, Undefeated, The Book of Books, In the Beginning,* and *From Slavery to Freedom.*

Goldmann, Naḥum (1895–1982) American statesman and Zionist leader. He was born in Lithuania and was taken to Germany as a child. In 1925 he helped to found the Eshkol publishing house in order to produce the *Encyclopaedia Judaica*. Together with Stephen Samuel Wise, he organised the World Jewish Congress in 1936. He became chairman of its executive board and later its president. He was also President of the Zionist Organisation. He played an important role in negotiating the reparations agreement with Germany after World War II. In 1962 he left the US and became an Israeli citizen.

Goldschmidt, Lazarus (1871–1950) German orientalist and bibliophile. He was born in Lithuania and lived in Berlin, later emigrating to London. His early studies dealt with the Ethiopian language and literature. He published an edition of the Sepher Yetzirah, a Hebrew translation of the Koran, and a translation of the Babylonian *Talmud* into German.

Goldschmidt, Meir Aaron (1819–1887) Danish novelist and journalist. He was born in Vordingborg, Zealand, and settled in Copenhagen, where he founded *Corsaren*, a satirical weekly. From 1847 to 1859 he published the periodical *Nord og syd*. He wrote novels and plays dealing with Jewish subjects.

Goldsmid, Albert Edward Williamson (1846–1904) English communal leader, nephew of Isaac Goldsmid. A soldier by profession, he adopted Judaism later in life. He was a leading member of the Ḥovevei Zion and administered the Jewish colonies in Argentina in 1892–94. He may have been the model for the protagonist in George Eliot's *Daniel Deronda*.

Goldsmid, Sir Isaac Lyon (1778–1859) English communal leader. In his business life he financed railway construction. Prominent in the struggle for Jewish Emancipation in England, he was one of the founders of University College, London. He also played a role in the establishment of the Reform synagogue. He was made a baronet in 1841 and in 1846 he was created Baron de Palmeira by the King of Portugal.

Goldstein, Israel (1896–1986) American conservative rabbi and Zionist leader. He was born in Philadelphia and served as a rabbi of Congregation B'nai Jeshurun in New York. He was President of the Jewish National Fund of America and the Zionist Organisation of America. He also served as a member and officer of various Jewish, interfaith and public organisations. In 1961 he settled in Israel, where he was World Chairman of the Keren ha-Yesod-United Israel Appeal. He wrote a history of his congregation in New York and also published collections of sermons and essays.

Goldziher, Ignaz (1850–1921) Hungarian scholar. He was born in Székesfehérvár. He became lecturer at the University of Budapest in 1872. He served as secretary of the Budapest Neolog Jewish community for 30 years, becoming Professor of Religious Philosophy at the Budapest Rabbinical Seminary in 1900. Four years later he was appointed professor at the university. He published studies of pre-Islamic and Islamic culture, the religious and legal history of the Arabs, and their ancient and modern poetry.

Golem An artificially created being, usually human, brought to life through a magical act or the use of holy names. The concept is connected with the

magical exegesis of the Sepher Yetzirah an the idea of the creative power of Hebrew letters. The *Talmud* records stories of the creation of a golem, and they are also found in Jewish literature from the 12th century. German Ḥasidim of the 12th–13th centuries viewed the creation of a golem as a symbolic ecstatic experience following a solemn ceremony. From the 15th century a golem was regarded as a real creature able to perform specific tasks.

Golgotha (from Hebrew: 'a place of a skull') Place outside Jerusalem, north-west of the city walls, where Jesus was crucified (Matthew 27:33).

Goliath Philistine giant from the city of Gath, who was killed by David in combat (I Samuel 17). Another tradition relates that he was slain by Elhanan the Bethlehemite (II Samuel 21:19).

Goll, Iwan (1891–1950) Franco-German poet and author. He was born in Saint-Dié, Vosges. He was initially active in German expressionist circles, but during World War I he moved to Switzerland. Later he settled in Paris, where he established the magazine *Surréalisme*. After living for a period in the US, he returned to Paris in 1947. Jewish themes frequently appear in his poetry.

Gollancz, Sir Hermann (1852–1930) British rabbi and teacher, brother of Israel Gollancz. He was born in Bremen and settled in London. He officiated at the Bayswater Synagogue (1892–1923) and taught Hebrew at University College, London (1902–24). He published critical editions and translations of Hebrew, Aramaic and Syriac texts. He was the first British rabbi to receive a knighthood.

Gollancz, Sir Israel (1864–1930) English literary scholar, brother of Hermann Gollancz. He was a lecturer in English at University College, London and then at Cambridge University. In 1903 he became Professor of English at

King's College, London. He published studies of Shakespeare and early English literature and philology. He served on the council of Jews College for several years.

Gollancz, Sir Victor (1893–1967) English publisher and writer. He founded his own publishing house in 1928 and later helped to establish the Left Book Club, whose aim was to expose Nazism. During World War II he campaigned for the National Committee for Rescue from Nazi Terror. From 1945 he endeavoured to secure the admission of Jewish refugees to Palestine. His writings include *The Brown Book of the Hitler Terror, My Dear Timothy, More for Timothy,* and *The Case for Adolf Eichmann.*

Golomb, Eliyahu (1893–1945) Palestinian Zionist. He was born in Belorussia and settled in Palestine in 1909. At the outbreak of World War I he helped to form an independent Jewish defence force. From 1921 he was a member of the Haganah Committee of the Histadrut and the following year he was sent abroad to purchase arms. Beginning in 1931, he attempted to establish a broad popular basis for the Haganah. He was one of the founders of the Palmaḥ.

Golus (Yiddish) Diaspora The word has connotations of restricted freedom and oppression.

Good According to the Bible, goodness is defined in terms of what is pleasing to God, one of whose attributes is absolute goodness. Human beings are granted free will to choose to do good or evil. Rabbinic psychology sees each person as driven by both good and evil inclinations ('yetzer ha-tov,' and 'yetzer ha-ra').

Goodman, Benny (1909–86) American musician. Born in Chicago, he studied at the Lewis Institute in Chicago. In 1933 he formed his own band. He played a blend of jazz and contemporary popular music. His band featured in various movies.

Goodman, Percival (1904–1989) American architect. He was born in New York and became Professor of Architecture at Columbia University. He designed numerous synagogues in the US.

Goor, Yehudah (1862–1950) Israeli educator and lexicographer. He was born in Belorussia and emigrated to Palestine in 1887. He was a co-founder of the first Hebrew Teachers' Association in Palestine, and was one of the pioneers of the Ivrit be-Ivrit method of teaching Hebrew. He wrote manuals on the study of Hebrew, Jewish history, natural sciences and the geography of Palestine, and translated classical literature into Hebrew. He also published several dictionaries, including the *Dictionary of the Hebrew Language.*

Gordin, Jacob (1853–1909) American Yiddish playwright and journalist. He was born in Ukraine. He taught at a russified Jewish school in Yelizavetgradka, and in 1880 he founded the Spiritual Biblical Brotherhood. In 1891 he emigrated to the US, where he worked as a Yiddish journalist and wrote more than 100 Yiddish plays.

Gordis, Robert (1908–1992) American rabbi and biblical scholar. He was born in New York. He served as rabbi of Temple Beth El in Rockaway Park, New York, from 1831 until his retirement in 1968. From 1940 he was a professor of Bible at the Jewish Theological Seminary. He served as editor of the journal *Judaism* and President of the Rabbinical Assembly and Synagogue Council of America. He published studies of wisdom, biblical poetry and the masorah.

Gordon, Aaron David (1856–1922) Palestinian Hebrew writer. He was born in Troyanov, Russia. He held a post in the financial management of Baron Horace Günzburg's estate for 23 years. In 1904 he emigrated to Palestine, where he worked as an agricultural labourer. In his writings he emphasised that self-realisation can be attained only through settlement on the land.

Gordon, David (1831–1886) Hebrew journalist and editor. He was born in Podmerecz and settled in Sergei, where he worked as a teacher. In the mid-1850s he emigrated to England, where he taught Hebrew and German. In 1858 he moved to Lyck, where he was assistant editor and later editor of the Hebrew weekly *Ha-Maggid*. He became one of the leading members of Ḥibbat Zion in the 1880s. He published several books and contributed to Hebrew and Yiddish journals.

Gordon, Lord George (1751–1793) English convert to Judaism. He was President of the United Protestant League and was implicated in the serious anti-Catholic riots of 1780; as a result he was tried for high treason but was acquitted. In 1787 he was circumcised and assumed the name Israel ben Abraham. He was later tried for libel and was imprisoned in Newgate, London, where he surrounded himself with foreign Jews.

Gordon, Judah Löb (1831–1892) Lithuanian Hebrew poet, writer, critic and allegorist. He was born in Vilnius, and taught in various government schools in the Kovno province. Later he became critical of Jewish religious life. In 1872 he went to St Petersburg as secretary to the Jewish community and Director of the Society for the Promotion of Culture among the Jews in Russia. Although his early poetry was romantic in character, his later work was full of disillusionment and despair. He is regarded as the creator of Hebrew realist poetry.

Gordon, Michel (1823–1890) Lithuanian Hebrew and Yiddish poet. He was born in Vilnius. He was influenced by the Haskalah circle of Abraham Dov Lebensohn. He wrote Hebrew books and articles as well as Yiddish songs. His later poetry is pessimistic in character.

Gordon, Samuel Löb (1863–1933) Palestinian writer and biblical scholar. He was born in Lithuania and emigrated to Palestine in 1898, where he taught at the boys' school in Jaffa. In 1901 he settled in Warsaw and established a Hebrew school for boys. In 1924 he returned to Palestine. He composed a commentary on the Bible, contributed poems, articles and translations to Hebrew periodicals, and wrote for children.

Goren, Shelomo (1917–94) Israeli rabbi of Polish origin. After settling in Palestine he joined the Haganah and fought in the War of Independence. He became Chief Chaplain of Haganah and was later responsible for the organisation of the military chaplaincy and regulations for religious observance in the army. In 1961 he received the Israel Prize for the first volume of his comprehensive commentary on the Jerusalem *Talmud*. He was elected Ashkenazi Chief Rabbi of Tel Aviv-Jaffa in 1968 and of Israel in 1972.

Gottheil, Richard James Horatio (1862–1936) American orientalist, son of Gustav Gottheil. He was born in Manchester, England, and was taken to New York in 1873. From 1886 he taught Semitic languages at Columbia University. He also served as Director of the Oriental Department of the New York Public Library from 1896. He was an active Zionist, and served as President of the American Federation of Zionists from 1898 to 1904. He published studies of Zionism and of Semitic languages.

Gottlieb, Adolf (1903–1974) American painter. He lived in New York and Tucson, Arizona, and created works of art for various synagogues.

Gottlieb, Jack (1930–2011) American composer and conductor. He taught at Loyola University and the Institute of Judaic Arts at Warwick, New York. He was appointed Music Director of the Congregation Temple Israel in St. Louis in 1970, then in 1973 became

Composer-in-Residence at the Hebrew Union College in New York. His compositions include *Love Songs for Sabbath, New Year's Service for Young People,* and *Verses from Psalm 118.*

Gottlober, Abraham bär (1810–1899) Hebrew and Yiddish writer and poet. He was born in Starokonstantinov and was taken to Tarnopol, Galicia, at the age of 17. Influenced by the Haskalah, he developed a hostility toward orthodoxy and Ḥasidism. During a period when he was living in Podolia, he wrote in Yiddish and Hebrew. From 1830 to 1850 he lived in Bessarabia, Berdichev and Kremenetz. Later he became an instructor in Talmud at the rabbinical seminary in Zhitomir. He published poems, dramas, stories, memoirs, translations and studies of the history of the Karaites, kabbalah and Ḥasidism.

Gottschalk, Alfred (1930–2009) American communal leader. He was born in Oberwessel, Germany. He served as President of the Hebrew Union College-Jewish Institute of Religion and professor of Bible and Jewish thought. He published works dealing with Aḥad ha-Am.

Gottschalk, Max (1889–1976) Belgian social scientist. He was born in Liège. He joined the Institute of Sociology of the Free University of Brussels as research professor in 1923. During World War II he taught at the New School for Social Research in New York but when the war was over he returned to the institute in Brussels. He served as President of the International Association of Social Progress and of the Brussels National Centre of Jewish studies.

Goudchaux, Michel (1797–1862) French banker and politician. He was born in Nancy. He worked as a banker and founded a working-class newspaper, *Le National.* After the revolution of 1848 he was mayor of his district of Paris, member of the general council of the department of the Seine, and pay-master general in Strasbourg. He later became Minister of Finance in the Second Republic, and was Vice-President of the National Assembly in 1849.

Goudsmit, Samuel (1884–1954) Dutch author. He was born in Kampen, at the mouth of the river Ijssel. His publications include *Dievenschool, In de grote leerschool, Jankefs jongste, Jankefs oude sleutel, Simcha, de knaap uit Worms,* and *De gouden kroon van Beiren.*

Government, Prayer for The duty to pray for the welfare of the civil authorities was first stated in the Book of Jeremiah (Jeremiah 29:7). The idea was reinforced in the Mishnah. In the synagogue prayers for the government became a regular feature from the 14th century. The prayer now used has a fixed form and is usually recited on the Sabbath after the reading of the law.

Goy (Yiddish) Non-Jew. Originally it was used to characterise a whole nation. Later it came to be applied to any individual who is not a Jew.

Grace after Meals (Hebrew 'Birkat ha-Mazon') Prayer consisting of four benedictions, recited after a meal where bread is eaten. If bread is not eaten, a shorter form of grace is recited. The benedictions praise God for providing food, express gratitude for his blessings, ask him for mercy and support, and thank him for his goodness.

Grace before Meals Prayer consisting of one or more benedictions recited before a meal or before the separate courses of a meal. The rabbis instituted separate blessings for various species of food. The blessing for bread ('Who brings forth bread from the earth') is based on Psalm 104:14, when recited at the beginning of the meal. It exempts one from the obligation to recite additional blessings for other courses.

Grade, Ḥayyim (1910–1982) Lithuanian Yiddish poet and novelist. He was born in Vilnius and became leader of the Yung Vilne literary movement. During World War II he lived in Soviet Russia, later settling in Poland. He subsequently moved to Paris, where he was active in revivifying Yiddish cultural life. Eventually he emigrated to New York, where he was associated with the Yiddish daily *Jewish Morning Journal*. His poetry reflects Jewish life in Eastern Europe.

Graetz, Heinrich (1817–1891) German historian and biblical scholar. He was born in Xions, in the district of Posen. He lectured in Jewish history and the Bible at the Jewish Theological Seminary in Breslau. In 1869 he was made an honorary professor at the university there. His multi-volume *History of the Jews* influenced subsequent Jewish historians.

Grammarians The study of Hebrew grammar was fostered by the Masoretes. The development of Arabic philology in the 8th and 9th centuries served as a model for Hebrew scholars such as Saadyah ben Joseph in Babylonia, and Menaḥem ben Saruk and Dunash ben Labrat in Spain. Other medieval scholars, such as Judah ben David Ḥayyuj of Fez, Jonah ibn Janaḥ of Córdoba, Abraham ibn Ezra and David Kimḥi, made further contributions to the study of Hebrew grammar. The scientific study of Hebrew began in the first half of the 19th century with Wilhelm Gesenius' *Elementarbuch*.

Granott, Avraham (1890–1962) Israeli economist of Bessarabian origin. He became secretary of the Jewish National Fund in 1919. After settling in Jerusalem in 1922 he became the fund's managing director and later chairman of its board of directors and president. He was elected to the Knesset in 1949 and served as chairman of its finance committee. He published studies of agrarian reform.

Gratz, Rebecca (1781–1869) American philanthropist. She is reputed to have been the model for Rebecca in Walter Scott's novel *Ivanhoe*. She lived in Philadelphia, where she aided in founding the Female Hebrew Benevolent Society, the Hebrew Sunday School Society, and the Philadelphia Jewish Foster Home and Orphan Asylum.

Grayzel, Solomon (1896–1980) American historian and editor. He was born in Minsk, Belorussia. He taught Jewish history at Gratz College from 1929. In 1939 he became editor-in-chief of the Jewish Publication Society of America. From 1966 he taught Jewish history at Dropsie College. He published studies of the relationship of Christians and Jews during the Middle Ages.

Great Assembly (Hebrew 'Keneset Gedolah') Religious body active at the beginning of the Second Temple period. It embodied Jewish leadership and served as the supreme authority in religious matters. According to tradition, it was composed of 120 prominent Jewish scholars. It has been identified with the great assembly of the people in the Temple court presided over by Ezra which accepted the authority of the Torah (Nehemiah 8–9).

Green, Gerald (1922–2006) American novelist. He was born in Brooklyn. His publications include *To Brooklyn with Love, An American Prophet, The Legion of Noble Christians,* and *Holocaust.*

Greenberg, Ḥayyim (1889–1953) American Zionist leader, essayist and editor. He was born in Todoristi in Russia. He edited the Russian Jewish weekly *The Dawn*, before moving in 1921 to Berlin, where he edited *Haolam*, the official weekly of the World Zionist Organisation. He had settled in the US by 1924, when he became editor of the Yiddish Zionist publication *Farn folk*. In 1934 he was appointed editor of the labour Zionist monthly the *Jewish Frontier*. During World War II he served as head of the American Zionist Emergency Council and after the war he was director of the Department of Education and Culture of the Jewish Agency in America. He published studies espousing Zionism.

Greenberg, Joanne (b.1932) Amercian novelist. She was born in Brooklyn. She served as adjunct professor at the Colorado School of Mines. Her novels include *The King's Persons, I Never Promised you a Rose Garden, The Monday Voices, In this Sign, Founders Praise,* and *A Sense of Delight.*

Greenberg, Leopold Jacob (1861–1931) English editor and Zionist. He was born in Birmingham. He served as Theodor Herzl's representative in his dealings with the British Government. In 1907 he and a group of his friends acquired the *Jewish Chronicle*, and he was appointed its editor-in-chief. He was a founder of a number of publications, including *The Jewish Year Book.*

Greenberg, Uri Tzevi (1894–1981) Israeli poet. He was born in Galicia and was taken as a child to Lemberg. After World War I he became a leader of a group of Yiddish expressionist poets. In 1924 he emigrated to Palestine, where he became a spokesman for the Revisionist movement. His *Book of Indictment and Faith* is an attack on the Jewish Agency's policy of self-restraint, and a defence of his conception of fighting Jewish youth. He supported underground movements that struggled against the British. He was a Ḥerut member in the first Knesset (1949–51). After World War II he published poems about the destruction of European Jewry.

Greenstone, Julius Hillel (1873–1955) American educator and author. He was born in Lithuania and emigrated to the US in 1894. In 1905 he joined the faculty of Gratz College, where he taught Jewish education and religion, and from 1933 to 1948 he was principal of the college. His writings include *The Jewish Religion* and *The Messiah Idea in Jewish History.* For 20 years he contributed a popular column to the Philadelphia weekly *Jewish Exponent.*

Greetings The general greeting 'Shalom aleikhem' (Peace be with you) is answered by 'Aleikhem shalom' (With you be peace). The word 'Shalom' is also frequently used alone. On the Sabbath the expression 'Shabbat shalom' (A Sabbath of peace) is used. On festivals the common greeting is 'Gut yomtov' (Good festival) or its equivalents 'Ḥag sameaḥ' or 'Moadim le-simḥah'. The greeting for the New Year is 'Le shanah tovah tikkatevu' (May you be inscribed for a good year). On the ninth of Av and in a house of mourning greetings are discouraged. On the completion of a religious duty, the Ashkenazim say 'Yishar koaḥ' (May your strength increase), while the Sephardim say 'ḥazak barukh' (Be strong, blessed).

Gregger Small rattle, with a toothed wheel that rotates against a wooden tongue. It is sounded in the synagogue on Purim when the name of Haman is mentioned during the reading of the Scroll of Esther.

Greidiker, Ephraim (fl. 18th cent.) Polish jester. Influenced by German and Italian motifs, his jokes resembled those of the German folk hero Till Eulenspiegel.

Greiner, Leo (1876–1928) Austrian author. He wrote poems and plays, edited literary journals and compiled anthologies.

Grinshpan, Yosl (1902–1934) Canadian Yiddish poet. He is known for two works, *Tsvishn vent* and *Lider un poemes.*

Grodzinoski, Hayyim Ozer (1863–1940) Lithuanian talmudic scholar. In 1887 he was appointed one of the dayyanim of the bet din of Vilnius. He was one of the initiators of the Vilnius Conference of 1909, which resulted in the formation of the Orthodox Keneset Israel organisation. He was also a sponsor of the conference of rabbis at Grodno in 1924, which founded the Council of the Yeshivot. He was an opponent of Zionism and secular education for Jews. His responsa were published in three volumes.

Gronemann, Sammy (1875–1952) German author and Zionist leader. he was born in Strasburg, West Prussia. He settled in Tel Aviv in 1936. An active Zionist, he was a member of the Zionist Action Committee in Germany and president of the Zionist Congress court. His novels depict the Eastern-European Jewish milieu; he also wrote comedies, which were adapted for the Hebrew stage.

Gross, Charles (1857–1909) American historian. He was born in Troy, New York. He became Professor of History at Harvard University. He published studies on medieval English administrative and economic history, and on the Exchequer of the Jews in England in the Middle Ages.

Gross, Haim (1904–1991) American sculptor and graphic artist. He was born in Galicia, studied in Budapest, and went to Vienna in 1920. In 1921 he emigrated to the US. His work is dominated by Judaic and biblical themes.

Gross, Heinrich (1835–1910) Bavarian rabbi and scholar. He was born in Szenicze, Hungary. He served as a rabbi in Gross-Strelitz, then from 1870 in Augsburg, Bavaria. He wrote studies of the lives of French rabbis and their communities in the Middle Ages. His *Gallia Judaica* is a geographical dictionary of France according to rabbinic sources.

Gorssman, David (b.1954) Israeli novelist. He was born in Jerusalem and worked as an editor and broadcaster on Israeli radio. His publications include *The Smile of a Lamb, See Under Love,* and *The Yellow Wind.*

Grossman, Elias Mandel (1898–1947) American artist. He was born in Poland and emigrated to the US in 1911. His works are based on Jewish life.

Grossman, Meir (1888–1964) Israeli Zionist leader. He was born in Russia. He lived in Copenhagen during World War I, where he began the publication of a Yiddish daily. At the suggestion of Vladimir Jabotinsky he published a periodical *Di Tribune,* which promoted the cause of a Jewish legion. After the Russian Revolution, he helped to establish the Jewish Correspondence Bureau. In 1934 he settled in Palestine. Initially a leader of the Revisionist and Jewish State parties, he joined the General Zionists in 1953. From 1948 to 1961 he was a member of the executive of the Jewish Agency.

Grossman, Vasily Semyonovich (1905–1964) Russian writer. He was born in Berdichev and moved to Moscow as a young man. He later worked as a chemical engineer in the coal mines of Donbas. His trilogy *Stepan Kolchugin* includes Jewish themes. His *Cartea neagră* provides documentary evidence of Nazi crimes against Jews in Soviet territory.

Grotius, Hugo (1583–1645) Netherlands statesman, jurist, theologian and historian. His report *Remonstrantie* described the conditions under which Jews could be allowed in the United Provinces. In his scholarly writings, he quoted from Josephus, Philo, medieval Jewish commentators, the Targum, *Talmud* and midrash. He was on friendly terms with Manasseh ben Israel.

Grumberg, Jean-Claude (b.1939) French dramatist. He was born in Paris and first worked in a tailor's shop. His plays include *Dreyfus*.

Grünbaum, Max (1817–1898)   German folklorist and philologist. He was born in Seligenstadt. He became Director of the Hebrew Orphan Asylum in New York in 1858, but in 1870 he returned to Europe and settled in Munich where he engaged in research about Jewish folklore. He wrote studies of Jewish folklore and the structure and evolution of the Yiddish language, as well as chrestomathy of Judeo-Spanish. He is regarded as one of the founders of Yiddish philology.

Grünbaum, Yitzhak (1879–1970)   Israeli Zionist leader and author of Polish origin. He was born in Warsaw, where he later edited several newspapers. During World War I he lived in St Petersburg, but he returned to Warsaw, where he became the leader of Polish Zionism. In 1919 he was elected to the Sejm. In 1933 he became a member of the executive of the Jewish Agency and settled in Palestine. As a representative of the General Zionist Party, he was minister of the interior in 1948–49. He published studies on Polish and Zionist history.

Grunwald, Max (1871–1953)   Israeli rabbi and folklorist of German origin. He was born in Hindenburg. He served as a rabbi in Hamburg and Vienna. In 1938 he settled in Jerusalem. He wrote studies of the communities he served and of Jewish folklore.

Grynszpan, Herschel (1921–?)   German Jewish activist. He was born in Hanover and moved to Paris in 1938. He killed Ernst von Rath, a German embassy official in Paris, in order to arouse public opinion in the West about Nazi persecution. This event served as a pretext for the pogroms of 9–10 November, 1938 (Kristallnacht) against Jews.

Güdemann, Moritz (1835–1918)   Austrian rabbi and historian. He was born in Hidesheim, Prussia. He served as rabbi in Magdeburg (from 1862) and Vienna. In 1869 he became head of the Vienna bet din, and subsequently Chief Rabbi. He wrote a study of trends and institutions in medieval Jewish life from the viewpoint of the non-Jewish environment. He was a leader of the opposition to Theodor Herzl's Zionism.

Guggenheim, Meyer (1828–1905)   American industrialist. When his father emigrated from Lengnau, Switzerland, to the US, he worked with him as a travelling salesman. Meyer became a manufacturer of polish, a shop owner and a spice merchant, as well as an importer of fine lace and embroidery. In 1877 he created the firm of M. Guggeheim's Sons in Philadelphia. Later he established the Guggenheim Exploration Company. In 1901 the Guggenheims bought the American Smelting and Refining Company.

Guggenheim, Peggy (1898–1979)   American art patron. The daughter of Meyer Guggenheim's son Benjamin, she had an important influence on modern art in Europe and the US. During the 1920s and 1930s she lived in Europe and opened the Guggenheim Jeune Gallery in London. When the Nazis invaded France, she shipped her collection to New York. Later she returned to Europe.

Guilds   Associations of artisans. Guilds are mentioned in the Bible and were established by the beginning of the Second Temple period (Nehemiah 3:8, 31–32). In the Mishnaic period (2nd and 3rd centuries) guilds existed throughout the Jewish world, but Jews were excluded from Christian guilds in European cities in the Middle Ages. In Eastern Europe a body of Jewish guilds developed from the 17th century.

Guilt offering   Sacrifice to atone for sin. Biblical ordinances concerning guilt offerings (Leviticus 5:14ff; 7:1–7) usually decree that a ram be sacrificed.

Gumplowicz, Ludwig (1838–1909)
Austrian sociologist. He was born in Kraków. He taught at the University of Graz from 1862. He converted to Christianity, but maintained an interest in Jewish affairs. He exercised an important influence on the development of sociology as a science.

Günzburg, Baron David (1857–1910)
Russian scholar and orientalist, son of Horace Günzburg. He was born in Kamenets-Podolskiy. He published studies on oriental subjects and linguistics and medieval Arabic poetry. He was active in the St Petersburg Jewish community and the Society for the Promotion of Culture among the Jews in Russia. In 1908 he established the Jewish Academy, where he taught rabbinics and Arabic literature.

Günzburg, Baron Horace (1833–1909)
Russian communal leader, son of Joseph Yosel Günzburg. He was born in Zvenigorodka in the province of Kiev, and became active as a banker in St Petersburg. During the blood libel case in Kutais in 1878 he encouraged Daniel Chwolson to write a book about the history of blood libel. In 1881–82 he attempted to establish an organisation of Russian Jews. Later he headed the Jewish community in St Petersburg and the Society for the Promotion of Culture Among the Jews in Russia.

Günzburg, Baron Joseph Yozel (1812–1878)
Russian banker and communal leader. He was born in Vitebsk and settled in Paris in 1857. In 1859 he founded the Joseph Yozel Günzburg Bank in St Petersburg. He was active in attempts to improve the situation of Russian Jewry. As a founder of the Society for the Promotion of Culture Among the Jews in Russia, he provided scholarships for Jewish youth to encourage higher education.

Günzburg, Mordecai Aaron (1795–1846)
Lithuanian Hebrew author and educationalist. He was born in Salantai and settled in Vilnius in 1835. Together with Solomon Salkind, in 1841 he founded the first modern Jewish school in Lithuania, where he served as headmaster. As a spokesman for the Vilnius Haskalah, he published studies of French and Russian history, translations and an autobiography (*Aviezer*).

Günzburg, Pesaḥ (1894–1947)
Palestinian writer and journalist. He was born in Volhynia and lived in the US (1912–14), Scandinavia (1914–17) and London (1917–22), before settling in Palestine. He published poems and stories, as well as translations from English and the Scandinavian languages into Hebrew.

Günzburg, Shimon (1890–1944)
Palestinian poet and critic. He was born in Volhynia and lived in the US from 1912 and in Palestine from 1933. He wrote poetry and edited the plays and letters of Moses Ḥayyim Luzzatto.

Gunzenhauser
The name of two German printers, Joseph ben Jacob Gunzenhauser (d.1490) and his son Azriel ben Joseph Gunzenhauser (fl. 15th cent.), active in Naples. They moved to Naples from Gunzenhausen in south Germany and set up a Hebrew press. From 1487 to 1492 they produced various books, including a Hagiographa with rabbinical commentaries, Avicenna's medical *Canon*, and Abraham ibn Ezra's commentary on the Pentateuch.

Günzig, Azriel (1868–1931)
Polish rabbi and scholar. He was born in Kraków and served as a rabbi in Czechoslovakia and Antwerp. He edited and published the literary journal *Ha-Eshkol* from 1899 to 1913. He wrote about the history of the Haskalah in Galicia.

Guri, Ḥayyim (b.1923)
Israeli poet, novelist and journalist. He was born in Tel Aviv and spent his early years in the Palmaḥ. In 1947 he went to Europe as an aliyah official. His writings include volumes of poetry and novels, dealing

with Holocaust survivors and memories of his Tel Aviv childhood. He has also made a documentary film about the Holocaust.

Gush Emunim (Hebrew 'The bloc of the faithful') Israeli spiritual and political movement. Founded in 1974, it aims to implement its conviction that the creation of a Jewish state constitutes the beginning of redemption. It actively supports the settlement of areas taken over in the Six-Day War.

Guston, Philip (1913–1980) American painter. His work was mainly abstract and was strongly affected by the horrors of the Holocaust.

Gutmacher, Elijah (1796–1874) Polish Zionist. He was born in Borek. He served as a rabbi in Pleschenitsy and Grodzisk Wielkopolski. His studies of the kabbalah led him to the view that the Jewish return to Palestine was necessary to purify Jewry from the pollution of exile. He took part in the Thron conference in 1860, which discussed the problems of Palestinian colonisation, and worked with Tzevi Hirsch Kalischer to encourage Jewish settlement in Palestine. He was the author of various rabbinic studies.

Gutman, Naḥum (1898–1980) Israeli artist. He was born in Romania and was taken to Palestine at the age of seven. He designed scenery for the Ohel theatre in 1935, and created a mosaic for the chief rabbinate building in Tel Aviv in 1961. He also wrote children's stories.

Guttman, Jacob (1845–1919) German rabbi and historian. He was born in Beuthen Silesia. He served as rabbi in Hildesheim from 1874 to 1892 and in Breslau from 1892. From 1910 he was President of the German Rabbinical Assembly. He published studies of medieval Jewish philosophers and the relation between Christian scholasticism and medieval Jewish philosophy.

Guttman, Julius (1880–1950) Israeli philosopher and historian of German origin. He lectured in philosophy at the University of Breslau (from 1910) and in Jewish philosophy at the Hochschule für die Wissenschaft des Judentums in Berlin (from 1919). In 1934 he settled in Jerusalem, where he became Professor of Jewish Philosophy at the Hebrew University. He published sociological studies of Jewry, philosophical investigations and explorations of the history of Jewish philosophy.

Guttmann, Michael (1872–1942) Hungarian talmudic scholar. He lectured on Jewish law at the Budapest Rabbinical Seminary from 1907 to 1921. He was then rabbi and Professor of Talmud and halakhah at the Breslau Jewish theological seminary (1921–33), of which he became head in 1933. He published studies of rabbinic literature and began work on a talmudic encyclopedia.

H

Melvin loved to brag and out-do his friends. Now it was time for his son Solomon's bar mitzvah. After studying a number of brochures, he decided to arrange an African safari. He hired a special flight to Africa. Then he chose a guide and his bearers. He phoned the guide and explained that he wanted the guests to see lions and tigers. The rabbi, he explained, would need a clearing for the service.

'Ok,' the guide said. 'No problem.'

Over 200 guests accepted the invitation and they were flown to Nairobi. On arrival the guide was waiting for them together with 20 elephants. They went to a luxurious hotel: the next day the guide arrived with enough elephants for the guests and they set off to the site for the bar mitzvah. But then, just five hours into the journey, the column of elephants came to a halt. The guide shouted: 'There will now be a delay of two hours.'

Melvin was furious. 'Why the delay?' he asked the guide.

'There's nothing I can do,' he said. 'There's another two bar mitzvah safaris ahead of us.'

* * * * *

Jewish jokes frequently satirise ostentation. Here the father wants to demonstrate how rich he is to his friends. He arranges an African safari to celebrate his son's bar mitzvah. He flies guests to Nairobi. They stay at a lavish hotel. Then elephants transport them to the place reserved for the ceremony. Yet, they are held up by two other bar mitzvah parties going to the same place. The joke shows up the ridiculous pretentiousness of Jews seeking to outdo one another.

Haan, Jacob Israel de (1881–1924)
Dutch poet and Orthodox leader. Born in Smilde, he initially rejected his Jewish background, but later reverted to an Orthodox lifestyle. In 1919 he left Holland for Palestine, abandoning his non-Jewish wife. He became a member of the Orthodox Agudat-Israel party and wrote articles for the Dutch and British Press. He was later murdered by opponents.

Ḥabad Ḥasidic movement. The name is based on the initials of the words 'hokhmah (wisdom), 'binah' (understanding), 'daat' (knowledge). Ḥabad was founded in the late 18th century by Shneour Zalman of Lyady, who was opposed by the Ḥasidic leaders of Volhynia and the mitnaggedim led by the Vilna Gaon. His teaching is contained in the *Tanya* in which he developed a theosophical doctrine based on the kabbalah of Isaac Luria. Originally the movement was centred in Belorussia, but after World War I it spread to other regions.

Habakkuk   Biblical book, one of the books of the 12 Minor Prophets. It records the prophecies of Habakkuk, who was active in the 7th century BCE. It consists of three chapters containing a protest against injustice in the world, a complaint about the victory of the Chaldeans, God's reply, a prayer, and a description of the Day of the Lord.

Habermann, Avraham Meir (1901–1980)   Israeli bibliographer and scholar of medieval Hebrew literature. He was born in Galicia. After serving as librarian at the Schocken library in Berlin, he emigrated to Palestine in 1934, where he was Director of the Schocken library in Jerusalem until 1967. From 1957 he taught medieval literature at Tel Aviv University and at the Graduate Library School of the Hebrew University. He wrote studies of Jewish bibliography, the history of Hebrew poetry, and medieval Hebrew poetry.

Habiru   Ancient poeople living in the Fertile Crescent in the second millennium BCE. The name appears in the Tel el Amarna tablets and other documents. Some scholars identify this group with the ancient Hebrews.

Ha-Cohen, Mordecai ben Hillel (1856–1936)   Hebrew author of Russian origin. He was born in Belorussia. He began publishing articles in Hebrew periodicals when he was 18. In 1875 he moved to St Petersburg, where he wrote a comprehensive survey of Jewish agriculturalists in modern Russia. In 1881 he joined the Ḥibbat Zion movement, and he later formed two societies for promoting settlement in Palestine He moved to Palestine himself in 1907 and was one of the founders of Tel Aviv. He played an active role in the economic and cultural life of the yishuv.

Ḥadash   In Jewish law, a term used to describe the new grain ripening in spring. It could not be eaten until a sheaf of the first fruits from the new harvest was offered by the priests in the Temple on the second day of Passover.

Hadassah [Women's Zionist Organisation of America]   It was founded in 1912 by Henrietta Szold to raise the standard of health in Palestine, to encourage Jewish life in the US, and to foster the Jewish ideal. In Israel it sponsors medical training, research, care and special education Its members in the US participate in fund-raising and Jewish educational activities.

Hadassi, Judah ben Elijah (fl. 12th cent.)   Turkish Karaite scholar. He lived in Constantinople. He wrote *Eshkol ha-Kopher*, an encyclopedic survey of Karaite belief and knowledge. It explains the mitzvot and the halakhot, and the reasons for their observance in accordance with specific commandments.

Ḥad Gadya ('An only kid')   Aramaic song chanted at the end of the Passover seder. It was adapted from a German folk song, itself based on a French nursery rhyme. It was included in the service so that children would not fall asleep before the end of the seder. The verse is as follows:

> *A father bought a kid for two zuzim.*
> *A cat came and ate the kid.*
> *A dog bit the cat.*
> *The dog was beaten by a stick.*
> *The stick was burned by fire.*
> *Water quenched the fire.*
> *An ox drank the water.*
> *A shoḥet slaughtered the ox.*
> *The shoḥet was killed by the Angel of Death, who was punished by God.*

Haganah   Underground military organisation of the yishuv in Palestine It succeeded Ha-Shomer in 1920 and operated until 1948, when its members transferred to the Israeli army, Tzeva Haganah le-Israel. In 1931 the movement split and a minority formed the Irgun Tzevai Leumi. The Haganah carried out underground training within individual settlements, organised illegal immigration and manufactured equipment. In 1941 military commando units (the Palmaḥ) were established. After World War II, Haganah's operations were directed agaisnt the British in order to secure the removal of the anti-Zionist White Paper of 1939. From 1947 it concentrated on defence against Arab attack.

Hagar (fl.? 19th–16th cent. BCE) Egyptian woman, maidservant of Sarah and mother of Ishmael. Since Sarah was barren, Hagar become Abraham's wife. When Hagar discovered she was pregnant, she fled to the desert to escape Sarah's anger, but she later returned. After Sarah had a son, Abraham banished Hagar, but she and her son were miraculously rescued in the wilderness (Genesis 16).

Hagbahah ('lifting') Term used in a liturgical context to mean the raising of the Torah scroll in the synagogue before or after the reading so that the congregation can see the writing.

Haggadah, Passover Ritual service performed in the home on the first Passover evening (or on the first two evenings in the diaspora). Originally a narrative of the Exodus from Egypt, it consists of a set form of benedictions, prayers, midrashic comments and Psalms, recited in the course of a festive meal. The order of the Passover Haggadah became an established custom and is recorded in the Mishnah. Later it took on a more elaborate form which is contained in the prayer books of Amram Gaon (8th century) and Saadyah ben Joseph (10th century). It has become the subject of various commentaries as well as manuscript illuminations.

Haggai Biblical book, one of the books of the 12 Minor Prophets. It records the prophecies of Haggai, which date from the second year of the reign of Darius I, King of Persia (c.520 BCE). They deal with the construction of the Temple, the restoration of the nation and the greatness of Zerubbabel.

Ḥagigah Twelfth tractate in the Mishnah order of Moed. It deals with the laws related to peace offerings made during the festivals, festival sacrifices, pilgrimage and ritual purity connected with sacred objects belonging to the Temple.

Hagiographa (Hebrew 'Ketuvim': lit. writings) The third section of the Hebrew Scriptures. It contains: Psalms, Proverbs, Job, the Song of Songs, Ruth, Lamentations, Ecclesiastes, Esther, Daniel, Ezra, Nehemiah, and I and II Chronicles.

Ḥagiz, Jacob (1620–1674) Palestinian scholar, son-in-law of Moses Ḥagiz. He lived in various communities in Italy as a youth. In 1658 he emigrated to Jerusalem, where he became head of the Bet Yaakov yeshivah. He was an opponent of Shabbetai Tzevi. His writings include a commentary on the Mishanh, a study of talmudic methodology and responsa.

Ḥagiz, Moses (1672–?1751) Palestinian scholar and Kabbalist. He was born in Jerusalem. He left Palestine in 1694 to collect money to found a yeshivah; he travelled to Egypt, Italy, Prague and Amsterdam, where together with Tzevi Ashkenazi he struggled against Sabbetaianism. Later he lived in Altona, and eventually settled in Safed. His writings include novellae on the Shulḥan Arukh, ethical works and responsa.

Ha-Gomel ('Blessing of Gomel'; from Hebrew 'gomel': he who makes recompense) Thanksgiving benediction recited by those who have been saved from danger. It should ideally be said in the presence of ten men (two of whom should be rabbis) within three days of the person's delivery from danger. It is customary to recite the blessing after being called to the reading of the Torah in the synagogue on Monday, Thursday or the Sabbath. After the benediction is said, the congregation responds: 'He who hath shown thee kindness, may he deal kindly with thee for ever'.

Ḥag sameaḥ ('Joyful feast') Greeting used on a religious holiday.

Hai Gaon (939–1038) Babylonian gaon, son of Sherira Gaon. Initially he assisted his father in administering and teaching in the academy at Pumbedita. He was appointed head of the bet din in 986 and gaon in 998. Under his leadership the Pumbedita academy became a centre of Jewish learning. He was the last gaon of Pumbedita. He issued thousands of responsa covering numerous areas of halakhic literature. In addition, he wrote a commentary on several tractates of the *Talmud*, poetry and a treatise on commercial transactions.

Haïm, Victor (b.1935) French playwright. He was born in Asnières. In 1954 he went to Paris, where he supported himself as a journalist. Some of his work integrates Jewish and universal themes.

Haimish (Yiddish) Informal, cosy, warm, or unpretentious.

Ha-kadosh barukh hu ('The holy one, blessed be he') Expression used in rabbinical literature in order to avoid mentioning God's name in non-liturgical contexts.

Ḥakham [Ḥaḥam] ('Sage') Title given to rabbinic scholars. Originally it was inferior to the title 'rabbi'. Later it was used to designate the third in rank after the nasi and the av bet din of the Sanhedrin. Sephardi Jews subsequently used the title for their local rabbis. In England the title 'Ḥaḥam' is applied to the rabbi of the Spanish and Portuguese congregation in London.

Ḥakham Bashi ('Chief sage') Title of the Chief Rabbi of the Turkish Empire. In 1836 the Ottoman authorities confirmed the first Ḥakham Bashi in Constantinople. The title was also used of chief rabbis in provincial towns.

Hakhnasat kallah ('bringing in the bride') The rabbis decreed that it is a duty to provide a dowry for brides and to rejoice at their weddings. This term is popularly applied to the provision of a dowry for poor brides. During the Middle Ages and later, communal societies (known as Hakhnasat Kallah socieities) were organised for this purpose.

Hakhnasat oreḥim ('entertaining wayfarers,' 'hospitality') The obligation to provide for travellers and strangers is a central commandment of the Jewish faith. Such hospitality is mentioned in the Bible in the narratives about Abraham, Laban, Jethro, and Rahab. In rabbinic literature it is frequently extolled. During the Middle Ages and later the custom arose of providing special lodging for the vagrant poor in a guest house.

Hakhsharah ('preparation') Intellectual and physical training for settlement in Israel. In the pioneering movements in the diaspora the word was applied especially to training in physical labour (such as farming).

Hakkaphot ('circuits') In liturgical and ceremonial use the term used for the circular route taken repeatedly by a procession. On the Feast of Tabernacles during the Hoshanah service, the reader and members of the congregation walk around the Torah carrying the lulav and etrog. This recalls the procession made in biblical times around the altar in the Temple. On Hosha-na Rabbah a similar circuit is made seven times. On the Feast of the Rejoicing of the Law, repeated hakkaphot take place. In Sephardi and Ḥasidic communities, mourners walk around a coffin seven times. In some communities the bride encircles the bridegroom several times before the wedding ceremony.

Ha laḥma anya ('This is the bread of affliction') Opening words of the introductory paragraph of the seder service. It is an invitation to all who are hungry to come and partake of the Passover meal.

Halakhah (lit. 'walking') The body of law comprising the rules and ordinances of Jewish religious and civil practice. It is identified with the Oral Law. It was first formulated by the scribes and was later refined and developed by rabbinic authorities. The law was passed down in this form from generation to generation, but eventually it became necessary to formulate it systematically. The most important early collection of halakhah was the Mishnah edited by Judah ha-Nasi. The next great compilation was the *Talmud*. After the talmudic period, the geonim interpreted and developed law in their responsa.

Halakhot Gedolot Codification of talmudic law arranged according to the order of the tractates. It was compiled in Babylonia during the 8th century by Simeon Kayyara. It was the first work that enumerated the 613 commandments.

Halakhot Pesukot The first known halakhic work of the geonim. It was written in Babylonia in the 8th century and is attributed to Yehudai Gaon. It confines itself to those halakhot that have a practical application. They are arranged according to their subject matter.

Halberstamm Ḥayyim (1793–1876) Polish rabbinic scholar. He was born in Tarnogrod, and was appointed rabbi of Nowy Sadz in Galicia in 1830. He became drawn to Ḥasidism and founded the Sanzer dynasty of Ḥasidic rabbis. He was the head of a yeshivah in Zanz which attracted both Ḥasidim and mitaggedim. In 1869 he was involved in a dispute with the Sadagora Ḥasidim. He published works on talmudic subjects as well as responsa.

Halberstamm, Solomon Zalman Ḥayyim (1832–1900) Polish Hebrew scholar and bibliophile. He was born in Kraków and became a successful merchant in Bielsko-Biala, Poland, where he collected rare books and manuscripts. In 1890 he published a catalogue of his manuscripts.

Halevai ('May it be so') Expression voicing a wish for a desirable outcome to any project, situation or circumstance.

Halévy, Élie (1760–1826) French Hebrew writer and poet. He was born in Fürth, Bavaria, and moved to Paris, where he served as a cantor, secretary of the Jewish comminity and teacher. From 1817 to 1819 he edited and published a weekly journal, *L'Israélite français*. His *Teachings of Religion and Ethics* is a textbook for Jewish religious instruction. His poem *Ha-Shalom* commemorates the ceasefire between France and England in 1802.

Halévy, Isaac (1847–1914) Polish rabbinic scholar. Born in Ivenets, he lived in various cities including Pressburg, Homburg and Hamburg, where he served as Klausrabbiner. His *Dorot ha-Rishonim* is a history of the Oral Law from biblical times to the period of the geonim.

Halvéy, Jacques François Fromental (1799–1862) French composer, son of Élie Halévy. He was born in Paris, and taught at the Paris Conservatoire from 1816, becoming Professor of Counterpoint and Fugue in 1833, and Professor of Composition in 1840. He composed operas, cantatas, and ballets. His opera *La Juive* is the story of a Renaissance prince in love with a Jewess.

Halévy, Joseph (1827–1917) French orientalist and Hebrew writer. He was born in Turkey and later taught in Bucharest. In 1868 he visited Ethiopia to study the Falashas. Later he explored southern Arabia and discovered numerous Sabean inscriptions. In 1879 he taught Ethiopic at the École-Pratique des Hautes Études in Paris, and became the librarian of the Société Asiatique. In 1893 he founded the *Revue semitique d'épigraphique et d'histoire ancienne*, to which he contributed articles on epigraphy and biblical studies. He was an ardent Hebraist and Zionist.

Halévy, Léon (1802–1883) French writer and dramatist, son of Élie Halévy. He was born and lived in Paris. He became Assistant Professor of French Literature at the École Polytechnique in 1831 and head of the antiquities department of the Ministry of Education in 1837. His writings include *Résumé de l'histoire des juifs anciens* and *Résumé de l'histoire de juifs modernes*.

Halitzah (lit. 'drawing off') Ceremony performed when a man refuses to marry his brother's childless widow (Deuteronomy 25:9–10). It involves her removing her brother-in-law's shoe and reciting the formula: 'So shall be done to the man who will not build his brother's house.' Without undergoing this ceremony, she is forbidden to remarry. The ceremony has become obligatory in Israel, where marriage between a man and his brother's widow is not permitted.

Halkin, Abraham (1904–1990) American orientalist and educator, brother of Simon Halkin. He was born in Russia and was taken to the US in 1914. From 1928 to 1950 he was a lecturer in Semitic languages at the City College of New York, and latterly Professor of Hebrew. He also taught at the Jewish Theological Seminary from 1930 to 1977. He edited Maimonides' *Epistle to Yemen*, and published studies of Judeo-Arabic literature.

Halkin, Shemuel (1897–1960) Russian Yiddish poet. He was born in Belorussia. He published a book of lyrics in 1922 and later Yiddish translations of English, American and Russian classics, as well as poetry and plays about Jewish history. Initially he supported Zionism and was criticised for his advocacy of Jewish nationalism.

Halkin, Simon (1898–1987) American Hebrew poet, novelist and educator, brother of Abraham Halkin. He was born in Russia and emigrated to the US in 1914. He taught at the Hebrew Union College School for Teachers in New York from 1925 to 1932, when he settled in Palestine. He returned to the US in 1939 and became Professor of Hebrew Literature at the Jewish Insitute of Religion in New York. In 1949 he was appointed Professor of Modern Hebrew Literature at the Hebrew University. He wrote novels and works of literary criticism, and made translations.

Hallah (i) ('dough offering') In the Bible the word is used of a portion of dough given to the priest (Numbers 15:17–21). It now refers to a special Sabbath loaf.

Hallah (ii) Ninth tractate in the Mishnah order of Zeraim. It deals with the setting aside of the Hallah ('dough offering').

Hallel ('Praise') In Jewish liturgical use the name of the group of Psalms (113–18). These psalms are expressions of thanksgiving and joy for divine redemption. They are recited in two forms. The full Hallel, consisting of Pslams 113–18, is chanted in the synagogue on Sukkot Ḥanukkah, the first day of Passover, Shavuot, and Israeli Independence Day. It is also recited at the Passover seder. The half Hallel, consisting of the full Hallel except Psalm 115:1–11 and Psalm 16:1–11, is recited on the new moon and the last six days of Passover.

Hallel ha-Gadol ('Great Hallel') In Jewish liturgical use the name given to Psalm 136. It is recited at the Sabbath and at festival morning services as well as the last day of Passover.

Hallelujah ('Praise ye the Lord') Word used as the refrain at the beginning and end of certain psalms. It was also the congregational response in the Hallel ha-Gadol during the talmudic period.

Halper, Ben Zion (1884–1924) American Hebraist, Arabist and editor. He was born in Lithuania and emigrated to Germany, from there to England, and finally to the US. From 1913 he taught at Dropsie College in Philadelphia, becoming Professor of Cognate Languages in 1925. He served as editor of the Jewish Publication Society of America from 1916 to 1924. He published studies of Hebrew and Arabic, an anthology of post-biblical Hebrew literature, and a catalogue of documents from the Cairo Genizah.

Halprin, Rose Luria (1896–1978) Amercian Zionist leader. She was born in New York. She served as President of the women's Zionist organisation, Hadassah, from 1932 to 1934, and 1947 to 1951. From 1934 to 1939 she was Hadassah's correspondent in Palestine. In 1947 she was elected to the Executive of the Jewish Agency for Israel, on which she served for over 20 years; in 1968 she became Chairman of the American section of the Jewish Agency.

Halter, Marek (b.1936) French artist and writer. Born in Warsaw, he escaped from the Warsaw Ghetto and lived in Soviet Uzbekistan. In 1945 he returned to Poland, but later moved to Paris, where he was appointed Director of the Centre du Judaisme. His writings include *The book of Abraham.*

Halukkah ('distribution') Financial support given to the inhabitants of Palestine by Jews in the diaspora. This type of charity flourished during the period of the tannaim, and from the 13th century the Jewish academies established in Palestine were supported in this fashion. Those sent from Palestine to collect money were known as 'meshullaḥim' or 'shadarim'. During the 17th and 18th century such emissaries were sent from Jerusalem, Hebron, Safed and Tiberias. The system of ḥalukkah continued into the 20th century.

Ḥalutz ('pioneer') Word used particularly of Jewish settlers in Palestine before the establishment of the State of Israel.

Ha-Makom yenaḥem ('May God comfort you') Opening words of the expression of consolation addressed to mourners before they leave the cemetery after a burial. The formula is also used by visitors to a house of mourning during Shivah when taking leave of the mourners.

Hamantash (Yiddish: 'Haman's hat') Triangular cake filled with poppy seeds or prune jelly. It is eaten during Purim.

Ha-Mavdil [Mavdil]. ('The one who distinguishes') Hymn sung in the Havdalah ceremony at the close of the Sabbath. It begins: 'May he who makes a distinction between holy and profane pardon our sins; may he mutliply our offspring as the sand and as the stars in the night'. It was probably composed for the concluding service of the Day of Atonement.

Hambro, Joseph (1780–1848) Danish financier. Born in Copenhagen, he became court banker to the king of Denmark and negotiated financial and trade agreements on behalf of the Danish government with Britain and Norway. He later settled in London where he founded a bank which was named after him.

Hammerstein, Oscar II (1895–1960) American composer. He was the grandson of Oscar Hammerstein who built theatres and opera houses in New York City. He collaborated with Richard

Rodgers and produced musicals including *Oklahoma, South Pacific, The King and I* and *The Sound of Music.*

Hamnuna (fl. 4th cent.) Babylonian amora. He was born in Harpabnia in Babylonia and lived in Harta of Argiz near Baghdad. He was a pupil and colleague of Ḥisda.

Hamnuna Saba (fl. 3rd cent.) Babylonian amora. He was a pupil of Rav and succeeded him as head of the academy at Sura.

Hamnuna Zuta (fl. 4th cent.) Babylonian amora. His confession of sin, which he recited on the Day of Atonement, is included in the liturgy for this holy day.

Ha-Motzi [Motzi] ('Who brings forth') Title of the blessing over bread. The blessing is 'Blessed art thou O Lord our God, king of the universe, who brings forth bread from the earth.'

Hanamel (fl. 1st cent. BCE) Israelite high priest (37–36 BCE, and again in 34 BCE). He was born in Egypt. He was appointed high priest by Herod who passed over Aristobulus III, the brother of Mariamne. Owing to the protests of Alexandra and Mariamne, Herod deposed Hanamel and appointed Aristobulus III. But after Aristobulus was murdered, Hanamel was restored to office.

Hananiah (fl. 2nd cent.) Babylonian tanna. In his youth he lived in Palestine, but later he settled in Babylonia, where he remained until his death. He was the greatest scholar in Palestine at the time of the Hadrianic persecutions. He established the calendar in exile, which was followed by the Jews of Babylonia. After Hadrian's death, the Sanhedrin was reconstituted and called on him to recognise its authority. He agreed and exhorted all Babylonian congregations to recognise the Palestinian Sanhedrin.

Hananiah ben Ḥakhinai (fl. 2nd cent.) Babylonian tanna. He lived in Palestine and was one of those who debated before the sages in Jabneh. He studied with Akiva in Bene-Berak for 12 years. Later he resided in Sidon. According to tradition, he was one of the Ten Martyrs under the Hadrianic persecutions.

Hananiah ben Teradyon (fl. 2nd cent.) Babylonian tanna. He was head of the yeshivah of Siknin in Galilee. He was sentenced to death for teaching the Torah in defiance of Hadrian's decree forbidding religious instruction. He was burned at the stake wrapped in a Torah scroll.

Hanging According to the rabbis hanging was not used as a method of capital punishment but only as a posthumous ignominy. This treatment was applied only to a person executed for blasphemy or idolatry, and the body was to be buried on the same day.

Ḥanina bar Ḥama (fl. 3rd cent.) Palestinian scholar. He was born in Babylonia and emigrated to Palestine, settling in Sepphoris, where he was a pupil of Judah ha-Nasi. He earned a living by trading in honey, and also practised medicine. He was a noted aggadist.

Ḥanina ben Dosa (fl. 1st cent.) Palestinian tanna. He lived in extreme poverty and was noted for his piety and his ability to perform miracles; his prayers for the sick had great efficacy. According to tradition, a divine voice proclaimed daily: 'The whole world is fed by the merits of Ḥanina my son, but Ḥanina himself is satisfied with a measure of carobs from one Sabbath eve to the next.'

Ḥankin, Yehoshua (1864–1945) Palestinian Zionist pioneer. He was born in Ukraine and went to Palestine in 1882. In 1897 he negotiated for the purchase of land in the Jezreel Valley, but not until 1909 was the sale completed. In 1915 he was exiled to Anatolia by the Turkish authorities, but he returned to Palestine three years later. In 1920 he purchased a second tract of land in the Jezreel Valley, on which many agricultural settlements were established. From 1932 he served as Director of the Palestine Land Development Corporation. He wrote *Jewish Colonization in Palestine*.

Hannah (fl. 11th cent. BCE) Israelite woman, wife of Elkanah and mother of Samuel. She was barren and in praying for a child she vowed to dedicate any son she had to the Temple. When her son Samuel was born, she left him with Eli the priest to serve in the Temple (I Samuel 1–2).

Hannover, Nathan Nata (fl. 17th cent.) Polish preacher, Kabbalist, lexicographer and chonicler. During the Chmielnicki massacres, he left his birthplace in Volhynia and wandered through Poland, Germany and the Netherlands. In 1653 he went to Italy. In 1662 he was appointed President of the bet din and head of the yeshivah in Jassy, Walachia. Later he moved to Moravia. He published sermons, a Hebrew-German-Italian lexicon, a Kabbalist prayerbook, and an account of the Chmielnicki persecutions.

Ha-noten teshuah ('He who gives salvation') Opening words of the prayer for government recited during the Sabbath and festival morning service.

Hanukkah ('Dedication') [Feast of Lights] Eight-day festival (starting on 25 Kislev) commemorating the victory of Judah Maccabee over Antiochus Epiphanes and the rededication of the Temple. It is associated with the miracle of the cruse of oil which kept the candelabrum burning for eight days in the Temple. During the festival one light is kindled every night in an eight-branched menorah until all eight are burning.

Haphetz Hayyim [Cahan [Kahan], Israel Meir] (1835–1933) Lithuanian talmudist and communal leader. He was born in Poland and became one of the leaders of Eastern-European Orthodox Jewry. He founded and was the head of a yeshivah at Radin, Lithuania, and was active in Agudat Israel. The name by which he is commonly known derives from his ethical and religious treatise *Haphetz Hayyim*.

Haphtarah ('conclusion') Section from the prophetic books of the Bible read in the synagogue on the Sabbath, festivals, and the afternoon of fast days after the reading from the Torah. The haphtarah is chosen because of its relevance to the Torah portion or the specific festival. It is chanted according to a system of cantillation and benedictions are read before and after it.

Ha-Reuveni, Ephraim (1881–1953) Israeli botanist. He was born in Ukraine and settled in Palestine in 1906. He founded the Museum of Biblical and Talmudical Flora in 1912 which was later transferred to the Hebrew University; he was appointed lecturer in biblical botany at the Hebrew University in 1935. He published (with his wife Hannah) studies of the flora of Palestine.

Harkavy, Albert (1835–1919) Russian orientalist. He was born in Belorussia. He became head of the department of Jewish literature and oriental manuscripts at the Imperial Library in St Petersburg in 1877. He published studies of the Khazars, the Karaites, and the history and languages of Russian Jewry. His writings on the ancient Jewish tombstones in the Crimea exposed the fabrications of Abraham Firkovich.

Harkavy, Alexander (1863–1939) American Yiddish lexicographer and writer. He was born in Belorussia and emigrated to the US in 1881. He first joined a collective agricultural colony, but after it failed he lived in numerous cities including Paris, New York, Montreal and Baltimore. He published textbooks and dictionaries for immigrants, including the *Yiddish-English-Hebrew Dictionary*.

Ḥaroset Paste made of fruit, spices, wine, and matzah meal, eaten at the Passover seder. The bitter herb is dipped into ḥaroset to make it less harsh. Ḥaroset symbolises the mortar which the Israelites used during their slavery in Egypt.

Harvest festivals In biblical times there were three harvest festivals: the Omer festival during Passover, when the offering of barley flour was brought to the Temple; Shavuot, the festival of the first fruits ('bikkurim') seven weeks later when the wheat ripened; and Sukkot, the feast of the ingathering, which concluded the entire harvest.

Ha-Shem ('the name') Term referring to God, used to avoid mentioning his name. It is found in phrases such as 'Barukh ha-Shem' (Blessed be God), 'Be ezrat ha-Shem (With the help of God), and 'Im yirtze ha-Shem' (God willing).

Hashkamah ('early rising') Early morning service held before the official morning prayers.

Hashkava (lit. 'lay to rest') The name given by the Sephardim to the memorial prayer. It corresponds to the Yizkor prayer in the Ashkenazi rite.

Hashkivenu ('Cause us to lie down [in peace]') Opening word of the second benediction following the evening Shema. It is a prayer for protection and peace during the night.

Ḥaside Ashkenaz ('Pious men of Germany') German medieval religious movement. The first centres of the movement were Regensburg and the communities of Speyer, Worms and Mainz. Its central figures included Samuel ben Kalonymus he-Ḥasid, his son Judah ben Samuel he-Ḥasid and Eleazar ben Judah of Worms. The teachings of these pietists (Ḥasidim) are collected in *Sepher Ḥasidim*. They advocated asceticism and the expurgation of sin by doing penance and practising physical mortification and fasting. They fostered humility by rejecting honours and accepting insults. They based their moral judgments on ethical considerations rather than strictly talmudic teaching.

Ḥaside umot ha-olam ('pious ones of the nations of the world') Expression used to designate righteous gentiles who have a share in the world to come. According to Maimonides, these are the pious gentiles who adhere to the seven Noahican Laws.

Ḥasidism Religious and social movement founded by the Baal Shem Tov in Volhynia and Podolia in the 18th century. He taught that all are equal before God, purity of the heart is superior to study, and devotion to prayer and God's commandments is of fundamental importance. He was succeeded by Dov Ber of Mezhirich, who systematised Ḥasidic teaching. Although the Ḥasidim were bitterly opposed by the talmudists (mitnaggedim), the movement spread throughout Eastern Europe and beyond. The great centres of Ḥasidism were wiped out during World War II, but several dynasties emigrated to the US, among them the Lubavicher and the Satmar. They established their own training colleges and schools and through them the movement continues to exert an important influence on world Jewry.

Haskalah ('Enlightenment') [Maskil] Hebrew social, spiritual and literary movement, which developed in the last quarter of the 18th century and continued to around 1880. It began in Germany and spread to Austria, Poland, and Russia. Its proponents (maskilim) believed that the Jews should reform their schools, learn the language of the land in which they lived, increase their knowledge of secular subjects, and adopt the manners of their gentile neighbours. The movement was challenged by leaders of orthodox Jewry, who regarded such innovations as a threat to the Jewish tradition.

Haskamah ('approbation') Authorisation prefixed to Hebrew books. Its use was established after the decision of the rabbinical synod of Ferrara in 1554 that Hebrew books should be approved by local Jewish authorities so as to avoid censorship by the civil authorities. Later the Haskamah was sought by an author as a seal of approval for his scholarship and the orthodoxy of his writings. Among the Sephardim, the term has come to refer to a communal regulation.

Hasmoneans Priestly dynasty founded in the 2nd century BCE by Mattathias of Modiin. He and his five sons (Judah Maccabee, Jonathan, Simon, John and Eleazar) led a revolt against the Hellenising policy of Antiochus Epiphanes. In 164 BCE they captured Jerusalem and rededicated the Temple. The Hasmonean dynasty of rulers lasted until 37 BCE.

Ḥas ve-shalom ('Forebear and [hold] your peace') Expression of apprehension used to restrain another from discussing an unwanted event.

Ha-Tikvah ('Hope') Anthem of the Zionist movement and national anthem of the State of Israel. The poem was written by Naphtali Herz Imber in 1878 and was first published in 1886. The words are:

As long as deep in the heart
The soul of the Jew yearns,
And towards the East
An eye looks to Zion,
Our hope is not yet lost,
The hope of two thousand years,
To be a free people in our land,
The land of Zion and Jerusalem.

The melody echoes a Sephardi hymn and a tune in Smetana's *Vltava*.

Hatraah ('warning') The *Talmud* stipulates that a person may not be sentenced

to capital or corporal punishment for a crime unless a warning has previously been given against committing the crime. This legislation was enacted to ensure that the person sentenced was being punished for an act committed willfully. If no specific warning had been given, the sentence was commuted to imprisonment.

Hatred Scripture commands that a person should not hate another (Leviticus 19:17). However, hatred of evildoers and enemies of God is allowed. The rabbis emphasised the duty of hating the sin rather than the sinner.

Hatvani, Lajos (1880–1961) Hungarian writer, literary critic and journalist. He was born in Budapest. He was a founder of the literary periodical *Nyugat* and served as the editor of the journal *Pesti Napló* before and during World War I. At the outbreak of the Communist Revolution in 1919 he went to Vienna, but he later returned to Budapest. He spent World War II in England and returned to Hungary in 1947. In his writings he dealt with the problem of the Hungarian attitude toward the Jews, as well as Jewish assimilation and nationalism.

Havdalah ('Differentiation') Ceremony marking the termination of the Sabbath. It consists of blessings recited over wine, spices and flame. The central blessing refers to the distinctions between the holy and profane, light and darkness, Israel and the nations, and the Sabbath and the other days of the week.

Ḥaver ('compassion') In the *Talmud* the term refers to the individual members of associations of pietists who appeared in the 2nd century BCE. They ate only tithed produce, strictly observed laws of ritual purity, and kept apart from the am ha-aretz. Subsequently the term came to refer to rabbinic scholars. It is now used to denote a friend.

Havlagah ('self-restraint') Name given to the policy adopted by the Jewish Agency and the Haganah during the Arab revolt of 1936–39 in Palestine. It involved self-defence and forbade attacks on Arabs not known to be implicated in the outbreaks.

Ḥayyim ben Isaac of Volozhin (1749–1821) Lithuanian talmudist. After the death of the Vilna Gaon, he became the leader of Lithuanian Jewry. He founded the Volozhin yeshivah in 1802 to counteract the influence of the Ḥasidim and the Haskalah movement.

Ḥayyon, Nehemiah (c.1655–c.1730) Kabbalist. He was born in Safed and became a rabbi at Uskub. Later he wandered from place to place and eventually joined the Sabbetaian movement. He then lived in Italy, Prague and Berlin. He published Kabbalistic studies, and advocated a new form of Sabbetaianism based on the doctrine of the Trinity, comprising the First Cause, the Infinite and the Holy Father (who was identified with Shabbetai Tzevi). He was involved in a controversy in Amsterdam, and his works were criticised and banned by European rabbis. He finally settled in north Africa.

Ḥayyuj, Judah ben David (c.945–c.1000) Spanish Hebrew grammarian. He was born in Fez but arrived in Córdoba in 960 and lived most of his life in Spain. He wrote a study of Hebrew punctuation, a philological commentary on the biblical books from Joshua to Ezekiel and two treatises on Hebrew verbs. A translation of his grammatical works form Arabic into Hebrew by Moses Gikatilla was the first of its kind.

Ḥazak ('Be strong') Greeting. It is based on Moses' address to Joshua: 'Be strong and of good courage' (Deuteronomy 31:7; 31:23). At the Torah reading in the synagogue a full version is recited when one of the Five Books of Moses is completed ('Be strong, be strong, and let us be strengthened'). In the Sephardi rite the person who returns to his seat after having been called up to the Torah is greeted with the expression: 'Be strong and blessed.'

Ḥazakah ('taking hold') Legal term expressing: (1) the mode of acquiring ownership; (2) the means of proving ownership or property rights; (3) the presumption of the existence of particular facts. In the first case ḥazakah creates a new legal reality; in the latter two cases it is instrumental in proving or presuming an already existing state of affairs.

Ḥazal Word formed by the initials of the phrase 'Hakhameinu zikhronam liverakhah ('our stages of blessed memory'). This expression refers to the teachers of the talmudic period.

Hazaz, Ḥayyim (1898–1973) Israeli writer. He was born in Zidorovichi and in his youth moved from one Russian city to another. During and after the Russian Revolution, he worked on the Hebrew daily *Ha-Am* in Moscow. In 1921 he went to Constantinople, and then lived in Paris and Berlin. He emigrated to Palestine in 1931 and settled in Jerusalem. In his novels he depicted Jewish life in different eras in various countries.

Ḥazzan Title given at different times to those performing certain liturgical or communal functions. In talmudic times the ḥazzan was a communal official, who performed certain duties in the synagogue. During the period of the geonim the term was used of the permanent representative of the congregation ('sheliaḥ tzibbur'). When piyyutim became part of the liturgy, the ḥazaan was the one who recited them and provided suitable melodies. In the Middle Ages the role developed into that of leading and chanting the service and the title became synonymous with cantor.

He Fifth letter of the Hebrew alphabet. Its numerical value is 5. As an abbreviation, the letter stands for the name of God.

Health The biblical command 'Only take heed to yourself and keep your soul diligently (Deuteronomy 4:9) is understood as enjoining care for one's health and physical well-being. Rabbinic law prohibits actions that endanger health. Many Jewish laws contribute to physical welfare and hygiene, for example, those forbidding any mutilation of the body such as tattooing.

Heaven [Paradise] (Hebrew 'Gan Eden') The abode of God, where he is surrounded by his court and by the souls of the righteous. In the Bible the location of Heaven is said to be the upper part of the universe, or the firmament dividing the upper from the lower waters. Later the word came to be used as a cognate for 'God' (as is reflected by such expressions as 'the fear of Heaven', 'the kingdom of Heaven', 'for the sake of Heaven'). Rabbinic literature refers to a plurality of heavens, where the various orders of the angelic host reside. It is the place where the righteous ascend after death.

Heave offering Offering made to the Sanctuary or to the priests. It refers to tithes, to the dough offering made to the priests, and to the half-shekel that had to be contributed to the Sanctuary.

Hebrew Hebrew belongs to the Canaanite brach of Semitic languages. It was used by the ancient Israelites until about 500 years after the Babylonian exile. Mishnaic Hebrew, an altered form of biblical Hebrew, was used by the tannaim from the 2nd century BCE to the 2nd century CE. Eventually it was superseded by Aramaic and Greek. In about 500 a literary revival of Hebrew began, which lasted throughout the Middle Ages. From 900 to 1400 Jews in north-western Europe wrote in Hebrew, while in Muslim countries (including Spain) Arabic was used. In eastern Europe Jews spoke and wrote in Yiddish. Though Hebrew continued in use as a religious language, for other purposes Jews used the vernacular. The Haskalah revived the use of Hebrew, and it was later adopted as the language of modern Israel.

Hebrew literature Biblical literature embraces various types of literary form, including narrative, poetry, prophecy and law. During the Second Temple period, the related writings collected together as the Apocrypha and Pseudepigrapha appeared. In the tannaitic and amoraic periods (roughly covering the 2nd century BCE to the 5th century CE), rabbinic literature consisted of the Mishnah, midrash, the Tosephta, and the Palestinian and Babylonian Talmuds. In the gaonic period (6th–12th centuries) much Hebrew writing took the form of legal lectures, collections, and inquiries; liturgical poems (piyyutim) and collections of midrashim were also written. Medieval rabbinic scholars wrote studies of grammar and works of lexicography, poetry, exegesis, philosophy, science and mysticism. The modern period witnessed an efflorescence of Hebrew literature by followers of the Haskalah, and Hebrew was used for writings of every kind. With the establishment of the State of Israel, modern Hebrew became the literary language of the country.

Hebrews Name given to various groups of Jews. In the Bible it is used of the descendants of Eber, grandson of Shem (Genesis 10:24), and of the people who came from beyond the River Euphrates. Abraham is referred to as 'the Hebrew' (Genesis 14:13). Later the term was used interchangeably with 'Israelites'

(Exodus 9:1). Some scholars identify the people known as Habiru with the Hebews. The word 'Hebrew' was frequently used in place of 'Jew' in the 19th century, but in Europe 'Israelite' was more common.

Hebrew University Israeli university. The proposal to establish a Hebrew university was made by Hermann Tzevi Schapira at the First Zionist Congress in 1897. In 1914 an area of land was purchased on Mount Scopus to the east of Jerusalem, and the foundation stones were laid in 1918. The university was officially opened in 1925. From 1925 to 1935 Judah Leon Magnes served as Chancellor. The university has faculties in many fields, now housed on several sites. It grants degrees in a wide variety of subjects.

Hecht, Ben (1893–1964) American novelist and playwright. Born in New York, he grew up in Racine, Wisconsin. He wrote plays and novels, including *Jew in Love*. In the 1940s he became an advocate of the Palestinian underground organisation Irgun Tzevai Leumi. His *A Guide for the Bedeviled* is an analysis of anti-Semitism.

Ḥeder ('school') The word is applied particularly to a school dedicated to teaching children the rudiments of Judaism. Many synagogues have a ḥeder attached to them.

Heidenheim, Wolf Benjamin (1757–1832) German Hebrew grammarian, masoretic scholar, exegete and commentator on the liturgy. He was born in Heidenheim. In 1800 he published the first volume of a nine-volume edition of the maḥzor. He also published other works in the field of liturgy.

Heifetz, Jascha (1901–87) American violinist, of Lithuanian origin. Born in Vilna, he performed in public from the age of seven. He studied at the St Petersburg Conservatory, and at 11 began performing throughout Europe.

The family escaped from Russia during the 1917 revolution, and he settled in California. He embarked on American tours as well as tours throughout the world.

Heilprin, Jehiel ben Solomon (1660–1746) Lithuanian talmudic scholar and historian. He served as a rabbi in Glussk, and in 1711 was appointed head of the yeshivah in Minsk. His *Seder ha-Dorot* contains a chronology of events and personages to 1696, an alphabetial list of tannaim and amoraim, and a catalogue of post-talmudic Hebrew authors and books.

Heine, Heinrich (1797–1856) German poet and essayist. He was born in Dusseldorf and settled in Berlin, where he published his first book of poetry. Influenced by Moses Mendelssohn and Leopold Zunz, he joined the Society for the Culture and Science of Judaism. In 1825 he embraced Christianity, but later he expressed regret for leaving the Jewish faith. In many of his works, such as *The Rabbi of Bacherach* and *Hebrew Melodies*, he exhibited an interest in Judaism. He later lived in Paris, where he worked as a journalist and poet. He influenced the development of the Haskalah movement as well as Hebrew and Yiddish poetry.

Heinemann, Yitzḥak (1876–1957) Israeli humanist and philosopher. He was born in Frankfurt am Main. From 1919 to 1938 he lectured in Jewish philosophy and literature at the Jewish Theological Seminary in Breslau. In 1939 he settled in Jerusalem. His writings deal with Hellenistic and medieval Jewish philosophy.

Hekdesh Property sanctified to God. It consisted of: (1) property owned by the Temple; (2) animals, wine, oil or flour set aside for sacrificial purposes; and (3) property set aside as a gift to the Temple. Such property was not to be handled by a person who was in a state of ritual impurity, and no benefit was to be derived from it. If anyone accidentally made use of it, he was obligated to offer a special sacrifice ('korban meilah') to the Temple. Hekdesh could be redeemed by payment of its value plus a fifth to the Temple treasury. The concept fell into disuse with the destruction of the Temple.

Hekhal [heikhal] ('shrine,' 'temple') The forward part of the central Temple building in Jerusalem (I Kings 7; II Chronicles 4). Among the Sephardim, the term denoted the Ark in the synagogue.

Hekhalot, Books of Collections of mystical midrashim of the amoraic and gaonic periods, attributed to Ishamel ben Elisha. They contain descriptions of the ascent to Heaven to behold the divine chairot ('merkavah'), heavenly places ('hekhalot'), and the throne of glory. Embracing ecstatic experiences and hymns in praise of God, some of this material has been incorporated into the Ashkenazi High Holy Day liturgy.

Helev ('fat') In the Bible the word refers specifically to certain portions of the intestinal fat of oxen, sheep and goats sacrificed on the altar (Leviticus 3:3–17); this was forbidden as food.

Hellenism The principles, ideals and way of life associated with classical Greek civilisation. Hellenism spread over the Mediterranean and the Middle East from the 4th century BCE. At this time Palestine was under Greek rule and Judea was surrounded by numerous Hellenised cities. In addition the Jewish diaspora was expanding into Egypt, Cyrenaica, Syria and Asia Minor, which were all under Hellenistic influence. By the Mishnaic period, Jewish life in Palestine and the diaspora was largely dominated by Hellenistic influences.

Heller, Bernhart (1871–1943) Hungarian Arabist and literary scholar. He was born in Nagybicse. He taught languages at high schools in Budapest and became Director of the Jewish High School. In 1922 he was appointed Professor of Bible at the Rabbinical Seminary. He published studies of ancient Jewish literature, Jewish folk literature and Muslim legends.

Heller, Chaim (1878–1960) American rabbinic and biblical scholar. He was born in Bialystok, Poland, and served as rabbi in Łomża. In 1917 he settled in Berlin, where he established a new type of yeshivah for research on the Bible and *Talmud*. In 1929 he joined the faculty of the Isaac Elchanan Theological Seminary in New York. He wrote studies of Syriac and Samaritan translations of the Bible and of halakhic issues. He also published an edition of Maimonides *Book of the Commandments*.

Heller, Joseph (1923–99) American novelist. Born in Brooklyn, he served in the American Air Force in World War II. He then studied at the Universities of New York, Columbia and Oxford. He worked for various magazines and published *Catch 22*, *Something Happened*, *Good as Gold* and *God Knows*.

Heller, Joseph Elijah (1888–1957) British Hebrew writer. He was born in Lithuania and lived in Russia and Germany. In 1938 he moved to London, where he edited the Zionist organisation's journal, *Tarbut*, and taught. He published studies of Jewish and general philosophy, and translated several of Plato's dialogues into Hebrew.

Heller, Yom Tov Lipmann (1579–1660) Bavarian talmudist. He became dayyan in Prague at the age of 18. In 1629 he was fined for libelling the state and Christianity, and was forbidden to act as a rabbi in Prague. Later he served several communities. During the Chmielnicki massacres of 1648–49 he lived in Kraków, where he composed penitential psalms and commemorative prayers for those who died. His *Tosephot Yom Tov* is a commentary on the Mishnah. He also wrote studies of religious subjects as well as works on mathematics and natural science.

Hellman, Lillian (1906–84) American playwright. Born in New Orleans, she worked as a manuscript reader. She then was a theatrical play reader and film scenario reader. In the 1930s she began to write her own plays, some of which were adapted for the screen. She also wrote three books of memoirs.

Henriques, Sir Basil Lucas Quixano (1860–1961) English social reformer and communal leader, son of Henry Straus Quixano Henriques. He was born in London. With the help of his wife he established the St George's Jewish Settlement in London after World War I. He served as a magistrate and later as Chairman of the East London Juvenile Court. He visited boys' homes and prisons, suggested reforms, and took an interest in Jewish offenders. After World War II he headed the anti-Zionist Jewish Fellowship. He wrote *The Indiscretions of a Warden*, *The Indiscretions of a Magistrate*, and *The Home Menders*.

Henriques, Henry Straus Quixano (1864–1924) English lawyer, communal worker and historian. He served as President of the Board of Deputies of British Jews from 1922 to 1925. He wrote *The Jew and the English Law* and *Jewish Marriages and the English Law*.

Hephker ('ownerless') In Jewish law it denotes any goods or chattels that have no owner. In most cases such goods are ownerless because they have been renounced or because they are unclaimed. The law stipulates that anyone may acquire such property by taking possession of it. In Yiddish the word means lawlessness.

Herberg, Will (1906–1977) American writer. He was active in the Young Communist League and edited Communist Party publications. In the 1940s he renounced communism and developed Jewish interests. His writings include *Judaism and Modern Man* and *Protestant, Catholic, and Jew*.

Ḥerem ('separated out') Term used in various senses to do with prohibitions and bans. In biblical times it applied to the prohibition against making use of spoils taken during war; these were destroyed. In the rabbinic period it came to mean the most serious form of ban, or excommunication, used as a punishment for individuals who committed offences harmful to Jewry.

Heresy Opinion or doctrine contrary to the orthodox tenets of a religion. Since Judaism does not have an official formulation of dogma, it has no clear definition of heresy. Nevertheless, rabbinic Judaism regards as heretics those who renounce the teaching of the Torah, and refers to them by such terms as 'min' (sectarian), 'apikoros' (epicurean), 'kopher' (freethinker), and 'mumar' (one who has changed). The punishment of heretics was justified as a means of preventing them from leading others into sin. In the Middle Ages heresy was punished by excommunication ('ḥerem').

Herman, Joseph (1911–2000) British painter. He was born in Warsaw and moved successively to Brussels, France and Glasgow; in 1944 he settled in Wales. His work of 1938–43 depicts the world of his Jewish childhood.

Hermeneutics, talmudic System or method of interpreting Scripture according to talmudic principles. Various collections of rules (referred to as 'middot' in rabbinic sources) governing the methodology of exegesis existed in the rabbinic period: the 7 rules of Hillel; the 13 rules of Islmael ben Elisha; and the 32 rules of Eliezer ben Yose ha-Galili. In addition Nahum of Gimzo developed a system of interpretation based on the assumption that the marking on every letter has a specific meaning; this was later developed by Akiva

Herod I [the Great] (fl. 1st cent. BCE) King of Judea (37–4 BCE), son of Antipater II. He was appointed Governor of

Galilee by his father in 47 BCE. When he successfully crushed a Galilean revolt, he was censured by the Great Sanhedrin. Later he was appointed tetrarch of Judea and subsequently king. As ruler he constructed a Greek theatre and amphitheatre in Jerusalem, transformed Samaria into a Greco-Samaritan city, built the port of Caesarea, and rebuilt the Temple in Jerusalem. During his reign he dealt harshly with any who he believed to constitute a threat to his power. He put many people to death, including his wife Mariamne and her sons.

Herod Agrippa I (10 BCE–44 CE)   King of Judea (41–44), son of Aristobulus and Berenice and grandson of Herod the Great. Educated in Rome, he served as market overseer in Tiberias and later returned to Rome, where he became a friend of Caligula. After being imprisoned for treachery, he was freed by Caligula, who appointed him King of Judea. He was sympathetic to the Pharisees and observant of Jewish law.

Herod Agrippa II (28–92)   King of Judea (50–92), son of Herod Agrippa I. He was the last king of the house of Herod. During the Jewish revolt against Rome he sided with the Romans. When Titus became emperor, he served under him. According to the New Testament, he was indifferent to the spread of Christianity (Acts 25–26).

Herod Antipas (20 BCE–c.40 CE)   Tetrarch of Galilee, and the Judean Transjordan, son of Herod the Great. He founded Tiberias in honour of the emperor. His forbidden marriage to Herodias (wife of his half-brother Philip) evoked the hostility of the population. John the Baptist was put to death when he denounced the marriage. During the reign of Caligula, Herod Antipas was accused of plotting against Rome and was exiled to Gaul.

Herod Archelaus (fl. 1st cent. BCE to 1st cent. CE)   Israelite, ruler of Judea (4 BCE–6 CE). He was a son of Herod

the Great and under Herod's will he was appointed king. When he went to Rome to ratify this appointment, the Jewish community protested. The emperor, Augustus, abolished the title of king, but confirmed him as ruler of Judea, Idumea and Sumeria. He was later removed from office and exiled to Gaul.

Herodias (fl. 1st cent.)   Judean queen, wife of Philip, the son of Herod the Great and Mariamne II. She bore Philip a daughter, Salome. In 31 she was divorced from her husband and married his half-brother Herod Antipas. This marriage violated Jewish law and angered the Jewish population. John the Baptist, who led the opposition, was imprisoned and, according to the New Testament, was killed at the request of Salome.

Herod of Chalcis (d.48)   King of Chalcis (41–8), son of Aristobulus and grandson of Herod the Great and Mariamne. He was granted the kingdom of Chalcis in 41. After the death of Herod Agrippa I in 44, he was given charge of the Temple administration and treasury and invested with the ability to appoint high priests.

Herschell [Hirschel], Solomon (1762–1842)   English rabbi. He was born in London. He served as a rabbi in Prussia, then in 1802 became rabbi of the Great Synagogue in London. He was recognised as Chief Rabbi by the Ashkenazi communities throughout Britain.

Herschmann, Mordechai (1888–1940)   American cantor. Born in Ukraine, he served as a cantor in Zhitomir, and in 1913 became chief cantor of Vilnius. In 1920 he emigrated to the US, where he became cantor of Beth El Temple in Brooklyn. Later he made concert tours in Europe, Palestine and the US.

Hertz, Henri (1878–1966)   French poet, novelist and critic. He was born in Norgent-sur-Seine. As a journalist, he discussed Jewish problems. In 1925 he became General Secretary of the French Zionist organisation, France-Palestine. His story *Ceux de Job* explores the aspirations and despair of the Jewish nation, and his poetry pursues themes of revolt against the Jewish condition.

Hertz, Joseph Herman (1872–1946) British rabbi. He was born in Slovakia and in 1884 was taken to New York. He served as a rabbi in Syracuse, New York, and Johannesburg, South Africa. In 1911 he returned to the US and became rabbi of Congregation Oraḥ Ḥayyim in New York. In 1913 he was appointed Chief Rabbi of Great Britain. He was critical of Russian anti-Jewish policies and liberal Judaism. He supported Zionism and later struggled against Nazism. His writings include the *Book of Jewish Thoughts* and commentaries on the Pentateuch and the Prayer Book.

Hertzberg, Abel (1893–1989) Dutch author and lawyer. He was born in Amsterdam. He became the editor of *De joodsche wachter,* the journal of the Dutch Zionist Federation. His publications include *Amor fati* and *Brieven ann mijn kleinzoon.*

Ḥerut Israeli political party, associated outside Israel with the Ḥerut Federation of Zionist Revisionists. It was founded in 1948 by members of the Irgun Tzevai Leumi, the Revisionist Party and the Betar movement; it was later led by Menaḥem Begin. It advocates a State of Israel on both banks of the Jordan, the mass ingathering of exiles, and liberalism in political and economic policies.

Herz, Henriette (1764–1847) German society leader, wife of Marcus Herz. She held a salon in her home in Berlin which attracted many of the leading figures in society, both Moses Mendelssohn and Solomon Maimon were frequent guests. She belonged to the Tugenbund, a youth group dedicated to encouraging ethical values. In 1817

she was baptised through the influence of Friedrich Schleirmacher.

Herz, Marcus (1747–1803) German physician and philosopher. He was born in Berlin and became a doctor at the Jewish Hospital there. He published philosophical works and corresponded with Immanuel Kant. As a friend of Moses Mendelssohn, he promoted the welfare of Prussian Jewry.

Herzl, Theodor (1869–1904) Austrian writer and journalist, founder of political Zionism. He was born in Budapest. From 1891 to 1895 he was the Paris correspondent for the *Vienna Neue Freie Presse.* In his play *Das neue Ghetto* he criticised Jewish assimilation, and after the Dreyfus case he wrote *Der Judenstaat* ('The Jewish State'), in which he advocated the establishment of a Jewish homeland. He convened the First Zionist Congress in Basle in 1897, at which the World Zionist organisation was established. Herzl was elected its president. He subsequently began negotiations with world leaders to create a Jewish state.

Herzog, Yitzḥak ha-Levi (1888–1959) Israeli rabbinic scholar. He was born in Poland and was taken by his family to Leeds, England, when he was nine. He served as a rabbi in Belfast and Dublin where he was Chief Rabbi of the Irish Free State. He became chief rabbi of Palestine in 1937. During World War II he attempted to rescue Jews from persecution in Europe, and after the war he travelled throughout Europe to find orphaned Jewish children. He published studies of the institutions of Jewish law and the *Talmud*, as well as responsa.

Heschel, Abraham Joshua (1907–1972) American theologian. He was educated in Berlin, then in 1938 deported by the Nazis to Poland; later he emigrated to England. From 1940 he taught philosophy and rabbinics at the Hebrew Union College in Cincinnati; in 1945 he was appointed Professor of Jewish Ethics and Mysticism at the Jewish Theological Seminary of America. He wrote studies of medieval Jewish philosophy, the Bible, kabbalah, Ḥasidism and the philosophy of religion.

Hess, Moses (1812–1875) German socialist. He was born in Bonn. In 1841 he helped found the socialist daily *Rheinische Zeitung* of which Karl Marx became editor. Subsequently he lived in Belgium, Switzerland and Paris. In 1862 he published *Rome and Jerusalem* which espoused Zionist ideals. Later he engaged in the work of the Alliance Israélite Universelle. His other publications include *The Holy History of Humanity* and *The European Triarchy.*

Hessaḥ daat (lit. 'removal of the mind') Expression conveying the idea of a lack of attentiveness in performing religious duties which require mental awareness. Because of this lack, such actions become invalid. The duties in which alertness is required include the separation from one's produce of the heave offerings due to the priests, the maintaining of the laws regarding ritual uncleanness, and the preparation of the ashes of the Red Heifer.

Hessen, Julius (1871–1939) Russian historian. He was born in Odessa. His scholarly and communal activities were concerned with the emancipation of Russian Jewry. He served as the secretary of the Union for Full Equality of the Jewish People in Russia in 1905–6. Later he initiated the publication of the Russian Jewish encyclopedia and served

as its first general secretary. His publications include studies of the history of the Jewish people in Russia.

Ḥet Eighth letter of the Hebrew alphabet. Its numerical value is 8.

Ḥevra [Havurah] Kaddisha ('Holy brotherhood') Mutual benefit society. The term now applies to associations devoted to visiting the sick, burying the dead and comforting the bereaved. Among the Sephardim such a society is generally called Ḥessed ve-Emet ('Kindness and truth').

Hezekiah (i) (fl. 8th–7th cent. BCE) King of Judah (713–687 BCE). Unlike his father Ahaz, he attempted to free Judah from Assyrian influence. He removed pagan images and altars from the Temple and reviewed the religions of Ancient Israel. These reforms were supported by Isaiah. When Hezekiah led a league of states against Assyria, Sennacherib invaded Judah, but did not occupy Jerusalem. As a consequence, Hezekiah was forced to pay tribute to the Assyrians.

Hezekiah (ii) (d. c.1058) Babyloinan exilarch and gaon. He served as exilarch from 1021. When Hai Gaon died in 1038, Hezekiah succeeded him as gaon and head of the academy at Pumbedita.

Ḥibbat Zion ('Love of Zion') International Zionist movement. It grew up in the 1860s and served as the focus of early Zionist aspirations from the middle of the 19th century, before the establishment of political Zionism. It had widespread appeal among the Jewish masses of Russia and Romania, and similar groups existed in Western Europe and the US. Its adherents (called Ḥovevei Zion) provided Theodor Herzl with wide popular support for his policies. When the World Zionist Organisation was founded in 1897, the members of Ḥibbat Zion joined the new movement.

Ḥibbut ha-kever ('torture in the grave') Belief that a person who has not lived a righteous and devout life is subjected to torture in the grave after burial unless he remembers his name; his tormentors are the Angel of Death and other demonic beings. To avert this judgment it was recommended that one learn by heart a biblical verse beginning and ending with the initial and terminal letters of one's name. The concept is found in eschatological aggadic passages and was developed by the Kabbalists.

Ḥidka, Feast of Rabbi Light meal eaten in addition to the three Sabbath meals. It is named after Rabbi Ḥidka, who asserted that four meals should be eaten on the Sabbath.

Higger, Michael (1898–1952) American talmudic scholar. He was born in Lithuania and emigrated to the US in 1915. He served as a consultant to the law committee of the Rabbinical Assembly of America. He edited minor treatises of the *Talmud* and compiled all of the baraitot and the non-Mishnaic tannaitic statements found in the Babylonian and the Palestinian Talmuds.

High holy day Term applied to the festivals of New Year and the Day of Atonement. The Ten Days of Penitence that fall between the two festivals are often known as the 'high holy day period'.

High place Place of worship built on a hill or mountain. Worship at such places was widespread until the establishment of the Temple in Jerusalem. They were eventually removed by Hezekiah and Josiah.

High priest Title given to the chief priest of the Jews from ancient times until the destruction of the Second Temple in the year 70. It is first found in reference to Aaron and his descendants., who were anointed with holy oil (Leviticus 21:10; Numbers 35:25, 28; Joshua 20:6). Later the title was applied to the chief priest of the First and Second Temples. In addition to the priestly garments (breeches, tunic, girdle, and miter), the high priest wore a robe, ephod, breastplate and frontlet; attached to the breastplate were the Urim and Thummim. On the Day of Atonement he wore white linen. The high priest was the principal officiant in the Temple and was entitled to be present at all sacrifices; among his responsibilities was the administration of the treasury. He also administered the divine oracle and the Urim and Thummim. He was the sole celebrant on the Day of Atonement, when he entered the Holy of Holies to offer incense. The office of high priest was brought to an end by the destruction of the Second Temple.

Hildesheimer, Azriel (1820–1899) German rabbi, scholar and leader of Orthodox Jewry. Born in Halberstadt, he served as secretary to the community there. In 1851 he became rabbi of the Austro-Hungarian community of Eisenstadt, where he set up a yeshivah. In 1869 he became a rabbi in Berlin and he later established a rabbinical seminary there. Together with Samson Raphael Hirsch, he was a leader of the Orthodox Jewish community of Germany. He assisted the victims of Russian pogroms from 1882, and was a supporter of the Jews in Palestine. His publications include an edition of the Halakhot Gedolot.

Hildesheimer, Meier (1864–1934) German rabbi, son of Azriel Hildesheimer. From 1899 he was a preacher at the Adass Jisroel Synagogue in Berlin. Subsequently he became Executive Director of the rabbinical seminary founded in Berlin by his father. He represented Orthodox German Jewry in numerous Jewish organisations. He published several studies on Jewish subjects and edited a collection of some of his father's writings.

Hillel (fl. 1st century BCE) Palestinian rabbinic scholar. He was born in Babylonia and settled in Palestine, where he studied with Shemaiah and Avtalyon.

He was later appointed President of the Sanhedrin. Together with Shammai, he was the last of the pairs (zugot) of scholars. He formulated seven hermeneutical rules for scriptural interpretation, and he was also the originator of the golden rule: 'Do not do unto others that which you would not have them do unto you.' He was the founder of the school known as Bet Hillel.

Hillel II (fl. 4th cent.) Palestinian patriarch (nasi) (330–65). After the revolt of the Jews against the emperor Gallus in 351–2, the Roman government attempted to restrict the privileges of the nasi. Hillel II agreed to limit his authority and functions. He later corresponded with the emperor Julian. In 358 he published a system of intercalation to equalise the solar and lunar years.

Hillel ben Samuel (fl. 13th cent.) Italian physician, talmudic scholar and philosopher. He lived in Rome, Naples and finally Capua, where he practised medicine. He played a major role in the controversies of 1289–90 concerning the philosophical writings of Maimonides, whom he defended. His *Tagmule ha-Nephesh* explores the nature of the soul and the concept of reward and punishment in the hereafter.

Hiller, Ferdinand (1811–1885) German composer. From 1828 to 1835 he was active as a music teacher and pianist in Paris. He subsequently converted to Christianity and held various positions in Germany and Italy. He founded the Conservatory of Cologne in 1850 which he directed. His compositions include the oratorios *The Destruction of Jerusalem, Saul,* and *Rebecca,* and settings of the Psalms.

Hillesum, Etty (1914–1943) Dutch writer. She was born in Middelburg. She was active in the left-wing, anti-Facist movement and in 1942 she began work at an office of the Jewish Council in Amsterdam. Later she was transferred to the Dutch transit camp, where she was assigned to care for people who were to go to extermination camps. She herself was killed in Auschwitz. Her letters describe life in the transit camp.

Hillul ha-Shem ('desecration' or 'profanation of the name') Expression used to designate any action that desecrates God's name. Such action must be avoided not only because it is itself a sin and is forbidden by the third of the Ten Commandments, but also because it sets a bad example to others. The phrase has also come to denote any action likely to bring disgrace on Judaism or the Jewish people. It is the opposite of kiddush ha-Shem.

Hinneni he-ani ('Behold the poor [in good works]') Opening words of a prayer recited at the beginning of the additional service on Rosh ha-Shanah and the Day of Atonement, according to the Ashkenazi rite.

Hiram (fl. 10th cent. BCE) Craftsman in metals. He cast the objects for Solomon's Temple (I Kings 7:13–45; II Chronicles 2:12–13; 4:11–16).

Hiring and letting (Hebrew sekhirut') Transactions in which parties contract for the use of property or the labour and skill of an individual. In Jewish law the hiring of one who offers a personal service is governed firstly by the relationship between master and servant, or employer and employee, as specified in the *Talmud,* and secondly by the specific terms of the contract. Hiring and letting of property is subject to the same laws as selling. The liability of the lessee extends to damage caused by neglect but not to that caused by normal use; due notice of the cessation of the arrangement must be given to the lessee if no date of termination of the lease is stated in the contract.

Hirsch, Emil Gustav (1851–1923) American rabbi, scholar and civic leader. Born in Luxembourg, he went to the US in 1866. He served as a rabbi in Baltimore and Louisville, and to the Chicago Sinai Congregation. He taught rabbinic literature and philosophy at the University of Chicago, and served as the editor of the section on the Bible in the *Jewish Encylcopedia*. He was a spokesman for the radical wing of Reform Judaism.

Hirsch, Baron Maurice de (1831–1896) German financier and philanthropist. He was born in Munich, moved to Brussels in 1851, and later settled in Paris. In 1873 he made contributions to the Alliance Israélite Universelle to establish Jewish schools in Turkey, and in 1891 he set up the Jewish Colonisation Association (ICA) to establish agricultural colonies in Argentina and elsewhere. He also founded the Hirsch Fund, the purpose of which was to open agricultural and crafts schools in Galicia, and the Baron de Hirsch Fund in New York for the technical and agricultural training of immigrants. His philanthropic activities were continued by his wife Baroness Clara de Hirsch after his death.

Hirsch, Samson Raphael (1808–1888) German rabbi and writer. He was born in Hamburg. He served as a rabbi at Oldenburg and Emden, and as chief rabbi of Moravia; from 1851 he was a rabbi in Frankfurt am Main. He was the founder of neo-Orthodoxy, which attempted to combine European culture with loyalty to traditional Judaism. His writings include *Nineteen Letters on Judaism* and *Horeb: Essays on Israel's Duties in the Diaspora*. He was the leader and foremost exponent of Orthodoxy in Germany in the 19th century.

Hirsch, Samuel (1815–1889) American Reform rabbi. He was born in Prussia. He served as a rabbi in Dessau and as Chief Rabbi of Luxembourg before emigrating to the US. There he became rabbi of the Reform congregation

Keneseth Israel in Philadelphia. In his *Die Religionsphilosophie der Juden* he depicted Judaism as an evolving religious system.

Hirschbein, Peretz (1880–1948) American Yiddish dramatist and novelist. He was born in Poland and lived in Warsaw from 1904. His first drama, *Miriam* (which is written in Hebrew), is the story of a prostitute. In 1908 he organised a dramatic group in Odessa to produce Yiddish plays. From 1912 to 1917 he wrote a series of folk dramas, which were later staged at the New York Yiddish Art Theatre. He eventually settled in the US, where he wrote numerous works, including the Yiddish novel, *Babylon*, describing Jewish life in America.

Hirschfeld, Georg (1873–1942) German playwright and novelist. Dissatisfied with a career in his father's factory in Berlin, he began to write plays. His *Die Mütter* depicts life among the Jewish bourgeoisie. A later play, *Agnes Jordan*, deals with Berlin Jewish society.

Hirschfeld, Hartwig (1854–1934) British orientalist. He was born in Thron, Prussia, and went to England in 1889. He first taught at Montefiore College in Ramsgate, then in 1901 became librarian and later Professor of Semitic Languages at Jews College, London. His publications include an edition of the *Kuzari* by Judah ha-Levi, a Hebrew translation of the *Book of Definitions* by Isaac ben Solomon Israeli, studies of the Koran, and works on Arabic and Hebrew philology.

Ḥisda (c.217–309) Babylonian amora. He was born in Kafri. He became wealthy as a brewer in 294 and rebuilt the academy at Sura at his own expense. During the last ten years of his life he was the academy's head. Numerous aggadic sayings are ascribed to him, many on the topic of health and hygiene. He and Huna were known as the pious men of Babylonia.

History and historiography The Hebrew Scriptures give an account of the early history of humanity as well as a detailed narrative of Jewish history. Accounts of the Hasmonean revolt are contained in the Apocrypha, and Josephus' *Jewish Wars* depict the Jewish revolt of 66–73 and the siege of Jerusalem. Medieval Jewish historiography was restricted to histories of tradition and stories of persecution. During the Renaissance historical interest in Jewish events revived and it has continued into the modern period. In the 19th and 20th century numerous Jewish scholars engaged in historical research, and their writings cover all periods of Jewish history.

Hivi al-Balkhi (fl. 9th cent.) Persian biblical commentator. He was born in Balkh. He wrote a polemical work containing 200 criticisms of the Bible, for which he was rebuked by both Rabbanite and Karaite scholars; among those who criticised his work was Saadyah Gaon.

Hiyya (fl. 2nd cent.) Palestinian tanna. He was born in Babylonia. He studied with Judah ha-Nasi and became an important halakhist. He and his pupil Hoshaiah were responsible for a collection of baraitot.

Hiyya bar Abba (fl. 3rd–4th cent.) Palestinian amora. He was born in Babylonia and settled in Palestine, where he was the outstanding pupil of Johanan. He was appointed by Judah ha-Nasi II as his emisaary to the diaspora.

Hod, Mordekhai (1926–2003) Israeli military leader. He was born in Deganyah. He became commander of the Israeli Air Force in 1966. He was in charge of the air strike at the beginning of the Six-Day War in 1967 which destroyed the Egyptian, Jordanian and Syrian air forces.

Hoffmann, David (1843–1921) German biblical and talmudic scholar. He was born in Verbo. He taught rabbinics at the Hildesheimer Rabbinical Seminary in Berlin, where he later became rector. He was regarded as the supreme halakhic authority of German Orthodox Jewry, and in 1918 he was awarded the title 'professor' by the German government. He opposed the Reform movement and attacked the Wellhausen school of biblical criticism. His publications include commentaries on parts of the Pentateuch and an introduction to tannaitic midrashim.

Hofsteyn, David (1889–1952) Ukrainian Yiddish poet. He wrote poems that acclaimed the achievements of the Communist Revolution of 1917. Later he protested against the banning of Hebrew and the persecution of Hebrew writers. He left the USSR but returned in 1926. When Israel became a state in 1948, he was an enthusiastic supporter; as a consequence he was arrested, transported to Siberia and executed.

Holdheim, Samuel (1806–1860) German Reform leader. He was born in Kempno near Posen. He served as a rabbi in Frankfurt an der Oder, Mecklenburg-Schwerin, and Berlin. He advocated radical reform at rabbinical conferences in Braunschweig (1844), Frankfurt am Main (1845) and Breslau (1846).

Hol ha-moed ('weekday of the festival') Name given to each of the days between the first and last days of the Passover and Sukkot festivals. The first and last days are holy days but on the intermediate days essential work may be done. However, no marriages may take place and mourning is forbidden.

Holiness (Hebrew 'kedushah') The Hebrew word for holiness denotes separation, in particular separation for holy purposes. As an aspect of moral life holiness is stressed in Leviticus 19: 'You shall be holy, for I, the Lord your God, am holy.' In ceremonial practice it is connected with the dietary laws, laws of ritual purity and spirituality. Special holiness is attributed to the Temple, Priests and Levites. Holiness is demanded of the entire people, who are referred to as a 'holy people'; the land of Israel is known as the 'Holy Land'.

Holocaust   The word originally meant a sacrificial burnt offering, but has come to mean great destruction or loss of life, especially by fire. It was used specifically of the extermination of six million Jews during the Nazi era. This chapter of history is also referred to as the Catastrophe, the Shoah (calamity), and the Ḥurban (destruction).

Holy days   In the Bible the following holy days are mentioned: the three pilgrim festivals Passover, Shavuot, and Sukkot, which in biblical times were harvest festivals as well as commemorations of historical events; and the days of solemnity, which are New Year and the Day of Atonement. On all holy days work is forbidden. (The first and last days of Passover and Sukkot are holy days when work is not allowed, but some work is permitted on the intermediate days.) Generally in the diaspora holy days (except the Day of Atonement) are observed for two days. Work may take place on the post-biblical festivals of Ḥannukah and Purim, which are the best known and most frequently observed of the many minor festivals.

Holy places   In modern Jewish tradition the principal holy places are the Western (or Wailing) Wall (a relic of the Temple of Herod) and the graves of biblical figures or famous sages from the mishnaic period until the present day.

Holy Spirit (Hebrew 'Ruaḥ ha-Kodesh')   In the Bible the Hebrew term means literally 'divine spirit' (Isaiah 63:10–11; Psalm 51:13). In rabbinic literature it refers to 'divine inspiration'; the criterion for determining the biblical canon was whether each book had been inspired by the Holy Spirit. According to rabbinic sources, the communication to an individual of the Holy Spirit takes place only after long religious discipline resulting in spiritual ascent.

Ḥomah u-migdal ('stockade and tower')   Name given to the pattern of settlements adopted in Palestine from 1936 to 1945. The camps were constructed in one day from pre-fabricated parts, with a watchtower and stockade. This construction enabled the settlers to meet Arab attack, but at the same time did not contravene the rules laid down under the British Mandate.

Homberg, Herz (1749–1841)   Bohemian educationalist and leading figure of the Haskalah. He was born in Lieben near Prague. He served as tutor to Moses Mendelssohn's son in 1779. In 1782 he moved to Vienna, and later in the 1780s taught at the Jewish school in Trieste. In 1787 he became superintendent of German-language schools in Galicia and assistant censor of Jewish books in Vienna. From 1814 he was government inspector of Jewish schools in Bohemia. He advocated the reform of Jewish education, the teaching of Hebrew grammar and German, and the purging of Jewish literature of superstition and hatred of the gentiles.

Ḥometz Botel   The removal of leaven from the house before Passover.

Homiletics   The art of preaching. Traditionally sermons began with a biblical verse which was illustrated in turn by another biblical verse and so on; eventually the preacher returned to his original text and expounded an ethical teaching or a ritual act prescribed by Jewish law. The preliminary biblical verses were chosen from sections of the Pentateuch, Prophets and Hagiographa associated with the week. The use of scriptural verse at the beginning of a sermon has continued to the present day.

Ḥoni ha-Meaggel ('Ḥoni the Drawer') (fl. 1st cent. BCE)   Palestinian miracle worker. His name originated from his habit of drawing a circle around himself, which he refused to leave until his prayer was granted. According to the *Talmud*, his prayers for rain were efficacious. During the war between Aristobulus II and Hyrcanus II, he was seized by the supporters of Hyrcanus and told to curse Aristobulus and his army; when Ḥoni ha-Meaggel refused to comply, he was stoned to death.

Hook, Sidney (1902–89) American philosopher. Born in Brooklyn, he studied at City College and at Columbia University. He taught at New York University and later at the New School for Social Research. His works include *Pragmatism and the Tragic Sense of Life*, *John Dewey, an Intellectual*, *Common Sense and the Fifth Amendment* and *Out of Step*.

Hophni (fl. 11th cent. BCE) Israelite priest, son of Eli. The Bible describes Hophni and his brother Phinehas as following an evil way and they died in battle against the Philistines (I Samuel 2–4).

Hora Israeli folk dance. It was originally from the Balkans, but became popular in Palestine after World War I.

Horayot ('Decisions') Tenth tractate of the Mishnah order of Nezikin. It deals with decisions in matters of religious law made in error by the high priest or the Sanhedrin (Leviticus 4:1–21).

Ḥorin [Chorin], Aaron ben Kalman (1766–1844) Hungarian Reform leader. He was born in Hranice and became rabbi of Arad in 1789. In 1803 he published *Emek ha-Shaveh*, which attacked those customs he believed had no basis in Judaism. He subsequently put his reforms into practice, and also endeavoured to improve the social and cultural status of Hungarian Jewry. He was bitterly criticised by the Orthodox for his views.

Horkheimer, Max (1895–1973) German sociologist. He was born in Stuttgart. He became Professor of Social Philosophy at the University of Frankfurt am Main in 1930. He emigrated to Paris in 1933 and the following year went to the US. From 1943 to 1947 he served as chief research consultant to the American Jewish Committee. In 1948 he returned to Germany and re-established the Institut für Sozialforschung in Frankfurt, which had been closed under Nazi rule. After 1954 he taught at the University of Chicago.

Horodetzky, Shemuel Abba (1871–1957) Israeli scholar of Ḥasidism and Jewish mysticism. He was born in Malin. After going as a delegate to the eight Zionist Congress in 1907, he remained in the West, living from 1908 to 1938 in Switzerland and Germany. He published studies of mysticism, Ḥasidism and the history of Polish Jewry, as well as biographies of medieval rabbis.

Horovitz, Bela (1898–1955) British publisher. He was born in Budapest. He set up the Phaidon Verlag in Vienna in 1923, then in 1938 transferred his publishing activities to London. In 1944 he founded the East and West Library, which published books of Jewish interest.

Horovitz, Marcus (1844–1910) German Orthodox rabbi, historian and halakhist. He was born in Hungary. He served as an Orthodox rabbi to the Frankfurt am Main general community after Reform had eliminated all Orthodox institutions. His publications include *Franfurter Rabbinen*, a study of the rabbis who served the Frankfurt community.

Horovitz, Saul (1859–1921) German talmudic scholar. He was born in Hungary. He became lecturer in religious philosophy and homiletics at the Breslau Rabbinical Seminary in 1896; later he served as religious tutor at the seminary. He wrote studies of Jewish and Islamic philosophy, and began to publish critical editions of the halakhic midrashim.

Horowitz, David (1899–1979) Israeli economist. He was born in Galicia and settled in Palestine in 1920. From 1935 to 1948 he was Director of the Economic Department of the Jewish Agency. From 1948 to 1952 he served as Director General of the Ministry of Finance. After he left his ministry post he worked to establish the Bank of Israel, of which he became the first governor in 1954. He published studies of economics and finance.

Horowitz, Eleazar (1803–1868) Austrian rabbi. He was born in Bavaria. He officiated as rabbi in Vienna from 1828. He engaged in disputes with anti-Semites and successfully advocated the abolition of the Jewish Oath. He contributed to Hebrew periodicals.

Horowitz, Isaiah (c.1565–1630) Scholar and Kabbalist. He was born in Prague. He became av bet din of Dubno in 1600, and av bet din and head of the yeshivah of Ostraha in 1602. He later served as av bet din of Frankfurt am Main and rabbi of Prague. After the death of his wife, he settled in Jerusalem, where he became the rabbi of the Ashkenazi community. His *Two Tablets of the Covenant* is a study of Jewish laws and customs influenced by the kabbalah. He was known as 'Sheloah', a name derived from the title of this work (*Shene Luḥot ha-Berit*).

Horowitz, Jacob Isaac [Rabbi of Lublin] (fl. 18th–19th cent.) Polish Ḥasidic rabbi. Originally from Galicia, he moved to Lublin at the turn of the century. He was believed by the Ḥasidim to be possessed of the Holy Spirit and was referred to as 'Ha-Hozeh' (the seer). He published studies of the Bible, stressing the importance of the tzaddik.

Horowitz, Leopold (1839–1917) Slovakian painter. He lived in Warsaw form 1869 to 1893, and then in Vienna. He painted the Austrian royal family as well as scenes from Jewish life.

Horowitz, Moses ha-Levi (1844–1910) American Yiddish playwright. He organised a Yiddish company in 1878, which performed plays throughout Europe. In 1886 he settled in New York, where he wrote for the Yiddish stage. He introduced operetta into the repertory of the American Yiddish theatre.

Horowitz, Phinehas (1730–1805) German rabbi. He was born in Czortkow, Poland, and served as a rabbi in Witkowo and Lachowicze. In 1771 he became a rabbi in Frankfurt am Main. He was an opponent of the Haskalah movement and criticised Moses Mendelssohn's German translation of the Pentateuch and its commentary. His *Haphlaah* consists of novellae on parts of the *Talmud*.

Hos, Dov (1894–1940) Labour leader in Palestine. He was born in Belorussia and emigrated to Palestine in 1906. At the beginning of World War I he was a founder of the Jaffa Group, which promoted military training. In 1919 he joined the Aḥdut ha-Avodah Party and became a member of its executive committee. He was also active in the Histadrut and the Haganah. From 1935 to 1940 he served as deputy mayor of Tel Aviv.

Hosea (i) (fl. 8th cent. BCE) Israelite prophet. He exhorted the Israelite nation to concentrate on religious and moral reform rather than dabble in international politics. Nonetheless he adopted a compassionate stance, using his own matrimonial difficulties as a symbol for God's love for his wayward people.

Hosea (ii) Biblical book, one of the 12 books of the Minor Prophets. It records the prophecies of Hosea.

Hoshaiah Rabbah (fl. c.200) Palestinian amora. He was the head of an academy at Sepphoris which was later transferred to Caesarea. He was a noted halakhist and aggadist, and the author of the opening homily of Midrash Rabbah.

Hosha-na ('Save now') Words used as the refrain in the liturgical poems recited during Sukkot in the daily procession around the synagogue; they are taken from Psalm 118:25. They also refer in popular usage to the willow branch used in the Sukkot ritual.

Hoshanah Rabbah Seventh day of the Sukkot festival. According to rabbinic teaching, God's decrees are sealed on this day. It became a widespread practice to spend the night before the festival in prayer. In biblical times on this day seven circuits were made around the altar in the Temple. Now seven circuits are made around the bimah of the synagogue. The Torah scrolls and branches of lulav, etrog, myrtle and willow are carried in the procession. When the seventh circuit is completed the willow branches are beaten.

Hoshanot Prayers recited during the Hakkaphot (circuits) of the Sukkot festival. They consist of brief lines, each of which opens and concludes with the response 'Hoshanah' (O deliver) spoken by the congregation.

Hoshea (fl. 8th cent. BCE) King of Israel (732–724). He secured the throne after his revolt against Pekah (II Kings 15:30). He later rebelled against Assyria and was imprisoned by Shalmaneser IV, who then captured Samaria (II Kings 17:1–6).

Houdini, Harry [Weiss, Ehrich] (1874–1926) American magician. He was the son of a religious leader from Budapest. He began his career as a trapeze artist and magician. He later attained fame as an escapologist.

Howe, Irving (1920–1993) American literary and social critic. He was born in New York and taught English literature at Brandeis University and Hunter College. He wrote studies of English

and Amercian novelists and Yiddish literature. His works include *A Treasury of Yiddish Stories* and *A Treasury of Yiddish Poetry*.

Huberman, Bronslaw (1882–1947) Israeli violinist, of Polish origin. He began performing at the age of ten. After World War I, he became active in the Pan-European movement. With the rise of Facism in Europe, he turned his energy to Palestine. He conceived of a comprehensive institute of music at the centre of which would be a symphony orchestra, a professional school of music, and additional ensembles. In the 1930s he concentrated on founding the Palestine Philharmonic Orchestra.

Hübsch, Adolph (1830–1884) Amercian rabbi and orientalist. He was born in Liptó-Szentmiklós in Hungary and served as a rabbi in Miawa and Prague. In 1886 he was appointed head of Congregation Ahawath Chesed in New York. He published an edition of the Syriac Peshitta on the Five Scrolls.

Ḥukkat ha-goy ('law of the gentile') Expression used of any non-Jewish practice that a religious Jew would seek to avoid.

Huldah (fl. 7th cent. BCE) Israelite prophetess. She is the only prophetess mentioned in the biblical account of the period of the monarchy (II Kings 22:14–20). She prophesied God's judgement on the nation after Josiah's death.

Ḥullin ('profane matters') Third tractate of the Mishnah order of Kodashim. It is also called Sheḥitat Ḥullin ('Slaughtering for profane use'). It discusses the laws of ritual slaughtering and other regulations connected with the preparation of animal food.

Humash (from the Hebrew root 'h-m-sh': five) The Five Books of Moses.

Humility According to the *Talmud* the verse 'And what doth the Lord require of thee but to do justly, to love mercy, and to walk humbly with thy God' (Micah 6:8) contains within it the entire Torah. Humility is viewed as the greatest Jewish virtue.

Humour The Bible contains many examples of satire and irony, and the *Talmud* and midrash contain humourous parables and anecdotes. A number of medieval works such as the Taḥ kemoni contain humorous passages. In addition Jewish figures such as Motke Ḥabad, Sheike Fifer in Lithuania, and Hershel Ostropoler in southern Russia were noted for their wit. In the modern period Sholem Aleichem and Mendele Mocher Sephorim are known as humorous storytellers, and Ephraim Kishon was a leading comic author in Israel. Jewish humour is today found in a wide variety of fields: literature, film, theatre, television and radio.

Huna (d. c.297) Babylonian amora. He became a leading authority in his time and served as the head of the academy at Sura from 256. His invitation 'He who is hungry, let him come and eat' is quoted in the Passover service.

Ḥuppah ('canopy') The word is used specifically of the canopy used in the marriage ceremony. Originally it referred to the bridal chamber, of which the modern canopy is a symbolic representation. In some communities a tallit is held as a ḥuppah over the bride and groom. In the *Talmud* the term indicates the legal domain of the man, to which the woman becomes subject on her marriage.

Hurwicz, Saul Israel (1860–1922) Russian Hebrew author. He was born in Uvarovichi and became a merchant and banker. He moved to Berlin after the 1905 revolution, but having returned to Russia in 1914 he lost his fortune in the Communist Revolution of 1917. Eventually he moved back to Berlin, where he became a prominent figure among émigré Hebrew writers. With Ḥayyim

Naḥum Bialik, he directed the Kelal Publishing House. He contributed stories and articles to Hebrew journals, and established his own periodical, *He-Atid.*

Hurwitz, Henry (1886–1961) American editor and Jewish educationalist. Born in Lithuania, he went to the US at the age of five. In 1906 he organised the Harvard Menorah Society, and in 1913 established the Intercollegiate Menorah Association, of which he was president and chancellor. In 1915 he founded the *Menorah Journal,* a magazine of Jewish opinion.

Ḥushi, Abba (1898–1969) Israeli labour leader. He was born in Galicia and emigrated to Palestine in 1920. He served as secretary of the Haifa Labour Council (1938–51), as Mapai member of the Knesset (1949–51), and as Mayor of Haifa (1951–69).

Ḥushiel ben Elhanan (fl. 10th–11th cent.) North African talmudist. He was head of the academy of Kairouan. According to tradition, he was one of four shipwrecked scholars from Bari who were ransomed in various communities. He developed new methods of study, stressing the importance of the Palestinian *Talmud* and the halakhic midrashim.

Husik, Isaac (1876–1939) American historian of Jewish philosophy. He was born in Russia and moved to Philadelphia in 1888. From 1898 to 1916 he taught at Gratz College in Philadelphia, later becoming Professor of Philosophy at the University of Pennsylvania. His publications include *A History of Medieval Jewish Philosophy.*

Husserl, Edmund (1859–1938) German philosopher. Born in Prossnitz, Moravia, he studied at the universities of Leipzig, Berlin and Vienna. He converted to Protestantism. He taught at the University of Halle, and then at the universities of Göttingen and Freiburg.

His writings have been published in 11 volumes.

Ḥutzpit ha-Meturgeman (fl. 2nd cent.) Palestinian tanna. He was the mouthpiece ('meturgeman') of Rabban Gamaliel of Jabneh. In the Tosephta he is described as one of the four elders who studied under Eliezer ben Azariah in Sepphoris. According to midrashic tradition, he was one of the Ten Martyrs executed under the Hadrianic persecutions of c.135.

Hyamson, Albert Montefiore (1875–1954) English administrator. From 1917 to 1919 he edited the *Zionist Review*. He served as Chief Immigration Officer in Palestine under the British Mandate, returning to England in 1934. He was President of the Jewish Historical Society of England from 1945 to 1947. He published studies of Palestine and Zionism as well as a history of the Jews of England.

Hyamson, Moses (1862–1949) American rabbi and scholar. Born in Lithuania, he was taken to England at the age of five. He served as a rabbi in England, Wales and the US. He taught the codes of Jewish law at the Jewish Theological Seminary of America from 1915 to 1940. His writings include translations of Maimonides' *Mishneh Torah* and Baḥya ben Joseph ibn Pakuda's *Duties of the Heart*.

Hygiene Many biblical prescriptions (such as those concerning circumcision, ablution and isolation of the sick) promote personal cleanliness. The *Talmud* amplifies these laws. In the Middle Ages such regulations ensured that the Jewish community had a relatively high level of hygiene.

Hypocrisy According to the *Talmud*, a hypocrite is a person who says one thing in his heart and another with his lips. Hypocrisy was condemned by the rabbis.

Hyrcanus II (fl. 1st cent. BCE) Judean high priest and ethnarch, elder son of Alexander Yannai and Salome Alexandra. He succeded his mother to the Judean throne but was driven out and had the high priesthood wrested from him by his brother Aristobulus II. With the help of Antipater, he resolved to overcome Aristobulus. The brothers appealed for arbitration to Pompey, who preferred Hyrcanus. After conquering Aristobulus and his supporters, Pompey appointed Hyrcanus high priest with limited political authority. Following Pompey's death Hyrcanus supported Julius Caesar, who elevated him to the position of ethnarch. When Judea was invaded by the Parthians, he was taken captive. He subsequently returned to Judea, where he was accused of treason by Herod the Great and executed.

I

Sam and Sylvia Horowitz live above a small grocery store in the lower East Side of New York. They are in bed, but Sam is tossing and turning. He wakes up his wife.

'What's wrong?' Sylvia asks.

'Oy,' says Sam. 'I'm really upset. I don't know how I'm going to pay Hymie Feinberg the loan I owe him.'

'Go back to sleep,' Sylvia says.

Ten minutes later, he says: 'It's a thousand bucks...'

'Go back to sleep,' his wife says again.

But Sam tosses and turns. He can't sleep, sits up in bed and exclaims: 'This is terrible!'

'Shut up, Sam,' his wife tells him.

'I can't take it,' he says. 'What will I do?'

Outside it is the middle of the night. Sylvia gets out of bed and opens the window and screams: 'HYMIE! HYMIE FEINBERG! WAKE UP, HYMIE!'

Finally, on the other side of the street, a window goes up and a sleepy head appears.

'Nu,' he says. 'What's going on?'

Sylvia yells in a loud voice: 'YOU KNOW MY HUSBAND SAM HOROWITZ? HE OWES YOU A THOUSAND BUCKS. HE CAN'T PAY!'

Sylvia slams down the window, gets back in bed, and turns to her husband. "Now," she says, 'let him worry about it.'

* * * * *

Sam Horowitz is consumed by guilt. He can't pay back the loan he owes. He can't sleep. So, to calm his nerves his wife wakes up their neighbour, tells him that he won't get back the loan, and says to her husband it is now their neighbour's problem, not her husband's. The joke emphasises that the husband is a 'schlemiel' (a hopeless fellow). He has no idea how to handle the situation. But his wife intercedes, temporarily removes the problem, and thereby rids her husband of his anxiety.

Ibn Abitur, Joseph ben Isaac (fl. 10th–11th cent.) Spanish scholar. After Moses ben Enoch's death in Córdoba, his place as rabbi and head of the yeshivah there was taken by his son Enoch. Ibn Abitur attempted to displace Enoch, causing a split in the community. He was forced into exile and travelled to north Africa, Pumbedita and Damascus. He wrote an Arabic commentary on the *Talmud*, a Hebrew commentary on the Psalms, and liturgical poetry.

Ibn Aknin, Joseph ben Judah (1150–1220)   North African philosopher and poet. He was born in Barcelona and moved to north Africa, where he lived as a crypto-Jew. He wrote studies of Jewish law and philosophy. He should not be confused with Maimonides' disciple Joseph ben Judah ibn Shimon, who is also referred to as Ibn Aknin.

Ibn Balam, Judah ben Samuel [Judah ibn Balam] (fl. 11th cent.)   Spanish biblical commentator and Hebrew grammarian. He was born in Toledo and lived in Seville. He wrote biblical commentaries, a study of the stylistic devices in the Bible, and works on Hebrew verbs and particles.

Ibn Barun, Isaac ben Joseph (fl. 11th–12th cent.)   Spanish Hebrew grammarian and lexicographer. He lived in Zaragoza and Málaga. He wrote Hebrew poetry, and developed the comparative linguistic studies begun by Judah the Kuraish, Dunash ben Tamim and Jonah ibn Janaḥ.

Ibn Daud, Abraham (c.1110–1180)   Spanish historian, philosopher, physician and astronomer. He was born in Córdoba and settled in Toledo. His *Emunah Ramah* ('Sublime faith') is a philosophical treatise based on Aristotelian principles. In this work he explores central problems connected with God, the soul, prophecy and creation, and free will. His *Sepher ha-Kabbalah* ('Book of tradition') relates the history of talmudic scholarship to his own day.

Ibn Ezra, Abraham (1089–1164)   Spanish poet, grammarian, biblical commentator, philosopher, astronomer and physician. Born in Toledo, he lived in Spain and later journeyed to Italy, France, England and Palestine. He wrote poetry, Biblical commentaries, grammatical works, philosophy and astrological studies.

Ibn Ezra, Moses (b.c.1055–after 1135)   Spanish Hebrew poet and philosopher. He was born in Granada and became a friend of Judah ha-Levi. After the Almoravides captured Granada in 1090 he led a wandering life. He wrote poetry, an examination of the methodology and meter of Hebrew and Arabic verse, an Arabic philosophical work based on Neoplatonism, and penitential prayers (seliḥot).

Ibn Gabirol, Solomon [Gabirol] (c. 1021–c.1056)   Spanish poet and philosopher. He was born in Zaragoza. He wrote secular and religious poetry and philosohical studies. His poem *Keter Malkhut* ('Crown of divine kingship') has been incorporated into the liturgy. Two of his philosophical works have survived: *Mekor Ḥayyim* ('Source of life') and *Tikkun Middot ha-Nephesh* ('Improvement of the moral qualities'). His philosophical investigations are based on Neoplatonic principles.

Ibn Ḥasan, Jekuthiel ben Isaac (d. 1039)   Spanish statesman and philanthropist. He served as vizier in the Muslim state of Zaragoza. He was a patron of Solomon Ibn Gabirol, who wrote three dirges in his memory after he had been deposed and executed.

Ibn Ḥasdai, Abraham ben Samuel ha-Levi [Abraham en Samuel Ḥasdai; Abraham ben Ḥasdai ha-Levi; Abraham ibn Ḥasdai; Ḥasdai] (fl. 13th cent.)   Spanish translator and Hebrew poet. He lived in Barcelona. He translated numerous Arabic works into Hebrew, and was an ardent defender of Maimonides.

Ibn Ḥaviv, Jacob [Habib] (?1445–1515/16)   Spanish rabbinic scholar. He was born in Zamora in Castile, and became head of a yeshivah in Salamanca. When the Jews were expelled from Spain in 1492, he went to Portugal and later settled in Salonica, where he was one of the leading scholars. His *En Yaakov* is a compilation of aggadic sections of the Palestinian and Babylonian Talmuds.

Ibn Ḥaviv, Levi (c.1480–1545) Palestinian rabbinic scholar, son of Jacob ibn Ḥaviv. He lived in Salonica. He completed his father's talmudic compilation, *En Yaakov.* Later he moved to Palestine, where he became Chief Rabbi in Jerusalem. He was an opponent of Jacob Berab's plan to revive rabbinic ordination.

Ibn Janaḥ, Jonah (fl. 11th cent.) Spanish Hebrew grammarian and lexicographer. Born in Córdoba, he settled in Zaragoza, where he was a physician. He wrote studies of biblical exegesis and Hebrew philology. His *Sepher ha-Dikduk* includes a list of roots of Hebrew words intepreted in the light of biblical and rabbinic literature, and compared with other Semitic languages. It was translated from Arabic into Hebrew by Judah ibn Tibbon.

Ibn Killis, Yakub ben Yusuf (930–91) Egyptian statesman. He was born in Baghdad and first settled in Palestine. Later he went to Egypt and converted to Islam. He served several caliphs, and as a vizier reorganised the administrative system of the Fatamid caliphate.

Ibn Kuraish, Judah (fl. 10th cent.) North African philologist. He was born in Morocco and became a physician. He wrote an Arabic letter to the Jewish community in Fez, protesting against the elimination of the recitation of the Aramaic Targum. In this letter he laid the foundation for a method which was later of considerable help in solving problems of biblical vocabulary.

Ibn Latif, Isaac ben Abraham (c.1220–1290) Spanish philosopher, Kabbalist and physician He spent the latter part of his life in Palestine. He established a new method of kabbalah based on Aristotelian philosophy and natural science. He also used a Kabbalistic terminology derived from philosophy and mathematics.

Ibn Migas, Joseph ben Meir ha-Levi (1077–1141) Spanish talmudic scholar. He served as the head of yeshivah in Lucena, as a successor to Isaac Alfasi. He wrote novellae to the *Talmud* and numerous responsa.

Ibn Polegar, Isaac ben Joseph [Ibn Pulgar; Ibn Pulkar] (fl. 14th cent.) Spanish theologian. He wrote a polemical reply to the anti-Jewish tract, *Minḥat Kenaot,* written by the convert Abner of Burgos. This work, *Ezer ha-Dat,* attempts to reconcile faith and philosophical reason.

Ibn Sahulah, Isaac ben Solomon (fl. 13th cent.) Spanish Hebrew writer. He worked as a physician at Guadalajara. He wrote a Kabbalistic commentary on the Song of Songs, and a book of fables, *Meshal ha-Kadmoni* ('Easterner's parable').

Ibn Shaprut, Ḥasdai [Shaprut] (c.915–c.970) Spanish statesman and physician. He served at the courts of the caliphs Abder-Raḥman III and Ḥakam II at Córdoba, and was employed on various foreign missions. He supported Jewish scholars and scholarship and defended Jewish communities. He wrote a well-known letter to the king of the Khazars expressing his joy at their independent Jewish kingdom. His scholarly activities included collaboration in translating a work of Dioscorides into Arabic.

Ibn Shaprut, Shemtov ben Isaac [Shaprut] (fl. 14th–15th cent.) Spanish scholar and physician. In 1375 he conducted a disputation in Pamplona with the future Pope Benedict XIII. He wrote a polemical work to combat apostasy (*Even Boḥan*), a commentary on Avicenna, a supercommentary to Ibn Ezra's Bible commentary, and a philosophical explanation of talmudic aggadah.

Ibn Shemtov, Joseph ben Shemtov (c.1400–c.1460) Spanish philosopher. He served in the Castilian court of King John II and his successor Henry

IV. In 1452 he was sent to Segovia to suppress an anti-Semitic movement. Later he wandered around the country giving lectures. His *Kevod Elohim* is a theological study which seeks to find a compromise between Maimonides and the anti-philosophical views of contemporary Jewish scholars.

Ibn Shemtov, Shemtov (c.1380–c.1441) Spanish Kabbalist. In *Sepher ha-Emunot* he criticised rationalists from Abraham ibn Ezra through Levi ben Gershom and Isaac Albalag. He was sharply opposed to the views of Maimonides and was particularly incensed by his *Guide for the Perplexed.*

Ibn Tibbon, Jacob [Don Profiat] (c.1230–1312) French astronomer, physician, writer and translator. He was born in Marseilles and lived at Montpellier, where he taught medicine at the university. He translated Euclid, Averroes and Al Ghazzali from Arabic into Hebrew. In addition he produced astronomical tables, which were translated into Latin and used by Dante for his *Divine Comedy.* He was a defender of Maimonides.

Ibn Tibbon, Judah ben Saul [Tibbon]. (c.1120–after 1190) Spanish physician and translator. Born in Granada, he settled in Lunel, France. He translated such Jewish works as Saadyah Gaon's *Beliefs and Opnions,* Baḥya's *Duties of the Heart,* and Judah ha-Levi's *Kuzari* from Arabic into Hebrew.

Ibn Tibbon, Moses ben Samuel [Tibbon] (d. c.1283) French writer and translator. He lived in Marseilles, where he practised medicine. He translated philosophical and scientific works from Arabic into Hebrew, and also wrote commentaries on the Bible and rabbinical studies.

Ibn Tibbon Samuel ben Judah [Tibbon] (c.1150–c.1230) French translator, scholar and physician. After travelling widely, he settled in Marseilles.

He translated Maimonides' *Guide for the Perplexed* from Arabic into Hebrew in collaboration with the author. He also translated other writings of Maimonides and wrote philosophical commentaries on the Bible.

Ibn Tzaddik, Joseph ben Jacob (c. 1075–c.1149) Spanish philosopher and poet. From 1138 he served as a dayyan at Córdoba. His philosophical study *Olam Katon* explores cosmology, the nature of man and his realtion to the external world. This work was influenced by Neoplatonism and Aristotelian concepts.

Ibn Verga, Joseph (c.1559) Turkish scholar, son of Solomon ibn Verga. When the Jews were expelled from Spain in 1492, he fled to Lisbon with his father. Later, he emigrated to Turkey, where he served as a rabbi and dayyan in Adrianople. He published his father's *Shevet Yehudah,* a collection of narratives describing persecutions and disputations, together with supplementary material. He also wrote a study of talmudic principles.

Ibn Verga, Solomon (fl. 13th–16th cent.) Spanish historiographer. After the conquest of Málaga in 1487, he was sent by Spanish Jewish communities to raise funds for ransoming Jews captured there. When the Jews were expelled from Spain in 1492, he settled in Lisbon. From 1497 he was compelled to live as a Converso, but he later emigrated to Italy. His *Shevet Yehudah* is a narrative describing the persecution of the Jews from the destruction of the Second Temple until his own time. It was published with additions by his son Joseph ibn Verga.

Ibn Yaḥia, David ben Joseph [Yaḥia] (1463–1543) Porguguese rabbi, grammarian and philsopher. Born in Lisbon, he became a leader of Portuguese Jewry and an adviser to the kings of Portugal. In 1525 he was appointed rabbi of Naples. After the Jews were expelled from Naples in 1540 he settled in Imola. He wrote studies of grammar and philosophy as well as poetry.

Ibn Yaḥia, David ben Solomon (c.1440–1524) Porguguese biblical commentator and grammarian. He was born in Lisbon, and served as a rabbi there. Later he lived in Naples and Constantinople. He wrote biblical commentaries, grammatical and legal studies, and a commentary on Maimonides' *Guide for the Perplexed.*

Ibn Yaḥia, Gedaliah ben Joseph (1515–1587) Italian historiographer and talmudist. He was born in Imola and lived in various cities in Italy before settling in Alexandria. His *Shalshelet ha-Kabbalah* consists of a history of the Jewish people, scientific tractates, and a chronicle of events from creation to the 16th century.

Ibn Yaḥia, Jacob Tam (d.1542) Portuguese scholar and physician, son of David ben Solomon ibn Yaḥia. He served as a rabbi and as court physician in Constantinople. He was the author of numerous responsa and completed *Tehillah le-David,* a study of the principles of Judaism begun by his father.

Ibn Yaḥia, Joseph (1494–1534) Italian biblical commentator and philosopher. He was born in Florence and moved with his family to Imola. He wrote biblical commentaries, a commentary on talmudic sayings, and studies of eschatology and the commandments.

Ibn Yaish, Solomon [Abenaes] (d.1603) Turkish statesman and merchant. Born a Portuguese Marrano, he reverted to Judaism in Turkey. He later became Duke of Mytilene and was the organiser of the Anglo-Turkish alliance against Spain.

Ibn Zabara [Zabara], Joseph (c.1140–c.1200) Spanish Hebrew poet. He was born in Barcelona and worked as a physician there. His *Sepher Shaashuim* (Book of amusements) contains a lit-

erary account of his journey to several countries, together with stories and proverbs.

Ibn Zeraḥ Menaḥem (d.1385) Spanish codifier. He was injured in the attack on the Jews of Navarre in 1328, and afterwards serttled in Toledo. His *Tzedah la-Derekh* is a handbook of essential Jewish laws for the use of Jews at the royal court.

Idel, Moshe (b.1947) Israeli scholar of Romanian origin. born in Targu Neamt, Romania, he emigrated to Israel in 1963. He served as Professor of Jewish Thought at the Hebrew University and as a visiting professor at Yale, Harvard and Princeton. His works include *Kabbalah: New Perspectives and Messianic Mystics, Hasidism: Between Ecstasy and Magic* and *From Midrash to Kabalah.*

Idelsohn, Abraham Zvi (1882–1938) American musicologist, of Lithuanian origin. He served as cantor in Leipzig, Regensburg and Johannesburg, and later settled in Jerusalem. There he worked as a cantor and music teacher at the Hebrew Teachers College. He later became Professor of Music at the Hebrew Union College in Cincinnati. He was the founder of modern Jewish musicology, and one of the pioneers of ethnomusicology.

Idolatry The worship of idols. Although biblical Judaism was opposed to idol worship, the Ancient Israelites engaged in idolatrous practices, which evoked the hostility ofthe prophets. Rabbinic law in the Mishnah treatise Avodah Zarah deals with prohibitions concerning contact with idolators. The rabbis forbade commercial transactions with an idolator before an idolatrous holiday in order to preserve the Jew from even indirect involvement in the festivities. It was also prohibited to sell or lease land or houses in Palestine to an idolator, to sell him animals, or eat with him. Further, it was forbidden to eat his bread, oil or wine.

Ignatov, David (1885–1954) American Yiddish author. He was born in Ukraine and was active in the revolutionary movement in Kiev in 1903–6 before he emigrated to the US. He was one of the founders of the eastern European literary group Di Yunge, and edited various literary journals. He was one of the creators of the modern Yiddish novel and also reworked Hasidic tales and medieval Jewish fables. His stories describe the lives of Jewish workers in the US.

Igrat Bat-maḥlat Name of an evil spirit of the night. According to the *Talmud*, it was rendered powerless by Abbaye.

Ikor, Roger (1912–1986) French novelist. He was born in Paris and became a teacher there. His novel *The Sons of Avron* is a depiction of Jewish immigrant life in Paris during the early decades of the 20th century.

Ikriti, Shemariah (1275–1355) Italian philosopher and biblical commentator. He was brought up in Crete and spent most of his life in Italy. In 1352 he went to Spain on an unsuccessful mission to reconcile Karaites and Rabbinites. He was accused of messianic pretensions and died in prison. His works include a philosophical commentary on the Bible, a cosmological polemic and a study of talmudic legends.

Illegitimacy In Jewish law the status of a child who is the product of any union prohibited in the Bible. Such a person is designated a 'mamzer'. He or she may not marry an Israelite (or Jew), except one of the same status, but is allowed to marry a proselyte. The children of mamzerim share the same prohibition with regard to marrying a true Israelite. These restrictions still pertain.

Illuy (Hebrew) Outstanding scholar of genius. The word is usually applied to a young talmudic scholar of extraordinary ability.

Imber, Naphtali Herz (1836–1909) American Hebrew poet. He was born in Galicia and went to Palestine in 1882, where he served as secretary and adviser on Jewish affairs to Laurence Oliphant (1882–8). He then returned to Europe and wandered as far as India, where he was wooed by missionaries. He was later accused of converting to Christianity. In 1892 he went to the US. His first volume of poems contained *Tekvatenu,* which (as *Ha-Tikvah*) later became the anthem of the Zionist movement and ultimately the Israeli national anthem.

Imber, Samuel Jacob (1889–c.1942). Galician Yiddish poet He was born in Ukraine. He became the pioneer and mentor of a generation of Galician Yiddish poets. His poetic romance *Esterke* recounted the 14th-century story of the love of the beautiful daughter of a Jewish blacksmith for the Polish King Casmir. After World War I he founded the literary monthly *Nayland.*

Imitation of God According to the rabbis, God's attributes should be seen as models for human behaviour. Human beings are to imitate his qualities of mercy compassion and loving-kindness. The doctrine of the imitation of God was important in the moral teaching of the Kabbalistic mystics.

Immanuel ben Solomon of Rome (c. 1261–after 1328) Italian poet and rabbinic commentator. He was born in Rome and lived in various cities in Italy. He wrote philosophical commentaries on the Bible, poetry and hymns. He introduced Spanish metrical forms into Italy and the sonnet form into Hebrew. His *Maḥberot Immanuel* contains poems on love, wine, and friendship, riddles, epigrams, epistles, elegies, religious poems, and an account of a journey through Hell and Paradise. The piyyut *Yigdal,* which is included in the daily prayer book, is an adaptation of one of his poems in this work.

Imma Shalom (fl. 1st–2nd cent.) Palestinian woman, wife of Eliezer ben Hyrcanus and sister of Rabban Gamaliel II.

She was praised for her learning and religious devotion. She is one of the few women mentioned in talmudic literature.

Immersion The statement 'He shall bathe his flesh in water' (Leviticus 15:16) is interpreted as referring to the total immersion of the body in a ritual bath ('mikveh') or flowing river water. Ritual immersion is the means of eliminating ritual impurity. In all cases the body must be scrupulously clean before immersion. Orthodox practice stipulates that women of childbearing age should practise immersion after menstruating, and that proselytes should immerse themselves as a sign of adopting Judaism. Among the very pious it is the custom to prepare for festivals by immersion, and some groups practise it daily before the morning prayer. Vessels that have been rendered unclean also require cleansing by this means, as do new or used vessels which have been purchased from a non-Jew.

Immortality of the soul The eternal existence of the soul after death. In the Bible the dead are depicted as living a shadow-like existence in Sheol. According to rabbinic literature human beings are described as having a body and a soul, which are parted at death but reunited in the resurrection of the dead. After the Day of Judgement, the righteous enter into Heaven (Gan Eden) and the wicked are punished in Hell (Gehinnom). In modern times this traditional view of physical resurrection, reward and punishment has been replaced in various branches of Judasim by belief in the immortality of the soul.

Imprisonment The rabbis legislated for imprisonment as punishment in the case of certain offences for which no other penalty is prescribed in Scripture. It was also to be used in special circumstances. The *Talmud* stipulates three sets of circumstances in which imprisonment is appropriate: to punish the incorrigible offender who has already received corporal punishment

for transgressing a prohibition involving excision or cutting off from the community; to punish someone who is guilty of murder but on whom the court cannot pronounce a death sentence because of legal technicalities; and to punish a person found guilty of murder by hiring an assassin.

Im yirtzeh ha-shem ('If the name [God] wills') Pious expression used in discussing future events.

Incense Gum, spice or other substance producing a sweet smell when burned. In biblical times the burning of incense accompanied all sacrifices in the Temple except the sin offering of the poor and the meat offering of the leper. It was burned by the high priest in the Holy of Holies on the Day of Atonement. Its ingredients are prescribed in Exodus 30:34–38 and elaborated in the *Talmud*.

Incest Sexual relationship between close kindred. Leviticus 18:6–18 lists prohibited sexual relationships between members of a family. The *Talmud* added other unions to those already defined as incestuous.

Incunabula Early printed books, especially those dating from before 1500. Approximately 150 Hebrew incunabula are known, about two-thirds of which were printed in Italy. The leading printers of early Hebrew books were the Soncino family.

Indemnity Security against or compensation for damage or loss. In Jewish law financial compensation and restitution are due if a person is injured or his property damaged. In cases of injury, indemnity consists of payment for the injury itself, the pain suffered, the medical expenses incurred, the loss of earnings arising and the indignity suffered. Since Jewish law states that two punishments may not be given for a single offence, a person who pays an indemnity should receive no further punishment. Offences punishable by the payment of an indemnity are not classified as criminal.

Informer One of the greatest crimes a Jew can commit against other Jews is to denounce them to the secular authorities. The attitude of the *Talmud* towards such individuals was one of extreme hostility. During the Middle Ages the incidence of betrayal by informers increased as a result of political and social conditions; the handing over of information to non-Jewish authorities about the lives, property and religious beliefs of Jews often had calamitous results. In response Jewish leaders and scholars tried offenders and imposed sentences on them.

Inheritance In biblical times the Jews adopted the principle of the right of primogeniture. The case of Zelolphehad's inheritance determined that daughters should inherit if there are no sons (Numbers 27:8–11). According to the rabbis, the order of legal heirs is: (1) sons and their descendants (the firstborn receiving a double portion; (2) daughters and their descendants; (3) the father; (4) brothers and their descendants; (5) sisters and their descendants; (6) the father's father; (7) the father's brothers; (8) the father's sisters and their descendants; (9) the father's father's father, and so on.

Innocence In Jewish law a person is presumed innocent until proven otherwise. Neither hearsay nor circumstantial evidence are allowed to overturn this presumption, and self-incrimination has no validity.

Inquisition Ecclesiastical tribunal of the Catholic Church dedicated to investigating and suppressing heresy. It was established in the 13th century under Innocent III. Initially it concerned itself only incidentally with Jews, but in Spain from 1478, operating under royal auspices and according to a papal bull, it dealt with Marrranos. The first

auto-da-fé was held in Seville in 1481 and in 1483 Tomas de Torquemada became Inquisitor-General. In 1540 the Inquisition spread to Portugal, and later was introduced into Spanish and Portuguese dependencies overseas.

Insanity According to the rabbis symptoms of insanity include going out alone at night, sleeping in a cemetery and destroying what is given to one. In addition a generally confused and irresponsible attitude is considered evidence of the condition. In Jewish law an insane person is exempt from all religious obligations and punishments, his dealings have no legal validity and he cannot marry. Any man who becomes insane after marriage cannot give his wife a bill of divorce, but a woman who becomes insane after marriage can be divorced, although the rabbis forbade such an act on humanitarian grounds.

Inspiration Divine influence affecting a written or spoken utterance. In Jewish sources the Holy Spirit or the 'Shekinah' is depicted as descending or resting upon human beings. Jewish philosophers in Alexandria compared the effect of divine inspiration on a man with a lyre, the strings of which are moved by wind. Rabbinic sources distinguish between the verbal inspiration of the Pentateuch and the lesser forms of inspiration found in other biblical books. The Pentateuch is regarded as the result of the highest form of inspiration, every letter, vowel and musical accent being of divine origin.

Insult In Jewish law an insult is viewed as an injury and must be compensated. Where bodily injury occurs, the insult involved is viewed as an additional factor in determining the damages. According to the rabbis, a person who insults another in public has no share in the world to come.

Intent The Hebrew word 'kavvanah' refers to a state of mental concentration which bestows religious intention on an act; in the medieval period it came to mean specific devotional intention as well as mystical meditation. The term denoting intention in the legal sense is 'zadon'. Intent must be proven for an individual to be culpable; when it is lacking the Bible prescribes compensatory ritual obligations in place of punishment in certain cases.

Intermarriage In Jewish usage marriage between a Jew and a non-Jew. Intermarriage was rare before the Emancipation of Jewry, but increased in the 19th century with the establishment of civil marriages. Although intermarriage is forbidden by Jewish law, a number of Reform rabbis in the US are willing to participate in mixed-marriage ceremonies.

Ionesco, Eugene (1912–94) Romanian-French playwright. He achieved fame wth a series of plays which mocked bourgeois life and the facist tendencies of his background. He was influenced by Franz Kafka and is viewed as the father of the Theatre of the Absurd.

Irgun Tzevai Leumi [Etzel] Jewish underground organisation in Palestine. Its alternative name is derived from the initial letters of the formal title. Founded in 1937 by members of Betar and Revisionists in the Haganah, its purpose was to retaliate against Arab attacks. When the White Paper advocating a joint Jewish–Arab State in Palestine was published in 1939, Irgun Tzevai Leumi attacked the British authorities in the country and was subsequently outlawed by the Mandatory Government. The Jewish Agency dissociated itself from the activities of the organisation. Its leader David Raziel was killed in 1941 and was succeeded by Menaḥem Begin. In 1944 the Irgun Tzevai Leumi renewed its anti-Jewish activities, and later it carried out attacks on Arab villages. When the State of Israel was proclaimed, its members joined the Haganah.

Isaac (i) (fl.? 19th–16th cent. BCE) Israelite, son of Abraham and Sarah. He was born when Abraham was 100 years old (Genesis 21:5). He was the heir of the Abrahamic tradition and covenant (Genesis 17:19; 21:12). In order to test him, God ordered Abraham to sacrifice Isaac, but the boy was saved at the final moment (Genesis 22). Isaac married Rebekah, who bore him two sons, Esau and Jacob.

Isaac (ii) (fl. 8th–9th cent.) Jewish merchant of Aachen. In 797 he was appointed by Charlemagne as guide and interpreter to an official delegation to Harun al-Rashid. When Charlemagne's ambassadors died on the way, Isaac completed the journey and was received by Charlemagne in audience when he returned after four years.

Isaac, Jules (1877–1963) French historian. He was born in Rennes. His *Cours d'histoire* served as a textbook for French schools and colleges. In 1936 he was appointed Inspector-General of Education for France. After his family was killed by the Nazis, he wrote about the Christian roots of anti-Semitism in *Jésus et Israel* and *Genèse de l'antisémitisme*.

Isaac ben Abba Mari (?1120–?1190) Franco–Spanish rabbinic scholar. Active in Provence and Spain, he corresponded with the important scholars of his generation. His *Sepher ha-Ittur* is a compilation of the main halakhic laws that have practical application. It was regarded as the authoritative code until the appearance of Jacob ben Asher's *Tur*, which superseded it.

Isaac ben Joseph of Corbeil [Baal ha-Ḥotem] (fl. 13th cent.) French codifier. His *Sepher Mitzvot* contains a compendium of halakhah, together with ethical homilies, parables and aggadot. This work, known from its initials as *Semak*, received recognition from scholars in France and Germany.

Isaac ben Meir of Düren (fl. 14th cent.) German codifier. His *Sepher Shearim* (also known as *Sharre Dura* or

Issur ve-Hetter) served as the authoritative code for dietary laws until the publication of the Shulḥan Arukh.

Isaac ben Moses of Vienna [Isaac Or Zarua]. (c.1180–c.1250) Bohemian halakhic authority. He became known as Isaac Or Zarua from the title of his halakhic work *Or Zarua*. This study is arranged on the basis of the *Talmud*, and contains commentaries on talmudic subjects, together with earlier codifications and responsa. It also includes material about medieval Jewish life in Germany, France and Italy.

Isaac ben Samuel of Acre (fl 13th–14th cent.) Spanish Kabbalist. In 1391 he left Acre for Italy, and then went to Spain where he met Moses de Leon. His publications include a commentary on Naḥmanides' mysticism, a mystical diary, a commentary on the Sepher Yetsirah, and a study of the composition of the *Zohar*.

Isaac ben Samuel of Dampierre (d. c.1185) French tosaphist. He lived in Ramerupt, assisting his teacher and uncle, Jacob Tam. Later he settled in Dampierre. Together with Jacob Tam, he was a central figure in the activity of the tosaphists.

Isaac ben Sheshet Perfet [Ribash] (1326–1408) Spanish rabbi and halakhic authority. He was born in Barcelona. After the persecution of the Jews in 1391, he left Spain and settled in Algiers, where he served as a rabbi. He wrote numerous responsa, which exercised considerable influence on later halakhah and contain information about popular customs in Spain and North Africa. He also wrote commentaries on talmudic tractates and the Pentateuch , as well as poetry.

Isaacs, Abraham Samuel (1852–1920) American rabbi, writer and educator. He taught Hebrew and German at New York University between 1885 and 1906. He served as a preacher at the East 86th Street Synagogue in New York and rabbi of the B'nai Jeshurun Congregation in Patterson, New Jersey. In 1878 he became editor of the *Jewish Messenger* and continued in that post until the journal merged with the *American Hebrew* in 1903. His publications include *A Modern Hebrew Poet: The Life and Writings of Moses Chaim Luzzatto* and *What is Judaism?*

Isaacs, Isaac (1855–1948) Australian Governor-General. Born in Melbourne, he worked as a teacher in local schools, and later studied law at Melbourne University. He initially worked as a lawyer, later serving as a member of the Victorian legislative assembly. He was Solicitor-General and Attorney-General. Subsequently he was a justice of the Federal High Court, becoming Chief Justice and Governor-General of Australia in 1931.

Isaacs, Samuel Myer (1804–1878) Preacher and communal leader. He was born in the Netherlands and first settled in London, where he served as principal of an orphan asylum. He emigrated to the US in 1839. He was the first cantor and preacher of the Congregation B'nai Jeshurun in New York. Later he became rabbi of Congregation Shaarei Tefila. He founded the first English-language Jewish weekly in the US, *The Jewish Messenger,* which supported the abolition of slavery and opposed Reform Judaism. In 1859 he was one of the organisers of the Board of Delegates of American Israelites, which advocated Jewish civil and religious rights.

Isaac the Blind (fl. 12th–13th cent.) Franco–Spanish Kabbalist, son of Abraham ben David of Posquières. He was one of the earliest kabbalists, in Provence and Spain. He transmitted his teachings orally and wrote a commentary on the Sepher Yetzirah. He has been referred to as the 'father of the kabbalah'.

Isaiah (i) (fl. 8th cent. BCE) Israelite prophet. He prophesied in Jerusalem from the death of Uzziah until the middle of Hezekiah's reign (740–701 BCE). He protested against unrighteousness and demanded justice for the poor and downtrodden. He opposed all treaties with neighbouring states and insisted that the people should put their trust in God. He proclaimed that the nation would be punished through Assyrian conquest and domination, but that a remanent of the people would return and continue the covenant.

Isaiah (ii) Biblical book, one of the books of the Later Prophets. It contains the account of Isaiah's prophecies. Most scholars believe that the book of Isaiah should be divided into two sections, chapters 1–39 and 40–66; they are believed to have been written by different authors, Isaiah and Deutero–Isaiah.

Ish-bosheth [Eshbaal] (fl. 11th cent. BCE) Israelite prince, son of Saul. After Saul and his other sons died in battle, Ish-bosheth was proclaimed king by Saul's general, Abner (II Samuel 2:8–9). Abner led the war against David (II Samuel 2:12–17; 3:6), but eventually abandoned Ish-bosheth. According to II Samuel 4, Ish-bosheth was murdered by Rechab and Baanah.

Ishmael (fl.? 19th–16th cent. BCE) Israelite son of Abraham and Hagar. After Hagar conceived, she was treated harshly by Sarah. She fled to the wilderness, but eventually returned. After the birth of Isaac, she and her son, Ishmael, were expelled by Abraham at Sarah's request (Genesis 21). According to tradition, Ishmael was the ancestor of the Arabs.

Ishmael ben Elisha (fl. 2nd cent.) Palestinian tanna. He lived at Kephar Aziz, south of Hebron. He disputed with Akiva about halakhic and aggadic matters and expanded to 13 the seven hermeneutical rules laid down by Hillel. He was also one of the leading aggadists of the period. According to legend, he was one of the martyrs who was killed in the persecutions that followed the Bar Kokhba revolt. Many mystical statements and literary works were ascribed to him.

Ishmael ben Nethaniah (fl. 6th cent.) Israelite soldier. After the destruction of Jerusalem by the Babylonians, he fled to Baalis, King of the Ammonites. When the Babylonians made the Israelite Gedaliah King of Judah, he gathered the scattered remnants of the people together and prepared to govern them. Ishmael murdered him and endeavoured to take the remaining Jewish community to Ammon, but was thwarted by Johanan ben Kareah (Jeremiah 40–41).

Ishmael of Akbara (fl. 9th cent.) Babylonian sectarian. He was the founder of the Akbaraites who seceded from the Karaite community. He did not recognise the masoretic emendations in the text of the Bible. He permitted the consumption on the Sabbath of food cooked or gathered on that day by non-Jews, and the use of the income of a business which operated seven days a week.

Ish-Shalom [Friedmann], Meir (1831–1908) Austrian scholar. He was born in Slovakia. He taught midrash at the Vienna Rabbinical Seminary and published editions of midrashic and aggadic literature.

Isidor, Lazare (1813–1888) French rabbi. He was born in Lixheim, Lorraine. He served as rabbi of Pfalzburg and Paris, and later as chief rabbi of France. During his time at Pfalzburg he refused to allow a member of the congregation of Saverne to pronounce the Jewish oath, *more judaico*. He was subsequently prosecuted, defended by Adolphe Cremieux and acquitted.

Isidore of Seville (c.560–636) Spanish theologian and encyclopedist, Archbishop of Seville. Born in Cartagena, he moved to Seville as a child. His *Contra Judaeos* attempts to demonstrate the fallacies of the Jewish faith, and provides evidence for the truth of Christianity in all the books of the Bible.

Islam Mohammed urged the spread of Islam by the sword, and the Jews of Arabia who failed to support the new faith were attacked. Later Jews living in Islamic lands enjoyed considerable freedoms, and a number of Jewish thinkers were deeply influenced by Islamic thought.

Israel Name used variously in Jewish history for the territory of the Jews and for the Jewish people. The name was given to Jacob after his struggle with the angel: 'Your name shall be called no more Jacob but Israel, for you have striven with God and with men and have prevailed' (Genesis 32:28–29). It is also used for the descendants of Jacob. with the division of the kingdom during the reign of Rehoboam (930 BCE). The southern kingdom was known as 'Judah' and the northern kingdom as 'Israel'. Subsequently the name 'Israel' was used in the books of the Bible written for the end of the northern kingdom and in rabbinic literature to denote the Jewish people as a whole. When a Jewish homeland was established in 1948 it was called the State of Israel.

Israel, Kingdom of [Samaria] The northern kingdom of the two kingdoms into which Palestine was divided after the revolt led by Jeroboam I against Rehobam in 930 BCE. The seceding tribes, led by Ephraim were Issachar, Zebulun, Naphtali, Asher, Dan, Reuben, Gad and part of Manasseh. During two centuries Israel had 19 kings. It was eventually captured by the Assyrians in 721 BCE (I Kings 12–II Kings 17).

Israel, Land of [Canaan; Eretz Yisrael; Holy Land; Jeshurun; Promised Land] Name of the land promised by God to Abraham and his descendants.

The area is indicated in the patriarchal covenant (Genesis 15:18–19). Other boundaries are described in Numbers 34:2–12 and other biblical books, as well as in talmudic sources. It is viewed as an inalienable divine gift to the Jewish people. Love of the land is expressed in the Bible, the *Talmud*, the liturgy, religious thought and Jewish law.

Israel, State of From the beginning of World War II, the creation of a Jewish state was the primary aim of Zionists. Although the Balfour Declaration of 1917 supported the creation of a Jewish homeland in Palestine, the British document known as the 1939 White Paper effectively rejected this proposal. After the end of the war the United Nations discussed the Palestinian problem. A plan to partition Palestine into areas for Arabs (Jordan) and Jews (Israel) was endorsed by the General Assembly of the United Nations on 19 November 1947. On 14 May 1948, in Tel Aviv, David Ben-Gurion read out the Israeli Scroll of Independence. In the years that followed Israel has repeatedly been at war with those of its Arab neighbours who have not recognised the legitimacy of the state (although some Arab states have recognised its legitimacy).

Israel ben Samuel Ashkenazi of Shklov (d.1839) Palestinian talmudic scholar of Lithuanian origin. He was born in Shklov, and during his years in Lithuania, he was entrusted with the publication of the Vilna Gaon's commentaries. He later settled in Safed. In 1816 he was chosen to succeed Menaḥem Mendel of Shklov, the leader of the Kolel ha-Perushim, in Safed. After an earthquake in 1837, he moved to Jerusalem. His *Peat ha-Shulḥan* supplements the Shulḥan Arukh with a codification of laws relating to life in Palestine, which had been omitted by Joseph Caro.

Israel ben Shabbetai of Kozienice [Kozienicer Maggid] (c.1737–1814) Polish Ḥasidic leader and scholar. He lived in Kozienice in central Poland.

He was know for his ability to perform miraculous cures by means of prayers and the use of amulets. Napoleon's Russian expedition of 1811 was due to Israel ben Shabbetai's prayers.

Israeli, Isaac ben Joseph (fl. 14th cent.) Spanish astromomer. He lived in Toledo and is known for his *Yesod Olam*, which deals with the geometrical problems of the earth in the Ptolemaic system of the universe.

Israeli, Isaac ben Solomon [Isaac Judaeus] (c.855–955) Physician and philosopher. He was born in Egypt; he later moved to Kairouan, where he served as court physician. He wrote eight medical works including treatises on pharmacology, fevers and ophthalmology, as well as studies of logic and psychology. He was one of the first Jewish medieval philosophers, and attempted to reconcile Jewish theology with Neoplatonism.

Israeli, Isaac d' (1766–1848) English author. He was the son of an Italian-born merchant. His first essays were among the earliest Jewish contributions to English literature. His writings include *Curiosities of Literature and Commentary on the Life and Reign of Charles I.* In 1813 he was fined by the Sephardi synagogue in London for refusing to serve as warden. He resigned from the congregation and had his children baptised. Benjamin Disraeli, later Prime Minister and Earl of Beaconsfield was his son.

Israels, Jozef (1824–1911) Dutch painter. He was born in Groningen, and earned his living in Amsterdam by painting portraits and historical subjects, including scenes from Jewish life and history. In 1885 he settled in Zandvoort, and later he moved to The Hague.

Isru Ḥag ('Bind the festival offering') Name given to the semi-festival days occurring after the festivals of Passover, Shavuot and Sukkot. On these days no applications or confessions are said, and fasting and funeral eulogies are forbidden.

Issachar (fl.? 19th–16th cent. BCE) Son of Jacob and Leah. His birth was considered by Leah to be a sign of divine favour after a long period of barrenness, as a reward for her having given her handmaid to Jacob (Genesis 30:18). Issachar was the ancestor of the tribe bearing his name.

Isserlein, Israel ben Pethahiah (1390–1460) German rabbi and talmudist. He was born in Regensburg and served as rabbi in Marburg and Wiener-Neustadt, where he was the leading halakhic authority of his time. His responsa were collected together in *Terumat ha-Deshen.*

Isserles, Moses [Rema] (c.1525–1572) Polish codifier. He was born in Kraków, where he later founded and mainained a yeshivah. When Joseph Caro's code, *Bet Joseph*, appeared, Isserles wrote the *Darkhe Mosheh,* which explained the views of Ashkenazi's scholars. After the abridgement of Caro's code, the Shulḥan Arukh was published, Isserles wrote the *Mappah*, which incorporated Ashkenazi practice. It was through these additions to the Shulḥan Arukh that the code was eventually accepted as authoritative among the Ashkenazim. He also wrote studies of philosophy and kabbalah.

Italia, Salom (c.1619–c.1655) Italian engraver, etcher and draftsman. He was born in Mantua, but lived and worked in Amsterdam. He produced engraved portraits and book illustrations, as well as copper-plate borders for the Ketubbah and Megillah.

Ithamar (fl.? 13th cent. BCE) Israelite, youngest son of Aaron. During the wanderings of the Israelites in the wilderness he was assigned special duties as leader over all the Levites (Exodus 31; 38:21).

The house of Eli traced descent to him (I Samuel 14:3; I Chronicles 24:3).

Itzig, Daniel Jaffe [Jaffe, Daniel (1723–1799) German financier, leader of the Berlin Jewish community He minted coins on behalf of the Prussian State during the Seven Years' War. In 1797 he was appointed court banker and inspector of road construction. He was also the chief representative of Prussian Jewry and responsible for the foundation of the Jewish Free School.

Ivrit be-Ivrit ('Hebrew in Hebrew') Method of teaching Hebrew by speaking the language. It was first practised in about 1874 in an Alliance Israélite Universelle school in Constantinople at the initiative of Nissim Behar. In 1883 he introduced his method into Palestine where it was adopted by various Jewish educational institutions under the leadership of Eliezer Ben-Yehudah. It was later widely accepted in many Jewish schools outside Palestine.

Iyyar Second month of the ancient Israelite calendar, and eight month of the modern Jewish calendar. 5 Iyyar is Israeli Independence Day. The second (or Little) Passover (celebrated in the Temple period by those who could not observe Passover in the usual month of Nisan) falls on 14 Iyyar, and Lag Ba-Omer on 18 Iyyar.

J

Saul Goldstein gets a new dog and can't wait to show him off to his friend Fred Feinberg. So when Fred comes for a visit, Saul calls the dog into the house. The dog quickly comes running, looks up at his master and wags his tail. Saul points to the newspaper on the couch and says: 'Fetch!'

The dog climbs on the couch and sits down. He looks at his master and whines: 'You think this is easy wagging my tail all the time? And do you think the dog food you give me is good? It's rubbish. You push me out the door every time I take a leak. I can't remember when you last took me out for a walk.'

Fred is astonished. 'What the hell is that all about?' he asks.

The dog looks up puzzled. 'Oh sorry,' the dog says. 'I thought you said KVETCH (complain).'

* * * * *

Jewish jokes often make fun of Jews complaining. The complainers are mothers, fathers or children. But here it is the dog who misunderstands his owner. The Yiddish for complain is 'kvetch'. The dog misheard the command and thought 'fetch' was 'kvetch'. But the dog is talented – he has a command of Yiddish even if his hearing is deficient.

Jabès, Edmond (1912–1991) French writer and poet. He was born in Cairo and settled in Paris in 1957. His works, most of which are theological, include *The Book of Questions* and *The Book of Resemblances*.

Jabotinsky, Vladimir (1880–1940) Russian Zionist leader, soldier and writer. He was born in Odessa. He first worked as a foreign correspondent in Berne and Rome. After returning to Odessa, he formed a Jewish self-defence group there. During World War I he advocated the recruiting of Jewish regiments to fight on the Palestinian front, and after the war, he supported the maintenance of a Jewish legion in Palestine to protect Jews from Arab hostility. In 1920 he organised a Jewish self-defence unit in Jerusalem, for which he was arrested, tried and punished by a British military tribunal. In 1925 he formed the World Union of Zionist Revisionists, and from 1936 he urged the evacuation of Eastern-European Jewry to Palestine. He was the spiritual father and head of the Jewish underground movement Irgun Tzevai Leumi, founded in 1937. Besides his military activities, he was also a translator, writer and poet.

Jachin Thae name of one of the two pillars set up by Solomon at the entrance to the Temple in Jerusalem (I Kings 7:15–22). The other was called Boaz.

Jacob [Israel] (fl.? 19th–16th cent. BCE) Israelite, son of Isaac and Rebekah. He bought the birthright of his brother Esau in exchange for food when Esau was faint with hunger, and later succeeded in securing the blessing Isaac intended to bestow on Esau. Fearing his brother's anger, Jacob left home and went to Haran, where he married Rachel and Leah, the daughters of his uncle Laban. By them and their handmaids Bilhah and Zilpah he had 12 sons and a daughter. After many years he made his way back to Canaan. During the journey he wrestled with an angel at the ford on the River Jabbok. In his old age, during a time of famine in Canaan, he was reunited with his youngest son, Joseph., who had been sold into slavery by his brothers and had become Pharoah's chief minister in Egypt (Genesis 23–50).

Jacob, Benno (1862–1945) German rabbi and biblical scholar. He was born in Breslau. He served as a rabbi in Göttingen and Dortmund before settling in Hamburg and then (in 1939) in England. He published studies of the Pentateuch, defending it against modern biblical criticism, and claimed that 'higher criticism' of the Bible was anti-Semitic. He was also opposed to Zionism, viewing it as a secularisation of Judaism and a basis for Jewish atheism.

Jacob ben Asher [Baal ha-Turim] (c. 1270–c.1343) Spanish codifier, son of Asher ben Jehiel. He was born in Germany and went with his father to Spain in 1303. He lived first in Barcelona and later in Toledo. His code, *Arbaah Turim*, contains the decisions found in both versions of the *Talmud*, and those of the geonim, as well as those given in earlier commentaries and codes. The work is divided into four parts: 'Orah Hayyim' deals with daily conduct, including prayers, Sabbaths and holidays; 'Yoreh Deah' lays down dietary laws; 'Even ha-Ezer' covers personal and family matters; and 'Hoshen Mishpat' describes civil law and administration.

Jacob ben Jacob Moses of Lissa (d.1832) Polish talmudist. He served as a rabbi at Kalisz, Lissa and Stryy. He was opposed to the Reform movement and to Hasidism. His *Derekh ha-Hayyim* is a compendium of Jewish practice.

Jacob ben Meir Tam [Rabbenu Tam] (c.1100–1171) French tosaphist, grandson of Rashi and brother of Samuel ben Meir. He lived at Ramerupt, and later settled at Troyes, where the first conference of French rabbis met under his leadership. His *Sepher ha-Yashar* contains many of his tosaphot and novellae. He wrote studies of grammar and biblical interpretation, and composed liturgical poetry.

Jacob ben Moses ha-Levi Mölln [Mölln, Jacob ben Moses] (c.1360–1427) German codifier. He served as a rabbi in Mainz and later in Worms. He was a leading authority on Jewish customs and liturgy. His religious practices were recorded by his disciple Zalman of St Goar in *Sepher Maharil*.

Jacob ben Reuben (fl. 12th cent.) Turkish Karaite biblical commentator. A native of Constantinople, he travelled to various countries to spread Karaism. His biblical commentary, *Sepher ha-Osher*, contains excerpts from Karaite authors.

Jacob ben Samson (fl. 12th cent.) French historian and scholar, pupil of Rashi. According to the tosaphists, he was the author of *Seder Olam*, a chronology of the tannaim and amoraim.

Jacobi, Frederick (1891–1952) American composer. He was assistant conductor at the Metropolitan Opera House in New York and taught composition at the Juillard School of Music from 1936 to 1951. Many of his works are based on Jewish themes.

Jacob Isaac of Przysucha (1766–1814) Polish tzaddik. He inaugurated a Hasidic approach to Judaism based on the speculative study of the Torah and

Ḥasidism. He was, however, opposed to the more popular form of Ḥasidism, with its belief in miracles.

Jacob Joseph of Polonnoye (d.1782) Ukrainian Ḥasidic scholar. He was a rabbi at Sharagrod, but left his position after he became a follower of the Baal Shem Tov. Later he served as a rabbi at Rashkov, Nemirov, and Polonnoye. His *Toledot Yaakov Yoseph* is a primary source for the teachings of the Baal Shem Tov; it led the Vilna Gaon to issue a ban against the Ḥasidim. His other works include the biblical commentaries *Ben Porat Yoseph*, *Tzaphenat Paneaḥ*, and *Ketonet Passim*.

Jacob Joshua ben Tzevi Hirsch Falk (1680–1756) Polish talmudist. He served as a rabbi in several Polish and German cities. His yeshivah at Lwów became the centre of rabbinic learning in Poland. In 1730 he became a rabbi in Berlin and later in Frankfurt am Main, through he resigned the latter post because of his support for the rabbinical scholar Jacob Emden. His *Pene Yehoshua* contains nevellae on the *Talmud*.

Jacobowski, Ludwig (1868–1900) German poet and author. He was born in Strelno, in the Posen district, and lived in Berlin. He edited a newspaper, wrote several volumes of poetry and published a number of novels. He was a significant Jewish figure in the last decade of 19th-century German literature; his writings sought to create a synthesis of Judaism with German culture.

Jacobs, Joseph (1854–1916) British historian, folklorist and scholar. Born in Australia, he settled in England, where he became active as an author and journalist. He was the founder (in 1896) and editor of the *Jewish Year Book*. His studies of medieval Anglo-Jewish history included *Jews of Angevin England*. In 1900 he settled in the US, where he was an editor of the *Jewish Encyclopedia* and taught at the Jewish Theological Seminary.

Jacobs, Louis (1920–2006) English rabbi and scholar. He was born in Manchester and served as a rabbi there and, later, in London. From 1959 to 1962 he was a tutor at the Jews College, but he was disqualified by Chief Rabbi Brodie as a candidate for the post of principal of the college because of his religious views. He subsequently founded the New London Synagogue, where he served as rabbi. He wrote on halakhic issues, Jewish theology and philosophy, and Jewish mysticism. His publications include *We Have Reason to Believe*, *Principles of the Jewish Faith*, and *A Jewish Theology*.

Jacobson, Dan (1929–2014) British novelist. He was born in Johannesburg, lived in Israel, and later settled in London. His novels deal with the problems of apartheid in South Africa and of Jewish identity in the modern world. His books include *The Trap*, *A Long Way from London and Other Stories*, and *Time and Time Again*.

Jacobson, Howard (b.1942) English novelist. He was born in Manchester. After a period spent in Australia as a lecturer in English literature at Sydney University, he returned to Britain to teach at Cambridge; he also worked as a publisher and retailer. In 1975 he became a lecturer in English at Wolverhampton Polytechnic. His novels deal with Jewish characters. His novels include *Kalooki Nights*, *The Finkler Question*, *Zoo Time*, and *Shylock is my Name*. He won the Man Booker Prize.

Jacobson, Israel (1768–1828) German Reform leader. He was born in Halberstadt. He was President of the Jewish consistory in Westphalia, where he worked for the reform of Jewish education and the synagogue liturgy. In 1801 he founded the Jacobson School for Jewish and Christian pupils in Seesen, Braunschweig. He set up a Reform Temple in Seesen in 1810. Later he moved to Berlin, where he held Reform services in his home.

Jacobson, Victor (1869–1935) Russian Zionist leader and diplomat. He was born in Simferopol in the Crimea. From 1899 he was a member of the Zionist General Council. In 1903 he opposed the Uganda Scheme and was one of the organisers of the Kharkov Conference in opposition to Theodor Herzl. He served as head of the Beirut office of the Anglo-Palestine Company from 1906, and later directed its branch in Constantinople. During World War I he ran the Zionist office in Copenhagen and, subsequently, he represented the Zionist organisation and the Jewish Agency in Paris and at the League of Nations.

Jacoby, Johann (1805–1877) Prussian politician. He was born in Königsberg. He advocated Jewish religious reform and emancipation. In 1848 he was elected to the Prussian Landtag, and in the following year to the German Nationalversammlung in Frankfurt am Main. From 1863 he served in the Prussian House of Representatives.

Jael (fl. 12th cent. BCE) Kenite woman, wife of Heber the Kenite. After the army of Jabin of Hazor was defeated by the Israelites, the commander Sisera sought refuge in her tent. She killed him in his sleep (Judges 4–5).

Jaffe, Leib (1876–1948) Russian Zionist leader and writer. He was born in Grodno in Belorussia. He participated in the First Zionist Congress in 1897. He edited Zionist periodicals in Russia, and later was called to Moscow to edit the monthly journal of the Zionist Organisation. He subsequently moved to Lithuania, where he was elected President of the Zionist Organisation and edited its newspaper. In 1920 he emigrated to Palestine, and became editor of the daily paper *Haaretz*. As a writer he published Zionist literature in Russian, Russian anthologies of Hebrew poetry, and a selection of world poetry on Jewish nationalist topics.

Jaffe, Meir ben Israel (fl. 15th cent.) German copyist and book binder. He wrote a Haggadah at the end of the 15th century. In 1468 the Nuremberg Council invited him to go to Nuremberg to bind a copy of the Pentateuch.

Jaffe, Mordecai ben Abraham (c.1535–1612) Talmudist, Kabbalist and communal leader. He was born in Prague. He studied in Poland under Solomon Luria and Moses Isserles, then returned to Prague, where he became head of a yeshivah. Later he settled in Venice but he eventually moved back to Eastern Europe and was appointed av bet din and head of the yeshivah of Gradno (now in Belorussia). He subsequently lived in Lublin, Kremenets, Prague and Posen. He is the author of *Levush Malkhut*, a comprehensive code of Jewish law which provoked widespread criticism.

Jaffe, Tzevi Hirsch (1853–1929) Russian mathematician. He wrote studies of mathematical theory and invented a calculating machine. He was also a talmudic scholar and an authority on the Jewish calendar.

Jair (fl. 12th cent. BCE) Israelite judge. He flourished in the generation preceding Jephthah and judged Israel for 22 years (Judges 10:3–5).

Jakobovits, Immanuel (1921–1999) British Chief Rabbi. He was born in Königsberg. He served as a minister in several London synagogues and became Chief Rabbi of Dublin in 1949. From 1958 he was a rabbi at the Fifth Avenue Synagogue in New York. In 1966 he was appointed Chief Rabbi of the United Hebrew Congregations of the British Commonwealth. He was subsequently knighted, and eventually created a peer.

James, Harry (1916–1983) American musician. He played with various bands, and eventually joined Benny Goodman's group. In 1939 he formed his own band. He was most popular for his skill as a jazz trumpet player.

Janco, Marcel (1895–1984) Israeli painter. He was born in Bucharest. Early in his career he was involved in Dadaism in Paris, but he left the movement and returned to Romania, where he worked as an architect. In 1941 he settled in Palestine and began to paint works that reflect the colours of the landscape and its picturesque aspects. In 1947 he was a founder member of the New Horizons group. Later he established Ein Hod, an artist's village outside Haifa.

Janner, Barnett (1892–1982) Welsh politician and communal leader. He served as a member of parliament: as a Liberal from 1931 to 1935, and as a Labour member from 1945 to 1970. He was also President of the Zionist Federation of Great Britain and Ireland (1950), and of the Board of Deputies of British Jews (1955–64). He was subsequently knighted and then created a life peer.

Janner, Greville (1928–2015) Welsh politician and communal leader, son of Barnett Janner. He was born in Cardiff. He became a barrister and served as a Labour member of parliament. He worked in various Jewish communal bodies and wrote and contributed to a number of books. He was accused of abusing children, but the case was not brought to court during his lifetime.

Janowsky, Oscar (1900–1993) American historian. He was born in Poland and was taken to the US in 1910. In 1948 he became Professor of History at New York City College. His writings include *The Jews and Minority Rights (1898–1919)*, *The American Jew: A Composite Portrait*, *the American Jew: a Reappraisal*, *The Education of American Jewish Teachers*, and *Foundations of Israel*.

Japheth Son of Noah. with his brothers, Shem and Ham, he travelled with

Noah in the ark. After the Flood, Noah planted a vineyard; the Bible recounts the story of Noah's drunkenness and of Shem and Japheth covering him with a garment as he lay naked in his tent (Genesis 9).

Japheth ben Ali ha-Levi (fl. 10th cent.) Palestinian Karaite scholar. He lived in Jerusalem. He wrote biblical commentaries, a translation of the Bible into Arabic and polemical tracts against Saadyah Gaon.

Jaques, Heinrich (1831–1894) Austrian lawyer and politician. He was born in Vienna, and worked as a lawyer and banker. In 1879 he entered the Reichstag as a German Liberal. He published a tract on Jewish Emancipation.

Jashar, Book of [Sepher ha-Yashar] Ancient work, one of the lost books mentioned in the Bible (Joshua 10–13; II Samuel 1:18; I Kings 8:53). It contained poems about individuals and events from the time of Joshua to the beginning of the monarchy (1250–1000 BCE). A medieval composition of biblical legends, based on midrashim to the Pentateuch, was known by the same title.

Jason (fl. 2nd cent. BCE) Israelite, high priest. He bribed Antiochus IV to depose his brother, Onias III, so that he could become high priest. But later he was dismissed from the high priesthood by the king, and Menelaus, who offered Antiochus IV a large sum of money, was appointed instead. Jason's Hellenizing policy contributed to the Hasmonean revolt (166–164 BCE), which freed Judea from the rule of the Seleucids.

Jastrow, Marcus (1829–1903) Amercian rabbi and philologist. He was born in Rogasen, in the Posen district. After serving as preacher to the progressive German congregation in Warsaw he became a rabbi in Worms. In 1866 he emigrated to the US and was appointed rabbi at Rodeph Shalom in

Philadelphia. His publications include *Dictionary of the Targumim, The Talmud Babli and Yerushalmi, and the Midrashic Literature.*

Jastrow, Morris (1861–1922) Amercian orientalist, son of Marcus Jastrow. Born in Poland, he was brought up in the US. He taught Semitics at the University of Pennsylvania, where he became Research Professor of Assyriology. He wrote studies of biblical and Assyriological topics.

Javits, Jacob (1904–1986) American politican. Born in New York City, he studied at Columbia University and New York University. He worked as trial lawyer and became a US senator in 1956. From 1969 he was a member of the Senate Foreign Relations Committee.

Jawitz, Ze'ev (1847–1924) Polish historian. He settled in Palestine in 1888 and worked as a teacher and writer. He left Palestine in 1894 and moved in succession to Vilnius, Germany and London. His *Toledot Yisrael* is a 14-volume history of the Jews.

Jedid al-Islam ('New Muslims') Name of a group of crypto-Jews, resident in Meshed, Persia. Their ancestors converted to Islam in response to persecution by the Muslims in 1839. The Jedid al-Islam lived as Muslims but secretly observed Jewish customs.

Jehiel ben Joseph of Paris (d. c.1265) French talmudist and tosaphist. He was the leading Jewish protagonist in the Disputation of Paris (1240) held at the court of Louis IX, which originated from the charges of the apostate Nicholas Donin. As a result of this disputation, copies of the *Talmud* were burned in Paris in 1242. Jehiel ben Joseph continued to lead the Jewish academy in Paris, but in 1260 he moved to Palestine and settled in Acre, where he opened a yeshivah.

Jehiel Michal of Zloczov [Maggid of Zloczov] (c.1731–1786) Galician Hasidic leader. He was born in Brody and served as a preacher there and, later, in Zloczov. He was one of the early propagators of Hasidism in Galicia. He was strongly opposed by the mitnaggedim. Toward the end of his life he settled in Yampol, Podolia. Miraculous tales are told of his asceticism and saintliness.

Jehoahaz (i) [Joahaz] (fl. 9th cent. BCE) King of Israel (c.814–800 BCE), son of Jehu. During his reign, Aram turned Israel into a tributary nation, reduced her army and controlled large parts of her territory (II Kings 13:1–9).

Jehoahaz (ii) [Shallum] (fl. 7th cent BCE) King of Judah, son of Josiah. His name was originally Shallum (Jeremiah 22:11), but it was changed to Jehoahaz when he was made king after his father had been killed in the battle against Pharaoh Necho II at Megiddo. Three months later Necho II deposed Jehoahaz and put his elder brother Jehoiakim in his place (II Kings 23:33–4; II Chronicles 36:3–4). Jehoahaz died in captivity in Egypt (II Kings 23:29–34).

Jehoiachin [Coniah; Jeconiah] (fl. 6th cent. BCE) King of Judah (597 BCE), son of Jehoiakim. He ascended the throne at the age of 18 during the rebllion against Babylon. He was exiled to Babylon by Nebuchadnezzar, together with his family and 10,000 captives (II Kings 24:12ff). He was released during the reign of Evil-Merodach (II Kings 24–25; II Chronicles 36:8–10).

Jehoiada [Joiada] (fl. 9th cent. BCE) High priest. After Athaliah assumed the throne and killed the royal family (II Kings 11:1), it was feared that the entire house of David would be eliminated. But Jehoiada's wife, Jehosheba, hid Joash, the baby son of King Ahaziah, in the Temple. Jehoiada later proclaimed Joash king, had Athaliah slain and acted as regent until Joash was seven. Under Jehoiada's influence, the cult of Baal was prohibited, and the Temple at Jerusalem restored.

Jehoiakim [Eliakim; Joiakim] (fl. 7th–6th cent. BCE) King of Judah (608–598 BCE), son of Josiah. He was made king by Pharaoh Necho II in succesion to his brother Jehoahaz (ii). During the first three years of his reign Judah was subject to Egypt. After Necho II was defeated in the battle of Carchemish in 605 BCE, Judah came under the Babylonian yoke; according to II Chronicles, Nebuchadnezzar bound him in fetters to take him to Babylon (II Chronicles 36:6ff). Jehoiakim was a vassal of Babylon for three years before he rebelled (II Kings 24:1), which brought about his downfall and death.

Jehoram (i) [Joram] (fl. 9th cent. BCE) King of Israel (853–842 BCE), son of Ahab. He joined Jehoshaphat of Judah in the war against Mesha of Moab. He engaged in battle with Aram and was wounded in the battle of Ramoth-Gilead; while he was recuperating in Jezreel, Jehu assassinated him. (II Kings 8–9).

Jehoram (ii) [Joram] (fl. 9th cent. BCE) King of Judah (851–843 BCE), son of Jehoshaphat of Judah. He was married to Athaliah who introduced the cult of Baal into Judah. During his reign, Edom rebelled against Judah and Judah was ravaged by the Philistines. (II Kings 8; II Chronicles 21).

Jehoshaphat (fl. 9th cent. BCE) King of Judah (874–850 BCE), son of Asa. He was the first king of Judah to make a treaty with Israel. He married his son Jehoram (ii) to Athaliah, the daughter of King Omri of Israel (II Kings 8:26). Together with Ahab, he waged war unsuccessfully against Aram. With Ahab's son Jehoram (i), he engaged in battle with Mesha of Moab.

Jehu (fl. 9th cent. BCE) King of Israel (c.842–814 BCE). He was commander-in-chief to Jehoram (i) but conspired with the army against the king. With the assistance of Elisha, he eliminated the royal family (including Jehoram, Ahaziah of Judah, and Jezebel), as well as the priests of Baal, whose worship had flourished under Jehoram's regin. He fought unsuccessfully against Aram and paid tribute to Shalmaneser III of Assyria for protection from the Arameans. His dynasty continued for 100 years (II Kings 9–11).

Jeiteles [Jeitteles], Baruch (1762–1813) Bohemian Hebrew writer and physician, brother of Judah Jeiteles. He maintained a yeshivah in Prague, but later became a supporter of the Haskalah movement. He wrote halakhic novellae as well as Hebrew poems and translations. In 1813 he persuaded leading individuals in the Prague community to open a hospital for wounded soldiers of all nationalities in the Jewish quarter.

Jeiteles [Jeitteles], Ignaz (1783–1843) Bohemian writer, son of Baruch Jeiteles. He studied law at Prague University before moving to Vienna, where he worked as a merchant. With his cousin Alois Jeiteles he published the short-lived Jewish periodical *Siona* in 1819. He wrote studies of literature, philosophy, history and statistics, as well as poetry.

Jeiteles [Jeitteles], Judah (1773–1838) Bohemian orientalist, brother of Baruch Jeiteles. He was one of the four chairmen of the Jewish community in Prague, where he supervised the German-language school. He was the first to use the word 'Haskalah' for the Jewish Enlightenment movement. In 1830 he settled in Vienna. He contributed to Hebrew periodicals, and was the author of an Aramaic grammar in Hebrew.

Jellinek, Adolf (c.1820–1893) Austrian preacher and scholar. He was born in Moravia and moved to Prague in 1838. He was a rabbi in Leipzig from 1845, and in Vienna from 1856, where he became a famous preacher. He published studies of the history of the kabbalah and medieval Jewish philosophy, editions of smaller midrashim in his *Bet ha-Midrash*, and bibliographical booklets on medieval Jewish history and literature.

Jephthah (fl. c.12th cent. BCE) Israelite judge. When Gilead was threatened by the Ammonites, he went to war against them. Before he engaged in battle, he vowed to sacrifice to God whatever came first from his house should he return safely. To his grief he was met by his daughter, who he subsequently sacrificed (Judges 11). Later he was victorious against the Ephraimites.

Jeremiah (i) (fl. 7th–6th cent. BCE) Israelite prophet. When he first emerged as a prophet he rebuked the nation for idolatry. After the religious revival that marked the reign of Josiah, Jeremiah warned the people to keep the newly made covenant with God. When Nebuchadnezzar became king in Babylonia, Jeremiah prophesied that he would conquer Judah. Later he foretold the defeat of Zedekiah and his anti-Babylonian alliance, and advocated surrender. After the fall of Jerusalem, he went to Egypt, where he condemned Egyptian Jewry for idol-worship.

Jeremiah (ii) Biblical book, one of the books of the Latter Prophets. It contains 52 chapters: chapters 1–18 contain prophecies from the time of Josiah; chapters 19–36 record prophecies and narrative from the reigns of Jehoiakim, Jehoiachin and Zedekiah; chapters 37–44 consist of historical narrative; chapters 45–51 contain prophecies concerning other nations; and chapter 52 recapitulates the Book of Kings.

Jeremiah (iii) (fl. 4th cent.) Palestinian amora. He was born in Babylonia and became head of the academy at Tiberias. He engaged in halakhic discussions with most contemporary sages.

Jeroboam I (fl. 10th cent. BCE) King of Israel (c.928–907 BCE). During Solomon's reign he was a superintendent of forced labour, and led a revolt against the monarchy. After Solomon's death, he led a delegation representing the northern tribes, which met Rehoboam at Shechem. The delegation demanded changes in the system of labour; when its request was refused, the northern tribes declared their independence and appointed Jeroboam king. He first made his capital at Shechem, but later move it to Penuel. He set up new shrines at Bethel and Dan, centred round the worship of golden calves (I Kings 11–15; II Chronicles 10,13).

Jeroboam II (fl. 8th cent. BCE) King of Israel (789–748 BCE), son of Joash. He was the greatest ruler of the dynasty of Jehu; during his reign the Northern Kingdom attained the height of its economic, military and political power. His rule was marred by corruption, which was denounced by the prophets Amos and Hosea (II Kings 14).

Jerusalem [City of David; Holy City; Salem] Capital of Israel. In the time of Joshua, Adoni-zedek, King of Jerusalem, was defeated by the Israelites at Aijalon (Joshua 10). Yet his city remained an independent enclave between the tribal areas of Benjamin and Judah. It was later captured by David and became the capital of a united Israel (II Samuel 5:6–8; I Chronicles 11:4–6). By transferring the Ark of the Covenant there, David made it also the religious centre of Israel.

Solomon enlarged the city by adding the Palace and the Temple. After his death, it remained the capital of Judah and the Davidic dynasty until it was destroyed by the Babylonians in the 6th century BCE. Subsequently Jewish exiles returned and rebuilt the Temple. The Temple and the city were devastated a second time by the Romans in the 1st century. In modern times Jerusalem has again become the capital of the Jewish State.

Jeshua ben Damna (fl. 1st cent.) Israelite, high priest (c.61–3). He was appointed by Herod Agrippa II but after a short period of office was displaced by Joshua ben Gamla. At the end of the Roman siege of Jerusalem (70 CE) he fled for refuge to the Romans, together with other members of priestly families.

Jeshua ben Judah (fl. 11th cent.) Palestinian Karaite scholar. He lived in Jerusalem. His principal works are an Arabic translation of the Pentateuch with a philosophical commentary, a study of the law of incest, and philosophical tracts.

Jesse (fl. 11th–10th cent. BCE) Israelite, father of David. He lived in Bethlehem but later settled in Moab for fear of Saul. The royal house of David is referred to in the Bible as growing from the root of Jesse (Isaiah 11:1,10).

Jesurun, Isaac (fl. 17th cent.) Dalmatian merchant. He was a merchant at Ragusa, where he was accused in 1622 of the ritual murder of a Christian girl. His suffering is described in Hebrew and Spanish accounts. Banished for his supposed crime, he died in Palestine.

Jesurun, Reuel (fl. c.1575–1634) Portuguese Marrano. He was born in Lisbon. In 1599 he travelled to Rome, intending to join a Christian monastic order; but on the journey he was persuaded to return to Judaism, and went back to Lisbon. In 1604 he settled in Amsterdam, where he worked as the administrator of the *Talmud* Torah rabbinical school. His *Diálogo dos montes* is a dramatic poem in praise of Judaism.

Jesus (fl. 1st cent. BCE–1st cent. CE) Palestinian religious leader, founder of Christianity. According to the New Testament, he grew up in Galilee and was baptised by John the Baptist. He performed various miracles and announced the coming of the Kingdom of God. He was arrested and crucified by order of the Roman procurator, Pontius Pilate, at the instigation of the Jewish authorities. His followers believed that he rose from the dead and ascended to Haven. They formed the core of the earliest Christian Church and actively spread the good news about Jesus, who they believed to be the Messiah (hence the addition to his name of 'Christ': the anointed one). According to Christian belief, Jesus was God Incarnate and is restored to the Godhead in the form of the Trinity.

Jethro [Reuel] (fl.? 13th cent. BCE) Midianite, father-in-law of Moses. Moses married Jethro's daughter Zipporah, and Jethro appointed him as shepherd of his flocks (Exodus 2:16–21; 3:1). After the Exodus, Jethro advised Moses on the reorganisation of the judicial system (Exodus 18). In Scripture Jethro is also referred to as Reuel.

Jew Member of the Jewish community. The word is derived from the Latin 'Judaeus,' which itself is from the Hebrew 'Yehudah,' meaning 'Judah'. Traditionally Jewish identity is dependent on maternal descent or conversion to Judaism. The term is also used to denote ethnic origin without reference to religious observance.

Jew Bill Name by which the Jewish Naturalisation Bill, debated in the English Parliament in 1753, was commonly known. The bill, which was passed in May 1753, facilitated the naturalisation of foreign Jews and encouraged immigration. It gave rise to considerable opposition and was repealed in December 1753.

Jewish oath [more judaico] Oath imposed on Jews involved in legal proceedings with non-Jews. It was current from the Middle Ages in central and Eastern Europe. The oath was sworn on the Sepher Torah (or tephillin), and invoked curses upon any who took it in vain. It was abolished in 1846 through the efforts of Issac-Adolphe Crémieux. Although it disappeared in Germany in the 19th century, it continued to be used in Eastern Europe.

Jezebel (fl. 9th cent. BCE) Israelite woman of Sidonite origin, wife of Ahab, and daughter of Ethbaal, King of Sidon. She introduced her native cult of Baal worship into Israel, thereby arousing the anger of Elijah. In I and II Kings she is portrayed as a callous woman who unjustly bought about the death of Naboth and persecuted the prophets (I Kings 16–II Kings 9). She was killed in Jehu's revolt against the monarchy.

Joab (fl. 10th cent. BCE) Israelite commander-in-chief, nephew of David. When David became king, Joab was appointed head of the army. He defeated the Ammonites and led the campaign against Absalom. During the revolt of Sheba, son of Bichri, he was replaced as commander-in-chief by Amasa, who he later murdered. He supported Adonijah's claim to succeed David, and was put to death by Solomon in accordance with David's wishes (II Samuel 2–3, 10–11, 14:17–21; I Kings 1–2; II Chronicles 11:18–21:27).

Joachim, Joseph (1831–1907) German violinist of Hungarian origin. He was born in Köpcsény and moved with his family to Budapest. He studied under Felix Mendelssohn, and later led Liszt's orchestra at Weimar. From 1854 to 1864 he was Concert Master and Conductor of the Royal Hanoverian Orchestra. During this period he converted to Christianity. In 1866 he settled in Berlin, where he was Director of the Hochschule für Musik, and founded the Joachim Quartet. His composition, mainly for violin, include *Hebrew Melodies.*

Joash (i) [Jehoash] (fl. 9th cent. BCE) King of Judah (835–798 BCE). His grandmother, Athaliah, seized the throne and murdered all members of the house of David when Joash was a year old. He was rescued by his aunt Jehosheba, wife of the high priest Jehoiada. Jehoiada later crowned him king, had Athaliah put to death, and acted as regent until Joash became king when he was seven. Joash restored the Temple, but he later deviated from following Jewish law. During his reign, Judah was invaded by Hazael of Aram. Joash was killed by conspirators (II Kings 11–14).

Joash (ii) [Jehoash] (fl. 9th cent. BCE) King of Israel (801–785 BCE). After Aram was defeated by the Assyrians, he recaptured several towns ceded by his father Jehoahaz. When Amaziah of Judah attempted to free his country from Israelite domination, Joash captuured Jerusalem, plundered the Temple and royal treasures, and reduced the country to vassaldom (II Kings 13:10–13).

Job Biblical book, part of the Hagiographa. It tells the story of Job, a righteous man, who questioned God's justice in allowing him to suffer. His friends argued that his suffering was a result of wickedness, but Job refused to accept their explanation. God eventually spoke from a whirlwind and stressed Job's finite knowledge compared with his designs for the universe.

Jochebed (fl.? 13th cent. BCE.) Israelite woman, wife of Amram and mother of Moses, Aaron and Miriam (Exodus 6:20).

Joel Israelite prophet, one of the 12 Minor Prophets. The Book of Joel depicts plague of locusts (chapters 1–2) and describes the Day of The Lord, when God will rescue the Jewish people from captivity and punish their enemies in the Valley of Jehoshaphat (chapters 3–4).

Joel, Manuel (1826–1890) German rabbi and scholar. He was born in Birnbaum, Poznania. In 1854 he joined the faculty of the Breslau Rabbinical Seminary and ten years later he became rabbi of the Breslau community. In the rabbinical assemblies of Kassel and Leipzig, he advocated moderation in reform practice. He published studies of Ibn Gabirol, Maimonides, Ḥasdai Crescas, and Levi ben Gershom; he also wrote a two-volume work on comparative religion.

Joezer (fl. 1st cent. BCE–1st cent. CE). High priest, son of Boethus. He was a brother of Herod's wife, Mariamne, and of Eleazar, who also served as high priest. He played a role in pacifying the people when they resisted the attempts of Quirinius (Governor of Syria) to conduct a census in Judea.

Johanan [Gadi] (fl. 2nd cent BCE). Israelite fighter, son of Mattathias the Hasmonean. He and his brothers fought in the uprising against the Syrians. He was killed while on a mission to the Nabateans.

Johanan bar Nappaḥa (c.180–c.279). Palestinian amora. He was born in Sepphoris. He studied with Judah ha-Nasi, and was the brother-in-law of Simeon ben Lakish. He founded his own academy in Tiberias. His teachings constitute a major part of the Jerusalem *Talmud*.

Johanan ben Kareaḥ (fl. 6th cent. BCE) Israelite military commander, active in Judah at the time of the destruction of the First Temple (Jeremiah 40–43). He supported Gedaliah and warned him of Ishmael ben Nethaniah's trechery; after Gedaliah's murder, he prevented Ishmael from carrying away prisoners. Out of fear of Babylonian reprisals, he went to Egypt along with other exiles including Jeremiah.

Johanan ben Nuri (fl. 2nd cent.) Palestinian tanna. Living in poverty, he influenced the formulation of laws and customs of the Jews in Galilee. He is often mentioned in the Mishnah as taking part in debates with Akiva.

Johanan ben Zakkai (fl. 1st cent.) Palestinian tanna. He was the leading sage at the end of the Second Temple period and in the years following the destruction of the Temple. During the rebellion against Rome (66–70), he was among the peace party in Jerusalem. According to legend, he was carried out of the city in a coffin, approached Vespasian and predicted his accession to the imperial throne. As a reward, he was allowed to continue his teaching. He founded an academy at Jabneh, which became the seat of the Sanhedrin after the fall of Jerusalem.

Johanan ha-Sandelar (fl. 2nd cent.) Palestinian tanna. He was born in Alexandria and became a pupil of Akiva. After Hadrian's reign (117–38), which saw widespread persecution of the Jews, and the death of Akiva, at Caesarea, Johanan transmitted Akiva's teachings.

Johlson, Joseph (1773–1851) German scholar and teacher. He taught at the Philanthropin school in Frankfurt am Main from 1813 to 1830. He based the teaching of Hebrew on the mastery of grammar and established a systematic plan for teaching Judaism. He published textbooks about Jewish history in biblical times, a biblical dictionary and a German translation of the Bible.

John Hyrcanus (fl. 2nd cent. BCE) High priest and ethnarch (135–104 BCE), son of Simon the Hasmonean. After the murder of his father and his two brothers by Ptolemy, he escaped to Jerusalem. In 135–134 BCE Antiochus Sidetes captured Jerusalem, and John

Hyrcanus was confirmed as high priest. Later he threw off Syrian domination, attacked the Samaritans, destroying their temple on Mount Gerizim, and forced the Idumeans to convert to Judaism. Although initially allied with the Pharisees, he subsequently drew closer to the Sadducees.

John of Giscala (fl. 1st cent.) Palestinian fighter, leader of the revolt against Rome (66–70). He was born in Giscala. He conducted retaliatory raids against the Syrians after they had destroyed his native city. In 66 when Josephus arrived as commander in Galilee, a controversy arose between the two military leaders. John suspected Josephus of disloyalty and advocated his removal. After Galilee was conquered by Vespasian, John fled to Jerusalem. He took control of the Temple from the Zealots, who subsequently fought under his command during Titus's siege. He was later captured by the Romans, sentenced to life imprisonment and died in a Roman prison.

John the Baptist (fl. 1st cent.) Palestinian religious leader, forerunner of Jesus. He preached repentance, proclaimed the coming of the messianic age, and practised baptism of those who accepted his preaching. Jesus was among those who he baptised. He was put to death by Herod Antipas at the behest of Herodias, his wife, whose marriage to Herod John the Baptist condemned.

Jonah (i) Biblical book, one of the 12 Minor Prophets. It relates God's command to Jonah, son of Amittai, to go to Nineveh and proclaim judgement upon its inhabitants for their wickedness. On a sea voyage Jonah was swallowed by a great fish and eventually spewed out on dry land. As a result of his prophecy, the inhabitants of Nineveh repented of their evil ways.

Jonah (ii) (fl. 4th cent.) Palestinian amora. He and Yose were heads of the academy in Tiberias. Discussions between these sages are contained in the Palestinian *Talmud*.

Jonathan (i) (fl. 11th cent. BCE) Israelite prince, eldest son of Saul. He was a devoted friend of David. Together with Saul, he was killed in a battle against the Philistines on Mount Gilboa. The news of their deaths caused David to compose his famous lament (II Samuel 1:17–27).

Jonathan (ii) (fl. 2nd cent. BCE) Israelite head of state (160–143 BCE), youngest son of Mattahias. Together with his brother Judah Maccabee, he fought in the battles at the beginning of the Hasmonean Revolt (166–145 BCE). On the death of his brother, he took over the leadership of the anti-Syrian campaign. Alexander Balas (a contender with Demetrius I for the Syrian throne) conceded to him the title of High Priest and recognised him as Governor of Judah. He was captured by the Syrian leader Tryphon at Acre and killed.

Jonathan ben Amram (fl. 2nd–3rd cent.) Palestinian sage. A pupil of Judah ha-Nasi, he lived during the period between the tannaim and the amoraim. The halakhot quoted by him concern laws of levitical cleanness.

Jonathan ben David ha-Cohen of Lunel (c.1135–after 1210) French talmudic scholar. He was active in Provence. He defended Maimonides in the controversy about him encouraged by Meir Abulafia. He wrote commmentaries on the Mishnah, the *Talmud* and Alfasi's Code.

Jonathan ben Eleazar (fl. 3rd cent.) Palestinian amora. He is the Jonathan ben Eleazar mentioned in the *Talmud* and midrash. Of Babylonian origin, he went to Palestine in his youth and became a pupil of Simeon ben Yose ben Lakunya. He lived in Sepphoris and was one of the great aggadists of his time.

Jonathan ben Uzziel (fl. 1st cent. BCE–1st cent. CE)   Palestinian translator. He was an outstanding pupil of Hillel and was responsible for the first translation of the biblical books of the prophets into Aramaic.

Jong, Erica (b.1942)   American feminist. Born in New York, she studied at Bernard College and Columbia University. Her works include *Fear of Flying, How to Save Your Own Life, Parachutes and Kisses,* and *AnyWoman's Blues.*

Joselman [Josel] of Rosheim [Loanz, Yoseph ben Gershom] (1480–1544)   German writer and communal leader. In 1510 he was elected warden and leader by the Alsatian Jewish communities. He represented German Jewry before secular authorities and interceded for the Jewish community in times of danger. In 1532 he attempted to curb the activities of the pseudo-messiah Solomon Molcho. Later he defended the Jews against the charges made by Martin Luther.

Joseph (fl.? 19th–16th cent. BCE)   Israelite, 11th son of Jacob and firstborn of Rachel. As his father's favourite son, he aroused the anger of his brothers, who sold him into slavery in Egypt. He was bought as a slave by Potiphar, a high official. Later he was imprisoned on a false charge made by Potiphar's wife. After interpreting Pharaoh's dreams, he achieved high office in Egypt. Eventually he was reconciled with his brothers and reunited with his father, after which his family settled in the Goshen region (Genesis 37–50).

Joseph, Morris (1848–1930)   English Reform rabbi. He served as Minister of the West London Synagogue for nearly 20 years. He also taught homiletics at Jewish College in 1891–92. His writings include *Judaism as Creed and Life, The Ideal in Judasim, The Message of Judaism,* and *The Spirit of Judaism.*

Joseph bar Ḥiyya (fl. 9th cent.)   Babylonian gaon. He was gaon of Pumbedita (828–33). During the controversy between the exilarch, David ben Judah and his brother Daniel, Joseph bar Ḥiyya and Abraham ben Sherira presided over the academy at Pumbedita. When peace was restored, Joseph renounced the office of gaon and temporarily resumed the position of av bet din at Pumbedita.

Joseph ben Abraham ha-Cohen [Joseph abu Jacob;Abu Yakub al-Basir) (fl. 11th cent.)   Babylonian or Persian Karaite scholar. He travelled widely, seeking converts to Karaism. Despite his blindness, he wrote religio-legal and philosophical works.

Joseph ben Gorion (fl. 1st cent.)   Palestinian military leader. He participated in the revolt against Rome. His name was associated with the authorship of the Hebrew historical narrative, *Josippon.*

Joseph ben Isaac ha-Levi (fl. 17th cent.)   Bohemian philosopher of Lithuanian origin. He lived in Prague, where he taught medieval religious philosophy. He wrote a commentary on Maimonides' *Guide for the Perplexed,* which was published by Yom-Tov Lipmann Heller with his own introduction and annotations. Joseph ben Isaac's *Ketonet Passim* treats the basic ideas of the *Guide.*

Joseph ben Jacob bar Satya (fl. 10th cent.)   Babylonian gaon. In 930 he was appointed gaon of Sura by the exilarch David ben Zakkai after the exilarch had become embroiled in a dispute with Saadyah Gaon. Saadyah was later reinstated but Joseph ben Jacob resumed the post after Saadyah's death. Some time after 943 he left Sura and settled in Basra.

Joseph ben Joshua ha-Cohen (1496–c.1575)   Italian historian. He was brought up in Italy and practised medicine in Genoa. His *History of the Kings of France and Turkey* describes the struggle between Christians and Muslims from the time of the crusades. In *Valley of Weeping* he recounts the trials of the Jews in the Middle Ages.

Joseph ben Nathan [Official, Joseph] (fl. 13th cent.) French writer, son of Nathan ben Joseph Official. He was born of a family who had close relations with the local nobility, and he himself was in the service of the Archbishop of Sens as a financial agent. His *Sepher ha-Mekanne* recounts the religious arguments he and his circle had with the Christian community.

Joseph ben Tanḥum Yerushalmi (b.1262) Egyptian Hebrew poet. At the age of 15 he composed a collection of poems in imitation of Moses ibn Ezra. On his father's death in 1291, he composed a lamentation in which he mentions the conquest of Acre by the crusaders. He was the most representative Hebrew poet of Egypt in the 13th century.

Josephus, Flavius [Flavius Josephus; Joseph ben Mattahias] (fl. 38–after 100) Palestinian historian and soldier. He was born in Jerusalem. In 764 he went to Rome on a mission to secure the release of several priests. At the outbreak of the Jewish rebellion against the Romans in 66 he was appointed Commander of Galilee, and, when the Romans attacked the province in 67, he directed the resistance. He surrendered to the Romans after Jotapata was captured; he accompanied Vespasian and Titus during the siege of Jerusalem. After the Roman victory he lived in Rome. His writings include *The Jewish War, The Antiquities of the Jews, Against Apion,* and an *Autobiography.*

Joshua (i) (fl.? 13th cent. BCE) Israelite leader. As Moses' successor, he was assigned the task of leading the people in the conquest of Canaan. He commanded the Israelites in the war with the Amalekites (Exodus 17:14–16). Later he was one of the 12 spies sent to

reconnoitre the land of Canaan. After the Israelites had crossed the Jordan, Joshua led them to victory over the alliance of southern kings, and then the northern kings. He subsequently brought the Tabernacle to Shiloh and divided the newly won territory among the 12 tribes.

Joshua (ii) Biblical book, one of the books of the Former Prophets. It describes Joshua's conquests and the division of the land of Canaan among the 12 tribes of the Israelites.

Joshua ben Gamla (d.69/70) High priest. He married one of the wealthiest women in Jerusalem. He established a universal system of education throughout Palestine. An opponent of the Zealots at the time of the Jewish rebellion against Rome, he was put to death by the Idumeans.

Joshua ben Hananiah (fl. 1st–2nd cent.) Palestinian tanna. During the siege of Jerusalem, he helped his teacher Johanan ben Zakkai to escape. Favoured by the Romans, he travelled repeatedly to Rome on national missions to aid the Jewish cause. After the death of Gamaliel II, he became av bet din at the Jabneh academy. His polemical debates with Christians are recorded in rabbinic literature.

Joshua ben Jehozadak (fl. 6th cent. BCE) High priest. He went to Jerusalem with Zerubabel. Encouraged by Zechariah and Haggai, he set up the altar as the first step in the restoration of the Temple. His descendants remained in office until the time of the Hasmoneans.

Joshua ben Korḥa (fl. 2nd cent.) Palestinian tanna. He studied under Johanan ben Nuri and Eleazar ben Azariah. He laid down the rule that where there is a difference of opinion the stricter view should be adopted with regard to a biblical injunction, but the more lenient view where the injunction is of rabbinic provenance. He engaged in disputations with sectarians and non-Jews.

Joshua ben Levi (fl. 3rd cent.) Palestinian amora. He was born in Lydda and later taught there, also concerning himself closely with communal needs. He was involved in affairs affecting the community in its relations with the Roman authorities, and travelled on various missions to Caesarea and Rome. He was a master of the aggadah, and some of his sayings are recorded in the Mishnah.

Joshua ben Perahyah (fl. 2nd cent. BCE) Palestinian leader, head of the Sanhedrin. Together with Nittai the Arbelite, he formed the second of the pairs ('Zugot') of sages. The Babylonian *Talmud* records that he was a teacher of Jesus.

Joshua Heshel ben Jacob of Lublin (1595–1663) Polish rabbi. Born in Lublin, he succeeded his father as rabbi of the community in 1650. Later he succeeded Yom-Tov Lipmann Heller as rabbi of Kraków. Subsequently he moved to Vienna and sought to exert pressure on the government in the interest of Jewry. He eventually returned to Poland, where he continued his educational activities. He was a noted halakhic authority.

Josiah (fl. 7th cent. BCE) King of Judah (640–609 BCE), son of Amnon. He was proclaimed king while still a child after his father was assassinated. His reign was marked by a great religious revivial: he removed foreign cults and re-established monotheism. During the restoration of the Temple, Hilkiah, the high priest, announced the discovery of a Book of the Law. This prompted Josiah to convene an assembly of the people, during which he made a covenant with God. He also discontinued worship in the high places and centralised it in the Temple at Jerusalem.

Josiah ben Zakkai (fl. 10th cent.) Babylonian exilarch. He was appointed exilarch after his brother David was deposed from office by Saadyah Gaon. The caliph intervened in David's favour. Josiah was then banished to Chorassan, where he died.

Josippon [Josephon] Hebrew historical narrative, describing the period of the Second Temple. Written in southern Italy in the 10th century, it was ascribed to Joseph ben Gorion. It is based on Josephus' writings.

Jost, Isaac Marcus (1793–1860) German historian. He was born in Bernburg. He served as head of a private high school in Frankfurt am Main. From 1835 he taught at the Philanthropin high school in Frankfurt, and in 1853 he founded an orphanage for Jewish girls there. He published a Pentateuch for young people, a vocalised Mishnah text with translations and notes, a textbook of English, a dictionary of Shakespeare, and a manual of German style. He was a pioneer in modern Jewish historiography and a supporter of the Reform movement.

Jotham (i) (fl. c.12th cent. BCE) Israelite, youngest son of Gideon. He was the sole survivor of Abimelech's massacre in which all his brothers died (Judges 9). He escaped to Mount Gerizim where he denounced the Shechemites for accepting Abimelech as king (Judges 9:8–15).

Jotham (ii) (fl. 8th cent. BCE) King of Judah (c.742–735 BCE), son of Uzziah. He defeated the Ammonites in battle (II Chronicles 27:5), and during his reign the country enjoyed considerable prosperity. He made repairs and additions to buildings in the Temple area in Jerusalem (II Chronicles 27:3; II Kings 15:35).

Journey, Prayer on Setting out on a The offering of prayers in preparation for travelling is enjoined in the

Talmud. Different versions of the prayer exist for land, sea and air journeys. They include appropriate biblical verses.

Joy According to the Bible (Psalm 100:2), joy is a prerequisite for true worship. Special occasions of joy include circumcision, bar mitzvah ceremonies, weddings, the Sabbath and festivals. Among the Ḥasidim it is a central feature of prayer.

Jubal Musician, son of Lamech. He is regarded as the father of all who handle the harp and pipe (Genesis 4:19–21).

Jubilees, Book of [Genesis Zutarta; Lesser Genesis] Pseudepigraphic work dating from the middle of the Second Temple period, it contains the secret revelation of the Angel of the Divine Presence to Moses on his second ascent to Mount Sinai. Some scholars believe it may have originated in an early Essene group.

Judah (fl.? 19th–16th cent. BCE) Israelite, fourth son of Jacob and Leah. When the sons of Jacob turned against Joseph, the 11th son, Judah convinced them to sell Joseph to travelling Ishmaelites rather than leave him to die in a pit (Genesis 37). Judah later received Jacob's patriarchal blessing (Genesis 49:8). David belonged to the tribe of Judah and his accession to the throne assured its supremacy. When the Israelite kingdom split after Solomon's death, the tribe of Judah supported Rehoboam and became predominant in the south.

Judah bar Ezekiel (d.299) Babylonian amora. He was the founder of the academy at Pumbedita, and was an authority on halakhah. His teachings are quoted extensively in the Babylonian and Jerusalem Talmuds.

Judah ben Asher (1270–1349) Spanish rabbi and talmudist, of German origin. He was born in Cologne, but left Germany with his family as a consequence of anti-Jewish outbreaks in 1283 and settled in Toledo. In 1321 he was appointed his father's successor and rabbi of the Toldedo community, and later became the head of the bet din and the Toledo yeshivah. His *Zikhron Yehudah* comprises 83 responsa. In *Iggeret Tokheḥah* he offered a testament to his children containing ethical sayings, an account of his family history, and instruction in the method of learning.

Judah ben Barzillai al-Bargeloni (fl. 11th–12 cent.) Spanish rabbi. He was rabbi of the community in Barcelona. He wrote numerous halakhic studies, incorporating summaries of talmudic discussions and gaonic material, as well as a commentary on the Sepher Yetzirah.

Judah ben Bathyra I (fl. 1st cent.) Babylonian tanna. He lived in Jerusalem in his youth, but left Palestine before the destruction of the Temple and settled in Nisibis in Babylon.

Judah ben Bathyra II (fl. 2nd cent.) Babylonian tanna, perhaps the grandson of Judah ben Bathyra I. He was born in Rome and studied in Palestine. Subsequently he went to Babylon and settled in Nisbis. At the time of the Hadrianic persecutions, he was regarded as an authority of equal rank with Akiva.

Judah ben Bava (fl. 1st–2nd cent.) Palestinian tanna. He was a leading sage in Jabneh, renowned for his piety. During the Hadrianic persecutions he was put to death by the Romans for ordaining five scholars, in transgression of the law forbidding ordination.

Judah ben Ilai (fl. 2nd cent.) Palestinian tanna. Born in Usha, he was a pupil of his father and of Tarphon and Akiva. His account of their teachings was used by Judah ha-Nasi in compiling the Mishnah. He was the original author of the *Siphra* and was a renowned aggadist. After the Hadrianic persecutions, he helped to establish the academy at Usha.

Judah ben Isaac [Sir Léon of Paris]
French tosaphist, grandson of Rashi.
He became the head of the Paris bet
midrash, which was reopened when
the Jews returned to France following
their expulsion in 1182. He composed
tosaphot to nearly all the *Talmud*, based
on the teachings of Isaac ben Samuel of
Dampierre.

Judah ben Kalonymos (d.1196/1199)
German scholar. He lived in Speyer.
His *Yiḥuse Tannaim va-Amoraim* provides biographical details of talmudic
rabbis and outlines their views.

**Judah ben Samuel he-Ḥasid of
Regensburg (c.1150–1217)** German
rabbi and mystic. He lived in Speyer
and later settled in Regensburg. He was
one of the most important scholars of
the Middle Ages in the fields of ethics
and theology, and was the main teacher
of the Ḥaside Ashkenaz movement. His
writings include magical treatises and
the *Book of Divine Glory*, a commentary on the prayers of the Jewish liturgy.
He was also the principal author of the
Sepher Ḥasidim. His teachings were
popularised by Eleazar ben Judah of
Worms.

Judah ben Simon (fl. 4th cent.) Palestinian amora. He was a leading aggadist.

Judah ben Tabbai (fl. 1st cent. BCE)
Palestinian sage. With his colleague
Simeon ben Setaḥ, he formed the third
of the pairs ('zugot') of sages during the
time of Alexander Yannai.

**Judah ha-Levi [Zionides] (before
1075–1141)** Spanish Hebrew poet
and philosopher. Born in Toledo, he
lived in various towns in Christian and
Muslim Spain, where he was active as a
physician. Eventually he left Spain for
Palestine. He wrote about 800 poems,
including eulogies and laments, covering such topics as love, Jewish festivals,
personal religious experience and longing for Zion. His philosophical work
The Kuzari describes a disputation con-

ducted before the King of the Khazars
by a rabbi, a Christian, a Muslim and an
Aristotelian philosopher.

Judah ha-Nasi (fl. c.2nd–3rd cent.)
Palestinian communal leader, son of
Simeon ben Gamaliel II. He lived most
of his life in Galilee, first at Bet Shearim
and then at Sepphoris. He was known
as 'Rabbenu ha-Kadosh' (our holy
teacher), and is referred to in rabbinic
literature as 'Rabbi'. He served as the
political and religious head of the Jewish community in Palestine. His major
contribution was the redaction of the
Mishnah.

Judah Ḥasid ha-Levi (?1660–1700)
Lithuanian Shabbetaian preacher. He
was born in Dubno. He was maggid in
Szydłowiec, and was active in preparing
the people for the second appearance of
Shabbetai Tzevi in 1706. He travelled
throughout the communities and urged
total repentance, mortifications and
fasts. He and hundreds of followers set
out for Palestine to await the Messiah.
He died a few days after arriving in Jerusalem in 1700.

**Judah Löw ben Bezalel [Höhe
Rabbi Löw; Maharal] (c.1525–1609)**
Bohemian rabbi, talmudist, moralist
and mathematician. He served as Chief
Rabbi of Moravia from 1553 to 1573,
and later settled in Prague. There he
founded a yeshivah, organised circles
for the study of the Mishnah, and regu-
lated the statues of the ḥevra kaddisha.
Revered for his piety and asceticism, he
was active in all aspects of communal life,
particularly education. He wrote studies
of halakhah, aggadah, ethics, philosophy
and homiletics, as well as rabbinic commentaries. According to legend, he was
the creator of the Prague golem.

Judah Maccabee (fl. 2nd cent. BCE)
Palestinian rebel leader, third son of
Mattathias the Hasmonean. He succeeded his father as leader of the revolt
against Antiochus IV Epiphanes. After
occupying Jerusalem in 164 BCE, he

purified the Temple and assisted Jewish communities in Transjordan and Galilee. He was later killed in battle at Elasa. He is celebrated as the prototype of Jewish heroism.

Judah Nesiah (fl. 3rd cent.) Palestinian nasi, son of Gamaliel III. He was the first nasi to settle in Tiberias. He was assisted by Johanan bar Nappaḥa and Resh Lakish.

Judah the Galilean (d. c.6 CE) Palestinian Zealot leader. He was born in Gamala in the Golan. He participated in the disturbances in the country following the death of Herod the Great. He was the head of a band of rebels active around Sepphoris, who had seized control of the armoury in Herod's palace there. Though the rebels were defeated, Judah escaped. Together with Zadok the Pharisee he founded the Zealots, and opposed the census conducted in Judea by Quirinius.

Judaism The Jewish religion originated with God's call to Abraham (Genesis 12). The Jewish faith has undergone numerous developments. Throughout its history various groups (Sadducees, Pharisees, Karaites, Ḥasidim, Conservative Jews, Reform Jews etc.) have claimed that their beliefs and practices are authentically Jewish. In the Middle Ages Maimonides formulated 13 principles of the Jewish faith, which are widely recognised as the central tenets of Judaism. In modern times the Jewish community is fragmented along religious lines. Groups ranging from the strictly Orthodox to the most liberal all claim to represent valid manifestations of Judaism.

Judge Before the settlement in Canaan, elders of the Israelite community acted as judges. Later leaders, priests and prophets assumed this position. The prophet Samuel administered justice (I Samuel 7:15–17), but after the creation of the monarchy this responsibility passed to the king (II Samuel 12:1–

16; 15:2). According to the Book of Chronicles, David appointed 6,000 Levites as officers and judges (I Chronicles 23:4). Jehoshaphat's court in Jerusalem consisted of judges selected from among the priests, Levites and heads of houses (II Chronicles 19:8–11). During the period of the Second Temple, the Great Sanhedrin in Jerusalem consisted of 71 judges. In addition lesser Sanhedrins of 23 judges sat in towns. Courts of three judges also settled civil disputes. In the Middle Ages and subsequently, tribunals of rabbis sat as judges in religious cases.

Judges (Hebrew: 'Shophetim') Biblical book, one of the books of the Former Prophets. It describes the period of the Judges from the death of Joshua until before the time of Eli and Samuel. Chapters 1–3:6 consist of an introduction; chapters 3:7–16:31 recount stories about the judges (particularly Othniel, Ehud, Deborah, Gideon, Jephthah and Samson); and chapters 17–21 relate the incident of the statue stolen by the Danites, and the story of the concubine of Gibeah.

Judith Apocryphal book. It recounts the story of Judith, a Simeonite woman, living in Bethulia in northern Samaria. During the siege of the city by the Assyrians she succeeded in beheading their general, Holophernes, as a result of which the besieging army took flight.

Jung, Leo (1892–1987) US Orthodox rabbi, of Moravian origin. He became rabbi of Congregation Kenesseth Israel in Cleveland in 1920, and later of the Jewish Centre in New York. He was Professor of Ethics at Yeshiva University from 1931 and later at Stern College for Women. In 1935 he was appointed Chairman of the New York Sate Advisory Board for Kashrut Law Enforcement. He was also a member of the supreme council of the Agudath Israel organisation. He started the series known as the Jewish Library in 1928 and edited eight of its early volumes himself.

Jus gazaga ('law of right by usage'; from Latin 'jus': law, and Hebrew 'hazakah': right by usage) Term used in Italy during the ghetto period (16th–18th centuries) to denote a tenant's rights. It applied to houses occupied but now owned by Jews.

Jus talionis (Latin: 'law of retaliation') Law exacting equality of punishment and crime; it is embodied in the phrase 'an eye for an eye, a tooth for a tooth'. The law is stated three times in Scripture: Exodus 21:24; Leviticus 24:20; Deuteronomy 19:21. According to rabbinic interpretation, these prescriptions were not to be taken literally; instead financial compensation was allowed.

Justice The Hebrew words for justice ('tzedek,' 'tzedakah' and 'mishpat') denote various types of just action. Justice is a cardinal principle of biblical ethics, based on a recognition of human rights and their protection. According to the rabbis, justice should be tempered with mercy, in imitation of God's nature and activity. The concept of justice is a central feature of biblical and rabbinic law.

K

Mordecai Cohen goes to see his rabbi. He tells the rabbi that he is depressed. His father died three weeks ago. The rabbi expresses his condolences.

'Did you want to talk to me about your loss?,' the rabbi asks.

'Actually, rabbi,' he says, 'my father left me millions.'

'I'm not surprised,' says the rabbi. 'Your father was a remarkable businessman.'

'I know, rabbi,' Mordecai continues. 'But what you don't know is that the week after my father died, my uncle also died, and he too left me millions. Then just last week, my cousin died of liver cancer, and he also willed me millions of dollars.'

'Well,' said the rabbi, 'all of those losses are terrible. You have my deepest condolences. I realise how sad you must be. It's not surprising that you are feeling depressed. But all that money left to you shows how much your family members must have cared for you, and there is so much good you can do with the money.'

'No, rabbi,' Mordecai says, 'you don't understand. I'm depressed because so far this week, NOTHING.'

* * * * *

Jewish jokes frequently satirise greed. Here a mourner goes to see the rabbi because he is feeling depressed. Three of his relatives have died, leaving him millions of dollars. The rabbi misunderstands the situation and offers consolation for his loss. The punchline, however, reveals that what he is upset about is the fact that nobody else has died leaving him more money. Jews laugh at themselves for their materialism, but the joke is also a warning against such callousness.

Kabak, Ahron Avraham (1880–1944) Lithuanian writer. Born in Smorgon in the province of Vilnius, he lived in Turkey, Palestine, Germany, France and Switzerland. In 1921 he settled in Palestine, where he taught at the Jerusalem Reḥavyah Gymnasium. His novel *By Herself* was regarded as the first Zionist novel in Hebrew literature.

Ka'b Al-Aḥbār (fl. 7th cent.) Yemenite scholar. Though born a Jew, he converted to Islam. He was one of the followers of the caliph Omar when he entered Jerusalem. At Omar's request, Ka'b Al Aḥbār pointed out the site where the Temple had stood. Many teachings of the rabbis and words of the aggadah are attributed to him in Muslim literature.

Kabbalah ('mysticism') The body of esoteric teachings of Judaism and Jewish mystical literature, particularly from the 12th century onward. The kabbalah draws on early rabbinic mystical traditions about the divine chariot ('maashe merkavah') and the mysteries of creation ('maaseh bereshit'). It is concerned with esoteric doctrines about God and creation, the problem of evil, the soul, and the mystic way. Important kabbalistic texts include the Bahir, the Shiur Komah, the Sepher Yetzirah, and the *Zohar*. In the 16th century, kabbalistic speculation was transformed by the teachings of Moses Cordovero and Isaac Luria. In Lurianic kabbalah the term 'tzimtzum' refers to the process whereby God contracts himself to form a vacuum in which creation can take place. The concept of 'tikkun' (cosmic repair) is also associated with Lurianic kabbalah. Kabbalistic thought also profoundly influenced the Sabbetaian movement. In modern times kabbalistic theories are subscribed to by various Ḥasidic groups.

Kabbalat Shabbat ('Reception of the Sabbath') Synagogue service marking the inauguration of the Sabbath. The Sabbath begins at nighfall; it is customary to prepare for it by bathing, putting on festive clothes, and reciting various prayers and hymns.

Kabronim (from 'kavar': to bury) Gravediggers in the Jewish community.

Kaddish [Prayers for the Dead] Doxology in Aramaic, recited at the end of individual sections of the funeral service and at its conclusion. There are four forms: the complete kaddish; the half kaddish; the scholar's kaddish ('kaddish derabbanan'); and the mourners' kaddish, which is recited by close relatives of the deceased at the end of the service. All four forms of the kaddish are recited standing, facing Jerusalem. In some communities the entire congregation stands; in others only the mourners. The prayer consists of praise and glorification of God, and expressions of hope for the establishment of God's kingdom on earth.

Kadoorie, Sir Ellis (1865–1922) Hong Kong philanthropist. He was born in Baghdad and settled in Hong Kong.

He bequeathed funds for the building of two agricultural schools for Jews and Arabs, one at Tulkarm and one near Mount Tabor. He also contributed to the Anglo-Jewish Association for Education.

Kadoorie, Sir Elly Silas (1867–1944) Hong Kong businessman, brother of Ellis Kadoorie. He was born in Baghdad and settled in Hong Kong, developing business interests in Shanghai and other cities. He was an active Zionist and served as President of the Palestine Foundation fund in Shanghai, established agricultural schools in Palestine, and contributed to the construction of the Hebrew University.

Kafka, Franz (1883–1924) German novelist of Czech origin. He was born in Prague and worked in a law office and then an insurance company, pursuing his writing in his spare time. His short stories (including *Metamorphosis*) were published in his lifetime. At his death, he instructed his friend Max Brod to burn his remaining manuscripts, but Brod succeeded in publishing three novels, *The Trial, The Castle* and *America*. Some commentators interpret Kafka's works as reflecting the Jew's isolation in society.

Kaftan [caftan] Long gown or undertunic. It was worn by oriental and Eastern-European Jews.

Kahal Congregation. In Eastern Europe the term was applied to the Jewish community, which had autonomous rights and was responsible for such civil matters as taxation.

Kahana (i) (fl. 2nd–3rd century) Babylonian amora. He and Assi were prominent scholars when Rav returned from Palestine to Babylonia. Later Kahana emigrated to Palestine, where he joined some of the last tannaim.

Kahana (ii) [Kahana, pupil of Rav] (fl. 3rd cent.) Babylonian amora. It is recorded that he read the weekly

Bible portion at Rav's academy. After executing a person who had threatened to denounce a fellow Jew to the Perisan authorities, he fled from Babylonia to Palestine. There he joined the academy of Johanan.

Kahana (iii) [Kahana, pupil of Rava]. (fl. 4th cent.) Babylonian amora. He taught at the academy of Pum Nahara; among his pupils was Ashi, the redactor of the Babylonian *Talmud.*

Kahana (iv). (d. c.414) Babylonian amora. He succeded Rafram ben Papa as head of the academy of Pumbedita from 396.

Kahana, Aharon (1905–1967) Israeli painter and ceramic artist. He was born in Stuttgart and lived in Berlin and Paris before settling in Palestine in 1934. In 1947–48 he was a founder member of the New Horizons group of artists. Initially his work was influenced by biblical themes, but later his painting became more abstract. Subsequently he returned to figurative painting.

Kahana, Avraham (1874–1946) Russian biblical scholar and historian. He emigrated to Palestine in 1923, where he served as a librarian at the Sh'ar Zion Library in Tel Aviv. From 1903 he worked on an edition of the Hebrew Bible, which was published with a critical commentary and introduction. He also edited the Apocrypha, wrote historical studies, published biographical works and contributed to Hebrew linguistics.

Kahane, Meir (1932–1990) Israeli rabbi and politician of American origin. He was ordained at the Mirrer Yeshiva, and received a law degree at the New York Law School. He was the founder of the Jewish Defence League, the Jewish Identity Centre and the organisation Shuva.

Kahanovitz, Phinehas [Der Nister] (1884–1952) Russian Yiddish author. He is chiefly known for his realistic historical novel of Ukrainian Jewish Life, *House of Crisis,* the first volume of which appeared in 1939.

Kahle, Paul (1875–1965) German orientalist, masoretic scholar and minister. He was born in East Prussia. After serving as a pastor in Cairo he taught at the universities of Halle, Giessen and Bonn. From 1923 he was Director of the Oriental Institute at Bonn. Later he settled in Oxford. He made pioneering contributions to the understanding of the emergence and development of the masorah, basing his studies on material from the Cairo Genizah. He also wrote articles on Muslim holy places in Palestine, and published studies of the Dead Sea Scrolls.

Kahn, Bernhard (1876–1955) German-American community leader. He was born in Sweden, but spent much of his life in Germany, where he became involved in Jewish affairs. He was appointed Secretary-General of the Hilfsverein der Deutschen Juden in 1904. In 1921 he became Director of the refugee department of the American Jewish Joint Distribution Committee (JDC), and later the JDC's European director, as well as managing director of the American Joint Reconstruction Foundation. In 1939 he emigrated to the US, where he served as honorary chairman of the JDC European Council.

Kahn, Louis (1901–1974) American architect, of Estonian origin. Born in Opel, Estonia, he came to the US at the age of four. He studied at the University of Pennsylvania, and worked in various architectural offices. He later taught architecture at Yale University. From 1957 to 1974 he taught at the University of Pennsylvania. He designed a range of buildings as well as synagogues and community centres.

Kahn, Zadok (1839–1905) French rabbi. He was born in Mommenheim, Alsace. He became Director of the

Talmud Torah of the École Rabbinique in Metz. In 1866 he became assistant to Chief Rabbi Isidore Lazare of Paris, who he succeeded in 1868, and in 1889 he became Chief Rabbi of France. He was active in the Ḥibbat Zion movement, and served as President of the Société des Études Juives. He served as editor of the French translation of the Hebrew Bible, and assisted Isidore Singer in preparing the American *Jewish Encyclopedia*.

Kaidanover, Aaron Samuel [Aaron Samuel ben Israel Kaidanover; Maharshak] (1614–1676) Polish talmudist. He was active as a religious leader in Polish and German Jewish communities. His publications include talmudic novellae, sermons and responsa

Kaidanover, Tzevi Hirsch (d.1712) Lithuanian writer, son of Aaron Samuel Kaidanover. He was imprisoned for four years in Vilnius on a false charge. After his release he published his father's writings in Frankfurt am Main. He was himself the author of an ethical treatise, *Kav ha-Yashar*, which he also translated into Yiddish.

Kalich, Bertha Rachel (1875–1930) American actress. She was born in Poland and settled in New York in 1895. In her youth she appeared at the Bucharest National Theatre and later in the Romanian Imperial Theatre. After emigrating to the US she became the first Yiddish-speaking actress to be recognised in the English-language theatre; she also appeared in Yiddish repertory.

Kalischer, Tzevi Hirsch (1795–1874) German rabbi and Zionist pioneer. He was born in Lissa in the Posen district, and settled in Thorn in 1824. An opponent of Reform Judaism, he advocated Jewish settlement in Palestine, and in *Derishat Zion* argued for the establishment of a Jewish agricultural society there. In 1864 he was responsible for the founding in Berlin of the Central Committee for Palestine Colonisation. He believed that Jewish redemption would come about through human endeavour before the coming of the Messiah. His publications deal with rabbinic topics and Zionism.

Kallah (i)   Bride

Kallah (ii) ('Bride')   Minor tractate appended to the fourth order, Nezikin, in the Babylonian *Talmud*. The tractate is known in two versions. The shorter version consists of one chapter and deals with betrothal, marriage, chastity and moral purity. The longer version, known as Kallah Rabbati, discusses betrothal and marriage, and also amplifies Derekh Eretz Rabbah and Derekh Eretz Zuta.

Kallah (iii)   During the talmudic and gaonic period, the name given to courses of study which took place at the Babylonian academies of Sura and Pumbedita in the months of Elul and Adar (the so-called 'kallah' months, when agricultural work was minimal and students had time to meet for study and discussion). During each kallah month a specific tractate of the *Talmud* was studied.

Kallir, Eleazar (fl. 7th cent.)   Hebrew poet. He lived in Tiberias. He was the greatest and most prolific of the early composers of piyyutim, writing examples for all the main festivals, special Sabbaths, weekdays of festive character and fasts.

Kalmanoivitch, Zelig (1881–1944) Lithuanian Yiddish writer, philologist, and translator. He was born in Latvia and settled in Vilnius in 1929, where he joined the YIVO Institute and served as editor of its journal. In 1943 he was deported to a concentration camp in Estonia, where he was killed the following year. He published studies on Yiddish philology, the influence of Hebrew on Yiddish syntax and Yiddish dialects. He also translated various works into Yiddish.

Kalonymos ben Kalonymos [Maestro Calo] (1286–after 1328) French Hebrew author and translator. He lived in various French cities and also in Rome. He translated philosophical and scientific works from Arabic into Hebrew and Latin for King Robert of Naples. His *Even Boḥan* is an ethical study of rhymed prose. In *Masekhet Purim* he presented a satirical parody of a talmudic tractate.

Kal va-Ḥomer ('Light and heavy') The name given to the first principle of rabbinic hermeneutics in the systems of Hillel and Ishmael ben Elisha. It consists of an *a fortiori* argument.

Kamatz Sign used to indicate two vowel sounds in Hebrew. 'Kamatz gadol' is sounded as an 'a' in Sephardi pronunciation, and as 'o' in Ashkenazi pronunciation. 'Kamatz katan' is sounded as an 'o' and occurs only in closed, unstressed syllables. The sign, which resembles a capital T in the Roman alphabet, is written below the consonant preceding the vowel sound.

Kaminer, Isaac (1834–1910) Ukrainian Hebrew writer. He was born in Lewkiow in Ukraine and from 1854 to 1859 taught at the government school for Jews in Zhitomir. Later he served as a physician in Kiev. He wrote verse satires for the Hebrew socialist papers, criticising supports of the Haskalah, the Ḥasidim and rich communal leaders. After the pogroms of the 1880s he joined the Ḥibbat Zion movement.

Kaminka, Armand Aharon (1866–1950) Austrian scholar. He was born in Berdichev in Ukraine. He served as a rabbi at Frankfurt an der Oder, and then as preacher at the Reform temple in Prague. After a period as rabbi to the Jewish community in Esseg, Slavonia, he moved to Vienna, where he became Secretary of the Israelitische Allianz. In 1924 he founded Maimonides College, and from 1924 lectured on the *Talmud*

and Jewish philosophy at the University of Vienna. After the annexation of Austria by Hitler in 1938, Kaminka settled in Palestine. His works include biblical and rabbinic studies, translations of Greek and Latin classics into Hebrew, and poetry.

Kaminski, Esther Rachel (1870–1925) Polish Yiddish actress, wife of Abraham Isaac Kaminski. She toured Poland acting in her husband's theatre company. In 1909–11 she appeared in the US, and in 1913 played in London and Paris.

Kaminski, Ida Kaminska (1899–1980) Polish Yiddish actress, daughter of Esther Rachel Kaminski and Abraham Isaac Kaminski. As a child she acted in her father's company, and later became the outstanding actress on the Yiddish stage in Poland. She left Poland in 1968 after anti-Semitic disturbances.

Kanah, Book of Kabbalistic work on the commandments. Composed in Spain during the 14th century, it was written in the form of a commentary on the commandments, containing the author's own mystical interpretation.

Kaniuk, Yoram (1930–2013) Israeli author. He was born in Tel Aviv. His publications include *The Acrophile, The Last Jew,* and *Confessions of a Good Arab.*

Kann, Jacobus Henricus (1872–1945) Dutch banker and Zionist. He was born in The Hague and became the owner and manager of his family's bank (Lissa & Kann) from 1891. As an aide to Theodor Herzl, he was one of the founders of the Jewish Colonial Trust in 1899. He was an active participant in the Zionist Congresses and was elected to the Zionist Organisation's executive in 1905. Later he worked on various projects in Palestine.

Kantor, Judah Leib (1849–1915) Lithuanian journalist. He was born in

Vilnius. After working as an editor on Jewish newspapers in Berlin and St Petersburg, in 1886 he founded the first Hebrew daily, *Ha-Yom,* which he edited until 1888. He later served as Crown Rabbi in Libau (1890–1904), Vilnius (1905–8), and Riga (1909–15).

Kaph Eleventh letter of the Hebrew alphabet. Its numerical value is 20.

Kaplan, Eliezer (1891–1952) Russian Labour Zionist. He was born in Minsk. He was one of the founders of the Tzeire Zion in Russia in the early years of the 20th century. He became active in the Labour Zionist movement in Europe, and from 1923 in Palestine. He was a member of the executive of the Jewish Agency from 1933, and served as head of its finance department until the establishment of the State of Israel in 1948. He then became Israeli Minister of Finance, and later was appointed Deputy Prime Minister.

Kaplan, Jacob (b.1895) French rabbi and author. He was born in Paris. He held rabbinical positions in Mulhouse, Alsace and Paris. During the German occupation of France he worked with the Resistance movement. In 1950 he became Chief Rabbi of Paris, and in 1955 was appointed Chief Rabbi of France. He was a lecturer at the Institut d'Études Politiques and a member of the Academie des Sciences Morales et Politiques in Paris.

Kaplan, Mordecai Menaḥem (1881–1983) American rabbi and founder of the Reconstructionist movement. He was born in Lithuania and at the age of nine emigrated with his family to the US. After his ordination he became rabbi of the Kehillath Jeshurun synagogue in New York. In 1909 he became Dean of the Teachers Institute of the Jewish Theological Seminary of America in New York. Later he taught homiletics, midrash and philosophy of religion at the seminary's rabbinical school. He developed a concept of Judaism known as

Reconstructionism, and in accordance with its ideas in 1922 set up a congregation known as the Society for the Advancement of Judaism. He also established the Jewish Reconstructionist Foundation, which published *The Reconstructionist* magazine. His writings include *Judaism as a Civilization, The Meaning of God in Modern Jewish Religion,* and *The Future of the American Jew.*

Kaplansky, Shelomoh (1884–1950) Israeli Zionist labour leader of Polish origin. He was born in Bialystok and lived in Vienna from 1903 to 1912. After moving to London, he was chairman of the finance and economics committee of the Zionist Executive in Jerusalem and the director of its Settlement Department (1929–31). In 1932 he was appointed director of the Haifa Technion.

Kapparah ('atonement') In Jewish practice the custom of transferring the sins of a person symbolically to a bird. In a ceremony performed on the eve of the Day of Atonement, a fowl is swung over the head of an individual, who prays that by its death it will serve as his substitute and bear his sins. The following prayer is said during the ceremony: 'This is my substitute, my vicarious offering, my atonement; this cock [or hen] shall meet death, but I shall find a long and pleasant life of peace.'

Kara, Abigdor ben Isaac (d.1439) Bohemian rabbi, Kabbalist and poet. He lived in Prague. There he witnessed the massacre of the Jewish community in 1389 as a result of the accusation that they had desecrated the Host; he wrote an elegy to commemorate their sufferings. His other writings include rabbinic studies and kabbalistic works. He also engaged in polemical debates with Christians. According to legend, he was a favourite of Wenceslaus IV, King of Bohemia, and played an important role in his court.

Kara, Joseph ben Simeon (c.1060–c.1130) French Bible commentator.

He lived in Troyes and Worms. He took part in theological discussions with Christians, wrote commentaries on most of the books of the Bible, and commented extensively on the piyyutim.

Karaites Jewish sect founded at the beginning of the 8th century and active in and around Persia. The Karaites denied the talmudic-rabbinic tradition. The most ancient Karaite text is the *Sepher ha-Mitzvot* of Anan ben David, the founder of the movement. In this work he interpreted the Bible literally and attempted to deduce from it a code of life without reference to the Oral Law. During the following centuries various Karaite groups flourished in Persia, Babylonia, Palestine, Egypt and elsewhere. Karaite scholars produced polemical works, grammars, Bible commentaries and codes. From the 12th century the movement went into decline.

Karkasani [Qirqisani], Abu Yusuf Yakub [Jacob; Kirkisani, Jacob] (fl. 10th cent.) Babylonian Karaite scholar. He came from Karkasan near Baghdad. He was the most important proponent of Karaism of his age. His *Book of Lights and Watch-Towers* is a systematic code of Karaite law. In *Book of Gardens and Parks* he commented on the non-legal parts of the Torah.

Karlitz, Avraham Yeshayahu [Hazon Ish] (1878–1953) Israeli rabbi and codifier, of Russian origin. He was born in the province of Grodno and lived in Vilnius. Later he settled at Bene Berak in Palestine, where he founded a yeshivah. Writing under the name Hazon Ish, he became one of the most important modern codifiers.

Karni, Yehuda (1884–1949) Hebrew poet of Russian origin. He was born in Pinsk. After settling in Palestine, he served on the editorial board of the daily *Ha-Aretz* from 1921. In his *Shirei Yerushalayim*, Jerusalem is presented as the eternal symbol of the people and their destiny. In later writings he lamented the victims of the Holocaust.

Karpeles, Gustav (1848–1909) German literary historian. He was born in Einwanowitz, Moravia. He edited the *Allgemeine Zeitung des Judentums* in Berlin from 1890 and also played an important role in establishing and running the Association of Societies for Jewish History and Literature. He wrote various literary studies, including a history of Jewish literature.

Kashe (Yiddish: 'a difficulty question') A problem, talmudic query or question.

Kasher, Menahem (1895–1983) American rabbi and halakhist. He was born in Warsaw. In 1925 he went to Palestine, and founded the yeshivah Sefat Emet in Jerusalem. From 1939 he lived in the US. His *Torah Shelemah* is an encyclopedia of the *Talmud* and midrash, in which all relevant material in the Oral Law is collected according to the scriptural verse to which it applies.

Kashrut ('dietary laws') The body of regulations governing Jewish diet. The laws enumerated in the Pentateuch were developed in the Oral Law and by rabbinic legislation. In the *Talmud* the tractate Hullin deals with the dietary laws, as does the section 'Yoreh Deah' in the Shulhan Arukh. Only food which is fit to be eaten in accordance with Jewish law ('kasher' or 'kosher') may be consumed. Food which is 'terephah' (unfit) is forbidden. The laws of kashrut deal with animals that are fit for consumption, methods of slaughter, the preparation of meat, the eating of milk and meat products together, vegetable foodstuffs, Passover regulations, and so on.

Kassovsky [Kossovsky], Hayyim Yehoshua (1873–1960) Israeli rabbinic scholar. His writings include concordances of the Bible, Targum Onkelos, the Mishnah, the Tosephta and the Babylonian *Talmud*.

Katz, Ben-Tziyyon (1875–1958)   Israeli journalist and author, of Russian origin. In 1903 he founded and edited the Hebrew periodical *Ha-Zeman*, which appeared first at St Petersburg and later at Vilnius. In 1916 he established a Hebrew weekly *Ha-Am*, in Moscow. After World War I he settled in Berlin and in 1931 moved to Palestine, where he continued his work in Hebrew journalism. He published studies of Russian Jewish history.

Katz, Jacob (1904–1998)   Israeli scholar of Hungarian origin. Born in Hungary, he studied at the University of Frankfurt. With the rise of Nazism he went to England and then to Israel where he became a professor at the Hebrew University. His work concerns Jewish gentile relations and modern Jewish society and includes *Tradition and Crisis, Exclusiveness and Tolerance* and *Out of the Ghetto.*

Katz, Menke (1906–1991)   American Yiddish poet. He was born in Tsvintsyan, Lithuania, and emigrated to the US in 1920. His publications include *Three Sisters, Burning Village, My Grandmother Moyne Speaks, Safad,* and *Aspects of Modern Poetry: a Symposium.*

Katzenelson, Isaac (1886–1944)   Polish Hebrew poet and playwright. He was born in Korelichi and later lived and taught in Łódź. He was one of the pioneers of the modern Hebrew theatre. During World War II he was active in Warsaw and other cities. His works of this period describe the catastrophe that befell European Jewry.

Katznelson, Berl (1887–1944)   Palestinian labour leader. He was born in Belorussia and emigrated to Palestine in 1909. He became an ideologist of the labour movement there. He was one of the founders of the Aḥdut ha-Avodah party in 1919, and of the Histadrut in 1920. He served in various positions in the Zionist Organisation and edited various labour journals, including the His-

tadrut daily *Davar.* He was a founder of Mapai in 1930.

Katzir, Ephraim (1916–2009)   He graduated from the Hebrew University and from 1951 was professor and head of the biophysics department at the Weizmann Institute of Science. He received the Israel Prize, the Rothschild Prize, and the Linderstrom-Lang gold medal. In 1966 he was the first Israeli elected to the United States National Academy of Sciences. In 1973 he became President of Israel.

Kaufman, Bel (1911–2014)   American author and educator, of German origin. Born in Berlin, she grew up in Russia. Her grandfather was Sholem Aleichem. She studied at Hunter College and Columbia University, and taught in New York high schools. From 1964 she taught in several New York colleges. Her works include *Up the Down Staircase.*

Kaufmann David (1852–1899)   Hungarian painter. He was born in Arad. He travelled throughout Galicia, Poland and Ukraine, making sketches of shtetl life. He was a pioneer in the depiction of Eastern-European Jewish life.

Kaufmann, Yeḥezkel (1889–1963)   Israeli biblical scholar and philosopher. He was born in Russia and settled in Palestine in 1920, where he later became Professor of Bible Studies at the Hebrew University. In *A History of Israelite Faith* he challenged numerous theories of biblical criticism.

Kautzsch, Emil Friedrich (1841–1910)   German scholar. He taught at Leipzig, Basle, Tübingen and Halle. He published a revision of Gesenius' Hebrew grammar, philological studies, works on the Apocrypha and apocalyptic literature, and a critical translation of the Bible into German.

Kaye, Danny [Kaminsky, David Daniel] (1913–1987)   American actor. Born in Brooklyn, he worked as an entertainer in the Catskill Mountains. He appeared in various films and plays including *The Secret Life of Walter Mitty*, and *Hans Christian Anderson*. Later he toured on behalf of the United Nations International Children's Emergency Fund and subsequently began to host his own musical variety show on television.

Kayserling, Meyer (1829–1905) German rabbi and historian. He was born in Hanover. He served as a rabbi in Switzerland and later in Budapest. He published studies of Jewish history, literature and religion, and a seminal study of Marrano history.

Kayyara, Simeon [Simeon ha-Darshan; Simeon Kahira] (fl. 19th century) Babylonian scholar. He was the compiler of the Halakhot Gedolot.

Kedeshah Sacred harlot. Cultic prostitution was regarded as an abomination and condemned under Jewish law (Deuteronomy 23:18), but it probably did not disappear until the end of the First Temple period. In the Bible both male and female prostitutes are mentioned (I Kings 14:24).

Kedushah ('Sanctification') The name given in the Mishnah to the third of the Eighteen Benedictions; in later rabbinic literature the title is used for an addition to the third blessing, in which the congregation responds to the cantor's introduction and alternates with his text by reciting prayers of praise to God. The Kedushah prayer takes different (sometimes amplified) forms, depending on the various liturgical traditions and the occasion on which it is used.

Kehillah. Congregation The term is applied to a Jewish community or to the congregation in the synagogue.

Kelal Israel ('the whole of Israel') Term used to mean the body of all Jewish people. The unity of the Jewish nation is viewed as a spiritual reality as well as a social concept.

Kelim ('Vessels') First tractate in the Mishnah order of Tohorot. It deals with the laws of ritual purity affecting different kinds of vessels (Leviticus 11:32; Numbers 19:14; 31:20).

Kellner, Leon (1859–1928) Austrian scholar and Zionist. He was a specialist in English literature, and after teaching in high schools, became a lecturer in literature at the University of Vienna. From 1904 to 1914 he was a professor at the University of Czernowitz. When World War I broke out, he returned to Vienna, and he later served as an English expert in the office of the Austrian president. He was one of Theodor Herzl's advisers and published a selection of Herzl's writings as well as the first part of a biography of Herzl.

Kelm, Maggid of (1828–1899) Lithuanian preacher. He studied under Israel Salanter at Kovno, and later became the envoy and preacher of the Musar movement. He travelled throughout the Pale of Settlement and also lived in London.

Kemelman, Harry (1908–1996) American novelist. His novels deal with an amateur detective, Rabbi Small, who solves murders by using talmudic logic. His publications include *Friday the Rabbi Slept Late, Saturday the Rabbi went Hungry,* and *Someday the Rabbi will Leave.*

Kempf, Franz (b.1926) Australian artist and printmaker. He was born in Melbourne. He became President of the Contemporary Art Society of the South Australian School of Art, and later head of the graphic art department at the school. Influenced by the Ḥabad movement, he became a practising Jew. His work contains biblical and Ḥasidic themes.

Kene-hora ('No evil eye') Expression used to ward off the evil eye.

Keneset Israel ('congregation of Israel') In rabbinic literature the phrase refers to the whole Jewish community. In modern times it was used as a title to the official Jewish community in Palestine when it was organised as a corporate entity in 1927. When the provisional council of the State of Israel was convened in 1948, the Keneset Israel was abolished and its powers transferred to the State.

Kepher avodah ('work village') A type of transitional settlement in Israel in which immigrants were placed on their arrival. The inhabitants were employed by the Jewish National Fund to develop the land. They built their own homes and received agricultural training. The kephar avodah then formed the nucleus for a permanent village.

Keritot ('Excisions') Seventh tractate in the Mishnah order of Kodashim. It deals with the biblical punishment of 'karet' (cutting off, that is temporary or permanent excommunication from the community) and lists the offence to which it applies.

Keri u-khetiv ('read and written') In rabbinic studies a term used of corrections to those words that are regarded as deviations from the original biblical text. Over 1,300 such corrections were transmitted orally and later noted by the Masoretes in the margins of Bible manuscripts. These manuscripts were not used in synagogues.

Kern, Jerome (1885–1945) American composer. Born in New York, he published his first song in 1902. Later he wrote his first hit song: *How'd You Like to Spoon with Me?* Until the outbreak of World War I, many of his songs were written for New York productions of London shows. During the 1920s he collaborated with Oscar Hammerstein II and Otto Harbach. Later he and Hammerstein won an Oscar for *The Last Time I Saw Paris.*

Kerovah (from Aramaic 'kerova'): precentor) Name given to several types of piyyut that form part of the Amidah prayer. They were written for Sabbaths, festivals, Purim and fast days. On Sabbaths and festivals they generally extend over the first three blessings. At other times they extend over all the Eighteen Benedictions.

Kesten, Hermann (1900–1996) German novelist. He was appointed literary adviser to the Berlin publishing house of Kiepenheuer in 1927. In 1933 he left Germany and became active in European refugee circles. He later settled in the US. After the collapse of Fascism in Italy he went to Rome. In *Spanish Fire* he recreated the period of the Jewish expulsion from Spain in the late 15th century. His *Die fremden Götter* portrays the return to Judaism of a father and daughter under the Nazis.

Kestenberg, Leo (1882–1962) Israeli pianist and music educator, of Hungarian origin. He served as Music Counsellor at the Ministry of Culture in Berlin, and from 1933 directed the Czech Society for Musical Education. He arrived in Palestine in 1938, where he became the general manager of the Palestine Orchestra. In 1945 he founded the Music Teachers' Training College in Tel Aviv, of which he became the director.

Keter malkut ('crown of royalty') The mark of the sovereignty of God, recognised by angels and men in worshipping him. It is also the name given by Solomon ibn Gabirol to his poem in praise of God, which is recited after the evening service on the Day of Atonement.

Ketubbah ('writing') Document recording the financial obligations a bridegroom undertakes toward his bride. Written in Aramaic, it contains various clauses which follow a stereotyped formula. The tractate Ketubbot in the *Talmud* deals with the document and its preparation. It was frequently embossed on parchment with illuminated borders; the art of illuminating ketubbot is especially associated with Italy.

Ketubbot ('Marriage contracts') Second tractate in the Mishnah order of Nashim. It deals with the money to be received by the wife in case of divorce or widowhood. In addition it contains a discussion of a father's rights regarding his daughter, as well as the mutual rights and duties of a husband and wife.

Kevutzah ('group') Cooperative agricultural group in Israel, working a common farm on national land. The earliest such group was Deganyah (1910). The kevutzah was responsible for health, housing and education; unlike the kibbutzim, its members excluded outside wage-workers. The kevutzot initially belonged to an organisation called Hever ha-Kevutzot; this later merged with an association of kibbutzim to form Ihud ha-Kevutzot Ve-he-Kibbutzim.

Khazars [Chazars; Hazars] Turkish or Finnish tribe which settled in the lower Volga region. From the 18th century a Judaising movement manifested itself among the peoples and their king, Bulan, and thousands of nobles converted to Judaism. The central theme of Judah ha-Levi's *Kuzari* is the legendary disputation which resulted in this conversion. Hasdai ibn Shaprut believed that the Khazars were one of the Ten Lost Tribes of Israel. According to tradition, he entered into correspondence with their king, Joseph, in the 10th century.

Kibbitzer (Yiddish) Person who offers unsolicited advice, busybody.

Kibbush avodah ('conquest of labour') Concept formulated in the early 20th century by pioneers in Palestine. The phrase is used principally to mean the acquisition of the skills of productive manual labour. It also refers to the process of obtaining work with Jewish employers. Such practices were central objectives of the Ha-Shomer movement and the Histadrut, which organised bodies (such as Yakhin and Solel Boneh) to encourage the employment of Jewish labour.

Kibbutz ('gathering in') Collective village in Israel. Similar to the kevutzot, kibbutzim originated during the Third Aliyah (1918–21). During this period the kevutzah concept was broadened to incorporate industry, wage labour and the removal of restrictions on the size of the group. Inspired by social ideas, the kibbutz movement has played a pioneering role in the economic, political and cultural activities of the country, and has contributed significantly to Israeli national security.

Kibbutz galuyyot ('ingathering of the exiled communities') The name given to the ideal of reuniting the Jewish people. It originated with the Babylonian exile (6th century BCE), and was intensified after the destruction of the Second Temple (70 CE). Linked to messianic aspirations, it was one of the aims of pseudo-messiahs such as Serenus, Shabbetai Tzevi and Judah Hasid. In modern times it became a central concept of Zionism and Israeli political philosophy.

Kibbutznik Member of a kibbutz. The word is Hebrew with a Russian suffix.

Kichel (Yiddish) A small, plain biscuit.

Kiddush ('Sanctification') The name of a prayer recited over a cup of wine in the home or the synagogue to consecrate the Sabbath or a festival.

Kiddush ha-Shem ('sanctification of the [divine] name') Descriptive term originally used of acts of martyrdom; later it was also applied to other acts of righteousness that reflect well on Jews and Judaism in the eyes of non-Jews. When a Jew willingly suffers death rather than violate God's commandments, he achieves Kiddush ha-Shem. If he fails to do so, he is guilty of Hillul ha-Shem.

Kiddushin ('Betrothals') Seventh tractate in the Mishnnah order of Nashim. It deals with the regulations regarding betrothal (including prohibited marriages).

Kidnapping According to the Bible kidnapping is a capital offence (Exodus 21:16; Deuteronomy 24:7). The *Talmud* states that the eighth commandment of the Decalogue refers to kidnapping rather than stealing property. To be liable to capital punishment for kidnapping four conditions must be obtained: the kidnapper must have taken the kidnapped person into his possession or domain; he must have sold him as a slave; he must have sold him to a stranger; and he must have treated his victim as a slave before selling him. Each condition must have been attested by at least two witnesses.

Kike A disparaging and offensive term for a Jew.

Kilayim ('Diverse kinds') Fourth tractate in the Mishnah order of Zeraim. It deals with the prohibitions concerning the mingling of different species of plants and animals, and of different textiles in fabric for clothing (Leviticus 19:19; Deuteronomy 22:9).

Ki lo naeh ('For to him it is befitting') Opening words of an alphabetic eulogy chanted at the end of the Passover seder service in the Ashkenazim liturgy.

Kimḥi, David [Redak] (?1160–?1235) French grammarian and exegete, son of Joseph Kimḥi. He was a teacher in Narbonne, Provence, where he was also active in public life. During the Maimonidean controversy of 1232, he undertook a journey to Toledo to gain the support of Judah ibn Alfakhar for the adherents of Maimonides. His *Mikhlol*, which assembled the researches of Spanish Jewish grammarians and philologists consists of a Hebrew grammar and biblical dictionary. He also wrote biblical commentaries, which combine Spanish speculative, philological and philosophical traditions with the rabbinic midrashic method of exegesis and the interpretations of Rashi.

Kimḥi, Dov (1889–1961) Israeli author, translator and editor, of Galician origin. He was born in Jaslo, Galicia, and emigrated to Palestine in 1908. He settled in Jerusalem, where he taught at the Reḥaviah Gymnasium. He wrote novels, short stories and essays, and produced numerous translations.

Kimḥi, Joseph [Joseph ben Isaac Kimḥi] (c.1105–c.1170) Spanish grammarian, exegete, translator and polemicist. As a refugee from the Almohad persecutions in Spain, he settled in Narbonne, Provence. His writings include grammars, commentaries on biblical books, religious poems, and translations from Arabic. His *Sepher ha-Berit* was one of the first anti-Christian polemical works written in Europe.

Kimḥi, Moses (d.1190) French grammarian and exegete, son of Joseph Kimḥi. He was active in Narbonne, Provence. His *Mahalakh Shevile ha-Daat* was the first printed Hebrew grammar (1489); translated into Latin, it was used by Christian scholars during the period of the Reformation. He was also the author of commentaries on Proverbs, Ezra and Nehemiah, as well as liturgical poems.

Kinah ('lamentation') [Elegy] Dirge for the dead. Kinot were recited at funerals and on other days of mourning in biblical, mishnaic and talmudic times. In the Middle Ages the term was applied to a special type of piyyut for the Ninth of Av, dealing with the loss of the Temple and national independence, contemporary persecutions, and the hope for the coming of the Messiah and redemption. The most famous author of kinot was Eleazar Kallir.

Kindling of lights Lights are kindled by the housewife at the beginning of

Sabbaths and festivals. This act is obligatory: if no woman is present, it must be done by a man. Before the lighting takes place, an appropriate blessing is recited. Other occasions for the kindling of lights are Ḥanukkah, the anniversary of the death of a near relative and the Day of Atonement.

Kingdom of Heaven Eschatological concept concerning a future state of perfection in the world. After the divine judgement the sinful order of the world will come to an end and God will create a new Heaven and a new earth, in which all creatures will be at peace with one another (Daniel 7:13–14). Eventually this notion was linked to the concept of the Messiah.

Kings The name of two biblical books, which form part of the group known as the Former Prophets. They relate the history of Israel and Judah from the death of David until the liberation of Jehoiachin during the Babylonian captivity.

Kings and kingship The Israelite monarchy replaced tribal chiefs of the earlier period, and from the 11th to the 10th centuries BCE ruled over the entire kingdom. In 931 BCE the nation divided into two kingdoms (Judah and Israel) with their own dynasties. With the destruction of these kingdoms (Israel in 722 BCE, Judah in 586 BCE), Israelite kingship came to an end. Under the Hasmoneans (2nd-1st centuries BCE), the monarchy was restored for a brief period but Jewish movements of the 1st-2nd centuries CE produced claimants to messianic kingship. The posi-

tions, rights and limitations of the king are elaborated in the Mishnah (Sanhedrin 2:2–5), as well as in Maimonides *Mishneh Torah.*

Kinnim ('Bird nests') Eleventh tractate in the Mishnah order of Kodashim. It deals with the regulations for the bringing of an offering after childbirth (Leviticus 2:8), and for the offerings made by the poor who might commit the offences listed in Leviticus 5. It also treats cases where sacrifices are interchanged.

Kipnis, Menachem (1878–1942) Polish singer, folklorist and writer. He was born in Ushomir, in Ukraine, and moved to Warsaw in 1901. From 1912 to 1932 he toured Poland, Germany and France, appearing with his wife, Zimra Seligsfeld, in lecture-recitals of Jewish folk songs. These he published in numerous collections. He also published articles on various aspects of Jewish music.

Kircheim, Raphael (1804–1889) German scholar. He was born in Frankfurt am Main and became a partner in a banking house. Initially he was an opponent of Reform Judaism, but under the influence of Abraham Geiger he became a supporter. His publications include editions of various medieval Hebrew works.

Kirschen, Ya'akov (b.1938) Israeli cartoonist. He was born in Washington DC and grew up in Brooklyn. In 1968 he settled in Israel. He created 'Dry Bones', a daily political comic strip which appeared in the *Jerusalem Post.*

Kisch, Alexander (1848–1917) Austrian rabbi and scholar. He was born in Prague. He served as a rabbi in Brüx, Bohemia (1874–7), Zurich (1877–81), Jungbunzlau, Bohemia (1881–6), and Prague (1886–1917). In Zurich he founded the first Swiss-Jewish weekly. In 1899 Franz Joseph I awarded him a gold medal for 25 years' service as a military chaplain. He was the first rabbi in Austria to be appointed a Government Professor of Religion and Inspector of Religious Education. His writings include studies of Bohemian Jewish history.

Kisch, Frederick Hermann (1888–1943) British soldier and Zionist. He was born in India. He joined the Indian Army and was posted to Baluchistan in World War I. Later he was appointed to the Directorate of Military Intelligence at the War Office, working in the section covering Russia, Persia, China and Japan. He was a member of the British delegation to the Paris Peace Conference (1919–21). In 1923 he became a member of the Zionist Executive in Jerusalem and head of its Political Department. Later he advised the Jewish community on security matters. During World War II he returned to active service in the British Army.

Kisch, Guido (1889–1986) American legal historian. He was born in Prague. He taught the theory and history of law at the universities of Leipzig, Königsberg, Halle and Prague. After emigrating to the US in 1935 he taught history at the Jewish Institute of Religion in New York. In 1962 he moved to Basle, where he taught at the university. He published studies on medieval law and German Jewry. He was also the founder and editor of the periodical *Historia Judaica*.

Kiska (Yiddish) Sausage containing a mixture of meat, flour and spices.

Kishon, Ephraim (1924–2005) Israeli humourist. He was born in Hungary and moved to Israel in 1949. From 1952 he wrote a column in the newspaper *Maariv*, which dealt with political and social issues. He published books, plays, flim scripts, satires and articles reflecting Israeli life.

Kislev Ninth month of the Hebrew calendar. Historical days during the month are 1 Kislev, the announcement of a series of public fasts in Judea in the intercession for rain in years of drought; 3 Kislev, the anniversary of a Hasmonean victory over the Greeks (164 BCE); 7 Kislev, the anniversary of the death of Herod the Great; 21 Kislev, the 'Day of Gerizim' which commemorates the legendary decision by Alexander the Great in favour of erecting the Temple in Jerusalem (against the Samaritan claim for siting it on Mount Gerizim; 25 Kislev, the beginning of the festival of Ḥanukkah.

Kiss, Joseph (1843–1921) Hungarian poet. He was born in Mezocsat. After the publication of several volumes of his poetry, he became acknowledged as a leading figure in Hungarian literature. In his writings he described social change, moral degeneration and the breakdown of traditional Jewish family life. The theme of anti-Semitism is a prevailing motif throughout his work.

Kissing The rabbis disapproved of kissing except in the case of a kiss given to a man when appointing him for a position of honour, a kiss given at meeting or parting, and a kiss exchanged between relatives. Sacred objects (such as fringes, the Scroll of the Law, the mezuzah, a religious book that has fallen to the ground) are kissed as a sign of respect. Among the Sephardim children kiss their parents' hands after receiving the parental blessing. Oriental Jews kiss the hand of the Ḥakham in salutation.

Kissinger, Henry (b.1923) American politician and scholar, of Barvarian origin. He lived in Fürth, Bavaria, as a child but went with his family to the US in 1938. He was drafted in 1943 and served in Germany as an interpreter, then as administrator of a civilian district. He studied at Harvard, later becoming a professor. He was a consultant to Presidents Eisenhower, Kennedy and Johnson before accepting a full-time position in 1968 in the Nixon administration. He helped negotiate a peace settlement in the Middle East after the

Yom Kippur War. He won the Nobel Peace Prize in 1973.

Kitaj, R. B. (1932–2007) American painter. He was born in Cleveland and later lived in England. From the 1970s he became concerned with Jewish identity as a conscious and subconscious impulse.

Kittel (Yiddish) White shroud-like garment worn by the officiant and many members of the congregation during the prayer service on the high holy days, and by the cantor at the musaph service on Shemini Atzeret and the first day of Passover. It is also worn by the person conducting the seder on Passover, and by the groom during the marriage ceremony. In some communities it is called a 'sargenes'.

Kittel, Rudolph (1853–1929) German Protestant theologian and Bible scholar. He taught at the universities of Tübingen (1879–81), Stuttgart (1881–8), Breslau (1888–98), and Leipzig (1898–1924). A follower of the Wellhausen school of biblical criticism, he published studies of the Jews in biblical times. He also translated into German several books of the Bible, the Apocrypha and apocalyptic literature. Together with other scholars, he published a critical edition of the Hebrew Bible (*Biblia Hebraica*).

Klaczko, Julian (1825–1906) Polish author, critic and historian. Raised in the atmosphere of the Lithuanian Haskalah, he wrote poetry in Hebrew and Polish. In 1840 he moved to Germany and then settled in Paris. After converting to Catholicism, he continued to live in France from 1849 to 1869. Subsequently he served in the Galician and imperial Austrian parliaments. From 1888 he lived in Kraków.

Klein, Abraham M. (1909–1972) Canadian author and poet. He was born in Montreal, and became a partner in a law firm. He is regarded as the first outstanding Jewish contributor to Canadian literature. In addition to writing his own poetry, he made numerous translations of Hebrew and Yiddish poems. His publications include *Hath not a Jew, the Hitleriad, Poems,* and *The Rocking Chair.* His work was influenced by Jewish themes, talmudic erudition and Yiddish folklore.

Klein, Melanie (1882–1960) Austrian psychoanalyst. Born in Vienna, she studied at the University of Vienna. After moving to Budapest she was drawn to the works of Sigmund Freud and was analysed by Sandor Ferenczi. She went to Berlin and later settled in London. She was the founder of the object relations school of psychoanalysis.

Klein, Shemuel (1886–1940) Hungarian historian and geographer of Palestine. He served as a rabbi in Dolnja Tuzla, Bosnia(1909–13), and Ersekujvar (1913–28). In 1929 he became Professor of Historical Topography of Palestine at the Hebrew University. In his writings he used the *Talmud* and midrash as primary sources of information on the country's topography and the history of its settlement.

Klemperer, Otto (1885–1973) German musician. Born in Breslau, he studied in Frankfurt and Berlin. He was chorus master and then conductor at the German theatre in Prague. In 1917 he became Music Director of the Cologne Opera. Later he led several German opera companies. When the Nazis came to power, he emigrated to the US. He directed the Los Angeles Philharmonic Orchestra and the Pittsburgh Symphony Orchestra. From 1947 to 1950 he was Director of the Budapest Opera. In 1954 he began conducting and recording with the Philharmonia Orchestra of London, becoming its principal conductor.

Klop (Yiddish) To hit (also a blow), to blab.

Klotz (Yiddish) A clumsy person, a bungler.

Klutznick, Philip Morris (1907–1999) American communal leader and diplomat. He was born in Kansas City. He held a succession of appointments connected with community planning. In 1935–6 he was a special assistant on housing to the US attorney general, in 1938–41 general counsel for the Omaha Housing Authority, and in 1944–46 federal housing commissioner. From 1961 to 1963 he served as Ambassador to the United Nations Economic and Social Council. He held several positions in Jewish organisations, including International President of B'nai Brith, General Chairman of the United Jewish Appeal, and Vice-President of the Jewish Welfare Board.

Knaydl (Yiddish) A dumpling made of matzo meal.

Knesset ('assembly') The Parliament of Israel. It consists of a single chamber of 120 members, who are elected by proportional representation for a four-year term. It is the supreme authority in the state. Created in 1949, the Knesset initially met in Tel Aviv but later moved to Jerusalem.

Knishes (Yiddish) Little dumplings. It is also used figuratively as a term of abuse.

Kobrin, Leon (1873–1946) American Yiddish dramatist and novelist. He was born in Russia, and emigrated to the US in 1892, where he worked in a sweatshop. His stories and plays describe Jewish life in the US during the period of immigration, depicting the problems of nationalism, assimilation, and relations between parents and children.

Kodashim ('Holy things') Fifth order of the Mishnah. It deals with the laws of ritual slaughter, sacrifice and other topics connected with the Temple ritual.

Koenig, Leo (1889–1970) British Yiddish author, critic and journalist. He was born in Odessa. He wrote art criticism for leading Yiddish periodicals in Paris before moving to London in 1914; he then worked for the Yiddish press in England and abroad. In 1952 he settled in Haifa.

Koestler, Arthur (1905–1983) English author. Born in Budapest, he travelled widely, settling in England in 1940. Initiallly a communist in the 1930s, he later repudiated communism. His works include novels, essays and reminiscences. *Thieves in the Night* portrays kibbutz life in Palestine, and *Promise and Fulfilment* deals with Zionism.

Kogan [Kahana], David (1838–1915) Ukrainian scholar. He was born in Odessa. He wrote numerous studies of Jewish history and literature, including *House of the Kabbalists, Sabbataians and Ḥasidim*.

Kohen, Tzedek ben Joseph (fl. 10th cent.) Babylonian gaon. He was gaon of Pumbedita from 917 to 936. He was appointed gaon by the exilarch David ben Zakkai I, but the scholars of the academy refused to recognise him and elected Mevasser Kahana instead. As a result both men served simultaneously as geonim, but after Mevasser's death in 926 Kohen Tzedek ben Joseph assumed the post alone.

Kohler, Kaufmann (1843–1926) American Reform leader. He was born in Fürth in Bavaria and emigrated to the US in 1869. He served as rabbi of the Congregation of Beth El in Detroit, Sinai Congregation in Chicago, and Temple Beth El in New York. He was a leading figure at the Pittsburgh Conference of Reform Jews in 1885, at which the Pittsburgh Platform (a statement of the tenets of American Reform Judaism) was adopted. In 1903 he became President of the Hebrew Union College. His publications include *Jewish Theology*.

Kohler, Max James (1871–1934) American attorney and communal leader. He was born in Detroit. He served as Assistant US District Attorney in the southern district of New York from 1894 to 1898, and then entered private law as a defender of the legal and public rights of immigrants, naturalised citizens and aliens. His writings include *Immigration and Aliens in the United States: Studies of American Immigration Laws and the Legal Status of Aliens in the United States.*

Kohn, Abraham (1807–1848) Ukrainian rabbi. He was born in Bohemia, and served as a rabbi in Hohenems. In 1844 he became a preacher in Lemberg, where his reforms aroused the opposition of Orthodox Jews. When he and his son died from food poisoning, Orthodox leaders were arrested, but they were later released for lack of evidence.

Kohn, Samuel (1841–1920) Hungarian rabbi and scholar. He was born in Baja, Hungary. He served as a rabbi in Budapest from 1866 to 1905, when he was appointed Chief Rabbi of Hungary. He was one of those responsible for the establishment of the Jewish Theological Seminary in Budapest. He published works on the Samaritans and the history of the Jews in Hungary.

Kohut, Alexander (1842–1894) American rabbi and scholar, of Hungarian origin. He served as a rabbi in Stuhlweissenburg, and later became Chief Rabbi of Fünfkirchen. In 1885 he left for the US, where he served as rabbi of Congregation Ahavath Chesed in New York. He helped to establish the Jewish Theological Seminary, where he taught midrash and talmudic methodology. His *Arukh ha-Shalem* is a lexicon of talmudic terms based on the talmudic dictionary of Nathan ben Jehiel.

Kohut, Rebekah (1864–1951) American educator and community leader, wife of Alexander Kohut. She was born in Kaschau. From 1897 to 1901 she was President of the New York Council of Jewish Women, and in 1914 was appointed head of the employment bureau of the Young Women's Hebrew Association. In 1942 she became President of the World Congress of Jewish Women. Her writings include. *My Portion, More Yesterdays,* and *George Alexander Kohut: His Memoir.*

Koigen, David (1879–1933) Ukrainian philosopher and sociologist. He lived in Germany until 1912, when he returned to Russia. In 1921 he was appointed Professor of Philosophy and Sociology at the Ukrainan University in Kiev. His writings include studies of the Jewish experience in history and culture.

Kokowzoff, Pavel (1861–1942) Russian orientalist. He was born in Pavlovsk. In 1894 he became Professor of Hebrew at St Petersburg University, succeeding his teacher Daniel Chwolson. He wrote studies of Aramaic, Syriac, Turkish and Ethiopic manuscripts and epigraphic material, and also published an edition of the 10th-century correspondence between Ḥasdai ibn Shaprut and the Khazar king, Joseph.

Kol Bo ('Compendium') Anonymous medieval Jewish legal codification. It contains 148 sections dealing with such topics as blessings, prayer, the synagogue, the meal, the Sabbath and festivals, marriage, money, vows and oaths, laws relevant to the land of Israel, forbidden foods, the redemption of the firstborn son, visiting the sick, and mourning.

Kollek, Theodor (1911–2007) Israeli politician. He was born in Vienna. In 1934 he emigrated to Palestine, where he became a member of kibbutz En Gev. From 1940 to 1947 he served in the political department of the Jewish Agency. He then represented the Haganah in the US and in 1951–52 served as Israel's Minister Plenipotentiary in Washington DC. He was Director of the Israeli Prime Minister's Office from 1952 to 1964, and Chairman of the Israel Government Tourist Corporation from 1956 to 1964. In 1965 he was elected Mayor of Jerusalem.

Kol Nidre ('All vows')   Opening words (and hence title) of the formula for the annulment of vows, recited on the eve of the Day of Atonement. The custom of annulling all personal vows and oaths made unwittingly or rashly during the preceding year originated in the early gaonic period. The practice gave rise to the accusation among non-Jews that a Jewish oath was not to be trusted. In the 12th century Jacob Tam changed the formula to refer to vows of this nature that might be made in the forthcoming year. It has become the most beloved ritual of the Day of Atonement.

Kompert, Leopold (1822–1886)   Austrian novelist. He was born in Bohemia. In 1840 he moved to Hungary, where he became editor of the German-language literary periodical *Pannonia* published in Pressburg. Later he settled in Vienna, where he worked as a journalist. His writings deal with Eastern-European Jewish life, mixed marriage and anti-Semitism. He was active in Jewish affairs and Viennese civil life, taking a special interest in education and the welfare of orphans.

Kook, Avraham Yitzḥak (1865–1935)   Palestinian rabbinic scholar of Latvian origin. He was born in Greiva, Latvia, and served as rabbi of Zaumel and Bauska, before emigragting to Palestine in 1904. An ardent Zionist, he became Chief Rabbi of the Ashkenazi community in Palestine in 1921. He believed that the return to Palestine marked the beginning of divine redemption. His writings include *Orot* (on holiness in the newborn nationalism), *Orot ha-Teshuvah* (on repentance), and *Halakhah Beruah* (on halakhic issues).

Koph   Nineteenth letter of the Hebrew alphabet. Its numerical value is 100.

Kops, Bernard (b. 1926)   English playwright and novelist. He was born in the East End of London, which became the subject of his work. His writings include *The World is a Wedding, Yes* *from No-Man's Land, By the Waters of Whitechapel* and *The Hamlet of Stepney Green*.

Korah (fl. 13th cent. BCE)   Levite, kinsman of Moses. Together with Dathan, Abiram of the tribe of Reuben, and 250 Israelite leaders, he rebelled against Moses and Aaron (Numbers 16). As a punishment, the earth opened and swallowed them (Numbers 26:11).

Korczak, Janos (1879–1942)   Polish author, educator and communal leader. He was born in Warsaw, where he worked as a physician and became concerned with the plight of the poor; his early writings depict the condition of homeless orphans in the cities. In 1911 he became head of a Jewish orphanage in Warsaw. He published theoretical studies about pedagogical method, as well as children's books. With the rise of Hitler, he became Poland's non-Zionist representative in the Jewish Agency. In 1952 he was deported to a concentration camp, where he was killed.

Korda, Alexander [Korda, Sandor Laszlo] (1893–1956)   British film producer and director, of Hungarian origin. Born in Hungary, he studied at the Royal University in Budapest. He initially worked as a journalist, but later turned to film production. He founded the trade journals *Post Movie, The Movie* and *Film Week*. He produced a number of Hungarian films. He eventually went to Hollywood, and later he settled in London where he founded London Films Limited.

Kovner, Abba (1918–1987)   Lithuanian resistance fighter and Hebrew poet. Born in Sevastopol, he grew up in Vilnius. He was a commander of the Vilnius ghetto and fought the Germans as leader of the partisan groups in the surrounding forests. In 1945 he settled in Palestine, but he was imprisoned in Egypt by the British when he attempted to return to Europe to continue Jewish rescue work. His poems and novels deal with Jewish partisans during the Nazi period and Israel's War of Independence.

Kovner, Abraham Uri (1842–1909) Russian Hebrew author. He was born in Vilnius. He published a collection of essays, *Ḥeker Davar,* in 1865, which condemned Haskalah literature, and in *Tzeror Peraḥim* he attacked Hebrew as a dead language. In 1870 he settled in St Petersburg, where he contributed weekly articles to the Russian journal *Golos.* Condemned to exile in Siberia for a criminal offence, he later adopted Christianity. His last years were spent in Łomża, Poland, where he worked as a government official.

Krakauer, Leopold (1896–1954) Israeli architect and designer, of Austrian origin. He was born in Vienna. He helped to design the parliament building in Belgrade. In 1924 he emigrated to Palestine, settling in Jerusalem. He designed public buildings and private houses, and later concentrated on writing.

Kramer, Jacob (1892–1962) British painter. He was born in Ukraine; his family emigrated to England in 1900 and settled in Leeds. His paintings include *The Day of Atonement,* and *Hear our Voice, O Lord our God.*

Krauskopf, Joseph (1858–1923) American Reform rabbi. He was born in Prussia and settled in the US in 1872. He served congregations in Kansas City and Philadelphia. A leader of radical reform, he was an important figure in the national organisation of Reform Judaism. He established the National Farm School in Doylestown, Pennsylvania, and in 1917 was appointed to direct food conservation among Jews for the US Food Administration.

Krauss, Samuel (1866–1948) Austrian historian, philologist and talmudic scholar, of Hungarian origin. He taught the Bible and Hebrew at the Jewish teachers' seminary in Budapest. In 1906 he was appointed to teach the Bible, history and liturgy at the Vienna Rabbinical Seminary; later he became head of the seminary and rector. When the Nazis came to power, he fled to England. He published studies in the fields of philology, history, the Bible, the *Talmud,* Christianity and medieval literature.

Krechtz (Yiddish) To grunt in pain, to fuss or complain (also a sound of complaint), to make gasping noises.

Krein, Alexander (1883–1951) Russian composer, brother of Grigori Krein. He studied at the Moscow Conservatory, where he served as professor (1912–17). He was then Secretary of the Russian Board of Education (1918–20), and a member of the board of the State Publishing Department (1918–27). He was one of the leaders of the Jewish musical movement and an active member of the Society for Jewish Folk Music. His music contains Jewish traditional folk motifs.

Krein, Grigori (1885–1955) Russian composer and violinist, brother of Alexander Krein. He studied in Moscow and later in Leipzig. From 1926 to 1934 he lived in Paris and later in Tashkent. A number of his compositions have a Jewish content.

Kreitman, Esther (1891–1954) Polish Yiddish author, sister of Israel Joshua Singer and Isaac Bashevis Singer. She was born in Bilgoraj, Poland. He publications include *Der sheydem-tants, Brilyantn,* and *Yikhes.*

Krementzky, Johann (1850–1934) Austrian Zionist leader. He was born in Odessa; he settled in Vienna in 1880 and built several factories. An ardent Zionist, he became an adherent of Theodor Herzl; he served as a member of the Zionist Executive and the Zionist General Council and was appointed Director of the Jewish National Fund.

Krenk (Yiddish) An illness.

Kreplach (Yiddish) Triangular or square dumpling containing chopped meat or cheese. It is usually served in soup.

Krimchaks The original Orthodox Jews of the Crimea. They spoke a Turkish dialect, wore Turkish dress, and adopted many Turkish customs.

Krochmal, Abraham (1818–1888) Galician-born writer and scholar. He lived in Lemberg, Brody, Odessa and Frankfurt am Main. In Galicia and Odessa he moved in Haskalah circles. He wrote studies of the *Talmud* and the Bible, philosophical works on Judaism, and articles advocating religious reform.

Krochmal, Naḥman (1785–1840) Galician philosopher and historian. He was born in Brody and lived in Zolkiew in Galicia. Later he returned to Brody, and eventually moved to Tarnopol. He was a leading figure in the Haskalah movement and the founder (in the 1830s) of Wissenschaft des Judentums. His *Guide to the Perplexed of the Time* is a philosophical investigation of the course of Jewish history.

Kubbutz Vowel sound in Hebrew. It is generally sounded 'oo', as in 'foot', but in some traditions it is sounded like the German 'u'.

Kugel (Yiddish) Pudding of noodles or potatoes.

Kulisher, Michael (1847–1919) Russian historian, ethnographer and communal worker. He studied at the rabbinical seminary in Zhitomir in Ukraine, and at the law faculty of the University of St Petersburg. From 1869 to 1871 he was on the editorial board of Russian Jewish newspaper *Den*. He published a life of Jesus as well as studies of gentile attitudes to the Jews.

Kumin, Maxine (1925–2014) American poet and writer. She was born in Philadelphia. She taught at Tufts, Columbia, and Princeton universities. Some of her poetry deals with her Jewish identity.

Kumsitz ('come and sit') Expression used in modern Hebrew to denote an impromptu party.

Kuntras (medieval Hebrew) Notebook. The word was applied by the tosaphists to Rashi's commentary on the *Talmud*. It was also used in France as a general term for collected commentaries.

Kuppah Poor box. Jews contribute to the poor box in the synagogue or at home on joyful, sad and solemn occasions, and at weekday services. The distribution of the collection was formerly supervised by a group of overseers. The term has come to refer to general relief.

Kurzweil, Baruch (1907–1972) Israeli literary critic. He was born in Moravia, and emigrated to Palestine in 1939. He was appointed Professor of Modern Hebrew Literature at Bar-Ilan University in 1955. His writings include *On the Novel, Our New Literature, Continuation or Revolution?, Bialk ve-Tchernichovsky, Massot al Sippurei S.Y. Agnon,* and *Between the Vision and the Absurd.*

Kusevitsky, Moshe (1899–1966) Polish cantor. Her served as chief cantor at the main synagogue in Warsaw. From 1947 he lived in the US and made concert tours abroad.

Kushner, Harold (b.1935) American rabbi. He has served congregations in New York and Massachusetts. His publications include *When Bad Things Happen to Good People.*

Kutim (i) Talmudic term for the Samaritans. The word was also used to denote any individual or group that rejected the Oral Law.

Kutim (ii) ('Samaritans') Minor tractate appended to the *Talmud*, which deals with the relationship between Samaritans, gentiles and Jews.

Kutscher, Eduard Yechezkel (1909–1971) Israeli linguist. He was born in Topoltshani, Slovakia, and went to

Israel in 1941. He taught at the Hebrew University, and later at Bar-Ilan University, specialising in Hebrew and Semitic languages. His publications include *The Language and Linguistic Background of the Isaiah Scroll,* and *History of the Hebrew Language.*

Kuznets, Simon (1905–1985)   American economist, of Russian origin. Born in Pinsk, he went with his family to Kharkov. He studied at the University of Kharkov and worked in the Division of Statistics of the Central Soviet of Trade. In 1922 he settled in the US and studied at Columbia University. From 1930 to 1954 he was Professor at the University of Pennsylvania. Later he taught at Johns Hopkin's University and Harvard. He received the Nobel Prize in 1971.

Kvell (Yiddish)   To fuss, to complain, to squeeze, to delay, to shrug, to exert. It can also refer to someone who complains, works slowly, or uses alibis for a lazy performance.

Kvitko, Leib (1890–1952)   Russian Yiddish writer. He worked in various cities in Ukraine as a dyer, shoemaker, porter and stevedore. In 1920 he settled in Germany, but he later returned to the USSR. He was arrested in the Stalinist purges in 1949, and executed with other Yiddish writers in 1952. He wrote novels and poetry, as well as stories for children.

L

The founder of Feinberg tool company decides to go on vacation in Las Vegas. He entrusts his company to his assistant Harry Schwartz and his son Mortimer who just graduated from Harvard with an MBA. After several days away, he phones to see how everything is going at the factory. Schwartz says he must come home immediately. He tells him he will understand the problem as soon as he is back on the highway. Anxiously he flys back, rents a car and on the highway sees a huge billboard with a picture of Jesus on the cross. Underneath it says: 'THEY USED FEINBERG'S NAILS.'

Feinberg is mortified. He spent years working on public relations. At the factory he is furious with his son. 'How could you be so stupid!', he exclaims. The son swears he will make it up to him and says he knows just what to do. His father is beside himself. The next day a new billboard goes up. On it is the same picture of Jesus on the cross. But underneath is the caption: 'THEY DIDN'T USE FEINBERG'S NAILS.'

* * * * *

Living in a Christian environment, Jews have been sensitive to their status as a minority group. In this joke, the owner of a factory is horrified to discover that, in his absence, a sign depicting Jesus' crucifixion was put up on the highway advertising the use of his factory's nails. When his son tries to fix the problem, he utterly fails and we are amused. Jewish jokes abound with stories about rabbis, priests, synagogues and churches. In general Jews come off badly, but we are good sports about it.

Laaz In medieval Jewish commentaries, a word in a foreign language, transliterated into Hebrew script and used as a gloss. In Rashi's commentaries on the Bible and the *Talmud* there are thousands of such glosses. The origin of the word 'laaz' is unknown.

Laban (fl.? 19th–16th cent. BCE) Israelite herdsman, brother of Rebekah and father of Leah and Rachel. He was a breeder of sheep and goats. He gave his sister Rebekah in marriage to Isaac (Genesis 24). Later he consented to the marriage of his daughter Rachel to Jacob, but deceived Jacob by substituting her sister Leah; he finally gave Rachel to Jacob as a wife in exchange for a further seven years of labour (Genesis 29).

Labour The Bible and *Talmud* praise physical work for its moral and spiritual value. The Bible prescribes fair treatment of labourers (Deuteronomy 24:14) and makes obligatory their payment on the day of work (Leviticus 19:13). These passages serve as the basis for further mishnaic and talmudic legislation concerning the relationship between employer and labourer. In modern times the Haskalah and Ḥibbat Zion movements stressed the importance of manual labour.

Lachover, Yeruḥam Fishel (1883–1947)   Israeli literary scholar. He was born in Chorzele, Poland. He began his literary career as a critic in 1904, and in 1908 moved to Warsaw, where he edited several journals and miscellanies. He settled in Palestine in 1927. His publications include a history of modern Hebrew literature, and a biography of Bialik.

Ladino   Judeo-Spanish dialect. It is spoken by the Sephardim of Mediterranean countries and written in Hebrew script.

Lagarde, Paul de (1827–1891)   German orientalist. He was a professor at Göttingen from 1869. He published studies of the Septuagint, and editions of the Targum to the Prophets and Hagiographa. He encouraged the emigration of Jews from Germany.

La Guardia, Florello (1882–1947)   American politician. Born in New York City, he was educated in Prescott, Arizona. Later his family went to Budapest where he obtained employment in the US consulate. On his return to the US, he opened a law office. He later became New York State Deputy Attorney General, and was elected to Congress in 1916. In 1932 he became Mayor of New York. Subsequently he became Director General of the United Nations Relief and Rehabilitation Administration.

Lag Ba-Omer   The 33rd day of the Omer period. It falls on 18 Iyyar. According to tradition, a plague among the pupils of Akiva ended on this date, and it is thus called the 'Scholars Feast'. It has been celebrated as a semi-holiday since the time of the geonim. Kabbalists observed this day as the anniversary of the death of Simeon ben Yoḥai.

Laguna, Daniel Israel Lopez (1653–1723)   Jamaican Marrano poet. As a child he was taken to Peyrehorade in the south of France. Later he was arrested by the Inquisition in Spain. He settled in Jamaica, where he practised

Judaism. In about 1720 he moved to London but he eventually returned to Jamaica. During his time in London he published a paraphrase of the Psalms in Spanish verse forms.

Lambert, Mayer (1863–1930)   French scholar. He was born in Metz. He lectured on Arabic, Syriac and Hebrew at the École Rabbinique and taught Hebrew at the École Normale Orientale of the Alliance Israélite Universelle. In 1903 he began teaching Hebrew and Syriac at the École Pratique des Hautes Études. His publications include studies of Hebrew grammar and the writings of Saadyah Gaon.

Lamdan   Talmudic scholar.

Lamdan, Yitzhak (1899–1954)   Hebrew poet. He was born in Milnov, in Ukraine, and witnessed the Ukrainian pogroms after World War I. In 1920 he emigrated to Palestine, where he initially worked as a labourer. From 1934 he published and edited the literary monthly *Gilyonot*. His poem *Masadah* reflects the spirit of the pioneers of the 1920s.

Lamed vav   Thirty-six righteous men. According to tradition, 36 righteous men live in every generation, and on their continued existence the world depends. Each one is referred to as a 'lamed-vovnik' or 'nistar' (secret saint).

Lämel, Simon von (1776–1845)   Bohemian merchant. He established a wool factory in Prague and was ennobled in 1812 for his services to Austria during the Napoleonic Wars. He was a benefactor of various Jewish causes.

Lamentations [Ekhah]   Biblical book, the third of the five scrolls in the Hagiographa. It contains elegies and mourning over the destruction of Judah, Jerusalem and the Temple by the Babylonians. It is read in the synagogue on the Ninth of Av.

Lamentations Rabbah [Ekhah Rabbati]   Aggadic midrash on the Book

of Lamentations. It contains homiletical interpretations of the text as well as
aggadot about the destruction of the
Temple. It was produced by Palestinian
amoraim.

Lamm, Norman (b.1927) American
scholar. He was born in Brooklyn. He
became Professor of Philosophy and
President of Yeshiva University. His
publications include *A Hedge of Roses,
The Royal Reach, Faith and Doubt, Torah
Lishmah,* and *The Good Society.*

**Lampronti, Isaac ben Samuel (1679–
1756)** Italian talmudist. Born in Ferrara, he taught in the *Talmud* Torah of
the Italian and Sephardi community in
the city. Later he became head of the
yeshivah there. His *Paḥad Yitzḥak* is a
talmudic encyclopedia.

Lamps Lamps and the symbol of light
play an important role in Jewish tradition. In biblical times a menorah
was placed in the Tabernacle and the
Temple; smaller lamps were used
for houses and public buildings. The
eight-branched Ḥanukkah lamp was
produced in a variety of forms from the
Middle Ages. In the synagogue the ner
tamid ('eternal light') is kept constantly
burning before the Ark. The custom of
lighting a lamp during mourning and
on the anniversary of a parent's death is
based on Proverbs 20:27.

Land, Edwin (1909–91) American
inventor. Born in Bridgeport, Connecticut, he studied at Harvard and in 1937
founded the Polaroid Corporation. In
1941 he developed a three-dimensional
motion-picture process based on polar-
ised light and worked on the possibil-
ity of instant photography. In 1948 the
Polaroid system was launched.

Landau, Adolph (1842–1902) Russian journalist, educator and publisher.
He was born in Lithuania. He contributed to the Russian liberal press, and
in 1871 began to publish a literary-
historical anthology, the *Jewish Library.*

In 1881 he founded the monthly journal
Voskhod later adding a weekly supple-
ment in which he attacked Ḥibbat Zion,
Zionists, and those who hated Jews.

Landau, Ezekiel ben Judah (1713–1793)
Bohemian halakhic authority. He was
born in Opatów, Poland, and served as
dayyan of Brody and rabbi of Yampol.
In 1754 he became rabbi of Prague and
the whole of Bohemia. He attempted
to mitigate the conflict between Jacob
Emden and Jonathan Eibeschütz,
fought against the Sabbetains, and
opposed Ḥasidism. He objected to
Moses Mendelssohn's German translation of the Bible. His *Noda bi-Yhudâh*
contains over 800 responsa.

Landau, Jacob (1892–1952) Austrian
journalist and publisher. He was born
in Vienna. In 1914 he established the
Jewish Correspondence Bureau, a news
agency, in The Hague. He later moved
his offices to London and renamed the
organisation the Jewish Telegraphic
Agency. Branch offices were opened
in Berlin, Warsaw, Prague, Paris, New
York and Jerusalem and headquarters
were subsequently established in New
York. In 1940 he helped to found the
Overseas News Agency.

Landau, Judah Leo (1866–1942) African rabbi, scholar, poet and playwright,
of Galician origin. He served as minister
of the North Manchester Hebrew Congregation (1900–1904) before moving
to Johannesburg to become rabbi of the
Johannesburg Hebrew Congregation.
In 1915 he became Chief Rabbi there
and Professor of Hebrew at Witwatersrand University. He wrote Hebrew
poems and plays, as well as stories of
modern Hebrew literature.

Landau, Zisho (1889–1937) American
Yiddish poet, of Polish origin. He settled in New York, where he published
an *Anthology of Yiddish Poetry in America
until 1919.* Deeply affected by Jewish suffering during World War I, he reverted
to Jewish themes in his later poetry.

Landauer, Gustav (1870–1919) German philosopher and writer. The son of a wealthy Karlsruhe merchant, he was attracted to anarchism in his youth and was twice imprisoned for political agitation. In 1918 he became editor of the theatrical periodical *Masken*, published in Düsseldorf. When the Bavarian Soviet Republic was proclaimed in 1919, he accepted an invitation to become Minister of Public Instruction. Following the overthrow of the government, he was murdered by counter-revolutionary soldiers in Munich. He published novels and philosophical and literary essays, and translated foreign literature into German.

Landauer, Samuel (1846–1937) German orientalist and bibliographer. He was born in Hürben. He taught oriental langauges at the University of Strasbourg from 1875, and in 1905 he became Director of the state and university library. Later he settled in Augsburg. He published the Arabic original of Saadyah Gaon's *Emunot ve-Deot.*, as well as a standard edition of the works of the Perisan poet Firdausi.

Landesmann, Heinrich [Lorm, Hieronymus] **(1821–1902)** German author. Born in Nikolsburg, he lived in Leipzig, Berlin, Vienna, Dresden and Brünn. Although he was both deaf and blind, he published fiction, works of philosophy and poetry. His novel, *Gabriel Solmar*, depicts a Jew's disillusionment with Emancipation and his return to the Jewish community.

Landman, Isaac (1880–1946) American rabbi, of Russian origin. He emigrated to the US in 1890 and served as a Reform rabbi in New York. He edited the *American Hebrew*, as well as the *Universal Jewish Encyclopedia*. From 1906 to 1916 he served as Executive Secretary of the National Farm School.

Landowska, Wanda (1879–1959) Polish musician. She studied with the Chopin interpreter, Michalowski, at the Warsaw Conservatory. In 1895 she went to Berlin to study counterpoint and composition. In 1900 she eloped with the musician Henry Lew to Paris. From 1909 she devoted herself to the revival of the harpsichord. She began playing the harpsichord in public in 1903 and taught harpsichord at the Berlin Hochschule für Musik. Later she went to Switzerland and settled in Paris. She began recording and embarked on a series of tours. In 1925 she founded the School for Ancient Music at Saint-Leu-la-Forêt. She eventually settled in the US.

Landrabbiner In Germany, a rabbi appointed (or recognised) by government. The term was used from the 17th century, and applied to rabbis who were invested with authority over a political region.

Landsmannschaft (German: 'compatriots' organisation') Aid organisation for immigrants from Eastern Europe. Such organisations were formed in the US, Israel, Latin America, the UK, South Africa and elsewhere, and were given names according to the place of origin of their members. They were established to deal with social, economic and cultural problems, and provided a social framework for mutual assistance.

Landsteiner, Karl (1868–1943) Austrian scientist. Born in Vienna, he studied at the University of Vienna and later in Würzburg, Munich and Zurich. He worked in laboratories and hospitals in Vienna and Berlin, and later at the University of Vienna and subsequently the Wilhelmina Hospital in Vienna. After World War I he moved to Holland, eventually settling in the US where he worked at the Rockefeller Institute of Medical Research in New York. In 1930 he received the Nobel Prize.

Landstone, Charles (1891–1978) British dramatist and novelist. He was taken to London from Vienna at the age of four. He was a founding member of the Jewish Drama League and later its secretary. He reviewed fiction for the *Jewish Chronicle* and subsequently became its theatre critic. His publications include *The Kernels of Hill End*, and *I Gatecrashed.*

Lang, Fritz (1890–1976) Austrian film director. He initially was a painter in Paris, but returned to Austria at the outbreak of World War I. In 1919 he began directing and produced a number of films. He was offered the directorship of the film industry of the Third Reich, but feared his Jewish origin would be discovered and fled to France. Later he went to Hollywood. During the war, he made a number of anti-Nazi films. He eventually returned to Germany.

Langer, Jiři (1894–1943) Czech poet and author. After a visit to Palestine in 1913, he stayed for some time at the court of the Rokeah dynasty of Ḥasidic rabbis in Galicia. Returning to Prague, he led a religiously observant life, became a teacher at a Jewish school, and wrote Hebrew poetry. In various studies he applied Freudian theories to the interpretation of certain aspects of Jewish literature and ritual. His *Nine Gates* is a volume of Ḥasidic tales.

Lansky, Meyer (1902–83) American gangster. He was associated with American gambling syndicates. He moved to Israel in 1970 when he faced criminal charges in the US, but his application to remain in Israel was rejected. He then went to South America, but later returned to Miami where he was arrested.

Languages of the Jews Hebrew is the original language of the Jews, but from the time of the first exile in the 6th century BCE, Jews have spoken the vernacular of the peoples among whom they lived in the diaspora. In some places, however, special dialects (such as Ladino and Yiddish) developed and Jewish communities never abandoned

Hebrew as a holy language and the language of the liturgy. With the founding of the State of Israel, modern Hebrew has become the language of the Jewish nation.

Lanzmann, Claude (b.1925) French writer and film maker. He was born in Paris. He produced the film *Shoah* on the subject of the Holocaust.

Laqueur, Walter (b.1921) American author. Born in Breslau, he served as Director of the Wiener Library, and at the Centre for Strategic and International Studies in Washington DC. His works include *Communism and Nationalism in the Middle East, Young Germany, Russia and Germany, The Road to War—1967, Europe since Hitler: A History of Zionism* and *Holocaust Encyclopedia.*

Lara, David Cohen de (1602–1674) German philologist, lexicographer, writer and translator. He was born in London, and became ḥakham of the Spanish-Portuguese community in Hamburg. He later lived in Amsterdam and then returned to Hamburg. His *Keter Kehunnah* deals with talmudic words which do not appear in the *Arukh* of Nathan ben Jehiel of Rome. He also translated ethical works from Hebrew into Spanish.

Lasker, Eduard (1829–1884) German Liberal politician. He was born in Posen. He took part in the Revolution of 1848. During 1853 he went to England to study the system of British parliamentary government. He was elected to the Prussian parliament in 1865, and later led the Liberal Party in the Reichstag. He was a champion of Jewish rights.

Laski, Harold (1893–1950) British political scientist. Born in Manchester, he studied at University College, London, and at Oxford. He worked as a journalist on the Labour newspaper *Daily Herald*. He taught at McGill University and then at Harvard. Eventually he returned to Britain and became a professor at the London School of Economics. He was invited to become President of Brandeis University, but refused since he believed it was important for him to remain in Britain. His works include *The Problem of Sovereignty, Authority in the Modern State, The Foundations of Sovereignty, A Grammar of Politics, The State in Theory and Practice, Parliamentary Government in England.*

Laskov, Ḥayyim (1919–1982) Israeli military commander. He was born in Borisov, Belorussia, and moved to Palestine in 1925. In 1944 he served with the Jewish Brigade Group in Italy. He joined the permanent staff of the Haganah in 1947, later becoming Commander of the Israeli Air Force. After the Sinai Campaign against Egypt in 1956 he was appointed commanding officer of the southern command of the Israeli forces, and in 1958 fifth chief of general staff. In 1961 he became Director General of the ports authority.

Latteiner, Joseph (1853–1935) American Yiddish dramatist. He was born in Romania, and emigrated to New York in 1884. Initially he chose biblical subjects for his plays, but later turned to contemporary sources. He produced more than 80 plays, comedies and musicals.

Lattes, Bonet (fl. 15th–16th century) Italian rabbi, astronomer and physician. He was born in southern France, and later settled in Rome, where he served as rabbi and dayyan of the community. He foretold the coming of the Messiah in 1505. In 1513 Johanns von Reuchlin asked Lattes to use his influence with Pope Leo X to support him in his controversy with the Dominicans.

Lattes, Dante (1876–1965) Italian writer, journalist and educator. From 1896 he worked for the paper *Corriere Israelitico* in Trieste. Subsequently he helped to found the weekly *Israel* in Florence and *La rassegna mensile di*

Israel. He also taught Hebrew language and literature at the Institute for Oriental Languages in Rome. He translated the work of writers of the Jewish national revival movement into Italian, and also produced commentaries on the Torah, the Prophets, and the Psalms.

Lattes, Isaac ben Jacob (fl.14th century) French rabbi and physician. He was active in Provence. His *Kiryat Sepher* explains passages of the Oral Law, the process of transmission of the oral tradition, and the basis of the Mishnah and Tosephta. This work also lists the 613 commandments in the order of their appearance in the Torah and interprets them according to Maimonides.

Lattes, Isaac Joshua ben Immanuel (d. c.1570) Italian rabbi. He was born in Provence, and emigrated to Italy, where he became a rabbi. He lived in Rome, Bologna, Mantua, Venice and Ferrara. He wrote responsa and poetry, and was associated with the printing of the Mantua edition of the *Zohar.*

Lattes, Judah ben Jacob (fl. 13th cent.) French scholar. He was educated at Béziers. His *Baal Asuphot* is a collection of rabbinical decisions and responsa.

Lattes, Moses (1846–1883) Italian scholar. He wrote works on Italian Jewish history, talmudic lexicography, and the historical writings of Elijah Capsali.

Latzky-Berthold, Jacob Wolf (1881–1940) Ukrainian socialist leader. He was born in Kiev. He became involved in socialist activities, and became Minister for Jewish Affairs in the government of the independent Ukraine in 1918. In 1920 he settled in Berlin, but later returned to Riga, where he edited the Yiddish daily newspapers *Dos folk* and *Frimorgn.* In 1935 he moved to Palestine.

Lauterbach, Jacob Zallel (1873–1942) American rabbinic scholar. He was born in Galicia, and went to New York in 1903. After working on the staff of the *Jewish Encyclopedia,* he served as a rabbi in Peoria, Illinois; Rochester, New York; and Huntsville, Alabama. In 1911 he became Professor of Talmud at the Hebrew Union College. His publications included an edition of the *Mekhilta d-Rabbi Ishmael* with an English translation.

Lavadores (Ladino) The name used by the Sephardim for members of the communal burial society (Ḥevrah Kadisha).

Laver Basin for ritual ablutions required of priests. In biblical times lavers were provided in the Tent of Meeting and in the Temple. They are used for washing the priests' hands before the priestly blessing in some synagogues.

Lavon [Lubianiker], Pinḥas (1904–1976) Israeli labour leader. He was born in eastern Galicia, and was one of the organisers of Gordonia in Galicia and Poland. In 1929 he settled in Palestine, where he was Secretary of Mapai in 1938–39, and later General Secretary of the Histadrut. He served in the government as Minister without Portfolio (1950–52) and Minister of Defence (1953–54). He was involved in the dispute with Mapai (known as the 'Lavron Affair'), which led to a split in the party.

Lavry, Marc (1903–1967) Israeli composer and conductor. He was born in Riga, and was active as a conductor in Riga, Saarbrücken and Berlin. In 1935 he settled in Palestine, where he conducted at the Opera Amamit and for the Palestine Broadcasting Service. In 1949 he became Director of the music section of the Kol Zion la-Golah broadcasting service. Later he settled in Haifa. His compositions include an opera, a Sabbath morning service, symphonic poems, oratorios and music for the stage.

Law The rules by which Jewish life is governed. The ultimate source of Jewish law is the Pentateuch, the Five Books of Moses. In addition the Oral Law was passed on from generation to generation. Discussions of the law were recorded in the Mishnah and *Talmud,* and decisions concerning it were collected in the codes. Later decisions based on individual laws are known as responsa.

Law, codes of The earliest compilations of Jewish law are the gaonic codes: Halakhot Pesukot and Halakhot Gedolot. In these works the order of the laws is based on the talmudic sequence. The later code of Isaac Alfasi, *Sepher ha-Halakhot* (11th–12th centuries), gives a synopsis of talmudic law, omitting legislation which is not applicable in post-Temple diaspora life. The *Mishneh Torah* of Maimonides includes all talmudic law. The code of Asher ben Jehiel, *Piske ha-Rosh* (13th–14th centuries), follows Alfasi's code with the addition of the views of later authorities. His son Jacob ben Asher compiled the *Arbaah Turim,* which formed the basis for the Shulḥan Arukh of Joseph Caro. Moses Isserles added supplementary notes *(Mappah)* to this code, incorporating Ashkenazi practices. Every generation produced posekim (religious leaders), who interpreted the meaning of the law in practice and thus contributed to its codification.

Law, reading of the The practice of reading passages from the Torah in the synagogue. The entire Pentateuch, divided into 54 sections ('sedarot'), is read in the course of a year, concluding on Shemini Atzeret, in according with the Babylonian rite. (In Palestine, the complete reading took three years.) Originally congregants read the section to themselves, but eventually a special reader read it aloud (though the Yemenites still keep to the older tradition). Three people are called up to say blessings before and after the reading on Mondays, Thursdays, Ḥanukkah, Purim, fast days and Sabbath afternoons; four on New Moons and intermediate days of the festivals; five on festivals; six on the Day of Atonement; and seven on Sabbaths.

Law, Scroll of the (Hebrew: 'Sepher Torah') The form in which the Pentateuch (Torah) is used for public reading in the synagogue. The law is written by a 'sopher' (scribe) on strips of vellum or parchment, which are sewn together to form a roll; each end is attached to a wooden stave and is rolled towards the middle. The Scroll of the Law is kept in the synagogue in the Ark.

Law, Tablets of the Two stone tablets on which were inscribed the Ten Commandments, received by Moses from God on Mount Sinai. When Moses descended from the mountain and found the people worshipping the Golden Calf, he shattered the tablets. Later he re-ascended Mount Sinai, where he received the Commandments a second time. The Tablets of the Law were placed in the Ark of the Covenant.

Layman In Temple times the word 'hedyot' was used to refer to a commoner who held no special office (as opposed to a member of the royal family or the priesthood). It was also used to refer to an ignorant or ill-mannered person, or an unskilled worker. After the destruction of the Temple, such distinctions disappeared, though priests retained a limited number of exclusive functions and were subject to various restrictions. In modern times the term 'layman' designates the members of a congregation in contrast to officiants.

Lazare, Bernard (1865–1903) French writer. He was born in Nîmes. He lived in Paris, where he was involved in Jewish affairs and worked on a number of Jewish periodicals. In *Anti-Semitism, its History and Causes* he argued that anti-Semitism could help to bring about the advent of socialism by teaching hatred of Jewish capitalism. After the Dreyfus Affair he changed his views.

Lazaron, Morris Samuel (1888–1979) American Reform rabbi. He was born in Savannah, Georgia. He served as a rabbi in Wheeling, West Virginia, and later to the Baltimore Hebrew Congregation. He was a founder and vice-president of the American Council for Judaism.

Lazarus, Emma (1849–1887) American poet. She was born into a New York Sephardi family. She wrote poetry, tragedies and numerous essays, as well as translating the works of medieval Spanish Jewish poets. Her sonnet, *The New Colossus*, was inscribed on the Statue of Liberty in New York.

Lazarus, Moritz (1832–1903) German philosopher and psychologist. He was born in Filehne, in the district of Posen. He became Professor of Philosophy at the University of Berne, and later rector of the university. In 1868 he moved to Berlin, where he lectured in psychology, political science and education at the military academy, and then became professor at the University of Berlin. Later he taught at the Hochschule für die Wissenschaft des Judentums in Berlin. His writings include *Ethik des Judentums*.

Leah (fl.? 16th cent. BCE) Israelite woman, elder daughter of Laban, and wife of Jacob. She was married to Jacob as a result of Laban's trickery in substituting her for her sister Rachel (Genesis 29:23–25). She gave birth to Reuben, Simeon, Levi, Judah, Issachar, Zebulun and Dinah (Genesis 29:32–35; 30:14–21).

Leaven (Hebrew' ḥametz') Fomenting dough made from flour and used as a raising agent in making bread. It was forbidden for use as a meal offering in most of the Temple sacrifices and is prohibited during Passover.

Leaven, search for On the evening preceding Passover a search is made by candlelight in Jewish households so that all foodstuffs containing yeast may be destroyed. This practice commemorates the institution of the Passover, when God commanded that no leaven be kept in the Israelites' households (Exodus 12:15; 13:7). In modern times small pieces of bread are placed in various parts of the house so that the search is not in vain. After the search the bread is burned and an Aramaic formula is recited.

Lebensohn, Abraham Dov [Adam ha-Cohen] (1794–1878) Lithuanian Hebrew poet. He was born in Vilnius, where he became a succesful borker. He was a central figure in the Haskalah movement in Lithuania, and an outstanding poet; his poetry was collected in *Shire Sephat Kodesh*. With Benjacob he published a Bible edition – Mikrae Kodesh – with Moses Mendelssohn's German translation – *Biur* – and his own notes. In 1847 he became a teacher of Hebrew, Aramaic and biblical exegesis at the government rabbinical school of Vilnius.

Lebensohn, Micah Joseph [Michal] (1828–1852) Lithuanian Hebrew poet of the Haskalah. He was born in Vilnius. His publications include a Hebrew translation of part of Virgil's *Aeneid*, but later he turned to subjects from Hebrew literature. His poems were published in *Songs of the Daughter of Zion* and the posthumous collection *Lyre of the Daughter of Zion*.

Lederberg, Joshua (1925–2008) American scientist. In 1947 he was appointed Professor of Genetics at the University of Wisconsin, and later at Stanford University. In 1961 he became Director of the Kennedy Laboratories for Molecular Biology and Medicine. He and a colleague at Yale University discovered that certain bacteria were capable of sexual reproduction and thus of genetic intermingling. In 1948 he won the Nobel Prize for Medicine and Physiology.

Lehman, Herbert Henry (1878–1963) American banker, politician, and statesman. He worked for his father's banking and investment firm, Lehman Bros. During his political career he served as Democratic Lieutenant-Governor of New York State (1928–32), Governor of New York State (1932–42), and Director of the Rehabilitation Agency (1943–46). From 1949 to 1957 he was US Senator for New York. He was active in Jewish and general social welfare, and a member of the American Jewish Committee.

Lehman, Irving (1876–1945) American jurist. He was born in New York. He served as State Justice in the Supreme Court until 1924 and then as Judge on the New York State Court of Appeals (1924–45). He was President of the Jewish Welfare Board (1921–40), Honorary Vice-President of the American Jewish Committee (1942), and a supporter of development projects in Palestine.

Lehmann, Behrend (1661–1730) German court Jew. He was born in Essen. He was a financial adviser to Augustus II of Saxony, who became King of Poland. He used his influence to improve the position of the Jewish community.

Lehmann, Marcus (1831–1890) German rabbi, scholar and writer. He was born in Verden. From 1854 he served as rabbi in Mainz, where he founded the weekly *Israelit*, the principle voice of German Orthodoxy. Lehmann became one of the leaders and spokesmen of modern German Orthodoxy. He wrote historical novels, short stories and Sabbath lectures, and made a German edition of the Haggadah.

Lehrer Leibush (1887–1965) American Yiddish writer and educator. He was born in Poland. After living in Belgium from 1906–1909 he emigrated to the US. He helped to develop the Shalom Aleichem schools and founded and directed the Yiddish-speaking Camp Boiberik. He taught in the Teachers Seminary of the Shalom Aleichem Folk Institute in New York, and from 1921 to 1947 was the director of the Shalom Aleichem Folk Institute in New York, and from 1921 to 1947 was Director of the Shalom Aleichem Secondary School. He wrote studies of literature, psychology, education and Judaism.

Leibowitz, Yeshayahu (1903–1994) Israeli scientist and writer. He was born in Riga. He emigrated to Palestine in 1935 and became Professor of Organic Chemistry, Biochemistry and Neurophysiology at the Hebrew University. He wrote studies of Maimonides, Jewish Orthodoxy and Israeli politics.

Leibzoll (German: 'body tax') Tax levied on Jews by states in central Europe from which they were normally excluded. By paying the tax a Jewish person could gain access to a ticket of passage or a limited residence, which guaranteed his safety. The Leibzoll was abolished in Prussia in 1787, in Bavaria in 1799, and in most other German states at the beginning of the 19th century. The Russian form of the tax ('Geleitzoll': escort tax) was abolished in 1862.

Leivick [Leyvick], H. [Halpern, Leivick] (1866–1962) American Yiddish poet and dramatist. He was born in Igumen, Belorussia. He was active in revolutionary politics and was exiled to Siberia as a result. He escaped to the US in 1913, where he worked in a sweatshop and as a paper-hanger. His writings include *Der goylem, Shmates, In Treblinka bin ich nit geven,* and *Di chasene in fernvald.*

Lekaḥ Tov ('Good teaching') Midrashic commentary on the Torah and the First Scrolls of the Hagiographa (Song of Songs, Ruth, Lamentations, Ecclesiastes and Esther.) It was composed by Tobiah ben Eliezer of Castoria in the 11th century.

Lekert, Hirsch (1879–1902) Russian revolutionary. A bootmaker by trade, he was a member of the Jewish socialist party, the Bund, in Dvinsk, Kovno, Yekaterinoslav and Vilnius. He was executed for shooting the Governor of Vilnius because he had ordered the flogging of 26 demonstrators on 1 May, 1902.

Lekhah dodi ('Come, my beloved') Opening words of a song of greeting for the Sabbath, written by Solomon Alkabetz in the early 16th century in Safed. It is customary, while reciting the final verse, to turn toward the synagogue entrance and bow.

Leku nerananah ('O come, let us exult') Opening words of Psalm 95, and hence of the group of six psalms (95–99 and 29) which are recited in the Ashkenazi rite for the inauguration of the Sabbath at the beginning of the Friday evening service. These six psalms describe God's grandeur in nature, and his righteous judgement of the world. The custom of reciting these psalms was introduced by kabbalists in Safed in the 16th century.

Lel Shimmurim ('Night of watching') The first night of Passover. Because it was believed that no danger could occur on this night it was the custom to leave the doors unbolted and to omit the recital of the night prayer.

Lemon, Hartog (c.1750–1823) Dutch physician and protagonist of Jewish rights. Living in Amsterdam, he was a central figure in the Felix Libertate society, which struggled for Jewish rights. He served as a deputy in the second national assembly of the Batavian Commonwealth, and was a delegate to the Napoleonic Sanhedrin in Paris in 1807.

Lensky, Ḥayyim (1905–?1942) Russian Hebrew poet. He was born in Slonim, a district of Grodno in Russia, and lived in Moscow and Leningrad. In

Moscow he wrote poems which he sent to literary periodicals in Palestine. Later he was sentenced to imprisonment in Siberia for writing in Hebrew, but in 1937 he was transferred to a forced-labour camp near the Soviet-Mongolian border. Although he returned to Leningrad on his release, he was again arrested; he is assumed to have died in captivity. His poetry describes his childhood and Siberian exile, as well as his faith in the Jewish people.

Leon Judah Messer [Judah ben Jehiel; Messer Leon] (fl. 15th cent.) Italian rabbi and author. He was the head of a yeshivah in Mantua. He engaged in a controversy with Joseph Colon which split the Jewish community there. Subsequently he lived in Venice, Bologna, Ancona and Naples, where he was the head of the yeshivah. His writings include *Nophet Tzuphim*, a Hebrew work based on the rhetorical rules of Aristotle, Cicero, and Quintilian.

Leon Templo, Jacob Judah Aryeh [Temple, Judah] (1603–1675) Dutch rabbi and scholar. He was born in Hamburg. He officiated at Middelburg in the Netherlands, and taught in Amsterdam from 1643. He constructed a model of Solomon's Temple and published an accompanying exposition in Spanish, which was translated into several languages. He also produced a model and exposition of the Tabernacle.

Leprosy In the Bible the term 'tzoraat' refers to an affliction of the skin which renders the person unclean. (The word is also applied to a blemish on the surface of an object, which similarly makes it unfit for ritual or sacred use.) Signs of leprosy are described in Leviticus 13. A person pronounced leprous by a priest is quarantined; when cured, the leper must undergo a service of cleansing and must bring offerings to the Temple. According to the rabbis, the disease is the result of scandalmongering and evil talk. The laws concerning leprosy are contained in the talmudic tractate Negaim.

Lerner, Max (1902–92) Amercian writer, of Russian origin. Born in Minsk, Russia, he went to the US at the age of five. He taught at Sarah Lawrence College, Harvard University, Williams College and Brandeis University. His works include *It is Later than You Think, Ideas are Weapons, Ideas for the Ice Age, American as a Civilization* and *The Age of Overkill*.

Leshon ha-ra ('tongue of evil') Expression denoting slander or unfounded malicious gossip.

Lessing, Theodor (1872–1933) German philosopher. He was born in Hanover. He converted to Lutheranism in 1908 and was appointed instructor at the Technische Hochschule in Hanover. He published studies of Schopenhauer, Wagner and Nietzsche. Later he returned to Judaism, and expressed his views in *Jewish Self Hate*. Towards the end of his life he lived in Marienbad, where he was murdered by the Nazis.

Lestschinsky, Jacob (1876–1966) German scholar. He was born in Horodicz in Ukraine, and left the USSR in 1921 for Berlin. In the 1920s he helped to establish the Institute for Research into Contemporary Jewry and Judaism. He was a pioneer in the study of the sociology, economics and demography of Jewish life and published studies of eastern European Jewry.

Letteris, Meir ha-Levi (?1800–1871) Galician Hebrew poet, writer and editor. He was born in Zolkiew. He worked as a copy-reader in Vienna, Pressburg and Prague. He published books of Hebrew poetry, translations and collections of Hebrew literature. Among his editions of Hebrew texts was the Bible, which he prepared for the British and Foreign Bible to Society.

Letters A notable group of letters from the biblical period are the so-called

Lachish Letters, inscribed on potsherds in the 6th century BCE (before the fall of Israel). Letters in Aramaic, dating from the 5th century BCE, were discovered at the site of the Jewish military colony at Elephantine. Official letters are included in the Books of Maccabees and the writings of Josephus, and a number of Hebrew letters written during the Bar Kokhba revolt survive. In the Middle Ages rabbinic responsa were written in the form of letters. Large numbers of Hebrew letters are preserved from the 16th century. From the 18th century onward Jews commonly wrote letters in the vernacular.

Levanda, Lev [Leib, Yehudah] (1835–1888) Russian author. He was born in Minsk, where from 1854 to 1860 he taught at a government Jewish school. In 1860 he became the Jewish adviser to the governor-general of Vilnius. After the pogroms of 1881, Levanda became a supporter of Hovevei Zion. His writings include Russian stories depicting Jewish life in the Pale of Settlement.

Levanon, Mordekhai (1901–1968) Israeli painter of Transylvanian origin. He went to Palestine in 1921 and worked as an agricultural labourer. From 1922 he studied painting in Jerusalem and Tel Aviv. His works include paintings of Jerusalem, the Sea of Galilee and Safed.

Levayah Funeral.

Leven, Narcisse (1833–1915) French public figure. He was born in Germany, and moved to Paris as a child. He was secretary to Isaac-Adolphe Crémieux during the Franco-Prussian War, and later practised law. One of the founders of the Alliance Israélite Universelle, he served successively as its secretary, vice-president and president. He was also President of the Jewish Colonization Association. His writings include *Cinquante ans d'histoire: l'Alliance Israélite Universelle.*

Levi (fl.? 19th–16th cent. BCE) Israelite, third son of Jacob and Leah. He was the founder of the tribe of Levites. He and Simeon, his brother, killed the men of Shechem who raped their sister, Dinah (Genesis 34). Because of this act they were rebuked by Jacob, who foretold that their descendants would be scattered throughout Israel (Genesis 49:7).

Levi, David (1742–1801) English Hebraist and polemicist. He was born in London, and worked as a hatter. He published translations of the Pentateuch for use in the synagogue, a Hebrew grammar and dictionary, and polemics in defence of Jews and Judaism.

Lévi, Israel (1856–1939) French rabbi. He was born in Paris. He began teaching Jewish history at the École Rabbinique in 1892, and *Talmud* and rabbinic literature at the École Pratique des Hautes Études in 1896. In 1886 he became editor of the *Revue des Études Juives.* From 1919 to 1938 he was the Chief Rabbi of the French Central Consistoire. He published studies of the Bible, Apocrypha, *Talmud*, midrash and Jewish history.

Levi, Primo (1919–1987) Italian author. He was born in Turin, and trained as a chemist. His works, many of which describe his experiences in Auschwitz, include *If This is a Man* and *The Truce.*

Lévi, Sylvain (1863–1935) French Indologist. He was born in Paris. He taught at the Sorbonne, the École des Hautes Études and the Collège de France. He also served as President of the Alliance Israélite Universelle and the Société des Études Juives. His publications include studies of Buddhism.

Levias, Caspar (1860–1934) American orientalist and lexicographer, of Lithuanian origin. He was an instructor in Semitic languages at the Hebrew Union College (1895–1905) and then (1910–20) Principal of the Plaut Memorial

Hebrew Free School in Newark, New Jersey. His writings include *A Grammar of the Aramaic Idiom Contained in the Babylonian Talmud.*

Leviathan　Sea monster described in Job 40–41. The aggadah and Apocrypha identify it with the male and female sea animals made by God on the fifth day of Creation; when they threatened to destroy the world, God emasculated the male but preserved the female. In the future God will make war on leviathan and the righteous will participate in the struggle. A similar legend is found in Ugaritic sources.

Levi bar Sisi (fl. 2nd–3rd cent.)　Palestinian and Babylonian amora. A pupil of Judah ha-Nasi, he settled in Nahardea in Babylonia. His baraitot are mentioned in the *Talmud.*

Levi ben Abraham ben Ḥayyim (c. 1245–c.1315)　French talmudist and philosopher. He was born in Villefranche-de-Confluent, and lived in various towns in southern France, earning his living as a teacher. His book *Livyat Ḥen* deals with various branches of science, and includes his theological and philosophical views. He was persecuted by opponents of Maimonides because of his rational interpretation of miracles, as well as his allegorical biblical exegesis.

Levi ben Gershon [Gersonides; Ralbag] (1288–1344)　French philosopher, mathematician, astronomer, biblical commentator and talmudist. He was born at Bagnols-sur-Cèze, and lived in Orange and Avignon. His *Milḥamot Adonai* deals with the immortality of the soul, prophecy, omnipotence, providence, astronomy, creation and miracles. He also wrote a study of the 13 hermeneutical rules of Rabbi Ishamael, and works on arithmetic, geometry, harmonic numbers and trigonometry. In addition he produced commentaries on Aristotle, Averroes and the Bible.

Levi ben Japheth (fl. 10th–11th cent.)　Palestinian Karaite scholar. He lived in Jerusalem. His *Book of the Precepts* deals with Karaite law.

Levi-Bianchini, Angelo (1887–1920)　Italian naval officer and member of the Zionist Commission. He was born in Venice. He lectured at the naval academy and the military school in Turin. He was appointed to the Zionist Commission and travelled to Palestine in 1918. In 1920 he helped to obtain the approval of the Italian Foreign Office for the British Balfour Declaration and the Mandate on Palestine, which was ratified at the San Remo Conference.

Levi Isaac of Berdichev (c. 1740–1810)　Polish Ḥasidic leader. A pupil of Dov Ber of Mezhirch, he was a rabbi in Zhelikhov, Pinsk and Berdichev. He founded Ḥasidism in central Poland, consolidated the movement in Lithuania, and expanded it in Ukraine. His *Kedushat Levi* contains his teachings.

Levin, Hanoch (1943–1999)　Israeli playwright. He was born in Tel Aviv. His plays include *You and I and the Next War, Ketchup, Queen of the Bathtub, Solomon Grip,* and *Yaacobi and Leidental.* In 1988 he became house playwright at Israel's Cameri Theatre.

Levin, [Loebel], Hirschel [Hirschel Levin; Lyon, Hart](1721–1800)　German rabbi, and author. He was born in Galicia. He served as rabbi at the Great Synagogue in London from 1756 to 1763, then officiated in Halberstadt, Mannheim and Berlin. He opposed Naphtali Herz Wesseley's reforms in Jewish education and was an advocate of Moses Mendelssohn's German translation of the Hebrew Bible, *Biur.*

Levin, Judah Leib [Yehalel] (1844–1925)　Russian Hebrew socialist poet and writer. In 1870 he became a tutor and secretary to the Brodskis, Jewish sugar magnates of Kiev. Between

1874 and 1880 he contributed poetry to the literary monthly, *Ha-Shaḥar,* which introduced socialist themes into Hebrew literature. After the pogroms of 1881, he joined Ḥibbat Zion as one of its founding members in Kiev. Later he settled in Tomashpol, where he continued his literary work. He published his memoirs in 1910. He eventually returned to Kiev.

Levin, Mayer (1905–1981) American novelist. He was born in Chicago, and became a reporter for the Chicago *Daily News.* In his writings he retold stories of the Ḥasidim and depicted his own generation of Chicago Jews. He also wrote various histories of Israel for young people and published books on the synagogue and the Jewish way of life. In 1958 he settled in Israel.

Levin [Lefin; Satanower], Mendel (1749–1826) Russian author, translator and educator, and a leading figure in the Haskalah movement. He was born in Satanev, Podolia,. From 1780 to 1784 he lived in Berlin, where he met Moses Mendelssohn through whom he came into contact with the leaders of the Haskalah. Later he lived in various Russian centres and became one of the chief advocates of the Haskalah in Galicia. His publications include studies of natural sciences, translations of classics, and a Yiddish translation of various books of the Bible.

Levin [Varnhagen von Ense], Rachel (1771–1833) German socialite. She was born in Berlin. Her home there was a meeting place for literary, intellectual and social leaders. She married Karl August Vernhagen von Ense, and converted to Protestantism.

Levin, Shemaryahu (1867–1935) Russian Zionist leader and author. He was born in Svisloch, Belorussia. He served as a rabbi in Grodno and Yekaterinoslav and as a preacher in Vilnius. At the Sixth Zionist Congress he was one of the leaders of the opposition to the project

to found a Jewish homeland in Uganda. Later he represented Vilnius in the Russian Duma. He left the USSR and lived first in Berlin, then, during World War I, in the US, where he promoted Zionism. From 1922 he worked in Berlin for the Devir Publishing Company. He finally moved to Palestine, and was one of the founders of the Haifa-Technion.

Levin, Yitzḥak Meir (1894–1971) Israeli activist and politician, leader of the Agudat Israel movement. He was born in Gora, Poland. He served in various offices in Agudat Israel. In 1940 he settled in Palestine, where he was active in rescue operations to help Jews escape from Nazi-controlled Europe. He was appointed Minister of Social Welfare in the first Knesset. In 1954 he became President of the World Actions Committee and Chairman of the World Executive of Agudat Israel.

Levinas, Emmanuel (1905–1995) French philosopher, of Lithuanian origin. He became head of the École Normale Orientale of the Alliance Israélite Universelle in Paris, and taught at the University of Paris at Nanterre. His writings include *De l'existence à l'existant, En découvrant l'existence avec Husserl and Heidegger, Totalité et infini, Difficile liberté,* and *Quartres lectures talmudiques.*

Levinthal, Bernard (1865–19532) American Orthodox rabbi of Lithuanian origin. He emigrated to the US in 1891 and became rabbi of Congregation B'nai Abraham in Philadelphia. He served as head of the United Orthodox Hebrew Congregations of Philadelphia and President of the Union of Orthodox Rabbis of the United States and Canada. In addition he helped to establish the Mizraḥi Organisation of America.

Levinthal, Israel Herbert (1888–1978) American rabbi. He served as rabbi of the Brooklyn Jewish Centre from 1919. Active in the Zionist movement, he was President of the

Rabbinical Association of America. His writings include *Judaism: an Analysis and an Interpretation, Point of View: an Analysis of American Judaism,* and *Judaism Speaks to the Modern World.*

Levinthal, Louis (1892–1976). American communal leader. He practised law in Philadelphia, eventually becoming Judge in the Philadelphia Court of Common Pleas. He served as President of the Zionist Organisation of America, chairman of the Board of Governors of the Hebrew University, and President of the Jewish Publication Society of America.

Levirate marriage. The marriage of a man with his brother's childless widow. Such a marriage is prescribed if the deceased brother has left no offspring (Deuteronomy 25:5). Release from the obligation of such a marriage may be obtained through performance of the ceremony of Halitzah (Deuteronomy 25:7–10). Regulations governing levirate marriage are contained in the tractate Yevamot in the *Talmud.*

Levi-Strauss, Claude (1908–2009) French anthropologist. Born in Brussels, he studied at the Sorbonne and became professor in São Paulo, Brazil, and later Director of Studies, École Pratique des Hautes Études in Paris and professor at the Collège de France. His works include *A World on the Wane, Structural Anthropology, The Savage Mind, Totemisme* and *Elementary Structures of Kinship.*

Levita, Elijah [Bahur, Elijah] (1468–1549) Italian Hebrew philologist, grammarian and lexicographer. He was born in Neustadt but spent most of his life in Italy, where he taught Hebrew. Numerous Christian humanists, such as Cardinal Egidio da Viterbo, were his students. He also served as a proofreader for the Protestant Hebraist Paul Fagius in Isny. He wrote studies of Hebrew grammar, lexicographical works, and a Yiddish-Hebrew dictionary. In addition he composed Hebrew and Yiddish poetry and produced various Yiddish translations.

Levites The descendants of the tribe of Levi. Moses consecrated them to serve in the Tabernacle and instruct the people; they were therefore in attendance upon the priests. Each family of Levites was assigned specific duties. The Book of Chronicles records that David divided them into separate groups with different functions in the Temple. According to Jewish law, the Levite is regarded as second only to the priest in the line of those who may read the law.

Levitical cities Name given to the 48 towns which God commanded Moses to set apart for the tribe of Levi (Numbers 35). They included the six cities of refuge. Joshua 21 records the decisions made by each of the other 11 tribes as to which cities should be assigned to the Levites.

Leviticus (Hebrew 'Va-Yikra') Biblical book, the third book of the Pentateuch. It was formerly known in Hebrew as Torat ha-Kohanim ('Law of the Priests'). It contains laws given to Moses concerning sacrifice, impurity, moral instruction and social legislation. Chapters 1–7 deal with sacrificial laws; chapters 8–10 with the installation of priests; chapters 11–16 with physical purity and unclean animals; chapter 17 with prohibitions against eating meat that has not been sacrificed; chapters 18–22 with moral instruction; chapter 23 with festivals; chapter 24 with regulations concerning the Tabernacle; chapter 25 with sabbatical and jubilee years; chapter 26 with blessings for observance and curses for non-observance of the law; and chapter 27 with valuations and devotion to sacred usage.

Leviticus Rabbah [Va-Yikra Rabbah] Homiletical midrash, the third part of the Midrash Rabbah. It dates from the 5th–6th centuries in Palestine. It contains 37 chapters dealing with topics based on the opening verses of the weekly Torah readings, according to the triennial cycle.

Levontin, Zalman David (1856–1940) Russian banker and pioneer of Jewish settlement in Palestine. He was born in Belorussia. In 1882 he went to Palestine, where he purchased land and founded the town of Rishon-le-Zion in the Judean costal plain. He subsequently served as branch bank manager in various towns in the Pale of Settlement. In 1901 he was summoned by Theodor Herzl to become one of the directors of the Jewish Colonial Trust in London. Two years later he returned to Palestine to establish the Anglo-Palestine Bank which he directed.

Levy, Asser (d.1681) Dutch merchant and landowner. He was among the first Jews to arrive in New Amsterdam in 1654, and became the most prominent member of the Jewish community there, defending the rights of Jews in the New World.

Levy, Benjamin (c.1650–1704) British merchant, founder of the Ashkenazi community in London. The son of Levy Moses of Hamburg, he arrived in London in about 1670. In 1697, in the course of the reorganisation of the Royal Exchange, he became one of the 12 original Jewish brokers of the City of London. In 1696 he purchased a cemetery for the Ashkenazi community.

Levy, Jacob (1819–1892) German rabbi and lexicographer. He was born near Poznán in Poland. He served as rabbi of Rosenberg, Upper Silesia, but then for a period devoted himself to scientific work. In 1857 he became assistant rabbi in Breslau, and later was appointed to the Breslau court to administer the Jewish oath. In 1878 he was appointed lecturer at the Mora-Salomon Leipziger Foundation. He compiled dictionaries of the Targum and of the *Talmud* and midrash.

Levy, Moritz Abraham (1817–1872) German scholar. He taught Semitic paleography and epigraphy at the Breslau Synagogen-Gemeinde. He wrote textbooks on Jewish history and religion, and a history of Jewish coins.

Levy, Reuben (1891–1966) English orientalist. He was born in Manchester. He was a lecturer in Persian language and literature at Oxford University, and then taught biblical literature at the Jewish Institute of Religion in New York. He later became Professor of Persian at Cambridge University. He edited and translated classical Persian and Arabic texts, wrote textbooks about Persian language and literature, and published studies of Islam.

Levy-Bruhl, Lucien (1857–1939) French philosopher. Born in Paris, he taught at Poitiers and Amiens. Subsequently he became Professor of Higher Rhetoric at the Lycée Louis-Le-Grand and a lecturer at the École Normale Superieure. He then moved to the Sorbonne and lectured at the École Libre des Sciences politiques. In 1925 he established the Institute d'Ethnologie. His works include *Ethics and Oral Science.*

Lewandowski, Louis (1821–1894) German choral director and composer. He was born in Wreschen, near Posen. After moving to Berlin he served as conductor of the choir at the Old Synagogue in the Heidereutergasse, and later at the New Synagogue. He also served as a singing teacher at the Jewish Free School and the Jewish Teachers Seminary. His compositions had a profound influence on Western Ashkenazi synagogue music, and his style was transferred to numerous Conservative and Reform congregations in the US.

Lewin, Benjamin Manasseh (1879–1944) Israeli rabbinic scholar, educator and authority on gaonic literature. He was born in Gorodets, Russia. In 1912 he went to Palestine, where he was a teacher and later head of the religious schools network, Netzaḥ Yisrael. His *Otzar ha-Geonim* is a collection of the teachings of the geonim of Sura and Pumbedita.

Lewin, Judah Leib (1894–1971)   Russian rabbi. Born in Yekaterinoslav, he became the rabbi of Grishino, and later of Yekaterinoslav. He then returned to Grishino where he worked as a religious scribe. In 1957 he was appointed principal of the yeshivah of the Moscow Great Synagogue. After the death of Solomon Schliefer he became the rabbi there.

Lewinski, Elhanan Löb (1857–1910)   Russian Hebrew writer and Zionist leader. He was born in Podberezye, Russia. He travelled to Palestine after the pogroms of 1881 and returned an ardent Zionist. He settled in Odessa and in 1896 became the representative in Russia of the Palestinian Carmel wine company. He was a founder of the Moriah publishing house and supported literary enterprises. He also served as treasurer and preacher in the Zionist synagogue in Odessa. His writings were published in various journals.

Lewis, Bernard (b.1916)   English orientalist. He was born in London. He was appointed assistant lecturer at the University of London in 1938. During World War II he served in the army and was seconded to the Foreign Office. In 1949 he became Professor of Near and Middle Eastern History in the School of Oriental and African Studies at London University. He published studies of Arab and Turkish history and translated Hebrew prose and poetry into English.

Lewisohn, Ludwig (1883–1955)   American author and translator. Born in Berlin, he was taken to Charleston, South Carolina, in 1890. He was Professor of Comparative Literature at Brandeis University. Between 1924 and 1940 he lived in Paris. His writings include novels on Jewish subjects: *The Island Within*

and *The Last Days of Shylock*. He also wrote books dealing with Judaism and Zionism, including *Israel, Mid-Channel, Theodor Herzl: A Portrait for this Age, The American Jew: Character and Destiny,* and *What is the Jewish Heritage?*

Lewy, Israel (1841–1917)   German rabbi and scholar. He was born in Inowroclaw, Poland. He became a lecturer in Talmud at the Hochschule für die Wissenschaft des Judentums in Berlin, then in 1883 took up an appointment at the Breslau Rabbinical Seminary. He published studies of Talmudic literature.

Libation   A drink offering or sacrifice. In biblical times oil and wine were used in nearly all sacrificial ceremonies. Oil was usually offered with the meal offering. Every animal oblation was accompanied by a wine libation, different measures being prescribed for the various types of animals (Numbers 15:1–16).

Liberman, Serge (b.1942).   Australian novelist and editor. He was born in Fergana in Uzbekistan, and went to Australia in 1951. He became the editor of the *Melbourne Chronicle*. His publications include *Ethnic Australia, Jewish Writing from Down Under, Joseph's Coat, An Anthology of Multicultural Writing,* and *Bibliography of Australian Judaica.*

Libin, Solomon (1872–1955)   American Yiddish writer. He was born in Russia and emigrated to London in 1891, later moving to New York. He wrote hundreds of stories about early immigrant life and the suffering of sweatshop workers. In addition he wrote about 50 plays.

Libraries   Jewish libraries existed in the academies of Babylonia after the completion of the *Talmud*. The first great Jewish public library was that of Samuel ibn Nagrela. Private libraries continued to exist throughout the Middle Ages and during the Renaissance. In modern times various scholars have established important collections of Jewish books and manuscripts. In addition Hebrew libraries are found in such institutions as the British Museum, the Vatican, the Palatine Library, the Bibliothèque Nationale in Paris, the Bodleian Library in Oxford, the University Library in Cambridge, the Hebrew University in Jerusalem, the Jewish Theological Seminary in New York,, the Hebrew Union College in Cincinnati, and Jews College London.

Lichtenstein, Hillel (1815–1891) Hungarian rabbi. He served as rabbi in Margarethen, Kolozsvar, Szikszó and Kolomyya in Galicia. He was an ardent critic of religious reform.

Lichine, David (1910–72) Russian dancer and choreographer. Born in Rostov-on-Don, he went to Paris as a boy. In 1932 he joined Colonel de Basil's Ballets Russes de Monte Carlo and began choreographing. In 1941 he and his wife, the ballerina Tatiana Riabouchinska, went to the US where they joined the American Ballet Theatre as guest artists. Eventually they moved to South America, but returned to the US in 1952 where they opened a school.

Lidzbarski, Mark (1868–1928) German Semitic philologist. He was born in Plock in the Russian part of Poland, and in adulthood converted to Protestantism. In 1896 he began lecturing in oriental languages at the University of Kiel. In 1907 he took up an appointment at the University of Greifswald, and in 1917 one at the University of Göttingen. He was the founder of Semitic epigraphy, and also published various studies and texts of the gnostic Mandeans.

Lieberman, Saul (1898–1983) Amercian scholar. He was born in Motol, near Pinsk, Belorussia, and settled in Jerusalem in 1928. In 1931 he was appointed lecturer in Talmud at the Hebrew University. He also taught at the Mizrahi Teachers Seminary, and was Dean of the Harry Fischel Institute for Tal-

mudic Research. In 1940 he became Professor of Palestinian Literature and Institutions at the Jewish Theological Seminary where he later served as dean and rector of the rabbinical school. He published studies of Jewish Hellenism, editions of the Tosephta, and works on the Palestinian *Talmud*.

Lieberman, Aaron Samuel (1845–1880) Lithuanian socialist and Hebrew writer. He was born in Lunna, Lithuania, and became secretary of Suwalki. Later he lived in Vilnius, where he worked with an insurance company and as a draftsman. From 1872 he was a leader of a local revolutionary group. He subsequently joined socialist circles in Berlin and became a pioneer of Jewish socialism. He lived successively in London (where he worked as a typesetter), Vienna (from where he was expelled to Germany), London again, and finally the US. He published various works about socialism.

Liebermann, Max (1847–1935) German painter. He was born in Berlin, and lived in various cities including Paris. His work includes *Judengasse*, a series of paintings of street scenes in the Jewish quarter of Amsterdam.

Liebman, Joshua Loth (1907–1948) Amercian Reform rabbi. He was born in Hamilton, Ohio. He served as a rabbi in Lafayette, Indiana, and as an instructor at the Hebrew Union College. Later he was rabbi to congregations in Chicago and Boston, where he also taught at Boston University and at Andover-Newton Theological Seminary. He published the book *Peace of Mind.*

Liebmann, Jost (c.1640–1702) Prussian court Jew. He was court jeweller and mint-master to Friedrich Wilhelm and Friedrich III of Brandenburg. Toward the end of the 17th century he was one of the richest Jews in Prussia. The owner of the only synagogue in Berlin, he played an important role in the Jewish community.

Lieme, Nehemiah de (1882–1940) Dutch economist and Zionist leader. He was involved in life insurance and education for Dutch workers. In 1913 he became Chairman of the Dutch Zionist Federation, and from 1919 to 1921 he served as President of the Jewish National Fund.

Liessin, Abraham (1872–1938) American Yiddish poet and editor. He was born in Minsk, and went to the US in 1897, where he became an active socialist. From 1913 he was editor of *Zukunft*, a Yiddish literary and cultural monthly. In his writings he described the heroes and martyrs of the Jewish past.

Life The Bible teaches that life is God's supreme blessing. According to the rabbis, all laws (except those that deal with idolatry, bloodshed and forbidden sexual liaisons) can be suspended if there is danger to life. Human life is viewed as infinitely valuable, and thus one is prohibited from hastening death. Rabbinic law also prohibits euthanasia.

Lifshitz, Nehama (1927–2017) Israeli Yiddish and Hebrew singer. Born in Kaunas, Lithuania, she went to Uzbekistan during World War II. In 1946 she returned to Soviet Lithuania and studied at the Vilnius conservatoire. She later travelled throughout the USSR giving concerts of Yiddish songs. In 1969 she emigrated to Israel.

Light It is the symbol of life, blessing, peace, knowledge, understanding, redemption, the soul and goodness. According to Genesis, it was God's first creation (Genesis 1:3–4). Light played an important role in kabbalistic mysticism. Its symbolic importance is reflected in the frequent use of candles and candelabra.

Lilien, Ephraim Moses (1874–1925) German artist. He was born in Drohobycz, Galicia. He first worked in Munich as a cartoonist, later in Berlin as a book illustrator. An active Zionist, he was a founder and editor of the Berlin publishing house Judischer Verlag. In 1902 he published *Juda*, a volume of ballads on biblical themes with his illustrations. He was a member of the committee formed to establish the Bezalel School of Arts and Crafts in Jerusalem. Among his works are a group of etchings that include impressions of Palestine.

Lilienblum, Moses Leib (1843–1910) Russian Hebrew writer, critic and political journalist. He was born in Kédainiai, near Kovno. He was initially attracted to the Haskalah and encouraged religious reform, but in his autobiography, *Hattot Neurim*, he criticised the impracticality of the Haskalah movement and expressed his socialist ideas. After the pogroms of 1881 he became an advocate of Zionism, and a leader and ideologist of Hibbat Zion. He published articles in Hebrew, Yiddish and Russian.

Lilienthal, Max (1813–1882) American educator and rabbi, of Russian origin. He was born in Munich, Bavaria. He served as Director of the Jewish school of Riga. In 1841 the czarist government invited him to initiate the creation of state schools for Jews. Encountering opposition from the Jewish community, he eventually realised that this proposal was aimed at the conversion of Jewry. He left Russian and settled in the US, becoming rabbi of the Bene Israel Congregation in Cincinnati.

Lilith Female demon. She is mentioned in Isaiah 34:14, and is depicted in the *Talmud* as having a human face, long hair and wings. In mystical sources she was the queen of demons and the consort of Satan-Samael. In kabbalistic literature she is the symbol of lust and temptation. It was common to protect women who were giving birth from her power by fixing amulets over their beds.

Lind, Jacob (1927–2007) Austrian writer. Born in Vienna, he went to the

Netherlands in 1938. During the Nazi period he worked as a gardener, and escaped deportation by acquiring false papers and finding employment in Germany. He lived in Palestine after the war, and later settled in London. His publications include *Soul of Wood,* and *Counting my Steps.*

Linetzki, Isaac Joel (1839–1935) Ukrainian Yiddish author. He was born in Podolia. Living in Odessa, he became a spokesman for the radical wing of the Haskalah. He published various works including *Dos poylische yingel,* which criticised Jewish life and satirised the Ḥasidim.

Lion of Wrath   Character mentioned in the Dead Sea Scrolls in the commentaries on Naḥum and Hosea. He took vengeance on his enemies by crucifying them. He has been identified with Alexander Yannai, who crucified 800 rebels in the 1st century BCE.

Lipchitz, Jacques (1891–1973) American sculptor. He was born in Lithuania and in 1925 became a French citizen. He left Paris in 1940 and settled in the US. In his work he often utilised biblical episodes and themes taken from Jewish life and history.

Lippe, Karpel (1830–1915) Romanian Zionist, of Galician origin. He was born in Stanislav, Galicia. He became a physician in Jassy, Romania. Active in Ḥibbat Zion, he was one of the initiators of the Zionist idea. In 1911 he returned to Galicia. He published scientific studies, Jewish apologetics, works on the rights of Romanian Jews and poetry.

Lipschütz, Jacob (1838–1922) Russian author. He was born in Vilkomir. He became the secretary and chief assistant of Isaac Elhanan Spektor, the rabbi at Kovno, and opposed the Haskalah and Zionism. His *Zikhron Yaaov* is a book of reminiscences which casts light on Russian Jewish history.

Lipsky, Louis (1870–1963) American Zionist leader, journalist, and author. He was born in Rochester, New York. He founded the Zionist periodical *The Maccabean* in 1901, and also edited the *American Hebrew.* From 1922 to 1930 he was president of the Zionist Organisation of America. He was a founder of Kerent ha-Yesod, the Jewish Agency, and the American and World Jewish congresses. His writings include *Thirty Years of American Zionism.*

Lipton, Seymour (1903–1986) Amercian sculptor. He trained as a dentist and practised in New York before devoting himself to sculpture. Some of his works are based on Jewish motifs.

Liptzin, Solomon (1901–1995) Israeli literary scholar. He was born in Satanov, Russia, and taken to the US at an early age. He was Professor of German at City College, New York. Later he settled in Israel. His writings include *Peretz, Eliakum Zunser, The Flowering of Yiddish Literature, The Maturing of Yiddish Literature,* and *The Jew in American Literature.*

Lisitsky, Ephraim E. (1885–1962) American Hebrew poet and educator of Russian origin. He was born in Minsk. He emigrated to the US and settled in New Orleans, where he became the principal of the city's Hebrew school. He wrote Hebrew poetry about Native American Indians, as well as Jewish themes.

Liturgy   The Jewish liturgy dates back to worship in the Temple in ancient Israel, when prayers were recited during the sacrificial ritual. During the Babylonian exile sacrifice was replaced by prayers recited in public assemblies. In time the Jewish liturgy followed a fixed pattern of three daily services: Shaḥarit (morning service), Minḥah (afternoon service), and Maariv (evening service). An additional prayer (Musaph) was recited on Sabbaths and festivals, and a special prayer (Neilah) was recited at the conclusion of the service on the

Day of Atonement. The central prayers of the Jewish liturgy are the Shema and the Amidah or Eighteen Benedictions. Prayers recited on weekdays and the Sabbath are contained in the siddur (the prayer book); those recited on festivals are found in the maḥzor (the festival prayer book). The prayer structure is based on the threefold division of adoration, thanksgiving and petition. There are two versions of the Jewish liturgy: the Ashkenazi ritual is used by Eastern-European Jewry and the Sephardi ritual by Jews of Spanish and Portuguese origin, as well as a number of oriental Jewish communities.

Litvakov, Moses (1875–?1938) Russian Yiddish writer. He was born in Cherkassy in Ukraine. He wrote in Russian, Hebrew and Yiddish on social and literary issues. After the revolution of 1905 he became a member of the central committee of the territorialist Socialist-Zionist Party. He edited periodicals in Vilnius, and after 1917 he contributed to Yiddish journals in Kiev. In 1919 he joined the Communist Party and became a leader of Moscow's Yevsektzia. From 1924 he edited *Emes*, the Yiddish organ of the Communist Party. He was arrested in the Stalinist purges of 1937 and died in prison.

Litvinovsky, Pinḥas (1894–1995) Israeli painter. He was born in Ukraine. He settled in Palestine and studied at the Bezalel School of Arts and Crafts in Jerusalem; later he studied at the St Petersburg Academy. After returning to Jerusalem in 1919 he participated in the first group exhibitions of Palestinian artists there from 1923, and in Tel Aviv from 1926. In his paintings he utilised various styles to depict traditional Jewish themes.

Loans According to Jewish law, whoever borrows money must return it at a fixed time. Otherwise the lender may recover the value of the loan in the form of the borrower's property. If the loan is made by a promissory note, it may even be recovered from property sold by the debtor after the date of the note. Originally a Sabbatical Year cancelled all debts, but the sage Hillel instituted the prosbul, a legal document which allowed the collection of debts to be postponed until after the Sabbatical Year. According to the Bible loans with interest are forbidden; nonetheless, permission was given to charge interest under certain conditions.

Loans [Loanz], Elijah ben Moses [Elijah Baal Shem] (1564–1636) German Kabbalist. He was born in Frankfurt am Main, and served as a rabbi in Fulda, Hanu, Friedberg and Worms. He was a writer of kabbalistic amulets and incantations. His *Rinnat Dodim* is a kabbalistic commentary on the Song of Songs.

Loch in kop (Yiddish: 'hole in the head') Expression used to designate something which is not needed.

Locker, Berl (1887–1972) Israeli Labour Zionist leader. He was born in Galicia and became the editor of the Lemberg Labour Zionist newspaper. Before World War I he organised the Poale Zion party in the Austrian Empire, and from 1916 he ran the world office of Poale Zion at The Hague. From 1931 to 1936 he was a member of the executives of the Zionist Organisation and the Jewish Agency in London. He settled in Palestine in 1936 and served as a member of the executive of Histadrut. From 1948 to 1956 he was Chairman of the Jewish Agency in Jerusalem. He wrote articles in Yiddish, German, Hebrew and English.

Loeb, Isidore (1839–1892) French rabbi and scholar. He was a tutor in Bayonne and Paris, and later served as a rabbi at St Etienne. In 1869 he was appointed secretary of the Alliance Israélite Universelle. From 1878 he taught Jewish history at the École Rabbinique. He wrote studies of biblical and talmudic literature, medieval historiography and Jewish history in Spain and France.

Loeb, Richard (1905–36) American criminal. He and Nathan Freutenthal Leopold were university graduates from wealthy Jewish families. They abducted and killed a 14-year-old boy in 1924. They were sentenced to life imprisonment. He was murdered in prison.

Loewe, Heinrich (1867–1950) German Zionist and scholar of Jewish folklore. He was born in Wanzleben. He founded Jung Israel, the first Zionist group in Germany, in 1892, and edited various Zionist publications. From 1899 he worked as a librarian in the University of Berlin, where he became a professor in 1915. In 1933 he settled in Palestine and worked as a librarian in Tel Aviv. He published studies in the filed of Jewish folklore.

Loewe, Herbert Martin James (1882–1940) English orientalist. He was born in London. He taught rabbinic Hebrew at Oxford, rabbinics at Cambridge, and Hebrew at the University of London. He published studies of rabbinics and Jewish history. With C.G. Montefiore, he edited the *Rabbinic Anthology*.

Loewe, Joel ben Judah Loeb [Brill, Joel ben Judah Loeb] (1762–1802) German Hebrew writer, grammarian and exegete. He was born in Berlin, and joined Moses Mendelssohn's Haskalah movement. In 1791 he was appointed Principal of the Wilhelms-Schule in Breslau. He published an introduction and commentary to Mendelssohn's German translation of the Psalms, a scientific grammar of biblical Hebrew, and epigrams in the style of the Book of Proverbs. He also translated the Passover Haggadah into German.

Loewe, Louis (1809–1888) British orientalist. He was born in Zülz, Germany, and settled in England. In 1837 he visited Egypt (where he deciphered various inscriptions) and Palestine. From 1839 he was Sir Moses Montefiore's secretary, as well as the director of the oriental department of the Duke of Sussex's library. He was Principal of Jews College in 1856–8 and later served as Principal of Ohel Moshe vi-Yhudit, the theological seminary founded by Montefiore. He published works on the life of the Montefiore and on oriental languages.

Loewisohn, Solomon (1788–1821) Austrian Hebrew poet and scholar. He was born in Hungary, and settled in Vienna, where he worked as a proofreader. He was one of the outstanding Hebrew authors of the Haskalah movement. His *Melitzat Yeshurun* is an exposition of biblical poetry, and his Meḥkere Aretz is the first modern Lexicon of biblical geography.

Logos (Greek: 'the word') The Word of God by which the universe was created. It was understood by Philo as divine reason, the mind of God manifested in and through the created universe. It is also linked to the concept of memra (also meaning 'word') in Targum literature. In Proverbs, Job and various apocryphal books the concept of divine wisdom ('ḥokhmah') shares some of the qualities of the logos. It later became a central feature of Christian theology. In kabbalistic literature concepts similar to the logos are found in the doctrine of the sephirot.

London, Meyer (1871–1926) American lawyer and socialist leader. He was born in Poland, and went to the US in 1891. In 1914 he was elected to the House of Representatives as a socialist from the immigrant district on the Lower East Side in New York. He opposed the US entry into World War I, and had little sympathy with Zionism.

Lonzano, Menaḥem di (1550–before 1624) Palestinian linguist, poet and Kabbalist. Born in Constantinople, he emigrated to Jerusalem, and later moved to Safed; 40 years later he went to Turkey and Italy, returning to Jerusalem in 1618. He wrote studies of the masoretic text of the Bible, Hebrew grammar, prosody and lexicography. His *Shete Yadot* contains original writings and midrashic literature.

Lookstein, Joseph Hyman (1902–1979) American rabbi, of Russian origin. He went to the US as a child. He served as a rabbi of Kehilath Jeshurun Congregation in New York and Professor of Homiletics and Sociology at Yeshiva University. In 1958 he became President of Bar-Ilan University in Tel Aviv.

Lopez, Aaron (1731–1782) American merchant shipper. He was born in Portugal, and settled in Newport, Rhode Island, in 1752. There he became a leader of the Yeshuat Israel Congregation. He built up an extensive transatlantic mercantile empire and became Newport's leading merchant. A supporter of the rebel cause, he moved to Leicester, Massachusetts, when the British captured Newport.

Lopez, Roderigo (1525–1594) British Marrano physician. Originally from Portugal, he settled in London during the reign of Queen Elizabeth. He was appointed physician to the Earl of Leicester and to Queen Elizabeth. In 1594 he was arrested, found guilty of plotting to poison the queen and executed.

Lorki [de Lorca], Joshua [Geronimo de Santa Fé) (d. c.1419) Spanish physician and writer. He was born in Lorca, Spain. He converted to Christianity in 1412 and assumed the name Geronimo de Sante Fé. He became a physician to anti-Pope Benedict XIII. He initiated the Disputation of Tortosa (1413–14) in which he was a participant. Subsequently he travelled widely, attempting to convert Jews to Christianity.

Lorre, Peter [Lowenstein, Ladislav] (1904–64) American actor, of Hun-garian origin. Born in Rozsahegy, Hungary, he moved to Austria as a child. He acted on the Berlin stage and in films until the rise of Nazism. He went to England and later worked in Hollywood. He appeared in such films as *M, The Man who Knew too Much, Mad Love, The Maltese Falcon, Casablanca, Arsenic and Old Lace,* and *The Beast with Five Fingers.*

Lot (fl.? 19th–16th cent. BCE) Israelite, nephew of Abraham. The Bible depicts his sojourn in Sodom, escape from the city, and the disaster that befell his wife who looked back at the destruction of Sodom and became a pillar of salt. After the devastation of the city, Lot lived in a cave with his two daughters, who plied him with wine and, when he was drunk, committed incest with him. Each daughter bore him a son, Ammon and Moab (Genesis 19).

Lothar, Ernst (1890–1974) Austrian writer and stage director. He was born in Brünn, Moravia, and became a civil servant. He was later active as a theatre critic and director. Although he converted to Catholicism, he had to leave Austria in 1938. He lived in the US, but later returned to Vienna. His publications include *The Angel and the Trumpet,* which discusses intermarriage.

Louvish, Simon (b.1947) Israeli author. He was born in Glasgow, and moved to Israel in 1949. His publications include *A Moment of Silence, The Therapy of Avram Blok,* and *The Death of Moishe Ganef.*

Love (Hebrew 'ahav') In the Bible the term 'ahav' refers to love of all kinds – that of men and women as well as moral and spiritual relationships. In rabbinic literature, the concept of the love of God is a central religious value. In the Middle Ages it acquired a mystical significance.

Löw, Eleazar (1758–1837) Polish rabbi. He was born in Wodzislaw and became dayyan there. Later he was rabbi of Pilcia, Třešt, Pilsen, Liptovsky Mikuláš, Slovakia and Santo. An opponent of religious reform, he published studies of the halakhah.

Löw, Leopold (1811–1875) Hungarian scholar. He served as a rabbi in several Hungarian communities. From 1850 he officiated at Szeged. He was an extreme reformer and engaged in controversy with the Orthodox. He wrote studies of the history of Hungarian Jewry. In addition, he was the publisher of a journal of Jewish studies (*Ben Hananiah*) from 1858 to 1867.

Lowenthal, Marvin (1890–1969). American author. He was born in Bradford, Pennsylvania. He organised the Zionist movement on the West Coast. From 1924 to 1929 he was the European editor of the *Menorah Journal*, and during this period wrote about literature, politics and Zionism. He served on the Zionist Advisory Commission (1946–9), and was editor of the *American Zionist*. He translated and edited *Memoirs of Glueckel of Hameln*, and edited *Henrietta Szold: Life and Letters*.

Lox (Yiddish) Smoked salmon.

Lozowick, Louis (1892–1973) American painter, graphic artist and art critic. He was born in Ludovinka, a small village in the Kiev district, and went to the US in 1906. He published articles in the *Menorah Journal* on the works of Jewish artists. His *Hundred American Jewish Painters and Scuptors* is a comprehensive study of modern American Jewish art.

Lublin, Meir ben Gedaliah of [Maḥaram Lublin] (1558–1616) Polish talmudist. He was born in Lublin and became head of the yeshivah there (1582–87). He later served as dayyan and head of the yeshivah at Kraków. From 1595 to 1613 he was a rabbi in Lemberg, and he was then appointed rabbi and head of the yeshivah in Lublin. His *Meir Ene Ḥakhamim* contains novellae on the entire *Talmud*. His responsa were published in *Manhir Ene Ḥakhamim*.

Lublinski, Samuel (1868–1910) German playwright, literary historian and philosopher of religion. He was born in east Prussia. As a young man he was apprenticed to a bookseller in Italy, and he eventually devoted himself to literature. He lived in Berlin, Dresden and Weimar. His writings include *Jüdische Charaktere bei Grillparzer, Hebbel, und Otto Ludwig, Die Enstehung des Judentums,* and *Der urchristliche Erdkreis und sein Mythos.*

Ludomir, Maid of Ukrainian Ḥasidic leader. Her real name was Hannah Rachel and she was the daughter of Monesh Werbermacher. After an illness, she followed Ḥasidic customs, built her own synagogue, and observed the religious duties of men (putting on talllit and tefillin when she prayed). She later emigrated to Palestine where she continued her mystical studies and practised rituals designed to hasten the coming of the Messiah.

Lueger, Karl (1844–1910) Austrian politician. He was born in Vienna. He qualified as a lawyer and was elected to parliament in 1885. In 1893 he united the different Christian factions into the Christian Social Party, which he led until his death. He became Mayor of Vienna in 1897. His administration pursued various discriminatory policies against the Jewish community.

Luftmensch (German) Rootless person. The expression was introduced by Max Nordau to describe the Jews in Eastern Europe, who lived by peddling and minor speculation.

Lukács, György (1885–1971) Hungarian philosopher and literary critic. He was born in Budapest, where he later became Commissar of Education. When Hitler came to power he fled to the USSR. After World War II he returned to Hungary, was elected to parliament, and was appointed a professor of aesthetics and cultural philosophy at the University of Budapest. He published Marxist interpretations of literature and was influenced by the socialist views of Moses Hess.

Lulav Palm branch. According to Leviticus, it is to be used ceremonially on the feast of Sukkot, together with the etrog, myrtle and willow (Leviticus 23:40). It is the custom to carry them during the recital of the Hallel and the Hoshanot. At particular points in the recitations the lulav is shaken in all directions.

Lunchitz, Solomon Ephraim (d.1619) Czech talmudist. He was the head of the yeshivah in Lwów. From 1604 he served as Chief Rabbi in Prague. He contributed to talmudic study and composed liturgical poems.

Luncz, Abraham Moses (1854–1918) Palestinian author, publisher and editor. He was born in Kovno, and emigrated to Jerusalem in 1869. Although he became blind, he published 12 volumes of a yearbook about Palestine, as well as a literary almanac, which appeared form 1895 to 1915. He also edited geographical works on Palestine.

Lunel, Armand (1892–1977) French novelist. He was born in Aix-en-Provence and taught philosophy in Monaco. He wrote novels about Provencal life, including portrayals of the regions Jewish inhabitants. He also wrote the librettos for Darius Milhaud's *Esther de Carpentras* and the oratorio *David*.

Luria, Isaac ben Solomon [Ari; Ashkenazi] (1534–72) Palestinian Kabbalist. He was born in Jerusalem and educated in Egypt. From 1570 he lived in Safed. His kabbalistic teachings were received by his disciples orally. They were later recorded by his pupil Ḥayyim Vital in *Etz Ḥayyim, Peri Etz Ḥayyim*, and *Sepher ha-Gilgulim*. His kabbalistic theories profoundly influenced the development of Jewish mysticism. In his teaching he propounded doctrines about divine contraction ('tzimtzum'), the shattering of the vessels ('shevirat ha-kelim'), and cosmic repair ('tikkun').

Luria, Solomon ben Jehiel [Maharshal] (?1510–1574) Polish codifier. He officiated in communities in Lithuania and Poland. His *Yam shel Shelomoh* was critical of the Shulḥan Arukh, which according to Luria relied on the codifiers instead of being based on the *Talmud*.

Luxemburg, Rosa (1871–1919) German revolutionary, of Polish origin. Born in Zamosc, eastern Poland, she studied at the University of Zurich. She was a leader of the Polish and Lithuanian Social Democratic Party, and sought to overthrow the czar. She became a German citizen and was one of the leaders of the militant left wing of the German party. In 1914 she helped form the Spartacus League. She was imprisoned for most of the war, and freed in 1918. She helped transform the Spartacus League into the German Communist Party. She and a fellow leader of the left, Karl Liebknecht, were arrested and murdered by army officers when they were being taken to prison.

Luz, Kadish (1895–1972) Israeli labour leader. He was born in Bobruisk, Belorussia, and served in the Russian army during World War I. He was a founder of the organisation of Jewish soldiers in Russia and of the Zionist pioneer movement. He settled in Palestine in 1920. From 1951 to 1969 he was a Mapai member of the Knesset. He was minister of agriculture (1955–59), and speaker of the Knesset (1959–69).

Luzki, Joseph Solomon ben Moses (d.1844) Crimean Karaite scholar. He was born at Kukizow, near Lemberg, and lived at Lutsk, Volhynia. In 1802 he moved to Yevpatoriya in the Crimea, where he became rabbi of the Karaites. He went with Simḥah Babovich to St. Petersburg to obtain exemption for the Karaites from military service. In 1831 he settled in Palestine, but he later returned to Yevpatoriya. He wrote religious poems, studies of Hebrew grammar and Bible commentary.

Luzki, Simḥah Isaac ben Moses (d.1766) Crimean Karaite writer and bibliographer. He was born in Lutsk and lived in Chufut-Kale in the Crimea, where he became head of a bet midrash. He was a copyist of early Karaite manuscripts, and wrote various studies of theology, philosophy, halakhah and kabbalah. His *Oraḥ Tzaddikim* is a history of the Karaites and Karaite literature.

Luzzatti, Luigi (1841–1927) Italian statesman and economist. He was born in Venice, where he founded a mutual aid society for the gondoliers. Expelled from the city as a revolutionary, he went to Milan where he became Professor of Economics at the Istituto Tecnico; he was later appointed Professor of Constitutional Law at the University of Padua. In 1869 he became General Secretary to the Ministry of Agriculture, Industry and Commerce. From 1871 he served in parliament in various posts, becoming Prime Minister in 1910. He acted on behalf of oppressed European Jews, and supported Zionist activities in Palestine.

Luzzatto, Moses Ḥayyim [Ramḥal] (1707–1746) Italian Kabbalist, Hebrew poet and writer. He was born in Padua. He engaged in mystical practices and gathered around himself a group of disciples. He believed he was in communion with a maggid who dictated secret doctrines to him. His messianic claims provoked the hostility of the rabbis. Forced to leave Italy, he settled in Amsterdam and subsequently went to Palestine. He wrote kabbalistic studies, ethical works, theological investigations, poetry and verse drama. He is regarded as the father of modern Hebrew literature.

Luzzatto, Samuel David [Shadal] (1800–1865) Italian scholar, philosopher, biblical commentator and translator. From 1829 he was professor at the Padua Rabbinical College. He wrote studies of the Bible, Hebrew grammar and philology, Jewish liturgy, Hebrew poetry, and philosophy. In addition he edited the poems of Judah ha-Levi, translated parts of the Bible into Italian, and composed poetry in Hebrew in the traditional Italian style. He was opposed to the kabbalah and criticised several Jewish philosophers including Maimonides, Ibn Ezra and Spinoza. His correspondence with other Jewish scholars is of historical importance.

Lying The act of lying is forbidden in the Bible (Leviticus 19:11) and the bearing of false witness is specifically prohibited in the ninth commandment. The talmudic scholar Jonah of Gerona lists nine types of lies: (1) untruths spoken in business; (2) deceit without causing harm; (3) lying with desire for benefit; (4) deliberate falsification of facts heard; (5) a promise made with the intention of not keeping it; (6) a promise which is not kept; (7) leading another to believe, falsely, that one has done him a favour; (8) priding oneself on qualities one does not have; and (9) the falsehoods of children.

Lyra, Nicholas de (c.1270–1349) French exegete. He published Bible commentaries in Latin, based largely on those of Rashi.

M

Christopher, George and Morris were at a Turkish bath talking about the control they have over their wives. Christopher and George were doing all the talking while Morris was silent. After a while, they said: 'What about you, Morris, are Jewish men any different? What sort of control do you have over your wife?'

'Just the other night,' Morris said, 'my wife Selma came to me on her hands and knees.'

Christopher and George were amazed. 'What happened then?' they asked.

'Well,' he replied, 'Selma said, "Get out from under the bed and fight like a man."'

* * * * *

Many jokes depict Jewish men as submissive husbands, frightened of their wives. Here the Jewish husband confesses that he hid under the bed from his wife who shouted at him that he should get up and fight like a man. Through amusing, the joke highlights the stark contrast between overpowering wives and submissive spouses.

Maamad One of the non-priestly Israelites who attended the Temple sacrifice. The whole people was divided into 24 groups of priests, Levites and Israelites, who were assigned specific times to attend in the Temple. The groups of Israelites sent only a few representatives (the maamadot) to be present at the sacrifices. The rest assembled in their own towns at the appointed time to read prayers and the first chapter of Genesis. In the post-Talmudic period the practice of reading these selections was partially retained.

Maaphilim Term applied to Jews who attempted to reach Palestine despite obstacles, in particular those who defied the restrictions imposed by the British Mandatory government. From 1934 transports were arranged by the Polish organisation He-Ḥalutz and the Revisionists. Immigration began in 1938,

but the British were quick to counter it by restrictive legislation.

Maariv [evening service] The service of evening prayer. According to tradition, it was ordained by Jacob. The *Talmud* relates a controversy about whether it is obligatory or optional; in time it became required. The service includes the Shema, its blessings, and the Eighteen Benedictions. during the medieval period, poems called 'maaravot' were composed for it.

Maaseh (Yiddish from Hebrew) A far-fetched story.

Maaseh bereshit ('work of creation') Mystical tradition concerning the Creation. Based on Genesis 1, it depicts the creation of the universe according to mystical doctrines. These views are expressed in the Sepher Yetzirah, in which the cosmos is said to have been created out of 32 secret paths of wisdom (consisting of 10 basic numbers, sephirot, and the 22 letters of the Hebrew alphabet).

Maaseh Book Name given to any of several collections of mostly miraculous stories, which provide ethical instruction. Derived from the *Talmud* as well as medieval folklore, they were written in Yiddish. A comprehensive English edition of the stories was published in 1934 by Moses Gaster. Similar collections were found among Mediterranean Sephardi communities under the title *Maaseh Nissim.*

Maaseh merkavah ('work of the chariot) [chariot mysticism] Mystical doctrine, based on the vision of the divine chariot in Ezekiel 1. It describes the mystic's ascent to Heaven, his vision of the divine palaces and personal experience of the divine presence. It formed the basis of a complex of speculations, homilies and visions connected with throne of glory and the divine chariot.

Maaserot ('Tithes') Seventh tractate in the Mishnah order of Zeraim. It deals with the tithe given to the Levites (Numbers 18:21).

Maaser Sheni ('second tithe') Eighth tractate in the Mishnah order of Zeraim. It deals with tithes eaten in Jerusalem (Deuteronomy 14:22–27). and how they can be redeemed for money.

Maccabee Name given to Judah, son of Mattathias, who led the revolt against Syria in 168 BCE. It was also applied to the Hasmonean dynasty, which lasted for about 120 years from the 2nd century BCE.

Maccabees (i) [Hannah and her seven sons] Name given in Christian tradition to the seven children of Hannah martyred by Antiochus Epiphanes when they refused to commit idolatry. Shrines to their memory, and to Hannah's, were established throughout the Christian world.

Maccabees (ii) Name of four apocryphal works (of which the first two only are included in the Apocrypha). I Maccabees coverts the period of 40 years from the accession of Antiochus Epiphanes in 175 BCE to the death of Simeon the Hasmonean in 135 BCE. II Maccabees focuses on the life and times of Judah Maccabee. III Maccabees is related in subject matter to other books. It explains why the Jews in Egypt have a Purim-like festival in the summer. It may have been grouped with I and II Maccabees because it relates a persecution of the Jews by a Hellenistic king and their miraculous deliverance. IV Maccabees depicts the story of the martyrs of the persecution preceding the Maccabean revolt in 168 BCE. It is a philosophical sermon on the theme of pious reason.

Macher (Yiddish) Important person, active member of an organisation.

Machetunim (Yiddish) Members of the extended family of one's spouse.

Mack, Julian William (1866–1943) American judge and Zionist leader. He was born in San Francisco. He began his career as a professor of law at Northwestern University, Illinois. He served as a judge in the circuit court of Cook County, Illinois, in the Chicago juvenile court, and in the US commerce court. In 1913 he was appointed to the US circuit court of appeals. He was President of the Zionist Organisation of America (1918–21), and was the first president of the American Jewish Congress. He was also the first chairman of the Comité des Délégations Juives at Versailles (1919).

Magen Avot ('A shield of our forefathers') Opening words of an abbreviated form of the seven benedictions of the Friday evening Amidah. It is recited by the cantor after the Amidah.

Magen David ('Shield of David') The name given in Judaism to the symbol consisting of two superimposed triangles forming a star (it is also known as the Star of David). Although it was used in the synagogue at Capernaum as early as the 3rd century, it was not commonly adopted as a Jewish symbol until much later. From the 13th century, the name figures in practical kabbalah, and the symbol (believed to have magical properties) is found in association with the pentagram (or Star of Solomon). The Magen David occurs in a Jewish context in Prague in the 17th century. In the 19th century it was adopted by the First Zionist Congress as its symbol, and it appears on the flags of the Zionist Organisation and the State of Israel. The Nazis employed a yellow six-pointed star as a Jewish badge.

Magen David Adom ('Red Shield of David') Israeli first-aid society. It was founded in Tel Aviv in 1930 as the medical wing of the Haganah.

Maggid ('preacher') Popular preacher. Such preachers spoke both on Sabbaths and on weekdays. Frequently they described the torments of hell to bring their congregations to repentance. But they also preached words of comfort and hope, and the promise of Messianic redemption. The Ḥasidim, in particular, produced many preachers who helped to spread the teachings of the Ḥasidic movement in Poland and Russia.

Magic The art of influencing events by the occult control of natural and spiritual forces. In the Bible sorcery, witchcraft and magic are prohibited (Exodus 22:17). Nonetheless the Bible, *Talmud* and later Jewish literature abound with examples of magical practices. Magical activities connected with divine names, the names of angels, permutations and combinations of Hebrew letters and scriptural quotations flourished under the influence of kabbalah. In the medieval period Jewish magicians were widely known.

Magister Judaeorum (Latin: 'Master of the Jews') Title given to a French palace official during the Carolingian period (8th–9th centuries). He was appointed by the sovereign to supervise and protect the Jewish community.

Magnes, Judah Leon (1877–1948) American rabbi and educator. He was born in San Francisco. He was the rabbi of Temple Israel in Brooklyn, and later assistant rabbi of Temple Emanu-El in New York. He was also President of the kehillah in New York. In 1922 he emigrated to Palestine, where he helped build up the Hebrew University; when the university opened in 1925 he became the chancellor and he was its president from 1935. He inspired the founding of the peace movement Berit Shalom and its successor, Iḥud.

Magnus, Lauire (1872–1933) English writer, son of Sir Philip Magnus and Lady Katie Magnus. He wrote various studies of Judaism, including *Aspects of the Jewish Question, Religio laici Judaici,* and *The Jews in the Christian Era and their Contribution to its Civilisation.* From 1917 he served as editor of the anti-Zionist *Jewish Guardian.* He was active in Jewish communal life.

Magnus, Philip, Sir (1842–1933) English Reform minister and politician. He was born in London. He served as minister of the West London Synagogue of British Reform Jews from 1866 to 1880. He lectured in applied mathematics at University College, London, and in 1880 he became the Organising Secretary and Director of the City and Guilds of London Institute. From 1906 to 1922 he served as London University's member of parliament. He was knighted in 1886 and created a baronet in 1917. He played an important role in Anglo-Jewish affairs.

Mahamad In Sephardi communities the name given to the governing body of the congregation of the synagogue. During the 18th and 19th centuries the term was also applied to the executive body of an autonomous Jewish community. The word is an alternative transliteration of the Hebrew word more often rendered 'maamad.'

Mahler, Eduard (1857–1945) Hungarian orientalist, mathematician and astronomer. He was born in Cziffer. He taught oriental history and languages at Budapest University, becoming professor there in 1914. In 1912 he was appointed Director of the Egyptological Institute in Budapest and in 1922 director of the Oriental Institute. His *Handbuch der jüdischen Chronologie* established the systems of the different Jewish calendars and chronologies in the light of ancient Near-Eastern and medieval calculations.

Mahler, Gustav (1860–1911) Austrian musician. Born in Kalischt, Bohemia, he studied at the Vienna Conservatory and worked in several operatic companies in Kassel, Prague and Leipzig. He later became Musical Director of the Budapest Opera and at the Hamburg Municipal Theatre. He converted to Catholicism and became Kapellmeister at the Vienna Court Opera, and later artistic director. Subsequently he became Guest Conductor of the Metropolitan Opera, and later the New York Philharmonic. His reputation is based largely on ten symphonies and song cycles.

Mahler, Raphael (1899–1977) Galician historian. He was born in Nowy Sadz in eastern Galicia. He served as a teacher in Jewish secondary schools in Poland. In 1937 he went to the US and taught in various educational institutions in New York. In 1950 he went to Israel, where he lectured on the history of Israel at Tel Aviv University. He was appointed professor there in 1961. He wrote various works about Jewish history from a Marxist perspective, including a history of the Jews in modern times, and studies of the Jews in Poland, the Karaites and Galician Jewry.

Mahloket ('division') Used figuratively, it signifies dissension as well as difference of opinion. Dissension was condemned by the rabbis, but differences of opinion based on principle were a central feature of rabbinic discussion.

Mah nishtannah? ('Why is it different?'). First of the four questions recited at the Passover seder.

Mah Tovu ('How goodly') Opening words of a prayer recited by Ashkenazim upon entering the synagogue. It consists of biblical verses taken from the Psalms. In the Sephardi ritual Psalm 5:8 is recited on entering and Psalm 5:9 on leaving the synagogue.

Mahzor Festival prayer book. Initially the term was applied to the collection of prayers for the entire year in chronological order. In later usage it came to refer to the festival prayer book as distinct from the daily prayer book ('siddur'). It contains additional prayers ('piyyutim') to those of the liturgy, written by various poets. Both the Ashkenazi and the Sephardi versions of the prayer book are based on the oldest mahzor, the Mahzor Vitry, compiled in the 11th century by Simhah ben Samuel of Vitry, a pupil of Rashi.

Maid of Ludomir (1805–92) Ukrainian Hasidic leader. Her real name was Hannah Rachel and she was the daughter of Monesh Werbermacher. After an illness, she followed Hasidic customs, built her own synagogue and observed the religious duties of men (putting on tallit and tefillin when she prayed). She later emigrated to Palestine where she continued her mystical studies and practised rituals designed to hasten the coming of the Messiah.

Mailer, Norman (1923–2007) American novelist. He was raised in Brooklyn and studied at Harvard. He published *The Naked and the Dead*, a novel about war in the Pacific. This was followed by *Barbary Shore* and *The Deer Park*. Other works include *Armies in the Night, Miami and the Siege of Chicago, A Fire* *on the Moon, the Executioner's Song* and *Ancient Evenings.*

Maimon, Solomon (1754–1800)   Polish philosopher. Born in Sukoviboeg, Poland, he was a child prodigy in the study of rabbinical literature. He initially supported his family by working as a tutor. In his spare time he studied Jewish philosophy and kabbalah, adopting the name Maimon in honour of Maimonides. He later left his home and went to Berlin, where he was a member of Moses Mendelssohn's circle. He subsequently lived in various cities, returning to Berlin in 1786. His work was praised by Immanuel Kant, and he published various studies of philosophical subjects.

Maimon [Fishman], Yehudah Leib (1876–1962)   Israeli rabbi and leader of Mizraḥi. He was born in Bessarabia, where he served as a rabbi and became active in the Zionist movement. In 1913 he moved to Palestine. After World War I he arranged for the executive of the World Centre of Mizraḥi to be based in Palestine and became its head. He was a member of the executive of the Jewish Agency from 1935 to 1948, and Israeli Minister for Religious Affairs from 1948 to 1951. Concurrently he was a Mizraḥi delegate to the Knesset (1949–51). He wrote on folklore, and talmudic and Zionist subjects. He was also the director of the Mosad ha-Rav Kook which he initiated.

Maimon ben Joseph (d. 1156/70)   Spanish rabbi and dayyan, father of Maimonides. He served as a dayyan in Córdoba, and wrote an Arabic commentary to the Bible. In 1148 he left Spain with his family because of persecution by the Almohades after their conquest of the city. For about ten years he wandered through Spain and possibly also Provence. In about 1160 he emigrated to Fez, Morocco; he later moved to Palestine, where he died. His writings include *Iggeret ha-Neḥamah*, a guide for forced converts to Islam.

Maimonides [Moses ben Maimon; Rambam] (1135–1204)   North African philosopher and halakhist. He is commonly referred to by the name Maimonides, though his given (Hebrew) name was Moses ben Maimon; the name Rambam is derived from the title Rabbi Moses ben Maimon. He was born in Córdoba, but left the city when it was captured by the Almohades. After several years of wandering, he settled in Fez. During this period he wrote treatises on the Jewish calendar, logic and halakhah. In 1168 he completed his commentary on the Mishnah. From 1170 to 1180 he worked on the *Mishneh Torah* (also own as *Yad Ḥazakah)*, a compilation of the halakhah. In 1190 he completed his philosophical study, the *Guide for the Perplexed*, which evoked a controversy that lasted for a century. The work was accused by some of expressive rationalism, which might lead to heresy, while others supported Maimonides' views. He also wrote medical studies and became physician to the Sultan of Egypt. Maimonides exercised a profound influence on Jewish scholarship; his codification of Jewish law remained a standard guide to the halakah and he is perceived as the principal Jewish philosopher of the Middle Ages.

Majority   According to the Bible, the decision of the majority does not excuse the individual for wrongdoing and a person should not follow the majority in doing evil (Exodus 23:2). On this basis the rabbis stress that a majority should be followed only in doing good.

Makhir ben Abba Mari (fl.? 14th cent.)   French exegete. His *Yalkut ha-Makhiri* is a collection of aggadot on the books of the Prophets and the Hagiographa.

Makhshirim ('Predisposings')   Eighth tractate in the Mishnah order of Tohorot. It deals with the laws of ritual impurity in connection with foods which are liable to become impure when wet (Leviticus 11:34,38).

Makkeph Hyphen. In Hebrew two, three or four words may be connected by hyphens. The vocalisation of some words alters when they are followed by a makkeph.

Makkot (Stripes') Fifth tractate in the Mishnah order Nezikin. It deals with the rules that govern flogging (Deuteronomy 25:1–3), false witnesses (Deuteronomy 19:15–21), and the cities of refuge (Numbers 35:9–28).

Malachi (i) (fl. 5th cent. BCE) Israelite prophet. He protested against the transgression of ritual laws concerning sacrifice and tithes, and also condemned mixed marriages and divorce. His eschatology embraced a vision of the Day of the Lord preceded by the coming of Elijah. According to rabbinic tradition, he was the last of the prophets.

Malachi (ii) Biblical book, one of the books of the 12 Minor Prophets. It records the prophecies of Malachi.

Malamud, Bernard (1914–1986) American novelist. He was born in New York. He taught at Oregon State University and Bennington College. A number of his novels deal with Jewish themes, including *Idiots First, the Assistant* and *The Fixer*.

Malbim, Meir Leibush (1809–1879) Rabbinic scholar. He was born in Volochisk and lived in Warsaw and Łęczyca. In 1839 he became rabbi of Wreschen, and then moved to Kempen. In 1858 he became Chief Rabbi of Romania. He attacked the Reform movement, was forced to leave the country, and subsequently wandered throughout Europe. He wrote a commentary on the Bible.

Malkhuyyot ('Sovereignty') The name of the first of the three sections of the additional Amidah service on Rosh ha-Shanah (the others are Zikhronot and Shopharot). It deals with the theme of God's sovereignty.

Mamet, David (b.1947) American playwright. Born in Chicago, his works include *Duck Variations, Sexual Perversity in Chicago, American Buffalo* and *Glengarry Glen Ross*.

Mammeloshen (Yiddish: 'mother tongue') Colloquial expression for Yiddish.

Mamran [mamrem] (Hebrew, ? from Latin 'membrana': parchment) Promissory note. First mentioned in the 12th century, the term came to mean the particular kind of promissory note used by Jewish merchants in their internal trade. It was a simple document. On one side was the signature of the debtor; the amount owed and the date that payment was due were written on the other side. Since it did not bear the name of the creditor, the mamran could be transferred from one person to another.

Mamzer A person born from certain forbidden relationships, or the descendent of such a person. A mamzer in modern Jewish culture is someone who is either born out of adultery by a married Jewish woman and a Jewish man who is not her husband, or born out of incest, or someone who has a mamzer as a parent.

Manasseh (fl. 7th cent. BCE) King of Judah (698–643 BCE), son of Hezekiah. He ascended to the throne at the age of 12 (II Kings 21:1). He revoked his father's reforms and reintroduced pagan practices. According to II Kings 21:11–17, the destruction of the Temple was due to his unrighteousness. He paid tribute to Esarhaddon and Assurbanipal of Assyria. According to II Chroniclers 33:11–19 he was taken captive to Babylon.

Manasseh, Prayer of Apocryphal book consisting of a penitential psalm supposedly by Manasseh, King of Judah.

According to II Chronicles 33:11ff. Manasseh repented of his sins when he was taken to Babylonia. In this prayer he praises God's compassion for the repentant. The prayer was written by an unknown author before the beginning of the Christian era.

Manasseh ben Israel (1604–1657) Dutch rabbi. Born a Marrano in Maderia, he was taken to Amsterdam as a child. He succeeded Isaac Uziel as preacher to the Neveh Shalom congregation in 1622. In 1626 he founded the earliest Hebrew printing press in Amsterdam and proceeded to publish numerous works in Hebrew, Spanish and Latin. He represented Jewish scholarship in the Christian world, corresponded with various gentile scholars and was a friend of Grotius and Rembrandt. In 1655 he presented a petition to Oliver Cromwell to allow the Jews to return to England.

Manasseh ben Joseph of Ilye (1767–1831) Lithuanian talmudic scholar. He was born in Smogron, and became a disciple of the Vilna Gaon. He was versed in both rabbinic and secular studies. In his writings he challenged the *Talmud* as well as Rashi's understanding of the Mishnah. An advocate of halakhic change, he was persecuted by the Orthodox. He later worked as a private teacher in Russia and Galicia, where he became acquainted with the maskilim.

Mandelkern, Solomon (1846–1902). German Hebrew poet and scholar, of Polish origin. He was born in Mlynow. He served as assistant to the government-appointed rabbi of Odessa from 1873 to 1880, then settled in Leipzig, where he devoted himself to research. A supporter of Ḥibbat Zion, he attended the First Zionist Congress at Basle in 1897. His publications include *Hekhal ha-Kodesh* (a Bible concordance), a history of Russia, a history of Russian literature, and a German-Russian dictionary.

Mandelstam, Osip (1891–?1938) Russian poet. He was born in Warsaw, and lived in Leningrad. In 1934 he was arrested and exiled to the eastern USSR, where he died in a prison camp. His writing is filled with Jewish self-hatred.

Mandelstamm, Benjamin (1805–1886). Lithuanian Hebrew author, brother of Leon Mandelstamm. He was born in Zagare. In the 1840s he settled in Vilnius, where he adopted an extremist stance in the Haskalah circles in which he moved. Critical of Russian Jewish life, he advocated governmental intervention to forbid the printing of the *Talmud,* remove kabbalistic and Ḥasidic works from circulation, and dissolve the traditional ḥeder system.

Mandelstamm, Leon (1819–1889) Russian writer, of Lithuanian origin, brother of Benjamin Mandelstamm. He was born in Zagare. He studied at St Petersburg University and was the first Jew to enrol in a Russian university. In 1846 he was appointed to take charge of Jewish affairs in the ministry of education and to establish a network of governmental schools for Jews. He also supervised the Jewish ḥeder and Tamud Torah schools, and prepared Jewish textbooks. His work obliged him to travel throughout the Pale of Settlement. Dismissed from his post in 1857, he lived in Germany, where he engaged in trade and contracting. He eventually returned to Russia and lived in St Petersburg.

Mandelstamm, Max Emanuel (1839–1912) Russian ophthalmologist and Zionist, of Lithuanian origin, nephew of Benjamin and Leon Mandelstamm. He was born in Zagare. He opened a clinic in Kiev, where his practice flourished, and lectured in ophthalmology at Kiev University. A founder of the Ḥibbat Zion movement in Russia, he became an associate of Theodor Herzl. At the Seventh Zionist Congress, he participated in the Founding Conference of the Jewish Territorial Organisation. He was the head of the emigration office established by the Territorialists in Kiev to organise the emigration of Jews to Galveston, Texas.

Mané-Katz (1894–1962) French artist. He was born in Russia, moved to France in 1921, and later lived in the US. His early subjects included biblical scenes and figures from the ghetto. There is a museum dedicated to his paintings in Haifa.

Manger, Itzik (1901–1969) Yiddish poet, dramatist and novelist. He was born in Czernowitz, and lived in Germany as a child. He learned Yiddish in Romania and published ballads and plays, which were influenced by German lyricists and such writers as Eliakum Zunser. During and after World War II he lived in London, later moving to the US. He finally settled in Israel.

Mani Leib [Brahinski, Mani Leib] (1883–1953) American Yiddish poet and journalist. He was born in Russia and emigrated to the US in 1905. He served on the editorial staff of *Forverts* from 1916 to 1953, and edited a number of journals of the Yiddish literary movement Di Yunge. He translated several Russian novels into Yiddish and published poems in Di Yunge's periodicals and anthologies. His ballads and tales for children were sung and recited in Yiddish schools.

Mankind According to the Bible, men and women are part of God's creation. They have responsibility for all created things, and are free moral agents. Through the covenant with Israel, God created a special bond between himself and human beings. The Bible views the human person as an indivisible whole, but the rabbis assert that each individual consists of a body and soul and is derived by both a good and an evil inclination. The kabbalah envisages humans as closely linked to

the divine and their life as vital to the entire cosmos.

Mankowitz, Wolf (1924–1998) English author. He was born in London, where he became an antique dealer. He wrote various books inspired by his childhood in the East End of London. His publications include *A Kid for Two Farthings, Make me an Offer, The Boychick,* and *The Mendelman Fire.*

Mann, Jacob (1888–1940) American scholar. He was born in Galicia. He studied in London, and subsequently taught history at the Hebrew Union College in Cincinnati. He utilised genizah material in a series of studies on the history and literature of the gaonic period. His publications include *The Jews of Palestine and Egypt under the Fatimids, Texts and Studies in Jewish History and Literature,* and *The Bible as Read and Preached in the Old Synagogue.*

Manna Food eaten by the Israelites in the desert (Exodus 16:4–35). It was discovered on the ground every morning except the Sabbath. A double portion was left on the day before the Sabbath. It was thin and white, and tasted like honey cake.

Manne, Mordecai Tzevi (1859–1886) Lithuanian Hebrew and artist. He was born near Vilnius, and studied art there. In 1889 he became a student at the Academy of Arts in St Petersburg, and began to write poems and articles. He later went to Warsaw, where he designed the covers for anthologies of works by Nahum Sokolow and Saul Phinehas Rabinowitz. His poem *Masat Nafshi* expresses his longing for Palestine.

Mannheim, Karl (1893–1947) Hungarian sociologist. Born in Budapest, he studied at the University of Budapest. He initially taught high school in Budapest, then at a teacher's training college of the University of Budapest and later at Heidelberg. In 1930 he was appointed

Professor of Sociology and Economy at the University of Frankfurt. With the rise of the Nazis, he emigrated to England and became a professor at LSE. His works include *Ideology and Utopia, Man and Society in an Age of Reconstruction* and *Diagnosis of Our Time*.

Mannheimer, Isaac Noah (1793–1865) Austrian preacher and liturgist. He was born in Copenhagen, where he taught religion and held services for adherents of Reform Judaism. In 1824 he became a preacher at the new Seitenstetten Synagogue in Vienna. He later adopted a more Conservative approach to Reform Judaism, and created a moderate Reform liturgy. He also translated the prayer book and the festival prayers into German. In 1848 he was elected to the Reichstag, where he advocated Jewish rights.

Man of Lies   Character who is described in the Dead Sea Scrolls as the opponent of the Teacher of Righteousness. He is said knowingly to have perverted the meaning of the law.

Mantino, Jacob (d.1549)   Italian physician and translator of Spanish origin He practised medicine in Bologna, Verona and Venice. During the debate on the annulment of the marriage of Henry VIII of England and Catherine of Aragon, he opposed Henry's supporters. He thus earned the gratitude of Pope Clement VII by whose influence he was appointed lecturer in medicine at Bologna University. In 1533 he was invited by the Pope to Rome where he took a stand against the messianic claims of Solomon Molcho. The following year he was appointed personal physician to Pope Paul III, and became Professor of Practical Medicine at the Sapienza in Rome. His scholarly work included translations of philosophical works from Hebrew into Latin.

Manuscripts   Early manuscripts of Hebrew sources, include the Dead Sea Scrolls, manuscripts from the Cairo Genizah, and the Nash Papyrus. The oldest complete manuscript of the Hebrew Bible is the Codex Petropolitanus from the 10th century. Numerous Hebrew manuscripts of European origin have survived from the 12th century onward, containing all kinds of literature. With the advent of Hebrew printing in 1475 manuscripts ceased to play such an important role. Great collectors of Hebrew manuscripts include David Oppenheim, G.B. de'Rossi, Elkan Nathan Adler, David Kaufmann and David Solomon Sassoon. Important collections are held in the libraries of Oxford and Cambridge Universities, the British Museum, the Bibliothèque Nationale, the Vatican and Parma Libraries, and the library of the Jewish Theological Seminary of America.

Maot ḥittim ('wheat monies'). Collections made before Passover to ensure that there is a supply of flour for unleavened bread for the poor. The maot ḥittim was a compulsory community tax from the period of the *Talmud*. In modern times the term denotes a collection of charitable donations to provide for all the holiday needs of the poor at Passover.

Maoz tzur ('O fortress, rock [of my salvation]')   Opening words of a hymn sung in the Ashkenazi ritual in the synagogue and at home after the kindling of the Ḥanukkah lights. The song originated in Germany in the 13th century and was composed by a poet named Mordecai.

Mapam   Israeli socialist party. It was formed in 1948 by the fusion of Ha-Shomer ha-Tzair and Aḥdut ha-Avodah-Poale Zion. Marxist in orientation, it stressed the importance of class conflict and initially sought an alliance with the Soviet bloc. In 1954 Aḥdut ha-Avodah-Poale Zion seceded from Mapam, and later a small group under Mosheh Sneh also broke away and joined Maki.

Maphtir ('one who concludes') Term referring both to the person who concludes the reading in the synagogue and to the reading itself. The maphtir first reads a portion of the Torah (usually a repetition of the last three verses of the portions assigned for the day) and then the Haphtarah.

Mappah ('cloth') The fabric strip used as a binder round a Torah scroll. The term is also used of the decorated cover of the reading desk in the synagogue. The term was used by Moses Isserles as the title of his commentary on the Shulḥan Arukh.

Mappik The dagesh (diacritical mark) inside the letter at the end of a word. It shows that the letter is sounded as h.

Mapu, Abraham (1808–1867) Lithuanian Hebrew novelist. He worked as a children's tutor and lived in various towns, including Slobodka, Georgenberg, Kovno, Rossyieny and Vilnius. His *Ahavat Tziyyon* is a historical romance set in the period of Hezekiah. In *Alyit Tzavua* he satirised contemporary Lithuanian Jews. His other novels include *Ashmat Shomron* and *Ḥozeh Ḥezyonot.*

Mar ('Master') Title given to some Babylonian amoraim and especially to exilarchs.

Marceau, Marcel (1923–2007) French mime. As a young man, he worked in the underground and helped smuggle Jewish children into Switzerland. He was regarded as the greatest exponent of mime.

Marcus, David [Stone, Micky] (1902–1948) American soldier. He was born in New York. He served in the US Attorney-General's Office, and later as Commissioner of Correction in New York. He joined the army, and was appointed head of its War Crimes Branch. In 1948 he was David Ben-Gurion's military adviser, taking the name Micky Stone. In the same year he

became commander of the Jerusalem front. He was killed by a sentry during the Israeli War of Independence.

Marcus, Jacob Rader (1896–1995) American rabbi and historian. He was born in Connellsville, Pennsylvania. He taught history from 1920 at the Hebrew Union College, where he founded the American Jewish Archives. He published numerous studies of American Jewry.

Marcus, Ralph (1900–1956) American scholar of Hellenistic Judaism. He was born in San Francisco. He taught at the Jewish Institute of Religion, Columbia University, and at the University of Chicago. He edited, translated and annotated four volumes of the works of Josephus and two of those of Philo in the Loeb Classical Library series.

Marcuse, Herbert (1898–1979) German philosopher. Born in Berlin, he studied in Berlin and Freiburg. He initially worked at the Frankfurt Institute for Social Research, but from the early 1940s he was an intelligence analyst in various US agencies. He was a fellow of Russian research centres at Columbia and Harvard, and became Professor of Philosophy and Politics at Brandeis University in 1954, and later at the University of California at San Diego. His works include *Reason and Revolution, Eros and Civilisation* and *One-Dimensional Man.*

Margolin, Eliezer (1874–1944) Australian military commander. He was born in Belgorod, Russia. He moved to Palestine in 1892 and settled in Rehovot. In 1900 he went to Australia and he served in the Australian army during World War I, later commanding the Second Battalion of the Jewish Regiment. In 1919 he became Commander of the Jewish Legion. When the legion was dismantled, he became Commander of the Jewish unit of the Palestine Defence Force. Subsequently he returned to Australia.

Margoliouth, David Samuel (1858–1040) English classical scholar and orientalist. He was born in London, and became a professor of Arabic at Oxford University He published studies in the fields of Islamic history and literature, and edited medieval Arabic texts. His writings include *The Origin of the 'Hebrew Original' of Ecclesiasticus*, and *Relations between Arabs and Israelites prior to the Rise of Islam.*

Margoliouth, George (1853–1952) English bibliographer. He converted to Christianity and became a priest. He was in charge of the Hebrew, Syriac and Ethiopic manuscripts in the British Museum from 1891 to 1914. His publications include *The Liturgy of the Nile, The Palestine Syriac Version of the Holy Scriptures*, and *Catalogue of the Hebrew and Samaritan Manuscripts in the British Museum.*

Margolis Max Leopold (1886–1932) American biblical and Semitic scholar. He was born in Russia, and went to the US in 1889. He taught at the Hebrew Union College, and in 1897 went to the University of California at Berkeley to teach Semitic languages. He then returned to the Hebrew Union College, but resigned in 1910, to become Professor of Biblical Philology at Dropsie College. He supervised the translation of the Bible published by the Jewish Publication Society of America, and collaborated with Alexander Marx on the *History of the Jewish People.*

Margoshes, Samuel (1887–1968) American Yiddish journalist. He was born in Galicia, and went to the US in 1905. He engaged in communal, educational and relief activities before, during and after World War I. Later he served as editor of the New York Yiddish daily. He supported Zionism in the US and took an active role in the American Jewish Congress and Zionist activities.

Marheshvan [Heshvan] Second month of the Jewish year (eighth of the civil year); it is often shortened to Heshvan. The name dates from post-exilic times and replaced the earlier name Bul (I Kings 6:38).

Mariamne (?60–29 BCE) Israelite queen, daughter of Alexander (son of Aristobulus II) and granddaughter of John Hyrcanus. She was the second wife of Herod the Great, though she hated him because he had killed nearly all the members of her family, and had replaced her own dynasty (the Hasmoneans) with his own. Herod eventually put her to death.

Mariamne II (d. c.20 BCE) Israelite queen, daughter of the high priest Simeon ben Boethus. She was the third wife of Herod the Great. Her son, also Herod, was designated to succeed to the throne after Antipater III (Herod the Great's son by his first wife, Doris). Although Mariamne knew of Antipater's intentions to kill his father, she held her peace because of the succession. When Antipater's plot was discovered, Herod divorced her and expunged her son's name from his will.

Marinoff, Jacob (1869–1964) American Yiddish poet and editor. He was born in Russia. He moved to London, where he worked in a tailor's shop; then he emigrated to the US and settled in Denver. From 1895 he contributed poems to Yiddish periodicals. He was a co-founder of the journal, *Der groyser kundas* and served as it editor.

Markish, Peretz (1895–1952) Ukrainian Yiddish poet, novelist and playwright. Born in Volhynia, he left Russia in 1921 and lived in Poland and France. From 1921 to 1926 he wrote poetry about the anti-Jewish pogroms in Ukraine. In 1926 he returned to the USSR, where he published epic poems and novels. He was accused of Jewish nationalism and executed.

Markon, Isaac Dov Ber (1875–1949)
Russian scholar and librarian. Born in
Rybinsk on the Volga, he was Professor of Jewish Studies at the University
of St Petersburg, and later professor
at the Belorussian University at Minsk.
In 1926 he settled in Berlin. Expelled
from Germany in 1938, he went to
Holland and then England, where he
joined the Montefiore College in Ramsgate. His publications deal with Karaite history and literature and associated
topics.

**Markova, Alicia [Marks, Lillian
Alicia] (1910–2004)** English prima
ballerina. Born in London, she appeared
with the Diaghilev company, and in
1933 founded her own together with
Anton Dolin. She was made a Dame of
the British Empire in 1963. The same
year she became Director of the Metropolitan Ballet in New York. In 1970
she became Professor of Ballet at the
University of Cincinnati.

Marks, Simon, Baron (1888–1964)
English industrialist and philanthropist. He was born in Manchester He
became chairman of the board of
Marks and Spencer. chain stores in
1917. He was an active Zionist and
served as Secretary of the Zionist delegation to the Versailles Peace Conference. Later he became Chairman of
the Keren ha-Yesod Committee, Vice-
President of the Zionist Federation,
and a member of the executive of the
Zionist Organisation.

Marmorek, Alexander (1865–1923),
French bacteriologist and Zionist
leader. He was born in Mielnice, Galicia. He became assistant and later senior
reseacher at the Pasteur Institute in Paris.
He was an associate of Theodor Herzl,
and served as a member of the Zionist
General Council at the first 11 Zionist
congresses. He was a co-founder of the
Paris Zionist monthly *L'écho Sioniste.*

Marmorek, Oscar (1863–1909) Austrian architect and Zionist leader. He
was born in Skala, Galicia. He built
important buildings in Vienna and Austria, and designed synagogues based on
old Jewish architecture. After the publication of Theodor Herzl's *Der Judenstaat,* Marmorek joined Herzl and was
elected to the executive of the Zionist Organisation at the first six Zionist
congresses. He was a co-founder of the
Zionist weekly *Die Welt.*

Marmorstein, Arthur (1882–1946)
British rabbi, scholar, and teacher. He
was born in Miskole, Hungary, and
served as a rabbi at Jamnitz, Czechoslovakia. From 1912 he taught at Jews
College in London. His publicatons
embrace a wide range of Jewish topics
and include *Doctrine of Merits in Old
Rabbinic Literature* and *Old Rabbinic
Doctrine of God.*

Maror ('bitter herb') Generic term
for a bitter-tasting herb. The children
of Israel were commanded to eat maror
with unleavened bread at the Passover
celebration in remembrance of the bit-
terness of slavery (Exodus 12:8; Numbers 9:11). A bitter herb is still eaten
during the Passover seder.

**Marranos (Hebrew 'Anusim'; the
coerced) [New Christians]** Term
applied in Spain and Portugal to the
descendants of baptised Jews suspected of adhering to Judaism. They
became numerous in Spain after the
Jewish massacres of 1391, and after
the Dominican campaign at the beginning of the 13th century. It was partly
to deal with such individuals that the
Inquisition was introduced into Spain
in 1480. Similarly in Portugal the
forced conversions in 1497 led to an
increase in the number of Marranos,
whose heretical tendencies were suppressed by the Inquisition, introduced
in 1540. Many Marranos fled to
Italy, north Africa and Turkey, and
large groups later settled in the Netherlands, the West Indies and North
America.

Marriage   The Bible stipulates that it is necessary for the human race to reproduce and ensure its continuance. Thus the first commandment of God to man in the Bible is 'be fruitful and multiply' (Genesis 1:22). Men are obligated to marry to fulfil this commandment. According to Judaism there are two stages in the marriage ceremony: betrothal ('erusin' or kiddushin') and marriage ('nissuim'). Betrothal is the ceremony at which a woman is promised as the wife of the betrother. The ceremony must take place before witnesses and can be contracted in three ways: by money; by deed; or by sexual intercourse (committed in private but with the knowledge of the witnesses). The second stage is 'marriage', which involves bringing the woman into the home in order to live a marital life with her. Until the 10th century, when monogamy became legally binding, the Jews practised polygamy. In modern Jewish tradition marriage continues to be a social, moral and religious ideal.

Marshalik   (Yiddish)   Name   given to a jester at Eastern-European weddings. He sang humorous songs and announced the gifts in verse.

Marshall, Louis (1856–1929)   American lawyer and communal leader. He was born in Syracuse, New York, and became a partner in the New York legal firm of Guggenheimer, Untermyer, and Marshall. He was the chief spokesman for the German-Jewish elite in Jewish affairs. In 1912 he became President of the American Jewish Committee. He also served as President of Temple Emanu-El in New York, and Chairman of the board of directors of the Jewish Theological Seminary. During World War I he was President of the American Jewish Relief Committee.

Martinez, Ferrand (fl. 14th cent.)   Spanish priest, Archdeacon of Écija. In sermons preached in public in Seville, he demanded that the synagogues in the city should be destroyed and the Jews confined to their own quarter. He later secured the right of jurisdiction over the Jews of Seville and its environs and demanded their expulsion. As a result of his agitation, riots broke out throughout Castile and spread to Aragon.

Martini [Marti], Raymund (1220–1285)   Spanish Dominican friar and polemicist. He was born in Subirat, Catalonia. He participated in the Disputation of Barcelona in 1263, which involved debates between Naḥmanides and representatives of the Church. In 1264 he was appointed a member of the first censorship commission to examine Jewish books. His *Pugio fidei* is an anti-Jewish polemic.

Martyrs   Prominent   among   early Jewish martyrs were the seven sons of Hannah, killed by Antiochus IV Epiphanes during the Hasmonean revolt (166–164 BCE). In the early rabbinic period the Ten Martyrs were killed during the Bar Kokhba revolt of 132 BCE. According to rabbinic Judaism a martyr is someone who dies willingly for the Jewish faith and thereby achieves the sanctification of the divine name ('Kiddush ha-Shem'). During the Middle Ages regulations governing the ways in which martyrs should comport themselves and the benedictions they were to recite were formulated by the rabbis.

Marx, Alexander (1878–1953)   German historian, bibliographer and librarian. He was born in Elberfeld, Germany, and emigrated to the US in 1903. He served as librarian and taught history at the Jewish Theological Seminary. He published studies of bibliography and history, and collaborated with Max Margolis on the *History of the Jewish People*.

Marx, Groucho (1895–1977) American comedian. He and his brothers were children of German immigrants. Together they were a vaudeville act. Later they became Broadway stars and appeared in several films. Groucho had his own quiz show, *You Bet Your Life,* and published several books.

Marx, Karl (1818–1883) German social philosopher, founder of modern communism. He was born in Trier, and converted to Protestantism at the age of six. He was the editor of the Cologne daily, *Rheinische Zeitung.* He moved to Paris in 1843, and then went to Brussels. In 1848 he and Friedrich Engels published *The Communist Manifesto.* In 1849 he settled in London, where he wrote *Das Kapital.* In his writings he expressed hostility towards Jews and Judaism.

Masekhet [massekhet] (lit. 'woven fabric') Term applied to a tractate of the Mishnah or *Talmud.*

Mashgiaḥ ('supervisor') Overseer who supervises the observance of the laws of kashrut.

Mashiv ha-ruaḥ u'morid ha-gashem ('who causes the wind to blow and the rain to fall') Phrase in the Amidah prayer added to the second of the benedictions It is recited during the winter season from the last day of Sukkot until the last day of Passover. A variant ('who causes the dew to descend') is recited during the summer months in Israel. Elsewhere it is used in the Sephardi ritual only.

Masliansky, Tzevi Hirsch (1856–1943) Polish-Amerian preacher. He was born in Slutsk, Belorussia, and taught at the Polish *Talmud* Torah and at the yeshivah of Pinsk. Active in Ḥibbat Zion, he left the country in 1894, and undertook a lecture tour of central and western Europe. In 1895 he settled in New York where he helped to popularise Zionism through Friday evening sermons at the Educational Alliance on East Broadway.

Masorah [massorah] Body of rules, principles and traditions developed in the 6th–9th centuries by textual scholars, known as 'masoretes', in order to preserve the authentic text of the Hebrew Bible. The masoretes divided the biblical text into words and sentences, as well as into segments of verse length. They added vowel signs to the Hebrew words and cantillation marks indicating the articulation and inflections of the text for chanting. They also indicated those cases where the written form of the word ('ketiv') differs from the pronunciation or even the actual word used when the texts is read aloud ('keri'). In addition they corrected spellings. The accepted text of the Bible is that determined by Aaron be Asher of the Tiberias school of Masoretes.

Massadah Israeli publishing house. Founded by Meir and Berakah Peli in Tel Aviv in 1931, it has published encyclopedias and the works of Yoseph Klausner, David Shimoni and Asher Barash.

Mathematics Jews engaged in mathematical studies from the early medieval period. In the 12th century such scholars as Abraham ibn Ezra and Abraham bar Ḥiyya made important contributions and later Jacob ben Maskhir, Levi ben Gershon and Immanuel ben Jacob of Tarascon added their discoveries. In the 15th century Simeon ibn Motot invented the pure equation of the 3rd and 4th degrees, and solved the problem of asymptotes. Modern mathematics is indebted to the work of numerous Jewish mathematicians.

Matmid ('one who persists')   A scholar devoted to the study of the *Talmud*.

Matriarchs   The wives – Sarah, Rebekah, Leah and Rachel – of the three patriarchs.

Matsa, Joseph (1919–1986)   Greek scholar and Hebrew folklorist. He was born in Ioannina and taught Greek literature at a high school there. His publications include *The Hebrew Songs of the Jannina Jews* and *The Names of the Jews of Ioannina*.

Matsas, Nestoras (1932–2012)   Greek author, painter and film director. Born in Athens, he was baptised into the Geek Orthodox Church during the Nazi occupation. Some of his stories and novels deal with Jewish themes.

Mattan Torah ('giving of the law')   Term applied to the giving of the law by God to Moses on Mount Sinai.

Mattathias (fl. 2nd cent. BCE)   Israelite priest and reel leader. He was priest of Modi' in and led the uprising of the Hasmoneans aganst Antiochus IV in 166–164 BCE. He led the revolt in the Judean hills, waging war on the Syrians. He was succeeded by his son Judah Maccabee.

Mattathias ha-Yitshari (fl. 14th–15th century)   Spanish scholar. A pupil of Ḥasdai Crescas, he wrote a commentary on Psalm 119, a commentary on Avot, and homiltical explanations of the Pentateuch. He played a role in the Disputation of Tortosa in 1413–15, representing the Zaragoza community.

Mattuck, Israel Isidor (1883–1954)   British Liberal rabbi, of Lithuanian origin. He went to the US as a child and served as a rabbi in Far Rockaway, New York, and Lincoln, Nebraska. In 1911 he became the leader of the Liberal Jewish Synagogue in London. He served as chairman of the World Union of Progressive Judaism. His writings include *What are the Jews?, Essentials of Liberal Judaism, Jewish Ethics,* and *Thoughts of the Prophets.*

Matyah ben Harash (fl. 2nd cent.)   Palestinian tanna. He left Palestine after the Hadrianic persecutions of 135–38 and settled in Rome, where he founded a rabbinical academy.

Matzevah   Monument. The word is usually used of a gravestone.

Maurois, André [Herzog, Emile] (1885–1967)   French novelist. Born in Elbert, Normandy, he studied at Rouen and Caen. He worked in the family business, but began to publish novels and short stories. Fleeing from France during the war, he went to the US and taught at Princeton University. He subsequently returned to France. A 16-volume collection of his collected works appeared in 1950–55.

Mausoleum   Large stately tomb. Tombs marked by freestanding monuments were common in Palestine in the Hellenistic period. From the Middle Ages mausoleums were rare in Jewish communities, but they were reintroduced in the 19th century in the US.

Maybaum, Ignaz (1897–1976)   British Reform rabbi and theologian. Born in Vienna, he was a rabbi in Bingen, Frankfurt an der Oder and Berlin. In 1939 he settled in England and served as a rabbi in London. He also lectured on theology and homiletics at Leo Baeck College. His writings include *Synagogue and Society, Jewish Mission, Jewish Existence, The Future of the Jewish Diaspora,* and *The Face of God after Auschwitz.*

Mayer, Leo Ari (1895–1959)   Israeli orientalist. He was born in Stanislav in Ukraine. He moved to Palestine in 1921 and became Inspector of Antiquities, and Librarian and Keeper of Records for the Department of Antiquities.

From 1932 to 1958 he was Professor of Near Eastern Art and Archeology at the Hebrew University. He published works on Islamic art, costume, epigraphy and numismatics.

Mayer, Louis [Mayer, Lazar] (1885–1957) American film producer, of Russian origin. Born in Minsk, Russia, he went to Canada with his parents. In 1904 he worked in the scrap-metal business in Boston. Several years later he invested in a small theatre in Haverhill, Massachusetts. This was followed by several other theatres and he branched out into film distribution. In 1918 he established his own studio in Los Angeles; subsequently he became head of Metro-Goldwyn-Mayer studios.

Mayzel [Meisel], Nahman (1887–1966) Polish Yiddish writer. From 1921 he edited Yiddish periodicals in Warsaw. He emigrated to New York in 1937 and became the central figure of the Yiddish cultural society Yiddisher Kultur Farband, and editor of its monthly journal, *Yiddisher kultur*. He wrote studies of Jewish life in Poland and Russia. In 1964 he settled in Israel.

Mazar [Maisler], Binyamin (1906–1995) Israeli archeologist and historian. He was born in Ciechanowiec in Poland, and settled in Palestine in 1929. In 1951 he became Professor of the History of the Jewish People in the Biblical Period and the Archeology of Palestine at the Hebrew University. In 1952 he became rector of the university, and the following year president. He directed various archeological excavations. His publications include numerous archeological studies, a historical atlas of the country, and a history of Palestine up to the period of the monarchy.

Mazzal Constellation. By astrological association the term refers to luck.

Mazzal tov ('Good luck') Phrase used in a greeting on festive occasions.

Mazzik ('one who causes harm') In Jewish folklore a demon. It is synonymous with 'shed (demon), and 'ruah' (evil spirit). It connotes the dangerous and harmful nature of demons.

Meal offering (Hebrew 'minhah') A sacrificial offering made with flour. The various types of meal offering are described in Leviticus 2. Made with oil and seasoned with salt, they were either unbaked, baked in an oven or on a griddle, cooked or parched with fire. Part was left on the altar, and the rest was given to the priests.

Meassephim Name adopted by the contributors to the Hebrew monthly, *Ha-Measseph*. The journal was founded in 1783 by Isaac Euchel, M.M. Bresselau and the Friedländer brothers. It was published in Königsberg (1784–86), Berlin (1788–90), Breslau (1794–97), and in Berlin, Altona and Dessau (1809–11). It published poetry, essays, interpretations of biblical passages, explanations of grammar, historical studies and book reviews.

Mechaieh (Yiddish) Pleasure, enjoyment.

Medals The midrash contains a fanciful account of medals struck to honour the patriarchs. The first modern medal was made for the physician Benjamin ben Elijah Beer in the 16th century. In the 17th century medals were made for important Jewish families. A medal with a portrait and Hebrew inscription was struck in 1735 when Eliezer Brody was appointed rabbi of Amsterdam. At the end of the 18th century medals were made on historic occasions or to honour important figures. A number of Jews were awarded medals for their services to the Jewish community by the governments who had employed them to further the causes of Emancipation and integration. In modern times medals have been issued in Israel by the Coins and Medals Department of the Prime Minister's Office.

Medicine   The Bible records the existence of physicians during the period of the First Temple (Jeremiah 8:22), and the *Talmud* contains extensive medical information. In the Middle Ages Jews often served as court physicians, and Jewish scholars translated Greco-Arabic medical treatises. Jewish physicians of this period include Asaph, Shabbetai Donnolo, Isaac Israeli and Maimonides. In the Renaissance noted Jewish physicians were active in Western Europe, but various restrictions meant that there were fewer prominent Jewish physicians in the 17th–18th centuries. After the Emancipation Jews made major contributions to medical science.

Medini, Ḥayyim Hezekiah (1832–1904)   Palestinian rabbi. He was born in Jerusalem. From 1867 to 1899 he was a rabbi in Karasubazar in the Crimean peninsula. He subsequently moved to Palestine and settled in Hebron, where he founded a yeshivah. His *Sede Ḥemed* is a halakhic encyclopedia.

Megged, Aharon (1920–2016)   Israeli writer and editor. He was born in Wloclawek, Poland, and went to Palestine in 1926 with his family. In 1950 he settled in Tel Aviv, where he edited the journal *Ba-Sha'ar*, and was a founder of the literary magazine *Massa*. From 1960 to 1971 he was Israel's cultural attaché in London. His stories and novels depict modern life in Israel.

Megillah (i)   Scroll. Parchment, scrolls were the traditional form of books in the ancient world. Letters were also written on scrolls. Biblical books used in the synagogue still take this form, notably the Scroll of the Law from which the Torah portions are read. In its plural form, 'megillot', the word is used specifically to refer to five biblical books: the Song of Songs, Ruth, Lamentations, Ecclesiastes and Esther.

Megillah (ii) ('Scroll')   Tenth tractate in the Mishnah order of Moed. It deals with the reading of the Scroll of Esther on Purim and enumerates scriptural readings for special Sabbaths, festivals, and fast days. It also contains regulations for the care of synagogues and holy objects.

Megillat Taanit ('Scroll of the fast')   Early tannaitic work compiled at the beginning of the 1st century. It lists the 36 days that commemorate miracles and joyous events and on which it is forbidden to fast.

Meḥitzah ('partition')   Screen in the synagogue separating men from women during public prayer. In Jewish law it is also a technical term for the partition fence, or wall which creates a separate domain.

Meḥuttan   Relative by marriage. The term also denotes a wedding guest.

Meijer, Jacob (1912–1993)   Dutch historian, author and poet. He was born in Winschoten, and taught history at the Jewish Lyceum in Amsterdam in 1941–43. He was deported to Bergen-Belsen in 1944. After the war he taught history in Amsterdam, and later in Haarlem. He published studies of the pre-war history of the Jews of the Netherland.

Me'il ('mantle')   The term used for the richly embroidered cloth covering in which a Scroll of the Law is wrapped.

Me'ilah ('Trespass')   Eighth tractate in the Mishnah order of Kodashim. It deals with the laws concerning trespass in the sense of using things consecrated for holy use in a profane way (Leviticus 5:15–16)

Meir (fl. 2nd cent.)   Palestinian tanna. A pupil of Akiva, he was a member of the Sanhedrin at Usha after the Hadrianic persecutions. He was sometimes known as Rabbi Meir Baal ha-Nes. His Mishnah was one of the main sources of the Mishnah of Judah ha-Nasi. His wife, Beruyah, was also an outstanding scholar.

Meir [Meyerson], Golda (1898–1978) Israeli politician. She was born in Kiev, and emigrated to the US in 1906. In 1921 she settled in Palestine. Active in Labour Zionism, she held important positions in the Histadrut and the Jewish Agency. After the establishment of the State of Israel in 1948, she was appointed Minister to Moscow. In 1949 she was elected to the Knesset as a member for Mapai. Later she was Minister of Labour in successive governments, and from 1956 to 1966 she served as Foreign Minister. She was Prime Minister from 1969 to 1974.

Meir, Yaakov (1856–1939) Palestinian rabbi. Born in Jerusalem, he was a Zionist and advocated the revival of spoken Hebrew. In 1906 he was elected Ḥakham Bashi. From 1908 to 1919 he served as Chief Rabbi of Salonica, and in 1921 he became Sephardi Chief Rabbi in Palestine.

Meir Baal ha-Nes, Rabbi ('Rabbi Meir the miracle worker') Appellation applied to Meir because of miracles he performed. Traditional charity boxes in the diaspora for collecting funds for poor Jews in Palestine were called after him.

Meir ben Isaac Nehorai (fl. 11th cent.) German religious poet. He lived in Worms and wrote hymns, including the acrostic poem Akdamut. According to tradition he was killed by the crusaders in 1096.

Meir ben Samuel (c.1060–c.1135) French tosaphist, son-in-law of Rashi. He lived with Rashi in Troyes, but later moved to Ramerupt where he founded a bet midrash. He wrote commentaries to the *Talmud*. Halakhic statements by him were quoted by his son Jacob Tam in his writings.

Meiri, Menaḥem ben Solomon of Perpignan (1249–1316) Fench talmudist. He was born in Perpignan. He was a participant in Solomon ben Adret's polemic against Maimonides, which led to Adret's excommunicating any person who read philosophical works in his youth. Later Meiri disassociated himself from Adret, and supported freedom of thought for the scholars of every country. He wrote studies of halakhah, customs, ethics and philosophy. His *Bet ha-Behirah* is a commentary on the *Talmud*.

Meir of Przemyslany (1780–1850) Polish Ḥasidic leader. He was a miracle worker. Thousands of Ḥasidim went to receive his blessing and hear his teaching.

Meir of Rothenberg (c.1215–1293) German teacher, scholar, tosaphist and communal leader. He was born in Worms. He became the outstanding rabbinic authority of his generation. He was imprisoned by Emperor Rudolf I at Ensisheim in 1286 for attempting to settle in Palestine; refusing to be ransomed lest European rulers begin to blackmail other communities in a similar way, he died a prisoner. His body was ransomed 14 years later. He wrote numerous responsa as well as tosaphot and novellae to 18 tractates of the *Talmud*.

Meisel, Mordecai Marcus (1528–1601) Bohemian financier, philanthropist and communal leader. He was a court banker to the Austrian imperial house, and built the Meisel Synagogue in Prague in 1597. He also financed the building of a hospital, a bet midrash and a mikveh. In addition he sent money to Jerusalem and granted loans to the Jewish communities in Kraków and Poznan.

Meisels, Dov Berush (1798–1870) Polish rabbi and patriot. He settled in Kraków where he opened a bank, and was later elected rabbi of the city. Rabbi Saul Landa and his followers did not, however, recognise this election and established their own bet din. Opposed to the Haskalah, Meisels played a major role in the life of the Kraków Jewish community. In 1846 he was elected to the senate of the Kraków Republic and two years later to the Austrian parliament. In 1856 he became Chief Rabbi of Warsaw. He participated in the events leading to the Polish rebellion of 1863. His writings include a commentary on Maimonides' *Sepher ha-Mitzvot*.

Mekhilta (lit. 'measure') Term applied to various midrashic works. It is also used as a synonym for 'masekhet' (tractate of the Mishnah or *Talmud*).

Mekhilta de-Rabbi Ishma'el Tannatic midrash on Exodus. It consists largely of a halakhic commentary on Exodus 12–23:19, and concludes with two sections on the Sabbath (related to Exodus 31 and 35).

Mekhilta de-Rabbi Simeon ben Yoḥai Tannaitic midrash on Exodus.

Mekhulleh (lit. 'destroyed') Bankrupt.

Melamed, Samuel Max (1885–1938) American writer and journalist. He was born in Lithuania, and in 1914 settled in the US where he edited periodicals including the *American Jewish Chronicle*. His writings include *Der Staat in Wandel der Jahrtausende*, *Psychologie des Jüdischen Geistes*, and *Spinoza und Buddha*.

Melammed ('teacher') Private teacher or assistant in a ḥeder.

Melavveh Malkah The meal eaten at the close of the Sabbath. Kabbalistic and Ḥasidic influence has led to the practice of prolonging the meal (and thus delaying the end of the Sabbath) by the singing of melodies.

Meldar Sephardi term for the reading of sacred literature.

Meldola, Raphael (1797–1853) British rabbi. He was born in Livorno. In 1804 or 1805 he became Ḥaham of the Sephardi community in London. In this capacity he reformed Jewish educational institutions, introduced a choir into the synagogue, and cooperated with Solomon Hirscher, the Ashkenazi Chief Rabbi. He published a handbook of the laws of marital life, as well as sermons, memorial poems and a catechism.

Melitzaḥ In biblical Hebrew the word means 'aphorism'. During the medieval period, it referred to an elegant literary style. In modern times it denotes a literary technique, popular during the Haskalah period, based on the artistic combinations of phrases from the Bible.

Mellaḥ The name given to the Jewish quarter in Moroccan cities.

Melnikoff, Avraham (1892–1960) Israeli sculptor. He was born in Russia, studied sculpture in Chicago, and in 1918 emigrated to Palestine. His work includes a monument to the soldier and pioneer Joseph Trumpeldor and his comrades.

Meltzer, Shimshon (1909–2000) Israeli poet. He was born in Tluste, and settled in Palestine in 1933. Initially he taught in a school in Tel Aviv, and later he engaged in editorial work. From 1959 he was on the editorial staff of the Zionist Library publications produced by the Jewish Agency. He published poems and ballads combining Ḥasidic tales and motifs. He also translated Yiddish literature into Hebrew.

Mem Thirteenth letter in the Hebrew alphabet. Its numerical value is 40.

Memmi, Albert (b.1920) French author and sociologist. He was born in Tunis. He fought with the Free French during World War II, and later became head of a psychology institute in Tunis. In 1966 he became a professor at the École Pratique des Hautes Études. His writings which concern north-African Jewry, include *Pillar of Salt, Agar: Portrait of a Jew,* and *The Liberation of the Jew.*

Memorbuch (German: 'book of memory') A type of community prayer book once common in Jewish communities in central Europe. It consisted of a collection of prayers, a necrology of distinguished persons, and a martyrology.

Menaḥem (fl. 8th cent. BCE) King of Israel (c.746/7–737 BCE). He seized the throne after assassinating Shallum, son of Jabesh. When the Assyrian king Tiglath-Pileser III invaded Israel, Menahem was forced to pay tribute to him.

Menaḥem ben Judah (fl. 1st cent.) Israelite rebel leader, son of Judah the Galilean. He led the group known as the Sicarii in the war against Rome (66–70), successfully attacking the stronghold of Masada, and gaining victory over the Romans in Herod's palace. Later he antagonised Eleazar ben Hananiah and his followers, who killed him.

Menaḥem ben Saruk (c.910–c.970) Spanish Hebrew lexicographer. He was born in Tortosa. He served as the secretary of Ḥasdai ibn Shaprut, but was dismissed and persecuted for his heretical views. His *Mahberet,* the first Hebrew dictionary, was attacked by Dunash ben Labrat.

Menaḥem Mendel of Chernobyl (1730–1789) Ukrainian Ḥasidic rabbi. Initially he engaged in ascetic practices and fasting. After studying with the Baal Shem Tov, he became a maggid, spreading Ḥasidism in Russia and Ukraine. He collected money for ransoming Jewish captives and for other charitable ends. He emphasised the importance of the spiritual state known as 'devekut' and upheld the position of the tzaddik.

Menaḥem Mendel of Przemyslany (fl. 18th cent.) Palestinian Ḥasidic leader. A pupil of the Baal Shem Tov, he went to Palestine in 1764 and settled in Tiberias. He was an extreme enthusiast among the first generation of Ḥasidic leaders, and emphasised the importance of prayer.

Menaḥem Mendel of Rymanov (fl. 18th–19th cent.) Galician Ḥasidic rabbi. His preaching attracted thousands of Ḥasidim to visit him in Rymanov, Galicia. During the Napoleonic Wars, he predicted the coming of the Messiah.

Menaḥem Mendel of Vitebsk (1730–1788) Polish Ḥasidic leader. A disciple of Dov Ber of Mezhirich, he became the head of a congregation in Minsk. In 1772 he went with Shneour Zalman to defend the Ḥasidic movement to the Vilna Gaon, but the Vilna Gaon refused to meet them. In 1773 he settled in Gorodok in Belorussia and later moved to Palestine, where he became the leader of the Ḥasidic community. He subsequently settled in Tiberias. He taught that God is present through the process of contraction ('tzimtzim'), whereby he makes a space in which creation can take place. His writings include *Peri ha-Aretz, Peri ha-Etz, Etz Peri,* and *Likkutei Amarim.*

Menaḥem the Essene (fl. 1st cent. BCE) Israelite seer. He prophesied that Herod would become king but that he would not act unjustly and be punished. Later Herod questioned Menaḥ em about how long he would reign.

Menaḥot ('Meal offerings') Second tractate in the Mishnah order of Kodashim. It deals with the preparation of the meal offering (Leviticus 2:1–14; 5:11–13), as well as the shewbread (Leviticus 24:5–9), and the two loaves brought to the Temple on the Feast of Weeks (Leviticus 23:17).

Mendelssohn, Erich (1887–1953) Israeli architect. He was born in Allenstein, Germany. From the 1920s he was a member of the revivalist movement in European architecture. He left Germany in 1933 and worked in Britain and Palestine. Between 1934 and 1939 he designed various buildings in Palestine, including the Anglo-Palestine Bank in Jerusalem, the Hadassah hospital on Mount Scopus, and the government hospital in Haifa. He subsequently built a number of synagogues in American cities.

Mendelssohn [Mendelssohn-Bartholdy], Felix (1809–1847) German composer, grandson of Moses Mendelssohn. He was baptised and later converted to Christianity. His compositions include the oratorio Elijah. He was also responsible for the revival of Bach's *St Matthew Passion*.

Mendelssohn, Moses [Biur] (1729–1786) German philosopher. He was born in Dessau. He lived in Berlin, where he studied philosophy, mathematics, Latin, French and English, and became a partner in a silk factory. In 1754, with the help of Gotthold Ephraim Lessing, he began to publish philosophical studies and in 1763 was awarded the first prize of the Prussian Royal Academy of Sciences for his philosophical work. He became embroiled in a dispute about Judaism, and from 1769 devoted his literary work to issues dealing with the Jewish faith. He published a German translation of the Pentateuch with a Hebrew commentary (*Biur*). His *Jerusalem* is an analysis of Judaism and a defense of tolerance. He was the hero of Lessing's *Nathan der Weise*.

Mendes, Henry Pereira (1852–1937) American Sephardi rabbi. He was born in Birmingham, England, and served as a rabbi to the new Sephardi congregation of Manchester from 1874 to 1877.

He then emigrated to New York, where he served as a rabbi to the Shearith Israel congregation. He was a founder of the Union of Orthodox Congregations of America, the Jewish Theological Seminary, and the New York Board of Jewish Ministers. He wrote about Jewish and general topics for the weekly paper, *American Hebrew*. His works include *Looking Ahead, Bar Mitzvah, Esther and Harbonah, Jewish Religion Ethically Presented, Mekhor Ḥayyim: Mourner's Handbook,* and *Derekh Ḥayyim: Way of Life.*

Menelaus (fl. 2nd cent. BCE) High priest. He obtained the priesthood in 171 BCE by means of bribery. An extreme Helleniser, he supported the persecution of the Jews by Antiochus IV Epiphanes. At the beginning of his tenure of office, he plundered the Temple. Later he lost favour in the Seleucid court and was put to death on the advice of Lysias.

Mene mene tekel u-pharsin The phrase in an unknown language that appeared miraculously on the wall during Belshazzar's feast (Daniel 5:25). It was interpreted by Daniel to mean that the king's deeds had been weighed and were found wanting. He explained the works as follows: *Mene*: 'God has numbered the days of your kingdom and will bring it to an end'; *tekel*: 'You have been weighed in the balance and found wanting'; *pharsin*: 'Your kingdom has been divided and given over to the Medes and Persians.

Menes, Abraham (1897–1969) American Jewish historian. He was born in Grodno, Poland, and founded a branch of the socialist party, the Bund, there; he later became Vice-Chairman of the Grodno Jewish community. In 1920 he moved to Berlin, and he subsequently settled in Paris, where he contributed to the Yiddish Encyclopedia. In 1940 he moved to the US. He published studies of the economic and social aspects of Jewish history.

Menorah, Candelabrum The golden seven-branched menorah stood in the Tabernacle and the Temple. The menorah from the Second Temple was taken to Rome by Vespasian and is depicted on the Arch of Titus there. The term also refers to the eight-branched Hannukah lamp.

Mensh (Yiddish) Literally a human being, but colloquially an honourable person, someone of consequence.

Menuhin, Yehudi (1916–99) American musician. Born in New York, he made his debut at the age of eight. He became a world famous violinist and served as president of the International Musical Council of UNESCO. He was knighted for his services to music in 1965 and received the Order of Merit in 1987.

Mephibosheth (fl. 11th cent. BCE) Name given to Meribaal, the son of Jonathan, in the Book of Samuel. When he was five his father was killed (I Samuel 4:4) and he fled with his nurse; in the haste of the journey he was dropped and the accident left him lame. When David was established in Jerusalem he restored Mephibosheth to favour. During Absalom's rebellion, Mephibosheth remained in Jerusalem, while his servant Zoba accompanied David. When the uprising was quelled, Mephibosheth pleaded that he had been misled by Zoba and David treated him leniently.

Merchant During the biblical period, although mercantile commerce was well developed, the Jews appear not to have acted as merchants; nor, according to Josephus, were Jews of his time engaged in trade. However, Jewish merchants are documented in Alexandria and elsewhere in the Roman Empire. During the Middle Ages, the Jews played an increasingly important role in international trade, but after the Crusades these activities were curtailed and in Western Europe, they turned instead to moneylending. In Eastern Europe the Jews continued to act as merchants, as did Marranos in north-west Europe and America. In the modern period, Jewish merchants have been active throughout the world.

Merits, doctrine of The belief that by performing works commanded by God a person may obtain divine favour, which benefits himself and his descendants.

Merits of the fathers According to Jewish doctrine, the blessings secured for their descendants by parents who perform worthy deeds. In particular the merits of the patriarchs (Abraham, Isaac and Jacob) are believed to have obtained benefits for future generations.

Mesharet The accent marks in Hebrew which indicate minor pauses.

Meshuga (Yiddish) Crazy.

Meshullah (lit. 'shadow') Emissary. The term is applied particularly to emissaries sent to raise funds for a charitable institution. In the early rabbinic period the rabbinical academies in the Four Holy Cities of Palestine (Jerusalem, Hebron, Safed and Tiberias) sent emissaries known as 'shadar' to Jewish communities in distant lands. Because they travelled widely meshullahim performed a useful function in linking communities throughout the world. Their accounts of their journeys serve as important historical sources.

Meshummad Convert to Christianity.

Messiah [Mashiah] Annointed one. In the Bible the term refers to kings, high priests and any individual who had a divine mission. After the exile, the prophetic vision of God's kingdom was associated with the ingathering of Israel under an anointed scion of the House of David. During the period of Roman rule, the expectation of a messiah who would free the Jews gained prominence. During this period various false messiahs appeared including Jesus, who the Jews refused to accept because he did not fulfil the role laid out for the

Messiah in the Hebrew Scriptures. In the 2nd century Simeon Bar Kokhba was viewed as the Messiah. In the 5th century a pseudo-messiah, Moses, appeared in Crete. Other false messiahs included Abu Issa al-Isfahani (8th century), Serene (8th century), Yudghan (8th century), David Alroy (12th century), Abraham Abulafia (11th–12th centuries), Moses Botarel (14th century), Asher Lamlein (16th century), Solomon Molcho (16th century), Shabbetai Tzevi (17th century), and Jacob Frank (18th century).

Metatron   The most important angel in aggadic and kabbalistic literature. He was identified with the Angel of the Presence and with Enoch after he ascended to Heaven. He served as the scribe of the divine court, the keeper of celestial secrets, and the heavenly archetype of man.

Meteg   Short vertical line placed on the left of a vowel sign in Hebrew. It denotes a secondary emphasis in a word (or series of words joined by a makkeph).

Metempsychosis (Hebrew 'gigul')   The migration of a soul from one body after its death to another. In kabbalistic Judaism the doctrine of the transmigraiton of souls appears in the Bahir and the *Zohar*. Eventually it became a commonly accepted belief among mystics and played an important role in Ḥasidic lore.

Methuselah   Patriarch, son of Enoch, father of Lamech, and grandfather of Noah (Genesis 5:21–5). According to the Bible, he lived 969 years (Genesis 5:25–7).

Metivta (Aramaic)   Yeshivah.

Metsieh (Yiddish)   Bargain, nothing to brag about.

Meturgeman (Aramaic: 'interpreter')   The title given to the spokesman for a talmudic rabbi. It was customary for sages to deliver their lectures through him: the rabbi spoke to the meturge-man who then addressed the assembled congregation.

Meyerbeer, Giacomo [Beer, Jakob Liebmann]   **(1791–1864)**   German composer. Born in Vogelsdorf, he was the son of a wealthy Berlin banker. He composed operas in Italy in the style of Rossini, and then moved to Paris where he produced *Robert le Diable.* Other works include *Les Huguenots.* In 1842 the King of Prussia appointed him General Music Director in Berlin.

Mezumman (lit. 'ready cash')   The word is used to refer to one of the quorum of three people whose presence is necessary for the public recitation of Grace after Meals.

Mezuzah (i) ('doorpost')   Parchment scroll placed in a container which is fixed to the doorpost of a room in a Jewish house; every doorway in the house carries a mezuzah. On the scroll are written verses from Deuteronomy (6:4–9 and 11:13–21). The practice is prescribed by Deuteronomy 11:20: 'You shall write [these words] upon the doorposts of your house and upon your gates'.

Mezuzah (ii) ('Doorpost')   One of the seven minor talmudic tractates. It deals with regulations regarding the writing and use of the mezuzah.

Mi addir al ha-kol ('He who is mighty above all')   Opening words of a hymn recited before the wedding service in the Ashkenazi rite.

Micah (i) (fl. 8th cent. BCE)   Israelite prophet. He lived in Judah, where he defended the people against the oppression of the ruling classes. He prophesied the destruction of the country and exile to Babylon, and also predicted the coming of a king of the House of David who would bring peace to the world.

Micah (ii)   Biblical book, one of the books of the 12 Minor Prophets. It records the prophecies of Micah.

Midrash Rabbah 285

Michael Archangel. With Gabriel he is the only angel mentioned by name in the Bible (Daniel 10:13). He is a divine messenger who executes God's judgements. In the Apocrypha and aggadic literature he is the guardian angel of Israel, the chief opponent of Satan, and the keeper of the celestial keys.

Michal (fl. 10th cent. BCE) Israelite princess and queen, daughter of Saul and wife of David. She helped her husband to escape from Saul's messengers, who had been sent to kill him. Subsequently she was given in marriage to Paltiel son of Laish, but was eventually restored to David. When David danced in front of the Ark, she rebuked him. She died childless (I Samuel 18–19; II Samuel 16; I Chronicles 15).

Michelson, Albert (1852–1931) American physicist of East Prussian origin. Born in Strelno, Germany, he went to the US at the age of three. His family moved to Nevada, and he studied at the US Naval Academy. He became an instructor in science there and later Professor of Physics at Case School of Applied Science in Cleveland, and later at Clark University. Subsequently he was Professor of Physics at the University of Chicago. In 1907 he received the Nobel Prize in Physics.

Microcosm A miniature representation or vision of something. In ancient philosophy humankind was regarded as a model or epitome of the universe. During the Middle Ages it was asserted that there is a correspondence between the human organism and the cosmos. In Jewish thought this concept is found in midrashic and philosophical works, such as *Olam Katan* by Joseph ibn Tzaddik, as well as in kabbalistic texts.

Middot ('Measures') Tenth tractate in the Mishnah order of Kodashim. It deals with the architecture, organisation and dimensions of the Second Temple.

Midrash ('study,' 'interpretation') [derash, ('enquiry,' 'exposition')] Interpretation of biblical texts. The interpretive approach known as 'midrash halakhah' aims to define the full meaning of biblical law; 'midrash aggadah' seeks to derive a moral principle, lesson or theological concept from Scripture. The rabbis formulated various rules to deduce hidden or new meanings. Rabbinic literature is replete with midrashic expositions.

Midrashic literature The body of rabbinic writings concerning the interpretation of biblical texts. It dates from the tannaitic period (beginning c.100 BCE) to the 10th century. Of works connected with the Bible, the best known is Midrash Rabbah on the Pentateuch and the five megillot. The Tanḥuma contains discourses on the portion of the law read weekly in the synagogue. Other homiletic works on the Bible include *Shoḥer Tov* on Psalms, and works on Proverbs and Samuel. Midrashim relating to festivals and special Sabbaths are called 'pesiktot'. The *Pesikta Rabbati* contain homilies for special occasions. *Avot de-Rabbi Natan* is an expansion of the Mishnaic tractate Avot. *Derekh Eretz Rabbah* deals with ethical teachings, and *Derekh Eretz Zuta* advises scholars about religious and pedagogic duties. The *Tanna de-ve-Elyahu* contains moral advice. *Seder Olam* is a work of historical aggadah, and *Pirke de-Rabbi Eliezer* contains numerous stories about biblical events. The *Yalkut Shimoni* is a collection of aggadic literature. In addition, there are large numbers of separate midrashim on books of the Bible, and short midrashim on various topics.

Midrash Rabbah Collection of aggadic midrashim on the Pentateuch and the five megillot. It consists of Genesis Rabbah, Exodus Rabbah, Leviticus Rabbah, Numbers Rabbah, Deuteronomy Rabbah, Song of Songs Rabbah, Ruth Rabbah, Lamentaitons Rabbah, Ecclesiastes Rabbah and Esther Rabbah.

Mielziner, Moses (1828–1903)   American Reform rabbi and scholar. He was born in Czerniejewo, and served as a preacher and teacher in Waren. From 1857 to 1865 he was head of the Jewish school in Copenhagen. He emigrated to the US, where he served as a rabbi in New York and later became a professor of *Talmud* and rabbinic literature at the Hebrew Union College. His writings include *Introduction to the* Talmud, *The Jewish Law of Marriage and Divorce and its Relation to the Law of the State,* and *The Introduction of Slavery among the Ancient Hebrews.*

Miesas, Matisyohu (1885–1945)   Galician Yiddish semiologist. He was born in Pshemeshl, Galicia. At a language conference held at Czernowitz in 1908 he gave a paper on the scientific analysis of Yiddish; this was the first such study to be written in the language itself.

Miggo (lit. 'since')   In talmudic studies the word denotes a type of legal proof.

Migration   The first major migration of the Jewish people was the deportation of Israelites to Babylonia after the destruction of the First Temple in the 6th century BCE. The Jews returned from exile in the 5th century BCE. The destruction of the Second Temple in the 1st century CE precipitated a new wave of migration to Mesopotamia, Asia Minor and Egypt. In later centuries Jews emigrated from Palestine to southern Italy, and then into France and Germany; from the Byzantine Empire up the valley of the Danube into central Europe; and under the Arabs from Mesopotamia and Egypt through Morocco into Spain. Later Western European Jewry moved from northern Europe into Poland, and from Spain to the Ottoman Empire. In the modern period Jewry has shifted from Europe to the US and Israel.

Mikhoels, Solomon (1890–1948)   Russian Yiddish actor. He was born in Dvinsk. He became the chief actor in Alexander Granovsky's drama group, and later succeeded him to the directorship of the Jewish State Theatre in Moscow. During World War II he visited Western countries on behalf of the Jewish anti-Facist Committee. He was assassinated by the Soviet secret police.

Mikvaot ('ritual baths')   Sixth tractate in the Mishnah order of Tohorot. It deals with regulations about ritual bathing (Leviticus 14:8; 15:5).

Mikveh   Ritual bath. According to Jewish law, individuals as well as various objects have to be immersed and ritually cleaned on certain occasions. The water in the mikveh must come from a natural spring or river. Such immersion renders a person ritually clean who has had contact with the dead or a defiled object, or who has become impure through an unclean flow from the body (it is, for example, practised by women after menstruation). In addition, ritual bathing is undertaken by pious individuals to add to their spirituality, and is prescribed for proselytes. Ritual cleansing is also used for vessels.

Milhaud, Darius (1892–1974)   French composer. He was born in Aix-en-Provence. He served as secretary to the French minister in Brazil in 1917–18. After returning to Paris, he wrote a wide variety of musical compositions including *David, Service sacré, Poèmes Juifs, Chants populaires Hébraïques, La création du monde,* and *Le candelabre à sept branches.* In 1940 he settled in the US, where he was appointed professor at Mills College in California. Later he was a professor of composition at the Paris Conservatory.

Military titles   In biblical times the following titles were used: 'sar' (commander), 'sar tzava (commander-in-chief), 'sar gedud' (unit commander), 'sar ha-rekhev' (captain of chariots), 'sar alaphim [meot], [ḥamishim], [asarot]' (captain of a thousand, a hundred, fifty, ten). The term 'sar ha-tabbaḥim' (captain of the body guard), and 'shalish' (charioteer) are also found. In modern Israel various other military titles are employed.

Milk The halakhic restrictions on the consumption of milk are that it be drawn from a permitted animal, and that milk or milk products not be mixed or cooked with meat or meat products.

Millennium A thousand years. In Jewish usage the word is applied specifically to the thousand-year period after the coming of the Messiah. This period, also referred to as the 'Days of the Messiah', will precede the last Judgement and the inauguration of the Kingdom of Heaven.

Miller, Arthur (1915–2005) American novelist and playwright. He was born in New York. His early works include *Focus*, a novel about anti-Semitism. He later wrote *Incident at Vichy*, which concerns the arrest of Frenchmen, including Jews, during the Nazi occupation of France.

Minhag Custom. The word is used of customs that became binding and assumed the force of halakhah. It also refers to local traditions and liturgical rites which developed in different Jewish communities.

Minḥah [afternoon service] The service of afternoon prayer. It was instituted in place of the afternoon Temple offering. On the Sabbath and fast days a portion of the Torah is read during the service.

Minim ('heretics') Talmudic term for heretical sects. It was applied to various groups, including early Christian and gnostics.

Minister In Jewish usage, an Orthodox Jewish spiritual leader in the British Commonwealth, functioning as a rabbi.

Minkowski, Maurice (1881–1930) Polish artist. Although he was deaf and dumb, he was an important chronicler of traditional Jewish life during the czarist period.

Minority rights Before and during World War I, various Jewish bodies struggled to protect the religious and civil rights of Jews in Eastern Europe. At the Versailles Peace Conference in 1919, they obtained the agreement of the principal allied powers that special treaties should be made with the successor states of the Austro-Hungarian and Czarist empires and the enlarged states of south-eastern Europe. Later a project to include an article in the covenant of the League of Nations concerning minority rights came to nothing. However, treaties were concluded with Poland, Romania, Hungary, Austria, Lithuania and Latvia. In addition, it was agreed that any member of the Council of the League of Nations had the right to bring an infringement of minority rights to the attention of the Council. The United Nations Charter encourages respect for human rights without distinction on grounds of race, religion or language.

Minyan ('number') Term applied to the group of ten male Jews (13 years or older), who constitute the minimum number for communal worship.

Minyan man A Jew who, for payment, attends synagogue services regularly to ensure that there is a minyan.

Miracle Extraordinary event attributed to divine intervention. In the Bible such occurrences are referred to as 'signs' and 'wonders'. The *Talmud* records miracles performed by men of God or brought about through their merits. In Jewish philosophy attempts were made to give a rational account of miraculous occurrences.

Mirandola, Giovanni Pico della [Pico della Mirandola] (1463–1494) Italian humanist. He studied Hebrew under Elijah del Medigo and became convinced that the kabbalah provided an access to the truths of Christianity. His writings mark the beginning of the study of Hebrew as an academic discipline by Christian scholars.

Miriam (fl.? 13th cent. BCE) Israelite woman, sister of Moses. According to Exodus 2:2–8, she advised Pharaoh's daughter, who had discovered the hiding place of the baby Moses, to call a Hebrew nurse for Moses and succeeded in having his mother engaged to care for him. Later, when she and Aaron challenged Moses' exclusive right to speak in the name of the Lord (Numbers 12), she was stricken with leprosy, but she was healed by Moses, who interceded with God on her behalf.

Miseh   An abnormal or violent death.

Mi she-berakah ('He who blessed') Opening words of a benediction recited on behalf of one called up for the reading of the Torah. After each reading it is customary for the cantor to ask God's blessing on the reader, his family and anyone he wishes to have mentioned. In many congregations the person called up for the Torah reading makes an offering for the synagogue or to charity. Additional forms of this prayer are recited after the birth of a son, after the birth and naming of a daughter, by the bridegroom before his wedding, and on behalf of a sick person.

Mishegoss (Yiddish) An irrational belief, nonsense.

Mishkovsky, Zelda (1914–1984) Israeli poet. She was born in Chernigov in Ukraine. She emigrated to Jerusalem at the age of 11, and taught in a religious school for girls. Her poetry contains ultra-Orthodox and modern sensibilities. She became known by her forename alone.

Mishnah ('Repetition,' 'Study,' 'Teaching') Early rabbinic legal code. Compiled by Judah ha-Nasi in the 2nd century, it is divided into six orders: (1) Zeraim ('Seeds'), dealing with laws regarding agriculture; (2) Moed ('Set feast'), regarding the laws of the Sabbath and festivals; (3) Nashim ('Women'), describing the laws of marriage, divorce and vows; (4) Nezikin ('Damages'), treating civil and criminal violations; (5) Kodashim ('Holy Things'), setting out the laws concerning ritual slaughter, sacrifices and consecrated objects; and (6) Tohorot ('Purities'), dealing with the laws of ceremonial purity.

Mishpokhe (Yiddish) Family, relatives.

Mission In a religious context, the sending out of persons to bring about the spread of religion. Medieval church bodies devoted to conversionist propaganda were the prototypes for Christian mission among the Jews. The earliest organisations to adopt this policy were established in the 17th century in the Netherlands. Later they spread to Germany, where the Institutum Judaicum was founded at Halle in 1728. In England the London Society for Promoting Christianity among the Jews was founded in 1809. Educational and medical facilities set up by these institutions in Europe and Near Eastern countries pursued similar ends. In recent years such activities have diminished and have been replaced by a more sympathetic attitude toward Judaism.

Mitnagged ('opponent') The term 'mitnaggedim' is applied specifically to opponents of the Ḥasidic movement. The Vilna Gaon gave the impetus to the development of opposition to Ḥasidism. His antagonism was based on the pantheistic tendencies of the Ḥasidim, their use of the Sephardi liturgy, their belief in tzaddikim, and the creation of Ḥasidic synagogues. Because of the ban issued against the Ḥasidim by the Vilna Gaon, Shneour Zalman of Lyady was arrested and held in the St Petersburg fortress in 1798. After he was released, the conflict abated. During the 19th century the two groups were generally reconciled.

Mittwoch, Eugen (1876–1942) German orientalist. He was born in Schrimm. He helped Paul Nathan to set up a school system in Palestine under the auspices of the Hilfsverein der deutschen Juden. He taught at the universities of Berlin and Greifswald, and in 1919 became a professor at the Seminary for Oriental Languages in Berlin, where he was eventually appointed director. In 1933 he directed the office of the Joint Distribution Committee in Berlin and in 1939 he moved to England. He published studies of the influence of Jewish prayer on the liturgy of Islam; Hebrew epigraphy; and Islamic art and politics. He was one of the editors of an edition of the works of Moses Mendelssohn.

Mitzvah ('commandment') In Jewish law commandments are either positive ('mitzvah ashe') or negative ('mitzvah lo taaseh'). According to tradition, there are 613 commandments in the Torah, and various scholars enumerated them. The *Talmud* differentiates between types of commandment: 'mishpatim', ordinances, that would have been deducible even if Scripture had not prescribed them; and 'hukkim', commandments that could not have been logically derived. Medieval scholars referred to the first type as rational ('sikhliyyot') and the second as revealed ('shimiyot'). The term 'mitzvah' is also applied to a good deed.

Mizpah Ancient place in the territory of Benjamin. Samuel gathered the Israelites there for prayer before they went into battle against the Philistines (I Samuel 7:5). After their victory, he visited Mizpah annually to judge the people. Later it was in the Kingdom of Judah and served as the residence of Gedaliah when he was governor. Judah Maccabee and his men also assembled there before engaging in battle.

Mizrah ('east') Decorated parchment or metal plate, hung on a wall to indicate, for the purposes of prayer, the direction of Jerusalem.

Mizrahi (from 'merkaz ruhani': spiritual centre) Religious Zionist organisation. It was founded in 1902 and its first conference took place in Pressburg. It encouraged a programme of religious Zionism within the framework of the Zionist movement. Since the establishment in 1948 of the State of Israel, it has formed part of successive Israeli governments. It also engaged in religious education at all levels, created an organisation for yeshivot, established the Mosad ha-Rav Kook publishing society, maintained economic enterprises (including banks and a house-building company), and ran an organisation to deal with refugee rabbis. Its women's section sponsors kindergartens, social welfare and children's homes in Israel. In 1955 it joined with Ha-Poel ha-Mizrahi to form the National Religious Party. The World Centre of Mizrahi and Ha-Poel ha-Mizrahi is the highest body of the religious Zionist movement and acts as the executive of both bodies.

Mizrahi, Elijah (c.1450–1526) Ottoman rabbinic authority. He was born in Constantinople, and became the foremost rabbinic authority in the Ottoman Empire. He adopted a more tolerant attitude to the Karaites than other rabbinic scholars. He wrote various responsa, a super-commentary on Rashi's commentary to the Pentateuch, and a mathematical treatise.

Moadim le-simhah ('Holidays for rejoicing') Greeting used among the Sephardim on religious holidays. The reply is 'Hagim u-zemanim le-sason' ('Festivals and festal periods for joy').

Mocatta, Frederick David (1828–1905) English philanthropist, scholar and communal leader. He was active in the Charity Organisation Society , and the Jewish Board of Guardians. An observant Jew, he was a member of Orthodox as well as Reform synagogues. He donated his library to University College, London, and the Jewish Historical Society of England. His writings include *The Jews and the Inquisition.*

Modeh ani ('I give thanks') Opening words of the prayer said upon waking in the morning.

Modena, Aaron Berechiah (fl. 17th cent.) Italian Kabbalist. He composed collections of material for liturgical use. His *Maavar Yabbok* contains prayers for the sick and the dead in addition to regulations concerning mourning.

Modena, Leone [Leon of Modena] (1571–1648) Italian rabbi, scholar and writer. Born in Venice, he initially became an elementary teacher and preacher there. In his autobiography, *Hayyei Yehudah,* he listed the various occupations he resorted to throughout his life. He was regarded by Christian scholars as the most distinguished Jewish scholar of his day. His writings include sermons, as well as polemics against the Oral Law, the kabbalah and Christianity.

Moed ('Set feast') Second order of the Mishnah. Its tractates deal with laws concerning the Sabbath, festivals and fast days.

Moed Katan ('Minor festival') [Mashkin 'One may irrigagte')] Eleventh tractate in the Mishnah order of Moed. It deals with the nature of work permitted during the intermediate days of the feasts of the Passover and Tabernacles, as well as mourning on holy days.

Mohilever, Samuel (1824–1898) Polish rabbi and religious Zionist. He was born in Glebokie, in the district of Vilnius, and became a rabbi there in 1848. Later he served in Szaki, Suwalki, and Radom. From 1874 he actively supported Jewish settlement in Palestine, and his views on this influenced Baron Emond de Rothschild and Baron de Hirsch. He formed the first society of Hovevei Zion in Warsaw, and later supported Theodor Herzl. In 1884 he was the Honorary President of the Kattowitz Conference.

Mohr, Abraham Menahem Mendel (1813–1868) Galician Hebrew scholar and maskil. He was born in Lemberg. His writings, in Hebrew and Yiddish, include a geography of Palestine and its Jewish inhabitants, Purim plays, and editions of *Mikveh Yisrael* by Manasseh ben Israel and *La-Yesharim Tehillah* by Moses Hayyim Luzzatto. He also published a Yiddish newspaper.

Moïse, Penina (1797–1880) American poet, hymn writer and teacher. She was born in Charleston, South Carolina, and became the superintendent of the Beth Elohim Congregation's Sunday school there. She was the author of the first American Jewish hymnal. Her hymns and poetry were published as *Secular and Religious Works* in 1911.

Moissis, Asher (1899–1975) Greek author, translator and communal leader. He was born in Trikkala. He became a lawyer and participated in Jewish communal and Zionist affairs. In 1917 he founded the Zionist monthly *Israel*, which he also edited. In the 1930s he published books on Jewish subjects, particularly Greco-Jewish relations through the ages. He served as President of the Jewish National Fund (1930–38), the Salonica Jewish community (1934–6), and the Greek Zionist Federation (1936–8). Later he was President of the Central Council of Jewish Communities in Greece (1944–9), and from 1948 served as Honorary Consul of Israel in Athens.

Molcho, Solomon (c. 1500–1532) Italian Kabbalist and pseudo-messiah. He was born in Lisbon of Marrano parents, and his given name was Diogo Pires. He became Secretary to the King of Portugal's council and recorder at the Court of Appeals. After meeting David

Reveni he circumcised himself and took his Hebrew name. He lived for a time in Salonica, where he studied kabbalah, then returned to Italy. Believing himself to be the Messiah, he preached about the coming of messianic redemption. Although he obtained the protection of Pope Clement VII against the Inquisition, he was accused by an inquisitional court of Judaising (trying to persuade converts to Christianity to return to Judaism) and was condemned to be burned at the stake. He was reprieved on this occasion but was condemned again after refusing to convert to Christianity and was burned in 1532. Many Jews and Marranos in Italy refused to believe that he had died, and thought he had been saved once more.

Moloch [Molech; Milcom]   Canaanite deity. The Canaanites sacrificed firstborn children to Moloch by passing them through fire. This practice was forbidden in Scripture (Leviticus 18:21; 20:3–5). Nevertheless in Jerusalem altars were built to Moloch at Topheth in the valley of Hinnom (Jeremiah 7:31; 19:1–5; II Chronicles 28:3).

Molodowski-Lew, Kadia (1894–1975) American Yiddish poet and novelist. She was born in Lithuania. She participated in the publications of the Kiev Yiddish Group after 1917, but soon moved to Warsaw to teach in Yiddish schools. In 1935 she settled in New York. Her verse reflects her experiences in Europe, America and Israel. After the establishment of the State of Israel, she wrote lyrics expressing joy at the restoration of Zion. She also wrote novels, short stories and plays, depicting Jewish life in Poland as well as biblical and historical themes.

Momigliano, Arnaldo (1908–1987) Italian historian. He was born in Caraglio. He taught in Rome, Turin, Pisa, London and Chicago. He wrote studies about ancient history, the Maccabees and Judaica, and the history of

the Second Temple period. His publications include *Alien Wisdom: The Limits of Hellenism.*

Monatsschrift für Geschicte und Wissenschaft des Judentums   German scholarly monthly publication which appeared from 1851 to 1939. It was founded in Dresden by Zacharias Frankel, and dealt with various Jewish subjects; after 1861 it was published mostly from Breslau.

Mond, Alfred Moritz, 1st Baron Melchett (1868–1930)   English industrialist and statesman. He entered his father's firm, which later became Imperial Chemical Industries. He was elected to parliament as a Liberal in 1906, and was appointed Commissioner of Works, and later Minister of Health. He subsequently became a member of the Conservative Party. He was made a baron in 1928. A dedicated Zionist and contributor to Zionist causes, he helped to found the Jewish Agency in 1929 and became the chairman of its council.

Mond, Henry, 2nd Baron Melchett (1898–1949)   English Zionist and communal leader, son of Alfred Moritz Mond. He was brought up in the Christian faith but converted to Judaism after the rise of Hitler. An ardent Zionist, he succeeded his father as Chairman of the council of the Jewish Agency. He also served as President of the World Union of Maccabi.

Mondays and Thursdays   These days of the week are characterised liturgically by the reading of the law and the recitation of additional penitential and supplicatory prayers during the morning service. In addition they are also the preferred days for voluntary fasts. The three voluntary fasts, known as 'Behab' (Monday, Thursday and Monday) are observed shortly after the feasts of the Passover and Tabernacles, and are intended to atone for unintentional sins and levity during the festive season.

Moneylending   The exacting of interest on a loan to a fellow citizen is prohibited in the Torah but it is permitted when the borrower is a stranger (Deuteronomy 23:20–21). Despite this exception, there was a tendency to forbid any lending at interest in biblical times. In the Middle Ages, Jews were frequently approached for loans; as they were excluded from trade and craftsmen's guilds in northern Europe, moneylending became a common Jewish activity, which performed an important function in medieval society. In southern Europe moneylending was the profession of a small Jewish minority. In central and northern Italy, the employment of Jews as municipal moneylenders was responsible for the establishment of new Jewish communities in the 13th–14th centuries. With the removal of civil and economic restrictions on Jewry in modern society, moneylending ceased to be concentrated in Jewish hands.

Monis, Judah (1683–1764)   American Hebraist. He is believed to have been born in Algiers or Italy. He was educated in Livorno and Amsterdam, and later settled in the US, where he was admitted as a freeman of New York in 1715. In 1722 he was baptised in the hall of Harvard College in Cambridge, Massachusetts. In the same year he was appointed instructor of Hebrew at the college. His essays are an apology for and defence of his new faith. His *Dickdook Leshon Gnebreet: a Grammar of the Hebrew Tongue* was published in 1735.

Montheism   The belief that there is only one God. Jewish monotheism is enshrined in the Shema (confession of faith): 'Hear, O Israel, the Lord our God, the Lord is one' (Deuteronomy 6:4). The doctrine of Jewish monotheism describes God as holy, transcendent, immanent, eternal, omnipresent, omniscient, omnipotent and all-good. As creator of the universe, he is also a redeemer of humanity, just, compassionate and merciful and ready to answer the prayers of humankind. In the Middle Ages Jewish theologians discussed a wide range of issues connected with this concept of God.

Monsky, Henry (1890–1947)   American communal leader of Russian origin. He lived in Omaha, Nebraska, where he was active in Jewish and communal organisations. An ardent Zionist, he was the principal organiser of the American Jewish Conference of 1943. In 1945 he served as a consultant to the US delegation to the United Nations Organising Conference in San Francisco. He was President of the Supreme Lodge of B'nai B'rith from 1943 until his death.

Montagu, Edwin Samuel (1879–1924)   English politician, son of Samuel Montagu. He was elected to parliament in 1906, and served as Parliamentary Under-Secretary of State for India from 1910 to 1914. In that year he became Financial Secretary to the Treasury, and in 1916 Chancellor of the Duchy of Lancaster and Minister of Munitions. From 1917 to 1922 he was Secretary of State for India. He was an opponent of Zionism and the Balfour Declaration.

Montagu, Edwin Edward Samuel (1901–1985)   English lawyer and communal leader, grandson of Samuel Montagu. He was Judge-Advocate of the Fleet and Chairman of the Middlesex Quarter Sessions. He served as President of the United Synagogues (the federation of Ashkenazi synagogues in tte UK) from 1954 to 1962.

Montagu, Lilian Helen (1873–1963)   English social worker and magistrate, daughter of Samuel Montagu. She founded the West Central Girls' Club in London in 1893. Together with Claude Goldsmid Montefiore, she established the Jewish Religious Union in 1902, and the World Union for Progressive Judaism in 1926.

Montagu, Samuel, 1st Baron Swaythling (1832–1911)   English banker and communal leader. He was born in Liverpool. In 1835 he founded the merchant bankers Samuel Montagu and Company. He served as the Liberal member of parliament for Whitechapel from 1885 to 1900. In 1894 he was made a baronet, and in 1907 a baron. He was the leader in Britain of Orthodox Russian Jewish immigrants, and in 1887 founded the Federation of Synagogues. He travelled to Palestine, Russia and the US on behalf of Jewry, but was an opponent of Zionism.

Montefiore, Claude Joseph Goldsmid (1858–1938) English theologian and leader of Liberal Judaism. He studied at Balliol College, Oxford, and the Hochschule für Wissenschaft des Judentums in Berlin. In 1888 he founded the scholarly journal the *Jewish Quarterly Review*. He was a founder of the Jewish Religious Union in 1902, which led to the establishment in 1926 of the Liberal Jewish Synagogue in London. In 1926 he was elected President of the World Union for Progressive Judaism. With Baron von Hügel, he founded the London Society for the Study of Religion. An opponent of Zionism, he served as President of the Anglo-Jewish Association. His writings include *Aspects of Judaism, The Synoptic Gospels, Liberal Judaism, Outlines of Liberal Judaism,* and *Rabbinic Literature and Gospel Teaching.* With Herbert Loewe he edited *A Rabbinic Anthology.*

Montefiore, Francis Abraham (1860–1935) English Sephardi leader. A supporter of Theodor Herzl, he was active in Ḥibbat Zion, and served as Chairman of the English Zionist Federation.

Montefiore, Sir Moses (1784–1855) British communal leader. He was born in Livorno, but grew up in London, where he worked as a broker. An observant Jew, he maintained his own synagogue in Ramsgate from 1833. He was an opponent of Reform Judaism. In 1837 he was Sheriff of the City of London, and he was the first Jew to be knighted in Britain. He went on a mission to the Levant with Isaac-Adolphe Crémieux in 1840 at the time of the Damascus Affair, and he intervened with their governments on behalf of the Jews of Russia, Morocco and Romania. He visited Palestine on several occasions and worked to improve the conditions under which the Jewish community lived there. From 1838 to 1874 he was President of the Board of Deputies of British Jews.

Months The months of the Jewish year are Nisan, Iyyar, Sivan, Tammuz, Av, Elul, Tishri, Ḥeshvan, Kislev, Tevet, Shevat and Adar.

Montor, Henry (1905–1982) American Zionist, of Canadian origin. He was assistant editor of the journal *New Palestine* from 1926 to 1930. He served with the United Palestine Appeal (1930–39), and was then Executive Vice-President of the United Jewish Appeal (1939–50). Later he was Vice-President and Chief Executive of the American financial and Development Corporation for Israel.

Moon, Blessing of the (Hebrew 'Kiddush levenah') Prayer of thanksgiving recited at the appearance of the new moon. According to tradition, a quorum ('minyan') of ten adult men is required to perform this rite, which usually takes place at the close of the Sabbath in the synagogue courtyard on any day between the 3rd and 15th days of the lunar month (when the moon is waxing).

Mor [Friedmann-Yellin], Nathan (1913–1980) Israeli public figure. He was born in Poland, and settled in Palestine in 1941. He joined the underground terrorist movement Loḥame Ḥerut Yisrael, which he headed from 1943. After the assassination of Count Bernadotte in 1948, he was sentenced to prison, but he was freed under the terms of the general amnesty of February 1949. He represented the Fighters' Party in the first Knesset. Later he was active in Semitic Action, which supported the idea of a Jewish-Arab federation.

Morais, Sabato (1823–1897) American rabbi. He was born in Livorno. At the age of 22 he became assistant ḥazzan to the Spanish and Portuguese congregation in London. In 1852 he became ḥazzan to the Mikveh Israel Congregation in Philadelphia. A leading opponent of Reform, he was an Abolitionist during the Civil War. In 1856 he helped to establish the Jewish Theological Seminary and he then served as President of its faculty.

Mordecai (fl. 5th cent. BCE) Persian palace official at Shushan during the reign of Ahasuerus. His niece Esther was part of the king's harem. Through her Mordecai informed the king of an assassination plot against him. Later when Mordecai refused to bow to the vizier Haman, the vizier resolved to avenge himself on the Jewish population. His plan was frustrated by Esther. Haman was hanged, and Mordecai assumed Haman's position as chief minister. These events are recorded in the Book of Esther.

Mordecai ben Hillel (fl. 13th cent.) German codifier. He lived in Numemberg, where he died a martyr's death in the Rindfleisch massacres along with his wife and five children. His *Sepher Mordekhai* is a compendium in the style of the tosaphot, dealing with talmudic problems. He also wrote responsa and liturgical poetry.

Morenu ('Our teacher') Title accorded to distinguished rabbis. Introduced to Germany in the 14th century, it spread to other countries.

Morgenstern, Julian (1881–1976) American biblical scholar. He was born in St. Francisville, Illinois. He served as a rabbi in Lafayette, Indiana, and later taught at the Hebrew Union College, where he became President in 1922.

He published studies of a wide range of biblical topics.

Morgenthau, Henry (1856–1946) American financier and diplomat. He was born in Mannheim, Germany, and settled in the US in 1865. Initially he practised law, but then became active in real estate and banking. From 1913 to 1916 he was US Ambassador to Turkey. He was active in secular as well as Jewish religious and philanthropic work.

Morpurgo, Samson (1681–1740) Italian rabbi and physician. He was born in Gradisca d'Isonzo, in Friuli. He became a member of the bet din of the Kabbalist Joseph Fiametta in 1709 and he later served as a rabbi in Ancona. He had contacts with all the great scholars of his generation, and his skills as a doctor widely recognised. In 1713 he was involved in the polemics of the rabbis against Nehemiah Ḥayyon. He published a polemic against the priest Luigi Maria Benetelli, who wrote an anti-Semitic work. He also published numerous responsa and a philosophical commentary on Jedaiah Bedersi's *Beḥinat Olam*.

Mortara, Marco (1815–1894) Italian rabbi and scholar. From 1842 he served as rabbi of Mantua. An advocate of reform, he published books on the principles of Judaism and a new edition of the prayer book. He produced a catalogue of the manuscripts in the library of the Mantua community, and a list of Jewish scholars who lived in Italy form the 1st to the 19th centuries.

Morteira, Saul Levi (c.1596–1660) Dutch rabbi and scholar, of Venetian origin. He became Ḥakham of the Beit Ya'akov community in Amsterdam, and founded the Keter Torah Yeshivah there. He was a member of the bet din that excommunicated Benedict Spinoza. His *Givat Shaul* is a collection of sermons. He also wrote responsa and Jewish apologetics.

Moser (betrayer')   Term used among the Ashkenazim to refer to an informer who denounces fellow Jews to the secular authority. In southern Europe the equivalent term is 'malsin'.

Moses (fl.? 13th century BCE)   Lawgiver, leader of the Israelites, and prophet. He was born in Egypt to Amram and Jochebed, who hid him in a basket among the reeds of the Nile to escape Pharaoh's decree to slaughter all newborn Jewish males. He was found by Pharaoh's daughter, who raised him in the royal household. In early manhood he killed an Egyptian who he discovered beating a Hebrew. He fled to Midian and became a shepherd to the local priest Jethro, whose daughter, Zipporah, he married. She bore him two sons. While keeping Jethro's sheep on Mount Horeb he encountered God, who spoke to him from the burning bush and commanded him to free the Hebrew slaves. He interceded with Pharaoh who eventually released the Hebrews after ten plagues had afflicted Egypt. Moses led the people across the Red Sea, which miraculously parted to let them pass, and guided them for 40 years in the desert. On Mount Sinai he recieved God's revelation of the law, embodied in the Ten Commandments written on tablets of stone. Before his death, he appointed Joshua his successor.

Moses, Adolph (1840–1902)   American rabbi, of Polish origin. He emigrated to the US in 1870 and served as rabbi to the Reform congregation in Louisville from 1882 until his death. With Isaac S. Moses and Emil G. Hirsch, he edited the German-language weekly *Zeitgeist*. A collection of his writings appeared posthumously as *Yahvism and Other Discourses*.

Moses, Assumption of   Apocryphal work. It relates the address given by Moses to Joshua in the form of a prophecy. It also includes a history of Israel to the time of Herod. In an additional section, which is now lost, the death of Moses and the war between Satan and the archangel Michael over his body are depicted.

Moses, Blessing of   Title given to Deuteronomy 33, which records the blessing of the tribes of Israel by Moses before his death. Poetic in form, this text consists of a blessing for each tribe (except Simeon) and a blessing for the entire people.

Moses, Seat of   Term used of a place in the synagogue which cannot be identified with certainty. According to Matthew 23:2 it was the seat occupied by the scribes and Pharisees. Some scholars maintain that it was either the place of the rabbi, or the stand where the Sepher Torah was placed.

Moses, Song of [Haazinu]   Title given to the speech made by Moses before his death; it is recorded in Deuteronomy 32. It foretells the disasters that will occur if the Torah is disobeyed, and describes God's love for Israel. It is also known by its initial word 'Haazinu' [Hearken].

Moses ben Enoch (fl. 10th cent.)   Spanish scholar. In the story of the Four Captives in *The Book of Tradition*, Abraham ibn Daud relates that four rabbis (including Moses ben Enoch) were captured by Saracen pirates after they sailed from Bari in southern Italy in 972. Moses ben Enoch was ransomed in Córdoba, and was appointed rabbi of the community.

Moses ben Isaac di Rieti [Rieti, Moses of] (1388–c.1460)   Italian physician, philosopher and poet. He worked as a physician at Rieti until 1422, and then lived in Perugia, Narni, Fabriano and Rome, where he was a rabbi and physician to Pope Pius II. His *Mikdash Me'at* is a moral and philosophical poem in *terza rima*. It contains a vision of Paradise, and an account of Jewish scholars down to his own time. He also wrote medical and other philosophical studies.

Moses ben Jacob of Coucy (fl. 13th cent.) French scholar. An itinerant preacher, he began his ministry in Spain in 1236, where he preached sermons that attracted a huge audience. Later he visited other countries, and participated in the Disputation of Paris in 1240. His *Sepher Mitzvot Gadol* (also known as *Semag*) contains the Oral Law presented as groups of positive and negative commandments. His other writings include the *Tosaphot Yeshanim* and a commentary on the Torah.

Moses ben Jacob of Russia (1449–1520) Ukrainian talmudic author. He was born in Seduva, Lithuania. He lived in Kiev, where he pursued his studies as a biblical exegete, talmudist, poet, linguist and Kabbalist. When the Tartars attacked the city in 1482 he escaped, but his children were taken captive to the Crimea. After ransoming them, he returned to Kiev. In 1495 the Jews of Lithuania and Ukraine were expelled, and he was forced to wander. In 1506 he was himself taken captive by the Tartars and was ransomed by the Jews of Salkhat. He then settled in Kaffa, where he became rabbi and head of the community. His writings include a liturgy according to the Crimean rite.

Moses ben Shem Tov de Léon (1250–1305) Spanish Kabbalist. He lived in Guadalajara and, from 1290, in Avila. He wrote some 20 kabbalistic works and is known for his revelation of the *Zohar*. According to kabbalistic tradition, the book (attributed to Simeon ben Yohai) was sent by Nahmanides from Palestine to Spain, where it reached Moses ben Shemtov, who made it known.

Moses ha-Darshan [Narboni, Moses] (fl. 11th cent.) French scholar. He lived in Narbonne. His writings, notably commentaries on the Bible, influenced Rashi.

Moses of London (fl. 13th cent) English grammarian, halakhist and Jewish scholar. His *Darkhe ha-Nikkud veha-Neginah* is a treatise on Hebrew punctuation and accentuation.

Moses of Narbonne [Maestro Vidal Blasom] (fl. 14th cent.) French philosopher, translator and physician. His commentary on Maimonides *Guide for the Perplexed* is based on an Aristotelian-Averroistic perspective.

Moses of Sodilkov [Ephraim Moses Hayyim of Sodilkov] (c.1737–c.1800) Ukrainian Hasidic leader, grandson of Israel Baal Shem Tov. He studied under Dov Ber of Mezhirich and lived as a rabbi and preacher in Sodikov in Volhynia. His *Degel Mahaneh Ephraim* is based on the doctrines of the Baal Shem Tov and teaches that the goal of Hasidism is humility and self-evaluation. The role of the tzaddikim is to reprove and reform those who are negligent, and to elevate the people through prayer and religious teaching.

Moshav zekenim Old people's home.

Moss, Celia (1819–1873) English writer. Together with her sister Marian Moss, she wrote *The Romance of Jewish History* and *Tales of Jewish History*.

Mosse, Rudolf (1843–1920) German publisher and philanthropist. He was born in Oraetz. He founded an advertising business in 1867, and several years later established the *Berliner Tageblatt*, one of Germany's leading newspapers. In 1880 he acquired the *Allgemeine Zeitung des Judentums*. His activities on behalf of the community included the setting up of a hospital in Graetz and the founding of an educational institute in Wilhelmsdorf.

Mother According to the Bible, and the *Talmud*, the mother has equal rights with the father in the moral and ethical sphere to the respect and defence of her children. The duty of honouring both parents is enjoined by the fifth of the Ten Commandments. Similarly the punishmnent for smiting or cursing parents applies to such actions against the mother as well as the father. Traditionally Jewish status is derived from the mother. The mother is the symbol of home and family life for which she is responsible. In Jewish tradition the four matriarchs (Sarah, Rebekah, Rachel and Leah) are to be revered equally with the patriarchs (Abraham, Isaac and Jacob).

Motke Ḥabad [Rakover, Mordecai] (fl. 18th cent.) Lithuanian jester. He was a famous figure among Lithuanian Jewry.

Motta, Jacob de la (1789–1845) American physician and communal leader. He was born in Savannah, Georgia. He served as an army surgeon in the War of 1812. He was prominent in Jewish communal life in Savannah and later in Charleston, South Carolina.

Motzkin, Leo (1867–1933) Ukrainian Zionist leader. He was born in Brovary, near Kiev. In 1887 he helped to found the Russian Jewish Scientific Society in Berlin, which included Jewish students from Russia and Galicia who supported the Ḥibbat Zion movement. A follower of Theodor Herzl, he was active in the Zionist movement. In 1901 he joined the Democratic Fraction, formed at the Fifth Zionist Congress. During World War I he directed the Zionist bureau in Copenhagen, and in 1919 he acted as Secretary and President of the Comité des Délégations Juives at the Paris Peace Conference. In 1925 he was appointed Chairman of the Zionist Executive. He served in this capacity and as head of the organisation of European National Minorities until his death in 1933. His publications include a history of Russian pogroms.

Mount Sinai Mountain in the wilderness of Horeb on the Sinai peninsula. The Book of Deuteronomy identifies Mount Sinai with Mount Horeb and they are thus sometimes confused. The Israelites camped at the foot of Mount Sinai after the Exodus from Egypt

(Exodus 19:1), and Moses ascended the mountain to receive the Ten Commandments (Exodus 20:1–24:8). According to rabbinic tradition, Moses received both the Written Law and the Oral Law there.

Mourning (Hebrew 'avelut') Mourning customs during the biblical period involved the rending of garments, wearing sackcloth, sitting on the ground, placing earth and dust on the head, and weeping. Other practices were added during the talmudic period. In contemporary practice mourning begins after the burial of a close relative. The bereaved person puts on splendid garments, takes off his shoes, remains in the home for seven days of mourning sitting on a low stool, refrains from attending the synagogue except on the Sabbath, and reads Scripture. No work may be done and sexual intercourse is forbidden. It is the duty of friends and relatives to visit the mourner during this period. Parents are mourned intensively for 30 days, during which the hair and beard are left uncut and no weddings or joyful ceremonies may take place. A lesser state of mourning continues until 12 months after the burial. In post-talmudic times some alterations to these mourning customs took place, but most continued to be observed. A major innovation was the kindling of a lamp during the mourning period, and the recitation of the Kaddish prayer for 11 months after the burial of a parent or child, and each year on the anniversary of the death.

Mühlausen, Yomtov Lipmann [Lipmann, Yomtov ben Solomon; Yomtov Lipmann] (fl. 14th–15th cent.) Bohemian scholar, philosopher, Kabbalist and polemicist. He lived in Prague, where he participated in a disputation with the apostate Peter (Pesaḥ), who alleged that the Jews blasphemed Christian beliefs. Eighty Jews were martyred as a consequence, but Muhlausen was saved. His *Sepher Nitzaḥon* contains a depiction of this disputation.

Mukdoni [Kappel], Alexander (1877–1958) American Yiddish essayist and theatre critic. He was born in Lyakhovichi in Belorussia. After World War I he edited the Yiddish daily *Nayes*, produced in Kovno. In 1922 he settled in the US where he wrote for the Yiddish daily *Jewish Morning Journal*. He wrote stories, essays and memoirs.

Muktzeh ('things' set aside') Objects that a Jews must not handle on the Sabbath or festivals. The *Talmud* specifies several categories of forbidden objects: (1) money and tools the nature of which renders them unfit for use on the Sabbath or Festivals because of their connection with work; (2) objects not normally used; (3) objects that were not in existence or were inaccessible at the beginning of the Sabbath or festival; (4) objects that at the beginning of the Sabbath or festival were being used as a support or base for others which it is forbidden to use.

Müller, Joel (1827–1895) Moravian rabbinic scholar. He was born at Mährisch Ostrau and served as a rabbi there, and later in Leipa, Bohemia. After teaching religion in Vienna, he took up a post at the Berlin Hochschule für die Wissenschaft des Judentums. He published studies of gaonic and French responsa.

Müller-Cohen, Anita (1890–1962) Austrian social worker. She was born in Vienna. She served as a relief worker in Galicia and Bukovina during World War I. She established hospitals for mothers, day nurseries, medical services for children, and institutions for the care of the aged. After the war she helped returning soldiers to readjust to civilian life and established milk stations for undernourished children in Austria. She also directed the placement of orphans in Jewish homes. In 1936 she settled in Tel Aviv.

Mumar Apostate. Although an apostate is regarded as a sinner under Jewish law

and is denied certain rights and privileges, he still retains his status as a Jew. A distinction is made between a 'mumar le-hakis' (who violates a precept in a spirit of rebellion and denial of its divine authority), and a 'mumar le-te'avon' (who violates the precept because he is unable to withstand temptation). The *Talmud* classifies apostates in various categories: (1) one who violates a single commandment; (2) one who regularly violates a particular precept; and (3) one who violates the whole Torah.

Muni, Paul [Weissenfreund, Muni] (1895–1967) American actor. He began acting at the age of 12 in Chicago and in 1918 joined the Yiddish Art Theatre in New York. He appeared in numerous plays on Broadway as well as in films.

Muñiz, Angelina (b.1936) Mexican novelist, of Fench origin. She was a lecturer in literature at the Colegio de México and the Universidad Nacional Autónoma de México His publications include *Morada interior, Tierra adentro, La guerra del unicornio, and Huerto cerrado, huerto sellado*. Her works deal with Jewish cultural and religious themes.

Munk, Salomon (1803–1867) French orientalist. He was born in Glogau, Silesia. He settled in Paris in 1828, where he took charge of Semitic manuscripts at the Bibliothèque Nationale. In 1840 he joined the delegation to Egypt led by Sir Moses Montefiore and Isaac-Adolphe Crémieux, and intervened in the Damascus Affair. He became blind in 1850, but was nevertheless appointed Professor of Hebrew and Syriac Literature at the Collège de France in 1864. His writings include studies of Hebrew and Arabic literature of the Golden Age of Spain, as well as an edition of the Arabic text of Maimonides' *Guide for the Perplexed*.

Münster, Sebastian (1849–1552) German Hebraist and reformer. He was born in Ingelheim. He taught Hebrew at Heidelberg, and became Professor of Hebrew at Basle University in 1528. One of the outstanding Christian Hebraists of the 16th century, he edited the Hebrew Bible, translated the Gospel of Matthew into Hebrew, wrote grammars of biblical Aramaic and rabbinic Hebrew, and translated the grammatical works of Elijah Levita into Latin.

Münz [Minz], Judah (c.1409–1509) German rabbi. After the Jews were expelled from Mainz in 1461, he settled in Padua, where he founded a yeshivah and taught philosophy at the university; he remained in Italy for the rest of his life. He wrote numerous responsa and engaged in a polemic with Elijah Delmedigo.

Münz [Minz], Moses (c. 1750–1831) Hungarian rabbi. He was born either in Podolia or in Galicia. He served as a rabbi in Vishravitz and Brody, then in 1789 was appointed rabbi of Alt-Ofen, where he represented the Jewish community at Royal ceremonies. In 1793 he became Chief Rabbi of the entire Pest region. Initially tolerant of reformers, he later became antagonistic towards them. He wrote responsa and published (with annotations) the *Peri Ya'akov* of Jacob ben Moses.

Murder [homicide] According to Hebrew law, the penalty for premeditated murder, witnessed by two individuals who warned the perpetrator of the seriousness of the crime before it was committed, is beheading. Yet the law requires such meticulous proof of the details of the act that, for practical purposes, it became impossible to impose capital punishment. Under these circumstances, the guilty person was sentenced to imprisonment. When the murder was not premeditated, the killer could flee to one of the cities of refuge.

Musaph ('additional sacrifice') Service comprising an additional Amidah which is recited on those days when an additional sacrifice was formerly offered in the Temple (Sabbaths, New Moons, the three pilgrim festivals, New Year and the Day of Atonement). It can take place at any time of the day before the seventh hour.

Musar In biblical Hebrew the word is used variously to mean punishment or chastisement and instruction. Later it came to signify morals, ethics and moral instruction. In the Middle Ages, a distinct branch of literature developed, known as 'musar literature', which dealt with moral and ethical matters. In the modern period the word has connotations of sermonising and denotes a type of literature of edification.

Muselman (German: 'Muslim') The word became a colloquial term for the victims of the concentration camps in the Nazi period who were resigned to their impending death.

Museums Jewish museums are a relatively new phenomenon resulting from the development of scholarly research into Judaica in Western and Eastern Europe and the US at the end of the 19th century and beginning of the 20th. From this period exhibitions of Judaica began to be organised, and the interest generated led to the founding of numerous Jewish museums through the world notably in Europe (Vienna, Frankfurt am Main, Gdansk, Berlin, London and Paris), the US (New York), and Israel (Jerusalem and Tel Aviv).

Music In early biblical history Jewish music and musical instruments are frequently mentioned. In the Temple the Levites organised the performance of the service, and trained singers, players and conductors. After the Babylonian exile, a decline in instrumental music took place, and with the destruction of the Second Temple, Jewish music was restricted to chanting in the synagogue. Services were sung in traditional chant by the ḥazzan (or cantor), who might, however, embellish the melodies. Jewish musical life in Eastern Europe culminated in the worship of the Ḥasidim, which placed emphasis on ecstatic religious music. In modern times there has been a resurgence of interest in the development of music in the Jewish world, and many works have been written for the concert hall that take Jewish events as their subjects, or use Hebrew words or melodies.

Myrtle   One of the four species of plant, branches of which are used ceremonially on the feast of Sukkot.

N

A Jewish dentist goes to see an Orthodox rabbi and asks for a mezuzah (a box with prayers normally fixed on a doorpost) for his Jaguar. The Orthodox rabbi is outraged, tells him that one doesn't put a mezuzah on a car, and says he should go see the Conservative rabbi whose synagogue is nearby. He arranges an appointment with the Conservative rabbi, only to be told the idea is utterly stupid. The Conservative rabbi then tells him to go see the Reform rabbi whose Temple is around the corner. When he meets with the Reform rabbi, he asks if he can have a mezuzah for his Jaguar. The rabbi tells him that he has a Jaguar too. It was a gift from his wife's parents. He asks what model the rich man has, and how many miles he gets to the gallon. Then the Reform rabbi asks: 'What's a mezuzah?'

* * * * *

There are numerous jokes about Orthodox and non-Orthodox rabbis. Often they make fun of the non-Orthodox rabbi's lack of knowledge about the tradition. Here the Reform rabbi is rudely depicted as not knowing what a mezuzah is. Such a caricature is amusing, but is a stinging critique of modern Jewish life.

Naaman (fl. 9th cent. BCE) Syrian commander-in-chief. He suffered from leprosy and was sent by his king to search for a cure in Israel. After Elisha had cured him he was overtaken on his return journey to Damascus by Elisha's servant Gehazi, who obtained gifts from him by pretending that Elisha would distribute them to the poor. When Elisha discovered this deception, he inflicted Naaman's leprosy on Gehazi (II Kings 5).

Nabal (fl. 11th–10th cent. BCE) Israelite landowner, husband of Abigail. He was a wealthy man, the owner of thousands of sheep and goats in Carmel. When ten young followers of David visited him he received them inhospitably. David gathered a band of 400 together to take revenge on Nabal, but was appeased by Abigail. However, Nabal did not escape. He was killed by God a few days later, and David married Abigail (I Samuel 25).

Naboth (fl. 9th cent. BCE) Israelite landowner. He possessed a vineyard, which Ahab coveted. When Naboth refused to give it up, Ahab's queen Jezebel plotted to bring about his downfall. She persuaded the local elders to honour Naboth and then to bring false evidence of blasphemy against him. Eventually he was stoned to death. This act led Elijah to predict the downfall of Ahab (I Kings 21: II Kings 9).

Nadab (i) (fl.? 13th cent. BCE) Israelite priest, eldest son of Aaron. With his brother Abihu, he ascended Mount Sinai to behold God's revelation (Exodus 24:1–11). Later they made a fire sacrifice on the altar against God's will and were struck dead by fire as a punishment (Leviticus 10:1–3).

Nadab (ii) (fl. 10th cent. BCE)   King of Israel (907–906 BCE), son and successor of Jeroboam I. He and the House of Jeroboam were assassinated by Baasha (I Kings 15:25–31).

Nadel, Arno (1878–1943)   German poet and musicologist. He was born in Vilnius. He became conductor of the choir at the synagogue in Pestlozzistrasse in Berlin, and later was the musical supervisor of the Berlin synagogues. He published poetry, collected synagogue music and Eastern-European Jewish folk songs, painted portraits and landscapes, and composed music.

Nadir, Moshe [Reiss, Isaac] (1885–1943)   American Yiddish writer. He was born in eastern Galicia, and emigrated to New York in 1898. He contributed to numerous literary publications, and wrote poetry, drama and essays.

Nagid ('prince')   Head of the Jewish communities in Islamic countries (except under Abbasid rule, 750–1258, when the Jews were led by the exilarch). From the 10th century there was a nagid in Spain, Kairouan, Egypt and Yemen, and from the 16th century to the 19th in Morocco, Algeria and Tunisia; the office was discontinued in the 19th century.

Nahmanides [Bonastruc de Porta; Moses Ben Nahman; Ramban] (1194–1270)   Spanish talmudist, kabbalist and biblical commentator. He is commonly known by the name Nahmanides, though his Hebrew name was Moses ben Nahman and his Spanish name Bonastruc de Porta. The name Ramban is derived from the title Rabbi Moses ben Nahman. He served as rabbi of Gerona. In 1263 he was challenged by Pablo Christiani to a religious disputation, which took place in Barcelona in the presence of King James I (1213–

1276). Later he was tried for blasphemy and forced to leave Spain. From 1267 he lived in Palestine, settling in Acre. Nahmanides was regarded as the foremost Spanish talmudist of his day. Among his works are *Torat ha-Adam*, which deals with the rites of mourning, and a popular Bible commentary.

Nahman of Bratzlav (1772–1811)   Ukrainian Hasidic leader, greatgrandson of the Baal Shem Tov. He was born in Medzhibozh and lived in Medvedevka in the province of Kiev, where he attracted many disciples. In 1798 he went to Palestine, but later emigrated to Zlatopol in the province of Kiev where he engaged in controversy with Aryeh Leib of Spola. In 1802 he moved to Bratslav. His various journeys are described in works by his disciple Nathan Sternhartz. In 1810 he settled in the Ukrainian city of Uman. In his teachings he emphasised simple faith and prayer, and developed the theory of the tzaddik as the intermediary between man and God.

Nahoum, Haim (1873–1960)   Turkish rabbi and scholar. He went to Abyssinia in 1907 to investigate the Falashas. From 1908 to 1920 he served as Hakham Bashi of Turkey, and from 1923 he was Chief Rabbi of Cairo; he was later appointed Chief Rabbi of Egypt. He also served as a member of the Egyptian Senate.

Nahshon (fl.? 13th cent. BCE)   Israelite, chief of the tribe of Judah during the Exodus and the wandering in the desert; he was the brother-in-law of Aaron. According to rabbinic tradition, he was the first Israelite to embark on the crossing of the Red Sea during the flight from Egypt.

Nahum ('Comfort')   The name of a prayer, instituted by Palestinian amoraim, which is recited in the Amidah of the afternoon service on the Ninth of Av. It consists of a supplication for comfort for those who mourn Zion, and a prayer for the rebuilding of the city.

Nahum   Biblical book, one of the books of the 12 Minor Prophets. It records the prophecies of the Israelite prophet Nahum (fl. 7th century BCE) concerning the fall of Nineveh.

Nahum of Gimzo (fl. 1st–2nd cent.)   Palestinian tanna. His system of exegesis was based on the view that in the Torah the untranslated Hebrew particle 'et' signifies that the word it precedes should be given a wide rather than a narrow connotation. This method was developed by his pupil Akiva. He was known for his saying 'gam zo le-tovah' (this is also for good) when confronting misfortune; this has been understood as the basis for the name 'Gimzo'.

Naiditsch, Isaac (1868–1949)   Russian philanthropist and Zionist. He was born in Pinsk, and lived in Moscow, where he was an alcohol industrialist. An ardent Zionist, he contributed to Hebrew periodicals. At the beginning of World War I he was a founder and Director of the Central Committee for the Relief of Jewish War Sufferers. After the Russian Revolution, he became a strong supporter of Hebrew culture. Later he emigrated to France, but fled to the US during the Nazi occupation. He returned to Paris in 1941. He was a friend and adviser of Chaim Weizmann.

Najara, Israel ben Moses (c.1555–c.1623)   Syrian Hebrew poet. Born in Damascus, he was secretary to the Jewish community there. In 1587 he published two collections of hymns, *Zemirot Yisrael* and *Mesaheket ba-Tevel*, in Safed. Later he served as a rabbi in Gaza.

Nakdanim   ('punctuators')   Name given to a group of scholars (active from the 9th to the 14th centuries), who provided biblical manuscripts with vowels and accents. Successors of the masoretes, they lived in the Orient and in England, France and Germany.

Nakhes (Yiddish)   Pleasure.

Name, change of   The Bible contains a number of accounts of God changing a person's name (Abram to Abraham, Sarai to Sarah, Jacob to Israel). According to the *Talmud*, a person's name is customarily changed if the individual is dangerously ill; this was regarded as a means of misleading the Angel of Death. The change is conferred at a short ceremony in which charity is given on behalf of the invalid, a blessing is recited, and a formula is read announcing the additional name. A prayer is then recited asking for renewed life for the person with the new name.

Names   Biblical names in the early period were based on Hebrew roots and often (for reasons which are not known) incorporated the name of Baal (e.g. Ishbaal). Later monotheistic attitudes were reflected in names based on such prefixes as El- or Jeho-(Eliezer etc.), and in suffixes such as -el, -eli, or -jahu. At the end of the Second Temple period, Greek names were often used in conjunction with Hebrew, and Aramaic forms were found in Palestine and Babylonia. In the Middle Ages vernacular equivalents (often based on the blessings of Jacob or Moses) were used alongside Hebrew names. Although surnames appeared in Italy and Spain in the medieval period patronymics were generally employed in Jewish communities. Surnames in the modern sense were used in Western European countries and in the US from the 18th century. Surnames were often patronymic, geographical or occupational in character. In the 19th century, it was usual for Jews to adopt names of a non-Jewish nature, whereas in Israel in the 20th century the opposite process has taken place.

Namier, Sir Lewis Bernstein (1888–1960)   British historian and Zionist. He was born in eastern Galicia. He was Professor of Modern History at Manchester University from 1931. An ardent Zionist, he served as Political

Secretary of the Jewish Agency from 1929 to 1931. He wrote studies of the social-political structure of England in the 18th century, the 1848 revolutions, the Habsburg monarchy, and the events leading up to World War II.

Namir, Mordekhai (1897–1975) Israeli politician. Born in Bratolinbovka, Ukraine, he settled in Palestine in 1924. From 1929–1935 he was the director of the statistical section of the Histadrut, and in 1936–43 he served as Secretary-General of the Tel Aviv Workers' Council. After the establishment of the State of Israel in 1948 he held diplomatic posts in Bulgaria, Czechoslovakia, Romania and the USSR. From 1951 he served in the Knesset, and became Minister of Labour. He was the first mayor of Tel Aviv.

Naomi (fl. 12th–11th cent. BCE) Israelite woman, wife of Elimelech. With her husband and sons (Mahlon and Chilion), she left Bethlehem for Moab during a famine. After several years, during which time Elimelech and her sons died, she returned with Ruth, her daughter-in-law, whom she helped to marry the Israelite landowner Boaz.

Naphtali (fl.? 16th cent. BCE) Israelite, sixth son of Jacob and second son of Bilhah, Rachel's maid (Genesis 30:7). The tribe of Naphtali was named after him.

Naphtali, Peretz (1888–1961) Israeli economist. He was born in Germany. He served as economic editor of the *Frankfurter Zeitung* (1921–26) and manager of the Labour Movement's Economic Research Bureau in Berlin (1926–33). He settled in Palestine in 1933 and directed the Workers' Bank from 1938 to 1949. He was then elected a Mapai member of the Knesset; during his ten years in parliament (1949–59) he was Minister without Portfolio (1951–52, 1955–59), and Minister of Agriculture (1952–55).

Nardi, Naḥum (1901–1977) Israeli composer. He was born in Kiev. After studying the piano and composition at the Kiev, Warsaw and Vienna conservatories, he emigrated to Palestine in 1923 where he gave piano recitals and began composing. His work was inspired by Arab bedouin and peasant songs, as well as Sephardi and Yemenite melodies.

Nash [nosh] (Yiddish) Snack.

Nashim ('Women') Third order of the Mishnah. It deals with betrothal, marriage, divorce, the relationship between husband and wife, vows and the law of the Nazirite.

Nashn [noshen] (Yiddish) To eat a little something between meals.

Nasi ('prince') The title accorded in the *Talmud* to the president of the Sanhedrin. He served as spiritual head, and subsequently political representative of the Jewish people. The second in authority to the Nasi was the av bet din ('president of the court'). From the 2nd century CE the nasi was recognised by the Roman authorities as Patriarch of the Jews. Later the title was used in some places to designate the lay leader of the Jewish community.

Nasi [Mendes], Gracia (c.1510–1569) Portuguese Marrano stateswoman and patroness. She was born in Portugal (as Beatrice de Luna), and married the banker Francisco Mendes. On his death she went to Antwerp in 1537. Fearing religious persecution, she escaped to Venice in 1545, but she was denounced and imprisoned there. Released 1549, she moved to Ferrara, where she was known as a Jewess and became a patron of writers. She also controlled an underground organisation which rescued Marranos from Portugal. In 1553 she went to Constantinople, where she became known as Gracia Nasi. Joined by her nephew Joseph Nasi, she became the leader of Turkish Jewry. She built synagogues, helped fugitive Marranos, and began a project for the colonisation of Tiberias.

Nasi, Joseph, Duke of Naxos (c.1524–1579) Portuguese statesman, active in Turkey. He was born a Marrano in Portugal, under the name Joao Micas. He accompanied his aunt Gracia Mendes when she went from Lisbon to Antwerp in 1537, but when in 1545 she fled to Italy, he remained behind to settle her affairs. In 1554 he joined her in Constantinople where he embraced Judaism publicly and married her daughter, Reyna. He became an intimate of Selim, the heir to the Turkish throne. In 1561 he obtained from the sultan the lease of Tiberias and control of an adjacent area, which he developed as a Jewish centre. He was eventually created Duke of Naxos and the Cyclades.

Nassy, David (fl. 18th cent.) Caribbean physician and communal leader. He was born in Surinam, and became President of the Jewish community there. His *Essai historique sur la colonie de Surinam* is a record of the Jewish role in the colony's history. Eventually he settled in Philadelphia and became the first Jewish physician to practise in the city. In 1795 he returned to Surinam, where he went into business. Later he published a tract supporting the emancipation of Dutch Jewry.

Nathan (i) (fl. 11th–10th cent. BCE) Israelite prophet. He prophesied during the reign of King David, and declared to David that his royal dynasty would be established perpetually. Yet he prevented David from building a Temple in Jerusalem and accused him of plotting the death of Uriah the Hittite. Subsequently he was instrumental in securing Solomon's succession. According to I Chronicles 29:29, he wrote an account of David' reign.

Nathan (ii) (fl. 2nd cent.) Palestinian tanna and son of the exilarch. He went to Palestine to study, but was forced to leave during the Hadrianic persecutions. Later he returned and became President of the Court at Usha. An expert judge in civil suits, he was opposed to fixing the calendar outside Palestine. The *Avot de-Rabbi Natan* is attributed to him.

Nathan, Isaac (?1790–1864) Australian composer, singer and writer. He was born in Canterbury, England, and began a career as a singer, composer and music teacher in London from 1810. He was a friend of Lord Byron who at his request wrote *Hebrew Melodies*, which Nathan set to music. In 1841 he emigrated to Australia and settled in Sydney. He was Australia's first resident professional composer.

Nathan, Paul (1857–1927) German philanthropist and public figure. He was the editor of the Berlin liberal publication *Die Nation*, and the founder of the Hilfsverein der Deutschen Juden. He was active at international Jewish conferences on emigration and the relief of Jewish victims of persecution and war. During the trial of Menaḥem Mendel Beilis in 1913 on a blood libel charge, Nathan helped to organise Beilis's defense outside Russia. Opposed to the Zionist movement, he advocated assimilation as a solution to anti-Semitism. After World War I, he fostered agricultural settlement among Russian Jewry.

Nathan ben Isaac of Baghdad [Nathan the Babylonian] (fl. 10th cent.) Babylonian chronicler. He lived in Baghdad and his *Akhbar Baghdad* is a book on the Jews of the city. This work is an important source for the history of Babylonian Jewry in the 10th century. It contains an account of the organisation of the gaonic academies in Mesopotamia as well as the disputes that occurred during this period.

Nathan ben Jehiel of Rome [Arukh] (1035–c.1110) Italian lexicographer. He was taught by his father, the head of the yeshivah in Rome. When his father died, he and his two brothers in turn succeeded him in that office. Nathan's *Baal he-Arukh* (by which name he was sometimes known) is a lexicon of the *Talmud* and the midrashim.

Nathan ben Joseph Official (fl. 13th cent.)   French talmudist. He engaged in religious controversies with Christians. These disputes were recorded by his son Joseph in his *Yosef ha-Mekanne.*

Nathan of Gaza [Ghazzati, Nathan Benjamin]. (1643–1680) Palestinian religious leader, disciple of Shabbetai Tzevi. He was born in Jerusalem, and lived in Gaza where he engaged in a kabbalistic study and practices. He met Shabbetai Tzevi in Gaza and proclaimed him to be the Messiah. After Shabbetai Tzevi converted to Islam, Nathan travelled through the Balkans and Italy, developing and preaching the theology of Shabbetainism, which was based on Lurianic Kabbalah. He was expelled by the rabbis of Venice, and returned to the Balkans. He died at Uskub near Salonica.

Nathansen, Henri (1868–1944)   Dutch playwright. He was born in Hjørring, Jutland, and trained as a lawyer. In 1909 he became the stage director of Copenhagen's Royal Theatre. Many of his plays deal with Jewish issues. In 1919 he protested against the persecution of Polish Jewry and later he called for the Copenhagen Jewish community to counteract Nazi anti-Semitism. In 1943 he fled to Sweden.

Nathanson, Mendel Levin (1780–1868)   Danish merchant and journalist. He was born in Altona, and moved to Copenhagen at the age of 12. From 1798 he was a wholesale draper. In 1838 he became editor of the newspaper *Berlingske Tidende.* He worked for the emancipation of the Jews and helped to establish the Jewish Free School for boys in Copenhagen in 1805 and later a similar school for girls. He wrote a history of the Jews of Denmark.

Nationalism   In biblical times the Ancient Israelites inhabited the Promised Land and established a monarchy. Forced into exile by the Babylonians in 586 BCE, many Jews never returned to Israel but made their homes elsewhere. Palestine ceased to be a Jewish centre after the destruction of the Temple by the Romans in 70 CE and the crushing of the Bar Kokhba rebellion in 132. Through much of the period of the diaspora the desire for a Jewish homeland permeated the religious and artistic expressions of Jews in all parts of the world. This nationalist feeling was grounded in the practice of the Jewish faith, such as the annual celebration of Passover which promised the return of the homeland in the greeting 'Next Year in Jerusalem!' The return to Zion was fostered by numerous writers such as Moses Hess, Judah Loeb Pinsker, Theodor Herzl and Ahad ha-Am. According to Zionist ideology, Jewish persecution would cease only when Jews were secure in their own land. After 2,000 years of living in the diaspora with no country of their own, the Jews re-established a Jewish state in modern Israel in 1948.

Natronai bar Hilai (fl. 9th cent.) Babylonian gaon of the academy at Sura (853–56). He was one of the most prolific writers of responsa among the geonim in the 9th century. His responsum to a query from the Lucena Jewish community as to how to fulfil the rabbinic dictum to recite 100 benedictions daily became the basis of the prayer book.

Natroni bar Nehemiah (fl. 8th cent.) Babylonian gaon of the academy at Pumbedita (719–30). He married into the family of the exilarch. He was known for his severity with scholars in the academy, some of whom left for Sura, returning to Pumbedita only after his death.

Natural law   The law of nature or the moral sense innate in the human mind, as opposed to that which results from revelation or legislation. The Noachian Laws may be construed as natural laws. In addition there are many rabbinic dicta which assume the existence of natural law. Medieval Jewish philosophers argued that God did not intend morality to be left to the vagaries of human reason; he therefore revealed a number of laws that are part of natural law (such as the prohibition against murder); he also revealed those rituals and precepts which would not otherwise occur to human beings. Non-philosophical Jewish theologians maintain that the purpose of the Torah is to lift the Jews above natural law.

Nature   Although the biblical writers recognised the regular workings of nature (as Psalms 104 and 148 show), they were primarily concerned with God's supervision of the universe. According to the rabbis, the regularity of natural phenomena is an expression of God's will, as are miraculous occurrences.

Naumbourg,   Samuel   (1815–1880) German musicologist. He was born in Dennelohe, near Ansbach. He became the first ḥazzan at the synagogue in the rue Notre-Dame-de-Nazareth in Paris in 1843. Two years later he published two volumes of *Zemirot Yisrael*, which contain musical settings of the entire liturgical cycle. His *Agudas Shirim* is a collection of traditional synagogue melodies.

Navigation   Under Solomon the Ancient Israelites collaborated with the Tyrians in maritime journeys (I Kings 9:26–28). During the period of the Second Temple, the symbols on Hasmonean coins suggest maritime knowledge, and from this time onward there seems to have been an interest in sea journeys. Naval engagements took place in the Mediterranean and the Sea of Galilee during the war of 66–70, and in the Mediterranean in the war of 132–35. During the Middle Ages Jewish merchants owned ships and a number of Jews were expert cartographers; others invented important navigational instruments. In modern times the State of Israel has established a navy and a merchant fleet.

Navon, Joseph (1852–1934)   Palestinian philanthropist. He was born in Jerusalem and became a merchant banker. He helped settlers in Palestine and supported popular housing schemes in Jerusalem. In 1888 he received a concession to construct a railway from Jaffa to Jerusalem.

Nazir ('Nazirite')   Fourth tractate in the Mishnah order of Nashim. It deals with the biblical prescriptions concerning Nazirite vows (Numbers 6:1–21).

Nazirite   [Nazarite]   Jewish   ascetic bound by a vow. The Nazirite is prohibited from drinking wine, cutting his hair, and contracting impurity by contact with a dead body (Numbers 6:2). The vow was usually taken for a limited period, but could also be for life (as in the case of Samuel and Samson). Taking the Nazirite vow was common in biblical times, but the practice ultimately disappeared.

Nebbish (Yiddish)   Interjection, expressing sympathy. The word also refers to an ineffectual or unfortunate person.

Necromancy   The art of divination by summoning and questioning the spirits of the dead. Although forbidden in Scripture (Leviticus 19:31; 20:6; Deuteronomy 18:11), it was widely practised in Ancient Israel.

Nedarim ('Vows') Third tractate in the Mishnah order of Nashim. It deals with regulations regarding vows as well as their annulment and interpretation.

Nedoveh (Yiddish) A charitable contribution.

Negaim ('Plagues of leprosy') Third tractate in the Mishnah order of Tohorot. It deals with the laws concerning leprosy (Leviticus 13–14).

Negligence In Jewish law an artisan or labourer is guilty of negligence when work is performed badly, when instructions are disregarded, or when materials are destroyed. In such cases full compensation is required of the artisan or labourer by the person who has commissioned the work. Jewish law also recognises other categories of negligence arising from intention and accident; in such cases the ordinary compensation does not apply (in the former it would be too lenient a penalty, in the latter too severe).

Nehemiah (i) (fl. 5th cent. BCE) Israelite, Governor of Judah. He was a cupbearer to the Persian king Artaxerxes I, of whom he asked permission to go to Jerusalem. The King agreed, and appointed him Governor of Judah. Nehemiah organised the repair of the walls of Jerusalem, and initiated various social and religious reforms. Later he returned to Susa, but subsequently settled in Jerusalem. He and Ezra took steps to discourage the Israelites from contracting mixed marriages.

Nehemiah (ii) Biblical book, part of the Hagiographa. It relates the events of the life of Nehemiah, Governor of Judah, and includes part of the story of the prophet Ezra.

Neher, André (1913–1988) French scholar. He was born in Alsace, and became Professor of Jewish Studies at the University of Strasbourg. He wrote works dealing with prophecy and with the teachings of Judah Löw ben Bezalel.

Nehunya ben ha-Kanah (fl. 1st cent.) Palestinian tanna. He was born in Emmaus in Judea. His students included Ishmael ben Elisha, who was influenced by his method of interpreting Scripture. He adopted the interpretive principle of 'kelal u-pherat' (a general followed by a particular), in opposition to the system of Nahum of Gimzo. A number of mystical works are ascribed to him, including the Bahir and the acrostic prayer *Anna be-koah.*

Nehushtan The name of the brass serpent which King Hezekiah broke into pieces in an attempt to reform its cult (II King's 18:4). According to tradition, it was created by Moses to prevent the fiery snakes from biting the people (Numbers 21:6–9; II King's 18:4). It probably stood in the Temple court.

Neilah ('Closing') The name of a prayer originally recited daily one hour before sunset and the closing of the Temple. It was also said on all public fast days and on the Day of Atonement. It now survives only as a service on the Day of Atonement. The Neilah concludes the rite for the day, symbolising the closing of the gates of Heaven after the Day of Judgement.

Neofiti (Italian: 'neophytes') The name given to the Jews forcibly converted to Christianity in southern Italy from the end of the 13th century. While living outwardly as Christians, many of the Neofiti remained secretly attached to Judaism.

Neoplatonism Late Greek philosophy combining Platonism with Oriental elements, expounded by Plotinus, Porphyry and Proclus. In the Middle Ages it had an important impact on the writings of Jewish theologians, including Isaac Israel, Solomon ibn Gabirol, Bahya ibn Pakudah, Abraham bar Hiyya, Joseph ibn Tzaddik and Abraham ibn Ezra. The kabbalah was also influenced by Neoplatonic ideas.

Ner tamid ('eternal light')   The name given to the light which is kept burning constantly in the synagogue. It is a symbolic reminder of the golden seven-branched candelabrum, or menorah, which burned continuously in the Temple. Originally this was placed in the niche in the Western Wall, but later was suspended in front of the Ark. The ner tamid has been interpreted alternatively as the symbol of God's presence and as the spiritual light emanating from the Temple. In ancient times it was created by a wick burning in olive oil, but in the modern period an electric light is used.

Nesekh   Wine intended or used for heathen worship. By extension, it is any wine made by a gentile. Wine produced by a non-Jew was always suspected of having been sanctified for a libation or a similar ceremonial act. In modern times the ban on drinking gentile wine is still binding. The prohibition also extends to unbottled wine that is no more than touched by a gentile; wine which has not been touched by a gentile before the bottle was sealed is kosher.

Neshamah yeterah ('extra soul')   According to tradition, God gave Adam a higher soul which elevated him on the Sabbath. This soul is given to all Jews during the Sabbath. The smelling of spices at the Havdalah service is meant to provide comfort for the loss of this extra soul when the Sabbath comes to an end.

Netanyahu, Benjamin (b.1949)   Born in Tel Aviv, he served as Deputy Chief of Mission at the Israeli embassy in Washington, Deputy Minister, and Prime Minister of Israel. His works include *Terrorism: How the West Can Win*, *International Terrorism: Challenge and Response*, *A Place Among the Nations: Israel and the World*, *Fighting Terrorism: How Democracies Can Defeat Domestic and International Terrorism* and *A Durable Peace*.

Netter, Charles (1826–1882)   French philanthropist. He was born in Strasbourg. He went into business in Lille, Moscow and London, and in 1851 settled in Paris, where he engaged in various public activities. One of the founders of the Alliance Israélite Universelle, he served as its treasurer. He established the Mikveh Israel Agricultural School near Jaffa, and was its first director (1870–73). He was also active in Jewish philanthropic work in Europe.

Neubauer, Adolph (1831–1907)   British bibliographer, of Hungarian origin. He went to Oxford in 1868 to complete the catalogue of Hebrew manuscripts in the Bodleian Library, which had been started by Moritz Steinschneider; he later became a sub-librarian. His writings include a series of medieval Hebrew chronicles, as well as studies of the geography of the *Talmud*.

Neuman, Abraham Aaron (1890–1970)   American rabbi, historian and educator. He was born in Brezan, Austria, and emigrated to the US in 1898. He taught history and later became President of Dropsie College. He was active in the Zionist movement. His writings include *The Jews of Spain*, *Cyrus Adler, a Biography*, and *Landmarks and Goats*.

Neumann, Emanuel (1893–1980)   American Zionist leader. He was born in Libau, Latvia, and was taken to the US as an infant. He founded the youth movement Young Judea in 1909, and served as Education Director of the Zionist Organisation of America. He subsequently was Director of the Keren ha-Yesod in the US, and Chairman of the executive committee of the United Palestine Appeal. In 1929–30 he was President of the Jewish National Fund in the US. He then moved to Palestine, where he worked for the Jewish Agency in Jerusalem. He was also President of the Zionist Organisation of America. In 1954 he founded the Herzl Foundation and served as its president. He was elected President of the World Union of General Zionists in 1963.

Neumann, John (1903–57) American mathematician of Hungarian origin. He studied at the University of Budapest and later at the University of Zurich. He was assistant professor at the University of Berlin, and later at the University of Hamburg. Subsequently he was professor at the Institute of Advanced Studies at Princeton.

Neumann, Robert (1897–1975) Austrian author. He was born in Vienna. He wrote poetry, parodies and anti-Nazi novels. After the war he settled in Switzerland, where he wrote documentary works dealing with the Nazi period.

Neumann, Solomon (1819–1908) German physician and public worker. He engaged in work on medical statistics and public hygiene. His refusal in 1845 to take the special form of medical oath for Jews led to its abolition in Prussia. Besides his professional work he was active in Jewish communal activities and was a patron of scholarship.

Neumark, David (1866–1924) American Reform scholar, of Galacian birth. He was a rabbi in Germany, and later Professor of Jewish Philosophy at the Veitel-Heine-Ephraimschen Lehranstalt in Berlin. In 1907 he became the professor of philosophy at the Hebrew Union College. His writings include *History of Jewish Philosophy* and *Essays in Jewish Philosophy*.

Neurath, Otto (1882–1945) Austrian philosopher and sociologist. Born in Vienna, he studied in Vienna and Berlin. He taught at the Handelsakademie, and later was in charge of planning the Bavarian Republic. He then returned to Vienna and founded the Social and Economic Museum. He was also part of the Vienna Circle of philosophers. In 1934 he went to Holland, and later settled in England.

Neusner, Jacob (1932–2015) American scholar. Born in Hartford, Connecticut, he taught at Columbia University, the University of Wisconsin, Dartmouth College, Brown University, and the University of Southern Florida. He wrote numerous books and received various scholarly awards. In 1968–69 he served as President of the American Academy of Religion.

Nevelson, Louise (1899–1988) American sculptor. Born in Kiev, she emigrated to the US in 1905. Her work includes *Six Million,* a work in memory of the victims of the Holocaust.

Newman, Barnett (1905–1970) American painter and sculptor. He was born in New York. Jewish themes are found throughout his work in such works such as *Covenant, Abraham* and *Adam.*

Newman, Louis Israel (1893–1972) American rabbi and writer. He was rabbi of Temple Rodeph Shalom in New York, and taught at the Jewish Institute of Religion. He published *Jewish Influence on Christian Reform Movements, The Jewish People, Faith and Life,* and *The Hasidic Anthology.*

New Moon, Blessing of the (Hebrew: 'Birkat ha-Hodesh') Formula for announcing the day or days on which Rosh Hodesh (the beginning of the lunar month) may be celebrated. It is recited after the reading of the Torah on the Sabbath preceding the new moon, by a reader holding a Torah scroll. The Ashkenazi rite is more complex than the Sephardi and includes a formal announcement, a supplication for national redemption, and a prayer for a prosperous month.

New Year The opening Mishnah of the treatise *Rosh ha-Shanah* lists four dates for New Year in the Jewish calendar: 1 Nisan is regarded as New Year for the purpose of dating the reigns of kings, for ordering religious festivals and for counting the months. 1 Tishri (Rosh ha-Shanah) is the start of the agricultural year, and from this date the years are counted to establish the observance of Sabbatical and Jubilee years. Cattle are tithed according to a year beginning on 1 Elul. Fruit is tithed according to a year starting on 15 Shevat.

Next Year in Jerusalem (Hebrew: 'La-Shanah ha-Baah bi-Yerusalalyim') Expression of communal hope, uttered at the end of the Passover Seder service by all participants. In some communities it is also used as the conclusion to the services on the Day of Atonement. Its purport is to remind Jews of the coming era of the Messiah when all nations will look to Jerusalem.

Nezikin ('Damages') [Yeshuot ('Deeds of help')] Fourth order of the Mishnah. It deals with money matters, damages decided by the courts, criminal law and oaths. It also contains an ethical treatise, *Pirke Avot.*

Niddah ('Menstrous woman') Seventh tractate in the Mishnah order of Tohorot. It deals with the ritual uncleanness created by menstruation (Leviticus 15:19–24) and childbirth (Leviticus 12:1–5).

Niemirover, Jacob Isaac (1872–1939) Romanian Chief Rabbi. He was born in Lemberg, and served as rabbi of Jassy. He became rabbi of the Sephardi community of Bucharest in 1911 and later Chief Rabbi of Romania. In 1926 he was elected to the Romanian senate, where he served as the representative of Romanian Jewry. Active in educational and Zionist circles, he also served as President of the Order of B'nai B'rith in Romania. He wrote studies of various Jewish topics.

Nieto, David (1654–1728) British rabbi and philosopher. He was born in Venice. He served as a rabbi in Livorno, and in 1702 became Haham of the Sephardi community in London. He wrote about the Inquisition and also produced anti-Sabbetaian polemics. His *Matteh Dan* is a philosophical defense of Judaism.

Niger, Samuel [Charney, Samuel] (1883–1955) American Yiddish literary critic. He was born in Russia, and began his career contributing to various Russian literary magazines. In 1909 he went to Berlin; several years later he edited a Yiddish monthly, *Di yidishe velt,* in Vilnius. In 1919 he emigrated to the US and settled in New York, where he became literary editor of *Der tog.* His studies of Yiddish literature appeared in various volumes.

Niggun ('air') Type of traditional song, cultivated particularly among the Ḥasidim.

Night (Hebrew: 'leilah') The Jewish day is reckoned from sunset to sunset. The period from sunset until sunrise constitutes night. The night is traditionally divided into three or four watches. According to Jewish law, certain activities (such as starting a court session or signing a document) may not be carried out at night.

Night Prayer (Hebrew 'Keriat Shema al ha-mittah'): *lit.* the reading of the Shema on the bed) Prayer recited before going to sleep. The central part of the prayer in the first paragraph of the Shema; the rest consists of blessings and prayers taken from the evening service. The talmudists and later authorities, including kabbalists added other prayers and scriptural texts to the Shema to form the Night Prayer liturgy. The substance of the Night Prayer is based on a saying of Joshua ben Levi that he who wishes to sleep should recite a certain portion of the Shema and the blessing to God.

Nikkur ('separating the fat') The act of removing the fat of animals bought for sacrifice in the Temple. According to Leviticus, fat taken from a sacrificial offering may not be eaten (Leviticus

7.25); generally it was burnt on the altar (Leviticus 3.3–4). Most of the forbidden fats could be easily removed, since much animal fat forms a separate solid surrounded by a membrane. However, some threads of fat run through the lean tissue and these had to be removed by a process known as 'porging'. Only someone familiar with this technique might undertake the preparation of an animal for sacrifice.

Nine Days (Hebrew: 'Bein ha-Mezarim'): *lit.* **'between the straits')** In the Ashkenazi rite a penitential period during the later part of the three weeks of mourning that lead up to the fast of the Ninth of Av. For the three-week period no festivities are celebrated, nor do marriages take place. During the period of Nine Days, pious Jews abstain from meat and wine. On the Sabbath before the Ninth of Av a prophetic portion is read from Isaiah (Isaiah 1.1–27).

Ninth of Av (Hebrew: 'Tisha b'Av') Fast day commemorating the destruction of the First and Second Temples and other Jewish tragedies. In the synagogue service Lamentations is read and dirges (kinot) are recited. A three-week period of mourning, which includes the nine days of penitential observance, lead up to the fast day.

Nisan. First month of the religious year (it is the seventh month of the civil year). In the Bible it is referred to as the month of aviv ('spring'). Passover occurs on 15 Nisan. No public mourning is permitted during the month, nor is the penitential taḥanun (the prayer for grace and forgiveness) recited during the daily prayers.

Nishmat ('The breath of every living thing') Opening words of the doxology recited at the end of the Pesuke de-Zimrah on Sabbaths and festivals. It is referred to as the 'Birkat ha-Shir' (Blessing of the song) in Talmudic literature. During the Mishnaic period it was recited after the Hallelujah on the Passover Seder night. It consists of three parts: the section known in Mishnaic days; a section which served as a thanksgiving for rain; and a gaonic addition. According to medieval legend, it was ascribed to the apostle Peter.

Nissenbaum, Isaac (1868–1942) Polish rabbi, author and Zionist. He was born in Bobruysk, Belorussia, and lived in Minsk, where he was an active Zionist. Later he became head of a secret nationalistic association formed by members of the yeshivah of Volozhin after it was closed. In 1894 he moved to Bialystok, where he became secretary to Samuel Mohilever. After Mohilever's death, he preached about Zionism throughout Russia, Poland, Lativa and Lithuania. In 1900 he settled in Warsaw, where he was active in the Mizraḥi organisation. He wrote numerous works about Zionism.

Nissenson, Hugh (1933–2013) American novelist and short-story writer. He was born in New York. His work explores the difficulties of sustaining religious belief in modern society; his fictional publications include *My own Ground* and *Tree of Life*. In 1961 he reported on the trial of Eichmann for the magazine *Commentary*. His *Notes from the Frontier* is a memoir of visits to a kibbutz before and during the Six-Day War.

Nissim, Yitzḥak Raḥamim (1896–1981) Israeli rabbi. He was born in Baghdad, and settled in Jerusalem in 1925. In 1955 he was elected Rishon le-Zion, Sephardi Chief Rabbi of Israel. He published and edited volumes of responsa.

Nissim ben Jacob ben Nissim [Ibn Shahin]. (c.990–1062) North African talmudist. Born in Kairouan, he became head of the academy there after the death of Hananel. He had close contacts with Samuel ha-Naggid, and corresponded with Hai Gaon. His *Kitab Miftaḥ Maghalik al-Talmud* (Key to the locks of the Talmud) is a commentary on the *Talmud* and its methodology.

Noachian Laws [laws of Noah] A series of laws, derived from Genesis 9:4–7, which according to the rabbis are binding on all human beings. They prohibit idolatry, blasphemy, murder, adultery, robbery and the eating of flesh cut from a living animal. They also require the establishment of courts of justice. According to tradition, gentiles can enter into the after-life as long as they observe these commandments.

Noah Son of Lamech, father of Shem, Ham and Japheth (Genesis 5:28–29; 6:10; I Chronicles 1:4). In the Bible he is described as a righteous and blameless man who walked with God (Genesis 6:9). At God's behest he built an ark, and placed in it members of his family, as well as representatives of the animal kingdom; when a great Flood came they were thus saved to perpetuate humankind and the animals. After the Flood, Noah disembarked from the ark and offered sacrifices to God, who blessed him and his sons, and established a covenant with them (Genesis 6–9).

Noah, Mordecai Manuel (1785–1851) American newspaper editor, politician and playwright. He was born in Philadelphia, and started his career as a clerk in the US Treasury. In 1809 he went to Charleston, South Carolina, where he edited the *City Gazette*. Later he became editor of the *National Advocate* in New York and established the *New York Enquirer*. In 1841 he became a judge of the court of Sessions. He was active in the congregations of Mikveh Israel in Philadelphia and Shearith Israel in New York. In 1825 he helped to purchase land on Grand Island near Buffalo, New York, which he planned to develop as a Jewish colony. After the failure of this project, he became an advocate of Palestine as the national home for the Jews.

Nobel Prize winners Since the prize was established listed in 1899, Jews in

a variety of fields (World Peace, Literature, Physiology and Medicine, Chemistry, Physics and Economics) have received the award. They include Henry Kissinger and Eli Wiesel (World Peace), Albert Einstein (Physics), Arthur Kornberg (Medicine), Melvin Calvin (Chemistry), and Isaac Bashevis Singer, Nelly Sachs and many others (Literature).

No-goodnik An unethical, irresponsible, or undependable person. It is also used of someone who does not earn and honest living.

Nomberg, Hirsch David (1876–1927) He was born in Mszczonów, near Warsaw, and from 1903 to 1905 wrote for the Warsaw Hebrew paper *Ha-Tzopheh*. He published a collection of Hebrew stories in 1905. This was followed by five collection in Yiddish. A disciple of Isaac Leib Peretz, he helped resolve the struggle between Hebraists and Yiddishists at the Czernowitz Yiddish conference in 1908. After 1910 he engaged in politics and journalism. In 1916 he was a founder of the Polish People's Party, and later was a member of the Polish Sejm. He was also President of the Society for Jewish Writers and Journalists.

Nordau, Max [Zidfield, Simeon] (1849–1923) Hungarian author and Zionist leader. He was born in Budapest. In 1880 he settled in Paris, where he practised as a doctor. In 1883 he published *Conventional Lies of our Civilization*; this was followed by *Paradoxes, The Malady of the Century* and *Degeneration*. An associate of Theodor Herzl, he participated in all the Zionist congresses until 1911. Later he was a political counsellor to the president of the Zionist Organisation, David Wolffsohn. After Wolffson's policy was rejected by the practical Zionists, Nordau joined the opposition circles within the Zionist movement, which worked against cultural Zionism advocated by, among others, Aḥad ha-Am.

Norman, Edward Albert (1900–1955)
American financier and philanthropist.
He was born in Chicago, and entered
his family's financial business. He
served as President of the American
Fund for Israel Institutions, President
of the American Economic Commission for Palestine, National Secretary for
the American Jewish Committee, and
Director of the Joint Distribution Committee. In addition he was President of
the Group Farming Research Institute.

**Norsa [Norzi], Raphael Ben Gabriel
(1520–?1583)**   Italian rabbi. He served
as rabbi at Ferrara and Mantua, and
wrote various studies of ethical issues
connected with religious questions.

Nossig, Alfred (1864–1943)   Polish
author, sculptor and musician. He initially belonged to the circle of assimilationist Polish Jews, but later he became
a supporter of Zionism and advocated
the establishment of a Jewish state in
Palestine. In 1908 he founded a Jewish
colonisation organisation. He published
studies about Jewish national problems,
and his work on Jewish statistics served
as the basis for the Jewish Statistical and
Demographic Institute. He also produced sculptures with Jewish themes.
He lived in Berlin, but was expelled to
Poland when the Nazis rose to power.
Suspected of collaborating with the
Nazis, he was sentenced to death by the
Jewish underground.

Notarikon (Greek)   System of abbreviation by shortening words or writing
only one letter of a word. The term is
derived from the system of shorthand
used by the notarii in Roman courts of
justice. In Hebrew studies notarikon is
one of the tools or methods of interpreting Scripture. It is the 30th of the 32
hermeneutical rules laid down in the
Baraita of 32 Rules.

Novellae (Latin; Hebrew 'ḥiddushim')
Commentaries on the *Talmud* and later
rabbinic literature, which attempt to
derive new principles or facts from the

text. Novellae of the early French and
German talmudists are incorporated
into the tosaphot, but in Spain novellae
were issued as separate works by such
scholars as Naḥmanides, Solomon ben
Adret and Yomtov ben Abraham of
Seville. From the 16th century Rashi's
commentary and the tosaphot were
printed in editions of the *Talmud*. This
practice gave rise to new novellae which
were printed either together with the
Talmud or as separate works.

Nu (Yiddish)   An ejaculation used in
many different contexts. It can express
the emotions connected with a sigh,
a frown, a grin, a grunt or a sneer. It
can be used fondly, acidly, tritely or
belligerently.

Numbers (i)   In Hebew the letters of
the alphabet stand also for numbers.
This attribute of the language has
given rise to the significance of numbers in some systems of Jewish thought.
Although the Bible does not generally attribute a particular significance
to numbers, talmudic literature uses
numbers mnemonically. In addition,
rabbinic sources regard the occurrence
of the same number in different contexts or events as indicating a connection between them. This concept was
later developed in the tradition of biblical exegesis known as gematria. In mystical sources numbers were regarded
as having special creative powers. The
concept of the magical significance and
use of numbers was developed in the
Jewish and (particularly) Christian traditions of the kabbalah.

Numbers (ii) (Hebrew 'Be-Midbar')
Fourth book of the Pentateuch. It traces
the history of the Israelites in the desert
after the Exodus.

Numbers Rabbah   Midrash on the
Book of Numbers. It is part of the Midrash Rabbah. The first 14 sections comprise a later aggadic composition on
Numbers 1–7. Sections 15–23 is largely
the Midrash Tanḥuma.

Numerus clauses (Latin: *lit.* **'Closed number')** Term applied to the restricted number of persons that may be admitted to specific professions, higher education, professional associations and positions of public office. Such restrictions frequently applied to Jews, particularly in czarist Russia.

Nun Fourteenth letter of the Hebrew alphabet. Its numerical value is 50.

Nuñez, Hector (1521–1591) Portuguese physician and merchant. He became leader of the Marrano community in England. His overseas trading activities enabled him to supply valuable information to the English government.

Nuñez, Maria (fl. 16th century) Portuguese Marrano communal leader. With other Marranos she escaped from Portugal on a ship bound for the Netherlands. Captured by a British vessel, they were diverted to London. According to one account, Nuñez was presented to Queen Elizabeth, who took her on a tour of London. She eventually settled in Amsterdam, where she founded a community that became a haven for other Marranos.

Nunsakh (*lit.* **'version')** Term used for the various rites of prayer in different communities of Judaism; for example, Nusakh Ashkenaz means the Ashkenazi rite or liturgy. It also refers to the different traditions of synagogal melody.

O

Manny Kaplan and Sidney Shapiro, who are in business together, are having a ferocious disagreement. They decide to go see the rabbi for his opinion. Manny goes first and explains the situation to the rabbi who makes copious notes. After listening for half an hour, the rabbi says: 'You're right.' Then it is Sidney's turn. He puts his point of view, and after a half hour the rabbi says, 'You're right.' Incensed, Manny objects: 'We can't both be right.' The rabbi strokes his beard and looks at his notes. 'You're right,' he sighs.

* * * * *

Many Jewish jokes concern the nature of Jewish culture. Underlying this joke about the rabbi's indecision is a reflection of the nature of rabbinic debate. In the Talmud, the opinions of rabbinic sages clash with one another. Frequently there is no solution to the problem being discussed. Instead, there are conflicting opinions with no solution.

Obadiah (i) (fl. 9th cent. BCE) Israelite official, governor of the house of King Ahab. He hid 100 prophets of God to save them from Jezebel's persecution (I King's 18).

Obadiah (ii) (fl. 6th cent. BCE) Israelite prophet. His life spanned the Babylonian conquest of Judah, and he spoke out against the Edomites for having refused to assist Jerusalem in her time of need.

Obadiah (iii) Biblical book, one of the 12 books of the Minor Prophets. It records the prophecies of Obadiah. It is the shortest book in the Hebrew Bible.

Obermann, Julian (1888–1956) American orientalist. He was born in Warsaw. He taught Semitic languages at the University of Hamburg from 1919 to 1922. After emigrating to the US he became Professor of Semitic Philology at the Jewish Institute of Religion in New York, and later Professor of Semitic Languages at Yale University. In 1944 he was appointed Director of Judaic Research and editor of the Yale Judaica Series. He wrote works on Semitic philology and epigraphy, Old Testament and Ugaritic studies, Islamic culture and Arabic philosophy.

Occupations Throughout the biblical and Second Temple periods the Israelites were largely farmers, herdsmen and craftsmen. Jews in the diaspora engaged in trade and in skilled handicrafts such as glass-making, silk weaving and dyeing. In Muslim lands they mostly worked the land. From the Middle Ages Southern European Jews continued the traditional occupations of trade and handicrafts, while in Northern Europe, many Jews became money-lenders. In Poland the majority of Jews were craftsmen, whereas in Salonica and other parts of the Turkish Empire, they were employed as menials. In Western Europe Jews were involved in trade and commerce. With the Emancipation such concentration on particular occupations began to be recorded and in the modern period Jews have engaged in all kinds of work.

Odel (fl. 18th cent.)   Polish matriarch, daughter of the Baal Shem Tov. She was the mother of several tzaddikim. In Ḥasidic literature she is presented as the ideal type of womanhood.

Odets, Clifford (1906–63)   American playwright. Born in Philadelphia, his family moved to the Bronx. In 1925 he began to present radio programmes that he wrote himself. In 1935 his play *Waiting for Lefty* was produced. This was followed by *Till the Day I Die*, *Awake and Sing* and *Paradise Lost*, *Golden Boy*, *Rocket for the Moon*, *Night Music* and *Clash by Night*. He also wrote screen-plays including *The General Died at Dawn*, *None But the Lonely Heart* and *The Sweet Smell of Success*.

Ofek, Abraham (1935–1990)   Israeli painter. He was born in Burgus, Bulgaria, and emigrated to Israel in 1949. He taught at the Bezalel School of Arts and Crafts and at the University of Haifa. His paintings cover the walls of Kfar Uriah, the Jerusalem Centre Post Office, the Agron and Stone schools in Jerusalem, the Tel Aviv University Library, and the entrance to the main building of the University of Haifa.

Offenbach, Jacques (1819–80)   French composer, of German origin. He was the son of a Cologne cantor. He became the conductor of the Theatre François in Paris. He composed over a hundred operettas including *The Tales of Hoffman*.

Ohalot ('Tents')   Second tractate in the Mishnah order of Tohorot. It deals with the ritual impurity caused by contact with a corpse (Numbers 19:13–20).

Ohel ('tent')   Structure over a grave. The Ḥasidim, in particular, venerate the tombs of their tzaddikim, visiting them on the anniversary of the death. An ohel is erected over the grave and a ner tamid is kept burning at its foot. It was formerly the practice to prostrate oneself upon the grave and place a note there asking for help.

Oholah and Oholibah   Sisters who represent Israel and Judah in an allegorical prophecy of Ezekiel (Ezekiel 23); their sexual promiscuity and depravity stand for the sins of the Israelites, and their downfall for the fate of Israel and Judah.

Oil   Oil plays an important part in the ritual, ceremonial and sacrificial practices of Judaism. Pure olive oil was used in the Sanctuary and Temple (Exodus 27:20), and among oriental Jews. This is still traditionally the only oil that may be used to fuel the ner tamid in the synagogue. Rabbi Tarphon declared that only olive oil could be used for Sabbath lamps, but the general ruling is that any oil may be used. Oil was also used to anoint high priests and kings, and formed part of certain sacrificial offerings.

Oistrakh, David (1908–1974)   Russian violinist. Born in Odessa, he studied at the Odessa Music School and later taught at the Moscow Conservatory. During the 1930s he won various competitions including the Ysaye competition in Brussels. During World War II he performed at the front, in hospitals and in factories. In 1953 he played in Paris and London, and later in New York.

Okhalah ve-Okhalah   Early collection of masoretic notes to the Bible, dating from before the 10th century. They are arranged partly alphabetically and partly in the order of the books of the Bible.

Oleh (*lit.* 'one who ascends')   The word is used specifically of an immigrant to Israel. It is also applied to a person visiting the Holy Land as a pilgrim for the observance of Passover, Shavuot, and Sukkot (Exodus 23:14–17).

Olgin, Moses Joseph (Novomski, Moissaye] (1876–1939)   American journalist and translator. He was born near Kiev, and began his career as a teacher. In 1913 he moved to Vienna, where he was co-editor of the Bundist Yiddish weekly *Di tsayt.* He emigrated to the US and settled in New York in 1914. He was a staff member of the Yiddish daily paper *Forverts,* and later edited the Communist Yiddish daily *Freiheit* and the monthly *Der hamer.* He wrote about political affairs, literature and the theatre.

Olivetti, Camillo (1868–1943)   Italian inventor, he opened a small factory in Ivrea, Italy, that manufactured electrical measurement instruments. This was followed by typewriters, including the Olivetti typewriter.

Olman, Israel (1883–1968)   Dutch composer and choirmaster. He studied music in Amsterdam and became choirmaster of the Santo Servicio choir of the Sephardi synagogue there. His compositions include J*igdal, Populus Sion, Jerusalem* for performance in the synagogue, as well as liturgical works for Jewish choirs.

Omer ('Sheaf') (i)   First sheaf cut during the barley harvest. It was offered in the Temple as a sacrifice on the second day of Passover (Leviticus 23:15). Until the sacrifice had been offered, it was forbidden to eat the new grain. The period of seven weeks between the

second day of Passover and the feast of Shavuot is known as the Counting of the Omer.

Omer ('sheaf') (ii)   Dry measure equal to the tenth part of an ephah.

Omer, Counting of the (Hebrew 'Sephirat ha-Omer')   The counting of the 49 days from the second day of Passover, when the first sheaf of the barley harvest – the omer – was offered in the Temple, until the feast of Shavuot. The time of counting is referred to as the Sephirah period, during which mourning customs are practised and marriages are forbidden. The kabbalists viewed the 49 days of the Counting of Omer as having mystical significance.

Omri (fl. 9th cent. BCE)   King of Israel (c.882–871 BCE). During his reign he transferred the capital of Israel from Tirzah to Samaria (I King's 16:21–8). According to the Moabite Stone, he conquered Moab.

Onaah (*lit.* 'overreaching')   In Jewish law a term meaning fraudulent representation or unfair profit. The biblical instruction 'You shall not wrong one another' (Leviticus 25:14) was interpreted by the rabbis as pertaining to transactions in which the profit was so great that the overcharging was tantamount to fraud. They decreed that if the seller of movable goods overcharged the buyer by one-sixth or more of the market value of the goods the buyer had grounds for cancelling the transaction. (The transaction could be regarded as fraudulent only if the seller concealed such profit.)

Onam Ken ('Yes it is true')   Opening words of a penitential piyyut for the Kol Nidre service on the eve of the Day of Atonement in the Ashkenazi rite. It was composed by Yom Tov ben Isaac of Joigny in the 12th century.

Onan (fl.? 19th cent. BCE)   Second son of Judah and Shua (Genesis 38:2–4;

46:12; Numbers 26:19). After the death of his brother Er, his father instructed him to marry his childless sister-in-law, Tamar. He refused to fulfil his duty, and would not consummate the marriage. His conduct was viewed as abhorrent, and God took his life (Genesis 38:8–10).

Oneg Shabbat ('Sabbath delight') Name given to an educational or cultural gathering that takes place on Saturday afternoon. The term has come to refer to any celebration during the Sabbath.

Onias I (fl. 4th century BCE) High Priest. According to I Maccabees 12:20–23, Aerios I, King of Sparta, sent a letter to Onias claiming that the Spartans and the Jews were both descended from Abraham.

Onias II (fl. 3rd cent. BCE) High Priest, grandson of Onias I. He wished to free the Jewish people from the yoke of Ptolemaic Egypt. In pursuit of this aim he conspired with the enemies of Ptolemy III and withheld the payment of taxes. Ptolemy threatened to expel the Jews, but was pacified through the intervention of Onias's nephew, Joseph, son of Tobias.

Onias III (fl. 2nd cent. BCE) High Priest, grandson of Onias II. Simeon, an official in the Temple, demanded from Onias the post of market commissioner, which was in his gift. When his petition was refused, Simeon revealed to Apollonius, the commander of the Syrian army, that the treasurers of King Seleucus of Syria were being held in the Temple vaults. Seleucus then sent his chancellor Heliodorus to remove them. When his mission failed, Onias fell out of favour with his Syrian overlords. After Antiochus IV Epiphanes ascended the throne, Onias was summoned to Antioch and his brother Jason became high priest in his place. Later Jason was replaced by Menelaus, who was an extreme Helleniser.

Onias IV (fl. 2nd cent. BCE) Son of Onias III. After he was ousted as high priest by Akimus, he went from Judea to Egypt. In 145 BCE Ptolemy VI Philometer granted him authority to build a temple in Leontopolis.

Onkelos (fl. 2nd cent.) Palestinian proselyte. He was a contemporary of Rabban Gamaliel II of Jabneh. He translated the Pentateuch into Aramaic.

Opatoshu, Joshua [Opatovsky, Joseph] (1886–1954) American Yiddish novelist, of Polish origin. He settled in the US in 1907. From 1910 he contributed stories to periodicals and anthologies. Later he joined the staff of the New York Yiddish daily paper *Der tag*. His novels deal largely with Jewish life in Poland and America.

Opferpennig (German: 'tribute penny') Poll tax introduced in 1342 throughout the Holy Roman Empire by Emperor Louis IV, the Bavarian. All Jews over 12 years old who possessed 20 guilders or more were to pay one guilder annually. The tax was regarded as a continuation of the traditional Temple tax which the Jews had paid to the Roman authorities after the destruction of the Second Temple.

Ophan Name give to a type of piyyut, incorporated into the morning service for the Sabbath and feast days. Based on the description of the ophan (traditionally identified with the cherubim) in Ezekiel 1, it describes the recitation of the doxology by the angels.

Oppenheim [Openheimer], David (1664–1736) German rabbi. He was born in Worms, and served as a rabbi in Nikolsburg and Prague. His library contained 7,000 volumes, including 1,000 manuscripts. They became the basis of the Hebrew section of the Bodleian Library in Oxford.

Oppenheim, Moritz Daniel (1799–1882) German painter. He was born in Hanau. In 1821 he went to Rome,

where he was influenced by a Christian group known as the Nazarenes, who painted pictures based on the New Testament. Later he returned to Germany and settled in Frankfurt am Main. He painted biblical scenes and pictures on Jewish themes, including confrontations between Christians and Jews.

Oppenheimer, Franz (1864–1943) German economist and sociologist. He was born in Berlin. From 1919 to 1929 he was a professor of sociology at the University of Frankfurt am Main. After Hitler's rise to power, he taught at the Hochschule für die Wissenschaft des Judentums in Berlin. In 1938 he settled in the US. He was associated with the Zionist movement. The Merḥ avyah cooperative settlement in Palestine was founded in accordance with his theories.

Oppenheimer, Joseph (c.1698–1738) German financier. His father was a merchant in Heidelberg and collector of taxes from the Jews of the Palatinate. In 1732 Oppenheimer became the finance minister of Karl Alexander of Württemberg. After the duke's death in 1737 he was accused of stealing state finances and was hanged at Stuttgart; he refused to save his life by accepting baptism. His life was the subject of the novel *Jud Süss* by Lion Feuchtwanger.

Oppenheimer [Oppenheim], Samuel (1630–1703) Austrian financier and philanthropist. He was Leopold I's agent and financier, and was the first Jew to be allowed to settle in Vienna. He helped to finance Leopold's wars with the Turks and the War of the Spanish Succession. In 1697 he was accused of conspiring to murder Samson Wertheimer, but was acquitted. Among his benefactions were support for the poor, Jewish scholars, and Judah Ḥasid ha-Levi's movement for a Jewish settlement in Palestine.

Oppert, Jules (1825–1905) French philologist, orientalist and archaeolo-

gist. Born in Hamburg, he settled in France early in his life. He became an authority on Old Persian and Assyrian, and in 1851 he went on an expedition to explore Mesopotamia, where he identified the site of Ancient Babylon. In 1874 he became Professor of Assyrian Philology and Archaeology at the Collège de France. He wrote studies on various aspects of oriental scholarship. He was an active member of various Jewish communal and scholarly literature bodies.

Oral Law According to tradition, the Oral Law was given to Moses on Mount Sinai (together with the Written Law). During the Second Temple period the Oral Law was upheld by the Pharisees (in opposition to the Sadducees). Later the Oral Law was studied in the academies and was eventually written down in the Mishnah, compiled by Judah ha-Nasi (2nd century). After further centuries of discussion, the Oral Law was recorded in the *Talmud* (6th century). After the redaction of the *Talmud*, the Oral Law was further studied in Talmudic academies. During the gaonic period, the Karaites rejected the authority of the Oral Law. Modern non-Orthodox Judaism (Reform, Conservative, Liberal), rejected the belief that the Oral Law was revealed to Moses on Mount Sinai, arguing instead that it originated through discussion and interpretation over the centuries.

Ordeal, Trial by Judicial method for determining the validity of an accusation. It usually involved the infliction of a painful physical test upon the suspected person. If the victim emerged unscathed, it was supposedly a sign of supernatural intervention and (in Jewish law) was seen as proof of innocence. In biblical times the text of bitter waters was imposed by the priest upon a 'sotah' (a married woman suspected of adultery; Numbers 5:11–31). In a ceremony involving a meal offering and ritual curses, a mixture of holy water and dust was administered to the woman. If her flesh swelled and became diseased, she was guilty, but if she was unharmed she was innocent. This practice was eventually abolished by Johanan ben Zakkai.

Ordination (Hebrew 'semikhah') [Hattarat Horaah ('Permission to lay down a decision')] In Jewish usage, the conferring of the title 'rabbi' on a man learned in Jewish law and the practice of religion. Traditionally teachers granted the title 'rabbi' to learned pupils, who thereby earned the right to give decisions about ritual and legal matters. The *Talmud* traces the origin of this institution to Moses, who conveyed leadership to Joshua by placing his hands on Joshua's head. Initially Jewish ordination was confined to Palestine. In Babylonia scholars received the title 'rav'. A new form of ordination was established in the 14th century in Germany by Meir ha-Levi of Vienna. He required that all newly qualified candidates should receive a 'ketav semikhah' (writ of ordination), and this practice spread to other countries. Later a distinction was made between ordination in the sense of granting 'Hattarat Horaah' (permission to lay down a decision), and the conferring of the title 'Morenu' (our teacher) as an honorary title. In modern times a candidate for the rabbinate undergoes a lengthy period of study in a seminary, at the end of which he is given the certificate of Hattarat Horaah. This usually includes the phrase 'yoreh yoreh, yadin, yadin' (he may surely give a decision and may surely judge). In some seminaries the graduation ceremony is described as 'ordination' and may involve the laying one of hands.

Oren (from Latin 'orare': to pray) Word used among German Jews, meaning to pray.

Orgad, Ben Zion (1926–2006) Israeli composer and educator. He was born in Germany, and in 1933 settled in Palestine, where he later became a superintendent of music education. His works are motivated by national ideology.

Organ According to the *Talmud* there was an organ of ten pipes in the Second Temple. In the 17th–19th centuries an organ was used in the principal synagogue in Prague. During the 19th century the use of the organ in synagogues became a point of conflict between Reform and Orthodox Jews. According to Orthodoxy, the organ is forbidden under the general ban on instrumental music in worship outside the Temple. Its use also contravenes the rabbinic ordinance against playing a musical instrument on the Sabbath. The organ is now used in services of worship in Reform and Conservative synagogues.

Orientalist An orientalist is one who studies the civilisation and culture of Eastern (especially Asiatic) countries. In Jewish usage the term is applied principally to those studying the countries of the eastern mediterranean, north Africa, and the Middle East. From the Middle Ages onward Jewish scholars studied Islamic theology, philosophy and religious law. In the 19th and 20th centuries, Jewish philologists, archaeologists, theologians and philosophers made important contributions to the study of oriental languages and civilisations.

Original sin Christian doctrine that all human beings live in a state of sin because of Adam's transgression. According to this view, humanity can be redeemed only by the atoning death of Jesus. Jewish theology, however, maintains that humans are not born in a state of sinfulness, but that each person is motivated by innate evil and good inclinations.

Orlah ('Uncircumcised fruit') Tenth tractate in the Mishnah order of Zeraim. It deals with the law forbidding the use of the fruit of trees or vineyards for the first three years after planting (Leviticus 19:23).

Orlinsky, Harry (1908–1992) American biblical scholar. He was born in Toronto, Canada, and went to the US in 1931. He was Professor of Bible at the Hebrew Union College from 1943, and served as President of the Society for Biblical Literature in 1969–70. He was also editor-in-chief of the Jewish Publication Society's translation of the Torah. His writings include *Understanding the Bible through History and Archaeology*.

Ormandy, Eugene [Blau, Jean] (1899–1985) American musician, of Hungarian origin. Born in Budapest, he studied at the Budapest Royal Academy where he became Professor of Violin. In 1921 he went to New York and eventually played with the Philadelphia Orchestra. Later he became Music Director of the Minneapolis Symphony Orchestra. In 1938 he became Music Director of the Philadelphia Orchestra.

Ornitz, Samuel (1890–1957) American author. He was born in New York, where he worked as a social worker from 1908 to 1920. An advocate of Jewish assimilation, he saw no virtue in Jewish immigrant life. His novels chiefly concern the Jewish immigrant generation of the 1880–1914 period and portray Jewish types in an unsympathetic light.

Orpah (fl. 12th cent. BCE) Moabite woman, wife of Chilion and sister-in-law of Ruth. When her mother-in-law Naomi, returned home to Judah, Orpah was persuaded to remain behind in Moab, while Ruth went with Naomi (Ruth 1).

Orphans According to the Bible, caring for orphans is an important act of charity and a duty (Deuteronomy 14:29; 24:19–21). Rabbinic law provided for the support of orphans and granted them special privileges. During the Middle Ages the number of orphans increased, owing to frequent massacres of the Jewish community. Many communities organised special bodies to care for their welfare. In the 19th century orphanages were established in many Jewish centres (such as the Jewish Orphanage in London).

Orthodoxy Applied to a particular strand of religious thought and practice in Judaism, the term was first used in 1795. From the beginning of the 19th century it passed into common usage to denote traditional Judaism, which adheres to the belief in the divine origin of the Written and Oral Law and insists on strict adherence to the laws of the Shulḥan Arukh.

Osiris, Daniel (1825–1908) French financier and philanthropist. He was born in Bordeaux. His beneficiaries include the French State, the Institute de France, and the Jewish community.

Ossuary Receptacle, usually in the form of a small chest, in which the bones of the dead are placed. The use of ossuaries is referred to in the Mishnah. Most surviving Jewish ossuaries originated in Palestine in the period from the 2nd century BCE to the 3rd century CE. They are decorated with geometrical patterns, rosettes, olive branches, palms, wreaths, columns and chalices, and carry the names of the dead whose bones they contain inscribed in Hebrew, Aramaic and Greek.

Ostracon (from Greek 'ostracon': potsherd) Fragment of pottery carrying an inscription. Such fragments were used for various purposes, as letters and receipts among others. Important finds of ostraca of Jewish interest have been made at Gezer, Samaria, Lachish, Elath, Elephantine and Edfu.

Ostropoler, Hirsch (fl. 18th cent.) Polish Yiddish jester. He was born in Balta, Podolia, and lived at Medzibozh. He derived his name from Ostropol in Poland, where he was the shoḥet. He later wandered throughout Podolia. Booklets recording his tales and anecdotes were published posthumously.

Oy (Yiddish)   Exclamations with a wide range of meanings. It may express surprise, fear, sadness, contentment, joy, relief, uncertainty, indignation, irritation, pain, revulsion, anguish, dismay, despair, regret or outrage.

Oz, Amos (b.1939)   Israeli novelist. He was born in Jerusalem. His works include *Where the Jackals Howl, Elsewhere Perhaps, My Michael, Unto Death, Touch the Water, Touch the Wind, A Perfect Peace, In the Land of Israel* and *The Black Box*.

Ozick, Cynthia (b.1928)   American novelist. She was born in New York. Her writings include *The Pagan Rabbi and other Stories* and *The Messiah of Stockholm*.

P

Benny Goldberg who has just immigrated from Russia is detained at Ellis Island before entering the United States. In his suitcase there are three sets of false teeth. They are all made of gold. The immigration officer is puzzled and tells Benny that he cannot bring in that much gold. Benny then explains that he is a religiously observant Jew and he needs all three sets for dietary reasons. The immigration officer says: 'I know something about Jews and kosher food. Why do you need three sets of gold teeth?' Benny explains that he is Orthodox. 'I use one set for milk products, and one for meat.' 'I see,' says the immigration officer. 'You are clearly very religious. But you only mentioned two occasions. What is the third?' 'The third?' Benny says. 'That's when I want a ham sandwich.'

* * * * *

Here a Jewish immigrant who enters the United States wants to avoid being impoverished. He hopes to escape detection by bringing gold in false teeth. When confronted by an immigration officer he provides a religious justification for bringing in the gold. But in doing so he reveals his true intention. Jews laugh at the idiocy of his justification. Yet there is a serious side to the joke: it highlights the predicament faced by Jewish immigrants when they arrived in the United States with few possessions.

Pacifico, David (1784–1854) Anglo-Portuguese merchant and diplomat. Born in Gibraltar, he was a British subject. He served as Portuguese consul in Morocco (1833–37) and Greece (1837–42). In a riot against the Jewish community of Athens, he was attacked and his house destroyed. When his claim for compensation was refused, the British blockaded the port of Piraeus and captured 200 Greek ships. The Greek Government then made financial reparations to Pacifico.

Padua [Katzenellenbogen], Meir [Maharam Padua] (1482–1565) Italian talmudist. He was born in Germany, studied in Poland, and served as a rabbi in Padua. An important codifier, he was frequently consulted about halakhic issues.

Pagis, Dan (1930–1986) Israeli scholar and poet. He was born in Bukovina, Romania. In his youth he was imprisoned by the Nazis. He settled in Israel in 1947 and later became Professor of Medieval Hebrew Literature at the Hebrew University. He published studies of Hebrew literature, an annotated anthology of Hebrew love poetry of the 10th–18th centuries from Spain, Italy, Turkey and the Yemen, and his own poetry.

Palache, Juda Lion (1886–1944) Dutch orientalist and teacher. He was born in Amsterdam, and in 1925 became Professor of the Bible and Semitic Languages at the University of Amsterdam. He also served as parnas (or head) of the Spanish and Portuguese congregation in the city. He published studies of

Judaism, Islam and comparative Semitic philology.

Palache, Samuel (d.1616)   Community leader. He was the first person to settle in Amsterdam as a declared Jew, and he obtained authorisation for other Jews to settle there. In 1596 he gathered the first minyan in Amsterdam at his home for prayers on the Day of Atonement. He also built the first synagogue in the Netherlands. In 1608 he was appointed Ambassador to The Hague by the Moroccan sultan Mulay Zidan, and in 1610 he negotiated an alliance between Morocco and the Netherlands – the first treaty of alliance between Christian and Muslim states. Later he assumed command of a small Moroccan fleet which sized some ships belonging to the King of Spain; he was charged with piracy, but was acquitted.

Pale of Settlement   Territory within the borders of czarist Russia where Jews were legally authorised to reside. It consisted of 25 provinces in Poland, Lithuania, Belorussia, Ukraine, Bessarabia and the Crimea, and was established in 1791 by a decree of Catharine II. Permission to settle outside the Pale was given only to certain groups (including members of the liberal professions, Jews with a secondary school diploma, successful businessmen, skilled artisans and former Cantonists). In 1882, under the May Laws, Jews were excluded from rural areas inside the Pale. In August 1915 the Pale was effectively abolished, though the laws concerning it remained in force until March 1917.

Palestine   One of the names of the territory also known as Israel or the Holy Land. The name Palestine is derived form the Hebrew 'Peleshet'; in classical antiquity Palestine was called 'Palestinian Syria', but in time 'Syria' was omitted and the first element of the name adjusted accordingly. It is probable that the Romans imposed the name Palestine on the territory because

of the strong Jewish associations connected with the name Judea. In modern times the name Palestine was changed to Israel with the founding of the Jewish State in 1948. Following the establishment of Israel, Palestinians have been in continual conflict with Israelis.

Palmaḥ   The mobilised striking force of the Haganah. Established on 19 May 1941, it was an underground movement until 1948, when it became a part of the Israel Defence Army. From 1945 to 1947 it struggled against the British. In November 1948 General Yaakov Dori, Chief of General Staff to the Israeli forces, ordered its disbanding.

Pann   [Pfefferman],   Abel   (1883–1963)   Israeli artist, of Russian origin. He trained in Vienna and Paris. In 1913 he moved to Palestine, where he was a teacher at the Bezalel School of Arts and Crafts. His paintings depict Bible stories and scenes of Israeli settlement life.

Panofsky, Erwin (1892–1968)   American art historian of German origin. Born in Hanover, he studied at the University of Freiburg and became professor at Hamburg. After the Nazi rise to power, he went to the US and became a professor at New York University, and later at Princeton University; subsequently he was professor at Harvard.

Pantheism   The doctrine that the universe is God and God the universe. All forms of pantheism are opposed to classical theism, which affirms the belief in a creator and a created order. Kabbalistic doctrines often exhibit pantheistic tendencies.

Pap,   Karoly   (1897–1943)   Hungarian writer, son of the chief rabbi of Sopron. He served in the Hungarian Red Army and later settled in Budapest. Some of his writings deal with the issue of Jewish identity and assimilation.

Pappa (c.300–375)   Babylonian amora. He studied under Rava and Abbaye.

He founded an academy at Neresh, near Sura, which he directed. He frequently participated in halakhic disputes. Besides his scholarly activities, he engaged in the sale of poppy seeds and the brewing of date beer.

Pappenheim, Bertha (1859–1936) German communal leader. She was born in Vienna, where she was treated by the neurologist Joseph Breuer, who viewed her case as important in the development of psychoanalysis. Later she settled in Frankfurt am Main, where she became the headmistress of an orphanage. In 1904 she founded the relief organisation Jüdischer Frauenbund and visited Galicia, Romania and Russia to carry out its work. In 1914 she established and directed an institute near Frankfurt for unmarried mothers, prostitutes and delinquent women. She translated Yiddish works into German and wrote under the name of Paul Berthold.

Papua and Julianus (fl. 2nd cent.) Juden patriots They were brothers. According to rabbinic tradition, they set up banks to assist wayfarers in Jerusalem. They were probably among the leaders of the Jewish revolt against Trajan (115–17), since they were captured by the Romans at Laodicea in Syria and executed.

Papyrus Ancient Egyptian writing material made from an aquatic plan of the sedge family; also a manuscript written on this material. Aramaic papyri from Elephantine contain information about the Jewish garrison community there in the 5th century BCE. The majority of Egyptian papyri are written in Greek and date from the 2nd century BCE to the 7th century CE. They include petitions, proclamations, ordinances, records of court proceedings, wills, official correspondence, contracts, registers of people and property, tax lists, receipts and private letters. Papyri of importance to Jewish studies include the Acts of the Pagan Martyrs and the Nash Papyrus.

Parah ('Heifer') Fourth tractate in the Mishnah order of Tohorot. It deals with regulations concerning the congregational sacrifice of the red heifer (Numbers 19).

Parashah ('section') Term applied to the entire weekly portion ('sidrah') of the Torah read in the synagogue on the Sabbath, or to one of the shorter passages into which the sidrah is divided. Each of these shorter sections is read by a different person.

Parashiyyot, Four Name given to the final positions (or 'maphtir') of the Torah, read in the synagogue on the four Sabbaths preceding Passover. They are followed by an appropriate conclusion (haphtarah). The names given to the passages are Shekalim (Exodus 30:11–16); Zakhor (Deuteronomy 25:17–19); Parah (Numbers 19:1–22); and Ha Hodesh (Exodus 12:1–20). A second Scroll of the Law is used for the reading of these portions.

Pardes Paradise. The Hebrew is derived from Greek 'paradeisos'. In the Middle Ages 'pardes' was used as an acronym for the four types of biblical interpretation 'peshat' (literal), 'remez' (allegorical), 'derash' (aggadic) and 'sod' (mystical).

Pardo, David (1718–1790) Palestinian rabbinical author and poet. He was born in Venice, and served as a rabbi in Spalato in Dalmatia and in Sarajevo. Between 1776 and 1782 he travelled widely, making his way to Palestine. He settled in Jerusalem where he became head of a yeshivah. He wrote commentaries and novellae on tannaitic literature, as well as liturgical poetry.

Parents The duty of children to respect their parents is laid down in the Ten Commandments (Exodus 20:12; Leviticus 19:3) , and is emphasised in rabbinic teaching. According to Jewish law, parents must be obeyed unless they order their children to transgress the Torah, or disagree with a son in his choice of wife. The *Talmud* decrees that a son should not stand or sit in his father's place or contradict him. He should provide for his father's material needs in old age and take him where he needs to go. A father has the duty to support his children up to the age of six. He is permitted to chastise them, but only while they are minors. Both the father and mother are equal with regard to the duties owed them by their children.

Parhon, Solomon (fl. 12th cent.) Italian lexicographer. He was born in Qal'a, Spain, and became a pupil of Judah ha-Levi and Abraham ibn Ezra. He settled in Italy, where he wrote a biblical lexicon (*Maḥberet he-Arukh*) in 1160 at Salerno.

Parker, Dorthy (1893–1967) American author. Born in West End, New Jersey, she initially wrote drama reviews for *Vogue* and *Vanity Fair*. Later she reviewed books and theatre for the *New Yorker*. Her works include *Not So Deep as a Well*, *Laments for Living*, *After Such Pleasures* and *Here Lies*.

Parnas ('provider', 'supporter') Head of the Jewish community. Originally he was a lay leader, but later (especially among the Ashkenazim from the Middle Ages onward) he was elected to office as president of the community or synagogue. Election was usually for a term of one or three years, but it could occasionally be for life. In the Middle Ages and the early modern period, a system existed whereby several parnasim led the community in rotation. In modern times the term refers to the president of the community or a congregation.

Parokhet The curtain used to veil the Sanctuary of the Tabernacle, which served as a temple for the Israelites during the years in the wilderness. It was made by Bezalel of scarlet, purple and fine linen with a woven design (Exodus 26:31). In modern times the term is used by the Ashkenazim to refer to the curtain hanging before the Ark in the synagogue.

Partnership In Jewish law the concept of partnership in business includes joint ownership and commercial partnership. A partnership is formed by join acquisition or through inheritance, and can be dissolved on demand. According to Maimonides, commercial partnership is a development of joint ownership: before a partnership can be established the parties to it must gain ownership of all the capital invested in the enterprise. But other authorities regard symbolic consent or verbal agreement as a sufficient basis for partnership.

Partos, Ödön (1909–1977) Israeli composer and violinist. He was born in Budapest. He became first violinist of the Lucerne Orchestra in 1924, and from 1936 to 1938 taught violin and composition at the conservatory in Baku. In 1938 he went to Palestine and joined the Palestine Orchestra as a viola player. He was appointed Director of the Israel Conservatory and Academy of Music in Tel Aviv in 1953. His compositions include *Song of Praise* for viola and orchestra and the symphonic fantasy *En Gev*.

Paschal lamb The name given to the lamb sacrificed in the Temple period, on the eve of Passover (14 Nisan). After the sacrifice the animal was roasted whole and eaten by the community (Exodus 12:1–28, 43:9; Deuteronomy 16:1–8).

Pasken (Yiddish: 'decide', 'declare the law') To give a ruling on a religious question.

Passover (Hebrew 'Pesaḥ' [Feast of Unleavened Bread]) The first of the three pilgrim festivals, beginning on 15

Nisan. It commemorates the Exodus from Egypt, and according to tradition, the Hebrew. The name is derived from the verb 'to pass over' (Exodus 12:13). The festival is observed for seven days. The first and last day are feast days. All leaven ('ḥametz') is removed from the home on the evening before the festival; during the Passover period it is forbidden to eat or possess leaven, and only unleavened bread ('matzah') is eaten. During the period of the First and Second Temples, the paschal lamb was slaughtered on the eve of the festival. After the destruction of the Temple, a home celebration ('seder') was instituted. This takes place on the first night of Passover, and the Passover Haggadah is read.

Passover, Second (Hebrew 'Pesaḥ Sheni') Passover sacrifice offered on 14 Iyyar by anyone who had been absent or ritually impure during Passover in the preceding month (Numbers 9:6–13).

Pasternak, Boris (1890–1960) Russian author. Born in Moscow, he wrote pastoral and romantic poems and translated classical poetry and drama. During the 1930s he began working on *Doctor Zhivago*. He was denounced by the Soviet literary establishment and expelled from the Union of Soviet Writers. In 1958 he was awarded the Nobel Prize for Literature.

Patai, Joseph (1882–1953) Hungarian poet and editor. He was born in Gyöngyöspata, and taught at a Budapest high school. He published a Hebrew verse collection, anthologies of Hungarian poetry, Hungarian versions of Hebrew poetry and memoirs. He was also the editor of a Zionist monthly. In 1938 he settled in Palestine.

Patai, Raphael (1910–1996) American anthropologist and biblical scholar, son of Joseph Patai. He was born in Budapest, and in 1933 moved to Palestine, where he became an instructor in Hebrew at the Hebrew University. In 1944 he founded the Palestine Institute of Folklore and Ethnology in Jerusalem and served as its director of research. In 1947 he settled in the US, where he taught anthropology at Dropsie College and later at Fairleigh Dickinson University. He published studies on the culture of the Ancient Hebrews and the modern Middle East.

Paternity Although it is impossible conclusively to prove the paternity of a child, it is of fundamental importance in Jewish civil and ritual law concerning inheritance, incest, forbidden marriages and claims to the priesthood.

Pater synagogae (Latin: 'father of the synagogue') Title found in Greek and Roman inscriptions of Jewish origin in the classical period. It occurs in inscriptions discovered in the diaspora, particularly in Rome. The term 'Mater synagogae' (mother of the synagogue) was also used. The nature of the office referred to by these titles is not known.

Patriarchs [avot] Term applied in Judaism to the three progenitors of the Jewish people, Abraham, Isaac and Jacob.

Patterson, David (1922–2005) English scholar. He was born in Liverpool. He was a lecturer in post-Biblical studies at Oxford University and President of the Oxford Centre for Postgraduate Jewish Studies. His publications include *Abraham Mapu, The Hebrew Novel in Czarist Russia*, and *A Phoenix in Fetters*.

Payess (Yiddish from Hebrew 'peah' (*sing.*), 'poet' (*plural*) Long ringlets of hair worn in front of the ears by Orthodox, Yemenite and Ḥasidic Jewish men. The practice is based on Leviticus 19:27.

Pe Seventeenth letter of the Hebrew alphabet. Its numerical value is 80.

Peace (Hebrew 'shalom') The Hebrew word 'shalom' carries connotations of wholeness. The ideal of peace was proclaimed by the prophets and the Messiah was heralded as the bringer of peace. The last of the Eighteen Benedictions is a prayer for peace. In spite of the emphasis placed on peace in Judaism, pacifism is not required of the Jewish people, since war is justified in certain circumstances.

Peace offering Sacrifice of cattle or sheep, given as a thanksgiving, in fulfilment of a vow, or as a free-will offering (Leviticus 3; 7:11). The priests sprinkled the blood of the animal on the altar, sacrificed parts of the fat, and took their own portion. Those making the sacrifice then ate the remains.

Peah (i) ('corner') Term used specifically of the corner of a field, in connection with the rules on gleaning. Gleanings are one of the obligatory gifts to the poor (Leviticus 19:9–10; 23:22), and the Bible specifies that they should be left as the corners of a field that is being harvested. The rabbis taught that at least one-sixtieth of the harvest should be left. In the event of a good crop or a large number of poor gleaners, the proportion should be increased.

Peah (ii) ('Corner') Second tractate in the Mishnah order of Zeraim. It deals with the setting aside of the corners of the field for the poor (Leviticus 19:9–10; 23:22), as well as other duties owed to them (Deuteronomy 24:19–21).

Peerce, Jan (1904–1984) American singer. He was born in New York. He sang at Radio City Music Hall from 1932, and later performed in numerous operas. He also gave recitals of cantorial music and recorded cantorial works and Jewish folk songs.

Peixotto, Benjamin Franklin (1834–1890) American lawyer, diplomat and communal leader, grandson of Moses Levy Maduro Peixotto. He was born in New York, and became a clothing merchant in Cleveland, Ohio. He was

Grand Sar (president) of the B'nai B'rith in 1863–64. In 1866 he moved to New York to practise law. In 1870 he was appointed the first US consul in Bucharest, where he argued for Jews to be allowed to emigrate to the US. He was US consul in Lyons from 1877 to 1885.

Pekah (fl. 8th cent. BCE) King of Israel (735–732 BCE). He gained the throne by killing Pekahiah. He formed an alliance with Rezin of Aram-Dammesek and together they attacked Judah. King Ahaz of Judah appealed to the Assyrian King Tiglath-Pileser III who invaded the allied kingdom, abolished Aram-Dammesek as a state, and stripped Israel of Galilee and Gilead. Pekah was later killed by Hoshea.

Pekahiah (fl. 8th cent. BCE) King of Israel (737–735 BCE). He reigned at the same time as Uzziah, King of Judah. According to II King's 15:24, he did what was evil in the sight of the Lord. He was killed by Pekah who took his place on the throne.

People of the Book Term used in the Koran to denote the followers of religions dependant on Scripture (Jews and Christians).

Pereira, Abraham Israel [Tomás Rodrigues] (d.1699) Spanish religious leader and writer. He escaped from the Spanish Inquisition to the Netherlands, where he founded a *Talmud* Torah in Amsterdam. He also established the Ḥesed Abraham yeshivah at Hebron. A member of the Sabbetaian movement, he wrote *La certeza del camino* to encourage Marranos to repent in preparation for the Messianic age. He set out for Palestine to meet Shabbetai Tzevi but stopped in Italy.

Péreire, Jacob Rodriguez (1715–1780) French educator and communal leader. He was born into a Marrano family in Berlangua, Spain, and went to France, where he embraced Judaism.

He was a teacher of deaf mutes, and his work was recognised by Louis XV. He was also an inventor. Active in Jewish spheres, he was a counsellor of the Sephardi community in Paris from 1749.

Perez Shirah ('Chapter of song') Collection of scriptural verses in which the praise of God is uttered by different parts of creation. The notion that God is praised by all creation in its several ways is expressed in Psalm 148. This prompted the selection and putting together of a 'hymnal of creation' consisting of scriptural verses that represent the praises of the universe offered to God. The Perek Shirah is recited as a private devotion after the morning service.

Perelman, Sidney Joseph (1904–79) American author. Born in Brooklyn, he grew up in Providence, Rhode Island. He studied at Brown University, and later lived in Greenwich Village where he drew cartoons for the weekly *Judge*. From 1934 he contributed to the *New Yorker*. His works include *Dawn Ginsberg's Revenge, Acres and Pains, Westward Ha!, Swiss Family Perelman, The Rising Gorge, Baby, It's Cold Inside* and *Vinegar Pass*. He wrote movie scripts and collaborated wth the Marx Brothers for *Monkey Business* and *Horsefeathers*. His screenplay for *Around the World in Eighty Days* won an Academy Award.

Peres, Shimon (1923–2016) Israeli politician, of Polish origin. He went to Palestine in 1934. He served as Chairman of the Labour Party from 1977. He was Activist Prime Minister in 1977 and Prime Minister of Israel in 1984–86. His publications include *From these Men, Tomorrow is Now* and *The Next Phase*.

Peretz, Isaac Leib (1852–1915) Polish Yiddish and Hebrew poet and author. He was born in Zamość. Educated in the Eastern-European religious tradition, he also came into contact with modern learning. He practised law and lived in Warsaw, where he was an employee in the Jewish Communal Bureau. He began writing at an early age, and eventually decided to use Yiddish as a means of making literary material available to the Jewish masses. He was a master of the Yiddish short story, in which he depicted the misery and virtues of Polish Jewry. He also wrote romantic and symbolic stories based on Jewish legend and mysticism, mystic dramas and poetry, and edited a number of literary compositors.

Perjury The act of swearing to a statement known to be false, or of giving false evidence while under oath. Perjury violates the third of the Ten Commandments and constitutes a desecration of God's name. It thus may bring devastation on the whole community. Jewish law does not require witnesses to swear to the truth of their evidence.

Perl, Joseph (1773–1839) Galician Hebrew author and maskil. He was born in Tarnopol. He was initially attracted to Ḥasidism, but later embraced the Haskalah. In 1813 he established the first modern Jewish school in Galicia (in Tarnopol), which he directed. He encouraged the creation of Jewish agricultural colonies, and opposed the Ḥasidim in his satirical language.

Perles, Felix (1874–1933) Austrian rabbi and scholar. He was active in the Zionist movement in Vienna. In 1899 he became a rabbi at Königsberg and taught at the university there. He wrote studies of Bible criticism, Hebrew and Aramaic lexicography, apocryphal and pseudepigraphical literature, medieval Hebrew poetry, liturgy and Jewish dialects.

Persky, Daniel (1887–1962) American Hebraist, educator and journalist. He was born in Minsk, and in 1906 moved to the US, where he worked for the Hebraist movement, which aimed to foster the Hebrew language and literature. From 1921 he taught at the Herzliah Hebrew Teachers' College in New York. He contributed articles to the Hebrew weekly *Hadoar.* A number of his books were based on these contributions. He also edited several children's magazines.

Pesahim ('Paschal lambs') Third tractate in the Misnah order of Moed. It deals with regulations regarding the Passover holiday.

Peshat The term applied to the basic type of scriptural interpretation, concerned with the simple, literal meaning of the words.

Pesher ('interpretation') The name given to a number of biblical commentaries found among the Dead Sea Scrolls. The term derives from the authors' method of introducing their commentaries with the phrase 'pishro al' (its interpretation refers to). Pesharim have been found on the books of Habbakuk, Isaiah, Nahum, Micah, Hosea and Psalms.

Peshitta (Syriac: 'Simple') Syriac translation of the Bible. It was called Peshitta because the text was translated directly from the Hebrew, in contrast to the Syrio-Hexapla, which is a literal translation from the Greek of the Septuagint in Origen's *Hexapla.* The Peshitta was begun in the 1st or 2nd century, and was intended for use by Jews in certain synagogues. By the 3rd century it had become the Bible of Syriac-speaking Christians.

Pesikta de-Rav Kahana Collection of midrashic homilies for holidays and special Sabbaths. Attributed to Rav Kahanah, it is the oldest midrash termed 'Pesikta' (Aramaic 'Section'); it is sometimes known by that title.

Pesikta Rabbati Collection of midrashic homilies for holidays and special Sabbaths. Its contents are drawn from numerous sources though more than half of the homilies are of the Yelammedenu type.

Pesuke de-Zimrah ('Passages of songs') The name given to a section of the Shaharit prayer recited between the morning blessings and the prayer that precedes the Shema. The ordering of these elements accords with the dictum that praise of God should precede prayer. The Pesuke de-Zimrah consists of Psalms 145–150, various verses, and the Song of Moses (Exodus 14:30–15:18). They are introduced by the blessing 'Barukh sheamar' and end with the blessing 'Yishtabbah' (which on Sabbaths and festivals is preceded by the doxology Nishmat). Among the Sephardim the Pseuke de-Zimrah are referred to as the Zemirot. In the Sephardi rite a different ordering is observed (some of the psalm verses precede the 'Barukh she-amar') and on Sabbaths and festivals more psalms are recited.

Pethahiah of Regensberg (fl. 12th cent.) German traveller. In about 1175 he set out on a journey, which took him to Tartary, Khazaria, Armenia, Kurdistan, Babylonia, Syria and Palestine. An account of his experiences are recorded by Judah Ben Samuel he-Hasid. It casts light on Jewish life, especially in Baghdad and the Holy Land.

Pevsner, Nikolaus (1902–83) British art historian, of German origin. Born in Leipzig, he became keeper of the Dresden Art Gallery, and later taught at the University of Göttingen. In 1934 he fled to England. He was Professor of Fine Art at Cambridge, and later Professor of the History of Art at Birkbeck College, London. His works include *Outline of European Architecture, Pioneers of Modern Design: From William Morris to Walter Gropius, Mannerism to Romanticism* and *Sources of Modern Art.*

Pharisees ('separatists') One of the three main sects of Judaism before the destruction of the Jewish state in 70 CE. The others were the Sadducees and the Essenes. It is probable that the Pharisees were the successors of the

Hasideans. They adhered strictly to the Oral Law and were skilful interpreters of the Torah. They believed in resurrection and immortality, the existence of angels, divine providence and the freedom of the will. The traditions of Pharisaic Judaism were continued by Talmudic and later rabbis, and the Pharisees' teachings formed the basis of rabbinic Judaism.

Phasael (fl. 1st cent. BCE) Judean prince, son of Anipater II and the brother of Herod the Great. He was appointed Governor of Jerusalem by Antipater when Herod became Governor of Galilee. Accompanied by Hyrcanus II, Phasael went to negotiate peace in the Parthian camp, but was imprisoned by the Parthians. According to tradition, he committed suicide. Herod called one of the towers on the wall of Jerusalem after him.

Philip (d.34) Judean tetrarch, son of Herod the Great He was educated in Rome. He was appointed tetrarch by the provisions of his father's will, and received the territories of Gaulanitis, Trachonitis, Bashan and the city of Paneas. He married Salome.

Phillipson, Franz (1851–1925) Belgian financier and communal leader, son of Ludwig Phillipson. He was born in Magdeburg. He established a bank in Belgium in 1871. Later he was President of the Belgian Congo railway company and a founder of the Belgian Congo Bank. He served as President of the Jewish community in Brussels and contributed to Jewish colonisation in Argentina and Brazil.

Phillipson, Ludwig (1811–1889) German rabbi and newspaper editor. He served as preacher to the Jewish community of Magdeburg and was instrumental in initiating Reform rabbinical synods in Germany. In 1837 he founded the *Allgemeine Zeitung des Judentums*, which he edited. He published a translation of the Bible, and helped found the Institut zur Förderung des Israelitischen Literature.

Phillipson, Martin (1846–1916) German historian and communal leader, born at Magdeburg. He taught at the University of Bonn, and later at the University of Brussels, where he became rector. Owing to anti-German attitudes in Brussels, he was forced to resign and settled in Berlin, where he became involved in Jewish affairs and served as head of the Lehranstalt für die Wissenschaft des Judentums. He published studies of modern history.

Philipson, David (1882–1949) American Reform rabbi. He was born in Wabash, Indiana, and served as a rabbi in Baltimore and Cincinnati. He was President of the Central Conference of American Rabbis, and taught at the Hebrew Union College. His writings include *The Reform Movement in Judaism, The Jew in English Fiction,* and *My Life as an American Jew.*

Philo (c.25 BCE–40 CE) Hellenistic philosopher. He lived in Alexandria. He combined Hellenistic thought with Jewish belief in Holy Scripture. His writings include a legal exposition, philosophical interpretation and a commentary on the Pentateuch. In 40 CE he was a member of the Jewish deputation which travelled to Rome to make representations to the Emperor Calligula, concerning anti-Jewish activities in Alexandria.

Philosophy Jewish philosophical reflection about religious belief began with with Philo of Alexandria who interpreted Judaism in Neoplatonic terms. Later Jewish writers were influenced by the revival of Greek philosophy by the Arabs. Prominent among such medieval thinkers were Saadyah Gaon, Solomon ibn Gabirol, Bahya ibn Pakudah, Abraham ibn Daud, Maimonides, Levi ben Gershon, Hasdai ben Abraham Crecas, Joseph Albo and Isaac Abravanel. The modern period of Jewish philosophy began with Moses Mendelssohn who was followed by such writers as Solomon Fromstecher, Samuel Hirsch, Naḥmanides Krochmal, Solomon Ludwig Steinheim, Hermann Cohen, Franz Rosenzweig, Leo Baeck, Martin Buber, Abraham Heschel and Mordecai Kaplan.

Phinehas (i) (fl.? 13th cent. BCE) Israelite priest, grandson of Aaron. He slew Zimri and as a reward he and his descendants were granted the priesthood (Numbers 25). He was also given a holding on Mount Ephraim. Phinehas continued to officiate and was still in office at the time of the campaign against Benjamin (Judges 20:28). The Zadokites traced their ancestry to him.

Phinehas (ii) (fl. 11th cent. BCE) Israelite priest, second son of Eli. He and Hophni, his brother, officiated at Shiloh but were guilty of conduct unworthy of priests. While accompanying the Ark of the Covenant into battle against the Philistines, they were killed (I Samuel 4).

Phinehas ben Abraham of Koretz (1726–1791) Lithuanian Ḥasdic rabbi. He lived in Volhynia, where he became under the influence of the Baal Shem Tov. An opponent of the tradition of legal interpretation known as 'pilpul', he preached simplicity and humility.

Piatigorsky, Gregor (1903–76) Ukrainian cellist. Born in Ekaterinoslav, Ukraine, he received his first music lessons from his father. He studied at the Moscow Conservatory and in 1919 became a member of the Lenin Quartet and principal cellist of the Bolshoi Theatre Orchestra. In 1921 he went to Warsaw, Leipzig and later Berlin. He subsequently became first cellist of the Berlin Philharmonic, but left to become a soloist and performed in major capitals throughout the world.

Picon, Molly (1898–1992) American actress. She was born in New York. She played Yiddish roles on Second Avenue, acted at Kessler's Theatre, and went on tour with her husband, Jacob Kalilch. From 1942 she managed the Molly Picon Theatre in New York. After World War II she visited displaced persons' camps and toured widely. Subsequently she appeared in plays and films and on television.

Pilgrimage Journey made to a holy city or site for the spiritual benefit of the traveller. Jews made pilgrimage to Jerusalem for the festivals of Passover, Shavuot and Sukkot until the destruction of the second Temple. In the Middle Ages, the institution was revived largely through Karaite influence. Special prayers were composed for pilgrims to recite in Jerusalem, as well as on visits to the graves of biblical figures and rabbinic sages.

Pilgrim festivals According to Scripture, male Israelites were enjoined to make a pilgrimage to Jerusalem on the festivals of Passover, Shavuot, and Sukkot (Exodus 23:17; Deuteronomy 16:16) which therefore became known as 'pilgrim festivals'. All pilgrims were to offer a sacrifice and give the second tithe of their produce to the Temple (this had to be consumed in Jerusalem). In modern times there is no longer a formal obligation to go to Jerusalem on the pilgrim festivals. Special prayers, including the Hallelujah, are recited in the synagogue, and each festival has its own special liturgical characteristics, ceremonies, and customs.

Pilichowski, Leopold (1869–1933) Polish painter. Born in Zadzin, he lived in Łódź, Paris and London. He painted work scenes of wool-dyers at Łódź, and shopkeepers and artisans in London's Whitechapel. He also executed portraits of Hayyim Naḥmanides Bialik, Albert Einstein, Aḥad ha-Am, Max Nordau and Chaim Weizmann.

Pilpul (lit. fine distinctions) A tradition of interpretation of the Oral Law involving dialectical reasoning. It was occasionally carried to extremes of legal casuistry and its unrestrained use aroused the disapproval of various scholars. Nonetheless, the pilpul approach to the study of the law was developed by tosaphists and in the yeshivah.

Pincus, Louis Arieh (1912–1973) Israeli lawyer and Zionist, of South African origin. He was a lawyer and served as Chairman of the South African Zionist Socialist Party. In 1948 he moved to Israel, where he became a legal adviser and General Secretary to the Ministry of Transportation. Later he was appointed Managing Director of El Al. In 1961 he became a member of the executive of the Jewish Agency. He was acting Chairman of the 27th Zionist Congress, and served as Chairman of the Board of Governors of Tel Aviv University.

Pines, Jehiel Michal (1843–1913) Russian author, Zionist and yeshivah leader. He was born in Ruzhany, Belorussia. He contributed to the Hebrew press, arguing against assimilation, and made plans to establish an agricultural school. He represented the Mazkeret Mosheh society in Palestine from 1878, and played an important role in the early stages of Jewish settlement. One of the founders of the Hebrew-speaking movement in Jerusalem, he opposed Halukkah and fanaticism. His attitudes gave rise to conflict with rabbis in Jerusalem.

Pinsker, Judah Loeb [Leo] (1821–1891) Russian Zionist. He was born in Tomaszów, Poland, and was one of the first Jews to enrol at Odessa University, where he studied law. Later he studied medicine at the University of Moscow, and returned to Odessa to set up practice in 1849. He was a founder of the first Russian Jewish weekly to which he contributed. Initially he was an advocate of the Haskalah movement, but after the wave of pogroms in 1881 he argued that only national, territorial rebirth could solve the Jewish problem. In his pamphlet *Auto-Emancipation* he called for the establishment of a Jewish territory, where the Jews could support and govern themselves. In 1884 he convened the Kattowitz Conference of the Hovevei Zion where he was elected president of Hibbat Zion's presidium.

Pinsker, Simhah (1801–1864) Galician scholar. He was born in Tarnów. He was the founder of the first successful modern Jewish school in Russia – in Odessa in 1826. He accumulated a collection of ancient Hebrew manuscripts, several of which were examined and described by the Karaite scholar Abraham Firkovich on a visit of Odessa. Eventually Pinsker moved to Vienna, where he published a history of Karaism and Karaite literature. He later returned to Odessa.

Pinski, David (1872–1959) American Yiddish dramatist and novelist. He was born in Mohilever on the Dnieper, and lived in Warsaw. In 1899 he emigrated to the US, where he wrote for the Yiddish stage. His early works deal with Jewish suffering in Russia, but later he wrote poetic and symbolic treatments of Jewish historic themes. His plays include *Treasure, The Eternal Jew* and *Shabbetai Tzevi*. He also wrote novels and short stories. Active in Jewish affairs, he served as President of the Jewish Workers' Alliance. Later he settled in Israel.

Pinter, Harold (1930–2008) British dramatist. Born in London, he studied at the Royal Academy of Dramatic Art. From 1949 to 1960 he was a professional actor. His works include *The Room, The Birthday Party, The Caretaker, The Homecoming, A Night Out, A Slight Ache, The Collection, Landscape, Silence, Old Times* and *Betrayal*. He won the Nobel prize in literature in 2005.

Pirbright, Lord [Worms, Henry de, Baron] (1840–1903) British statesman. He was active in London Jewish communal life, serving as President of the Anglo-Jewish Association from

1874 to 1886. He was then Undersecretary of State for the colonies.

Pirke de-Rabbi Eliezer Tannaitic midrash on Genesis and the first chapters of Exodus. The first two chapters consist of biographical details of Eliezer ben Hyrcanus, for whom the midrash is named.

Pisher (Yiddish) An inexperienced young person, a nobody.

Pissarro, Camille (1830–1903) French painter. Born in St Thomas, Virgin Islands, he studied in Paris and returned to St Thomas to work in his family's store. He left to paint in Venezuela; in 1855 he moved to Paris. He became an important figure in the French Impressionist group.

Pittum ha-Ketoret ('The compound forming the incense') Title of the baraita on the preparation of incense in the Temple. Among the Ashkenazim it is recited on Sabbaths and festivals at the end of the musaph prayer. In the Sephardi ritual it is recited every morning and afternoon. In mystic circles importance was attached to the meticulous recital of this text.

Piyyut Liturgical poem, specifically one added to a statutory prayer. Originating in Palestine, possibly in the 5th century, piyyutim were also composed in Babylonia, Germany, France, Spain and Italy. The oldest known paytanim (authors of such poems) are Yose ben Yose, Yannai and Eleazar Kallir. Later important writers included Saadyah Gaon, Meshullam ben Kalonymos, Amittai ben Shephatiah, Rashi, Solomon ibn Gabirol, Judah ha-Levi, Solomon ben Judah ha-Bavli, Moses ben Kalonymos, Jekuthiel ben Moses and Meir ben Baruch of Rothenburg. The chief groups of piyyutim are: the yotzer, inserted in the first blessing before the Shema in the morning service; the ophan, inserted in the middle of the same blessing; the zulat, inserted in the Emet ve-yatziv prayer said after the Shema in the morning service; and the kerovah, accompanying the first three blessings of the Amidah. piyyutim for the evening service are known as 'maaravot'. Special groups of piyyutim were written for the Day of Atonement ('selihot') and the Ninth of Av ('kinot').

Plagues, Ten [Plagues of Egypt] The afflictions suffered by the Egyptians because of Pharaoh's refusal to allow the Israelites to leave Egypt (Exodus 7:14–12:34). The waters of the Nile were turned to blood; infestations of frogs, lice and flies occurred; the cattle were smitten with disease, and both men and animals with boils. A fierce hailstorm was sent; a swarm of locusts devastated the crops; for three days Egypt was blanketed in darkness; and finally, the firstborn were killed in the night.

Pledge Object given to a lender as security for a loan. According to Scripture, vessels used for the preparation of food should not be used in this way. If the lender accepts as a pledge a garment in which the borrower sleeps, it must be returned to its owner at night. The principle of returning the pledge when its owner has need of it also applies to any object taken from a poor man as security for a loan (Deuteronomy 24:10–17).

Plotst (Yiddish) To split, burst or explode; figuratively to be aggravated beyond endurance.

Podhoretz, Norman H. (b.1930) American writer and editor. He was born in Brooklyn. In 1960 he became editor of the intellectual monthly *Commentary* published by the American Jewish Committee. His writings include *Doings and Undoings: the Fifties and After in American Writing*, *The Commentary Reader*, and *Making it*.

Poetry Biblical poetry consists of epic poems, popular lyrical poetry and prophecies. It is characterised by 'parallelism', a technique in which the verse is divided into two halves, the second repeating the content of the first or forming an antithesis to it. Poetry is also found in the Dead Sea Scrolls and in the prayer book. Thought the medieval period liturgical poetry (piyyutim) was composed by numerous poets (paytanim); piyyutim are characterised by the use of rhyme, meters, strophic organisation, refrains and acrostics. Hebrew poetry was revived by the Haskalah movement, and has enjoyed a further renaissance in modern Israel.

Pogrom (Russian) Organised massacre of a body or class of people. The term has come to be used particularly of attacks against the Jews, carried out by the Christian population between 1881 and 1921. Three waves of pogroms occurred, in 1881–84, 1903–1906, and 1917–21. Such attacks involved destruction of property, looting, rape, bloodshed and murder.

Polanyi, Michael (1891–1976) Hungarian chemist and philosopher. He studied at the University of Budapest and worked on the chemistry of liquids and thermodynamics. He later emigrated to Germany and worked at Karlsruhe University and subsequently the Kaiser Wilhelmina Institute. When Hitler came to power he went to Manchester, England and became a professor of chemistry at the University of Manchester. Later he became Professor of Social Studies there. His works include *The Concept of Freedom: The Russian Experiment and After, Full Employment and Free Trade, Science, Faith and Society, Personal Knowledge, Beyond Nihilism* and *Knowing and Being.*

Polemic Controversial discussion or writing, especially in theology. In Talmudic literature there are references to Jewish polemics in the discussions between rabbis and heretics ('minim'). Christians also produced polemical literature aimed at convincing Jews of the truth of Christianity and proving the dogmas of the Trinity, the Virgin birth and the messiahship of Jesus. In the Middle Ages anti-Jewish polemics were encouraged by the Dominicans, and various public disputations between Christians and Jews took place, such as the Disputation of Paris (1240), and the Disputation of Barcelona (1263). In addition, Jewish writers produced polemics on particular subjects: of importance are the satirical letter of Profiat Duran, the *Sepher ha-Berit* by Joseph Kimḥi, the *Sepher Nitzaḥon* by Yomtov Lipmann Muhlhausen, and the *Ḥizzuk Emunah* by Isaac of Troki, Polemnical works were also produced by Marranos.

Poliakov, Léon (1910–1997) French historian. He was born in St Petersburg, and moved to France in 1920. He was on the staff of *Pariser Tageblatt* until 1939, then served in the French Army during World War II. After the war he became head of the research department of the Centre de Documentation Juive Contemporaine, and in 1952 research fellow at the Centre National de la Recherche Scientifique. He was appointed to a post at the École Pratique des Hautes Études in 1954. His writings include *History of Anti-Semitism.*

Pollak, Jacob (1460/1470–after 1552) Polish rabbi and halakhic authority. He was born in Bavaria, and became a rabbi in Prague, where he was a member of the bet din. Later he went to Kraków, where he opened the first yeshivah in Poland, and instituted the interpretive method known as 'pilpul' (fine distinctions). In 1503 he was appointed by King Alexander as the rabbi of the whole of Poland.

Poll tax A tax levied on every person. In biblical times a poll tax of half a shekel was imposed on all male Israelites (Exodus 30:12–16). During the period of the Second Temple, this was an annual levy. The Romans imposed a poll tax which caused a rebellion led by Judah the Galilean. After the destruction of Jerusalem in 70, the voluntary contribution of half a shekel per year that Jews had formerly made for the upkeep of the Temple was transformed into the contribution *ficus judaicus*, which was levied until the 4th century. During the Middle Ages the poll tax on the Jews was renewed by the Holy Roman Emperors in Germany under the name 'Opferpfennig'.

Polygamy   In biblical times Jewish society was polygamous. However, certain passages in the Bible, such as the image of the housewife in Proverbs 31, appear to reflect the values of a monogamous community. In the *Talmud* monogamy is extolled. The takkanah of Gershom ben Judah (c.1000), forbidding polygamy, gave formal sanction to the state of affairs that already existed among Ashkenazi Jewry. Among Spanish and oriental Jews polygamy continued to be accepted under religious law, though in modern times civil law enforces monogamy.

Pomi, David de (1525–1588)   Italian physician, linguist and philosopher. He was born in Spoleto. He was a rabbi and physician at Magliano, and later settled in Venice, where he published most of his works. Pope Pius IV gave him permission to attend Christians, but this concession was revoked by Pius V, though it was later restored by Pope Sixtus V. He published a treatise on gynaecology, a historical defence of Jewish physicians, and a Hebrew-Latin-Italian dictionary (*Tzemaḥ David*) containing scientific and historical information.

Pool, David de Sola (1885–1970)   American rabbi, communal leader and historian. He was born in London. After moving to the US he became minister of Congregation Shearith Israel in New York in 1907. He wrote studies in the fields of American Jewish history, religion, education and Zionism, and edited and translated liturgical works.

Porge [purge]   To remove the sinews of the hind legs of an animal slaughtered according to ritual law.

Portaleone, Abraham ben David (1542–1612)   Italian physician and author. He graduated from the University of Pavia in 1563, and later served as physician to the ducal house there. In 1591 he was given papal authorisation to attend Christian patients. He wrote a Latin work containing guidance for physicians, and a study of the application of gold in medicine. His *Shield of the Mighty* is a study of the Temple and its service.

Post-mortem [autopsy]   An examination (usually medical or forensic) made after death. In Jewish law a post-mortem must be carried out on all animals after slaughter to ensure the absence of physical defects and thus conformity with the dietary regulations. The halakhah objects to post-mortem operations on human beings, but this ruling may be overridden where such an examination might lead to the saving of other lives. Thus, for example, post-mortems are allowed in cases of obscure or hereditary diseases, where the findings may yield information of value in the treatment of patients suffering from the same or similar diseases.

Potok, Chaim (1929–2002)   American novelist. He was born in New York. He taught at the University of Judaism in Los Angeles and the Jewish Theological Seminary. In 1965 he became editor of the Jewish Publication Society. His novels include *The Chosen, The Promise, My Name is Asher Lev, In the Beginning, The Book of Lights*, and *Davita's Harp*.

Pottery   The earliest pottery remains found in Palestine date from the Neolithic period. The Philistines were making pottery on the coastal plain the 12th century BCE, and from the period of the monarchy the Israelites are known to have used earthenware storage jars with handles and bowls. Greek glazed ware from the 7th century BCE has been found in the region, as has black-glazed and brown-slipped ware of the Hellenistic period. During the Roman era red-glazed pottery was imported, and later was imitated locally by Jewish craftsmen. In the 4th century colour-coated pottery was developed. The *Talmud* records numerous names for different types of vessels. The tractate Kelim in the Mishnah deals with the ritual cleanliness of earthen vessels.

Poverty   According to the Bible, poverty is an ever-present misfortune (Deuteronomy 15:11), and its relief is a religious duty. Although various institutions have been founded throughout history to sustain the poor, and the giving of alms is enshrined in Jewish law and practice, the Jewish tradition stresses that the aim of charitable giving and social welfare should be to help the poor to become self-supporting.

Praag, Siegfried van (1899–2002)   Dutch novelist. He was born in Amsterdam. He became a schoolteacher and settled in Brussels; later he lived in London, where he worked for the BBC. A number of his novels deal with Jewish topics and his later writings recall the Jewish life of Amsterdam that was destroyed by the Nazi invasion.

Praefectus Judaeorum ('Prefect of the Jews')   Title of the lay representative of Hungarian Jewry in the 15th–16th centuries.

Prawer, Siegbert Salomon (1925–2012)   British scholar. He was born in Cologne, and went to England in 1939. He taught at the University of Birmingham, and later became a professor of German at London University. In 1969 he was appointed Taylor Professor of German at the University of Oxford. His publications include *Heine's Jewish Comedy: A Study of his Portraits of Jews and Judaism*.

Prayer   The offering, in public worship or private devotion, of petition, confession, adoration or thanksgiving to God; also the form of words in which such an offering is made. In the Bible prayers are mentioned as being made by individuals as well as in a cultic context. At the beginning of the Second Temple period a formal pattern of daily worship, consisting of prayer, was determined by the Great Assembly. Following the pattern of sacrifice, it took place in the morning (Shaharit), afternoon (Minhah) and evening (Maariv), and an additional prayer (Musaph) was recited on Sabbaths and festivals. On the Day of Atonement a further prayer (Neilah) was added. The original version of the prayer service included the Eighteen Benedictions (or Amidah) and the Shema. Over the centuries other prayers were added. From the gaonic period compilations of prayers were made in the daily prayer book ('siddur') and the festival prayer book ('mahzor').

Predestination   The doctrine that all events are predetermined by God. The biblical doctrine of predestination was amplified by the rabbis. Human beings have free will, but God controls the course of history and directs it to its final end.

Pre-existence   The doctrine that souls and objects existed before the creation of the world or before they came into being on earth. The concept is found in Apocryphal literature and was believed by the Essenes. In the *Talmud* various sages asserted that souls pre-existed in an abode called 'guph', that the Torah and the Messiah existed before creation, and that certain objects (such as the staff of Aaron) were pre-created. Some Jewish philosophers accepted the theory and it became a central kabbalistic doctrine associated with metempsychosis.

Preil, Gabriel (1911–1993)   American Hebrew poet. He was born in Dorpat, Estonia, and went to the US in 1922. He published essays, translated Hebrew texts into English and wrote Hebrew poetry.

Preminger, Otto (1905–86)   American film director, of Austrian origin. Born in Austria, he succeeded Max Reinhardt at a Vienna theatre. In 1935 he left Europe for the US. He directed the film *Laura;* his other films include *The Moon is Blue, The Man with a Golden Arm, Anatomy of a Murder, Exodus, Carmen Jones* and *Porgy and Bess.*

Presbyter Judaeorum   Secular head of the Exchequer of the Jews in 13th-century England. He supervised the collection of taxes and fees for the Crown, was called on by the King to advise on Jewish matters, and was responsible for the administration of justice in the Jewish community. The names of six holders of the office are known: Jacob of London, Josce fil'Isaac, Aaron of York, Elias de Eveske, Hagin, son of Master Moses of Lincoln, and Cok Hagin, son of Deulecresse of London.

Presser, Jacob (1890–1970)   Dutch writer and historian. He was born in Amsterdam, and became Professor of Modern History at the university there. His writing includes *The Destruction of Dutch Jewry.*

Priesand, Sally (b.1946)   American rabbi. A graduate of the University of Cincinnati, and the Hebrew Union College, she was the first woman to be ordained as a rabbi in the US.

Priest (Hebrew 'cohen')   In Judaism the position of priest is hereditary, and is based on descent from the family of Aaron. The duties of the priests were originally connected with the sacrificial service in the Temple at Jerusalem. The High Priest served as the spiritual head of the people and in some cases was also the secular head of the community. After the destruction of the Temple in 70 CE, the duties of the priest were limited to pronouncing the Priestly Blessing on festival days, redeeming first-born males on the 31st day after birth ('pidyon ha-ben'), and taking precedence at functions such as the Torah reading. While theoretically the priesthood continues to exist, the identity of those entitled to claim membership of it is obscure.

Priestly Blessing   Formula of words ordained by God and given to the priests by Moses for the blessing of Israel (Numbers 6:24–26): 'The Lord bless you and keep you; the Lord make his face to shine upon you and be gracious to you; the Lord lift up his countenance upon you, and grant you peace'. It was recited by the priests in the Temple each day, and eventually became part of the synagogue service.

Prilutski, Noyakh [Prylucki, Noah] (1882–1941)   Polish Yiddish scholar and political leader. He was born in Berdichev, and grew up in Kremenetz. He was active in the campaigns for Jews to gain access to higher education. In 1909 he set up a private law practice in Warsaw and founded a Yiddish daily newspaper. The following year he was elected to the Warsaw city council, and later served as a member of the Polish parliament. He helped establish Yiddish-speaking schools in Poland, organised the country's first Yiddish cultural conference, and helped to set up schools and libraries in rural areas. He published various works on Yiddish scholarship. Later he became Professor of Yiddish at the University of Vilnius.

Printing   In the 15th century Davin de Caderousse studied the art of printing in Avignon. The first dated example of Hebrew printing was produced in 1475 at Reggio di Calabria. About 150 Hebrew incunabula were produced in Spain, Italy and Portugal. The most important family in the early history of Hebrew printing was that of Soncino. Daniel Bomberg established Venice as a centre of Hebrew printing, and in the 16th century other cities with important presses were located in Germany, Poland and the Levant. In 1627 Manasseh ben Israel introduced Hebrew printing to Amsterdam, which became the major centre in the 17th–18th centuries. This role moved to various cities in Eastern Europe in the 19th century and has been taken over by Israel in the modern period.

Prinz, Joachim (1902–1988) American rabbi and communal leader. He was born in Burchartsdorf, Germany, and became the rabbi of the Berlin Jewish community in 1926. He attacked Nazism from the pulpit and was expelled from Germany. In 1939 he became rabbi at Temple B'nai Abraham in Newark, New Jersey. Active in Jewish affairs, he served as President of the American Jewish Congress form 1958 to 1966.

Profanation The desecration of holy things. Anyone committing such an act was required to bring a sacrifice and pay for the value of whatever was profaned with an increment of a fifth (Leviticus 5:14). If an animal donated for sacrifice was found to be unfit through a physical blemish, the donor could redeem it by paying the value of the animal plus the same increment. A house which had been consecrated to the sanctuary could also be redeemed (Leviticus 27:13–15). The priest was not allowed to marry a divorcee or harlot. The term is also used in a wider, non-cultic context, in such expressions as 'profanation of God's name' and 'profanation of the Sabbath'.

Property According to Jewish law property can come into an individual's possession through 'meshikhah' (drawing an object toward oneself), 'hagbahah' (raising an object), and 'hazakah' (taking possession). It can also be acquired through what is accepted by local custom as achieving the transfer of property. All these methods lead to what is termed 'kinyan' (possession). Change of ownership may also take place through inheritance. An individual has the right to abandon his property, which may then be taken over by another person.

Prophet (Hebrew 'navi' [seer]) A person who speaks through divine inspiration, gives warning of the future and expresses his will. Prophets existed in the Ancient Near East, and were of particular importance in Ancient Israel. Several major periods of prophecy may be traced in biblical times: Mosaic prophecy (?13th century BCE), charismatic prophecy (including Deborah and Samuel; 12th century BCE), early solitary prophesy (including Elijah and Elisha; 9th century BCE), classical prophecy (including Amos, Hosea, and Isaiah; 8th–7th century BCE), later pre-exilic prophecy (including Micah and Jeremiah; 7th century BCE), and post-exilic prophecy (Deutero-Isaiah, Nehemiah, and Ezra; 6th–5th centuries BCE). Some prophets predicted disaster. Others provided words of comfort and consolation. Prophetic utterances were oral or written, and were sometimes demonstrated by symbolic actions. In Scripture the title 'Former Prophets' applies to the historical books of Joshua, Judges, I and II Samuel, and I and II Kings. The books of the 'Latter Prophets' are divided into the 'Major Prophets', Isaiah, Jeremiah and Ezekiel, and the '12 Minor Prophets', Hosea, Joel, Amos, Obadiah, Jonah, Micah, Nah um, Habakkuk, Zephaniah, Haggai, Zechariah and Malachi.

Prosbul (Greek *lit.* 'for the court') Legal document enabling a creditor to claim debts after the Sabbatical Year. (The Sabbatical Year gave automatic release from debts, as set down in Deuteronomy 15.) The prosbul was instituted by Hillel (1st century BCE). Since there was a tendency not to make loans as the Sabbatical Year approached, Hillel issued an enactment by which a lender would not lose his money if he made a declaration that he wished to collect his debts after the Sabbatical Year.

Proselyte (Hebrew 'ger') A convert, especially a gentile converted to

Judaism. According to tradition, candidates for conversion are to be warned of the dangers of becoming a Jew. During the Second Temple period there was widespread proselytisation around Judea, particularly in Galilee and Idumea. In Roman times the number of converts to Judaism became so great that Hadrian and later emperors forbade conversion. Similarly, it was a capital offence in Christian Europe in the Middle Ages, though this did not prevent some individuals from joining the Jewish faith, including Obadiah the Norman, active in Palestine and neighbouring countries in the 12th century, and Robert of Reading, an English Dominican, who was burned at the stake in Oxford in 1222. In the modern period conversion to Judaism has become increasingly frequent. Converts often join the non-Orthodox denominations which are easier to enter than Orthodox Judaism. The traditional rites of conversion are for the male circumcision and 'tevilah' (complete immersion in a ritual bath), and for the female tevilah.

Prossnitz, Löbele (c.1670–1730) Moravian preacher and miracle worker. Born in Uherský Brod, he settled in Prossnitz. He underwent a spiritual transformation, and studied the Mishnah, the *Zohar*, and kabbalistic writings. He claimed that in his study of kabbalah he was accompanied by the souls of Isaac Luria and Shabbetai Tzevi, and predicted the return of Shabbetai Tzevi in 1706. He was criticised by the Moravian rabbis, but continued to preach in Austria and Germany. Later he claimed to be the Messiah ben Joseph, the precursor of the Messiah ben David. He subsequently lived in Hungary.

Prostration The act of lying face down, as in submission. As a gesture of reverence, prostration was practised in the Temple. Four types of obeisance are referred to in the *Talmud*: 'berikhah' (bending the knee), 'kidah' (bowing with the face to the ground), 'keriah' (kneeling), and 'hishta-havvayah' (full prostration with outstretched hands and feet). The last was performed by the priests and people at 13 different places in the Temple when the high priest pronounced the Tetragrammaton during the service on the Day of Atonement. A form of prostration is still practised by Ashkenazim during the recital of the Avodah on the Day of Atonement, and during the Aleinu prayer at New Year and on the Day of Atonement. A modified form (in which one is seated with the head resting on the arm) is performed when the Tahanun prayer is recited in the presence of a Scroll of the Law.

Proust, Macel (1871–1922) French novelist. He was born in Paris. Although he was raised as a Catholic, he retained Jewish sympathies. His *À la recherche du temps perdu* contains three major Jewish characters: the actress Rachel, intellectual Albert Bloch and Charles Swann. The work also alludes to the Dreyfus Affair.

Proverbs (Hebrew 'Sepher Mishlei') Biblical book, part of the Hagiographa, consisting of a collection of moral maxims. The first section (chapters 1–9) contains an introduction and a depiction of wisdom. The second section (10:1–22:16) and the fifth (25–39) are ascribed to Solomon and consist of collections of sayings. The third section (22:17–24:22) and the fourth section (24:23–24) consists of long stanzas on various themes. And the sixth section (chapter 30), attributed to Agur ben Jakeh, contains riddles, the sayings of King Lemuel, and a poem praising a virtuous wife.

Proverbs, Midrash to Medieval midrash on the Book of Proverbs, based on material from earlier midrashic collections and mystical sources (such as the Hekhalot).

Providence The divine attribute demonstrating God's foreseeing care for his creatures. According to the Bible, God directs the course of human history and the destiny of his chosen people. During the medieval period, Jewish philosophers, including Saadyah Gaon, Judah ha-Levi and Maimonides, discussed various issues connected with this doctrine.

Psalm, daily A different psalm is recited on each day of the week at the conclusion of the morning service. They are, on Sunday Psalm 24, on Monday Psalm 48, on Tuesday Psalm 82, on Wednesday Psalm 94, on Thursday Psalm 81, on Friday Psalm 93, and on Saturday Psalm 92. The practice, as well as the same choice of psalms, dates back to the Temple service, in which the Levites recited the daily psalm; the custom was continued in the synagogue after the destruction of the Temple.

Psalms (Hebrew: 'Tehillim') Biblical book, part of the Hagiographa, containing 150 songs. It is subdivided into five books, beginning with Psalms 1, 42, 78, 90 and 107. Each section concludes with a benediction of thanksgiving. The psalms include poems of thanksgiving and praise, didactic songs, songs in honour of kings, war songs, songs connected with festivals and historical events, and songs concerning events in individuals' lives. According to tradition, they are attributed to David.

Psalms, Midrash on Collection of homilies on the Book of Psalms. It is poularly known as 'Midrash Shoḥer Tov'.

Psalms of Solomon Pseudepigraphical book, thought to have been written in Palestine after the fall of Pompey in 48 BCE. It contains 18 poems attributed to Solomon, describing the desecration of the Temple by the enemy. It also condemns immorality and looks forward to the coming of the Messiah.

Pseudepigrapha Collective title given to a group of works of Jewish religious literature written between the 2nd century BCE and the 2nd century CE. Like the books of the Apocrypha, these works were not included in the canon of the Hebrew Scriptures. They are primarily apocalyptic in content and comprise the Psalms of Solomon, the Testament of the Twelve Patriarchs, the Book of Jubilees, the Apocalypse of Baruch, the Book of Enoch, the Assumption of Moses, the Ascension of Isaiah and the Sibyline Oracles.

Psychology The scientific study of behaviour or (more loosely) the mental make-up of an individual which gives rise to his actions. Various cases of mental disorder are described in the Bible. The *Talmud* specifies criteria for analysing human behaviour and identifies signs by which mental deficiency can be recognised. A number of medieval Jewish philosophers wrote about psychology, including Isaac Ben Solomon Israeli, Baḥya ben Joseph ibn Pakudah, Solomon ibn Gabirol, Joseph ibn Pakudah, Solomon ibn Gabirol, Joseph ibn Tzaddik, Judah ha-Levi, Abraham ibn Daud and Maimonides. Responsa literature also deals with mental diseases. In the 18th century the Ḥasidic movement introduced suggestive therapy. In the modern period a number of Jews (such as Kurt Lewin, Joseph Breuer, Sigmund Freud, Alfred Adler and Otto Rank) have made important contributions to the development of psychology.

Puah (fl.? 19th cent. BCE) Israelite midwife. She disobeyed Pharaoh's orders to kill all Hebrew male children at birth (Exodus 1:5).

Publishing As early as the 15th century Jews were involved in trade and commerce in the written word. In that century Jewish booksellers in Naples exported large quantities of books, and in the next books produced by the Venetian Hebrew press were exported to Poland and Turkey. Hebrew books were also sold at the fair at Frankfurt am Main. Many works were published

with the help of patrons or were sub-
sidised by their authors. The first catalogue of publications by a Jewish printer
was produced by Manasseh ben Israel
in Amsterdam in 1652. In the 19th century Jews entered into the general publishing field, and in the modern period
there are numerous publishing firms
throughout the world which produce
books of Jewish interest.

Pulitzer, Joseph (1847–1911)   American newspaper publisher, of Hungarian origin. Born in Mako, Hungary, of
a Jewish father and a Roman Catholic
mother, he studied in Budapest. At the
age of 17 he went to the US. He served
with Lincoln's Calvary. He became a
reporter for the *St Louis Westliche Post*
and was elected to the Missouri state
legislature. In 1874 he purchased the *St
Louis Staats-Zeitung*. In 1878 he bought
the *St Louis Dispatch* and merged it with
the *St Louis Evening Post*. In 1883 he
purchased the *New York World*. Later he
founded the *New York Evening World*.

Pulpit   Raised platform in a place of worship reserved for the preacher or other
leader of the service. The traditional
synagogue did not have a pulpit. The
sermon was delivered from the almemar
in the middle of the synagogue or from a
position in front of the Ark. In the modern period pulpits are found in many
synagogues and are often positioned
close to the reading desk and the Ark.

Punishment.   Biblical law makes provision for both physical and financial penalties for crime and wrongdoing. Physical penalties include stoning, burning,
beheading, strangulation and flogging,
as well as exile. Material penalties
included restitution, reparation for any
loss inflicted and financial compensation. All these penalties were supple-
mented by rabbinic law. Wilful violation
of rabbinic prescriptions was dealt with
by disciplinary flogging, and the punishment of excommunication enabled
courts to apply pressure on those who
would not respect its authority.

Pupik (Yiddish)   Navel.

Purification after childbirth   According to Jewish law a mother is regarded
as ritually impure for 33 days after the
birth of a male child, and 66 days after
the birth of a girl. After this period she
must offer a sacrifice of purification
(Leviticus 12:1–8). From the 15th century it was a custom among European
Jews for a mother to visit the synagogue
after recovering from childbirth.

Purim ('Lots')   Festival, celebrated on
14 and 15 Adar, commemorating the
rescue of Jewry through the mediation
of Esther from the threat of annihilation
planned by Haman. (The name derives
from Haman's casting lots to fix a date
for his massacre of the Jews.) The Book
of Esther (Megillat Ester) is read in the
synagogue on the eve and morning of
Purim; whenever the name Haman is
mentioned, rattles are sounded. An
account of the story of Purim is inserted
into the Amidah on that day, and a passage referring to the defeat of Amalek is
read from the Pentateuch. It was customary in Jewish communities to wear
fancy dress or masks at Purim, and
plays were enacted based on the story
of Esther. In modern times a Purim car-
nival takes place in Israel.

Purim, special   Name given to any
annual celebration instituted by a Jewish
community or individuals to commemorate a deliverance from danger. The oldest special festival of this kind was the
Purim of Narbonne, which celebrated a
deliverance of the Jews of the town on
21 Adar 1236. The Purim of Zaragoza
commemorated an event of 1380 or
1420, and there were other Purim celebrations in Cairo (23 Adar 1524), Buda
(10 Elul 1684), and Livorno (22 Shevat
1743). In southern France celebrations
in Avignon, Carpentras and Cavaillon
were called 'the yom-tov' ('good day',
i.e. 'festival') of the community.

Purim Katan   Name given to the 14th
and 15th days of the first month of Adar

in a leap year, when Purim is celebrated during the second month of Adar. Fasting and funeral eulogies are prohibited on Purim Katan, and the Taḥanun prayer is not recited.

Purim plays   The custom of presenting plays on the festival of Purim originated in Europe during the Middle Ages. The topic of the plays was the story of the Book of Esther. The earliest recorded Purim play took place in the Venice ghetto in 1531, and the oldest known text was written in Portuguese by Solomon Usque in 1559. It became the custom for itinerant actors to go from one community to another to perform the plays during the festival.

Purity, ritual   Biblical and Mishnaic law contain strict regulations on ritual purity (the prerequisite for worship) and impurity. Ritual bathing was regarded as sufficient to remove the impurity resulting from sexual intercourse or the emission of semen (Leviticus 15:16–18). Purification after childbirth required not only ritual bathing but also a sin offering and a burnt offering (Leviticus 12:6–8; 15:13–15; 28–30). Ritual impurity resulting from contact with a corpse required the sprinkling of water mixed with the ashes of the Red Heifer (Numbers 19:17–19). After menstruation women had to offer sacrifices; in post-Talmudic times a ritual bath (mikveh) was required. After the destruction of the Temple, laws connected with the Temple cult were no longer carried out, but practices associated with menstruation and childbirth, impurity through contact with the dead, and ritual bathing for various other purposes persist. The term tohorah (purification) has been transferred to the ritual washing of a corpse before burial.

Q

Shirley and Rose were playing cards at the Jewish country club. Shirley says: 'So, Rose, how's Julie, that daughter of yours?'

Rose says: 'Julie's fine, thanks. She married a fantastic person. He's got such a good job in the bank that she gave up being a secretary. She stays at home but never needs to cook. He always takes her out. She doesn't need to clean the house, because he got her a maid. And there's no need to worry about the grandchildren, because he got her a live-in nanny.'

Then Rose asks Shirley: 'How's your son, Max?'

Rose sighs and says: 'His life is awful. He married a real bitch. She never cooks anything. She makes him take her out to dinner every night. God forbid she should vacuum a carpet. She made Max get her a maid. He has to work like a dog because she refuses to get a job. And she never takes care of the grandchildren because Max got her a nanny.'

* * * * *

Here a mother is proud of her daughter for marrying a rich man who can support her so she does not have to do much at home. But she is fiercely critical of her daughter-in-law who behaves in exactly the same way. Jewish jokes often portray mothers as ambitious for their daughters. They are to marry money. At the same time they are overly protective of their sons, and frequently despise their daughters-in-law. The joke pointedly ridicules such attitudes.

Querido, Israel (1872-1932) Dutch novelist. He was born in Amsterdam, and in his novels portrayed Jewish diamond workers and the life of poor Jews of his native city. He also wrote plays with biblical backgrounds (including *Saul en David*).

Querido, Jacob (c.1650-1690) Greek religious leader. His sister became the last wife of Shabbetai Tzevi. After Shabbetai's death in 1676 she returned to Salonica and claimed that her brother was the recipient of her husband's soul. In 1683 there was a mass apostasy to Islam of a large group of Salonica families, who nevertheless continued to observe Sabbetaian and Jewish rites in secret. This group formed the nucleus of the Dönmeh sect. Taking the Turkish name Abdullah Yacoub, Querido became the most important leader of these sectarians.

R

Two Texans were sitting on a plane going to New York with an old Jewish man sitting next to them.

The first Texan says, 'My name is Butch. I own 250,000 acres, and 3,000 head of cattle and they call my place "Big Butch's Ranch".'

The second Texan says, 'My name is Billy. I own 350,000 acres. And I have 5,000 head of cattle. They call my place "Big Billy's".'

They both look at the little old Jewish man who says with a Yiddish accent: 'My name is Benny Plotkin, and I only own 300 acres'.

Both men shake their heads, and Butch says: 'Three hundred acres? What do you raise?'

'Nothing,' says Benny.

'Well, then, what do you call it?' asks Billy.

'Downtown Dallas'.

* * * * *

Many Jewish jokes deal with money. Here two Texans brag about how rich they are. But they are shown up by an old rich Jew. Although these two non-Jewish men are satirised, so indirectly is the Jew who belittles their wealth.

Raaya, Mehemena ('The faithful shepherd') Kabbalistic work on the commandments, dating from the 14th century. It was later incorporated into the *Zohar*. It is called after Moses, the faithful shepherd, who revealed secret knowledge to the Kabbalists.

Rabb, Maxwell Milton (1910–2002) Amercian lawyer, government official and communal leader. He was born in Boston. He served as Associate Counsel to President Eisenhower in 1953–54, and later as Secretary to the Cabinet. Active in Jewish affairs, he became Chairman of the government division of the United Jewish Appeal.

Rabbah bar Ḥanah (fl. 3rd cent.) Babylonian amora. He studied at the academy of Johanan ben Zakkai in Palestine. Later he returned to Babylonia, where he transmitted Johanan's teachings. Legends about his journeys are recorded in the tractate Bava Batra.

Rabbah bar Naḥmani [Rabbah] (c. 270–330) Babylonian amora. He studied under Huna at Sura and Judah bar Ezekiel at Pumbedita. Known for his interpretation of the Mishnah, he was knowledgeable about ritual purity. He was nicknamed Oker Harim ('uprooted of mountains') because of his dialectical ability.

Rabban Variant of the title 'rabbi'. It was used as an honorific title during the Mishnaic period, especially for heads of the Sanhedrin.

Rabbi ('My master') [Marbitz Torah ('Teacher of the Law'); Rav] Title originally used during the 1st century to refer to ordained members of the Sanhedrin. It was employed only in Palestine until the 5th century. Scholars in Babylolnia were addressed by the equivalent title 'rav'. Later, Jews distinguished in learning were referred to as 'rabbi', and the title was also conferred on the appointed spiritual heads of Jewish communities. Rabbis were not salaried until the 15th century. In large communities they maintained yeshivot, and various functions were performed under their supervision: dayyanim adjudicated lawsuits and arranged divorces, the shoḥet carried out ritual slaughter, and members of the community were purified by ritual bathing. In the eastern Mediterranean, the rabbi was called Marbitz Torah. In modern times rabbis have adopted pastoral, social and educational responsibilities. A rabbi is appointed by the congregation to act as its spiritual leader, to organise services, to supervise the religious education of the young, to visit the sick and bereaved, and to preside over life-cycle events.

Rabbi Binyamin [Ha-Talmi, Yehoshua; Radler-Feldman, Yehoshua] (1880–1957) Israeli journalist. He was born in Zborov, Galicia, and went to London in 1906. The following year he travelled to Palestine, where he worked as a labourer and later served as secretary of Herzlia high school in Tel Aviv. In 1910 he taught high school. After World War I he was active in the Mizraḥi party, and edited the national monthly *Ha-He'd* (1926–53). He was a founder (in 1926) of Berit Shalom, a society that advocated a bi-national state for Jews and Arabs. He published numerous books, articles and essays.

Rabbinical conference Synod of rabbis. In the 2nd century conferences were held at Lydda and Usha to deal with problems arising from the Bar Kokhba revolt of 132–35 and the persecution of the Jews under Hadrian. In the amoraic and gaonic periods, conventions were held in the Middle East twice a year. In the Middle Ages a number of rabbinical conferences took place in Western Europe, including an assembly at Troyes in 1165 and councils at Mayence in 1223 and 1245. At the beginning of the 19th century the Napoleonic Sanhedrin was convened, and in Germany rabbinical conferences were held from the mid-19th century onward. In modern times the rabbis of the various divisions of Judaism hold national and international conferences but there is no governing body of the worldwide Jewish community.

Rabbinites [Rabbanites] Name given by the Karaites to their rabbinical opponents.

Rabbinovitz, Raphael Nathan (1835–1888) Galician Talmjudic scholar. He was born in Novo-Zhagory, in the Kovno district. He lived in Lemberg and Pressburg, and travelled widely. His *Dikduke Sopherim* consists of 16 volumes of variant readings from *Talmud* manuscripts. He also wrote a study of the printed editions of the *Talmud*.

Rabbinowitz, Israel Michael (1818–1893) French writer and scholar. He was born in Gorodets, Lithuania. He became a physician and settled in Paris, where he devoted himself to scholarship. He participated in the Kattowtiz Conference of Ḥibbat Zion in 1884, and was head of the Benei Zion of Paris. In 1889 he went to Russia, and he eventually lived in London. His publications include *Législation criminelle du Talmud, La médicine du Talmud,* and *Le traité des poisons de Maimonide.*

Rabin, Chaim (1915–1996) Israeli scholar. He taught at the University of Oxford and later was Professor of Hebrew Language at the Hebrew University. His major contribution is in the field of linguistics; his publications include a thesaurus of Hebrew words, and studies of Qumran Hebrew, Aramaic, Biblical Hebrew, and modern Hebrew.

Rabin, Yitzhak (1922–1995) Israeli soldier and diplomat. He was born in Jerusalem. He joined the Palmah in 1940 and participated in underground activities against the British Mandatory government. In 1947 he became deputy commander of the Palmah, and later chief of operations of the Southern Command. From 1956 to 1959 he was chief of operations of the Northern Command. He subsequently became head of the General Staff Branch, deputy chief of staff, and eventually chief of staff. In 1968 he became appointed Israeli ambassador to the US. He was appointed Prime Minister in 1974, and re-elected in 1992.

Rabbinovich, Joseph (1837–1899) Bessarbian missionary. He was active in Kishinev. Initially attracted by the Haskalah, he joined Hibbat Zion in the 1880s and visited Palestine. In 1883 he founded a sect known as the Children of Israel of the New Testament, which accepted the tenets of Christianity while retaining Jewish nationalism and traditions. Two years later he converted to Protestantism. His writings include *Prayers and Principles of Faith of the Children of Israel of the New Testament* and *Words of Comfort*.

Rabinovich, Ossip (1817–1869) Ukrainian journalist. He was born in Kobelyaki. In 1845 he settled in Odessa, where he was an adviser and pleader at the commercial court, and later a notary. He founded the first Russian weekly, *Rasviet*, in Odessa in 1860. He advocated reforms in Jewish life, the acceptance of Jews as Russian citizens, and the integration of Jewry into Russian society.

Rabinowitz, Alexander Süsskind (1854–1945) Palestinian Hebrew scholar, also known as Azar. He was born in Lyady, Belorussia. He taught in Poltava in Ukraine, and became active in the Hibbat Zion movement. In 1906 he moved to Palestine, where he became a teacher and librarian. He wrote stories, monographs, translations of world literature and Judaica into Hebrew, and textbooks.

Rabinowitz, Louis Isaac (1906–1984) South African rabbi. He was born in Edinburgh, and served as a rabbi in various London congregations. In 1945 he became Chief Rabbi of the United Hebrew congregation of Johannesburg and the Federation of Synagogues of Transvaal and the Orange Free State. He also served as Professor of Hebrew at the University of Witwatersrand. His writings include *The Social Life of the Jews of Northern France, Jewish Merchant Adventures, Soldiers from Judea,* and *Far East Mission.*

Rabinowitz, Saul Phinehas [Shepher] (1845–1890) Polish Hebrew writer and Zionist leader, of Lithuanian origin. He lived in Warsaw, where he was initially attracted to Jewish nationalism and later to Zionism. After the pogroms of 1881, he helped to organise the emigration of Jewish refugees. He was Secretary of the Kattowitz Conference of Hibbat Zion in 1884, and subsequently Secretary of the movement's Warsaw office. He contributed to Hebrew journalism, edited the annual *Keneset Yisrael* in 1886–88, translated Heinrich Graetz's *History of the Jews* into Hebrew, and wrote studies of the Jews exiled from Spain in the 1490s.

Rachel (i) (fl.? 19th–16th cent. BCE) Israelite woman, daughter of Laban and wife of Jacob. Her father was a herdsman in Haran, for whom Jacob worked. Jacob wished to marry Rachel but was tricked into marrying her elder sister Leah. Subsequently Rachel also became his wife and bore him two sons, Joseph and Benjamin (Genesis 29–35).

Rachel (ii) [Blovstein, Rachel] (1890–1931) Palestinian Hebrew poet, of

Russian origin. In 1909 she emigrated to Palestine, where she worked as a labourer. Her poetry is imbued with love for the countryside of Palestine and the Jewish pioneers.

Racialism   The belief that races have distinctive hereditary characteristics that render some intrinsically inferior to others. In the 19th century racial theories developed according to which the Jews were regarded as an inferior homogenous group. In Germany this doctrine became a central tenet of the anti-Jewish movement and was a fundamental doctrine of Nazism.

Radanities   Jewish merchants. In the 9th century they travelled between southern France and China. Their activities are known about from the writings of the Arab geographer Ibn Khordadbeh. The origin of the name is obscure; it may derive from a Persian expression meaning 'knowing the way' or from the Latin Rhodanus (the name for the River Rhone).

Ragoler, Elijah Ben Jacob (1794–1850)   Lithuanian talmudist. He was born in Sogindat in the Zamut region, and became known throughout Lithuania for his talmudic knowledge; he was also an expert on kabbalah. He served as rabbi of Slobodka in Ukraine, and later Kalisz in Poland. He was a fierce opponent of religious reform. He produced manuscript studies in all spheres of Torah study.

Rain, prayer for   Petition in the musaph service on Shemini Atzeret, the last day of the festival of Sukkot. Liturgical poets (such as Eleazar Kallir) wrote special prayers to be recited on this occasion.

Rainbow   According to Scripture, God set a rainbow in the clouds after the Flood as a sign that he would never again destroy the earth in that way (Genesis 9:8–17). The rabbis decreed that when a rainbow is seen, the following prayer is recited: 'Blessed are thou, O Lord our God, King of the universe, who remembers the covenant, is faithful to his covenant, and keeps his promise.'

Raisin, Max (1881–1957)   American rabbi and author, of Polish origin. He served as rabbi of Congregation B'nai Jeshurun in Paterson, New Jersey, from 1921 to 1953. His writings include *Mordecai Manuel Noah: Zionist, Author and Statesman, Israel in America, A history of the Jews in Modern Times*, and *Great Jews I Have Known*.

Rank, Otto (1884–1939)   Austrian psychoanalyst. Born in Vienna, he met Sigmund Freud and studied at the University of Vienna. His works include *The Trauma of Birth*. He subsequently went to the US and developed the theory and technique of 'will therapy'.

Ransom   It is the duty of a Jew to ransom a fellow Jew captured by slave dealers or robbers, or unjustly imprisoned. Jewish law specifies several rules for the ransoming of captives: (1) women should be given preference over men; (2) a person captured with his father and teacher may ransom himself first but is then bound to ransom his teacher, and then his father; (3) preference should be given to a scholar; (4) the court has the power to compel a husband to ransom his wife; (5) money set aside for charity or the building of a synagogue may be used to ransom captives; (6) a person who delays ransoming a captive is regarded as if he has spilled the captive's blood.

Raphael   Archangel and divine messenger. He had the special function of healing. He is first mentioned in the books of Enoch and Tobit. In the *Talmud* he is named as one of the three angels who visited Abraham after he had circumcised himself. Jewish traditions regarding Raphael were eventually taken over by Christian angelology and syncretisation magic.

Raphael, Frederic (b.1931) British novelist and screenwriter. He was born in Chicago, and moved to England as a boy. Some of his novels deal with Jewish themes. His publications include *The Limits of Love, Lindmann, A Wild Surmise, Orchestra and Beginners,* and *The Glittering Prizes.*

Raphael ben Jekuthiel Cohen [Cohen, Raphael] (1722–1803) Polish talmudist. He served as a rabbi at Minsk, Pinsk, Posen and Altona. He was an opponent of Moses Mendelssohn, critical of modernism. His *Torah Yekutiel* is a commentary on the first part of the Shulḥan Arukh.

Rapoport, Solomon Judah [Shir] (1790–1867] Galician rabbi. He was born in Lemberg. He was a rabbi in Tarnopol from 1837 to 1840, when he was appointed Chief Rabbi of Prague. He was attacked by the Ḥasidim and the ultra-Orthodox for his enlightened approach to Jewish study, which laid the foundations for modern Jewish scholarship. He wrote studies of Jewish scholars of the gaonic period, began a talmudic encyclopedia, and translated European poetry into Hebrew. He was also known as Shir, a name derived from his initials.

Rappoport, O. Yehoshua (1895–1971) Australian Yiddish essayist, translator, and editor, of Polish origin. He was born in Bialystok and emigrated to Australia in 1947. He wrote about the Bible and the *Talmud* and translated works from Russian, German, French, and Hebrew into Yiddish. In Australia he was the editor of the newspaper *Yidishe neies.*

Rashi [Solomon Ben Isaac; Solomon [Saloman] Yitzḥak ben Isaac] (1040–1105) French rabbinic scholar. He was born in Troyes. After studying in the Rhineland he returned to Troyes, where he established a school. He published responsa, composed penitential hymns, and wrote commentaries on the Bible and the *Talmud*. His commentary on the *Talmud* established the correct text, defined numerous terms, and explained unusual words and phrases. His Bible commentary served as the basis for later interpretations of Scripture. Both works include numerous examples of the type of textual gloss known as a 'laaz' – an explanatory work in French (or another language) transliterated into Hebrew script.

Rathenau, Walter (1867–1922) German statesman. His father, Emil Rathenau, was a co-founder of the German Edison company. He succeeded his father as head of the AEG electricity trust and during World War I was in charge of Germany's war economy. In 1922 he became Minister of Foreign Affairs, but was assassinated by nationalists the same year.

Ratosh, Yonatan (1909–1981) Israeli poet, of Russian origin. He emigrated to Palestine in 1921. His poetry portrays Hebrew youth as strong and heroic, in contrast to the downtrodden Jews of the diaspora. He is best known for his championship of the anti-Zionist nationalist ideology known as 'Canaanism' and for his 'Manifesto to Hebrew Youth.'

Rav [Abba Arikha] (fl. 3rd cent.) Babylonian amora, also known as Abba Arikha. He was born at Kafri in southern Babylonia. He went to Palestine, where he studied under Ḥiyya and joined the academy of Judah ha-Nasi. Later he returned to Babylonia. He declined the position of head of the Nehardea academy at Sura, which flourished for eight centuries. He and Samuel are the two sages whose teachings figure most prominently in the *Talmud*. According to tradition, he was the author of the Alenu prayer.

Rava (fl. 4th cent.) Babylonian amora. He was born in Maḥoza, and established an academy there when Abbaye became head of the academy at Pumbedita.

After Abbaye's death, Rava succeeded him at Pumbedita, which he amalgamated with Maḥoza. His controversies with Abbaye were famous; with six exceptions the ordinances of halakhah were determined in accordance with his views.

Ravitsh, Melekh (1893–1976) Canadian Yiddish poet and essayist, of Galician origin. He was born in Radymno, eastern Galicia. He travelled widely, and in Warsaw during the 1920s he was a member of the poetic group known as Khalyastre. In 1941 he settled in Montreal, though he spent 1953–56 in Israel. In addition to poetry, he published a three-volume biographical working on Yiddish literary figures.

Ravnitzky, Yehoshua Ḥana (1859–1944) Palestinian Hebrew and Yiddish author and editor. He was born in Odessa. He became a member of a group of Ḥovevei Zion and was one of the founders of Bene Mosheh. In 1899 he was appointed editor of the Yiddish periodical *Der Yid*, and later was co-founder of the publishing house Moriah. In 1922 he emigrated to Palestine where he helped to establish the Devir publishing house. Together with Ḥayyim Naḥmanides Bialik, he published *Sepher Aggadah*.

Rawidowicz, Simon (1897–1957) American philosopher of Polish origin. He taught at Leeds University, the Chicago College of Jewish Studies, and Brandeis University. He published studies of philosophical thinkers and subjects as well as works on contemporary Jewish topics. From 1927 to 1930 he was co-editor of the scholarly journal *Ha-Tekuphah;* he was also editor of the scholarly and literary journal Metzudah, and a founder of Berit Ivrit Olamit.

Ray, Man (Radnitsky, Emanuel) (1890–1976) Amercian photographer. Born in Philadelphia, he studied at the Francisco Ferrer Centre and the Art Students League. In 1921 he went to Paris and became involved with the Dada movement. He worked as a photographer and also produced short films. In 1940 he went to Los Angeles but returned to France in 1951.

Raziel, Book of Collection of mystical, cosmological and magical Hebrew works. It contains mythical teachings, letter mysticism, descriptions of the heavens, angelology, magical recipes, and formulas for amulets.

Raziel, David (1910–1941) Palestinian underground fighter. He was born in Smorgon, near Vilnius, and went to Palestine with his parents at an early age. During the 1929 Arab riots he joined the Haganah. He was a founder and commander of the underground organisation Irgun Tzevai Leumi. Captured by the British in 1939, he was later released. In 1941 he was killed in a German air-raid while on a mission for the British to Iraq.

Real Estate Landed property. According to Jewish law it can be acquired by purchase, presumptive right or deed. If intention is demonstrated or proved, all movable property within the area of the real estate is automatically transferred without a separate deed. Real estate can serve as security for a loan contracted by deed, but not for one contracted verbally. No oath may be taken on claims involving real estate, and the laws of bailment do not apply to it. Only if the purchase price exceeds the value of the land by more than half, can a claim of overcharging be brought against the seller. Real estate cannot be stolen, thus no mater how many times it may have been sold, and despite whatever improvements have been made to it, if it has been sold without the permission of the original owner it reverts to him and no compensation is due to those who have had possession of it in the interim.

Rebbe (Yiddish) Rabbi. The title is also accorded to a teacher, and among the Ḥasidim to their spiritual leader.

Rebbitsen Wife of a rabbi.

Rebekah (fl.? 19th–16th cent. BCE)
Israelite woman, wife of Isaac. When
Abraham sent his servant Eliezer to
Aram Naharaim to seek a wife for his
son, Isaac, Eliezer chose Rebekah. She
bore Isaac twin sons, Esau and Jacob
(Genesis 24–28).

Rebellious son According to the Bible,
a son who rebels against his parents
may be sentenced to death on their
complaint (Deuteronomy 21:18–21).
The rabbis redefined the law of the
rebellious son so that it was inapplica-
ble in practice.

**Recanati, Menaḥem ben Benjamin
(fl. 13th–14th cent.)** Italian kabbalist and halakhic authority. He lived in
Recanati. He introduced German mysticism and the study of the *Zohar* into
Italy.

Rechabites Ancient Jewish sect, identified in Jeremiah 35, they traced their
descent to Jehonadab (or Jonadab) ben
Rechab (II King's 10:15–17). According
to the precepts laid down by Jehonadab,
the Rechabites abstained from drinking
wine, and were forbidden to own fields
or vineyards and to build houses. Jeremiah was commanded by God to put
them to the test by taking them to one
of the chambers of the Temple and
serving wine. The Rechabites refused
drink and were rewarded by God for
their steadfastness by a promise of his
favour. After Nebuchadnezzar invaded
Israel, they fled to Jerusalem.

Reconstructionism Religious   and
social movement, established by Mordecai Menaḥem Kaplan. According
to Kaplan, Jewish theism should be
rejected, and Judaism should be understood as an evolving religious civilisation. He called for a reconstruction of
Judaism, in which synagogues should
serve as centres for all aspects of Jewish
culture. His congregation, the Society
for the Advancement of Judaism, was
formed in 1922 and served as a vehicle
for his thought. In 1935 he established
the Jewish Reconstructionist Foundation in New York and began to publish
the magazine *The Reconstructionist*. In
1954 a congregational organisation was
created, and the Reconstructionist Rabbinical College opened in 1968.

Redemption Religious quest for salvation. In the Bible it is spoken of primarily as an historical event, involving the
entire nation. In the rabbinic period
the concept underwent various trans-
formations, involving the coming of
the Messiah and the restoration of the
world. Later redemption was understood in Kabbalistic literature as involving a metaphysical change in the order
of creation, whereby the identity of the
Godhead would be wholly restored in
the universe. After the failure of the
Sabbetaian movement, redemption
was more widely understood in terms
of personal salvation. In modern times,
a purely secular concept of redemption
has been related to the Zionist longing
for a Jewish homeland.

**Red heifer (Hebrew 'parah
adummah')** A young cow used for
sacrifice in accordance with the instructions laid down in Numbers 19. The
animal should be unblemished and
should never have been yoked. Its ashes,
mixed with water, formed a substance
that would remove impurity created by
contact with the dead. On the occasion
of the institution of the sacrifice it took
place outside the Israelite camp, and
those who handled it required purification. Thereafter the red heifer was
sacrificed in Jerusalem on the Mount
of Olives.

Reform [Liberal] Judaism Religious
movement, established in Europe in
the early 19th century. It began with
the formation of synagogues by laymen
such as Israel Jacobson. In the 1840s
Reform rabbis convened rabbinical
councils to determine the principles of

the movement, which involved modifications of traditional belief and practice to meet contemporary needs. The first congregation in the US was Beth Elohim in Charleston, South Carolina; its synagogue was built in 1840. Reform Judaism in the US received its central impetus from Isaac Mayer Wise, who founded the Union of American Hebrew Congregations (1873), the Hebrew Union College (1875), and the Central Conference of American Rabbis (1889). Reform Judaism has become a central force in Jewish life, with congregations throughout the world. It advocates the harmonisation of the Jewish tradition with modern life and culture.

Refugees   After World War I the protection of refugees was accepted as an international responsibility. In 1921 Dr Nansen was appointed by the League of Nations as High Commissioner for Russian and Armenian Refugees. Later this responsibility passed to the Nansen Office of the League. In 1933 another high commissioner of the League was appointed for Jewish and other refugees from Germany. In 1938 President Roosevelt convened a conference at Evian to arrange for the emigration and resettlement of refugees. During World War II the High Commissioner for German Refugees worked to help those who were outside the Nazi-occupied territories, and to improve conditions of emigration. In 1947 the League office and Committee were replaced by an instrument of the United Nations.

Refusenik   Term used in the USSR for a dissident Jew.

Reggio, Isaac Samuel [Yashar] (1784–1855)   Italian scholar and mathematician. He was born in Gorizia. His inspiration led to the funding of the Collegio Rabbinico Italiano in Padua in 1829. He published an Italian translation of the Pentateuch with a commentary in Hebrew. In 1846 he became the rabbi of Gorizia.

Rehoboam (fl. 10th cent. BCE)   King of Judah (930–908 BCE). He was the son of Solomon by his wife Naamah. When he refused to moderate his policy of taxation, the country split into the kingdoms of Israel and Judah. Only the tribes of Judah, Simeon, and most of Benjamin remained loyal to Rehoboam. Subsequently Shishak of Egypt invaded Judah and plundered the Temple (I King's 11ff.)

Reich, Steve (b.1936)   American composer, conductor and percussionist. He was born in New York, and lived in San Francisco, where he wrote music for the San Francisco Mime Troupe and presented concerts at the San Francisco Tape Music Centre. His compositions include *Tehilim*, based on pseudo-biblical cantillation.

Reich, Wilhelm (1897–1957)   Austrian psychoanalyst. Born in Galicia, he studied at the University of Vienna and joined the Vienna Psychoanalytic Society. He emphasised sexual repression as a source of pathology. An avid communist, he moved to Berlin in 1930 and founded Sexpol which promoted communism and sexual liberation. In 1939 he went to the US.

Reifmann, Jacob (1818–1895)   Polish Hebrew scholar. He engaged in historical and philological research and corresponded with the major scholars of his time. His publications include studies of the *Talmud* and other areas of Judaica.

Reik, Ḥavivah (1914–1944)   Palestinian resistance fighter, of Slovak birth. She joined Ha-Shomer ha-Tzair, and settled in Palestine in 1939. In 1944 she volunteered to join the allied forces as a parachutist. She was dropped in Poland, where she organised radio communications with the allies and Jewish partisan groups, and aided the escape of refugees. She was eventually captured and shot.

Reina, Joseph della (fl. 15th cent.)   Palestinian Kabbalist. According to tradition, he attempted to hasten the coming of redemption by breaking the power of the angel Samael, but his failure postponed the event. According to one tradition, he failed because he took pity on Samael. Another tradition holds that he was too preoccupied with the mystical combination of divine names to carry out the instruction to slay Samael.

Reinach, Joseph (1856–1921) French politician, brother of Solomon and Theodore Reinach. In 1881–82 he served as head of Leon Gambetta's cabinet, and he later served as a deputy. He attempted to establish the innocence of Alfred Dreyfus, to which end he published a seven-volume history of the affair. He also wrote works on politics and history, including several on Gambetta.

Reinach, Salomon (1858–1932) French archaeologist and historian, brother of Joseph and Theodore Reinach. He directed the excavations at Carthage in 1883, and three years later was appointed curator of the French national museums. He lectured at the Louvre School, and from 1902 directed the Musée des Antiquités Nationales de Saint-Germain-en-Laye. He was the author of authoritative works on Ancient Greece and the history of religions. He served on the council of the Jewish Colonization Assocation and on the central committee of the Alliance Israélite Universelle.

Reinach, Theodore (1860–1928) French historian and numismatist, brother of Joseph and Solomon Reinach. After working as a lawyer, he edited the scholar journals *La revue des études grecques and La gazette des beaux arts.* He taught at the Sorbonne, the École des Hautes Études, and the Collège de France. He was active in the Société des Études Juives, and some of his work deals with Hellenism and Judaism. He also edited the French translation of the works of Josephus.

Reines, Isaac Jacob (1839–1915) Lithuanian rabbi and Zionist. He officiated as a rabbi in various Lithuanian centres, evolving a method of talmudic study based on abstract rules of logic. In 1882 at a rabbinical conference in St Petersburg, he advocated the introduction of secular studies into the syllabus of yeshivah training. He was one of the first rabbis to join the Zionist movement, and helped to found the religious Zionist Mizraḥi movement in 1902.

Reinhardt, Max (1873–1943) German producer and director. Born in Baden, Austria, he was an actor and Assistant Director of the Salzburg State Theatre. In 1894 he went to Berlin. In 1903 he began directing, and in 1905 he became Director of the Deutsches Theatre. When the Nazis came to power, he left Germany and toured Europe. In 1933 he went to the US.

Reisen, Abraham [Reyzen, Avrom] (1876–1953) American Yiddish poet and story writer, brother of Zalman Reisen. He was born in Koydenev, Belorussia. Initially he wrote tales and simple lyrics. He advocated the recognition of Yiddish as the Jewish national language, and helped to convene the Yiddish Language Conference at Czernowitz in 1908. He travelled throughout Europe and America supporting Yiddish cultural activities. In 1914 he settled in New York, where he contributed to Yiddish papers and magazines.

Reisen, Zalman [Reyzen, Zalman] (1888–1941) Lithuanian Yiddish editor and scholar, brother of Abraham Reisen. He was born in Koydenev, Belorussia. In 1915 he moved to Vilnius, where he became a leader of the new Yiddish cultural movement. He edited the Yiddish daily *Vilner tog* and was a lecturer in Yiddish and Yiddish grammar at the Folk University and the Vilnius Yiddish Teachers' Seminary. His writings include a grammar of

Yiddish, a study of the origins of modern Yiddish literature, and a biographical Encyclopedia of Yiddish literature.

Religious parties After the Fifth Zionist Congress in 1901, Isaac Jacob Reines founded a religious wing of the Zionist Organisation, which he called Mizrahi. In 1912 the Agudat Israel was formed in opposition to political Zionism. From each of these movements there emerged a socialist group, the Poale Mizrahi and the Poale Agudat Israel. In addition a small extremist religious group, the Natore Karta, was formed in 1937 by members of Agudat Israel. The two Mizrahi groups eventually merged as the National Religious Party, but the two Agudat parties have remained separate.

Remez [Drabkin], David (1886–1951) Israeli labour leader, of Russian origin. He settled in Turkey in 1911, and later in Palestine. He was active in the labour movement, serving as Secretary General of Histadrut, Chairman of the Vaad Leumi, and a Mapai member of the Knesset. He served as Minister of Communications in 1948–50, and Minister of Education in 1950–51.

Remnant of Israel The Bible demonstrates, through its account of history, that even when the nation or its leaders deserted the faith there remained a 'remnant' whose faithfulness prevailed. The Bible teaches that after God destroys the sinners of Israel as a prelude to the Day of Judgement, he will leave the righteous remnant who will serve as his kingdom on earth. The concept is found in the biblical prophetic books from Amos (8th century BCE) onward.

Renaissance The name given to the art, culture, science, and thought of the period in European history that marked the waning of the Middle Ages and the rise of the modern world. It is normally regarded as having begun in Italy in the 14th century. During the Renaissance Jewish scholars such as Elijah Delmedigo advocated Aristotelian ideas and translated classical texts. In Florence a number of Jews were part of the circle of Pico della Mirandola, who was largely responsible for the revival of the study of Hebrew. In this milieu the *Dialoghi di amore* by Judah Abravanel became a popular work. At the end of the period Salomone de'Rossi of Mantua was actively involved in the musical revival, and Leone de'Sommi influenced the development of the theatre. In addition Jewish loan bankers patronised the arts, supported scholars and commissioned illuminated manuscripts. However, the Counter-Reformation in the 16th century put an end to the artistic and intellectual commerce of the Jews with the non-Jewish community by the introduction of the ghetto.

Rending of clothes Mourning custom. It is first mentioned in the Bible in connection with Joseph (Genesis 37:29,34). According to rabbinic law, it is obligatory after the death of a father, mother, son, daughter, brother, sister, wife or husband. The tear must be a hand's breath wide; when the dead person is a parent the rent should never be completely resewn. The rending of clothes is performed before the funeral when the Barukh dayan emet blessing is recited.

Reparations In international law the payment exacted by a victorious state from a defeated one to compensate for injury or damage caused. The related concept of restitution involves the restoration of property wrongly taken from the owner. Both reparation and restitution were exacted from Germany after the Nazi persecution of the Jews before and during World War II. In 1951 the Federal Republic of Germany agreed to make good material damage caused to Jewish property and to pay compensation for costs incurred in the integration of Jewish refugees in the various countries to which they had fled. The amount to be paid was set out in an agreement signed in 1952 by the German Chancellor and the Israeli Foreign Minister.

Repentance   (Hebrew   'teshuvah') The renunciation of sin, appeal for forgiveness, and return to righteous living. Repentance is a central idea in the Bible, and serves as the theme of the Ten Days of Penitence. On the Day of Atonement prayers focus on this doctrine. Forgiveness is dependent on true repentance and if another person has been wronged rectification and restitution must also take place. In the Middle Ages Jewish writers dealt extensively with this subject. During the modern period religious leaders have created movements (such as the Musar movement) that focus on moral improvement.

Resh Twentieth letter of the Hebrew alphabet. It's numerical value is 200.

Resh kallah ('Head of the kallah') Title of the second in authority to the gaon in the academies of Babylonia. He was especially active in the study courses that took place during the months of Adar and Elul.

Resnick, Judith (1949–86) American astronaut. Born in Cleveland, she grew up in Akron, Ohio. She studied at Carnegie-Mellon University and the University of Maryland. She was a design engineer for RCE, biomedical engineer at the National Institute of Health, and senior systems engineer for the Xerox Corporation. In 1978 she was selected to become an astronaut. In 1989 she died aboard the US space shuttle *Challenger* when it exploded in space.

Responsa   (Latin   'responses') Hebrew 'she'elot u-teshuvot'). Written replies ('teshuvot') given to questions ('she'elot') on all aspects of Jewish law by authorities from the time of the geonim to the present day. More than a thousand volumes of responsa have been written. Their influence is found in various codes, in novellae, and in compendium of the tosaphists.

Resurrection   (Hebrew   'tehiyat hametim') The coming back to life of the dead. Belief in the resurrection of the dead is part of the Messianic hope. It became a central feature of postexilic Judaism, particularly in Pharisaic circles. According to the *Talmud*, it is a central feature of the Jewish faith, and Maimonides included it among his thirteen principles of faith. In the modern period it has ceased to play as important a role in Jewish thought.

Retaliation Retributive action whereby injury or wrong is returned in kind. The concept is expressed in Scripture: 'Eye for eye, tooth for tooth, hand for hand, foot for foot, burn for burn, wound for wound, bruise for bruise' (Exodus 21:24–25; Leviticus 24:19–20; Deuteronomy 19:21). According to Jewish law, the one who has inflicted injury may compensate his victim financially and thus avert the literal application of this legislation.

Retribution   (Hebrew   'zedekah') The just requiring of each person according to their actions. According to the Bible, divine justice is meted out according to merits. Prosperity is seen as proof of righteous action, while misfortune is regarded as the result of wickedness. Rabbinic theology insisted that God's retribution was always tempered by mercy ('hesed'). At the same time, the rabbis extolled the vicarious suffering of righteous martyrs. In rabbinic literature the belief in reward and punishment in the afterlife is combined with the doctrine of retribution.

Reuben   (fl.?   19th–16th cent.   BCE) Eldest son of Jacob and Leah. He opposed his brothers' plot to kill Joseph (Genesis 37). When Jacob learned of Reuben's incestuous relations with Bilhah, he transferred his rights as firstborn to Joseph (Genesis 48–49).

Reuveni [Reubeni], David (fl. 16th cent.) Italian adventurer. He claimed to be the son of a King Solomon and brother of a King Joseph, who ruled the lost tribes of Reuben, Gad and half Manasseh in the desert of Habor. After travelling through Palestine and Egypt, he appeared in Venice in 1523. Later he settled in Rome, and Pope Clement VII gave him letters of recommendation. In 1525–27 he lived in Portugal where he was greeted by Marranos (including Solomon Molcho) who believed him to be the herald of the Messiah. In 1532 he and Molcho appeared before Charles V. Molcho was burned at the stake, and Reubeni was taken to Spain where he died. He left a diary which records these events.

Revel, Bernard (1885–1940) American educator and scholar. He was born in Kovno, Lithuania, and settled in the US in 1906. Initially he ran an oil-refining business in Oklahoma. In 1915, as rosh yeshivah, he reorganised the Isaac Elhanan Yeshiva, and in the following year founded the Talmudical Academy in New York. In 1928 he founded Yeshiva College which he directed as President. He wrote studies of Targum Jonathan, Josephus, Jubilees, the development of ancient exegesis, and Karaism.

Revelation (Hebrew 'nir'ah') Divine disclosure. The Bible account is concerned, essentially, with God's revelation of his nature and purposes to humankind. According to Scripture, God revealed himself to individuals, and on Mount Sinai provided the nation with a code of moral and ritual law. In the Middle Ages Jewish philosophers discussed the relationship between revelation and human reason. In modern times Reform Judaism has adopted the belief in progressive revelation, maintaining that revelation is a continual process throughout history.

Revisionism Zionist political movement, founded in 1925 by Vladimir

Jabotinsky under the name World Union of Zionist Revisionists or Ha-Tzohar. It advocated the establishment of a Jewish state on both sides of the Jordan. Initially it opposed the official Zionist policy toward British Mandatory rule, and encouraged political action. In 1935 the Revisionists seceded from the World Zionist Organisation and formed the New Zionist Organisation. The Irgun Tzevai Leumi and Loḥame Ḥerut Yisrael originated from the Revisionst section of the Haganah.

Ribalow, Menaḥem (1895–1953) American Hebrew critic and editor. He was born in Chudnov, Volhynia. He studied in Odessa and began to publish poems and essays at an early age. In 1921 he emigrated to the US, where he became editor of the Hebrew weekly *Ha-Doar,* and edited anthologies of American Hebrew literature.

Riboyne shel o'lem (Yiddish) O God in Heaven! Or God willing. The phrase is used as an expression of amazement or hope.

Ricardo, David (1772–1823) English economist. He was born in London. He was a member of the Stock Exchange until 1814, when he retired to devote his energies to economics. Although he left Judaism when he married a Quaker, he advocated the removal of Jewish disabilities.

Ricchi, Immanuel Ḥai (1668–1743) Italian rabbi, Kabbalist, and poet. He was born in Ferrara and raised in Rovigo. At the age of 20 he traveled to various Italian cities. He was ordained a rabbi in 1717; the following year he emigrated to Palestine and settled in Safed, where he studied kabbalah. Because of a plague, he left the country and moved to Livorno. He later travelled to Smyrna, Salonica, Constantinople, and London, before returning to Palestine, and finally to Livorno. He wrote various Kabbalistic works.

Richler, Mordecai (1931–2001) Canadian novelist and journalist. He was born in Montreal, and moved to London in the 1950s. His *Son of a Smaller Hero* and *The Apprenticeship of Dudley Kravitz* depict Jewish life in Montreal. In later novels he contrasted Jewish and gentile culture.

Rickover, Hyman (1900–86) American naval engineer of Russian origin. Born in Makov, Russia, he was the son of a tailor. He went to the US with his family when he was six. He was commissioned in the US navy. Later he studied electrical engineering. During World War II he was in charge of the electrical side of naval shipbuilding. After the war, he conceived the idea of nuclear-powered submarines. He became a vice-admiral.

Ridbaz, Yaakov [Slutzker Rav] (1845–1913) Russian rabbi. After serving as a rabbi in Russia, he lived in the US from 1900 to 1905. He subsequently emigrated to Palestine, where he founded and directed a yeshivah in Safed.

Riesser, Gabriel (1806–1863) German lawyer and politician. He was born in Hamburg. After he was refused permission to practise as a notary in his native city because of his faith, he published a series of memoranda and articles demanding civil equality for Jewry. He became an important advocate of Emancipation for German Jews. From 1832 to 1837 he edited *Der Jude*. He was elected to the parliament at Frankfurt am Main in 1848 and was a member of the 1850 'Union' Parliament at Erfurt. In 1859 he became the first Jewish judge in Germany.

Righteousness Uprightness, virtue, honesty, freedom from wickedness. According to Jewish teaching, a 'tzaddik' (righteous man) is one who lives according to the divine law. Righteousness is a central theme of biblical legislation and prophetic teaching. Jewish tradition holds that in every generation

there are 36 perfectly righteous men ('lamed vav') on whose account the world continues to exist. In rabbinic and medieval Hebrew the word 'tzedakah' denotes alms giving and charity.

Rimmonim ('pomegranates') Word used by the Sephardim to refer to the filial ornaments on the wooden staves on which the Scroll of the Law is rolled. Originally these were shaped like pomegranates; later they were in the shape of towers.

Ringelbaum, Emanuel (1900–1944) Galician historian. He was born in Buchach, in eastern Galicia, and became a high-school history teacher. Active in the Poale Zion movement, he was sent by the American Jewish Joint Distribution Committee to Zbaszyń in 1938 to direct relief work and collect testimonies from Jews who had been deported there. During World War II he assembled a secret archive of events in the Warsaw Ghetto; it later came too light and constitutes an important source of information on what took place there.

Rishonim ('first ones') Older authorities. The *Talmud* uses the term to distinguish the earlier from the later prophets, as well as the former from the later generations in the talmudic period. In modern times the term refers to all commentators and codifiers of talmudic law of the gaonic period, up to the time of the compilation of the Shulḥan Arukh (i.e., c. 600–1300 CE).

Rivers, Larry (Grossberg, Yitzroch Loiza) (1923–2002) American painter and sculptor. Born in the Bronx, he studied at New York University, and was a figurative artist. In 1952 he began producing sculpture.

Robbery (Hebrew 'gezelah') The unlawful removal of another person's property. According to the Bible, the penalty for the crime of robbery is restitution of the property or its value; the latter provision pertains if the stolen property no longer exists, has been seriously altered, has been incorporated in a structure that will have to be demolished if it were removed, or is regarded by its owners as lost. A penitent robber should be treated leniently.

Robbins, Jerome (1918–98) American choreographer. He was born in New York. He began his career as a dancer, appearing with the New York City Ballet. His choreography for Broadway shows includes *Fiddler on the Roof.*

Robinson, Edward G. (Goldenberg, Emanuel)   (1893–1973) American film actor. Born in Bucharest, Romania, he went to the US in 1902. He was a student at the American Academy of Dramatic Art. He appeared in *Little Caesar, Five Star Final, Dr Ehrlich's Magic Bullet, Double Indemnity, The Woman in the Window, Scarlet Street* and *Key Largo.*

Rogers, Bernard (1893–1968) American composer and educator. He was born in New York. He taught at the Hartt School of Music and at the Eastman School of Music. Some of his work was influenced by biblical themes.

Rogers, Richard (1902–79) American composer of musicals. He began writing songs at an early age. He studied at Columbia University and collaborated with Lorenz Milton Hart on a variety show. Later they produced a variety of musicals. When Hart died, he collaborated with Oscar Hammerstein III on musicals including *Oklahoma!, South Pacific, The King and I* and *The Sound of Music.*

Rodkinson [Frumkin], Michael (1845–1904) American Hebrew writer and editor. He was born in Dubrovno, Belorussia, and initially wrote tales of the Ḥasidim. He later moved to Königsberg, where he published Hebrew periodicals from 1876 to 1880. In 1889 he settled in the US and devoted himself to translating the *Talmud* into English.

Rojas, Fernando de (fl. 16th cent.) Spanish Marrano author. He was born in Puebla de Montalbán near Toledo. He was the author of one of the earliest Spanish tragedies, *La Celestina.* Members of his family suffered under the Inquisition.

Rokaḥ, Yisrael (1896–1959) Israeli communal leader and politician. He was born in Jaffa. He was a member of the Tel Aviv city council from 1922, the city's Deputy Mayor from 1919 and Mayor from 1937 to 1953. He was elected to the Knesset in 1949 as a General Zionist member, and later served as Minister of the Interior, and Deputy Speaker of the Knesset.

Romm Family of Lithuanian Hebrew printers. The first member of the family to be active as a printer was Baruch ben Joseph Romm (fl. 18th century), who established the first Hebrew printing press in Lithuania at Grodno. It was later transferred to Vilnius. His son Menaḥem (d. 1841) was responsible for the publication of the first 'Vilna Talmud'. Menaḥem's son Joseph Reuben (d.1848) and grandson David (d.1860) developed the firm. At the end of the 19th century the imprint of 'the widow and brothers Romm' was to be found on many Hebrew works.

Rosales, Jacob [Jacob Hebraeus] (c. 1588–1668) Marrano physician and author. He was born in Lisbon, and became a physician there. Later he settled in Rome, where he came under the influence of Galileo. During the 1630s he went to Hamburg. Emperor Ferdinand III bestowed on him the title of Count Palatine on him in recognition of his scientific achievements. Later he lived as a Jew in Livorno, assuming the name Jacob Hebraeus. He published works on medicine and astronomy.

Rosanes, Solomon Abraham (1862–1938) Bulgarian historian. He was born in Ruschuk. He was a businessman, but devoted himself to Jewish studies, and during World War I settled in Sofia, where he became librarian of the Jewish community. He published studies of Jewish history, including *A History of the Jews in Turkey and in the Orient.*

Rose, Billy (Rosenberg, William Samuel (1899–1966) American impresario. Born in New York City, he became a shorthand stenographer. Determined to become a songwriter, he began to write songs. In 1924 he became a nightclub owner. During the 1940s he produced shows. After World War II he wrote a syndicated column and began investing in art and real estate. In 1965 he donated his sculpture collection to Israel.

Rosen, Joseph (1877–1949) American agronomist. He was born in Moscow, and emigrated to the US in 1903. In 1921 he returned to Russia for the American Jewish Joint Distribution Committee on a relief mission to the Jews. In 1924 he initiated a landsettlement project in Ukraine and Crimea for Jews who had been deprived of Soviet citizenship. In 1940 he directed Jewish Colonisation in the Dominican Republic.

Rosen, [Rosenblüth], Pinḥas (1887–1978) Israeli and Zionist leader, of German origin. He was born in Berlin. He served as Chairman of the Zionist Organisation of Germany, and after living in Palestine joined the Zionist Executive in London. In 1931 he returned to Palestine, where he practised law. He was active in the Aliyah Ḥadashah party, and in 1948 he became President of the Progressive Party. From 1949 to 1968 he was a member of the Knesset, serving as Minister of Justice in successive coalition cabinets.

Rosenbach, Abraham Simon Wolf (1876–1952) American bibliophile. He was born in Philadelphia, where he founded the Rosenbach Company, a rare-book company, a rare-book business. He wrote *An American Jewish Bibliography* and a historical study of Congregtion Mikveh israel in Philadelphia. He served as president of the American Jewish Historical Society, and was a benefactor of Graetz College.

Rosenbaum, Simon (1860–1934) Polish jurist and Zionist. He was born in Pinsk, and practised law there and in Minsk. Active in the Ḥibbat Zion movement, he was a delegate to the Zionist Congresses until World War I. He was an opponent of the Uganda plan. During World War I, he worked for an independent Lithuania, and later became the country's Deputy Foreign Minister. Subsequently he served as Minister of Jewish Affairs. In 1924 he settled in Palestine, where he was Chairman of the Supreme Peace Court.

Rosenberg, Isaac (1890–1934) English poet and painter. He was born in Bristol. Some of his poetry (such as *Chagrin*) expresses the rootless condition of the diaspora Jew.

Rosenblatt, Joseph (1822–1933) American cantor and composer. He was born in Belaya Tserkov' in Ukraine, and in his youth toured Eastern Europe as a child prodigy. He was initially cantor in Mukachevo, then moved to Bratislava in 1901, and to Hamburg five years later. In 1912 he emigrated to the US where he became ḥazzan of the Ohab Zedek Congregation in New York. He was the most popular cantor of his time. His collection of sacred songs, *Zemirot Yosef*, contains many of his best known works.

Rosenfeld, Isaac (1918–1956) American writer. He was born in Chicago. Some of his essays deal with Jews, Judaism and Jewish life in America and Europe.

Rosenfeld, Morris (1862–1923) American Yiddish poet. He was born in Bolikshein in the Russian part of Poland, and grew up in Warsaw. After learning tailoring in London, he went to New York in 1886, where he worked in a sweatshop. Initially he published socialist poems. In 1894 he began editing a satirical weekly, and in 1905 the daily *New Yorker Morgenblat*. By this time he was recognised as a pioneer of Yiddish poetry and in 1908 he went on a tour of Galicia and Western Europe. He wrote poems on proletarian, national and romantic themes. He also published studies on Heinrich Heine and Judah Halevi.

Rosenheim Jacob (1870–1965)   Orthodox leader, of German origin. He was born in Frankfurt am Main. He first worked in a bank, and later founded the Hermon Publishing House. In 1906 he transferred publication of the weekly *Israelit* from Mainz to Frankfurt where it became an influential organ of German Orthodoxy. He was a founder and leader of Agudat Israel, of which he was president from 1929. From 1940 he lived in the US and Israel; he helped to secure permission for Agudat Israel to participate in the Israeli government and Knesset. He wrote on various religious themes.

Rosenthal, Erwin Isak Jakob (1904–1991)   British orientalist. He was born in Heilbronn, Germany, and settled in England in 1933, where he became a lecturer in Hebrew at University College, London. He taught Semitic languages and literature at Manchester University and later at Cambridge University. He wrote studies of Judaism, biblical exegesis, medieval philosophy, and Islam.

Rosenthal, Herman (1843–1917)   American writer and pioneer of Jewish settlement in the US. He was born in Friedrichstadt, near Kiel, and initially worked as a printer in Ukraine. During the Russo-Turkish War, he served with the Red Cross. After the pogroms of 1881, he organised a group of 70 people and set out for the US, where he attempted to establish an agricultural

settlement for Russian Jews on Sicily Island, near New Orleans. In 1891 he participated in the establishment of an ICA colony in Woodbine, New Jersey. From 1898 he was the head of the Slavonic department of the New York Public Library.

Rosenthal, Leser (1794–1868)   German bibliophile and biographer. He was born in Nasnelsk, Plock, Russia. He taught at Paderborn, Germany, and later was Klausrabbiner at Hanover. His library contained 32 manuscripts and 6,000 printed volumes, including incunabula and rare books.

Rosenwald, Julius (1862–1932)   American merchant and philanthropist. He was born in Springfield, Illinois. He first worked in his uncle's clothing store in New York, but later opened his own store. He began to manufacture summer clothing and in 1885 moved his business to Chicago. He became President of Sears, Roebuck and Company, and subsequently Chairman of the Board. He was president of the Associated Jewish Charities of Chicago, and contributed to Jewish war relief during World War I and in the post-war period. He also supported the Hebrew Union College and the Jewish Theological Seminary.

Rosenwald, Lessing Julius (1891–1979)   American merchant, bibliophile, and philanthropist, son of Julius Rosenwald. He was born in Chicago, where he later worked for Sears, Roebuck and Company. In 1943 he helped to found the American Council for Judaism, and served as its president. Opposed to Zionism, he campaigned against the establishment of Israel.

Rosenwald, William (1903–1996)   American philanthropist and financier, son of Julius Rosenwald. He was a director of Sears, Roebuck, and Company, but later concentrated on his own investments. He was Chairman of the National United Jewish Appeal Campaign, and Vice-Chairman of the

Joint Distribution Committee, and played an important role in the American Jewish Committee and United HIAS Service.

Rosenzweig, Franz (1886–1929) German theologian. He was born in Kassel. He studied at various universities, and eventually considered converting to Christianity. After attending an Orthodox high holy day service in Berlin, he embraced Judaism. Later he served in the German army; he wrote *Star of Redemption* while confined to military hospitals in Leipzig and Belgrade. After returning home he established an institute for Jewish studies, the Freies Jüdisches Lehrhaus, in Frankfurt am Main. In 1921 he became partially paralysed, but he continued to write. Together with Martin Buber he translated the Hebrew Scriptures into German.

Rosh Ha-Shanah ('Head of the Year') **(i)** New Year. The Jewish New Year begins on the first day of Tishri, and marks the start of the Ten Days of Penitence, which end on the Day of Atonement. In the Bible Rosh Ha-Shanah is referred to as falling on the first day of the seventh month (Leviticus 23:24). During the rabbinic period, it came to be regarded as a day of judgement for the entire world, on which each person's fate is inscribed in the Book of Life. During the festival service, which is traditionally celebrated in white vestments, the shofar is blown and other rituals are introduced.

Rosh Ha-Shanah ('Head of the Year') **(ii)** Eighth tractate in the Mishnah order of Moed. It deals with the regulations regarding the sanctification of the new moon, the blowing of the ram's horn (or shofar) on Rosh Ha-Shanah, and the special order of prayer for that occasion.

Rosh Ḥodesh ('Sanctification of the month') The celebration of the appearance of the new moon, which marks the beginning of the month. A special sacrifice was offered in the Temple on this day, at which musaph was recited (Numbers 28:11–15). The Bible mentions various observances that should take place on the day of the new moon; during the Talmudic period these became more elaborate and included a proclamation of the new moon's appearance, communicated throughout and beyond Palestine by a system of beacons. In modern times the formal celebration is confined to the recital of the half Hallel and the addition of the musaph service to the Amidah on the first day of the month. It is announced in synagogues on the preceding Sabbath in a special ceremony.

Rosh yeshivah ('Head of the yeshivah') Originally, the title accorded to one who directs an institution for the study of the *Talmud*. In modern times the title is used not only for the principals of yeshivot but also for the permanent members of the teaching staff.

Rosowsky, Shlomo (1878–1962) Israeli composer. In St Petersburg he was an active member of the Society for Jewish Folk Music. In 1925 he emigrated to Palestine, where he composed music for the Hebrew theatre. Besides composing, he studied Jewish music and published work on the cantillation of the Bible. He later lived in the US and taught at the Jewish Theological Seminary.

Rossi, Azariah ben Moses dei [Adummim; Azariah dei Rossi] (c.1511–1578) Italian scholar. He was born in Mantua, and lived in Bologna, Ferrara, and Mantua. His *Meor Enayim* shows how classical sources (such as the Letter of Aristeas) cast light on Jewish history and literature in the classical period. In the third part of this work ('Imrei Binah') he examined Ancient Jewish history by comparing Hebrew texts with classical Jewish and non-Jewish sources.

He also wrote poetry in Italian, Hebrew, and Aramaic. His writings provoked the hostility of a number of rabbis.

Rossi, Solomon de' (fl. 17th cent.) Italian composer. He came from Mantua. He was the leading Jewish composer of the late Italian Renaissance, and a court musician of the Gonzaga rulers of Mantua. In 1587 he entered the service of the Duke of Vicenzo I as a singer and viola player. Later he became the leader of the duke's musical establishment and directed an instrumental ensemble. He published secular, instrumental, and vocal music, including a collection of Hebrew religious songs.

Rosten, Leo (1908–1997) American humourist. He was born in Lodz in Poland, and went to the US as a child. He later served in the US government. Under the pen name Leonard Q Ross, he wrote *The Education of H*y*m*a*n K*a*p*l*a*n*, and *The Return of H*y*m*a*n K*a*p*l*a*n*. He also wrote the *Joys of Yiddish*.

Rotenstreich, Natan (1914–1993) Israeli philosopher. He was born in Sambor, Poland, and emigrated to Palestine in 1932. In 1955, he became Professor of Philosophy at the Hebrew University, and later Dean of the Faculty of Humanities and Rector. He wrote studies of Jewish thinkers and a survey of modern Jewish thought.

Roth, Cecil (1899–1970) English historian. He was born in London. He was reader in Jewish studies at Oxford from 1939 to 1964, when he settled in Jerusalem and became Visiting Professor at Bar Ilan University. His publications include histories of the Jews of England and Italy, Jewish biographies, a history of the Marranos, a study of Jews in the Renaissance, and studies of Jewish art.

Roth, Henry (1906–1995) American novelist. He was born in Austria, and went to the US as a child. He worked as a high-school teacher, precision metal grinder, and farmer. His *Call it Sleep* deals with Jewish immigrant life in New York's East Side.

Roth, Joseph (1894–1939) Austrian novelist. He was born near Brody in eastern Galicia. He worked from 1923 for the *Frankfurter Zeitung.* Later he lived in Paris. His novel *Job* describes Eastern-European Jewish life, and in *Juden auf Wanderschaft* he deals with the social position of Jews in Eastern Europe.

Roth, Leon (1896–1963) English philosopher. He was a lecturer in philosophy at Manchester University from 1923 to 1927. He settled in Palestine and became Professor of Philosophy at the Hebrew University, rector of the university, and Dean of the Faculty of Humanities. He returned to England in 1951. He wrote philosophical studies, translated philosophical classics into Hebrew, and published a study of the Jewish religion.

Roth, Philip (b.1933) American novelist. He was born in New Jersey. Many of his novels and short stories depict the struggle of American Jewish men, especially the conflict between their Jewish background and the attractions of American Christian culture. His writings include *Goodbye Columbus, Letting Go, Portnoy's Complaint, The Antaony Lesson, The Breast, My Life as a Man, The Ghost Writer, Zukerman Unbound, The Counterlife, The Professor of Desire, The Great American Novel,* and *Reading Myself and Others.*

Rothenberg, Morris (1885–1950) American Zionist leader. He was born in Dorpat, Estonia, and was taken to the US in 1893. During World War I he was a member of a federal commission charged with fixing the price of bread. In 1937 he became city magistrate of New York. He was a founder and executive committee member of the Jewish Welfare Board, a founder of the Joint Distribution Committee, and an executive committee member of the Council for German Jewry. He also served as President of the Zionist Organisation of America.

Rothenstein, William, Sir (1872–1945) English artist. He was born in Bradford. He studied in London, Paris and Oxford. During World War I he served as a war artist, and then became Professor of Civic Art at the University of Sheffield. From 1920 to 1935 he was principal of the Royal College of Art. He painted portraits, still lifes, and landscapes, as well as Jewish subjects and synagogue interiors.

Rothko, Mark (1903–70) American artist. Born in Dvinsk, Russia, he went to the US at the age of seven. He studied at Yale and later at the Arts Student League. He taught art to children at a school in Brooklyn and later at Brooklyn College. He painted huge spaces of colour in which he floated soft-edged rectangles.

Rothschild, Edmond de, Baron (1845–1934) French philanthropist and art collector, son of James de Rothschild. He and his wife, Adelaide, were interested in Jewish affairs. When the first Zionist pioneers in Palestine appealed to Rothschild for assistance, he supported the colonisation of Palestine. He sent agricultural experts and officials there to help in the settlement process, visited Palestine himself five times, and purchased 125,000 acres of land in the country. In 1900 he transferred the management of the colonies to the ICA. Later he served as the honorary president of the Jewish Agency.

Rothschild, Lionel (1808–1879) English banker. He was head of the family banking house at New Court in London. He was elected to parliament as a Liberal in 1847 but took his seat only in 1858, after the passing of the Jews' Disabilities Bill.

Rothschild, Mayer (1744–1812) German banker. He studied at a rabbinical school in Fürth. He set up in business as a general trader and money changer. In 1792 he attempted to establish a Jewish school with a modern curriculum. He served as intermediary for Prince William and other members of the royalty. In 1800 he became an imperial crown agent. In 1796 he took his two older sons, Amschel Mayer and Salomon Meyer, into partnership and later his other boys, Nathan Mayer, Carl Mayer and James Mayer also became partners. They subsequently created an international banking syndicate.

Rothschild, Nathaniel, 1st Lord (1840–1915) English banker. He was head of the English branch of the Rothschild banking house, and became the first Jewish peer. He served as President of the United Synagogue.

Rov (Yiddish) Rabbi.

Rovina, Hanna (1892–1980) Israeli actress, of Russian origin. She was born in Berezino, Minsk, and first worked as head of an institute for refugee children at Saratov. In 1917 she joined a Hebrew theatrical studio in Moscow and became one of the founding members of the Ha-Bimah Theatre Company. In 1928 she went to Palestine with the company and became the country's leading actress.

Rozin, Joseph [Rogochover, Gaon] (1858–1936) Latvian talmudist. He was born in Rogochover and became rabbi of the Ḥasidic community of Dvinsk in 1889. During World War I he fled to St Petersburg, where he was the rabbi of a Ḥasidic community for ten years. He subsequently returned to Dvinsk. He wrote responsa and a commentary on Maimonides *Mishneh Torah*. His collected works appeared under the title *Tzaphenat Paaneaḥ*.

Rubens, Bernice (1927–2004) British novelist. She was born in Cardiff. She was first a schoolteacher, and later a writer and director of documentary films. Her early novels deal with middle-class Jewish life.

Rubenstein, Richard L. (b.1924) Amercian theologian. He was born in New York. He served as Chaplain to Jewish students at the University of Pittsburgh, and in 1970 became Professor of Religion at Florida State University. His writings include *After Auschwitz*, *The Religious Imagination* and *The Cunning of History*.

Rubin, Solomon (1823–1910) Galician Hebrew writer. He was born in Dolnia. He became one of the most prolific writers of the Haskalah period, publishing studies of Jewish folklore, customs, and superstitions, and works about Spinoza.

Rubinstein, Anton Grigoryevich (1829–94) Russian pianist and composer. Born in Vykhvatinetz, Podolia, his family moved to Moscow. In 1844 the family moved to Berlin; when his father died the family went to Russia, but Anton spent two years in Vienna giving piano lessons. In 1848 he went to Moscow and with Elena Pavlovna helped found the Russian Musical Society, later the St Petersburg Conservatory. Subsequently he resumed his solo career.

Rubinstein, Helena (1871–1965) American cosmetics manufacturer. Born in Poland, she went to Australia at the age of 20 and began marketing cold cream. Later she went to London where she opened her own beauty salon. In 1914 she went to the US. Her innovations included a waterproof mascara, medicated face cream, and the selling technique of home demonstration.

Rubinstein, Isaac (1880–1945) Polish communal leader. He was born in Dotnuva, Lithuania. He was a rabbi in Genichesk, Ukraine, from 1906, and later became the government-appointed rabbi of Vilnius. In 1920 he was Minister of Jewish Affairs in Vilnius, and from 1922 to 1939 was a member of the Polish senate. He was also a leader of the Mizraḥi and active in the World Zionist Organisation. In 1941 he emigrated to the US and taught at Yeshiva University.

Rukeyser, Muriel (1914–1980) American poet, writer and translator. She was born in New York, and taught at Sarah Lawrence College. Her poetry includes works about Rabbi Akiva.

Ruppin, Arthur (1876–1943) Palestinian Zionist, economist, and sociologist. He was born in Rawicz, in the Posen district, and initially worked in the grain trade. From 1903 to 1907 he directed the Bureau for Jewish Statistics and Demography in Berlin. In 1907 he went to Palestine as a representative of the Zionist Organisation. Later he founded various settlement companies and helped to establish labour colonisation in the country. He was deported by the Turks in 1916, but returned in 1920. Subsequently he became Director of the Zionist Executive's colonisation department in Jerusalem. From 1926 he taught sociology at the Hebrew University. His writings include sociological studies of Jewry.

Rutenberg, Pinḥas (1879–1942) Palestinian engineer and Zionist teacher, of Ukrainian origin. He was born in Romny, in Ukraine. He participated in the 1905 Russian Revolution, and after living for a time in Italy and the US, returned to Russia in 1917. He was again involved in revolutionary activities, but he left Russia in 1919 and settled in Palestine, where he founded the Palestine Electric Company. He was elected Chairman of the Vaad Leumi in 1929.

Ruth (fl. 12th cent. BCE) Moabite woman. After her husband, Mahlon, died she went with Naomi (her mother-in-law) to Bethlehem, where she married Boaz. The Book of Ruth is one of the Five Scrolls, and is read during Shavuot.

Rutherston, Albert Daniel [Rothenstein, Albert Daniel] (1881–1953) English artist and illustrator. He designed an important Haggadah.

Ruth Rabbah Aggadic midrash, part of the Midrash Rabbah. It is exegetical in character. It utilises earlier sources including the Palestinian *Talmud*, Genesis Rabbah, Leviticus Rabbah and the Pesikta de-Rav Kahana.

Ruzhin, Israel of (1797–1851) Russian Ḥasidic rabbi. He established a Hasidic centre at Ruzhin, where he lived in luxury. In 1838 he was accused of giving the order to put to death two Jewish informers. Imprisoned for 22 months, he was later released and settled in Sadagora in Bukovina, which also became a Ḥasidic centre.

Ryback, Issachar (1879–1935) Russian artist. He was born in Yelizavetgradka in Ukraine. He helped to establish an art section of the Jewish Culutral Leage in Kiev. From 1921 to 1925 he lived in Berlin, where he illustrated children's books in Yiddish. In 1926 he moved to Paris.

Rybakov, Anatolii (1911–1998) Ukrainian writer. He was born in Chernigov, and moved to Moscow in 1919. He was arrested and sentenced to imprisonment in Siberia. After his release in 1935 he worked as a ballroom-dancing teacher, automobile mechanic and driver. Later he served in the army and began writing. His novel *Heavy Sand* deals with the Russian Jewish past and the Holocaust in the USSR.

S

A rich Jewish banker, Stanley Greenstein, lives next door to John D. Rockefeller. Both have enormous estates, and the Jewish neighbour has the same fleet of Rolls Royces as Rockefeller. He also has the same landscaping, and a replica of his neighbour's swimming pool. This copycat behaviour irritates his neighbour, and one day Rockefeller angrily says to Greenstein: 'Are you trying to be my equal? Do you actually think you can be like me by copying what I do?'

'I am not your equal,' Greenstein says. 'I am better than you!'

'And why is that?'

'Because,' says Greenstein, 'I don't have a Jew living next to me.'

* * * * *

Many Jewish jokes deal with anti-Semitism. Here Rockefeller expresses his hostility to Jews. He regards his neighbour as undesirable and vulgar. In response to his insult, Greenstein turns the tables, and says that he is superior to Rockefeller because he does not have a Jew living next door. The irony of this response highlights the predicament of Jews living in a gentile environment.

Saad al-Daula (fl. 13th cent.) Persian physician and statesman. He served as a physician in government service in Baghdad, and later became Governor of Baghdad and Iraq. In 1289 he was appointed Vizier by Arghun, the Mongolian ruler.

Saadyah Gaon [Saadyah ben Joseph] (882–942) Babylonian gaon. He was born in Pithom in the Faiym district of Egypt, and settled in Babylonia in 921. In 928 he became Gaon of Sura, but two years later he was deposed by the exilarch, David ben Zakkai. He was reinstated in 936. His earliest work was a polemic against the Karaite scholar Anan ben David. *Beliefs and Opinions* is his main philosophical treatise. His other scholarly works include a translation of the Bible into Arabic, Arabic commentaries on most biblical books, a Hebrew lexicon and grammar, and a list of biblical *hapax legomena*. He also produced a systematic compilation of the prayer book, and wrote liturgical poetry. His *Sepher ha-Galui* is an account of his personal tribulations.

Sabbath (Hebrew 'Shabbat') Day of rest. It is observed weekly from before sunset on Friday until after nightfall on Saturday. According to tradition, the Sabbath is a memorial of the day of rest enjoyed by God after the Creation. Its observance was enjoined by God, in one version of the Ten Commandments, to commemorate his bringing the Israelites out of Egypt. Work must cease on the Sabbath and rabbinic legislation stipulates 39 types of action which are forbidden. However, these regulations may be set aside if human life is in danger. The Sabbath day is an occasion for prayer, study and refreshment of the spirit. Synagogue services include readings from the Torah and the Books of the Prophets, and the day concludes with the Havdalah service.

Sabbath, Great (Hebrew 'Shabbat ha-Gadol') The name given to the Sabbath before Passover. On that day a special haftarah (Malachi 3:4–24) is read after the Torah portion, and a rabbinic discourse dealing with the laws of the approaching festival is delivered. The Ashkenazim read part of the Passover Haggadah during the afternoon service.

Sabbath lamp Oil lamp kindled in the home on Friday night to symbolise the light of the Sabbath. Made of brass, copper, pewter, or silver, it was bowl-shaped and hung from the ceiling. In modern times candles have been substituted for oil.

Sabbath prayers On Friday evenings the Maariv service is preceded by a special service in the synagogue known as 'Kabbalat Shabbat' (Reception of the Sabbath). At home the kiddish prayer is recited before the meal, and Sabbath songs ('zemirot') are sung after it. The prayers recited on the Sabbath follow the same basic structure as on other days. However, the Amidah consists of only seven benedictions, and a fourth prayer service (musaph) is added to the three regular daily prayers. In addition many extra psalms and poetic compositions are included in the morning service. At the end of the Sabbath, Maariv is recited as on weekdays, and is followed by the Havdalah service.

Sabbaths, special Four Sabbaths are named after the special Torah readings that replace the ordinary maphtir (or concluding portion) of the weekly reading from the law: (1) 1 Adar or the preceding Sabbath is known as Shekalim from Exodus 30:11–16; (2)

the Sabbath before Purim is known as Zakhor from Deuteronomy 25:17–19; (3) The Sabbath before Purim is known as Parah from Numbers 19:1–22; and (4) 1 Nisan or the preceding Sabbath is known as Ha-Ḥodesh from Exodus 12:1–20. In addition, three Sabbaths are named after the first word of the portion from the Books of the Prophets assigned to the day: (1) Sabbath Ḥazon (the Sabbath before the Ninth of Av) from Isaiah 1:1; (2) Sabbath Naḥamu (the Sabbath after the Ninth of Av) from Isaiah 40:1; and (3) Sabbath Shuvah (the Sabbath between New Year and the Day of Atonement) from Hosea 14:2. Similarly Sabbath Bereshit and Sabbath Shirah are named for the weekly biblical portions. Finally, the Sabbath during the intermediate days of Passover or Sukkot is known as Sabbath Ḥol ha-Moed, the Sabbath before Passover as Shabbat ha-Gadol.

Sabbatical year (Hebrew 'Shemittah') [Year of Release] Name given in Jewish law to every seventh year, when, according to Leviticus 25:3ff, no agricultural work should be done. All crops in this year are the property of the community. The Sabbatical year was also marked by the rescinding of debts, hence the alternative name 'Year of Release'. The year following seven Sabbatical years (this is every 50th year) is a Jubilee (Leviticus 25:8), when cultivation is prohibited, slaves are freed, and land purchased since the preceding Jubilee reverts to its original owner. The laws relating to Sabbatical and Jubilee years are treated in the Talmudic tractate Sheviit. They are now observed only by strict Orthodox Jews living in Israel.

Sabbetaians [Shabbetaians] Name given to the followers of the messianic leader Shabbetai Tzevi. After his death in 1676, they believed he would reappear as the saviour of Israel. They eventually split into various sects, including the Dönmeh sect (followers of Shabbetai Tzevi's successor, Jacob Querido), the Cardoza sect (disciples of Abraham Miguel Cardoza), and the Mokiah sect (centred on Mordecai Mokiah).

Sabra (Arabic) Native of Israel.

Sachar, Abram Leon (1899–1993) American educator and historian. He was born in New York. He taught history at the University of Illinois, and later served as National Director of the Hillel Foundaiton. In 1948 he became the first president of Brandeis University, subsequently becoming its chancellor. His publications include *History of the Jews*, and a history of Jewish life between the two world wars.

Sachs, Michael Jehiel (1808–1864) German rabbi and preacher. He was born in Glogau, Silesia. He was a preacher in Prague, and later in Berlin, where he also served as dayyan of the bet din. He was an opponent of the reforming influence of Samuel Holdheim and his Berlin congregation. He translated the liturgy and parts of the Bible into German.

Sachs, Nelly (1891–1970) German poet. She was born in Berlin. She escaped to Sweden at the beginning of World War II. Some of her writing was inspired by the Holocaust. She received the Nobel Prize for literature.

Sackler, Harry (1883–1974) American Hebrew and Yiddish author. He was born in Bohorodczany, Galicia, and went to the US in 1902. He worked as an attorney and served as an officer of various Jewish organisations. In his stories novels, plays and essays he recreated Jewry through the ages. His novel *Festival at Meron* depicts the period of the Bar Kokhba revolt (132–35 CE).

Sacks, Jonathan (b.1948) English rabbi. He was born in London. He deserved as principal of Jews College, and in 1991 became Chief Rabbi of the United Hebrew Congregations of the British Commonwealth. His publications include *Traditional Alternatives, Tradition in an Untraditional Age,* and *The Persistence of Faith.*

Sacrifice Ritual act involving an offering to a deity. In Judaism sacrifice was made to God to obtain his favour or atone for sin. The Canaanites sacrificed human beings (II Kings 3:27) but the story in Genesis of the binding of Isaac (22: 1–19) teaches God's displeasure with this type of sacrificial act. In Ancient Israel three types of sacrifice were offered in the Temple: animal sacrifice ('zera'), made as a burnt offering for sin, meal offering ('minḥah') and libations. The rituals and practices prescribed for the Temple sacrifice are set down in Leviticus 2 and 23, and Numbers 28–29.

Sacrilege (Hebrew 'me'ilah') The misuse or desecration of anything regarded as sacred or worthy of great respect. In biblical times it was regarded as sacrilege to appropriate Temple property for secular use, to put to secular use the formula for sacrificial incense, and to copy the design of the Temple candelabrum or other vessels for non-cultic purposes. Later it was decreed anti-religious to use the synagogue improperly, to treat the Scroll of the Law with disrespect, to imitate Holy Writ for secular purposes, and to recite the Song of Songs as secular poetry. Concerning matters pertaining to death and burial, it is sacrilege to misuse a cemetery or to derive private gain from any activity involving a body or a shroud.

Sadan, Dov (1902–1989) Israeli Yiddish and Hebrew writer. He was born in Galicia, and emigrated to Israel in 1925. He first worked on the newspaper *Davar* and for the Am Oved publishing company. In 1952 he was appointed to teach Yiddish literature at the Hebrew University. He also taught Hebrew literature at Tel Aviv University. He was elected to the Knesset in 1965. He translated many works from Polish, German and Yiddish, and published several collections of literary criticism.

Sadducees One of the three main sects of Judaism before the destruction of the Jewish state in 70CE. The others were the Pharisees and the Essenes. The group comprised the priestly class, who officiated in the Temple. Unlike the Pharisees, the Sadducees did not subscribe to a belief in the resurrection of the dead. Encouraging adherence to the Written Law, they dispensed with an oral tradition. They were supporters of the Hasmonean kings, but lost influence under Salome Alexandra and suffered persecution at the hands of Herod the Great. After the destruction of the Temple in 70, the sect died out.

Sadeh, Pinḥas (1929–1994) Israeli writer. He was born in Tel Aviv. He has written in a wide variety of genres, including children's books, poetry, and literary articles; he also published an autobiography and a novel, *Al Mazzavo Shel ha-Adam.*

Sadeh, Yitzḥak [Landsberg, Yitzḥak] (1890–1952) Israeli labour and military leader. He was born in Lublin, Poland. He served in the Russian army, then in 1920 left for Palestine, where he became the head of Joseph Trumpeldor's Labour Battalion. In 1941 he organised the Palmaḥ, which he commanded until 1945. Later he served on the staff of the Haganah. After the creation of the State of Israel, he commanded the Eighth Armoured Brigade. He published stories, plays and memoirs.

Sahl ben Matzliah (fl. 11th cent.) Palestinian Karaite. He travelled extensively, spreading his teaching. His writings incorporate information on the Karaites and Palestinian Jewry. They include polemics against the rabbis and an Arabic commentary on the Torah.

Salaman, Nina (1877–1925) English poet, wife of Redcliffe Salaman. She translated medieval Hebrew poetry. Her own writings included the collection *Apples and Honey.*

Salaman, Redcliffe (1874–1955) English pathologist and geneticist. He was the director of the Pathological Institute of the London Hospital from 1901 to 1904. In 1926 he became Director of the potato virus research station in Cambridge. His writings include *Jewish Achievements in Medicine* and *Racial Origins of Jewish Types.* During World War I he served in Palestine, and published *Palestine Reclaimed.*

Salant, Samuel (1816–1909) Palestinian rabbi, of Polish origin. He was born near Bialystok. He set out for Palestine in 1840, but was delayed in Constantinople, where he met Sir Moses Montefiore. In 1841 he reached Jerusalem, where he became rabbi of the Ashkenazi community. In 1878 he became Ashkenazi Chief Rabbi. He served various Jewish organisations and travelled widely in Europe to collect money for religious institutions in Jerusalem. A number of his novellae were published in Talmudic journals.

Salanter, Israel [Lipkin, Israel] (1810–1883) Lithuanian scholar. He was born in Zhagory. He founded the Musar movement in Lithuania and Russia from around 1830, and set up 'Musar houses' for the study of ethical literature. He also published a journal, *Tevunah,* to promote his views. His pupils helped to spread the Musar movement, particularly among the Torah students of Lithuania. Salanter also travelled to Western Europe to propagate his ideas. Isaac Belzer collected his ethical writings in *Or Israel.*

Sale According to the *Talmud,* a sale of any property is not legally binding until a 'kinyan' (act of agreement or possession) has been drawn up. An oral agreement is not binding. In the case of movable property, the vendor may void the sale, even after money has been paid by the buyer, as long as a formal kinyan has not been exchanged. A sale is effected in cases of immovable property by payment of the full cost or by writing a kinyan.

Salk, Jonas (1914–95) American scientist. He was a research professor at the University of Pittsburgh. He developed the anti-polio vaccine which is used worldwide. He served as an adviser on virus diseases to the World Health Organisation, and founded the Salk Institute for Biological Studies in California.

Salome (fl. 1st cent.) Palestinian princess, daughter of Herod's son Philip and Herodias. She is identified with the daughter of Herodias who was responsible for John the Baptist's death (Matthew 14:3–6; Mark 6:17–29). She married her uncle the tetrarch Philip, and subsequently Aristobulus, King of Lesser Armenia.

Salome, Alexandra [Shelom Tziyyon, Alexandra] (fl. 1st cent. BCE) Queen of Judea (76–67 BCE). She succeeded her husband Alexander Yannai. Reversing his policy toward the Pharisees, she gave them internal control of the country, while retaining responsibility herself for the army and foreign policy. When she appointed her son Hyrcanus, as high priest and heir, his younger brother Aristobulus denounced her action.

Salomon, Gotthold (1784–1862) German preacher and reformer. After an Orthodox education, he was sent to Dessau, where he was influenced by modern trends, such as new approaches to biblical criticism. He became a teacher and preacher in Dessau, and was later appointed rabbi of the Hamburg Reform temple. The publication of his new version of the liturgy in 1841 provoked considerable controversy.

Salomons, Sir David (1797–1873) English banker and communal leader. He was a founder of the joint stock banking system in England. An advocate of the admission of Jews into English public affairs, he was the first Jewish sheriff, alderman, and Lord Mayor of London. He was elected to parliament in 1851, and took his seat without taking the Christian oath. As a result he was ejected, which drew public attention to the problem of Jewish parliamentary disabilities.

Salt In the Bible salt is used as a symbol of the eternal covenant between God and his people (Numbers 18:19; II Chronicles 13:5). According to ritual practice all sacrifices and meal offerings had to be salted before being placed on the altar in the Temple (Leviticus 2:13); salt for this purpose was stored in the Salt Chamber on the north side of the Temple court. After the Temple was destroyed, the meal table in the Jewish home became a symbol of the altar; salt is placed on it for all meals. Bread is to be dipped into salt after the Ha-Motzi blessing. Jewish law stipulates that all meat must be soaked in water and salted before it may be eaten.

Salten, Felix [Zalzmann, Felix] (1869–1945) Austrian novelist and critic. He was born in Budapest. He lived in Vienna, where he was a contributor to the *Neue Frei Presse*. He also wrote plays, essays and stories, including the famous children's story *Bambi*. His Jewish interests are reflected in his novel *Simson*, and in essays about his visit to Palestine. In 1938 he settled in Hollywood, but after World War II returned to Europe to live in Zurich.

Salvador, Joseph (1796–1873) French historian. He was born in Montpellier. He initially studied medicine, but after settling in Paris he began to work on the history of religions. In *Paris, Rome, Jerusalem, ou la question religious extremism au 19e siècle*, he propounded a universal creed of religion. He also wrote a history of Roman rule in Judea, a study of the institutions of Moses and the Jewish people, and a work about Jesus.

Salvation (Hebrew 'yeshuah') Devine deliverance. The term 'yeshuah' (also 'teshuah') occurs in biblical and liturgical texts, where it generally refers to deliverance from suffering, oppression, and exile. It is also linked with the concept of messianic redemption.

Samael   Prince of demons. He is identified with Satan and his wife Lilith is the queen of demons. He is mentioned in the Slavonik Book of Enoch and in midrashic and Kabbalistic texts.

Samaritan   The language of the Samaritans is the Hebrew of the Torah, but it is pronounced differently from the Hebrew of the Ashkenazi and Sephardi rites. Modern Hebrew is a development of the Samaritan language. The old Defter liturgy is in Samaritan Aramaic as is the Midrash Memar Marka. The Samaritans also possess a literature in Arabic.

Samaritans   Ancient people descended from the tribes of Ephraim and Manasseh (II Chronicles 34:9; Jeremiah 41:5) who intermarried with the non-Israelite colonists (II King's 17:24–41). Their capital was at Samaria. During the Persian period, Nehemiah foiled the Samaritan ruler Sanballat, who attempted to obtain political and religious influence over Judah. When his son-in-law was driven from Jerusalem (Nehemiah 13:28), Sanballat built a rival Temple on Mount Gerizim. It was destroyed by John Hyrcanus in the 2nd century BCE. In modern times the Samaritans continue to live in Israel. Their synagogue, housing a Torah that is claimed to date from ancient times, is at Mount Gerizim, where they hold an annual Passover sacrifice.

Saminsky, Lazare (1882–1959)   American composer, of Russian origin. He studied at the University of St Petersburg and with Rimsky-Korsakov at the conservatory there. A founder of the Society for Jewish Folk Music, he went to the Caucasus in 1913 as a member of the ethnological expedition. In 1923 he settled in New York, where he became Music Director of Temple Emanu-El.

He wrote symphonies, including *Jerusalem, City of Solomon and Christ*, liturgical choruses, and Hebrew services. His writings include *Music of our Day*, *Music of the Ghetto and the Bible*, and *Living Music of the Americas*.

Sampter, Jessie (1883–1938)   American poet and Zionist writer. She grew up in the US, but later settled in Palestine, where she established evening classes for Yemenite working girls in Jerusalem. In 1920 she helped to organise the country's first camp for Jewish scouts. Subsequently she moved to Rehovot, where she did social work. In *The Emek* she portrayed kibbutz life in a series of prose poems. She also wrote books, articles and poems about Zionism and Jewish subjects.

Samson (fl. 12th–11th cent. BCE)   Israelite judge, son of Manoah of the tribe of Dan (Judges 13–16). He was a Nazirite of enormous strength, but when his mistress Delilah revealed the secret of his strength as laying in his hair, he fell into the hands of the Philistines. His hair was cut, his eyes were put out, and he was forced to turn the prison mill. When he was taken to Gaza to be mocked for the entertainment of Philistines at a festival, his strength returned to him and he destroyed the palace, killing all those assembled there.

Samson ben Abraham of Sens (fl. 12th–13th cent.)   French tosaphists. During the first Maimonidean controversy (1202), he spoke on behalf of the French rabbis. He opposed the teachings of Maimonides' *Mishneh Torah* and attacked his view of resurrection. The founder of the academy at Sens, he was one of the leaders of 300 rabbis who settled in Palestine at the beginning of the 13th century. He wrote Talmudic commentaries (*Tosaphot Sens*) and liturgical poetry.

Samuel (i) (fl. 11th cent. BCE)   Israelite prophet and judge. He was consecrated as a Nazirite by his mother before his birth, and served in the Sanctuary at Shiloh. There he foretold the destruction of the House of Eli. After the death of Eli and his sons, and the defeat of the Israelites by the Philistines, Samuel attempted to restore traditional religious worship. He lived at Ramah and judged the Israelites in Bethel, Gilgal and Mizpah. Later he acceded to the Israelites' demand for a King and selected Saul. When Saul lost favour with God, Samuel was sent to Bethlehem, where at God's behest he anointed David as Saul's successor (I Samuel 1–16).

Samuel (ii) Biblical book, part of the group known as the Former Prophets. It relates the history of the Israelites from the end of the period of the judges to the last days of David. It includes the biographies of Samuel (I Samuel 1–7), Saul (I Samuel 8–II 3), and David (I Samuel 16ff).

Samuel (iii) [Mar Samuel] (fl. 1st–2nd cent.) Babylonian amora. He was born at Nehardea, and became head of the academy there. He was acknowledged the outstanding authority on civil law. His debates with Rav about halakhic problems are recorded in the *Talmud*. He was also an expert astronomer, whose opinion on questions concerning the Hebrew calendar was often sought. He was on friendly terms with King Sapor I of Persia.

Samuel, Herbert Louis, Viscount (1870–1963) British statesman and philosopher. He was born in Liverpool. He entered parliament in 1902, becoming a privy council or six years later. He served as Postmaster-General and later Home Secretary. From 1920 to 1925 he was the first High Commissioner for Palestine. He was leader of the Liberal Party in both the House of Commons and the House of Lords. He was also President of the Council for German Jewry from 1936, and in 1939 founded the Children's Movement to bring refugee children from Germany to Britain. He wrote various philosophical works.

Samuel, Maurice (1895–1972) American author and translator. He was born in Macin, Romania, and was taken to England, where he grew up in Manchester. In 1914 he settled in the US. His writings include *You Gentiles, I the Jew, Jews on Approval, The Great Hatred, The Gentleman and the Jew, Harvest in the Desert, The Second Crucifixion, On the Rim of the Wilderness, The World of Shalom Aleichem, Prince of the Ghetto, Certain People of the Book, Blood Accusation,* and *In Praise of Yiddish.* He translated Hebrew and Yiddish works.

Samuel, Midrash to Midrash to the Book of Samuel. It was compiled in the 11th century from old midrashim.

Samuel ben Ali ha-Levi (fl. 12th cent.) Babylonian gaon. He was the head of the academy in Baghdad, and engaged in polemics with Maimonides about halakhic issues and about Maimonides' view of the resurrection of the dead.

Samuel Ben Avigor (1720–1793) Lithuanian rabbi. Between 1719 and 1746 he served (in succession) as rabbi of Pruzhany, Zelwa, Volkovysk, and Ruzhany. In 1750 he became rabbi of Vilnius, succeeding his father-in-law, Judah ben Eliezer. In 1777 the community decided to remove him from office because he was suspected of nepotism, but a compromise was reached. In 1782 the controversy broke out again, and the dispute was brought before Jewish and gentile courts. Samuel ben Avigdor was dismissed from his post and Vilnius was left without a rabbi. He was an ardent opponent of the Ḥasidim.

Samuel ben Hophni (fl. 10th–11th cent.) Babylonian gaon. He was appointed gaon of Sura in 997. One of the most prolific writers of the gaonic period, he wrote responsa, talmudic treatises, biblical exegesis, philosophy, theology and polemics.

Samuel ben Meir [Rashbam] (c.1085–1175) French biblical and talmudic commentator, grandson of Rashi. He was born in Ramerupt in northern France, and was a disciple of his grandfather. He engaged in sheep-farming and viticulture. His commentaries expound the simple and natural meaning of the Bible and *Talmud* texts. He completed Rashi's commentary on Bava Batra and Pesaḥim, and his works were quoted by the tosaphists.

Samuel ha-Katan (fl. 1st cent.) Palestinian tanna. His prayer Birkat ha-Minim expresses anathema against Judeo-Christians, sectarians, and informers. It was written at the request of Gamaliel II and was incorporated into the Amida.

Samuel ibn Adiya (fl. 6th cent.) Arabian poet. He lived in Tamya in Herjaz, northern Arabia. His poetry is similar to that of other pre-Islamic poets.

Samuel ibn Nagrela [Ha-Nagid; Ibn Nagdela; Ibn Nagrela; Samuel ha-Nagid] (933–1055) Spanish statesman, scholar and military commander. Born in Córdoba, he was forced to flee the city in 1013 and opened a spice shop in Malaga. He joined the staff of King Habbus, the Berber ruler of Granada, and was later appointed Vizier of Granada. In 1027 he became the nagid of Spanish Jewry. When Habbus died in 1037, Samuel ibn Nagrela supported his son Badis, taking on the administration of the kingdom and command of the armies. He composed poetry, wrote grammatical works, and completed an introduction to the *Talmud*. He was also a patron of numerous scholars.

Sanctuary (Hebrew 'bet ha-mikdash') The most holy part of a place of worship. The term is applied to the Tabernacles at Shiloh, Jerusalem and elsewhere. In Shiloh and Jerusalem, the sanctuary contained the Ark; in the Temple at Jerusalem the sanctuary was the Holy of Holies, where the Ark was kept, and the part of a modern synagogue where the Ark is positioned retains the name 'sanctuary'. The term also denotes a place of refuge for accidental killers. In ancient times, up to the period of the monarchy, this function was fulfilled by the altar (Exodus 21:14; I King's 1:51; 2:28). Moses set aside six cities of refuge where accidental killers could flee. The monarchy later took over the responsibility of dealing with such cases.

Sandalphon Angel. In the kabbalah he plays an important role as the guardian of prayers and of Israel in exile. He is also depicted as the divine messenger at the time of the resurrection.

Sandmel, Samuel (1911–1979) American biblical scholar. He was born in Dayton, Ohio. He served as a Hillel rabbi at Yale University and was Professor of Jewish Literature and Thought at Vanderbilt. In 1952 he became professor of Bible and Hellenistic literature at the Hebrew Union College. He published studies of Philo and the relationship between Judaism and Christianity.

Sanhedrin ('Assembly') (i) In the early rabbinic period an assembly of 71 scholars, which acted as a Supreme Court and legislature. It was headed by the nasi and an av bet din. Before the year 70 it convened in the Temple chamber called the Hall of Hewn Stone. Later it met at various centres. Its duties consisted of proclaiming the new moon, declaring leap years, and reaching decisions on State offences and questions of Jewish law. It was discontinued before the 4th century. During the 16th century Jacob Caro and Jacob Berab unsuccessfully attempted to revise ordination in Palestine and to establish a new Sanhedrin. Under Napoleon a modern form of the Sanhedrin was created.

Sanhedrin ('Assembly') (ii) Fourth tractate in the Mishnah order of Nezikin. It deals with courts of justice and judicial procedure, particularly related to criminal law. It also includes a list of sins which exclude a person from entering into the afterlife.

Sanhedrin, Great (French 'Grand Sanhedrin') Body of 71 members, convened by Napoleon to confirm the decisions of the Assembly of Jewish Notables. It comprised 45 rabbis and 26 lay members. Under the presidency of David Sintzheim, it met from 9 February to 9 March 1807.

Santa Maria, Paul de [Paul of Burgos; Solomon ha-Levi of Burgos] (c. 1352–1435) Spanish churchman. As Solomon ha-Levi he served as a rabbi in Burgos. After converting to Christianity, he became Bishop of Cartagena, and then of Burgos. He was partly responsible for the anti-Jewish legislation enacted in Castile in 1412. His writings include biblical commentaries.

Sapir, Pinhas (1907–1975) Israeli labour leader. He was born in Suwalki, Poland, and in 1924 went to Palestine, where he worked in the citrus groves. He later became head of the Negev settlement's Civil Defence. In 1953 he served as Director-General of the Ministry of Finance, and from 1955 he was Minister of Commerce and Industry. He became Minister of Finance in 1963, and General Secretary of the Israel Labour Party and Minister without Portfolio in 1965. The following year he was again appointed Minister of Finance.

Sapir, [Saphir], Yaakov (1822–1885) Palestinian writer and traveller. He was born in Oshmiany in the province of Vilnius. He was taken to Palestine in 1832 by his parents, who settled in Safed. In 1836 he moved to Jerusalem, where he became a teacher and scribe. In 1857 he travelled to orientalist countries as an emissary of the Perushim community to raise funds for the construction of a synagogue. After returning to Jerusalem he recorded his travels in *Even Sappir*, which contains important information about Yemenite Jews.

Sapir, Yoseph (i) (1869–1935) Moldavian Zionist leader. He was born in Kishinev, and became a doctor. A sup-porter of Hibbat Zion, he founded a publishing house, Di Kopeke Bibliotek, to publish Zionist literature. In 1903 he wrote a popular study of Zionism. He also edited a Russian-language Zionist weekly. After the 1917 Revolution, he became Chairman of the South Russia Zionist Organisation. Following the Bolshevik Revolution he moved to Bessarabia, then to Palestine, where he served as Director of a department of the Bikkur Holim hospital in Jerusalem.

Sapir, Yoseph (ii) (1902–1972) Israeli communal worker. He was born in Jaffa. He was active in the Farmers' Federation of Israel and worked for the Pardes citrus fruit Company. In 1940 he became Mayor of Petah-Tikvah, and later he served as a member of the Knesset; he was Minister of Transportation (1952–55), and Minister of Commerce and Industry. In 1968 he was elected Chairman of the Liberal Party.

Sarah [Sarai] (fl. 19th–16th cent. BCE) Israelite woman, wife of Abraham and mother of Isaac. After many years of barrenness, she gave Abraham her maid-servant Hagar, who bore him a son, Ishmael. Later Sarah gave birth to Isaac. She is one of the four matriarchs of Judaism.

Sarasohn, Kasriel Hersch (1835–1905) American newspaper proprietor. He was born in Russia, and was active as a rabbi and merchant before settling in the US in 1971. He founded the weekly *Die New Yorker yiddishe zeitung,* and *Die yiddishe gazetten,* which paved the way for the first Yiddish daily paper in the US, the *Yiddishes tageblatt.* He also published a Hebrew weekly (*Ha-Ivri*), and was a founder of HIAS.

Sarnoff, David (1891–1971) American broadcasting executive, of Belorussian origin. Born in Minsk, he went to the US with his family in 1901. He worked as an office boy at Commercial Cable Company. Later he became Commercial Manager of the Marconi Wireless and Telegraph Company of America. Subsequently he became President of RCA, and eventually Chairman and Chief Executive Officer.

Saruk, Israel (fl. 16th–17th cent.) Egyptian Kabbalist. He created his own version of Isaac Luria's doctrines. From 1594 to 1600 he propounded his views in Italy and founded a school of Kabbalists. Subsequently he lived in Ragusa and Salonica. He produced various Kabbalistic works.

Sasportas, Jacob (1610–1698) North African rabbi. He was born in Oran, North Africa. He became rabbi of the Tlemcen community, and subsequently wandered throughout Europe. In 1664 he became Hakham in London, and later in Amsterdam. He was a critic of Shabbetai Tzevi, and in his *Tzitzat Novel Tzevi* reprinted certain Sabbetaian letters and pamphlets with his responses to their teaching.

Sassoon, David Solomon (i) (1792–1864) Indian businessman and philanthropist. He took over his family's business in Baghdad. In 1828 he went to Bushehr on the Persian Gulf, and later settled in Bombay. There he built a synagogue, contributed to various cultural and welfare organisations, helped to publish a Judeo-Arabic newspaper and supported Jewish scholarship. In 1863 he built a synagogue in Poona, where he had his summer residence.

Sassoon, David Solomon (ii) (1880–1942) English Hebraist and bibliophile, son of Flora Sassoon. His collection included 1,000 Hebrew and Samaritan manuscripts. His writings include *History of the Jews of Baghdad.*

Sassoon, Sir Edward (1856–1912) English communal leader, grandson of David Solomon Sassoon. In 1889 he was elected to parliament as a member of the Conservative Party. He was involved in various aspects of English Jewish life.

Sassoon, Flora (1859–1936) English Hebrew scholar, daughter-in-law of David Solomon Sassoon. Initially she managed her husband's firm in Bombay. Later she settled in England. In 1924 she gave a discourse on the *Talmud* at Jewish College, and subsequently published an essay on Rashi in the *Jewish Forum.*

Satan The name of the devil. In the Bible he is referred to as a member of the divine household who functions as God's adversary (Job 1:6). Later he was conceived of as an evil spirit. In rabbinic literature he is identified with the tempter, the accuser, the Angel of Death, and the arch-enemy of Israel. In Kabbalistic texts other names are used for demonic rulers and princes of evil.

Satanov, Isaac (1732–1804) German Hebrew writer. He was born in Satanov, Podolia, and in 1771 settled in Berlin, where he was the director of a printing press of the Society for the Education of the Young. He wrote a Hebrew-German dictionary and thesaurus, studies of the liturgy, a collection of proverbs, an encyclopedia of arts and sciences, and commentaries on Maimonides' *Guide for the Perplexed,* and Judah Ha-Levi's *Kurzari.*

Satire The use of ridicule or irony to describe folly and wrongdoing in such a way as to expose them to contempt. Satire is found in the Bible, midrash and *Talmud.* In medieval Spain it became a fashionable literary genre among Jewish writers, and in Northern Europe it was a feature of compositions for Purim. In the modern period it has been used by such writers as Joseph Perl, Isaac Erter, Mordecai D. Brandstätter, J. L. Gordon, Peretz Smolenskin and Mendele Mocher Sephorim.

Saul (fl. 11th cent. BCE.) King of Israel. He was the first king of Israel, selected by Samuel in response to the request of the people for a king. He organised an army, undertook expeditions against the Philistines, Moabites, Ammonites, and Arameans. Eventually a rift developed between Saul and Samuel (I Samuel 13). Saul persecuted David after his triumph over Goliath and drove him from the country. Saul fell in battle against the Philistines on Mount Gilboa together with three of his sons (I Samuel 8–II Samuel 3).

Schaeffer, Susan Fromberg (1941–2011) American novelist and poet. She was born in Brooklyn, and taught at Brooklyn College. Her novel, *Falling*, deals with young a Jewish woman who attempts suicide. In *Anya* she tells the story of a victim of the Holocaust.

Schalit, Heinrich (1886–1976) Amercian composer and organist. He was born in Vienna, and lived in Munich, where he was organist at the Munich Liberal synagogue. In 1932 he wrote *Freitagabend Liturgie*, a complete Sabbath Eve Service. He emigrated to the US and served various Jewish congregations. In 1948 he moved to Evergreen, Colorado. His works on Jewish themes include *Chassidic Dances, Builders of Zion, Sabbath Morning Liturgy*, and *Songs of Glory*.

Schapira, Hermann Tzevi (1840–1898) Lithuanian Zionist. He was born in Erswilken, and was initially rabbi and rosh yeshivah in a Lithuianian townlet. He later lived in Kovno, Berlin, and Heidelberg, where he taught mathematics at the university. After the pogroms in Russia in 1881, he joined the Ḥibbat Zion movement, and was a delegate to the Frist Zionist Congress in 1897. At the Congress he proposed the foundation of the Jewish National Fund and the Hebrew University.

Schapiro, Israel (1882–1957) American bibliographer, orientalist and librarian. He was born in Sejny, Poland. From 1907 to 1910 he taught at the Jerusalem Teachers Training College. He then emigrated to the US and in 1913 he was appointed head of the Semitic division of the Library of Congress in Washington. He also lectured on Semitics at George Washington University from 1916 to 1927. He left his post at the Library of Congress in 1944, and in 1950 settled in Israel. He published studies of Jewish history and bibliography.

Scharfstein, Zevi (1884–1972) American Hebrew educator and publisher, of Ukrainian origin. He devoted himself to educational work and was the head of a Hebrew school in Tarnów, Galicia, from 1900 to 1914. After settling in the US, in 1916 he became an instructor at the Teachers Insitute of the Jewish Theological Seminary in New York, where subsequently he became Professor of Jewish Education. He published educational texts dealing with Hebrew language and literature, Jewish education, and the Bible.

Schary, Dore (1905–80) American film producer. Born in Newark, New Jersey, he worked as a newspaperman and stage actor, director and writer. Later he wrote screenplays. In 1938 he joined MGM, winning an Academy Award for *Boys Town*. Later, he was in charge of low-budget productions. Eventually he became head of RKO. Subsequently he wrote plays for the theatre. In 1970 he became New York's first commissioner of cultural affairs.

Schatz, Boris (1867–1932) Palestinian painter and sculptor of Lithuanian origin. He was born in Varna, in the province of Kovno. He studied sculpture in Paris, and in 1895 became court sculptor to Prince Ferdinand of Bulgaria. At the Zionist Congress of 1905 he proposed the idea of an art school in Palestine. In 1906 he went to Jerusalem, where he established the Bezalel School of Arts and Crafts. He produced sculptures dealing with Jewish religious practices, biblical subjects and Jewish leaders.

Schechter, Solomon (1847–1915) British rabbinic scholar. He was born in

Foscani, Romania. He became tutor in rabbinics to Claude Goldsmid Montefiore in London. In 1890 he became a lecturer in rabbinics at Cambridge University, and two years later reader. He was also Professor of Hebrew at University College, London, from 1899. During this time he discovered the Cairo Genizah, the contents of which he took to Cambridge. In 1901 he was appointed Executive President of the Jewish Theological Seminary of America. His writings include *Studies in Judaism* and *Some Aspects of Rabbinic Theology*.

Scheftelowitz, Isidor (1876–1934) British orientalist, of German origin. He was born in Sandersleben in the Duchy of Anhalt. He worked at the British Museum in London and at the Bodleian Library in Oxford. In 1908 he returned to Germany and until 1926 was a rabbi and teacher of religion in Cologne; in 1923 he became Professor of Sanskrit and Iranian Philology at Cologne University. He later settled permanently in England and taught at Oxford University. He published studies of Sanskrit and Iranian philology and history, as well as comparative religion.

Schenirer, Sarah (1883–1935) Polish educationalist. Born in Kraków, Poland, she worked as a seamstress and became concerned with the lack of education for Orthodox women. During World War I she went to Vienna, but returned to Kraków in 1917 and opened a school in her home. In 1918 Agudat Israel adopted the programme for schools for girls. Under the name Bais Yaakov, it developed a network of institutions. In 1923 Schenirer began to train teachers for these schools. She also founded the Bnos Youth Organisation.

Schiff, David Tevele (fl. 18th cent.) German rabbi. He was born in Frankfurt am Main. He served as maggid in Vienna, head of the bet midrash in Worms, and dayyan in Frankfurt. In 1765 he became rabbi of the Great Synagogue in London. A volume of his responsa, *Leshon Zahav*, was published by his son.

Schiff, Jacob Henry (1847–1920) American financier and philanthropist. He was born in Germany, and went to the US in 1885, where he became head of the banking firm of Kuhn, Loeb, and Co. He was a founder of the American Jewish Committee, and contributed to a wide range of secular and Jewish organisations.

Schiff, Meir [Maharam] (1605–1641) German talmudist. He was born in Frankfurt am Main. He was rabbi of Fulda, where he also directed a yeshivah. His novellae on the *Talmud* are recorded in *Maharam Schiff*.

Schildkraut, Rudolph (1862–1930) German actor. He was born in Istanbul, and grew up in Romania. He was an actor in Vienna, Hamburg and Berlin. In 1911 he settled in America, where he appeared in the Yiddish theatre; later he acted in German and English productions in the US.

Schiller-Szinessy, Solomon Mayer (1820–1890) British scholar of German origin. He was born in Alofen. He had a faculty appointment in Hebrew at Eperjes, where he also served the local community as its rabbi. In 1845 he attacked the Reform resolutions brought before the Frankfurt Rabbinical Conference. He was appointed rabbi of Manchester in 1851, and later taught talmudic and rabbinic literature at Cambridge University. His publications include the *Catalogues of Hebrew Manuscripts Preserved in the Cambridge University Library*.

Schindler, Alexander (1925–2000) American Reform leader. He was born in Munich, but left Germany in 1932, eventually settling in the US. He served in various congregations and became President of the Union of American Hebrew Congregations. In 1976 he became Chairman of the Conference of Presidents of Major American Jewish Organisations.

Schipper, Ignacy (1884–1943) Polish historian and communal worker. He was born in Tarnów, Galicia. He was a member of the General Zionists from 1922. From 1922 to 1927 he served as a deputy in the Polish Sejm. Latter he lectured on the history of Jewish economy at the Institute of Jewish Sciences in Warsaw., His writings include *The Economic Conditions of Medieval Polish Jewry, The History of Jewish Economy,* and *History of Jewish Theatrical Art and Drama.*

Schlessinger, John (1926–2003) British film director. He began as an actor. His films include *A Kind of Loving, Billy Liar, Darling, Far from the Madding Crowd, Midnight Cowboy, Sunday Bloody Sunday, Marathon Man, Madame Sousatka* and *Pacific Hights.*

Schlettstadt, Samuel ben Aaron (fl. 14th century) Alsatian rabbi. He was born in Schlettstadt and became rabbi of Strasbourg. After sentencing an informer to death, he was forced to flee from Strasbourg because of a controversy surrounding the affair. He lived in a castle near Comar, and later wandered to Babylonia and Jerusalem, before eventually returning to Strasbourg. He wrote an abridgement of *The Book of Mordecai* by Mordecai ben Hillel.

Schlossberg, Joseph (1875–1971) American journalist and trade union leader. He was born in Belorussia and emigrated to the US with his family when he was a child. He worked in the sweatshops of New York and was prominent in the Garment Workers Union. In 1913 he was elected Secretary of the Brotherhood of Tailors and in 1914 was a member of the group which seceded from the United Garment Workers of America to form an Amalgamated Clothing Workers of America. After his retirement in 1940 he devoted himself to community and Zionist affairs.

Schnabel, Artur (1882–1951) Austrian pianist. Born in Lipnik, Austria, he went to Vienna with his family at the age of seven. He taught music in Berlin. With the rise of Nazism, he went to Switzerland and later settled in the US. He achieved renown for his interpretation of Beethoven, Mozart and Schubert.

Schneersohn, Isaac (1879–1969) French communal leader. He was born in Kaments-Podol'sky in Ukraine. He was a crown rabbi in Gorodnya from 1906. Later he settled in France, where he founded the Centre de Documentation Juive Contemporaine during World War II. He also encouraged the establishment of a memorial to the unknown Jewish martyr in Paris. This initiative came to fruition in 1956.

Schneersohn, Menachem (1902–94) Amercian Hasidic leader, of Russian origin. Born in Nikolayev, Russia, he went to the US as a young man. He married the daughter of the sixth Lubavitcher rebbe, and in 1950 became the seventh Lubavitcher rebbe. His headquarters on Eastern Parkway, Brooklyn served as a centre of pilgrimage. Many of his followers regarded him as the Messiah.

Schneiderman, Harry (1885–1975) American administrator. He was born in Saven, Poland, and went to the US in 1890. From 1909 he was a member of the staff of the American Jewish Committee and from 1914 to 1928 he served as its chief administrator. He was also editor of the *American Jewish Year Book (1920-48).*

Schnitzler, Arthur (1862–1931) Australian playwright and author. Initially he practised medicine in Vienna, only later devoting himself to writing. His views about the position of Jews in modern society are found in the play *Professor Bernhardi* and the novel *Der Weg ins Freie.*

Schocken, Gustav Gershom (1912–1990) Israeli publisher. He was the owner and chief editor of *Ha-Aretz* from 1939, and director of the family publishing house in Israel. He served in the Knesset from 1955 to 1959.

Schocken, Shelomoh Salman (1877–1959) German Zionist, publisher and bibliophile. He was born in Margonin, in the province of Posen. A collector of rare books and manuscripts, he established the Research Institute for Medieval Hebrew Poetry in 1929 in Berlin, which was later transferred to Jerusalem in 1936. He also founded a publishing house in Berlin, branches of which were later opened in Tel Aviv and New York. In 1934 he went to Jerusalem, but he eventually settled in the US.

Schoenberg, Arnold (1874–1951) Austrian composer. He was born in Vienna, and held teaching positions in Vienna, Berlin and Amsterdam. In 1924 he settled in Berlin. He left Germany in 1933, and lived in the US. His compositions include the opera *Moses and Aron,* the Psalm *De profundis* to the original Hebrew words, and two works for chorus, speaker and orchestra: *Kol Nidre* and *A Survivor from Warsaw.*

Scholem, Gershom Gerhard (1897–1982) Israeli scholar. He was born in Berlin, and emigrated to Palestine in 1923, where he worked as a librarian in the Judaica collection at the Hebrew University. Subsequently he was appointed Professor of Jewish Mysticism at the university. His writings include *Major Trends in Jewish Mysticism, The Messianic Idea in Judaism and Other Essays in Jewish Spirituality,* and *From Berlin to Jerusalem.*

Shor, Ilya (1904–1961) American artist and silversmith, of Polish origin. He studied in Warsaw and Paris. In 1941 he settled in the US, where he worked as a silversmith, creating religious objects, and as a book illustrator. His art reflects Eastern European Jewish life.

Schorr, Joshua Heshel (1818–1895) Galician scholar, editor and leader of the Haskalah. He was born in Brody, and worked as a merchant there. In 1852 he established the periodical *He-Ḥalutz,* which he edited until 1887. In numerous articles he espoused religious and social reform. He engaged in satirical diatribes against Orthodox Judaism, and scholarly polemics against talmudic and rabbinic law. To the Jewish masses of Eastern Europe, he became a symbol of heresy.

Schorr, Moses (1874–1941) Polish rabbi and scholar. He was born in Przemyśl, Galicia. He was appointed a lecturer in Jewish religious studies at the Jewish Teachers Seminary in Lemberg in 1899. He eventually became Professor of Semitic Languages and Ancient History at Lemberg University, and later taught at Warsaw University. In 1928 he was one of the founders of the Institute for Jewish Studies, which served as the rabbinical seminary of Poland; he taught there and became the institute's rector. In 1935–38 he was a member of the Polish Sejm. He wrote studies of Polish Jewish history, Semitic history and philology, and the history of Babylonian and Assyrian culture.

Schreiber, Abraham Samuel Benjamin [Ketav Sopher] (1815–1875) Hungarian rabbi, son of Moses Sopher. He succeeded his father as head of the Pressburg yeshivah, and became a leading critic of religious reform. He was known as Ketav Sopher after his collection of responsa, Bible commentaries, and Talmudic glosses of that name.

Schreiner, Martin (1863–1926) Hungarian scholar. He was born in Nagyvárad. He was a rabbi in Csurgó (1887–92), and an instructor at the Jewish Teachers Training Institute in Budapest (1892–94). From 1894 to 1902 he was professor at the Lehranstalt für die Wissenschaft des Judentums in Berlin. He spent the rest of his life in a sanatorium. He wrote studies of the Islamic influence on medieval Jewish thought, interfaith polemics, Jewish philosophy and Karaism.

Schulman, Kalman (1819–1899) Polish Hebrew writer. He was born in Stari Bichov, Belorussia, and in 1843 settled in Vilnius, where he worked as a tutor. Later he taught Hebrew language and literature in the high school attached to the State rabbinical school. He eventually devoted himself to literary work. His writings, including translations, were intended to spread the Haskalah. He also published a history of Palestine and its environs.

Schulmann, Eleazar (1837–1904) Lithuanian Hebrew writer. He was born in Salantai, Lithuania, and lived in Odessa and Kiev. Financially independent, he devoted himself to research, publishing studies of Yiddish language and literature.

Schutzjude (German: 'protected Jew') Term used in the 17th and 18th centuries in Germany to refer to Jews who were given special privileges, such as being permitted to live outside the ghetto.

Schwab, Moise (1839–1918) French scholar. He was born in Paris. He served as secretary to Solomon Munk, then from 1869 worked at the Bibliothèque nationale. He translated the Palestinian *Talmud* into French, and described the Hebrew manuscripts and incunabula in the library of the Alliance Israélite Universelle and other libraries. His writings include *Abravanel et son époque* and *Histoire des Israélites*.

Schwabe, Mosheh David (1889–1956) Israeli scholar, of German origin. He was born in Halle. After World War I he was head of the department of schools in the Lithuanian ministry of Jewish affairs. In 1923 he settled in Jerusa-

lem, where he taught at the Hebrew University; he served there as dean of the faculty of humanities and rector. He was an authority on Greek and Greco-Jewish inscriptions.

Schwartz, Delmore (1913–1966) American poet, author and critic. He was born in Brooklyn. He became a member of the literary political group centred on the journals *Partisan Review* and *Commentary*. From 1940 to 1947 he taught at Harvard and Princeton universities. His writings include *Genesis*, which depicts the Jewish immigrant's experience of America.

Schwartz, Joseph J. (1899–1974) American communal leader and scholar. He was born in Russia, and went to the US in 1907. During World War II he negotiated the rescue of Jews from Germany and the occupied territories. After the war he directed the transfer of Jews to Israel form Europe, North Africa, and the Middle East. He also helped Jewish refugees emigrate to the US, Canada and Latin America. He served as Director-General of the American Jewish Joint Distribution Committee, Vice-Chairman of the United Jewish appeal, and Vice-President of the State of Israel Bond Organisation. He published studies of Semitics and Jewish affairs.

Schwartz, Maurice (1890–1960) American Yiddish actor. He was born in Ukraine, and went to the US in 1901. In 1918 he launched the Jewish Art Theatre in New York. He subsequently acted throughout the Yiddish-speaking diaspora. In 1960 he went to Israel to establish a Yiddish art theatre.

Schwarz, Adolf (1846–1931) Hungarian rabbi and scholar. He served as a rabbi at Karlsruhe from 1875, then in 1893 he became head of the Israelitsch-Theologische Lehranstalt in Vienna. His writings include studies of Talmudic hermeneutics.

Schwarzbard, Shalom (1886–1938)
Russian Yiddeish poet. He was born in
Izmail, Bessarabia. He was active in the
revolutionary movement of 1905 and in
1906 fled from Russia to Paris, where
he worked as a watchmaker. In World
War I he served in the French Foreign
Legion, but in 1917 he returned to
Russia, where he joined the Red Guard.
In 1920 he went on a mission to Paris
to assassinate Simon Petlyura, who
had carried out pogroms in Ukraine.
His autobiography *Inem loyf fun yoren*
describes his experiences.

Schwarz-Bart, André (1928–2006)
French author. He was born in Metz, and
served in the Free French army before
the Liberation. His novel *The Last of
the Just* reinterprets the Jewish legend
of the 36 righteous men ('lamed vav')
in terms of the martyrdom of European
Jewry.

**Schwarzbart, Isaac Ignacy (1888–
1961)** Polish Zionist leader. He was
born in Chrzanów, Galicia. He was the
founder in 1929 of the World Union of
General Zionists and served as its chairman. In 1938 he helped to establish a
committee to coordinate the activities of
the Zionists in western Galicia and Silesia. In the same year he was elected to
the Polish Sejm. During World War II he
was a member of the Polish government-
in-exile in Paris and London. From 1946
he lived in the US, where he was active
in the World Jewish Congress.

Schweid, Eleazar (b.1929) Israeli
scholar. He was born in Jerusalem,
and became a professor at the Hebrew
University. He published studies in the
field of Jewish philosophy and Hebrew
literature.

Schwinger, Julian (1918–1994) American physicist. Born in New York, he
studied at Columbia University. Later
he became professor at Harvard. In
1975 he was awarded the Nobel Prize
for Physics for his work on quantum
electrodynamics.

Sciaky, Leon (1893–1958) Greek-
American writer. He was born in
Salonica, and went to New York in
1915. His novel *Farewell to Salonica*
deals with the Jewish community of his
birthplace.

Science Within certain Orthodox circles all non-fundamentalist biblical criticism, theories of evolution, and other
scientific views are considered heretical.
Non-Orthodox branches of Judaism,
however, have generally accepted the
authority of the sciences. There have
been many eminent Jewish scientists.

Scouts International youth organisation
founded by Lord Baden-Powell in England in 1908. Jewish youth movements
adopted the current organisational
structures in their various countries.
The Israeli scouting organisation was
based on the Baden-Powell scouting
programme but emphasised, in addition, the values of self-management and
pioneering labour. There are Jewish
members of scout troops throughout
the world. But there are also exclusively
Jewish scouting organisations, affiliated
to the worldwide movement, in France,
Swizerland, Italy and Mexico, besides
Israel.

Scribe (Hebrew 'sopher') Originally
one who copies documents, but in Jewish usage a recognised scholar of the
law. Under the Judean monarchy the
king's scribe was the highest official of
his household. Ezra is depicted as the
'scribe' (that is , learned expert) of the
law of the God of Heaven (Ezra 7:6).
In the Book of Ecclesiasticus the scribe
is described as a literate man, occupied
with the study of the law. The New
Testament links the scribes with the
Pharisees. In the Mishnah the phrase
'words of the scribe' refers to post-biblical legislation. Rabbinic sources reserve
the term for those who write Torah
scrolls and preserve textual traditions.
The tractate Sopherim in the *Talmud*
describes the rules for writing sacred
documents.

Script The Ancient Israelites adopted alphabetic script from the Canaanites in the 12th or 11th century BCE; the Gezer Calendar from the late 10th century BCE is the earliest known Hebrew inscription. In the *Talmud* the early script is called 'ketav ivri' (Hebrew script). After the Babylonian exile a square script, based on Aramaic, came into use; the *Talmud* refers to this as 'ketav ashuri' (Assyrian script). Most talmudic scholars hold that Scripture was originally written in the ancient script, but was rewritten by Ezra. Detailed regulations are prescribed in the *Talmud* as to the ink and parchment to be used for writing sacred scrolls, as well as the writing to be employed. From the square script other cursive scripts later developed.

Seal A device impressed on wax or some other substance, fixed to a document as a mark of authentication. The Bible refers to the process of sealing, and numerous seals from the period of the monarchy have been discovered. They were used not only for documents but also to secure and attest the contents of the jar. Seals continued to be used, often in the form of signet rings. During the Middle Ages they frequently bore the name of a person or his emblem. Jewish communities also had their own seals.

Second day of festivals Before the days of scientific prediction, the regulation of the calendar depended on the verbal testimony of witnesses, who come to the Sanhedrin in Jerusalem to report that they had seen the new moon. Messengers were then sent out every month to announce this, but because it took some time to reach communities in the diaspora, there was some doubt as to which of two days was the first of the month, and thus which day marked the actual beginning of a festival.

Seder (lit. 'order') Ceremony that takes place on the first night of Passover in the home. The structure of the ritual is based on the Mishnah and its essential features are: the recitation of the Kiddush prayer, the reading of the Haggadah, the partaking of the special foods matzah and maror, the eating of the festival meal, the drinking of four cups of wine at specified intervals, the recitation of the Hallel, and the singing of songs.

Seder Olam Rabbah ('Major order') The earliest post-biblical chronicle. It contains a chronological record from the Creation to the time of Alexander the Great (4th century BCE). It also includes an appendix that extends the account to Simeon Bar Kokhba (d. 135).

Seder Olam Zuta ('Minor order') Chronology dating from the 8th century CE. It lists the names and dates of 50 generations from Adam to Jehoiakim, and those of 39 exilarchs in Babylonia from Jehoiakim to Zerubbabel.

Segal, George (1924–2000) American sculptor. He was born in New York. He began as a painter, then integrated freestanding plaster sculptures with his paintings, and eventually worked in sculptural forms alone. Some of his works refer to his Jewish background, and others to biblical subjects. He has also produced sculpture based on the Holocaust.

Segal, Lore (b.1928) Amercian novelist. She was born in Vienna. She taught creative writing at the University of Illinois at Chicago Circle. Her novel *My First American* explores the experiences of Jews and blacks. She has also written a collection of Bible stories, *The Book of Adam to Moses*.

Segal, Mosheh Tzevi Hirsch (1876–1968) Israeli Hebraist and Bible scholar. He was born in Myshad, Lithuania. He was a journalist in London, then in 1901 moved to Oxford, where he was minister to the Jewish congregation. In 1918 he went to Palestine as a member of the Zionist Commission.

He settled there and became Professor of Bible and Semitic Languages at the Hebrew University. His writings include *Grammar of Mishnaic Hebrew, Introduction to the Hebrew Bible,* and *The Pentateuch: its Composition and Authorship.*

Segall, Lasar (1891–1957) Brazilian painter, of Lithuanian origin. He was born in Vilnius, and settled in Brazil in 1923. His works on Jewish themes include *Pogrom, Ship of Emigrants,* and *Concentration Camp.*

Segol Sign indicating the short 'e' vowel in Herbrew. It consists of three dots arranged in an inverted triangle, and is placed beneath the consonant preceding the vowel sound.

Segrè, Emilio (1905–89) Italian physicist. During the 1930s he helped Enrico Fermi with his research into the neutron bombardment of uranium atoms. Later he bombarded molybdenum with deuterons and located small quantities of element number 43. In 1938 he emigrated to the United States and worked at the University of California. In 1959 he shared the Nobel Prize for Physics for the discovery of antiprotons.

Segrè, Joshua ben Zion (c.1705– c.1797) Italian dayyan and rabbi. He was born in Casale, Monferrato. He was engaged as a children's tutor in Scandiano, but pretended to be a fully qualified rabbi, claiming to have graduated from the Mantua yeshivah. This led to a dispute with the rabbis under whose authority he worked. His *Asham Talui* a polemic against Christianity.

Seixas, Gershom Mendes (1746– 1816) American communal leader. He was born the first Jewish minister to have been born in the US. In 1768 he became ḥazzan of Congregation Shearith Israel in New York. During the American Revolution he moved to Connecticut, and then to Philadelphia, but in 1784 he returned to New York. He was one of the 13 clergy to participate in George Washington's inauguration.

Selah Word found in the Book of Pslams. Its meaning is unclear. It has been interpreted as meaning 'forever'; as indicating a change in rhythm or tune when the pslam is chanted; as a eulogistic response to the words of the psalm; and as an acrostic of the Hebrew phrase meaning 'return to the beginning'.

Seleucids Hellenistic royal dynasty. It was founded by Seleucus Nicator, one of Alexander the Great's generals, and flourished from the 4th to the 1st centuries BCE. The Seleucids governed a vast empire comprising much of Asia Minor.

Self-defence The law regarding the killing of a burglar in the act of breaking in (Exodus 22:1–2) is interpreted in the *Talmud* as the basis for its theory of justifiable homicide. Where a criminal act gives rise to a direct threat to life or reasonable certainty of such a threat, it is permitted to kill the criminal in defence or in defence of another. This course of action, however, should be adopted as a last resort. Moreover if the attacker is killed without an attempt having been made to restrain him, his death is viewed as murder, though this is punishable only by an act of God.

Seligmann, Caesar (1860–1950) German leader of Liberal Judaism. He was born in Landau, and became the preacher of the Liberal synagogue in Hamburg in 1889. He then officiated as a rabbi in Frankfurt am Main. He published a two-volume prayer book, and edited the periodical *Liberales Judentum.* In 1929 he helped to publish the unified prayer book, which included traditional and newly composed Liberal prayers. Among his other publications are a collection of lectures and a history of the Reform movement. He moved to London in 1939.

Seligson, Esther (1942–2010) Mexican novelist. She was editor of the bimonthly review of Jewish culture *Aqui* *estamos* in Oaxaca. Some of her writings deal with Jewish subjects.

Seliḥot ('penitential prayers'; *sing.* 'Selihah') Prayers recited during the high holy day period and on fast days. Some date to the 1st century, but most were written by the Hebrew poets of Spain or by the liturgical poets of the 12th and 13th centuries. They deal with Jewish suffering, martyrdom, the destruction of the Temple, human weakness, confessions, and God's forgiveness and mercy.

Sellers, Peter (1925–80) British actor. Born in Portsmouth, he worked at a seaside theatre in Devon. He then served in the Royal Air Force. After World War II, he began to work in comedy, and later on radio. With Spike Milligan and Harry Secombe he produced *The Goon Show.* He subsequently appeared on film in *The Ladykillers* and *I'm Alright Jack.* By 1960 he was in Hollywood and appeared in *Lolita, Dr Strangelove, The Pink Panther* and *What's New Pussycat?*

Selznick, David O. (1902–65) American film producer. Born in Pittsburgh, he and his brother, Myron, became Hollywood agents. In 1926 he worked at MGM as a script reader. He then moved to Paramount, later becoming RKO's Vice President in charge of production. In 1933 he returned to MGM before forming his own company, Selznick International. His films include *Gone with the Wind.*

Semites The name given to a group of ancient peoples, originating in the Arabian peninsula. They settled in various areas from the Mediterranean coast to the mountains of Iran and Armenia. They included the Arabs, Hebrews, Phoenicians, Arameans, Babylonians, and Assyrians. The Bible attributes the origins of these peoples to Noah's son Shem.

Semitic languages A branch or sub-family of the Afro-Asiatic family of languages, comprising various groupings. Eastern Semitic consists of Old Akkadian, Babylonian and Assyrian; North-western Semitic of Amorite and Ugaritic; Cannanite of Hebrew, Phoenician, Punic, and Moabite; Aramaic of Old Aramaic, Imperial Aramaic, Biblical Aramaic, Nabaean, Palmyrenian, Palestinian Jewish Aramaic, Samaritan Aramaic, Christian Palestinian Aramaic, Jewish Babylonian Aramaic, Mandean, Modern Syriac, and Modern Aramaic of Malula; and Southern Semitic of Proto-Arabic, Arabic, ancient and modern southern Arabian languages, ancient Ethopic, Amharic, Tigre, Tigrinya, Harari, Gafat Gurage, and Agobba. The word 'Semitic' derives from the name of Noah's son Shem, mentioned in Genesis 10.

Senator, Ronald (1926–2015) English composer. He was born in London. He became Professor of Music at London University, the University of Europe, and the Guildhall School of Music. His works on Jewish themes include *Kiddush Terezin.*

Senior, Abraham (c.1412–c.1493) Spanish courtier. During the reign of Henry IV he was chief tax officer of Castile. From 1476 he was rabbi to the Jews of Castile and the assessor of Jewish taxes. He was appointed Treasurer of the Hermandad, a military organisation. He eventually converted to Christianity.

Sephardim One of the two main divisions of Jewry in the diaspora. The word comes from the Hebrew Sephard, the name, originally, of an area to which the Jews were deported after the destruction of the First Temple. It was first used in the Middle Ages of the Jews of Spain. After the expulsion from Spain in 1492 the Sephardim settled in north Africa, Italy, Egypt, Palestine, Syria, the Balkans, and the Turkish Empire. Subsequently these communities were reinforced by refugees from Portugal. Sephardi congregations were established later in Amsterdam, London, Hamburg, Bordeaux, Bayonne, Western Europe, the West Indies and North America. In Mediterranean countries the Sephardim spoke Judeo-Spanish (Ladino). The Sephardim are distinguished from the Ashkenazim. Aspects of liturgical practice and the pronunciation of Hebrew differ in the two groups.

Sepher Ḥasidim ('Book of the pious') Devotional work of the medieval German religious movement known as Ḥaside Ashkenaz. It incorporates the teachings of Samuel ben Kalonymus he-Ḥasid, his son Judah ben Samuel he-Ḥasid of Regensburg, and Eleazar ben Judah of Worms. It consists of three sections dealing with piety, humility, and the fear of God. It was intended to serve as a guide to everyday religious conduct, stressing asceticism, humility, and strict ethical standards.

Sepher Yetzirah ('Book of Creation') Early Babylonian or Palestinian mystical work, dating from the 3rd–6th centuries. According to this treatise, the cosmos is derived from the Hebrew alphabet, and the ten sephirot (manifestations of God). Knowledge of these mysteries, including significant letter combinations, allegedly conferred magical powers on the initiated. Thus the golem (an artificially created human being) was created by means of formulae from this volume. It greatly influenced later Kabbalists, and from the gaonic period various commentaries were written on it.

Sephirot Kabbalistic term meaning the emanation or manifestations of God. Ten sephirot are referred to. The concept, coloured by Neoplatonism and Gnostic thought, was used to explain how a transcendent, inaccessible godhead (En Soph) can relate to the world. In Kabbalistic literature the nature of the sephirot is a matter of controversy. In the Kabbalah a distinction is frequently made between the first three

sephirot (regarded as the highest) and the remaining (lower) seven. The ten sephirot are: (1) the Supreme Crown; (2) Wisdom; (3) Intelligence; (4) Love; (5) Power; (6) Beauty; (7) Endurance; (8) Majesty; (9) Foundation; (10) Kingdom.

Septuagint (from Latin 'septuaginta': 70) The principal Greek translation of the Bible (including the Apocrypha). According to tradition, the Pentateuch was translated into Greek at the command of Ptolemy II in the 3rd century BCE by 70 Jewish scholars, each of whom worked independently. The manuscripts of the Septuagint comprise the Great Codices (including the Alexandrinus, the Sinaiticus, and the Vaticanus), and the numerous Minor Codices.

Seraph Supernatural being, depicted variously as a winged human or serpent-like figure. In Isaiah 6:12 the seraphim are members of the celestial court surrounding the divine throne in the Temple. In medieval literature they comprise one of the 10 hierarchical classes of angels.

Serekh Word meaning 'rule' or 'order,' used in the Dead Sea Scrolls.

Serene (Severus) (fl. 8th cent.) Syrian pseudo-messiah. He declared himself the Messiah in Syria in about 720, and attracted numerous followers. He was put to death by the Muslim authorities.

Sereni, Enzo (1905–1944) Italian pioneer of settlement in Palestine. He was born in Rome, and was one of the first in Italy to support settlement in Palestine. He went to Palestine in 1927, and worked on an orange grove. Initially a pacifist, he joined the British army during World War II. As a parachutist, he was dropped in occupied Italy, captured and killed. His writings include *Arabs and Jews in Palestine* and *The Holy Spring*.

Serkes, Joel ben Samuel [Baḥ] (1561–1640) Polish codifier. He served as a rabbi in Polish and Lithuanian communities. His *Bayit Ḥadash* is a commentary on the *Arbaah Turim* of Jacob ben Asher. He also wrote responsa and Talmudic glosses.

Serlin, Yoseph (1906–1974) Israeli politician, of Polish origin. He emigrated to Palestine in 1933 and was a founder of the General Zionist Party there. Elected leader of the Knesset in 1946, he served as Deputy Speaker and Minister of Health.

Sermon An address of religious instruction or exhortation, usually delivered in a service of worship. The institution of the sermon goes back to the time of the prophets. During the Second Temple period, there was felt to be a need for a system of teaching and preaching, and this was provided by scholars, who read from the Torah and the prophetic books on Sabbaths and festivals. One method of teaching involved the translation of the biblical text into the Aramaic vernacular. After the destruction of the Temple, discourses in the form of midrashim were delivered in the synagogue. Eventually the sphere of the sermon was increased to include discourses for special events. During the medieval period preaching played an increasingly important role in Jewish life; in the 11th century professional preachers were known as 'darshanin.' The sermon became central to synagogue worship in Western Europe, but in Eastern Europe it was increasingly replaced by an ethical discourse preached by a 'maggid' (official or itinerant preacher). In the modern world, the sermon has become a prominent feature of the synagogue service.

Serpent Literary or dialect word for 'snake'. In Genesis 3 the serpent persuaded Eve to eat from the Tree of Knowledge. As a consequence of its role in the fall of man, God condemned it to a state of enmity with humans. Moses made a brass serpent, which cured people from snake bite. It was destroyed by Hezekiah because the Israelites worshipped it (II King's 18:4). In Leviticus the serpent is forbidden as food (Leviticus 19:26).

Servant of the Lord Title used in the Book of Isaiah, and variously interpreted. According to Isaiah 41:2–4, the Servant was chosen by God to convey divine truth to Gentiles. In Isaiah 52:12–13 he is described as suffering vicariously. The Servant of the Lord has been variously identified as the Jewish people, the Messiah, the prophet Isaiah, and Jesus.

Seter, Mordekai (1910–1994) Israeli composer. He was born in Novorossisk, Russia. He went to Palestine in 1926, and taught at the Israel Academy of Music in Tel Aviv. His compositions include *Sabbath Cantata, Tikkun Hatzot,* and *The Legend of Judith.*

Seth Third son of Adam. According to the Bible, he lived 912 years.

Setzer, Samuel Hirsch (1882–1962) American Yiddish and Hebrew journalist, of Polish origin. He was the literary editor of Naḥum Sokolov's Hebrew journal *Ha-Tzephirah* in Warsaw. Later he served as editor-in-chief of the Warsaw daily newspaper *Der Telegraph.* He lived in New York from 1912 to 1960, when he settled in Israel. He wrote studies of the German socialist writer Lassalle, Judah ha-Levi, the Baal Shem Tov and Naḥman of Bratzlav.

Seudat shelishit Third meal. During the Talmudic period it was customary for Jews to eat two meals a day. On the Sabbath, however, the rabbis stipulated that three meals should be eaten. Among the Polish Ḥasidim, the seudah shelishit was a major feature of religious life. At the table of the tzaddik the faithful would spend hours listening to his discourse and singing hymns.

Seudat havraah Meal for mourners. It was traditionally provided by neighbours for the family and friends of one who had died on their return from the funeral.

Seudat maphskeket   Last meal taken before the fasts of the Day of Atonement and the Ninth of Av.

Seven Benedictions (Hebrew 'Sheva Berakhot')   The benedictions recited at the wedding ceremony after the bridegroom places the ring on the bride's finger. The first benediction is said over the cup of wine. The following three praise God. The fifth celebrates the restoration of Zion. The sixth refers to the joy of the first couple in Paradise. The seventh thanks God for having created joy and gladness, and for the bride and bridegroom. During the seven days following the marriage, the Seven Benedictions are recited during grace after every meal.

Sevoraim ('Reasoners')   Name given to Babylonian scholars of the period c. 500–700 (between the amoraim and the geonim).

Sexual intercourse   Jewish law stipulates that sexual relations must take place only within marriage. Homosexuality, prostitution and various illicit sexual unions are forbidden. It is the duty of men to marry and procreate. Any form of physical contact between a man and his wife is forbidden during the menstrual period and for seven days afterward. The wife must take a ritual bath before sexual relations are resumed. Refusal of sexual relations by either partner is a ground for divorce in Jewish law.

Sforno, Obadiah ben Jacob (c.1470–c.1550)   Italian biblical commentator. He was born at Cesena, Sforno. He taught Hebrew to Johannes Reuchlin in Rome. After living in various cities, he settled in Bologna, where he helped to re-establish a Hebrew printing house and organise the Jewish community. He founded and ran a bet midrash there. He wrote commentaries on the Pentateuch, Song of Songs, Ecclesiastes, Pslams,

Job, Jonah, Habakkuk, and Zechariah. He also wrote a commentary on Avot, a number of grammatical works, and a philosophical treatise

Shaatnez   Fabric made of a mixture of wool and flax (the word is probably of Egyptian origin). The Bible prohibits the wearing of this material (Leviticus 19:19; Deuteronomy 22:11).

Shabbat ('Sabbath')   First tractate in the Mishnah order of Moed. It sets out the general rules of the Sabbath and its observance, the 39 categories of work, and the regulations concerning the Sabbath Lamp.

Shabbas goy (Yiddish)   Non-Jew employed by Jews on the Sabbath to carry out tasks that they themselves are forbidden to perform.

Shabbazi, Shalom (fl. 17th cent.)   Yemenite Jewish poet. He lived in a period of persecution and messianic expectations among the Yemenite Jews. According to legend he was a tzaddik and miracle worker. His poetry deals with exile and redemption, the Jewish people and God, wisdom and ethics, the Torah and the afterlife.

Shabbetai ben Meir ha-Cohen [Cohen, Shabbetai; Shak] (1621–1662)   Lithuanian rabbi. He was born in Amstivov and near Vilkaviškis, and became dayyan in the bet din of Moses Lima in Vilnius. He published *Siphte Kohen*, a commentary on *Yoreh Deah*. The alternative name, Shak, by which he was known is derived from the initials of the title *Siphte Kohen*.

Shabbetai Tzevi (1626–1676)   Turkish scholar and pseudo-messiah. He was born in Smyrna. He devoted himself to talmudic and Kabbalistic studies. In 1665 he met Nathan of Gaza, who recognised him as the Messiah and became his prophet. In December of that year Shabbetai proclaimed himself the Messiah in the synagogue at Smyrna. The Jewish world was seized with enthusiasm. He went to Constantinople in 1666 to claim his kingdom from the sultan, but he was arrested and imprisoned at Abydos, which his followers regarded as the Migdal Oz ('Tower of Strength') of the kabbalah. Eventually Shabbetai was summoned to appear before the sultan and adopted Islam to save his life. His apostasy caused great dismay, but a number of his followers (Sabbetaians) believed that his conversion was part of a divine plan.

Shabtai, Jacob (1934–1981) Israeli novelist and short-story writer. His most famous work, *Zikhron Devanim*, describes nine months in the protagonist's life, beginning and ending with a death. Despite its somber theme, it is notable for its wit and penetrating insight.

Shaddai ('Almighty') One of the names of God, used in the Bible. It later appeared in Kabbalistic formulae and on amulets. It is also frequently inscribed on the mezuzah.

Shadkhan ('negotiator') Marriage broker. The shadkhan negotiated marriages, settlements and dowries. The institution dates back to antiquity, and in the Middle Ages played an important role in Jewish life. It is still part of Jewish social custom in some communities.

Shaffer, Peter (1925–2016) English dramatist. He was born in Liverpool, and first worked as a coal miner. He spent some time in the US, where he worked at the New York Public Library. Later he was active as a literary and music critic in London. His play *The Salt Land* is set in a kibbutz in Israel. In *Yonadah* he adapted *The Rape of Tamar* by Dan Jacobson.

Shah (Yiddish) Exclamation, ordering someone to be quiet.

Shaham, Natan (b.1925) Israeli author. He was born in Tel Aviv. He served with the Palmah during the War of Independence, and later joined kibbutz

Bet Alpha. He wrote fiction, plays, and stories for children.

Shahar, David (1926–1997) Israeli novelist. He was born in Jeruslaem, and took part in the War of Indpendence. A number of his stories deal with the childhood recollections of a narrator who lived in Jerusalem between British Mandatory rule. Between 1929 and 1986 he published a series of five novels, *The Palace of Shattered Vessels.*

Shaharit [morning service] The service of morning prayer. It consists of: the dawn benedictions, biblical verses related to the sacrificial system, and passages of rabbinical writings for study; the Pseuke de-Zimrah with their bendictions, the Shema with its bendictions, the Amidah; the Tahanun; and concluding prayers, including the Alenu. On Mondays, Thursdays and occasions the Tahanun is followed by the reading of the law, but on Sabbaths and festivals, when the Tahanun is not recited, the reading of the law takes place after the Amidah.

Shahin (fl. 14th cent.) Persian poet. He lived in Shiraz. He based his work on the Bible. His *Sepher Sharh Shahin al-Torah* is a political paraphrase of the Pentateuch.

Shahn, Ben (1898–1969) American painter and graphic artist. He was born in Kovno, Lithuania. He settled in the US, but later travelled to Europe and North Africa. He made an early series of paintings based on the Dreyfus Affair. His later works include *Concentration Camp* and *This is Nazi Brutality.* He also produced works based on Hebrew letter forms and commissions for the decoration of synagogues.

Shaikevitch [Shomer], Nahum Meir (1849–1905) Russian Yiddish novelist and dramatist. He was born in Nesvizh, Belorussia, and settled in Pinsk. He wrote Hebrew short stories and longer narratives, as well as about 200 Hebrew lyrics. Later he moved to Vilnius, where he wrote novels of suspense, and plays for the Yiddish stage. His plays were produced in the US, where he settled in 1889.

Shaked, Gershon (1929–2006) Israeli scholar. He was born in Vienna, and settled in Palestine with his family at an early age. From 1959 he taught Hebrew literature at the Hebrew University, where he became professor in 1978. He published various studies of Hebrew literature and drama.

Shaliaḥ Emissary. The term (which is a synonym for meshullah) applies particularly to an emissary sent from Israel to Jewish communities in the diaspora.

Shallum (fl. 8th cent. BCE) King of Judah (747 BCE). He slew Zechariah, son of Jeroboam II and seized the throne (II King's 23:29–34). He was subsequently killed and succeeded by Menaḥem.

Shalom Word meaning well-being of various kinds: security, contentment, good health, prosperity, friendship, and peace of mind and heart. It is also used in greetings and farewells when the meaning is 'peace [be with you]'.

Shalom [Sholem] aleikhem [aleichem] Jewish greeting meaning 'Peace be with you.'

Shalom bayit ('domestic peace') Term used specifically of harmonious relations between husband and wife. The rabbis formulated various regulations to bring about this situation.

Shamgar (fl. 13th cent. BCE) Israelite judge. He defeated the Philistines, killing 600 men with an ox-goad (Judges 3:31).

Shamir According to legend, the name of a worm that could split stone and metal. It was used by Moses to engrave the names of the tribes on the high priest's breastplate. Later Solomon used it as an engraving tool in the construction of the Temple.

Shamir, Mosheh (1921–2004) Israeli author. He was born in Safed. He served in the Palmaḥ in 1944–45, and later was a member of the Knesset. He edited various Hebrew literary magazines. His works include novels describing Israel's struggle for independence and historical novels, which make indirect criticism of modern Israel.

Shamir, Yitzḥak (1915–2012) Israeli statesman. He was born in Ruzinoy, Poland. He emigrated to Palestine in 1935 and joined Irgun Tzevai Leumi. He later helped to reorganise the Central Committee of the Loḥame Ḥerut Yisrael. He was elected to the Knesset in 1973 and served as Foreign Minister, Vice-Premier and Prime Minister.

Shammai (fl. 1st cent. BCE) Palestinian scholar. He was a contemporary of Hillel, and together they were the last of the zuggot. He adopted a rigorous standpoint in moral and religious matters. The School of Shammai later disputed legal issues with the School of Hillel.

Shammash ('beadle') Caretaker or sexton in the synagogue. The term also refers to the candle used in kindling the Ḥanukkah lights.

Shapero, Harold (1920–2013) American composer. He was born in Lynn, Massachusetts, and became Professor of Composition at Brandeis University. Some of his works deal with Jewish themes.

Shapira, Constantin Abba (1840–1900) Russian Hebrew poet. He lived in St Petersburg, where he worked as a photographer. He converted to Christianity, but wrote Hebrew poetry and intended to settle in Palestine and return to Judaism. He died before he was able to carry out these plans.

Shapira, Moses Willliam (c.1830–1884) Polish dealer in antiquities. He was born a Jew but converted to Christianity. He dealt in antiquities in

Jerusalem. In 1882 he offered what he claimed to be ancient manuscripts of parts of Deuteronomy to the British Museum. When they were pronounced forgeries by C.S. Claremont-Ganneau, Shapira committed suicide.

Shapiro, Harvey (1924–2013) American poet and editor. He was born in Chicago. He was editor of the *New York Times Book Review*. His poetry was influenced by Jewish, and in particular, Ḥasidic themes.

Shapiro, Lamed (1878–1948) Polish Yiddish short-story writer. He was born in Rzhishchev, in the district of Kiev. He lived in Warsaw, where he came under the influence of Isaac Leib Peretz. In 1906 he went to the US, but he returned to Warsaw and worked for the Yiddish newspaper *Der fraynd.* Later he settled in Zurich and finally in the US. He wrote stories about Eastern-European pogroms and Jewish life in New York. He also published a study of Yiddish literature and language.

Shapiro, Phinheas (fl. 18th cent.) Polish Ḥasidic writer. He lived in Koretz. A pupil of the Baal Shem Tov, he wrote *Midrash Pinḥas.*

Sharansky, Natan [Shcharansky, Anatoly] (b.1948) Israeli human-rights activist, of Russian origi. He trained as a mathematician, but Israel's near defeat in the Yom Kippur War of 1973 provoked him into political activity. His ardent campaigns on behalf of Soviet refuseniks led to his imprisonment in 1978. After serving eight and a half years of a 13-year sentence he was released. He emigrated to Israel to join his wife, Avital, herself a constant campaigner for the rights of Soviet Jews. Sharansky continued to argue throughout the world on Zionist issues and for wider human rights. In 1987 he received the Simon Wisenthal Centre's annual humanitarian award. His autobiography, *Fear No Evil,* was published in 1988.

Sharett [Shertok], Moshe (1894–1965) Israeli statesman and Zionist leader, brother of Yehudah Sharett. He was born in Kherson, in Ukraine, and settled in Palestine in 1906. Active in socialist circles, he became head of the Jewish Agency's political department in 1933. He was a leader of the campaign against the policy set out by the British in the White Paper of 1939. In 1946 he was interned at Latrun. Later he was appointed Foreign Minister of the provisional government of Israel, and led the Israeli delegation to the United Nations Assembly (1949–50). He subsequently served as Foreign Minister, and from 1953 to 1955 was Prime Minister. He was appointed Chairman of the executive of the Jewish Agency in 1961.

Sharett [Shertok], Yehudah (1901–1979) Israeli composer, brother of Moshe Sharett. He was born in Kherson, in Ukraine, and went to Palestine as a child. He composed music, including children's songs, for his kibbutz, and published the *Yagur Passover Seder Service.*

Sharon, Ariel (1929–2014) Israeli soldier and politician. He was born in Kephar Malal. He joined the Haganah, fought in the War of Independence, and later led a commando group. In the Six-Day War his brigade broke through the Egyptian positions. In 1969 he was appointed GOC Southern Command, and in the Yom Kippur War he commanded a division. He was elected to the Knesset in 1973 and served as Minister of Agriculture and Minister of Defence. He became Prime Minister in 2001.

Shas Abbreviation of the words 'shishah sedarim' (six orders) referring to the six orders into which the Mishnah is divided and which form the basis of the *Talmud*. From the 16th century the term was used to refer to the *Talmud*.

Shaving According to biblical law, it is forbidden to shave the 'corners' of the head and the beard (Leviticus 19:27).

The rabbis state that the corners are five in number, but they differ as to where on the head they are. The *Talmud* interprets shaving as removal of the hair with a knife or razor. Other methods are not forbidden in the Bible or according to rabbinic teaching. Thus the beard may be clipped with scissors and an electric razor may be used. It is forbidden to shave on holy days and during a period of mourning, as well as during the Counting of the Omer and the three weeks before the Ninth of Av.

Shavuot [Feast of Weeks; Pentecost]   One of the three pilgrim festivals. It is observed on 6 and 7 Sivan. According to tradition, it commemorates the giving of the law on Mount Sinai. It is also known as Pentecost because it begins on the 50th day after the completion of the seven-week period of the Counting of the Omer.

Shaw, Irwin (1913–84)   American novelist. Born in New York, he studied at Brooklyn College. He worked as a journalist and later went to Europe where he wrote novels, short stories and plays. In the 1930s he wrote screen plays, radio scripts and stories for the *New Yorker*. His works include *The Young Lions*.

Shayner Yid (Yiddish: lit. 'beautiful Jew')   Term used of a Jew who other Jews esteem.

Shazar, Zalman (1899–1974)   Born in Mir, Belorussia, he studied at the Academy of Jewish Studies in St Petersburg. In 1907 he joined the Poale Zion and edited its publications. He was arrested by tsarist authorities and imprisoned for his Zionist activities. During World War I he edited *Judische Rundschau* and organised the labour movement in Germany. He emigrated in 1924 and was an editor of the labour daily, *Davar*, and later its editor-in-chief. He was a member of the Palestinian Jewish delegation to the 1947 United Nations General Assembly. He was elected to the Knesset and served as Minister of Education and Culture. In 1963 he became President of Israel.

Sheeny (Yiddish)   Disparaging or contemptuous word for a Jew.

She-heḥeyanu.   Opening words of a benediction, blessing God for preserving the speaker 'until this season'.

Sheḥita   Term used for the ritual slaughter of animals. It is carried out, using a special knife ('ḥallaph'), by a shoḥet, who must be qualified to practise. The method is governed in detail by Jewish law.

Sheitel (Yiddish)   Wig worn by Orthodox women. Jewish law requires married women to cover their hair, and the sheitel is used in some very traditional circles for this purpose.

Shekalim ('Shekels')   Fourth tractate in the Mishnah order of Moed. It deals with the half-shekel tax, which was used to maintain Temple worship during the period of the Second Temple.

Shekinah   Divine presence. The Bible refers to God's dwelling in the midst of the children of Israel (Exodus 13:21–22; 40:34–38). Later the concept of the shekinah embodied God's presence in the world with the people as a whole and with individuals, sharing in Israel's suffering and exile. In Kabbalistic sources the term 'shekinah' refers to the tenth sephirah (or manifestation of God), representing God's feminine aspect.

Sheliaḥ tzibbur ('Emissary of the congregation')   The title given to the one who leads the public prayer in a synagogue. The term also refers to the ḥazzan.

Sheloshim ('30')   Thirty-day period of mourning that follows the death of a relative. Some of the customs of mourning observed during the shivah (seven-day) period continue in force for the duration of Sheloshim. A public discourse was sometimes delivered at the end of the period.

Shem Son of Noah. According to the Bible, the nations of Elam Asshur, Arpachshad, and Aram originated from him (Genesis 10:22). Arpachshad was the father of Eber and the ancestor of Abraham. Shem is thus regarded as the father of the Semitic peoples.

Shema ('Hear!') Opening word (and hence the name) of a central prayer of the Jewish liturgy, incorporating a confession of faith. It is recited in the evening and morning. It consists of three passages from the Pentateuch (Deuteronomy 6:4–9; 11:12–21; Numbers 15:37–41), preceded by two blessings, and followed by a further benediction in the morning and two (sometimes three) benedictions in the evening. The Shema is also recited before going to sleep. Many martyrs met their death with the Shema on their lips.

Shemaiah (i) (fl. 5th cent. BCE) Israelite false prophet. During the rebuilding of the walls of Jerusalem Shemaiah was hired by Tobiah and Sanballat to persuade Nehemiah to hide from his enemies in the Temple. Their plan was to expose him as an irreligious coward (Nehemiah 6:10), but Nehemiah saw through Shemaiah and refused to follow his advice.

Shemaiah (ii) (fl. 1st cent. BCE) Palestinian rabbi. He was the head of the Sanhedrin in Palestine. He and Avtalyon were the fourth of the zugot.

Shema koli ('Hear my voice') Opening words of a rhymed hymn ascribed to Hai Gaon. It is recited in the Sephardi ritual before the Kol Nidre prayer on the eve of the Day of Atonement.

Shemini Atzeret ('Eighth day of solemn assembly') The final day of the festival of Sukkot. It takes its name from the regulations in Leviticus 23:36 on how it should be observed (that is, as a day of 'solemn assembly'). In the diaspora it is celebrated for two days (22–23 Tishri); in Israel on a single day (22 Tishri), which is also Simhat Torah. A special prayer for rain is recited during the musaph service. Among the Ashkenazim, the yizkor memorial prayer is said on this day.

Shenhar [Shenberg], Yitzhak (1905–1957) Israeli author. He was born in Voltshisk on the border of Galicia and Ukraine, and settled in Palestine in 1921. From 1942 he was an editor for the publisher Schocken. His novels deal with Jewish life in Eastern Europe and Israel. He also translated works from European literature into Hebrew.

Sheol The dwelling place of the dead, according to the Bible (Genesis 37:35; Isaiah 38:10). It is located below the earth (Isaiah 57:9).

Shephatiah ben Amittai (fl. 9th cent.) Italian liturgical poet and religious leader. He lived in Oria in southern Italy. When Abu Aaron came to Italy, he passed on to Shephatiah Kabbalistic secrets which Shephatiah used in performing deeds, as recorded in the *Chronicle of Ahimaaz*. In about 873 Shephatiah travelled to Constantinople to plead for the annulment of anti-Jewish decrees. His poem *Yisrael Nosha* is included in the Neliah service on the Day of Atonement in the Ashkenazi liturgy.

Sherira Gaon (906–1006) Babylonian gaon. He was gaon of Pumbedita in succession to his father, Hanina, and his grandfather, Judah. With his son, Hai Gaon, Sherira maintained contact by means of responsa with Jews in North Africa, Spain, and elsewhere. In an important epistle in response to an inquiry from Kairouan, he described the origins of the Mishnah and the *Talmud*, and the traditions of the sevoraim and the geonim. He also wrote commentaries on the Bible and Talmudic tractates. During the last years of his life he was imprisoned by the caliph Kadir.

Sheshet (fl. 3rd–4th cent.) Babylonian amora. He lived at Shilhi on the Tigris. Although he became blind, he was still able to teach, since he could cite tannaitic sources from memory.

Shestov, Lev [Schwarzman, Lev Isakavich] (1866–1938) French philosopher, of Ukrainian origin. He was born in Kiev. He lived in France after the Russian Revolution of 1917. In 1922 he became Professor of Russian Philosophy at the University of Paris. His writings include *Speculation and Revelation* and *Athens and Jerusalem.*

Sheva In Hebrew script, a sign resembling a colon, which indicates the absence of a vowel or the presence of a very short vowel.

Sheviit ('Seventh year') Fifth tractate in the Mishnah order of Zeraim. It deals with the laws of the Sabbatical year (Exodus 23:11; Leviticus 25:1–7). The release from debts (Deuteronomy 15:1–6) and the rabbinical institution of the prosbul are discussed in the last chapter.

Shevuot ('Oaths') Sixth tractate in the Mishnah order of Nezikin. It deals with different types of oaths (Leviticus 5:4), and the laws applying to a person who becomes aware of being unclean (Leviticus 5:2–3).

Shewbread [showbread] (Hebrew 'hapannim', 'leḥem pannim') The name given to the 12 loaves which were laid in two rows on the golden table in the inner shrine of the Temple. They remained there from one Sabbath to the next, and were then divided among the priests (Leviticus 24.1–9).

Shiddukh ('marital match') In the *Talmud* the words are used to refer to the conversations between a prospective bridegroom or his parents and a possible bride or her parents, in preparation for betrothal. It has come to mean betrothal or marriage.

Shikkun (from 'shakken': to house) Term applied to a housing project, building development or residence in Israel.

Shikseh (Yiddish) Non-Jewish woman.

Shimoni [Shimonovitz], David (1886–1956) Israeli poet, of Russian origin. He was born in Bobruisk, in the district of Minsk. He settled in Palestine in 1909, but later went to Germany to study, and returned to Russia at the outbreak of World War I. In 1921 he moved permanently to Palestine and taught at the Herzliyyah secondary school. He wrote poetry, parables, satires, meditations and memoirs.

Shin Shalom [Shapira, Shalom (1904–1990) Israeli poet, of Ukrainian origin. He was the son of the Hasidic rabbi of Drohobycz. From 1914 to 1922 he lived in Vienna, and then settled in Palestine. He wrote mystical religious poetry, and autobiographical novel, stories and plays. He also translated the sonnets of Shakespeare into Hebrew.

Shirayim ('leftovers') Food left by the tzaddik It is competed for by the Ḥasidim during the Sabbath and festival meals. According to Ḥasidim, these remains partake of the same holiness that traditionally resided in the part of a sacrifice which was not consumed upon the altar.

Shir ha-Kavod ('Song of glory') [Anim zemirot] Hymn of praise. Among the Ashkenazim it is recited after the morning service and after the additional service on the Sabbath. The Ark is opened during its recitation. It takes the form of an alphabetic acrostic. Its opening words are 'Anim zemirot'. (I shall sing songs).

Shir ha-Yiḥud ('Song of unity') Ashkenazi hymn. It is a product of the 13th-century German religious movement of the Ḥasidei Ashkenaz, and has been attributed to Samuel ben Kalonymus he-Ḥasid. It is divided into seven sections, one of which is read on each day of the week by the Ashkenazim. It glorifies the attributes of God.

Shitreet, Bekhor Shalom (1895–1967) Israeli politician. He was born in Tiberius. He was commander of the police in Lower Galilee and between 1935 and 1948 served as a magistrate in several towns. After the establishment of the State of Israel, he served as Minister of Police and Minister of Minorities, as a representative of Sephardi and Oriental communities. Subsequently he was a member of the Knesset for Mapai.

Shiur Komah ('The measure of the body') Mystical work concerning the nature of God. It dates from the gaonic period or earlier. It attributes colossal dimensions to God. It was denounced by various authorities as grossly anthropomorphic, but its defenders maintained that it should not be understood literally.

Shivah ('seven') Seven-day period of mourning that follows the death of a relative. It is also known in the *Talmud* as 'avelut ('mourning'). During this period ordinary work is prohibited; sexual intercourse is also forbidden. The mourners sit without shoes on low stools or on the floor, a custom known as 'sitting shivah'. It is usual for friends to make visits to the mourners' home to offer prayers and condolences. The prohibitions of sheloshim also apply to this period.

Shivah Asar be-Tammuz (*lit.* '17th day of the month of Tammuz') Fast day, originally commemorating the breach of the walls of Jerusalem three weeks before the fall of the city and the destruction of the Temple in 586 BCE. It is the 'fast of the fourth month' mentioned in Zechariah 8:19. The Mishnah names four other events to be commemorated on this date, all associated with the destruction of the Temple in 70 CE: (1) the breaking of the two Tablets; (2) the cessation of the daily sacrifice; (3) the burning of the Scrolls of the Law by Apostomus; and (4) the erection of an idol in the sanctuary.

Shlemiel (Yiddish) A foolish or unfortunate person, or a simpleton.

Shlep (Yiddish) To drag, pull or lag behind.

Shlimazel (Yiddish) An unlucky person.

Shlock (Yiddish) A shoddy, cheaply made or fake article.

Shlonsky, Avraham (1900–1973) Israeli poet. He was born in Karyokov, in Ukraine. He settled in Palestine in 1921, and in 1928 joined the staff of the newspaper *Ha-Aretz*. In 1943 he joined the editorial staff of the journal *Mishmar*, and subsequently edited the quarterly *Orlogin*. Associated with the Mapam party, he participated in the activities of international world peace movement of the 1950s. From the 1950s he criticised the Soviet attitude to Israel and Jewish culture in the USSR. In addition to writing poetry, he translated classics from several languages into Hebrew.

Shlump (Yiddish) A tiresome person, or 'wet blanket'.

Shmaltz (Yiddish) Cooking fat. It is also used figuratively, particularly of music, to mean sugary and sentimental.

Shmatte (Yiddish) A rag or cheap junk. Figuratively a person not worthy of respect.

Shmendrick (Yiddish) A person of no account.

Shmeruk, Chone (1921–1997) Israeli Yiddish scholar. He was born in Poland and emigrated to Palestine as a young man. From 1961 until his retirement he was Professor of Yiddish Literature at the Hebrew University. He is the chief editor, with H. H. Paper, of a complete edition of the works of Sholem Aleichem, and co-editor of the *Penguin Book of Modern Yiddish Verse*.

Shmo (Yiddish) A hapless fool; a 'fall guy'.

Shmuck (Yiddish) Penis; colloquially a foolish or stupid person.

Shmuss (Yiddish) To chat, or a chat.

Shnaps (Yiddish) Brandy.

Shneersohn, Dov Baer of Liubavich (1773–1827) Russian Ḥasidic leader. He was the successor of Shneour Zalman of Lyady. He founded the Ḥabad settlement at Hebron in Palestine, and advocated the establishment of Jewish settlements in Kherson province, in Ukraine.

Shneersohn, Joseph Isaac (1880–1950) Russian Ḥasidic leader. He was imprisoned for his religious activities, and after his release in 1927 moved to Otwock in Poland. Later he emigrated to the US and settled in New York, where he founded yeshivot and schools in the Ḥabad tradition.

Shneersohn, Menaḥem Mendel (1789–1866) Russian Ḥasidic leader. He was the successor of Dov Ber Shneersohn of Liubavich (who was his father-in-law). He composed the halakhic work *Tzemaḥ Tzedek.*

Shneour Zalman (1887–1959) Russian Hebrew author. He was born in Belorussia, and lived in Vilnius, Berlin, Paris, the US, and Israel. In his poetic cycle *Luḥot Genuzim* he criticised the moral development of Judaism as found in biblical literature. His collections of stories, *People of Shklow* and *Noah Pandre*, deal with Jewish life in the Pale of Settlement.

Shneour Zalman (ben Baruch) of Lyady (1747–1813) Russian Ḥasidic leader, founder of the Ḥabad movement. The pupil of Dov Ber of Mezhirich, he joined the Ḥasidim at the age of 20. In 1777 he succeeded Menaḥem Mendel of Vitebsk as the movement's leader, and became involved in controversy with the mitnaggedim. He was arrested by the Russian authorities and imprisoned in St Petersburg; although he was released, he was later re-arrested. His teaching emphasised a rational approach and stressed the importance of study and contemplation. He wrote a liturgy, a code of laws, a mystic commentary on the Pentateuch, and a Kabbalistic work, *Likkute Amarim* (also known as the *Tanya*).

Shnoder (Yiddish) To make an offering in the synagogue.

Shnook (Yiddish) An ineffectual person, a person to be pitied.

Shnorrer (Yiddish) Beggar.

Shnoz (Yiddish) Nose

Shoḥet Ritual slaughterer. The *Talmud* decrees that any normal person who is not a minor may slaughter animals and poultry, as long as the act is performed in accordance with Jewish law. Subsequently a shoḥet had to be correctly trained. In the modern period those who assume this role still have to be qualified and must in addition be learned in matters of halakhah.

Shokhen ad ('He who inhabits eternity') First words of the final section of the Nishmat prayer. In the Ashkenazi rite the service of morning prayer on Sabbath and festivals begins at this point.

Sholem Aleichem [Rabinovitz, Solomon] (1859–1916) Ukrainian Yiddish author. He was born in Pereyaslav, and began writing novels, poems and plays at an early age. In 1888–89 he published the literary annual *Die yiddishe folksbiblyotek.* He subsequently created the character of Tevye the milkman, who exemplifies the experience of Jewish life in Eastern Europe. He supported himself entirely by writing between 1900 and 1906, when he went to New York. He returned to Europe the following year. Many of his stories are set in an imaginary place called Kasrilevke, which was modelled on Voronkov, where he spent his childhood.

Shomer Yisrael ('Guardian of Israel') Liturgical poem (piyyut), first found in a 13th century manuscript among the penitential prayers (selihot) for 10 Tevet. Originally recited only on fast days, in the Ashkenazi and Hasidic rituals it was later incorporated into the Tahanun. In other rites it is still reserved for fast days, and an additional stanza is used on the Ten Days of Penitence.

Shool (Yiddish) Synagogue.

Shophar ('horn') Ceremonial wind instrument, originally made of a ram's horn. The Bible stipulates that it should be sounded on the New Year and to proclaim the Year of Release (Leviticus 25:9). During certain periods it was also blown on fast days in the ceremony of excommunication, before the start of the Sabbath, and at times of a famine or plague. The blowing of the shophar during the synagogue services in the month of Elul, on Hoshanah Rabbah, and at the conclusion on of the Day of Atonement was introduced later.

Shopharot The name of the last of the three central sections of the additional Amidah service on Rosh ha-Shanah (the others are Malkhuyyot and Zikhronot). It is composed of ten biblical verses that mention the shophar. It expresses hope for the messianic redemption, which will be heralded by the sound of the great shophar.

Shoshanat Yaakov ('The lily of Jacob') Opening words of the final section of the piyyut 'Who brought the counsel of the heathen to nought' by Asher Heni. It is recited on Purim after the reading of the Scroll of Esther at the evening and morning prayer services.

Shtadlan (Hebrew from Aramaic: 'persuader') Title given to a representative of the Jewish community, skilled in negotiation and with access to dignitaries of state who worked at royal courts. In 18th-century Poland the position of shadkhan was a formal appointment and was sometimes salaried.

Shtetl (Yiddish) Small Jewish town in Eastern Europe.

Shtif, Nochum [Baal Dimyon] (1879–1933). Ukrainian Yiddish critic and philologist. He was born in Rovno, Volhynia, and settled in Berlin in 1922. He was one of the founders of the Yiddish Scientific Institute (YIVO) in Vilnius in 1925. From 1926 he was in charge of the work of the linguistic section of the Institute for Yiddish Proletarian Culture in Kiev. Eventually he was appointed to the Chair of Yiddish at the Kiev State Academy.

Shtik (Yiddish) A piece or part of a larger whole; figurative a prank or trick, or misconduct.

Shtille (Yiddish), khuppeh (Hebrew) Secret wedding. Such a marriage is conducted in conformity with Jewish law, but does not follow civil regulations.

Streimel (Yiddish) A broad-brimmed black hat, trimmed with velvet or edged with fur. It is worn by religious Jewish men, particularly in Galicia and Poland.

Shtunk (Yiddish) An objectionable or offensive person, a fool, or an ungrateful individual. Also a scandalous mess.

Shtup (Yiddish) To push, thus to fornicate. The act of copulation.

Shtuss (Yiddish) Foolishness or nonsense.

Shul (Yiddish) Synagogue.

Shulklapper (Yiddish) The title of the official who knocked on the doors of Jewish houses to wake worshippers for early morning services in the synagogue. In Eastern Europe he used a special hammer for this purpose.

Shum   Word derived from the initial letters of the German place names Speyer, Worms and Mainz, and used to refer collectively to their Jewish communities which were prominent in the Middle Ages. The regulations of their join synod were called 'takkanot Shum' and we're binding on all German Jewry.

Shuruk   The name given to the long vowel sound 'u' in Hebrew.

Shvartzer (Yiddish)   The colour black, or a black person.

Shvitzer (Yiddish)   Literally one who sweats; figuratively a braggart.

Shylock   Jewish moneylender, the central character in William Shakespeare's *The Merchant of Venice*.

Sibylline Oracles   The name given to a series of prophecies in Greek hexameters, composed between the 5th century BCE and the 4th century CE. They are of pagan, Jewish, Christian, and mixed Jewish-Christian authorship. They sketch the history of the Mediterranean world in prophetic language, attack Israel's enemies, threaten disaster, and foretell messianic judgement and redemption.

Sicarii   Group of Jewish rebels active during the Second Temple period. They were called after the dagger ('sica') they carried under their clothes. They killed their political enemies who advocated peace with Rome. Their numbers included Menaḥem ben Jair and Eleazar ben Jair.

Sick, prayers for the   The eighth benediction of the weekday Amidah is a petition for the healing of the sick. In addition any person may offer prayers for sick friends or relatives. These may be added to the eighth or the 16th benediction of the Amidah, or they

may be offered anywhere at any time in the words of the worshipper. Prayers for the sick may also be offered in the synagogue after the reading of the law, and it is customary to read psalms on behalf of the sick. It also became usual for a special form of prayer (including psalms, petitions, and a brief confession of sin) to be recited by a sick person. A special prayer, including the change of name, was composed for those very serious ill.

Sick, visiting the (Hebrew 'bikkur ḥolim')   Bringing comfort to those who are ill is an important duty in Judaism. According to the rabbis it derives its importance from God's visit to Abraham (Gensis 18:1) during his illness caused by circumcision.

Siddur ('order')   The term used by Ashkenazi Jews for the book containing daily prayers. Sephardim used the term 'tephillah'. The Maḥzor contains the prayers for festivals.

Sidrah ('order')   Portion of the Pentateuch read in the synagogue on the Sabbath. Each sidrah has a distinctive name, taken from the first important word in the text. The Pentateuch is divided into 54 sedarot so that the entire Pentateuch is read annually.

Sieff, Israel Moses, Baron (1889–1972)   English industrialist and Zionist. He was born in Manchester. He was a collaborator of Chaim Weizmann and served as Secretary of the Zionist Commission to Palestine in 1918. In 1934 he founded the Daniel Sieff Research Institute at Rehovot. He contributed to various Zionist organisations.

Sieff, Rebecca (1890–1966)   English Zionist, wife of Israel Moses Sief. She was born in Leeds. She was a founder of the Woman's International Zionist Organisation (WIZO) in London in 1920 and served as its president until 1963.

Siegel, Benjamin [Bugsy] (1906–47)   American gangster. Born in New

York, he bossed his own criminal gang at the age of 14. He joined Meyer Lansky to form a gang which sold protection, engaged in robbery and hijacking, and handled killings for bootleg gangs. In the 1930s he went to California to operate the syndicate's West Coast operations. During the war years he borrowed syndicate money to build the Flamingo in Las Vegas.

Silberman, Eliezer Lipmann (1819–1882) Prussian Hebrew journalist and editor. He lived in Lyck in East Prussia, where he worked as a shoḥet and cantor. He started the first Hebrew newspaper, the weekly *Ha-Maggid*, in 1856, and in 1862 helped to found the periodical *Mekitze Nirdamim*.

Silberschalg, Eisig (1903–1988) American Hebrew poet and critic. He grew up in Metri, Galicia. After emigrating to the US, he became Professor in Hebrew Literature at the Hebrew Teachers College in Boston. He published poetry, wrote critical studies in Hebrew and English and translated Greek classics.

Silent prayer No mention is made of silent prayer in the Bible. In the rabbinic period it became the custom for the members of the congregation to recite the Amidah silently before its repetition by the reader. Private prayers may be added to the 16th benediction of the silent Amidah.

Silkiner, Benjamin Naḥum (1882–1933) American Hebrew poet. He was born in Vikija, Lithuania. He went to the US in 1904 and later taught at the Teachers Institute of the Jewish Theological Seminary in New York. He published texts for Hebrew schools, helped to produce an English-Hebrew dictionary, and wrote narrative poetry.

Silva, Antonio José da (1705–1739) Portuguese playwright. He was born in Rio de Janeiro, Brazil, and was of Converso origin. He moved to Lisbon, and studied at the University of Coim-

bra. While he was a student he wrote a satire, which led to his arrest. He was charged with Judaising, but was later released. He became an important Portuguese dramatist. He was arrested by the Inquisition in 1737 and killed two years later.

Silva, Francisco Maldonado da [Nazareno, Eli] (c.1592–1639) Chilean Marrano martyr. He worked as a physician in Chile, where he converted to Judaism, circumcised himself, and adopted the name Eli Nazareno. He was arrested by the Inquisition, but continued to practise Jewish rites even in prison. He was burned at an auto-da-fé in Lima.

Silver, Abba Hillel (1893–1963) American Reform rabbi. He was born in Sirvintos, Lithuania, and was taken to the US in 1902. He served as a rabbi in Wheeling, Virginia, and Cleveland, Ohio. In 1938 he became Chairman of the United Palestine Appeal and Joint Chairman of the United Jewish Appeal. He led the meetings of the American Zionist Emergency Council in 1943, and later was appointed Chairman of the American section of the Jewish Agency. His writings include *History of Messianic Speculation in Israel from the First through the Seventeenth Centuries*, *The Democratic Impulse in Jewish History*, *Religion in a Changing World*, *Where Judaism Differed* and *Therefore Choose Life*.

Simeon (i) (fl. 19th–16th cent. BCE) Israelite, second son of Jacob. To avenge the rape of his sister Dinah, he and Levi tricked the citizens of Shechem, captured the town, killed the male inhabitants, and took the women and children captive (Genesis 34).

Simeon (ii) (fl. 1st cent.) Palestinian Zealot leader, known as Simeon son of Judah the Galilean. He and his brother Jacob led the Zealots after their father's death. They were captured and crucified by the procurator Tiberius Julius Alexander.

Simeon ben Eleazar (fl. 2nd cent.)
Palestinian tanna. A contemporary of
Judah ha-Nasi, he lived in Tiberias. He
is mentioned only infrequently in the
Mishnah, but plays an important role in
the Tosephta. He was a noted halakhist,
aggadist, and polemicist.

**Simeon ben Gamaliel I (fl. 1st
cent.)** Palestinian nasi. He was leader
of the Sanhedrin at the time of the
destruction of the Second Temple in
70 CE. When the revolt against Rome
began, in 66, he was among its leaders,
but he later adopted a moderate policy.
He is listed among the Ten Martyrs.

Simeon ben Gamaliel II (fl. 2nd cent.)
Palestinian nasi son of Rabban Gamaliel of Jabneh and father of Judah ha-
Nasi. After the Romans destroyed the
house of the nasi in revenge for the Bar
Kokhba revolt (132–35), he was one of
the few survivors. He was forced to go
into hiding, but later became nasi of the
Sanhedrin at Usha. Many of his decisions are quoted in the Mishnah and the
Tosephta.

**Simeon ben Isaac ben Abun [Simeon
the Great] (d. c.1015)** German liturgical poet. He lived in Mainz. Many of
his hymns are included in the Ashkenazi
liturgy, notably that for the New Year.
According to legend, he was the father
of the pope Elhanan.

**Simeon ben Lakish [Resh Lakish]
(fl. 3rd cent.)** Palestinian amora. In
his youth he sold himself to men who
hired participants in gladiatorial con-
tests. According to legend, Johanan bar
Nappaha persuaded him to study the
Torah, and gave him his sister in marriage. Eventually Simeon became one
of the most important sages in the Tiberias academy.

Simeon ben Setah (fl. 1st cent. BCE)
Palestinian scholar. He was active during the reign of Alexander Yannai and
Salome Alexandra (who was his sister).
He and Judah ben Tabbai together
formed one of the zugot. He was largely
responsible for ensuring that the Pharisees were dominant in public and private life during the Second Temple
period. He managed to change the Sanhedrin into a Pharisaic body.

Simeon ben Yohai (fl. 2nd cent.) Palestinian tanna. He was among the five
pupils of Akiva who survived the failure of the Bar Kokhba revolt (132–35).
When he expressed political opinions
which were regarded by the Romans as
seditious, he was forced to flee for his
life. He is said to have hidden in a cave
for 13 years. He was noted as a miracle
worker, and was sent on a mission to
Rome, where he succeeded in obtaining
the withdrawal of a persecutory decree
against the Jews. The authorship of the
Zohar has been attributed to him, and
he is frequently quoted in the Mishnah
by his pupil Judah ha-Nasi. His tomb
at Meron is a centre of pilgrimage on
Lag Ba-Omer (the traditional date of
his death).

**Simeon ha-Tzaddik (fl.? 4th–5th
cent. BCE)** High priest. He played an
important role in the Keneset Gedolah, which formulated the liturgy,
established the canon of Scripture,
and formed the Sanhedrin. Scholars
have suggested that he belonged to the
Hasideans and supported the Seleucids.
He has also been credited with ensuring
the central role of study in the Jewish
tradition and stemming the influence of
Hellenisation.

Simhat ben Samuel of Vitry (d.1105)
French scholar. He was a pupil of Rashi.
He compiled the Mahzor Vitry, which is
regarded as an authoritative source for
the prayer book, synagogue customs,
and the hymnology of medieval French
Jewry.

**Simhat Bet ha-Shoevah ('Festival
of the Water-drawing')** Festival
observed at the end of the first day of
Sukkot (15 Tishri). Its ceremonies are
described in the Mishnah (Sukkah 5).
Water was poured out in offering to

God, huge bonfires were lit, and there was joyful dancing and singing. It ceased to be observed after the destruction of the Second Temple.

Simḥat Torah ('Rejoicing in the law') Holy day on which the annual completion of the reading of the Torah is celebrated. It is observed on Shemini Atzeret (22 Tishri) in Israel (on the second day of Shemini Atzeret [23 Tishri] in the diaspora). It is customary to carry the Scrolls of the Law round the synagogue seven times or more. The last section of Deuteronomy is read by the Bridegroom of the Law (Ḥatan Torah), and the first section of Genesis is read by the Bridegroom of Genesis (Ḥatan Bereshit).

Simon, Ernest Akiva (1899–1973) Israeli educator and writer, of German origin. He was born in Berlin, where he co-edited the monthly journal *Der Jude* with Martin Buber. He settled in Palestine in 1928, and became a teacher and co-director of secondary schools and seminaries. He later was appointed Professor of Philosophy and History of Education, and Director of the School of Education at the Hebrew University. He was an editor of the *Educational Encyclopedia* and wrote books on education and philosophy.

Simon, James (1851–1932) German merchant and philanthropist. He helped to found the Hilfsverein der Deutschen Juden in 1901 and served as its chairman. He was an art collector and patron, and also financed archaeological expeditions to Jericho and Tel el Amarna.

Simon, Sir John (1818–1897) British lawyer and politician. He was born in Jamaica, and went to England in 1833 where he studied law. He returned to Jamaica to practise as a lawyer, but eventually settled permanently in England, where he became a Queen's Counsel. From 1868 to 1888 he was a Liberal member of parliament and championed the cause of oppressed Jewry.

Simon, Julius (1875–1969) Zionist leader, of German origin. He was born in Mannheim, and engaged in banking in Switzerland and Alsace during World War I. Later he was invited by Chaim Weizmann to direct the economic activities of the Zionist Organisation, but his report was not accepted by the Zionist Congress and he resigned from the organisation. Between the wars Simon lived in Palestine and the US, and headed the Palestine Economic Corporation.

Simon, Sir Leon (1881–19645) English civil servant, brother of Maurice Simon. He was born in Southampton. His brother was Director of Telegraphs and Telephones in the General Post Office and later Director of the National Savings Bank. An ardent Zionist, he was active in the establishment of the Hebrew University. He lived in Jerusalem from 1946 to 1953 and worked in the Israel Ministry of Posts. He subsequently returned to England. His writings include *Studies in Jewish Nationalism, The Case of the Anti-Zionists: A Reply* and *Zionism and the Jewish Problem*. He also translated Aḥad ha-Am's writings into English.

Simon, Maurice (1874–1955) South African Hebraist and translator, brother of Leon Simon. He was born in Manchester. He moved to South Africa and later was associated with the Soncino Press. He was the co-translator into English of the *Zohar* and Midrash Rabbah, and helped with the Soncino translation of the *Talmud*.

Simon, Neil (b.1927) American playwright. Born in New York, he studied at New York University. He initially wrote for a number of television shows. Subsequently he wrote shows for the theatre including *Come Blow Your Horn, Plaza Suite, The Sunshine Boys, California Suite, The Odd Couple, Last of the Red Hot Lovers, The Prisoner of Second Avenue* and *I Ought to Be in Pictures*.

Simonsen, David Jacob (1853–1932) Danish rabbi. He was born in Copenhagen, and served as a rabbi there. During World War I he assisted war victims and took an interest in the Palestine Jewish community. His library of books about Judaism contained about 40,000 volumes. He published various works of oriental studies.

Simon the Hasmonean [Simeon ben Mattahias] (fl. 2nd cent. BCE) Palestinian ruler and high priest, second son of Mattathias the Hasmonean. In 142 BCE he succeeded his brother Jonathan as head of the Jewish State. He captured Gezer, secured the evacuation of Greek troops from the Jerusalem area, and gained from Demetrius II exemption from the tribute previously paid to the Seleucids. Elected high priest (an office which then became hereditary), ethnarch and general, he renewed the treaty with Rome and defeated Antiochus VII at Jabneh. He was killed by his son-in-law Ptolemy, and was succeeded by his son John Hyrcanus.

Simon the Just (fl.? 4th–2nd cent. BCE) High priest. According to Josephus, he is identifiable with Simeon I, the son of Onias I (4th–3rd cent. BCE). However the *Talmud* identifies him as the father of Onias, who built a temple at Leontopolis in Egypt. According to this account he was Simeon II (the father of Onias II; 200 BCE). In rabbinic literature he is described as one of the last members of the Great Assembly.

Sin (i) [shin] Twenty-first letter of the Hebrew alphabet. Its numerical value is 300.

Sin (ii) Transgression of God's commandments. There are three main categories of sin: 'het' (sin committed in ignorance); 'avon' (sin committed knowingly); and 'pesha' (sin committed in a spirit of rebellion). No individual is without sin, but repentance leading to forgiveness by God cancels sin. For a sin against another person restitution and placation are necessary.

Sinai Inscriptions The name given to a series of inscriptions on stone tablets in a Semitic alphabet script, dating from about 15th century BCE. The were discovered by Flinders Petrie in 1906 in the southern Sinai Peninsula. The script used is a prototype of the ancient Hebrew script.

Sinclair, Clive (b.1948) English author. He was born in London. His novel *Blood Libels* combines an account of the Israeli invasion of Lebanon and its repercussions in Israel with fantasies about the rise of anti-Semitism in England. His *Brothers Singer* is a biography of Isaac Bashevis Singer, Israel Joshua Singer and Esther Kreitman.

Singer, Isaac Bashevis (1904–1991) American author, brother of Israel Joshua Singer and Esther Kreitman. He was born in Leoncin, Poland, and moved to Warsaw in 1923. In 1935 he settled in New York, where he worked for the Yiddish daily newspaper *Forverts*. In 1978 he won the Nobel Prize for Literature. He has written numerous novels about Eastern-European Jewish life.

Singer, Isidore (1859–1939) American writer and editor. He was born in Weisskirchen, Moravia. After working as an editor and as literary secretary to the French ambassador in Vienna, he settled in Paris in 1887, and took a post in the press bureau of the French Foreign Office. He was active in the defence of Alfred Dreyfus and founded and edited the short-lived periodical *La vraie parole*. He went to New York in 1895 where he became managing editor of the *Jewish Encyclopaedia*.

Singer, Israel Joshua (1893–1944) Polish Yiddish novelist and playwright, brother of Isaac Bashevis Singer and Esther Kreitman. He was born in Bilgoraj, Poland, and lived in Warsaw and Kiev. He settled in the US in 1937. His writings include *Yoshe Kalb* and *The Brothers Ashkenazi*.

Singer, Simeon (1848–1906) English rabbi. He was headmaster of Jews

College School, and later served as minister of the New East End Synagogue. He edited and translated the siddur as *The Authorised Daily Prayer Book*.

Sinkó, Ervin (1898–1967) Yugoslav author. He initially wrote verse, fiction and drama. After engaging in revolutionary activities, he fled to Paris, where he wrote *The Optimists*. He returned to Yugoslavia in 1939, and wrote novels, short stories, essays and literary studies. His novel *The Love of Aaron* deals with a Jewish revolutionary who fought in the Spanish Civil War. In 1959 he became Professor of Hungarian Language and Literature at the University of Novu Sacz.

Sin offering (Hebrew 'ḥatta't') Sacrifice for a sin committed unwittingly (Leviticus 4:1–3). A sin offering was also made after childbirth, the curing of leprosy, and the taking of the Nazarite vow. The offering consisted of either an animal or a bird.

Sintzheim, Joseph David (1745–1812) French rabbi. He was born in Trier. He was head of the yeshivot in Bischheim and Strasbourg. During the Reign of Terror he fled from France, but later returned to Strasbourg, where he served as rabbi. In 1806 he was appointed to the French Assembly of Jewish Notables, and formulated the replies to the 12 questions put by Napoleon to the Assembly. In 1807 he became President of the Great Sanhedrin and in 1808 Chief Rabbi of the Central French Consistory. His *Yad David* consists of responsa on sections of the *Talmud*.

Siphra (Aramaic: 'Book') [Siphra de-ve Rav] ('Book of the School of Rav'); Torah Kohanim ('Law of the Priests') Halakhic midrash on Leviticus. It is a product of the school of Akiva, and dates for the 2nd century.

Siphre to Deuteronomy Exegetical midrash on Deuteronomy, dating from the 2nd century. It expounds the text chapter by chapter and verse by verse. Although primarily an halakhic midrash, its aggadic section is extensive. It contains a collection of various interpretations of the following passages of Deuteronomy: 1:1–30; 3:21–4:1; 6:4–9; 11:10–26; 15; 31:14; and 32:1ff.

Siphre to Numbers Exegetical midrash on Numbers, dating from the 2nd century. It expounds the text chapter by chapter and verse by verse. It contains a collection of various interpretations of the following passages of Numbers: chapters 5–12; 15; 18–19; 25:1–13; 26:52–31:24; and 35:9–34.

Siphre Zuta (Aramaic: 'Small books') Halakhic midrash on Numbers, dating from the 2nd century. It is a product of the school of Akiva, and records differences of opinion between the schools of Shammai and Hillel.

Sirota, Gershon (1874–1943) Lithuanian cantor. He was born in Podolia. He became ḥazzan in Odessa, and later served in Vilnius and Warsaw. He undertook concert tours in Europe and the US.

Sivan Third month of the Jewish year.

Six hundred and thirteen commandments (Hebrew 'Taryag mitzvot') The laws as found in the Pentateuch. There are 248 positive commandments (traditionally relating to the number of bones in the body), and 365 negative commandments (equal to the number of days in the year). The first classification of the 613 commandments was made by Simeon Kayyara, and is set out in the Halakhot Gedolot. Maimonides later classified them in his *Sepher ha-Mitzvot*, and Moses of Coucy made a compilation of them in his *Sepher Mitzvot Gadol*.

Siyyum ('termination') Term applied to the completion of the copying of a Torah scroll. It also refers to the completion of the study of a tractate of the *Talmud*. To celebrate either of these events a special meal is held ('seudah mitzvah'), where a concluding lecture ('hadran') is given.

Skoss, Solomon Leon (1884–1953) American Arabic and Hebrew scholar. He was born in Chusovoi, Serbia. He served in the Russian army, then in 1907 settled in the US. Later he taught at Dropsie College. His publications include a study of early Hebrew philology and an edition of the dictionary of the Karaite David Alfasi.

Slander (Hebrew 'leshon ha-ra') False report uttered maliciously to damage another person; the spreading of such a report. According to tradition, slander is a serious offence, and listening to slander is also forbidden. Rabbinic law empowered the courts to fine offenders, and to excommunicate them until they apologised to the satisfaction of the person injured. In certain instances fasting was also imposed as a punishment.

Slavery The condition of a person who is the legal property of another and is bound to absolute obedience to his owner. Scripture stipulates that an Israelite can be made the slave of another Israelite for only a limited period. A manumission must take place in the seventh year of service, or in a Jubilee year. After the Babylonian exile, the institution of Israelite slavery disappeared, but non-Jewish slaves could be purchased from neighbouring peoples. Male slaves had to undergo circumcision and all slaves were subject to Jewish law. A slave's marriage was arranged by the owner and the offspring of such a marriage became his property. During the Middle Ages some Jewish merchants engaged in the slave trade. Eventually Jews were prominent in the struggle that led to the abolition of slavery.

Sliosberg, Henry (1863–1937) Russian jurist and communal leader. He was born in Mir, Belorrussia, and settled with his family in Poltava, in eastern Ukraine. In 1889 he became legal counsel on Jewish affairs to Baron Horace Günzburg. He intervened with the Russian Government in Jewish affairs, and was involved in several Jewish legal disputes. He also served as Chairman of the Jewish community of St Petersburg. In 1920 he moved to France, where he became head of the Russian Jewish community in Paris. His memoirs, *Bygone Days*, present an account of Jewish life in Russia before the Revolution.

Slonimski, Hayyim Selig (1810–1904) Polish Hebrew writer and editor. He was born in Bialystok. During the Haskalah he wrote articles on popular science, and in 1834 he published the first part of a mathematics textbook. Later he wrote a work on astronomy. He also invented a calculating machine and in 1862 founded a Hebrew newspaper, *Ha-tzephirah*, devoted to popular science.

Slouschz, Naḥum (1871–1966) Israeli scholar archaeologist, and historian, of Lithuanian origin. He was born in Smorgon, near Vilnius, and as a child went to Odessa, where he later became involved in political and cultural activities. In 1904 he was appointed to the Chair of the Hebrew Language and Literature at the Sorbonne in Paris. He also taught at the École Normale Orientale of the Alliance Israélite Universelle. He wrote various studies of Jewry in North Africa. In 1919 he settled in Palestine, where he participated in archaeological explorations.

Smilansky, Moshe (1874–1953) Israeli writer. He was born in Ukraine and in 1890 emigrated to Palestine, where he started a farm near Rehovot. He was a frequent contributor to the Zionist press. He also wrote a set of six autobiographical novels and several histories of the early days of agricultural settlement in Israel.

Smilansky, Yizhar [Yizhar, S.] (1916–2006) Israeli author. He was born in

Rehovot. He worked as a teacher and principal in various schools and served in the Knesset. His writings include the novel *The Days of Ziklag.*

Smolenskin, Peretz (1840–1885)   Russian Hebrew novelist and editor. He was born in Monastyrshchina, in the province of Mohilev, Belorussia. He wandered for several years before settling in Odessa and later Vienna. In 1868, in Vienna, he founded the Hebrew monthly *Ha-Shaḥar*, which served as a central organ of Hebrew literary actives and Jewish national thought. Ten years later he established the weekly *Ha-Mabbit.* He wrote numerous stories and romances about Eastern-European Jewish life. His articles promoted a Jewish national theory opposed to religious Orthodoxy and the Haskalah. After the pogroms in Russia in 1881, he supported the Ḥibbat Zion movement.

Sneh, Mosheh [Kleinbaum, Mosheh] (1909–1972)   Israeli politician. He was born in Radzyn, Poland. He joined the General Zionists in 1935. After the outbreak of World War II, he fled form Warsaw to Vilnius and then to Palestine. From 1941 he served as chief of the national command of the Haganah. He became a member of the executive of the Jewish Agency in 1945, but later resigned and joined the Mapam party. Eventually he established the Socialist Left Party, which later joined the Israeli Communisty Party (Maki). He was editor of the communist newspaper *Kol ha-Am* and wrote *Conclusions of the Jewish Problem in the Light of Marxism.*

Sobol, Yehoshua (b.1939)   Israeli playwright. He was born in Tel Mond. He contributed to the leftist Israeli newspaper *Al Hamishmar.* From 1984 to 1988 he served as an art director at the Haifa Municipal Theater. His plays mostly explore life in modern Israel, but *Ghetto* depicts the existence of the Jewish community in the Vilnius Ghetto.

Socialism   Political and economic theory that advocates ownership and control by the community of the means of production, distribution and exchange. Many Jews participated in the development of socialism in the 19th century. However, some socialists expressed a hostile attitude toward the Jewish community since they viewed Jews as an incarnation of social parasitism. Later in the century anti-Semitism came to the fore in certain socialist circles. Jewish socialists mostly espoused one of four approaches to the Jewish problem. According to the assimilationist view Jews should be fully integrated with the communities in which they live in the diaspora. The Territorialists were dedicated to the procuring of land where Jews could establish self-governing settlements. The Bundists believed that Jewish problems would be solved by the establishment of a socialist revolution, but that notwithstanding political circumstances Jewish cultural autonomy should be maintained. Zionist socialists aimed to establish a socialist territory in Palestine.

Social justice   The concept of equity for all members of society in matters of civil and social rights, access to social amenities, and so on. It is a central theme of biblical legislation and a primary concern of the prophetic books of the Bible. Rabbinic, medieval and modern Jewish communal legislation continued to emphasise its importance.

Sod   ('secret')   Esoteric allegorical method of scriptural exegesis. It is based on the belief that the Torah has more than one level of meaning. It was used to interpret the Creation account in Genesis 1 (maaseh Bereshit) and Ezekiel's vision of the divine chariot in Ezekiel 1 (maaseh merkavah).

Sodom [Sedom]   Ancient Israelite city. Most important of the five cities (Sodom, Gomorrah, Admah, Zeboiim and Zoar) of the Jordan plain. Lot settled there, but escaped when the city was destroyed because of the wickedness of its inhabitants (Genesis 19).

Sokolow, Naḥum (1859–1936) Polish Zionist leader. He was born in Wyszogrod, near Plock, Poland. He joined the editorial board of the journal *Ha-Tzephirah* in Warsaw in 1884, later becoming its manager. From 1905 to 1909 he served as Secretary of the World Zionist Organisation. During this period he edited the organisation's journal *Die Welt* and also founded its Hebrew weekly *Ha-Olam*. At the outbreak of World War I he moved from Berlin to London, where he became involved in the negotiations concerning the Balfour Declaration. After the war he presided over the Comité des Délégations Juives during the Versailles peace conference in 1919. He was Chairman of the Executive of the Zionist Organisation, and President of the World Zionist Organisation and the Jewish Agency. His writings include a study entitled *History of Zionism*.

Sola, David Aaron de (1796–1860) British rabbi. He was born in Amsterdam. He became ḥazzan of the London Sephardi community in 1818. His writings include *Forms of Prayer According to the Custom of the Spanish and Portuguese Jews* and *Eighteen Treatises of the Mishnah*.

Solis-Cohen, Solomon (1857–1948) American physician and poet. He was a professor of clinical medicine at Jefferson Medical College, Philadelphia, and was also active in Jewish and Zionist organisations. He translated Hebrew poetry into English, including Ibn Ezra's *Selected Poems*.

Solomon (fl. 10th cent. BCE) King of Israel (965–931 BCE), son of David and Bathsheba. He became king before his father's death, through the influence of Bathsheba and Nathan, who promoted his accession to the throne in place of Adonijah, his elder brother.

Solomon built the Temple in Jerusalem, constructed fortresses, store cities and chariot cities, and built a harbour at Elath. He also made administrative innovations, including the division of the country into 12 districts. The biblical books Song of Songs and Ecclesiastes are attributed to him, as is Psalm 72. According to the Bible, he was known for his wisdom.

Solomon, Solomon Joseph (1860–1921) English painter. He painted portraits and figure compositions using Jewish motifs.

Solomon ben Jeroham (fl. 10th cent.) Palestinian Karaite scholar. He lived in Egypt and Jerusalem. His writings include Arabic commentaries on the Bible and a Hebrew polemic against Saadyah Gaon.

Soloveichik, Ḥayyim (1853–1918) Lithuanian talmudist, son of Joseph Baer Soloveichik. He was born in Volozhin, and taught at the yeshivah there from 1880 to 1892. Later he lived in Brest-Litovsk, where he served as rabbi. He developed a new trend in talmudic study based on conceptual analysis. He also wrote novellae on talmudic tractates and on Maimonides' *Mishneh Torah*.

Soloveichik, Isaac Ze'ev (1886–1956) Lithuanian rabbi and halakhist, son of Ḥayyim Soloveichik. He was born in Volozhin and became rabbi of Brest-Litovsk in 1918 after the death of his father. During World War II he fled to Vilnius, and he later settled in Jerusalem, where he founded an academy for advanced study of the *Talmud*.

Soloveichik, Joseph (1903–1993) American talmudic scholar, son of Isaac Ze'ev Soloveichik. He was born in Pruzhany, Poland, and grew up in Hasloviz, Belorussia. In 1932 he emigrated to the US, where he served as a rabbi in Boston. He became Professor of *Talmud* at the Isaac Elhanan Yeshiva in 1941. He was also Professor of Jewish Philosophy at the university's Bernard Revel Graduate School. His writings include *Ish ha-Halakhah.*

Soloveichik, Joseph Baer (1820–1892) Lithuanian talmudist. He lived in Volozhin, where he served as joint rosh yeshivah with Naphtali Tzevi Judah Berlin. Later he became rabbi of Slutsk, and after a period spent in Warsaw, of Brest-Litovsk. His *Bet ha-Levi* contains novellae on the *Talmud*, responsa, and sermons.

Sommerstein, Emil (1868–1946) Austrian soldier. He was born in Bukovina. He fought in Galicia during World War I, and later commanded the Austrian army that captured Burgenland. He served as head of the Austrian organisation for Jewish war veterans. After the Anschluss he was put under house arrest, and in 1921 he was deported to Theresienstadt. He returned to Vienna at the end of the war. Later he settled in the US.

Sommi, Leone de (1527–1592) Italian dramatist and poet. He was born in Mantua. He wrote and staged plays for the Gonzaga court theatre, and eventually became renowned throughout Europe as a dramatist and director. In 1585 he bought property in Mantua on which he built a synagogue. His writings include plays, poems, canzones, and satires. His greatest works are the *Dialoghi*, an exposition on stagecraft, and his Hebrew comedy of betrothal, *Zahut Bedihuta de-Kidushin.*

Soncino, Israel (d.1492) Italian printer. He was a physician. He set up a Hebrew press in Soncino, Italy, with his son. They produced a tractate of the *Talmud* in 1484. Later they produced a complete Hebrew Bible with illustrations. Moving to various towns in Italy, the family began to print in Latin and Italian.

Song of Degrees (Hebrew 'Shir ha-Malalot') Title found at the head of each of the 15 psalms from 120–134. Various interpretations of the description have been advanced. It is as though the word 'degrees', having to do with ascent, may imply that the Psalms were recited as the Jews returned form Babylon to Palestine, or that they are the songs of pilgrims on their way to Jerusalem. It has also been suggested that 'degrees' should be interpreted more literally and that this group of psalms was recited in the Temple by the Levites on the 15 steps leading from the Court of the Israelites to the Women's Court at the Water-Drawing Festival.

Song of Songs (Hebrew 'Shir ha-Shirim') [Song of Solomon] Biblical book, part of the Hagiographa. It is attributed to Solomon, and consists of a series of love poems. It was interpreted in the *Talmud* and by medieval Jewish commentators as an allegory depicting the love between God and Israel.

Song of Songs Rabbah (Hebrew 'Shir ha-Shirim Rabbah') [Midrash Hazita] Midrash to the Song of Songs, dating from about the 9th century. It is also known as Midrash Hazita after the opening word of its first verse (Proverbs 22:29).

Sonntag, Jacob (1905–1984) British scholar and editor. He was born in Wiznitz, northern Bukovina, and grew up in Vienna. He emigrated to England in 1938. In 1953 he founded the scholarly journal the *Jewish Quarterly,* which he edited.

Songs of God (Hebrew 'Benei Elohim') Term used variously in the Bible to designate demi-gods, angels, and mythological beings, as well as humans who have a special relationship with God. In the Apocrypha, it also refers to the Messiah. Rabbinic literature applies the term to Israel or to man generally.

Sons of Man (Hebrew 'Benei Adam') Term used variously in the Bible to mean ordinary men or men of God. In

Ezekiel 2:1 the prophet is called the Son of Man in the vision of the divine chariot. In the Book of Daniel the expression is first used in an apocalyptic context (Daniel 7:13), but is then applied to Daniel himself by the Angel Gabriel (Daniel 8:17). The name later passed into eschatological usage as a messianic title.

Sons of Light   Term found in the Dead Sea Scrolls, denoting the godly (in contrast to the Sons of Darkness – the ungodly). In the Qumran community, where the scrolls originated, the members of the community and their sympathisers were designated 'Sons of Light'.

Sopher [Schreiber], Moses [Ḥatam Sopher] (1762–1839)   Slovakian rabbi. From 1903 he served as rabbi at Pressburg, where he founded a yeshivah. He was an influential preacher, halakhic authority, and opponent of Reform Judaism. His *Ḥatam Sopher* (after which he was known) contains responsa and novellae.

Sotah ('errant wife') (i)   A married woman suspected of adultery (Numbers 5:11–31). The Bible prescribed a procedure to prove her innocence or guilt.

Sotah ('errant wife') (ii)   Sixth tractate in the Mishnah order of Nashim. It deals with the laws concerning a woman suspected of adultery (Numbers 5:11–31); the liturgical readings which may be recited in any language as opposed to those which must be recited in Hebrew; and the rite of breaking the neck of a heifer, performed when a murder by an unknown hand has been discovered (Deuteronomy 21:1–9). It also contains a discussion of declining standards after the destruction of the Temple, and depicts the chaos that will precede messianic redemption.

Soul   The spiritual, immaterial part of man, held to survive death. There are three biblical words translated as 'soul': 'nephesh', 'ruaḥ', and 'neshamah'. All derive from the words meaning 'breath' or 'wind'. The Bible makes an intimate connection between the soul and life itself, and speaks of the soul as the means by which the body is animated. After death the soul has only a shadow existence in Sheol. During the Hellenistic period the concept of the soul existing independently of the body became current. It was understood as originating in Heaven and was believed to join the body at the moment of birth. In Kabbalistic Judaism metempsychosis ('gilgul') was an important doctrine.

Soutine, Chaim (1893–1943)   French painter. Born in Similovitchi, Lithuania, he studied in the School of Fine Arts in Vilna and later went to Paris. He shared rooms with Amedeo Modigliani. With the Nazi occupation, he fled to a small French village and continued painting.

Spassky, Boris (b.1937)   Russian chess champion. Born in Leningrad, he was the son of a Jewish mother and gentile father. He became a grandmaster at the age of 18. In 1969 he became world champion.

Spector, Mordecai (1858–1925)   Ukrainian Yiddish novelist and editor. He was born in Uman. Initially he wrote sketches and novels, including *Der yidisher muzhik*, which advocated the return of the Jews to productive labour in Palestine. In 1857 he settled in Warsaw, where he wrote travel sketches, short stories, and novels, and also edited a series of anthologies. In 1894 he helped to set up the important anthology *Yontev bletlekh*. He moved to New York in 1921, and shortly before the end of his life wrote a volume of memoirs, *Mayn lebn*.

Spektor, Isaac Elhanan [Isaac Elhanan] (1817–1896)   Lithuanian rabbi. He was born in the province of Grodno, Russia. He served as a rabbi in various towns, eventually settling in Kovno, where he officiated until his death. He established a yeshivah in Kovno, and organised aid for stricken communities; he was the only rabbi invited to attend the conference of Jewish leaders held in St Petersburg in 1881–82 to discuss the plight of Jewry. Subsequently he supported the Ḥibbat Zion movement. The Isaac Elhanan Yeshiva in New York was named for him.

Sperber, Manes (1905–1984) Austrian author. He was born in Zabolotov, Galicia, and moved to Vienna in 1916. He taught in Berlin from 1927 to 1933 and then settled in Paris. His novels about shtetl life include *Like Tears in the Ocean* and *All our Yesterdays.*

Spices Aromatic woods were used in producing incense for the Temple. At the close of the Sabbath it is the custom to smell fragrant spices, and the spice boxes used for this practice have become a form of Jewish ritual art. Specific benedictions are prescribed to be recited on smelling aromatic woods or cloves. In the Middle Ages Jews were involved in the spice trade between Asia and Europe.

Spiegel, Shalom (1899–1984) American scholar and educator. He was born in Romania, and educated in Vienna. From 1923 to 1929 he taught in Palestine, but then settled in New York, where he was Professor of Medieval Hebrew Literature at the Jewish Theological Seminary. His publications include studies of the biblical prophets, and an edition of the liturgical compositions of Eleazar Kallir.

Spiegelman, Art (b.1948) Amercian cartoonist, of Swedish origin. His cartoon strip *Maus* is a depiction of the Holocaust based on the metaphor of the Nazis as cats and Jews as mice.

Spielman, Sir Isidore (1854–1925) English communal leader. He was the founder and director of the art exhibits branch of the Board of Trade. In 1887 he organised an exhibit on British Jewry under the title the Anglo-Jewish Historical Exhibition. He also served as President of the Jewish Historical Society.

Spielvogel, Nathan (1874–1956) Australian author. He was born in Ballarat, in the state of Victoria. He was a country schoolteacher and travelled frequently in the eastern Australian outback. In his writing he portrayed Jewish immigrants who arrived in Australia from England and Europe.

Spinoza [De Spinoza; Espinoza], Benedict (1632–1677) Dutch philosopher. He was born in Amsterdam. He had a traditional equation, but his heretical views led to his excommunication in 1656. From 1660 he lived away from Amsterdam, earning his living as a lens polisher. His *Thelogico-Political Treatise* initiated modern biblical criticism. In his *Ethics* he applied Euclidean methods to demonstrate a metaphysical concept of the universe with ethical implications.

Spire, André (1868–1966) French poet and Zionist leader. He was born in Nancy. He became a member of the Conseil d'État in 1894, specialised in employment problems at the French Minstry of Labour, and served as Inspector-General in the Ministry of Agriculture. He played an active part in the Dreyfus Affair. He became an advocate of Zionism, and in 1919 represented the French Zionists at the Paris Peace Conference. During World War II he lived in the US. His writings include *Poèmes juifs* and *Quelque Juifs et Demi-Juifs.*

Spitz, Mark (b.1950) American swimmer. Trained as a dentist, he won seven gold medals at the 1972 Olympics.

Sport The Bible records the use of lances, swords and slings for sport or training. In the 2nd century BCE a gymnasium was established in Jerusalem to train Jewish youths. Herod the Great constructed stadia and organised Palestinian teams to take part in the Olympic Games. In Talmudic and post-Talmudic times physical training was not regarded as a priority. In the modern period, however, Jews have been involved in a wide range of sport activities. Since 1932 international gatherings of Jewish athletes have been held under the auspices of the Maccabiah.

Sprinzak, Yoseph (1885–1959) Israeli politician. He was born in Russia where he was one of the founders of the socialist youth movement Tzeire Zion. He settled in Palestine 1908 where he became active in labour politics. A founder of the Histradrut and Mapai, he represented Mapai in the Knesset, and later became Speaker of the Knesset.

Stamps The first postage stamps issued by the State of Israel appeared on 16 May 1948. Special stamps have been issued for anniversaries, congresses, and memorial days, and for each Jewish New Year and Independence Day.

Starer, Robert (1924–2001) American composer. He was born in Vienna. He fled the Nazis in 1938 and settled in Palestine, where he became staff pianist for the BBC Palestine. Later he taught at the Juilliard School in New York and became Professor of Composition at Brooklyn College. His compositions include setting of the Psalms, and liturgical cantatas such as *Kohelet, Ariel,* and *Joseph and his Brothers.*

Starr, Joshua (1907–1949) American historian and communal worker. He was born in New York. He was Secretary of the Commission for European Jewish Cultural Reconstruction in 1947–49. He published studies of Byzantine and post-Byzantine Jewish history.

Statistics The Bible records several instances of a census (as in the Book of Numbers). Subsequently attempts were made from time to time to number Jewry. In the 12th century Benjamin of Tudela estimated the Jewish population in each place he visited. The scientific gathering of statistical information about Jewish communities took place from the 18th century onward. For example, the German Büro für Statistik der Juden in Berlin published a journal giving such information until the mid-1920s. Statistics on the population of the State of Israel are maintained by the Statistical Bureau.

Steinberg, Ben (b.1930) Canadian composer, conductor, organist, and educator. He was born in Winnipeg. He taught music in public schools in Toronto, and from 1988 he served as Director of Music at the city's Temple Sinai. He has written Jewish liturgical music, and *Echoes of Children* commemorating the children who died during the Holocaust.

Steinbeck, Isaac Nachman (1888–1957) Russian revolutionary and writer. He was born in Dvinsk, and worked as a lawyer in Moscow before World War I. He was arrested and exiled because of his revolutionary activities, but returned to Russia in 1910. In 1917–18 he was Commissar for Law. Later he lived in Berlin, London, and New York. He was prominent in the Yiddish and Territorialist movements, and published studies of the Russian Revolution and Jewish issues.

Steinberg, Judah (1863–1908) Bessarabian writer and educator. He was born in Lipkany. His early works include a writing manual, a book of proverbs, and a children's storybook. In 1897 he became a teacher in Leovo, Moldavia, and later settled in Odessa, where he was the correspondent of the New York daily *Di warheit.* He published textbooks, children's stories, feuilletons, and fables. A number of his stories deal with Hasidic life.

Steinberg, Milton (1930–1950) American rabbi and novelist. He was born in Rochester, New York, and became rabbi at New York's Park Avenue Synagogue. His publications include *As a Driven Leaf*, *The Making of the Modern Jew*, *Basic Judaism*, *A Partisan Guide to the Jewish Problem*, and *A Believing Jew*.

Steinberg, Yaakov (1887–1947) Hebrew author. He lived in Warsaw, Switzerland, and Palestine. His stories, set in Ukraine, illustrate the difficulties of life in the diaspora.

Steiner, George (b.1929) British scholar. He was born in Paris. He became Professor of Comparative Literature at Geneva University and a fellow of Churchill College, Cambridge. Many of his writings deal with Jewish themes. They include *The Death of Tragedy*, *After Babel*, *In Bluebeard's Castle*, and *The Portage to San Cristobal of A.H.*

Steinhardt, Jakob (1887–1968) Israeli artist. He was born in Zerków, Poland, and in 1933 settled in Palestine, where he became Director of the Bezalel School of Arts and Crafts in Jerusalem. He produced woodcuts dealing with Jewish and biblical themes, as well as Palestinian landscapes.

Steinheim, Solomon Ludwig (1789–1866) German philosopher. He was born in Bruchhausen, Westphalia, and practiced as a physician in Altona from 1813 to 1845. Later he settled in Rome. His writings include *Revelation According to the Doctrine of the Synagogue* and *The Doctrine of the Synagogue as Exact Science*.

Steinman, Eliezer (1892–1970) Israeli writer. He was born in Obodovka, in Ukraine, and became a part-time Hebrew teacher in Odessa. In 1920 he left Russia, and settled in Warsaw, where he wrote stories, essays, articles, and a novel; he also published collections of Yiddish essays and stories about the pogroms against Ukrainian Jews. In 1924 he settled in Tel Aviv, where he wrote for *Ha-Aretz* and *Ha-Olam* and published stories and novels. He later became a columnist for *Davar*.

Steinschneider, Moritz (1816–1907) German bibliographer and orientalist. He was born in Prossnitz, Moravia. He taught in Prague and Berlin, where he also preached, officiated at weddings, worked as a translator and wrote Hebrew textbooks. He was appointed lecturer at the Veitel-Heine-Ephraimsche Lehranstalt in 1859, and taught there for 48 years. From 1869 he was also assistant librarian at the Berlin State Library. He produced catalogues of the Hebrew books at the Bodleian Library, Oxford, and of the Hebrew manuscripts at Leyden, Munich, Hamburg, and Berlin. His other publications include studies of the history of Jewish literature and Hebrew typography.

Steinthal, Heymann (1823–1899) German philologist and philosopher. He studied in Berlin and was appointed lecturer in philology and mythology at Berlin University in 1850. In 1872 he became Professor of Biblical Studies and Philosophy of Religion at the Hochschule für die Wissenschaft des Judentums. He and Moritz Lazarus were the originators of the science of racial psychology.

Stencl, Avrom-Nokhem (1897–1983) Polish Yiddish poet. He was born in Czeladzy, Poland. He went to the Netherlands in 1919, then moved to Germany, and eventually settled in England. His publications include *Londoner sonetn* and *Vaytshepl shtetl d'Britn*.

Sterilisation The Bible contains prohibitions against castration and against the marriage of a man 'crushed or maimed in his privy parts'. (Deuteronomy 23:2). On the basis of these laws, the rabbis concluded that it is forbidden to impair the reproductive organs in humans, beasts, or birds. In males this includes the multiplication of the penis, testicles or seminal ducts (even after any previous impairment). The use of oral contraceptives and of sterilising agents is also forbidden, as is the sterilisation of females. The marriage ban applies only to those injured by human means rather than through an act of God or through illness.

Stern, Abraham Jacob (1762–1842) Polish maskil and mathematician. He was born in Hrubieszów, and lived in Warsaw. He invented a calculating machine and a threshing machine, and acted as government censor for Hebrew books.

Stern, Avraham [Yair] (1907–1942) Palestinian underground fighter. He was born in Suwalki, Poland. He went to Palestine in 1925 and became active in the Irgun Tzevai Leumi. In 1940 he formed an underground organisation, Lohame Herut Yisrael (known as the Stern Gang). He was killed by the British police while he was being arrested.

Sternberg, Erich Walter (1891–1974) Israeli composer. He was born in Berlin, and settled in Palestine in 1932. His early compositions incorporated material from Eastern European Jewish folklore. Many of his works are based on biblical themes and Jewish liturgical traditions.

Stern-Taübler, Selma (1890–1989) American historian, wife of Eugen Taübler. She was archivist of the American Jewish Archives in Cincinnati from 1947 to 1956. She wrote about the history of German Jewry and about court Jews.

Stiebel (Yiddish: 'small room') Side room in a synagogue, used for public prayer. The term is also applied to the meeting place of Hasidic Jews.

Stieglitz, Alfred (1846–1946) American photographer. Born in Hoboken, New Jersey, he studied at the Berlin Polytechnic. He was a pioneer of photographic techniques and helped gain acceptance of photography as an art form.

Stoicism Philosophical doctrine founded in c. 300 BCE in Athens. The sto-

ics made virtue the highest good, advocated control of the passions, and inculcated indifference to pleasure and pain. Stoicism flourished during the Greco-Roman period. It exercised an influence on Hellenistic Jewish thought, as well as on medieval Jewish theology.

Stone worship The use of stones in religious worship was current from ancient times, but is forbidden in the Bible. The Israelites were commanded not to erect a pillar or bow down to figured stone (Leviticus 26:1). Stones however were used as memorials of historic events (Joshua 4:9; 8:32; I Samuel 7:12) and as markers (Genesis 31:48–52).

Stranger (Hebrew 'nokrim,' 'zarim') According to the Bible, strangers must be shown consideration and should be treated like native-born Israelites (Leviticus 19:33–34). The rabbis asserted that in order to qualify for the protection offered by Jewish law, the stranger must adhere to the Noachian Laws.

Strasberg, Lee (1901–82) American actor. Born in Austria-Hungary, he went to the US at the age of seven. He grew up on the Lower East Side of New York. He joined the Chryssides Street Settlement House's drama club. He later studied at the Clare Tree Major School of Theatre. Subsequently he helped form the Group Theatre company. In 1948 he joined the Actor's Studio, becoming artistic director. He founded the Lee Strasberg Theatre Institutes in New York and Los Angeles.

Strashun [Zaskovitzer], Samuel (1794–1872) Lithuanian Talmudic scholar. He was born in Zaskovitzer. He was initially named after his birthplace, but later adopted the name of his father-in-law, David Strashun. He lived in Vilnius, where he devoted himself to scholarship. He wrote annotations and glosses on almost all the tractates of the Mishnah and the *Talmud*.

Straus, Nathan (1848–1931) American merchant and philanthropist, brother of Oscar Solomon Straus. He was commissioner first for parks then for health in New York, and a member of the New York Forest Preserve Board. He established a milk pasteurisation laboratory and milk distribution stations in New York, an emergency relief system to distribute coal and food to the poor, and a chain of boarding houses for the destitute. He also established the Pasteur Institute in Palestine and endowed child welfare stations and health centres there.

Straus, Oscar Solomon (1850–1926) American diplomat and jurist, brother of Nathan Straus. He served as American Minister in Turkey and later was appointed to the International Court of Arbitration at The Hague. He was Secretary of Commerce and Labour in the US, and then Ambassador to Turkey. He helped to found the American Jewish Committee, served as an officer of the Baron de Hirsch Fund, and was president of the American Jewish Historical society. In his writings he illustrated the impact of Hebrew concepts on American culture.

Strauss, Leo (1899–1973) American philosopher and political scientist, of German origin. After emigrating to the US, he taught at the New School for Social Research in New York and was appointed Professor of Political Science at the University of Chicago. He wrote studies of political philosophy and the relations between philosophy and theology.

Strauss, Levi (1829–1902) American manufacturer of German origin. Born in Buttenheim, Germany, he went to the US in 1847. He initially began peddling in New York City. Later he went to Louisville, Kentucky. In 1853 he went to San Francisco and established a store, Levi Strauss and Company. In 1873 he became a partner with Jacob W. Davis, a tailor from Nevada. They developed Levi jeans.

Streisand, Barbara (b.1942) American singer and actress. She was born in Brooklyn. She appeared in Broadway musicals and in films, some of which have Jewish subjects.

Stricker, Robert (1879–1944) Austrian Zionist leader and journalist. He was born in Brünn, and became an engineer for Austrian state railways. Before World War I he edited the Vienna *Jüdisches Zeitung*, and in 1915 he founded the Jewish War Archives. He became President of the Jewish People's Party, and in 1919 was elected to the Constituent National Assembly of the Federal Austrian Republic. From 1919 to 1928 he edited the *Wiener Morgenzeitung* and later *Die Neue Welt*. In 1931 he joined the Union of Zionist Revisionists, then in 1933 was one of the founders of the Jewish State Party.

Stroock, Alan Maxwells (1907–1985) American lawyer, son of Solomon Marcuse Stroock. He started his career as a law clerk to Supreme Court Justice Benjamin Cardozo, then joined the Stroock family legal firm Stroock and Stroock, where he became a partner. He served as Chairman of the Board and later President of the corporation of the Jewish Theological Seminary in New York, and was also active in various other Jewish organisations.

Stroock, Solomon Marcuse (1874–1945) American communal leader. A specialist in constitutional law, he was the chairman of various legal committees. He served as President of the New York branch of the Young Men's

Hebrew Association, the Federation for the support of Jewish Philanthropic Societies in New York, and the American Jewish Committee.

Stutschewsky, Joachim (1891–1981) Israeli cellist, composer and historian, of Ukrainian origin. He worked as a cellist in Switzerland and in Vienna, where he contributed essays on Jewish music to the periodical *Die Stimme*. In 1938 he settled in Palestine. He organised concerts of Jewish music in Tel Aviv. He composed works for cello, numerous songs, and arrangements of folk songs. He also engaged in historical research on Ḥasidic musicians.

Suarès, André (1866–1948) French author, of Portuguese Jewish descent. He was born near Marseilles. Although he adopted a negative attitude to Judaism, he rallied to the defence of the Jews after the advent of Nazism.

Subbotniki Name of a group of Russian Sabbatarians, which emerged at the end of the 18th century. Most of the Subbotniki practised Jewish customs but acknowledged the New Testament in addition to the Hebrew Scriptures; others accepted the Hebrew Scriptures but not the *Talmud*. Under Nicholas I they were banished to Siberia and conscripted into the army, but from 1905 they enjoyed religious freedom. Some of their descendants reverted to traditional Judaism and settled in Palestine.

Suffering The problem of human suffering occupies a central place in the Bible and the *Talmud*. A theme of the Book of Job is that the righteous person may be forced to endure suffering in order to prove that he is capable of piety. Other books of the Bible assume a different relationship between suffering and sin. The rabbis also adopted this view, but conceded that suffering can come upon an innocent person without explanation or apparent justification. Central to Jewish theology is the belief that the righteous will be rewarded in the world to come.

Suicide Taking one's own life is regarded in the Jewish faith as a crime equivalent to murder. A person who committed suicide was denied normal burial and mourning . Suicide is clearly differentiated from martyrdom which is extolled in Judaism.

Sukenik, Eliezer Lipa (1889–1953) Israeli archaeologist. He was born in Bialystok, and settled in Palestine in 1912. He became Professor of Archeology at the Hebrew University. He excavated the Third Wall of Jerusalem, the city of Samaria, and the synagogue in the town of Beth Alpha.

Sukkah ('tabernacle') (i) Booth erected during the festival of Sukkot. According to Leviticus, Jews are obliged to dwell or at least eat in it for the seven days of Sukkot (Leviticus 23:42). It symbolises God's protection of the Israelites during their 40 years of wandering in the desert. According to custom, it is decorated with curtains, fruits, and symbols of the holy day. In modern times it is usually constructed near the synagogue, and a token meal is eaten there after the service on each day of the festival.

Sukkah ('Tabernacle') (ii) Sixth tractate in the Mishnah order of Moed. It deals with the laws concerning the festival of Sukkot, and it also contains a description of the Festival of the Water-Drawing which in the first and second Temple periods was celebrated at the same time.

Sukkot ('Tabernacles') [Ḥag ha-Asiph; Ingathering Festival] One of the three pilgrim festivals. It begins on 15 Tishri and lasts for seven days (eight days in the diaspora). The eighth day (22 Tishri) is a separate holy day, Shemini Atzeret. Work is prohibited on the first day of Sukkot (or two days in the diaspora), and on Shemini Atzeret. The festival is also known as 'Ḥag ha-Asiph' (Festival of the Harvest) or simply 'Ḥag', and marks the end of the agricultural year (hence the English name Ingathering Festival, derived from Exodus 23.16). During the Temple period the first day of Sukkot was also celebrated as a water libation festival. Sukkot is celebrated by taking four species of plant – palm (lulav), citron (etrog), myrtle and willow – and carrying them in procession in the synagogue. According to Leviticus (23–42), it is also required to dwell or at least eat all meals in the sukkah.

Sulzberger, Mayer (1843–1923) American jurist and communal leader. He was born in Heidelsheim, Germany, and emigrated to the US in 1849. He became a lawyer in Philadelphia, and was later elected a judge of the Court of Common Pleas. He lectured on Hebrew jurisprudence and government at Dropsie College and the Jewish Theological Seminary. He served as President of the American Jewish Committee and the Young Men's Hebrew Association of Philadelphia. His writings include *The Am ha-Aretz – the Ancient Hebrew Parliament: a Chapter in the Constitutional History of Ancient Israel, The Policy of the Ancient Hebrews, The Ancient Hebrew Law of Homicide,* and *The Status of Labour in Ancient Israel.*

Sulzer, Solomon (1804–1890) Austrian cantor. He was born in Hohenems, in the Tyrol, and served as a cantor in Vienna from 1826. He sought to revive traditional cantorial music by incorporating modern musical innovations. His *Shir Tziyyon* purified many melodies from their later embellishments and included recitatives in the original Polish tradition.

Summerfield, Woolfe (1901–1976) English lawyer and author. He was born in Manchester. Under the pseudonym Ben Mowshay he published two novels set in Kidston (Manchester) about the life of a Jewish hero, Abraham Bear Davis.

Sumptuary laws Regulations limiting private expenditure. In Jewish communities laws that restricted extravagance in dress and festivities were known in Talmudic times, and became common in the Middle Ages. They governed matters such as the number of guests that could be invited to private festivities, the dishes that could be served, the jewellery and dress that could be worn, and the nature and number of wedding gifts.

Sun, Blessing of the (Hebrew 'Birkat ha-Ḥammah') Blessing recited once in every 28 years on the first Wednesday of Nisan, when the sun is believed to be in the same place in the heavens as at the time of Creation.

Superstition Credulity about the supernatural or mysterious. The Bible forbids divination and magic. In the *Talmud* superstitious practices and beliefs are frequently referred to, including the belief in demons, amulets and sorcery, and the significance of dreams and chance occurrences. In the Middle Ages a number of Jewish authorities declared all forms of superstition to be nonsense. Nonetheless, such beliefs, enhanced by Kabbalistic influences, have persisted in the form of folk customs.

Susannah, History of [Susannah and the Elders] Apocryphal book. It describes a plot by two elders against the virtue of Susannah and how Daniel exposed their guilt by uncovering contradictions in their account of the event.

Sussmann, Heinrich (1904–1986) Austrian painter. He was born in Tarnopol, Galicia, and went to Vienna in 1914. He later lived in Berlin and (from 1933) Paris. His later work deals with themes of the Jewish diaspora, including memories of his childhood in Galicia.

Sutskever [Sutzkever], Avraham (1913–2010) Polish Yiddish poet. He was born in Smorgon, Belorussia. His family moved to Siberia then to

Vilnius. He belonged to the 'Yung Vilne' school of Yiddish poet. In 1941–43 he was incarcerated in the Vilnius ghetto, but escaped and joined the partisans. He settled in Paris in 1949. Many of his poems deal with European ghetto life and the Holocaust.

Suzman, Helen (1917–2009) South African politician. She was a lecturer in economics and became a member of parliament in 1953. She spoke for non-white races who were not given representation.

Swine Pig (or collectively pigs). According to the Bible, the meat of the pig is forbidden as food for Jews (Leviticus 11:7; Deuteronomy 14:8).

Symmachus (fl. 2nd cent.) According to various traditions, he was an Ebionite, a Samaritan proselyte to Judaism, or a pupil of Meir. He translated the Bible into Greek.

Synagogue Meeting place of a Jewish congregation, where services of public prayer are held. The synagogue originated in the 6th century BCE among the Babylonian exiles as a substitute for the Temple. It served as a place of prayer, study, and public assembly. By the 1st century it had become an established institution in Jewish life. From the 3rd century synagogues were decorated with figured carvings, mosaics, and frescoes. In the Middle Ages they became centres of study and most had a rabbinical school ('bet midrash') attached. Although synagogues are built to different plans they have certain common features: the Ark containing the Scrolls of the Law is built into the wall facing Jerusalem and the reading desk is placed on the bimah, or platform, before the Ark; in the past men and women sat separately, and they still do so in Orthodox Judaism. The officers of the synagogue include the gabbai, ḥazzan, and shammash. In the 19th century the Reform movement introduced the organ into the synagogue, abolished the

women's area, and moved the reader's platform from the centre of the building to the east wall. Reform Judaism also altered the synagogue liturgy and changed the name of the institution to 'temple'.

Syncretism Attempt to unify or reconcile different schools of thought, beliefs, or principles. The term is applied specifically in the mixing of Greek and oriental religions during the Hellenistic period.

Synod Religious council responsible for the government of organised religion. The most important Jewish synod in ancient times was that held in 138 at Usha in Lower Galilee, to reorganise Jewish life after the Hadrianic persecutions. Local and regional rabbinical synods were held during the Middle Ages. In the 15th century a series of synods was held in Italy to combat anti-Jewish legislation by the Church. The Council of Four Lands served as the central governing body for Jewry in Poland and Lithuania from the 16th to the 18th centuries, though Lithuania had its own independent council from 1623. During the 19th century Reform rabbinical conferences were held in Europe. In the US conferences of the Reform, Conservative, and Orthodox rabbinate take place annually.

Syrkin, Marie (1899–1988) American author and educator. She was born in Berne, Switzerland, and was taken to the US as a child. She became the editor of the Labour Zionist monthly *Jewish Frontier*, and taught English at Brandeis University. Her writings include *Woman with a Cause* and *Blessed is the Match*.

Syrkin, Nachman (1868–1924) American leader of Socialist Zionism. He was born in Mohilev, Belorussia, and moved with his family to Minsk in 1884. Later he lived in Berlin, where he helped to found the Russian-Jewish Scientific Society, and participated in the first Zionist congresses. In 1907 he settled in New York and became active in Zionist work. He also contributed to Yiddish journals. During World War I he helped to establish the American Jewish Congress. He was a member of the Comité des Délégations Juives at the Paris Peace Conference in 1919. He published studies of Socialist Zionism.

Szenes, Hannah (1921–44) Palestinian poet and resistance fighter. She was born in Budapest, and moved to Palestine in 1939. She joined Kibbutz Sedot Yam, and began to write poetry. In 1942 she became one of a group of parachutists organised by the Haganah to rescue prisoners of war and organise Jewish resistance in Europe. She was dropped in Yugoslavia, and crossed the border into Hungary, where she was arrested and executed by the Nazis.

Szichman, Mario (b.1945) Argentine novelist. In 1967 he went to Colombia and later settled in Venezuela. He served as foreign reporter for Jacobo Timerman's *La opinión* and as a correspondent for the Italian news agency. In 1980 he moved to the US, where he continued to work as a correspondent. His novels trace the history of an Eastern-European family's attempt to adapt to life in Argentina.

Szigetti, Imre (1879–1975) Australian graphic artist and illustrator, of Hungarian origin. He was born in Budapest and emigrated to Australia in 1939. A number of his drawings depict Hungarian Jewish life.

Szold, Henrietta (1860–1945) American Zionist and philanthropist. She was born in Baltimore. She was Secretary of the Jewish Publication Society, in which capacity she edited and translated many books and edited the *American Jewish Year Book*. In 1912 she organised Hadassah, the Women's Zionist Organisation of America. She was the first woman to become a member of the executive of the Zionist Organisation, in which she took responsibility for education and health. After the rise to power of the Nazis, she worked as a leader of Youth Aliyah.

Szomory, Dezsö (1869–1944) Hungarian writer. He trained as a musician, studying at the Academy of Music in Budapest, before turning to writing. He later settled in Paris. Some of his works explore the problem of Jewish assimilation.

Szyk, Arthur (1894–1951) American artist. He was born in Łódź. After studying in Kraków and Paris, he specialised in book illumination. He produced illuminated versions of the Passover Haggadah and the Israeli Declaration of Independence. He lived in France and England, before settling in the US, where he produced book illustrations, and anti-Nazi caricatures.

T

An old Jew who has been praying at the Western Wall is known to have gone there every day for years. An enthusiastic young American reporter is anxious to write a story about him. He goes to the Wall and sees the man bent in prayer. Eventually once the old man has finished, he approaches him and asks him his name.

He says he is Leonard Finkelstein.

The reporter then asks him how long he has been praying at the Wall.

'Sixty-three years,' he says.

'What do you pray for?' the reporter asks.

'Peace between Jews and Arabs,' he says.

'So,' the reporter asks, 'what's it been like all these years?'

'Like talking to a wall,' he replies.

* * * * *

The Palestinian-Israeli conflict dominates Jewish life. Despite its seriousness, it is also a topic for humour. Here the seeming futility of the clash between Jews and Arabs is highlighted. In the face of this seemingly insurmountable problem, a pious Jew prays at the Western Wall. But he admits it does no good.

Taanit ('Fast') Ninth tractate in the Mishnah order of Moed. It deals with the designation of fast days during times of drought, as well as with the timing and form of prayers for rain. Other communal fasts are also discussed.

Tabatznik, Mendel (1894–1975) South African Yiddish essayist and poet. He was born in Kletsk, in Belorussia, and became the director of a Yiddish elementary school in Mir. In 1927 he settled in Johannesburg, South Africa, where he taught Yiddish and published articles about pedagogical issues. He also wrote poetry and an autobiographical novel.

Tabernacle [booth] (Hebrew 'sukkah') Portable habitation used as the sanctuary during the Israelites' years of wandering. Set up by Moses in the wilderness (Exodus 26–27), its chief architects were Bezalel and Oholiab. It was constructed of acacia wood overlaid with gold, and contained layers of curtains and animal skins, which gave it a tent-like appearance. Inside the Tabernacle was the Holy of Holies, containing the Ark of the Covenant, the seven-branched menorah, the table where the shewbread was laid, and the golden altar for incense. The term 'tabernacle' is also used of the booth constructed for the festival of Sukkot.

Tachlis (Yiddish) Achievement, or the substance of the matter.

Tadshe Opening word (and hence title) of a midrash dating from the late 2nd century and attributed to Phinehas ben

Jair (it is also known as the 'Baraita of Phineas ben Jair'). It deals with the symbolism of numbers.

Tag ('crown') The name given to a short vertical stroke added to the top of various Hebrew letters when they are used in the Torah and other parts of Scripture. According to the Masorah, the letters shin, ayin, tet, nun, zayin, gimel and tsadeh require three crown strokes. Other letters require one or none. The kabbalah stresses the mystical meanings of the tagin.

Taḥanun ('Supplication') The name of a prayer for grace and forgiveness. It is recited daily (except on Sabbaths, festivals and days of celebration) after the morning and afternoon Amidah. Its wording was established after the gaonic period.

Takkanah ('directive') The name given to any of the regulations which supplement the law as laid down in the Torah. The *Talmud* attributes to Moses the takkanah of reading the Pentateuch on Sabbaths, festivals, the New Moon and the intermediate days of festivals. The Amidah is traditionally regarded as a takkanah issued by men of the Great Synagogue. Tannaitic takkanot include the provision that a wife's marriage settlement is to be a general mortgage on the whole of the husband's property, that communities must appoint elementary school teachers, that a father must support his minor children, and that compulsory education is to be provided for children from the age of six. In the Middle Ages Gershom ben Judah issued 25 ordinances which were accepted as binding in Ashkenazi custom. Takkanot prescribed by a bet din remain valid even if the reason for their enactment no longer exists; only another bet din of greater authority can annul them. Notwithstanding the status of the takkanot, many lapsed with the passing of time.

Tal [Grünthal], Yoseph (1910–2008) Israeli composer and teacher. He was born in Pinne, in the Poznan district. He moved to Palestine and in 1937 joined the faculty of the Academy of Music in Jerusalem. Later he became head of the department of musicology at the Hebrew University. Many of his compositions are based on biblical motives and liturgical poetry.

Tallis Prayer shawl. It is worn by adult males during morning prayer, at the afternoon service in the Ninth of Av, and at all services on the Day of Atonement. The shawl is a four-cornered garment usually made of wool. Fringes are knotted on the corners in accordance with the biblical law (Numbers 15:37–41). Often the area that is draped over the head is adorned with a strip of silver or gold referred to as the 'atarah' (crown). A smaller garment, the 'tallit katan' (small talllit) also referred to as 'Arab kanphot' (four corners), is worn at all times under the outer clothes.

Talmon, Jacob Leib (1916–1980) Israeli scholar. Her was born in Rypin, Poland. In 1934 he went to Palestine, where he became Professor of Modern History at the Hebrew University. His writings include *The Origins of Totalitarian Democracy, The Nature of Jewish History: its Universal Significance; The Unique and the Universal, Romanticism and Revolt,* and *Political Messianism: the Romantic Phase.*

Talmud ('Study') Name given to each of the two collections of records of the discussion and administration of Jewish law by scholars and jurists in various academies in the period c.200–500. The two Talmuds are the Babylonian and the Palestinian (also known as the Jerusalem *Talmud*), and although they are distinguished from each other their contents overlap to a considerable degree. Both Talmuds contain the Mishnah together with Gemara (a commentary and supplement to the Mishnah text); both also contain aggadic digressions. The authorities referred to in the Palestinian *Talmud* lived before c.400; those mentioned in the Babylonian *Talmud* lived before c.500. The Babylonian *Talmud* contains more material than the Palestinian, and is regarded as more significant.

Talmud, burning of the   From the Middle Ages the attempted suppression of Judaism led at intervals to the wholesale destruction of copies of the *Talmud* and other Jewish texts. The first official burning of the *Talmud* took place in Paris on 17 June 1242, in response to the Disputation of Paris of 1240. On 9 September 1533 vast numbers of rabbinic texts were destroyed in Rome; this was followed by similar attacks throughout northern Italy. In the 18th century thousands of copies of the *Talmud* were burned in Poland after a disputation in 1757.

Talmud commentaries   The first commentaries on the *Talmud* consist of textual comments found in the writings of the later geonim. The earliest full commentaries are those of Sherira Gaon, Hai Gaon and Samuel ben Hophni, from the 10th to 11th centuries. In the 11th century Nissim ben Jacob of Kairouan and Hananel ben Hushiel produced important commentaries. The focus of talmudic study then moved to Germany and France. The early 11th-century commentary by Gershom ben Judah laid the foundation for the work of Rashi, who was followed by the Tosaphists. Later important commentaries were written by Nahmanides and Solomon ben Adret, and in the 16th century Solomon Luria, Samuel Edels and Meir Lublin produced significant works. In the modern period scientific studies of the *Talmud* have been prodded by various Jewish scholars.

Talmud Torah ('study [of the] law')   Term which refers to religious study. The term was adopted by a name (Hevra *Talmud* Torah) by voluntary associations that fostered religious education; it was also applied to their schools, and ultimately to Jewish religious schools in general. The institution of the *Talmud* Torah flourished in Europe and among immigrant communities in Western countries. It should be distinguished from the elementary school (heder) and advanced academies for talmudic study.

Tamar (i) (fl.? 19th cent. BCE)   Israelite woman, wife of Er, the eldest son of Judah, and later wife of Er's brother, Onan. After Onan's death, Judah refused to allow Tamar to marry his third son, Shelah. In protest she disguised herself as a prostitute and bore twins by Judah (Genesis 38).

Tamar (ii) (fl. 10th cent. BCE)   Israelite woman, daughter of David. She was raped by Amnon, her stepbrother (II Samuel 13), who was killed in revenge by her brother Absalom.

Tamid ('perpetual offering') (i)   The name given to the whole offering or sacrifice made twice daily (in the morning and the evening) in the Temple (Numbers 28:1–8).

Tamid ('perpetual offering') (ii)   Ninth tractate in the Mishnah order of Kodashim. It deals with the regulations for the daily burnt offerings in the Temple (Exodus 29:38; Numbers 28:1–8), and with the organisation of the Temple in general.

Tammuz, Benjamin (1919–1989)   Israeli writer. He was born in Khar'kov, in Ukraine, and went to Palestine in 1924. From 1965 he was the editor of the weekend literary supplement of *Ha-Aretz*, for which he wrote art criticism. In 1971 he became Cultural Attaché at the Israeli embassy in London. He wrote short stories, novels and children's books, and translated several books into Hebrew.

Tanakh   The Hebrew Bible. The name derives from the initial letters of the words 'Torah', 'Nevim', and 'Ketuvim' (Pentateuch, Prophets, Hagiographa).

Tanḥum ben Joseph of Jerusalem (c.1220–1291)   Palestinian philologist and biblical exegete. He lived in Palestine and Egypt. He wrote a lexicon to Maimonides' *Mishneh Torah*.

Tanḥuma [Midrash Tanḥuma; Yelamedenu']   Palestinian midrashic collection attributed to Tanḥuma bar Abba. It covers the entire Pentateuch and contains discourses, usually based on the opening verse of the portion of the week according to the triennial Palestine cycle. It is also known as 'Yelammedenu' from the opening phrase of each sermon: 'Yelammedenu Rabbenu' (Let our teacher pronounce).

Tanḥuma bar Abba (fl. 4th cent.)   Palestinian amora. He developed the art of homiletics and, according to tradition, was their author of many midrashim which begin 'Yelammedenu Rabbenu' (Let our teacher pronounce), including those that make up the Midrash Tanḥuma.

Tanna (Aramaic, from 'teni'; to teach)   Term used of a teacher in the mishnah or baraita, during the 1st–2nd centuries CE. The tannaitic period begins with the death of Hillel and Shammai, and ends with the generation after Judah ha-Nasi. The term was also applied during the talmudic period to a reader of tannaitic texts in the academies.

Tanna de-ve Eliyahu [Seder Eliyahu]   Ethical religious text consisting of Eliyahu Rabba and Eliyahu Zuta. The work is comprised of a series of moral homilies emphasising the love and study of the Torah, love of Israel and social justice. Although it is assigned to the talmudic period, it was probably copied in the 10th century.

Tanya (i)   Opening word and hence the title of a code of laws extracted from Zedekiah ben Abraham Anau's *Shibbole-ha-Leket*. It was prepared in Italy, probably in the 14th century.

Tanya (ii) [Likkute Amarim]   Ḥasidic Kabbalistic work written by Shneour Zalman of Lyady. It guides the believer to the attainment of devekut. Based on the kabbalah, it is also deeply influenced by talmudic literature and medieval Jewish philosophy.

Tappuḥim ('apples')   The fruit-shaped ornaments used to decorate the staves of the Torah scroll, particularly in Spain.

Targum (Aramaic, from Assyrian 'targumanu'; interpreter)   The name given to any Aramaic translation of the Bible or book of the Bible, oral or written. According to the *Talmud*, the custom of adding an Aramaic translation to the public reading of Scripture goes back to Ezra and became established in the Second Temple period. This oral Targum was both a translation and an interpretation of the text. The three written Targums to the Pentateuch are: Targum Onkelos; Targum Jonathan; and Targum Yerhushalmi. The Targum to the Former and Latter Prophets is called after Jonathan ben Uzziel. The Targums to the books of the Hagiographa are midrashic in character, especially that to the Five Scrolls.

Targum Sheni ('Second Targum')   Aramaic paraphrase of the Book of Esther, dating from c.500–1000. Additional to the ordinary Targum (hence its name), it is more midrashic in character.

Tarphon (fl. 1st cent.)   Palestinian tanna. He served with his priestly family in the Temple, and studied with Jonanan ben Zakkai and Gamaliel I. He was active in discussions at the academy at Jabneh. The Mishnah refers to differences of opinion between him and Akiva regarding the halakhah.

Tartakower, Aryeh (1897–1982)   Israeli sociologist and communal leader. He was born in Brody, in eastern Galicia, and taught at the Institute of Jewish

Sciences in Warsaw. In 1939 he went to the US, where he was Director of Relief and Rehabilitation for the World Zionist Action Committee. He settled in Palestine in 1946 and taught at the Hebrew University. From 1948 to 1971 he was Chairman of the Israeli section of the World Jewish Congress. He wrote studies of the Jewish labour movement, emigration problems, the history of Polish Jewry, anti-Semitism and the Jewish communities of the diaspora.

Tas ('plaque') A silver plaque placed on the Torah scroll to indicate the festival for which the scroll had been made ready.

Tashlikh ('Thou shalt cast') Custom practices on the first day of the New Year (or the second when the first takes place on the Sabbath). Prayers are recited near a stream or a body of water, preferably where there are fish. The term derives from Michah 7:19 ('thou shalt cast all their sins into the depths of the sea').

Tashmishei kedushah ('appurtenances of holiness') Religious articles and objects pertaining to the practice of the liturgy in the synagogue. They include the tallit, shophar and Torah ornaments.

Tata (Yiddish) Papa.

Täubler, Eugen (1879–1953) American historian and biblical scholar. He was born in Gostyn, in the district of Poznań. He taught at the universities of Berlin, Zurich and Heidelberg, where he was a professor. He emigrated to the US, where he taught at the Hebrew Union College in Cincinnati. He wrote studies of Jewish history.

Taxation According to the Book of Exodus, a poll tax was imposed on the Israelites during their years in the wilderness (Exodus 30:11–16). Later a system of tithes was used to maintain the Temple and the priesthood, and additional levies were used to help the poor. After the destruction of the Temple, the Romans imposed the Fiscus Judaicus on the Jewish community. This was revived during the Middle Ages as the Opferpennig. In the 17th–18th centuries in Italy, Jewish communal dues were exacted by a tax on capital ('capella'). In modern times such special Jewish taxes have disappeared, except in some countries where the Jewish community has the right to impose taxes on all its members to maintain communal institutions.

Tcherikover, Avigdor (1894–1958) Israeli historian, of Russian origin. He settled in Palestine in 1925 and became Professor of Ancient History at the Hebrew University. He published studies of the Jews in Palestine and Egypt during the Hellenistic and Roman periods.

Tchernowitz, Chaim (1871–1949) American talmudic scholar. He was born in Sebesh, Russia. He founded a yeshivah in Odessa and adopted the pseudonym 'Rav Tzair'. In 1923 he settled in the US and taught *Talmud* at the Jewish Institute of Religion in New York. He published studies of rabbinic literature, an abridgement of the *Talmud* and histories of Jewish law.

Teacher of Righteousness In the Dead Sea Scrolls, the title given to the organiser of the sect of the Qumran community. The name appears as in the Zadokite Fragments and from Qumran commentaries on books or sections of the Bible.

Tehinnah ('supplication') Any prayer of private devotion, or a prayer composed for private use. During the talmudic period private prayers were said after the Amidah: they were later replaced by the recital of the Tahanun. Tehinnot from the talmudic period include prayers for the forgiveness of sin, for divine blessing and protection, and for blessing in the study of the Torah. Many were subsequently incorporated into the prayer book. From the gaonic period many tehinnot were composed in the vernacular. Collections of such private devotions include prayers to be said when visiting the sick or at a cemetery, supplications for the blessing of scholarly and pious children, and prayers for use when baking Sabbath cakes or lighting Sabbath candles. Devotional books in Yiddish for women were also known as tehinnot.

Teitel, Jacob (1851–1939) Russian jurist and communal worker. He was born in Cherny Ostrov, Podolia. He was one of the first Jews in Russia to be employed in the judicial service during the czarist regime. Devoted to communal work, he helped Jews who were oppressed by the authorities, and was a founder of a relief enterprise which supported Jewish youth. In 1921 he left the USSR and became President of the Union of Russian Jews in Germany. When the Nazis came to power, he moved to France, where his memoirs were published.

Teitelbaum, Moses (1759–1841) Galician Hasidic leader. He was born in Przemýsl and served as a rabbi at Sieniawa and Ujhely. He was among the first to spread Hasidism in the northern and central districts of Hungary, and became known as a wonder-working tzaddik. He wrote a homiletics work (*Yismah moshe*) and responsa.

Teixeira, Abraham Senior (1581–1666) Portuguese Marrano financier and diplomat. He was born in Lisbon, the son of Dom Francisco de Melo and Donna Antonia de Silva Teixeira, lady-in-waiting to the queen. In 1643 he moved to Antwerp, where he became Consul and Paymaster for the Government of Spain. After moving to Hamburg, he and his sons were circumcised. This caused a scandal, and led to an (unsuccessful) attempt by the Imperial Viennese court to confiscate his property. Teixeira established an international banking house in Hamburg and took a leading role in Jewish affairs there, serving as the head of the city's Sephardi congregation. From 1655 he was Resident Diplomatic and Financial Minister for the Swedish crown in Hamburg.

Teixeira, Isaac Hayyim Senior (1625–1705) Dutch communal leader, son of Abraham Senior Teixeria. He became head of the Portuguese community in Amsterdam. He was unsuccessful in his attempt to intercede on behalf of the Jews of Austria when they were threatened with expulsion in 1670.

Temple (i) (Hebrew 'bet ha-mikdash', 'hakhal') In Jewish usage the name given to the principal place of worship of the Jews in Jerusalem until 70CE. The First Temple was built by Solomon c.950 BCE. It served as a shrine for the Ark of the Covenant and the sacred vessels, and as a place for the offering of sacrifice and prayer. It consisted of an outer court opening into a hall, behind which was the shrine; beyond the shrine was the inner sanctum (the Holy of Holies). These areas were surrounded by cells and rooms used for storing vessels and treasure. Worship was performed in the shrine, which was entered from the hall through two cedar doors. The Holy of Holies, where the Ark was kept, had a raised floor and was windowless. A small altar made of cedar overlaid with gold stood in the shrine at the entrance to the Holy of Holies. The main bronze altar was in the court before the hall and was surrounded by a ditch. On the south-east side of the court stood a huge cauldron resting on figures of bulls; close by were bronze bases for the lavers. At the entrance from the court to the hall were two columns, Boaz and Jachin. Solomon's Temple was destroyed in 586 BCE by the Babylonian troops of Nebuchadnezzar. The Temple was rebuilt in the Persian period, and completed and dedicated in 515 BCE. Herod the Great completely reconstructed the building, beginning in 55 BCE and (according to St John's Gospel) continuing for 46 years. The Temple was destroyed by the Romans in 70 CE. The only part surviving is the Western Wall.

Temple Scroll One of the Dead Sea Scrolls. It originated in the community of Qumran around the 2nd century BCE. It contains quotations from the Bible, rewritten so that God speaks throughout in the first person. The text describes the Temple, various festivals and the king's army; it also contains halakhot on a number of topics.

Temple tax According to Exodus 30:13, each Israelite paid half a shekel for the maintenance of the sanctuary. During the Second Temple period the half-shekel was levied as an annual tax on Palestine and the diaspora; the tractate Shekalim in the Mishnah deals with its collection. After the destruction of the Temple in 70, the Romans replaced this tax by a compulsory levy paid into the 'fiscus judaicus'. The Zionist Organisation revived the tax by a decree passed at the First Zionist Conference in 1897.

Temurah ('Exchange') Sixth tractate in the Mishnah order of Kodashim. It deals with the regulations concerning the exchange of an animal consecrated for sacrifice and associated problems (Leviticus 27:9–10).

Tenant One who occupies land or property under a landlord. According to talmudic law, a distinction is made between agricultural and urban tenancy. In the former case, the types of tenant are recognised: the 'aris' and the 'ḥokher'. The aris gives the landlord a percentage of the produce from the land; the ḥokher pays a fixed amount in rent. In both kinds of agricultural tenancy local custom served as the prime factor determining the law regarding landlord and tenant relationship. In the Mishnah urban tenancy is treated separately. The provisions of the lease grant him possession of the property for the duration of the lease. Acceptance of advance payment has the binding character of a lease. If a term is not specified for the duration of the lease, it is presumed that the rental is for the winter season or from the summer period. However, in large towns tenancies were assumed to be of 12 months' duration.

Ten Commandments [Decalogue] Ten laws proclaimed by God to Moses on Mount Sinai (Exodus 20:2–14; Deuteronomy 5:6–18). Moses wrote them on two stone tablets, which he later broke in anger when he found the Israelites worshipping the Golden Calf. He re-ascended Mount Sinai and brought down a second set of tablets inscribed with the Ten Commandments, which were placed in the Ark of the Covenant.

Ten Days of Penitence [Hebrew 'Aseret Yeme Teshuvah'] The name given to the first ten days of Tishri, from the beginning of the New Year to the close of the Day of Atonement. According to tradition, individuals are judged at the New Year and the judgement is proclaimed on the Day of Atonement. Clemency may be obtained through sincere repentance during the Ten Days of Penitence. Penitential prayers ('seliḥot') are said daily, fasts take place, and there are alterations to the liturgy emphasising God's kingship.

Ten Lost Tribes of Israel The ten tribes consistute the population of the northern kingdom of Israel from the time of Jacob until they were taken into captivity by the Assyrians in the period

721–715 BCE. They never re-emerged from this captivity and are assumed to have intermarried with the Assyrians. Those who remained in Israel intermarried with the Canaanites and became Samaritans. It was hoped that the lost tribes would be rediscovered intact. Ezekiel associated such a rediscovery with the final redemption of the Jews, involving the reunion of the whole house of Israel (Ezekiel 37:16). Various travellers reported their discovery. Eldad ha-Dani claimed that they were in the mountains of Africa. Benjamin of Tudela heard of them in Central Asia. David Reuveni stated that he was the brother of one of their rulers in the region of Arabia, and Antonio de Montezinos reported that he had found them in South America. Shabbetai Tzevi appointed rulers over the various tribes.

Ten Martyrs The name given to ten rabbis, who according to tradition were executed by the Roman Government after the Bar Kokhba revolt. They were killed for defying the prohibition against Jewish observances and Jewish religious teaching. Their identity is uncertain and not all of those usually named among the ten lived at the time of the Bar Kokhba revolt. The following names are those most commonly found in the various sources that list the Ten Martyrs: Akiva ben Joseph, Ishmael ben Elisha, Eleazar ben Dama, Ḥanina ben Teradyon, Judah ben Bava, Ḥutzpit the Interpreter, Yeshevav the Scribe, Eleazar ben Shammua, Ḥanina ben Ḥakhinai, Simeon ben Gamaliel I and Ishmael the high priest.

Tephillah A prayer, or especially, the Amidah or Eighteen Benedictions. The term is also used by the Sephardim to mean a prayer book.

Tephillat ha-Derekh ('Prayer for the journey') Prayer recited before setting off on a journey. Its original text ran: 'May it be Thy will that Thou leadest me in peace and settest my steps. Blessed be Thou who hearest prayer'. Under Kabbalistic influence, additional verses were interspersed with the phrases of the prayer

Tephillin ('phylacteries') (i) Name given to two small leather boxes each containing four passages from the Torah written on parchment (Exodus 13:1–10; Exodus 11–16; Deuteronomy 6:4–9; Deuteronomy 13–21). In accordance with Deuteronomy 6:8 they are worn by adult male Jews, bound by leather straps to the arm and the head. Their purpose is to remind the wearer to keep the law. Tephillin are worn on weekdays, but not on Sabbaths and festivals. Custom differs regarded their use on the intermediate days of festivals. Originally they were worn all day, but they are now worn only during morning prayer (only during afternoon prayer on the Ninth of Av).

Tephillin ('Phylacteries') (ii) Minor pseudo-talmudic tractate It discusses regulations regarding the wearing of tephllin and their preparation.

Terah, Father of Abraham He left Ur of the Chaldees with his son and nephew Lot. Intending to journey to the land of Canaan, they stopped at Haran, where Terah died at the age of 205 (Genesis 11:31–2).

Teraphim Household gods. According to Genesis, images of the household gods were stolen by Rachel from her father's house (Genesis 32:19). Teraphim were denounced by the Israelite religion, but were nevertheless frequently used perhaps for divination.

Tere Asar (Aramaic: '12') Traditional name for the books of the 12 Minor Prophets.

Terephah ('unfit') Term applied to food that is not kosher. The Sephardi word is 'tareph'.

Terumot ('Heave offerings') Sixth tractate in the Mishnah order of Zeraim. It deals with the heave offering due to the priest from the Israelite (Numbers 18:8; Deuteronomy 18:4), and the Levite (Numbers 18:25ff).

Testaments of the 12 Patriarchs Pseudepigraphic work. Dating from the Second Temple period, it purports to give the testaments of the sons of Jacob to their descendants. The testaments are modelled on the blessing of Jacob to his sons (Genesis 49). Each of the patriarchs describes the merits and sins of his own life and instructs his children to live righteously. Most of the testaments contain an apocalyptic ending.

Tet Ninth letter of the Hebrew alphabet. Its numerical value is nine.

Tetragrammaton (Greek: 'four letters') A word of four letters, especially the Hebrew name of God. Because the Jews would not pronounce the divine name itself, God was referred to by various other names descriptive of his attributes.

Tetrarch Subordinate ruler. The title was given to minor rulers in the provinces of Judea and Syria during the Roman period. They were appointed by the Roman emperor and were subject to him. Important tetrarchs of Jewish history include Phasael, Herod Antipas and Herod Philippus.

Tevel Agricultural produce which has not been tithed and which therefore may not be put to profane use. On the basis of Deuteronomy 26:13 the rabbis ruled that liability for tithes begins only when the crop is gathered in. Thus tevel could be eaten by the agricultural worker in the field.

Tevet Tenth month of the Jewish year. Tevet (the Fast of Tevet) commemorates the besieging of Jerusalem by Nebuchadnezzar (II King's 25:1).

Tevel Yom ('one who has bathed that day') Tenth tractate in the Mishnah order of Tohorot. It deals with the minor degree of ritual uncleanness which remains after ritual bathing until sunset.

Thank offering Sacrifice offered in the Temple as a token of thanks to God. The regulations for such an offering are contained in Leviticus 7:12–15.

Thanksgiving (Hebrew 'berakhah') Biblical expressions of thanksgiving frequently begin with the word 'Barukh' (Blessed be). Thus the statutory opening formula of benedictions said in thanksgiving to God before enjoying anything in the world is 'Blessed art thou, O Lord our God, King of the universe'. Other prayers of thanksgiving are recited on special occasions, on hearing good news, on the occurrence of joyful events, and on deliverance from evil. Thanksgiving is the theme of many of the psalms included in the liturgy.

Thanksgiving Psalms One of the Dead Sea Scrolls. It contains many prayers, beginning with the words 'I thank thee, O Lord'.

Theatre Jewish playwrights are known to have been active in Alexandria as early as the 2nd century BCE, but during the Roman period, Jewish sages denounced the theatre. From the medieval period Purim farces were performed in central and Western Europe. In the 16th century Marrano poets wrote plays in Spanish and Portuguese, and Jews in Italy took an active role in the theatre. An attempt was made in Venice in the 17th century to establish a ghetto theatre. From the 18th century there were outstanding Jewish actors in Western Europe, and German Jewry produced famous theatre critics and dramatists. In Eastern Europe and later the US, Yiddish theatre played an important role in Jewish life. In the modern period Jews have been involved in drama, film and television.

Theft (Hebrew 'genevah') In Jewish law, theft is distinguished from robbery:

a thief is one who appropriates another person's property secretly, while a robber steals without attempting to hide the deed. The convicted thief must pay double the value of the stolen property (Exodus 22:3). It is not permissible to buy stolen property, or property which the prospective buyer has reason to believe may have been stolen (for example, from an employer).

Theism (from Greek 'theos': god) Belief in the existence of gods, or (specifically) a god; having an existence independent of the world which he has created, and sustaining a personal relationship with his creatures.

Theocracy (from Greek 'theos': god) Form of government directly by God or through a priestly order; the term is used specifically of the Jewish commonwealth from Moses to the time of the monarchy. Josephus used the term to describe the government of the Jewish people under Moses. Samuel was reluctant to create a monarchy because he feared it might undermine the recognition of God as ruler and his commandments as law. According to tradition, Jewish kings were ruled by God's appointment and were pledged to heed the voice of the prophet who spoke in God's name. Persian and Hellenistic kings recognised the high priest as the supreme Jewish authority and the Torah as the basis of law. This belief was supported by the Maccabees but ended by Herod.

Theodicy (from Greek 'theos': god; and 'dikē': justice) Vindication of God's justice in the face of human suffering. The problem of the suffering of the righteous exercised biblical writers, rabbis, medieval philosophers, Kabbalists and modern Jewish thinkers.

Theology The study of the existence and nature of the divine. Although Jews have traditionally been more concerned with religious practice than orthodox beliefs, theological speculation has been current among Jewish thinkers from early times. Particularly in the Middle Ages Jewish scholars produced systematic expositions of theology. Prominent among them were Saadyah Gaon's *Beliefs and Opinions,* Judah ha-Levi's *Kuzari,* and Moses Maimonides' *Guide for the Perplexed.* The theological tradition was continued in modern times by such thinkers as Moses Mendelssohn, Leo Baeck and Franz Rosenzweig.

Therapeutae (Latin: 'Healers') Jewish religious sect in Egypt in the 1st century. It was described by Philo. Its members (both male and female) lived in solitude, poverty and (so far as possible) celibacy, spending their time in meditation on sacred writings. Every 50th day they gathered for a meal, and spent the night in religious singing and dancing.

Theudas (fl. 2st cent) Palestinian religious leader and pseudo-messiah. He persuaded the people to gather up their possessions and follow him to the Jordan, where at his command he claimed the river would part. The Roman procurator Cuspius Fadus sent cavalry after them. Theudas was caught and decapitated, and his head was taken to Jerusalem.

Thirteen attributes of mercy The attributes of God, according to Exodus 34:6–7. Before the Tablets of the Law were given to Moses a second time, God proclaimed himself: (1), the Lord (2), God (3), merciful (4), gracious (5), long-suffering (6), or abundant in loving kindness (7), and truth (8), keeping mercy unto the thousandth generation (9), forgiving iniquity (10), transgression (11) and sin (12) and able to clear the guilty (13). Alternative enumerations of the attributes have been formulated. The 13 attributes are of importance in the liturgy, especially in the penitential prayers recited on fasts, in the seliḥot days before and after the New Year, and in the service of the Day of Atonement.

Thirteen principles of faith   Principles of the Jewish faith enumerated by Maimonides. They state that: (1) God the Creator exists; (2) God is one; (3) God is incorporeal; (4) God is eternal; (5) prayer is for God alone; (6) the prophets are true; (7) Moses is supreme above all other prophets; (8) the Pentateuch was given to Moses; (9) the Torah is immutable; (10) God is omniscient; (11) divine retribution will be carried out; (12) the Messiah will come; and (13) the dead will be raised. These principles are reproduced in the prayer book.

Thirty-two paths of wisdom   Mystical concept, originating in the Sepher Yetzirah. The '32 Paths of Hidden Wisdom' used there refers to a system based on the 22 letters of the Hebrew alphabet and the ten elementary and primordial numbers that constitute the elements of Creation. In Kabbalistic sources the notion of the 32 paths was re-interpreted in terms of the doctrine of the sephirot: the highest sephirah emanates or descends into the lower sephirot by way of 32 paths or channels.

Thomashefsky, Boris (1866–1939)   American Yiddish actor, of Ukrainian origin. He went to the US in 1881. He produced, wrote, adapted and acted in many plays performed at New York's Yiddish theatres. He also initiated the visit of a Yiddish theatre company from London.

Thon, Osias (1870–1936)   Polish rabbi and Zionist, brother of Yaakov Thon. He was born in Lemberg. He became an associate of Theodor Herzl, who he assisted in preparing the First Zionist Congress. From 1897 he was a rabbi in Kraków. In 1919 he was appointed Vice-President of the Comité des Délégations Juives at the Paris Peace Conference; in the same year he was elected to the Sejm, where he served until 1935 and was head of the Jewish members'

organisation. He wrote a biography of Herzl and essays on Zionism.

Thon, Yaakov (1880–1950)   Palestinian communal leader, brother of Onias Thon. He was born in Lemberg, and in 1907 went to Palestine, where he became Arthur Ruppin's deputy in the management of the Palestine Office of the Zionist Organisation; he took Ruppin's place during his exile in Turkey (1916–20). In 1917 Thon organised the Jewish community council in Jerusalem, which he served as its chairman. Later he prepared a report on conditions in Palestine during World War I. In 1921 he became Managing Director of the Palestine Land Development Corporation.

Three Weeks (Hebrew 'Bein ha-Mezarim': lit. between the straits)   Period of mourning observed from 17 Tammuz (when the walls of Jerusalem were breached by Nebuchadnezzar) to 9 Av (the anniversary of the destruction of the Temple). The celebration of marriages, other festive occasions, and cutting of the hair are forbidden during this time; during the latter part of it the eating of meat and the drinking of wine are proscribed except on the Sabbath. On the three Sabbaths the prophetical readings in the synagogue consist of prophecies of doom (Jeremiah 1,2, and Isaiah 1).

Throne of God   Visions of the throne of God are recorded in various books of the Bible (1 Kings 22:19; Isaiah 6:1; Ezekiel 1). Ezekiel's vision gave rise to the tradition of chariot mysticism (maaseh merkavah); this evoked ecstatic states, in which the mystic's soul left the body, ascended to heaven, and there beheld the vision of the Throne of God.

Ticho, Anna (1894–1980)   Israeli artist. She was born in Brünn, Moravia, and went to Jerusalem in 1912. She made numerous drawings of the Judean landscape.

Tik Sephardi term for the wood or metal case in which the Scroll of the Law is kept.

Tikkun ('passage') (i) Name given to any of several collections of biblical, Mishnaic and Kabbalistic passages instituted by Kabbalists for reading on special occasions. The Tikkun Ḥatzot ('Midnight service') consists of selections of psalms, Lamentations and petitions recited at midnight in memory of the destruction of the Temple. The Tikkun lel Shavuot is read on the night of Shavuot. The Tikkun Hoshanah Rabbah includes readings from Deuteronomy, Psalms and the *Zohar*, and special Kabbalistic prayers recited on the night of Hoshanah Rabbah. A similar tikkun is observed on the night of 7 Adar (the anniversary of the birth and death of Moses) and 5 Av (the anniversary of the death of Isaac Luria).

Tikkun sopherim ('scribal emendation') Term used specifically of any of the 18 emendations of the Bible attributed to the scribes; they deal mostly with pronominal suffixes. The term is also applied to an unpainted copy of the printed Pentateuch, which is used for practice in reading of the Scroll of the Law.

Tiktin, Gedaliah (c.1810–1886) German rabbi, son of Solomon Tiktin. He became Landrabbiner in Breslau in 1854. He joined his father in a feud with Abraham Geiger.

Tiktin, Solomon (1791–1843) German rabbi. He became a rabbi in Breslau. In 1838 he opposed the appointment of the reformer Abraham Geiger as assistant rabbi, preacher and dayyan in Breslau. He and his son, Gedaliah Tiktin, engaged in a campaign against Geiger, which divided the community.

Timerman, Jacobo (1923–1999) Argentine journalist. He was born in Russia, and went to Argentina in 1942. He became a political journalist and founded *La opinión* in Buenos Aires.

Tiomkin, Vladimir (1860–1927) Russian Zionist leader. He was born in Yelizavetgrad in Ukraine. He was a founder of the Ahavat Zion Society in St Petersburg, and later became head of the executive committee of the Russian Ḥovevei Zion in Jaffa. He returned to Russia and joined the Zionist movement, participating in Zionist congresses. During World War I he directed relief projects in southern Russia. After the 1917 Revolution, he resumed his Zionist activities. In 1920 he settled in Paris and joined Vladimir Jabotinsky's Revisionist Zionist movement.

Tirado, Joseph (c.1560–1625) Portuguese religious leader. He was born in Portugal into a family of Converos. He settled in Amsterdam, where he returned to Judaism. In c.1608 he helped to found the first Sephardi community in the city. Before 1616 he went to Palestine and settled in Jerusalem.

Tish (Yiddish: lit. 'table') In Ḥasidic tradition, a meal taken by the tzaddik with his followers. Three such meals are held on Sabbaths, holidays and the anniversaries of the deaths of tzaddikim. During the tish the tzaddik gives a discourse, sings hymns with his followers, and distributes shirayim; on the Sabbath the proceedings conclude with dancing.

Tishby, Isaiah (1908–1992) Israeli scholar. He was born at Sándor Schwartz in Sanislo, Hungary. In 1933 he settled in Palestine, where he became a professor at the Hebrew University. His publications include studies of the kabbalah.

Tishri Seventh month in the Jewish calendar. The following festivals take place during Tishri: 1 Tishri (1 and 2 Tishri in the diaspora), Rosh ha-Shanah (New Year); 10 Tishri, Yom Kippur (Day of Atonement); 15–21 Tishri, Sukkot

(Tabernacles); 22 Tishri, Shemini Atzeret (Eighth Day of Solemn Assembly; in the diaspora it is observed also on the 23rd as Simḥat Torah (Rejoicing in the Law). The Fast of Gedaliah takes place on 3 Tishri.

Tithe (Hebrew 'maaser')   Tenth part of one's produce, set aside as a religious offering. According to Jewish law, there are various types. The 'first tithe' (Numbers 18:24) was given to the Levites after the heave offering ('terumah') for the priests had been separated from it. During the Second Temple period the first tithe was given as a whole to the priests. This subject is dealt with in the tractate Maaserot in the Mishnah. The 'second tithe' (Leviticus 27:30–31; Deuteronomy 14:22–26) was a tenth part of the first tithe, and was consumed by the owner himself in Jerusalem; it applied in the 1st, 2nd, 4th and 5th years in the Sabbatical cycle, and is dealt with in the tractate Maaser Sheni in the Mishnah. The 'poor tithe' (Deuteronomy 14:28–29; 26:12) was calculated in the same way as the second tithe and was paid in the 3rd and 6th years of the Sabbatical cycle; it was given to the poor. The 'tithe of the animal' (Leviticus 27:32) took place three times a year when the animals were counted; the selected animal was sacrificed. The animal tithe is dealt with in the tractate Bekhorot in the Mishnah. The Levites also paid a tithe from what they received (Numbers 18:26), in the form of an offering to God.

Tobiads   Name given to the descendants of Tobiah (fl. 3rd cent. BCE), a landowner who married the sister of the high priest Onias III. In the struggle over Palestine between Egypt and Syria, Hyrcanus, the younger son of Tobiah's son Joseph, supported the Ptolemies, whereas Joseph's other sons supported the Seleucid Antiochus III. When Antiochus IV Epiphanes came to power, Hyrcanus committed suicide. The other Tobiads encouraged the Hellenising movement that supported Antiochus IV, who replaced the high priest Onias III with Jason. Later Antiochus deposed Jason in favour of Menelaus. Jason endeavoured to regain power, but Menelaus and his followers reported that an anti-Seleucid revolt was taking place in Jerusalem. This led to Antiochus' persecution of the Jews. The Hasmonean uprising (c.160 BCE) put an end to the Tobiads as an important influence in Jewish life.

Tobiah ben Eliezer (fl. 11th cent.) Bulgarian talmudist and poet. He wrote *Lekaḥ Tov* (or *Pesikta Zutarta)*, a midrashic commentary on the Pentateuch and the five Scrolls.

Tobiah ben Moses (fl. 11th cent.) Turkish Karaite scholar, biblical exegete and liturgical poet. After studying in Jeruslaem under Yeshurah ben Judah, he lived in Constantinople. He translated the Arabic works of his sect into Hebrew. His writings include *Yehi Meorot* on the biblical commandments, *Otzar Neḥmad* on Leviticus, and *Zot ha-Torah* on the Pentateuch.

Tobit   Apocryphal book. It describes how Tobit, a blind exile at Nineveh, sent his son Tobias to Persia to collect a debt. On his journey, Tobias visited a relative, whose daughter Sarah had been married seven times, but each of whose bridegrooms had been killed on the wedding night by the demon Ashmedai out of jealousy. With the assistance of the Archangel Raphael, the demon was exorcised. Tobias then married Sarah and Tobit's blindness was cured.

Tochis (Yiddish)   Buttocks.

Todd, Michael [Goldbogen, Avrom] (1907–58)   American film producer. Born in Minneapolis, Minnesota, he became a building contractor. He worked as a theatrical producer and later formed the Magna corporation. His first film was *Oklahoma!* And he also produced *Around the World in Eighty Days*.

Tohorah [taharah] ('purification')
Ceremonial washing of the dead before
burial. the ceremony is performed by
the Ḥevra Kaddisha. The body is laid
on a board and thoroughly rubbed and
cleansed with lukewarm water. The
head and the front part of the body are
scrubbed with a beaten egg, and nine
measures of water are poured over the
body while it is held upright. The body
is then dried and dressed in a shroud.

Tohorot ('purifications') (i) The
rules of ritual cleanliness. The term is
also applied to foods that may be eaten
only by those who are in a state of
cleanliness.

Tohorot ('purifications') (ii) Sixth
order of the Mishnah. It deals with the
laws concerning purity and impurity.

Tohorot ('purifications') (iii) Fifth
tractate in the Mishnah order of
Tohorot. It deals with minor degrees of
ritual unleanliness, the effects of which
last only until sunset.

Tokheḥah ('reproof') The name
given to two sections of the Pentateuch
(Leviticus 26 and Deuteronomy 28),
which prophesy a series of punishments
to be visited upon the Israelites if they
forsake the Torah.

**Toledano, Yaakov Mosheh (1880–
1960)** Israeli rabbi. He was born in
Tiberias. He served as a rabbi in Alexandria, and in 1941 was appointed
Chief Sephardi Rabbi of Tel Aviv. He
served as Minister for Religious Affairs
in the Israeli Government.

**Toledot, Yeshu ('Histories of
Jesus')** Medieval Hebrew work on
the life of Jesus. It describes Jesus as the
illegitimate son of Joseph Pandera. It
records that he performed miracles but
was conquered by an emissary of the
rabbis and condemned to death.

**Toleranzpatent (German: 'edict of
toleration')** Law issued by Emperor
Joseph II on 2 January 1782. It relieved

the Jews in the Austrian dominions
from various disabilities, and encouraged them to engage in agriculture and
handcrafts.

Tombs Jewish tombs in Palestine initially consisted of rock-cut chambers.
In the Hellenistic and Roman periods,
the tomb was commonly one of a series
of such chambers linked by doors or
passages, in which bodies were placed
in cists or sarcophagi on ledges or in
galleries; arched niches containing
cists began to be used in the 3rd century. Large structures of this type are
known as catacombs. Tombs or mau-
solea above ground also originated during the Hellenistic period. Later individual tombs became common; they
were marked by upright or recumbent
tombstones bearing inscriptions (often
in Hebrew).

Topol, Ḥayyim (b.1935) Israeli actor.
He was born in Tel Aviv. He appeared
at the Hafia Municipal Theatre, and
later in *Fiddler on the Roof* in Tel Aviv.
Subsequently he starred in the film production of the play.

Torah ('Law') [Pentateuch] In the
narrow sense the term is synonymous
with Pentateuch. The Pentateuch (also
known as the Five Books of Moses) is
the Written Law. The five books are
Genesis, Exodus, Leviticus, Numbers and Deuteronomy). According
to tradition, they were given by God
to Moses on Mount Sinai. Along with
the Written Law, God gave Moses a
detailed explanation of its commandments (known as the Oral Law or Oral
Torah). Thus, in its broad sense the
term Torah refers to both the Written
and Oral Law.

**Torah, study of the (Hebrew 'talmud
Torah')** The study of the Torah is
a religious duty; the blessing preceding the reading of the Shema in the
morning and evening services asks for
grace to carry out this duty. Rabbinic
Judaism stresses that when groups (or

individuals) engage in such study, the divine presence dwells among them.

Torah ornaments General term for the covering and decoration of the Scroll of the Law. Special coverings for the scroll are mentioned in the *Talmud*; they assumed their present form in the Middle Ages. The binder ('mappah') is used to fasten the scroll and a mantle ('me'il') is placed over it. The mantle is surmounted with a silver crown ('keter', 'atarah'). In medieval Spain it was common to decorate the ends of the staves on which the scroll was rolled with fruit-shaped ornaments known initially as 'tappuḥim' (apples), and later as 'rimmonim' (pomegranates). In Italy, the crown and rimmonim were used together. In Ashkenazi communities a silver plaque ('tas') was placed on the scroll, and a pointer ('yad') made of precious metal and used in the reading of the law, was hung over it. In oriental and Sephardi communities the Torah scroll was kept in a wooden or metal case ('tik').

Torres, Luis de (fl. 15th–16th cent.) Spanish explorer. He was interpreter to Christopher Columbus on the expedition of 1492 which led to the discovery of the New World. Born a Jew, Torres was baptised before the expedition set sail.

Tort In legal usage, an act that damages a person, his property or his reputation, and which demands compensation; default on a contract is also a tort. The talmudic tractate Nezikin deals with legislation regarding tort in Jewish law.

Tosaphot ('addenda') Critical and explanatory notes on the *Talmud*, composed by French and German scholars from the 12th century to the 14th. These scholars, known as tosaphists, initially produced supplements to Rashi's commentary on the *Talmud*, but eventually evolved their own method of talmudic study. The first tosaphists were Rashi's

two sons-in-law, Meir ben Samuel and Judah ben Nathan. The greatest was his grandson Jacob ben Meir, known as Rabbenu Tam. Other important tosaphists were Samuel ben Meir, Samson ben Abraham of Sens, Judah ben Isaac of Paris, and Samuel of Falaise.

Tosephta ('Addition') Tannaitic work that parallels and supplements the Mishnah. It dates from around the 2nd century. It has six orders with the same names as those of the Mishnah. Some of its paragraphs (known as 'baraitot') are alternative versions of Mishnaic paragraphs; others supplement the Mishnah or provide elucidation; and still others are independent of Mishnaic law. Many of the baraitot in the Tosephta are identical to or are versions of baraitot quoted in the *Talmud*.

Touro, Abraham (1774–1882) American philanthropist, brother of Judah Touro. He was born in Newport, Rhode Island, and with his brother helped to support Newport's synagogue. His will made possible the building of residential units in what later became the new city of Jerusalem.

Touro, Judah (1775–1854) American philanthropist, brother of Abraham Touro. He was born in Newport, Rhode Island. He worked as a merchant and supported Christian and Jewish charities.

Touroff, Nissan (1877–1953) American educator. He served as Director of the Bureau of Hebrew Education in Palestine from 1914 to 1919. He was Dean of the Boston Hebrew Teachers' College (1921–26), and taught at the Jewish Institute of Religion.

Tradition Teachings and laws passed on from one generation to another. This oral tradition was collected and recorded in the Mishnah and Gemora and in later rabbinic responsa. Orthodox Judaism regards itself as the upholder of the Jewish tradition.

Trani, Isaiah (ben Mali [Elijah] di (fl. 12th cent.) Italian talmudist. He was born in southern Italy but lived in the north. His commentaries on the *Talmud* carried the conception of contemporary French tosaphists to Italy.

Trani, Joseph di (1568–1639) Palestinian rabbi and scholar, son of Moses ben Joseph di Trani. He was born in Safed and founded a yeshivah there. Later he settled in Jerusalem, where he did research on the design and plan of the Temple. He returned to Safed and became head of the Sephardi community. Eventually he moved to Constantinople, where he directed a yeshivah, and became Chief Rabbi of Turkey.

Trani, Moses ben Joseph di (1505–1585) Palestinian rabbi. He was born in Salonica. He was one of the four scholars ordained by Jacob Berab in his attempt to reintroduce ordination and establish an authoritative Jewish leadership. Trani served as a rabbi and dayyan for 54 years, eventually becoming spiritual head of the Safed community.

Translations The rise of communities of Aramaic- and Greek-speaking Jews during the Second Temple period created the need for translations of the Bible, the Apocrypha and the Pseudepigrapha from Hebrew into those languages. Until 1200 the bulk of translations from other languages into Hebrew was of Arabic works, and in the 13th century translators turned their attention to Arabic philosophical and scientific texts. After 1250 a number of Latin texts were translated. During the Renaissance and the Reformation period the process was reversed and Hebrew works, such as mystical writings, grammars and rabbinic texts were translated into Latin. Scientific translations from many languages into Hebrew flourished from the 18th century. The creation of a Jewish State stimulated the translation into modern Hebrew of a variety of works of all kinds, from fiction to scholarship.

Travellers From the earliest period of the diaspora Jews have, sometimes perforce, sometimes voluntarily, travelled widely. The memoirs of some Jewish travellers are valuable sources of information about the traditions of the various communities they visited. In the 8th century a deputation sent by Charlemagne to the caliph Haroun al-Raschid included a Jew named Isaac. Jewish merchants known as Radanites, undertook journeys from Europe to the Orient in the 9th century, and at about that tine Eldad ha-Dani made numerous journeys in Spain and North Africa. In c.970 the Caliph of Córdoba sent a deputation to Germany including Ibrahim ibn Jakub. Perhaps the best-known Jewish traveller was Benjamin of Tudela, who in the 12th century journeyed widely in Europe and the Middle East. A later notable Jewish traveller was Pethahiah of Regensburg, and others of the medieval period include Abraham ibn Ezra, Judah al-Harizi and Estori ha-Parḥi. In the 15th–17th centuries some Jews went on English and Portuguese expeditions of exploration. Like many of his predecessors, the late 18th century traveller Samuel Romanelli of Mantua left a written account of his experiences. In the 19th century a number of Jewish explorers were active in Africa and Asia: Joseph Wolff travelled to Bokhara, Nathaniel Isaacs explored Zululand and Natal, Arminius Vámbéry went to Central Asia, and Emin Pasha travelled to central Africa.

Trayf (Yiddish) Any food which is not kosher. An animal which is not slain according to ritual law.

Treason The Bible recounts a number of instances of rebellion and regicide (as in II Samuel 18:14; II Kings 11:1). The imposition of the death penalty for disobedience to the King is based on the declaration made by the people to Joshua that whoever rebelled against his word should be put to death (Joshua 1:18). Rabbinic law has transferred rights previously enjoyed by the king to the State.

Tree of Life   One of the two trees mentioned in the biblical account of the Creation as growing in the Garden of Eden (Genesis 2:9). Whoever ate from it lived forever. After Adam and Eve broke God's commandment and ate fruit from the second of the trees, the Tree of Knowledge of Good and Evil, they were expelled from the garden.

Treinin, Avner (1928–2011)   Israeli poet. He was born in Tel Aviv and taught chemistry at the Hebrew University. His poems are concerned with the Holocaust and recent events in Jewish history.

Trespass   Legal term applied in Jewish usage to a variety of acts, including offences against another person's rights or property, transgressions against divine law and certain specific offences that require a particular form of sacrifice.

Trespass offering   Sacrifice required of a person guilty of certain offences or trespasses. The acts for which such an offering was laid down were: perjury committed in denying a robbery; profane use of sacred objects; and violations of a betrothed handmaid. In cases of doubt concerning the commission of a trespass, the offering might be suspended. A trespass offering was also brought by a Nazirite after being cleansed from ritual defilement and by a leper after his purification. The sacrifice consisted of a two-year-old ram, which was consumed by the priests.

Trèves, Johanan (b.1429)   French rabbi, son of Mattathias ben Joseph Trèves. When his father died he became Chief Rabbi of Paris. Later Isaiah ben Abba Mari claimed the sole right of appointing rabbis in France and of conducting a yeshivah. With the help of Meir ben Baruch of Vienna, he attempted to remove Johanan from

his post. The expulsion of Jews from France in 1394 ended the dispute, and Johanan went to Italy.

Trèves, Mattathias ben Joseph (c.1325–c.1385)   French rabbi. He was born in Provence, and lived in Spain. He returned to France when the edict of expulsion of the Jews was repealed in 1361. He founded a yeshivah in Paris, and in 1363 became the city's Chief Rabbi.

Tribes of Israel   The 12 tribes into which the Ancient Israelites were divided. They derived from the sons of Jacob: Reuben, Simeon, Levi, Judah, Issachar, Zebulun, Joseph, Benjamin, Dan, Naphtali, Gad and Asher (Genesis 49). Moses conferred the priestly office on the tribe of Levi, and divided the tribe of Joseph into Ephraim and Manasseh. After Solomon's death the country split into two kingdoms: the tribes of Judah and Simeon, and most of the tribe of Benjamin peopled the southern kingdom of Judah, and the remaining tribes the northern kingdom of Israel. After the invasion of the Assyrians under Tiglath-Pileser III and Sargon in the 8th century BCE, the northern tribes were exiled. A large part of the population of the southern kingdom was exiled by Nebuchadnezzar to Babylon in 586 BCE.

Tribunal   Court of justice, or a judicial body. During the biblical period, the tribunals of the Israelites were constituted by rulers of groups of 10, 50, 100, and 1,000 families (Exodus 18:21–26). After the institution of the monarchy, elders sitting at the city gateway served as a tribunal subject to the authority of the judges. Eventually by the Second Temple period the bet din of three persons (or 23 in the cases of regional tribunal acting in major cases) constituted the tribunal. The Sanhedrin of 71, also established in the Second Temple period, had overriding authority. Throughout the Middle Ages a bet din of three scholars served as the normal Jewish tribunal. During the ghetto period, lay leaders of the community occasionally constituted a tribunal to arbitrate civil cases.

Trietsch, Davis (1870–1935) German Zionist writer. He was born in Dresden. During a period spent in the US (1893–99), he wrote several works on Jewish migration. He participated in the First Zionist Congress (1897), advocating Jewish settlement in Cyprus and the Sinai peninsula. Later he published schemes for Jewish settlement in Palestine. He himself moved to Palestine in 1932.

Troki, Isaac ben Abraham (c.1533–c.1594) Lithuanian Karaite scholar. He was born in Troki. He wrote an apologia for Judaism *Ḥizzuk ha-Emunah* ('Strengthening the faith').

Trope Traditional formula to which the Torah is intoned.

Trotsky, Leon [Bronstein, Lev Davidovich] (1879–1940) Born in Yanovka in Ukraine, he was involved in revolutionary groups and arrested in 1898 and exiled. He escaped in 1902 and went to London where he joined Lenin. He then moved to Geneva. In 1905 he returned to Russia and was again arrested and exiled in Siberia. He escaped and went to Vienna. During World War I he was in Paris. He then went to New York but returned to Russia in 1917. He was elected to the Central Committee of the Bolshevik party and was an organiser of the October Revolution. Later he came into conflict with Stalin and was exiled.

Trumpeldor, Joseph (1880–1920) Palestinian soldier. He was born in Pyatigorsk in the northern Caucasus. He volunteered for the Russian army and became an officer. In 1912 he moved to Palestine, where he attempted to found a cooperative agricultural settlement. In Egypt during World War I he and Valdimir Jabotinsky tried to establish a Jewish unit to fight against the Turks in Palestine. In 1917 Trumpeldor went to Russia to organise Jewish groups who would settle in Palestine Two years later he returned to Palestine as leader of a pioneer group and organised volunteers to protect Jewish settlements in Upper Galilee.

Tsadeh Eighteenth letter of the Hebrew alphabet. Its numerical value is 90.

Tschernikhovski [Tchernikovski], Shaul (1875–1943) Palestinian Hebrew poet, of Russian origin. He was born in Mikhailovka, and during World War I served in the Russian medical corps. From 1922 to 1931 he lived in Germany, and later moved to Palestine. He wrote poetry, stories, essays and philological studies, and translated ancient and modern verse. His poetry had an important impact on Jewish youth.

Tschlenow, Jehiel (1863–1918) Russian Zionist leader. He was born in Kremenchug in Ukraine, and became a physician. Active in the Ḥibbat Zion movement, he was one of the leaders of the Tziyyone Zion group founded in opposition to the plan for the Jewish homeland in Uganda. In 1906 Tschlenow convened the Helsingfors Conference. He later lived in Copenhagen and London, where he was an active Zionist. After the 1917 Revolution, he returned to Russia and convened a Russian Zionist Conference.

Tsimmes (Yiddish) Side dish of mixed cooked vegetables and fruits, or a dessert of stewed fruits.

Tsinberg, Yisrael (1873–1939) Russian literary historian. He was born in a village near Lanovits, Volhynia, and lived in St Petersburg, where he became head of a chemical laboratory. He published a popular science book in Yiddish, critical and literary-historical studies, and a history of Jewish literature.

Tsuris (Yiddish) Troubles, suffering, or problems.

Tubal-Cain   Son of Lamech. According to Genesis, he was the first craftsman in iron and copper (Genesis 4:22).

Tuchman, Barbara (1912–89)   American historian. She studied at Radcliffe College and was a research assistant at the Institute of Pacific Relations in New York. She then worked for the *Nation*. From 1943 to 1945 she worked at the US Office of War Information. Her works include *Bible and Sword, The Zimmerman Telegram, The Guns of August, The Proud Tower, Stilwell and the American Experience in China, Notes from Asia, The March of Folly* and *A Distant Mirror: The Calamitous 14th Century*.

Tucker, Richard (1916–1975)   American tenor. He was a successful synagogue cantor. From 1945 he made a career as an opera singer at the Metropolitan Opera in New York.

Tucker, Sophie (1889–1966)   Amercian entertainer. She was born in Russia, and went to the US as a child. The songs for which she was known included *My Yidishe Momma*.

Tudesco   (Ladino: 'German')   Sephardi expression applied to the Ashkenazim.

Tugendhold, Jacob (1794–1871)   Polish author. He was born near Kraków. He founded a modern Jewish school in Warsaw, which alienated Orthodox Jews. He served as vice-censor of Hebrew books, and was head of the government rabbinical seminary in Warsaw.

Tumarkin,   Yigal   (b.1933)   Israeli painter and sculptor. He was born in Dresden, and went to Palestine as a child in 1935. Later he lived in Germany, the Netherlands and Paris. He constructed a number of sculptural monuments in Israel.

Tunkel,   Joseph   (1881–1949)   Russian Yiddish humorist and cartoonist. He was born in Bobruisk, Belorussia.

In 1906 he went to the US, where he edited the comic magazines *Der kibitzer* and *Der groyse kundes*. He returned to Warsaw in 1910 and became editor of *Der moment*. In 1939 he fled to France and in 1941 to the US. He wrote under the pseudonym 'Der Tunkeler'.

Tur-Sinai, Naphtali Herz [Torczyner, Harry] (1886–1973)   Israeli philologist and Bible scholar. He was born in Lemberg. In 1933 he went to Palestine, where he taught at the Hebrew University. He wrote commentaries to the Book of Job, a study of Proverbs, essays on Biblical texts, rabbinic Hebrew, and problems in the history of the Hebrew language, and a work on the Lachish Letters.

Twersky   Dynasty of Ḥasidic tzaddikim, active in Chernobyl from around 1750. It was founded by Menaḥem Naḥum, the maggid of Chernobyl. Its influence declined after the Russian Revolution.

Twersky, Menaḥem Naḥum (1730–1783)   Lithuanian Ḥasidic leader. He was a pupil of Israel ben Eliezer Baal Shem Tov and Dov Ber of Mezhirich. He practised as an itinerant preacher, stressing the importance of purifying moral attributes. He was the founder of a dynasty of tzaddikim. His son, Mordecai of Chernobyl (1770–1837), lived in splendour and was greatly revered.

Twersky, Yoḥanan (1900–1967)   Israeli novelist. He was born in Shpikov in Ukraine. He went to the US in 1926 and taught at the Hebrew College in Boston. In 1947 he settled in Israel, where he served on the editorial staff of the Dvir Publishing House in Tel Aviv. His novels include *Uriel Acosta, Aḥad ha-Am, Alfred Dreyfus, Rashi* and *Rom u-Tehom*.

Twilight (Hebrew 'bein ha-arbayim', 'bein ha-shemashot')   The soft light occurring when the sun is just below the horizon, especially after sunset. The period of evening when this light occurs.

For halakhic purposes, it is deemed that as long as only two stars of medium size are visible, it is still twilight; the appearance of the third star marks the onset of night.

Tzaddik ('righteous man') Word used to describe a person of faith and piety. Such figures are praised in the Bible (Habakkuk 2:4; Proverbs 20:7), and the *Talmud* states that the world depends for its continued existence on the presence in every generation of 36 tzaddikim. In the Ḥasidic movement the concept of the tzaddik was developed by Dov Ber of Mezhirich and Jacob Joseph of Polonnoye into one of a spiritual leader. Regarded as the intermediary between God and man, he brought down divine blessings. Individuals frequently visited the tzaddik for advice, and on Sabbath and festivals multitudes of Ḥasidim gathered at his festival table for a meal known as a 'tish'.

Tzarfati [Zafartti], Samuel (fl. 15th–16th cent.) Italian physician. He was in the service of the Medici family in Florence, and of several popes in Rome. He was active in Jewish affairs.

Tzedakah box Box in the synagogue for gifts of money for charity. Located near the door, the contributions left there are used for local and Jewish charities. A box is also passed among the congregation for collections during weekday services and at funerals.

Tzemaḥ, Naḥum David (1890–1939) Theatre producer. He formed a Hebrew dramatic group in Vienna, which became the Ha-Bimah company. From 1930 to 1937 he directed the Tel Aviv Bet Am.

Tzemaḥ, Shelomoh (b.1886) Israeli author, of Polish origin. He lived in Palestine in 1903–09, and again from 1921. His stories describe life in Israel.

Tzaddik ha-din ('justification of the judgement') Term used to acknowledge the justice of any evil occurrence that can be accounted for, including death. By extension it has come to refer to the burial service.

Tzimtzum ('divine contraction') Kabbalistic doctrine which teaches that God makes a space in which the process of creation can take place.

Tzitzit ('fringes') The Bible commands the wearing of fringes on the corners of garments (Numbers 15:37–41). Initially all garments had fringes, but later an undergarment with fringes on the corners ('tallit katan') was devised for daily use.

Tzom ('fast') Term used as a component in the titles of particularly fast days, such as 'Tzom Gedaliah' (Fast of Gedaliah).

Tzur mi-Shello ('Rock from whose store we have eaten') Song sung at the Sabbath table. Its four stanzas correspond to the four benedictions of the Grace after Meals.

Tzur, Yaakov (b.1906) Israeli diplomat and public figure. He was born in Vilnius, and emigrated to Palestine in 1921. He worked in the head office of the Jewish National Fund from 1929 to 1948. After the establishment of the State of Israel, he represented Israel in Argentina and other South American countries, as well as in France. He later returned to Israel where he became Director of the Jewish National Fund.

U

A Jewish couple try for years to become members of an exclusive gentile country club. Finally Melvin and Selma gain membership because they have donated 2 million dollars to the building campaign. Now that they are members, Selma is excited to go to their first dinner. She wears a full-length mink coat and her finest and most expensive flashy jewellery. Upon entering she sees modestly and underdressed women with only the most tasteful jewellery. She realises how out of place she is compared to these gentile women, and loudly exclaims 'GEVALT' (the Yiddish word for shock). Looking around at the other women she says 'Vatever dat means.'

* * * * *

Many Jewish jokes satirise social aspirations. Here a Jewish couple attain membership of an exclusive country club. On their first visit to the club, the wife overdresses. In her embarrassment she utters a Yiddish expression of alarm. Then attempting to disguise her Jewishness, she pretends not to know what she said but expresses her ignorance with a Yiddish accent. The joke mocks social ambition, and stresses that Jewish identity cannot really be hidden.

Uktzin ('Stalks') Twelfth tractate in the Mishnah order of Tohorot. It deals with the transference of ritual impurity to a harvested plant when its roots, stalks or pods come into contact with an unclean person or thing.

Ullendorff, Edward (1920–2011) British scholar. He was born in Zurich. He lectured in Semitics at the University of St Andrews and was later professor at the universities of Manchester and London. He published numerous works on aspects of Semitics, notably in the field of Ethiopian studies.

Ulpan ('study') Institute for advanced study. The term is also used to refer to intensive course in Hebrew for new immigrants to Israel.

Unbeshrieen (Yiddish: lit. 'without evil omen') Exclamation made after praising someone, in order to ward off the evil that is thought to result from good fortune.

Universalism The claim of a religion that it is true for all humankind; it is contrasted with particularism. Judaism combines aspects of both universalism and particularism, since, although it advocates the vision of a united humanity, it perpetuates the survival of the Jewish people as a distinct entity. Jewish universalism is based on the recognition of the absolute sovereignty of God and the doctrine of the messianic redemption of humankind. The theme of the liturgy on high holy days is God's rule over all people, and the second section of the Alenu prayer intercedes for the perfection of humanity in the kingdom of God. Some Jewish thinkers have attempted to reconcile universalism and particularism in the Jewish faith by emphasising Israel's mission as a herald of the divine promise for all people.

Universities   As in other areas of life, Jews have been excluded from university education for much of the history of the Jewish community in the diaspora. Not until Emancipation in the 18th century did Jews begin to be admitted on equal terms with other students to universities in Europe. According to legend, Jews attended the medical school at Salerno during the Middle Ages. In the 14th century a few Jews studied medicine in universities such as that at Montpellier. In 1466 Sicilian Jews obtained royal authorisation to set up their own university, but this does not appear to have occurred. The University of Padua admitted Jews from Italy and elsewhere, again to study medicine, from the 16th century. Dutch universities accepted Jews in the 17th century, German universities in the 18th, and British universities in the 19th. In the US Jewish graduates were not known until the American Revolution. In modern times Jews attend universities throughout the world, and several universities have been founded in Israel.

Unterfirer (Yiddish)   Person (usually a close relative) who, during the marriage ceremony, conducts the bride or groom under the wedding canopy.

Unterman, Issar Yehudah (1886–1976)   Israeli rabbi and scholar. He was born in Brest-Litovsk, Belorussia. He served as rosh yeshivah in Vishova, Lithuania, and later as a rabbi in various Lithuanian communities. After moving to England, he became rabbi of Liverpool in 1924. In 1946 he was appointed Chief Rabbi to the Ashkenazi community in Tel Aviv-Jaffa, and in 1964 Ashkenazi Chief Rabbi of Israel. His writings include *Shevet Mi-Yehudah* on problems of Jewish law.

Urbach, Ephraim Elimelech (1912–1991)   Israeli scholar. He studied at Breslau Rabbinical Seminary and at the universities of Breslau and Rome. He later taught at the Breslau seminary (1935–38). In 1938 he settled in Palestine, where he became a schoolteacher and headmaster of grammar schools in Jerusalem. In 1958 he became Professor of *Talmud* at the Hebrew University. His publications include a study of the tosaphists and their methods.

Uri, Phoebus ben Aaron Levi [Witzenhausen, Joseph] (1623–1715)   Dutch printer. In 1658 he established a press in Amsterdam, which published rabbinical and religious works in Hebrew and Yiddish. He also published the first Yiddish newspaper, *Dienstagishe und Freytagishe Kurant*, from 1680. In 1692 he moved to Zholkva, Poland, where he is supposed to have been invited by the King, John Sobieski, to print Hebrew books.

Uriah ben Shemaiah (fl. 7th cent. BCE)   Israelite prophet. A contemporary of Jeremiah, he foretold the destruction of Jerusalem and Judah. He was persecuted by Jehoiakim and fled to Egypt. Later he was brought back and put to death (Jeremiah 26:20ff).

Uriah the Hittite (fl. 10th cent. BCE)   Israelite soldier. He was in the service of David, who, when he had taken Bathsheba, Uriah's wife, for his mistress, sent Uriah to the front line where he was killed in battle. David's sin was denounced by the prophet Nathan (II Samuel 11–12).

Uriel   According to mystical literature, one of the four Angels of the Presence.

Urim and Thummim   Instruments of divination attached to the breastplate of the high priest. Their form is uncertain. The process of divination involved the use of two stones or tablets by means of which an answer of 'yes' or 'no' could be obtained to important questions (I Samuel 23:10–12; 30:8).

Uris, Leon (1924–2003)   American novelist. He was born in Baltimore. His novels include *Exodus*, which tells the story of the birth of the State of Israel, and *Mila 18*, about the uprising in the Warsaw Ghetto.

Ury, Lesser (1861–1931)   German artist. He was born in Birnbaum, Prussia, and went to Berlin at the age of 12. He studied art in Düsseldorf, Brussels, Paris and Italy, later returning to Berlin. Some of his paintings deal with Jewish themes.

Ushpizin ('visitors')   According to the *Zohar*, the term refers to seven guests (Abraham, Isaac, Jacob, Joseph, Moses, Aaron and David) who in succession visit the sukkah or booth of every pious Jew during the festival of Sukkot to partake of a meal with him.

Usque, Abraham [Pinhel, Duarte] (fl. 16th cent.)   Portuguese printer. He fled from the Inquisition around 1543 to Ferrara, where he became associated with the Hebrew and Italian press established by Yom-Tov ben Levi Athias. His name appears in connection with the translation of the Bible into Italian.

Usque, Samuel (fl. 16th cent.)   Portuguese poet and historian. He was born in Spain, but his family emigrated to Portugal in 1492. His *Consolation for the Tribulations of Israel* was designed to persuade Marranos to return to Judaism.

Usque, Solomon [Lusitano, Salusque] (c.1530–1595)   Portuguese poet. He lived in Italy and Turkey. In collaboration with Lazzaro di Graziano Levi, he wrote the earliest known Jewish drama in the vernacular, a Purim play in Spanish. He also published a Spanish translation of the final part of Petrarch's sonnets. In Constantinople he engaged in Hebrew printing.

Ussishkin, Menaḥem Mendel (1863–1941)   Russian Zionist leader. He was born in Dubrovno in the district of Mohilev in Belorussia. He moved to Moscow in 1871. He was a founder of the Zionist youth group Bilu in 1882, and of the Bene Zion society in 1884. In 1897 he attended the First Zionist Congress as a delegate. He published a pamphlet, *Our Program*, in 1903, advocating a policy of political activity and practical work in Palestine. In the same year he convened an assembly of Palestinian Jews at Zikhron Yaakov and a teachers' conference. After returning to Russia, he organised the Tziyyone Zion in opposition to the proposal for a Jewish homeland in Uganda. In 1906 he went to Odessa, where he became leader of the Ḥovevei Zion. He later settled in Palestine, where he was appointed Chairman of the Jewish National Fund.

U-va-le-Zion ('And a redeemer shall come unto Zion')   Opening words of a prayer used in various services. It is one of the concluding prayers in the morning service. On Sabbaths and festivals it is recited in the afternoon service. On the Day of Atonement it occurs in the concluding service, and except for the first section, it is incorporated in the Saturday evening service. The prayer consists of Isaiah 59:20–21; Isaiah 6:3; a prayer based on verses from I Chronicles, the Book of Psalms and Micah; and a prayer for enlightenment in understanding the law (made up of verses from Psalms, Jeremiah and Isaiah).

Uziel, Ben Zion Meir Hai (1880–1954)   Israeli rabbi. He was born n Jerusalem. He became Ḥakham Bashi at Jaffa in 1912, and Rishon le-Zion in 1939. His writings include studies of Jewish law.

Uziel, Isaac ben Abraham (fl. 17th cent.) Dutch rabbi. He was born in Fez and in 1610 was appointed rabbi of the Neveh Shalom synagogue in Amsterdam. He wrote poetry, a Hebrew grammar, and a translation of legends and fables.

Uzziah [Azariah] (fl. 8th cent. BCE) King of Judah (c.780–c.740 BCE). He conquered Philistia and led a league of kings opposed to Tiglath-Pileser of Assyria. He also rebuilt the port of Elath. He eventually fell victim to leprosy and ceded power to his son Jotham.

V

Sandy Plotnik has been elected the next President of the United States – the first Jew to reach the White House. He phones his mother. 'Mom, guess what! I've just been elected President. You have to come to my inauguration?'

'Sandy! You know I hate trains. I can't face the journey all the way to Washington. Maybe next time.'

'Mom, you will take no train. Air Force One will collect you. The journey will be over in thirty minutes.'

'Sandy, I hate hotels. The non-kosher food. No, maybe next time.'

'Look Mom, you will stay in the White House, with a kosher chef all to yourself. Please come.'

'Sandy! I have nothing to wear.'

'I'll have someone on his way over to you now to take you shopping. You must come.'

'OK, OK, I suppose I'll come.'

At the Inauguration Sandy's mother is in the front row, next to the Secretary of State. Sandy is called up to take the oath of office as President. Sandy's mother digs the Secretary of State in the ribs and says, 'Do you see that boy Sandy? His brother is a very successful doctor.'

* * * * *

Many Jewish jokes ridicule the idea that being a doctor is the highest ambition in the Jewish world. In this joke the newly elected Jewish President of the United State pleads with his mother to attend his inauguration. Eventually she concedes. But at the ceremony, she proudly boasts to the Secretary of State that her other son is a doctor – he is the one she is clearly proud of.

Va-ani tephillati ('And as for me, may my prayer') Opening words of verse 14 of Psalm 69, which is recited at the opening of the afternoon service on the Sabbath. The verse is also included in the Mah Tovu prayer recited when entering the synagogue at the beginning of morning prayer.

Vajda, George (1908–1981) French Arabist and Hebraist. He was born in Budapest. In 1928 he settled in Paris, where he became Professor of Bible and Theology at the Séminaire Israélite. He also lectured at the École Pratique de Hautes Études, and was active in the oriental department of the Institut de Recherches et d'Histoire des Textes. From 1950 he edited the scholarly journal *Revue des Études Juives*. In 1970 he became a professor at the University of Paris. His writings include studies of

Arabic and Jewish philosophy, the kabbalah, and Arab manuscripts.

Vakhnakht (Yiddish: 'Watchnight') Feast celebrated on the night preceding the circumcision ceremony, or (later) on the Sabbath eve before. Formerly called 'Shavua ha-Ben', it is spent in feasting and reciting special prayers. The feast is also called 'Zakhar' (or 'Shelom Zakhar') after the first word of a hymn recited on the occasion.

Vámbéry, Arminius (1832–1913) Hungarian orientalist and traveller. He was born in Dunajska, Streda, on the island of Schütt, and lived in Constantinople, where he worked as a tutor in European languages. After becoming a Muslim, he became secretary to Mehmet Fuad Pasha. In 1863–64 he travelled through Armenia, Persia and Turkestan, disguised as a Sunnite dervish. He published an account of his experiences as *Travels and Adventures in Central Asia*. He later became a Protestant and taught oriental languages at the University of Budapest. His writings include studies of oriental languages and ethnology.

Vashti (fl. 5th cent BCE) Persian queen, wife of King Ahasuerus. According to the Book of Esther, she was divorced after refusing to answer the king's summons to appear before him at a banquet. Her place in the royal household was taken by Esther.

Vav Sixth letter of the Hebrew alphabet. Its numerical value is six.

Va-yekhullu ('And they were completed') Opening word (and thus the name) of the concluding paragraph of the Creation account in Genesis (Genesis 2:1–3). The paragraph is recited on Friday evening during and after the Amidah and in the Kiddush at home.

Vazsonyi, Vilmos (1868–1926) Hungarian politician and lawyer. He founded the club of Junior Democrats in Budapest around 1890. In 1894 he was elected to the Budapest municipal

council and in 1901 to the lower house of the Hungarian parliament. During World War I he served as Minister of Justice. He advocated assimilation of the Jews in the diaspora and was an opponent of Zionism.

Vecinho, Joseph (fl. 15th cent.) Portuguese scientist and physician. A pupil of Abraham Zucato, he translated his teacher's astronomical tables into Spanish. Together with Martin Behaim and the court physician Rodrigo, he participated in a commission investigating navigation. He was forcibly converted in 1497, adopting the name Diego Mendes Vecinho.

Vegetarianism According to the rabbis, the permission to eat animal food was not part of the original dispensation given by God to Adam at the time of the creation. Humankind was given dominion over the animals, but was allowed to eat only fruit and vegetables. However, the covenant made with Noah after the Flood permitted human beings to eat 'every moving thing that liveth ... even as the green herb' (Genesis 9:3). Jewish law dictates that only those animals that have been specifically permitted may be eaten, and that they must be killed according to established ritual practice.

Ve-hu rahum ('And he, being merciful') Opening words of verse 38 of Psalm 78. The verse occurs in the prayer book as the introduction to the weekday evening service, and the opening of a selihah recited before the Tahanun prayer on Mondays and Thursdays.

Venetianer, Lajos (1867–1922) Hungarian rabbi and historian. He was born in Kecskemét. He served as rabbi in Csurgó and Lugos, and from 1897 as Chief Rabbi in Ujpest. He was also professor at the Budapest Rabbinical Seminary. His publications include studies of Christian liturgy and Judaism, the history of Hungarian Jewry, and the organisation of Jewish communities.

Vengeance (Hebrew 'nekamah') Different attitudes to vengeance are expressed in biblical, rabbinic, moral and legal texts. In the Bible it is regarded as a divine prerogative and part of the system of divine retribution. It is thus restricted as a human act. The Bible and the *Talmud* contain numerous instances of forbearance and abstention from vengeance.

Veprik, Alexander (1899–1952) Russian composer. He was born in Balta. He taught orchestration at the Moscow conservatory from 1923 to 1942. His works include *Songs and Dances of the Gehetto, Jewish Songs,* and *Kaddish.*

Verbitsky, Bernado (1902–1979) Argentine novelist and academic. He was born in Buenos Aires. He wrote prose fiction and essays; some of his work deals with the problem of Jewish identity.

Vermes, Geza (1924–2013) British scholar of Hungarian origin. He taught at the University of Newcastle, and later became Professor of Jewish Studies at the University of Oxford. He published studies of the Dead Sea Scrolls, early Jewish biblical exegesis, and the Jewish background to the New Testament.

Ve-shameru ('And they shall keep') Opening word of the passage from Exodus 31 (verses 16–17) recited before the Amidah in the Friday evening service, and on the Sabbath during the Amidah in the morning service and the Kiddush after the service.

Vessels, sacred (Hebrew 'kelei kodesh') Term applied originally to vessels and other implements and furnishings used in the tabernacle during the wilderness years, and in the Temple. They include the Ark, seven-branched menorah, veil, table, laver, altar, coal shovels and large shovel. The vessel chambers, which surrounded the temple, contained vessels of silver and gold which were taken to Babylon when the Jews were exiled there (II Kings 25:13–17). According to Cyrus' edict, the vessels were returned to Jerusalem with the homecoming exiles. Later they were looted from the Second Temple by Titus and taken to Rome. The term 'sacred vessels' is used in modern times to refer to synagogue appurtenances.

Vidal-Naquet, Pierre (1930–2006) French historian. He was born into an assimilated Jewish family, but his attitude to Judaism was changed by the Holocaust, in which his parents were killed. He led a campaign against Revisionist historians, who claim that the Holocaust did not take place.

Vigée, Claude (b.1921) French poet and essayist. He was born in Bischwiller. He was active in the Jewish Resistance in France during World War II, but in 1942 escaped to Spain and the following year emigrated to the US. He taught at various American universities, before becoming a professor at the Hebrew University in 1963. He wrote poems, stories and recollections, many of which deal with Jewish themes.

Vimpel [wimpel] (Yiddish) Fabric strip used as a binder round a Scroll of the Law. A vimpel was frequently presented to a synagogue to commemorate the brith of a male child.

Virtue (Hebrew 'middot tovot') In the Jewish tradition virtue is regarded as consisting of practices, actions and states of mind that conform to God's will. Certain types of virtue, as well as the virtuous life, are exalted in the Bible. In rabbinic and medieval literature, the moral virtues such as humility, patience and contentment, are discussed according to various principles of classification. They are treated in the context of halakhic law or as mental and temperamental qualities conducive to the good life.

Vishniac, Roman (1897–1990) Russian photographer. Born in St Petersburg, he studied zoology at Moscow University. After the Russian Revolution he settled in Latvia and then Berlin. He later embarked on a sustained journey though the Jewish communities of Poland, Lithuania, Latvia, Hungary, Czechoslovakia and Germany recording the lives of Eastern-European Jewry. Later he went to France and then to the US where he was a portrait photographer. His works include *A Vanished World.*

Vision A mystical or religious experience in which a supernatural event or person is seen, or knowledge beyond normal human understanding is gained. A vision may be sought by mystical practices or may occur spontaneously. It may reveal terrestrial events removed in space and time, or spiritual realities and symbols. On the highest level in the Jewish tradition visions are the means by which God's will and purpose are made known to prophets. Visionary accounts occur frequently in apocalyptic literature, and are discussed in talmudic texts, though the *Talmud* does not itself generally record visions. Visionary experiences were cultivated in mystical circles among the ancient rabbis and medieval Kabbalists.

Vital, Ḥayyim (1543–1620) Palestinian kabbalist. He was a student of Moses Cordovero and Moses Alshekh, and was associated with Issac Luria during his last years in Safed. After Luria's death, Vital claimed that he alone had an accurate account of Luria's teaching. He boasted that his soul was that of the Messiah, son of Joseph, and he became known in oriental countries as a miracle worker. His notes on Lurianic Kabbalah were transcribed and published as *Etz Ḥayyim.* From 1590 he lived in Damascus, where he wrote Kabbalistic works and preached the coming of the Messiah.

Vital, Samuel (fl. 17th cent.) Syrian rabbi and Kabbalist, son of Ḥayyim Vital. He lived in Damascus and later went to Cairo. He edited his father's works on Lurianic kabbalah.

Viterbo, Carlo Alberto (1889–1974) Italian Zionist. He was born in Florence. He became President of the Italian Zionist Organisation in 1931. He was imprisoned in the Sforzacosta concentration camp during World War II and released by the Allies in 1944. After the war, he relaunched the periodical *Israel,* which continued until his death.

Vitkin, Yoseph (1876–1912) Palestinian Zionist pioneer. He was born in Mogilev, Belorussia. In 1897 he went to Palestine where he worked as a labourer, and later as a schoolteacher and headmaster. His writings include a number of pamphlets on pioneering, such as *A Call to the Youth of Israel whose Hearts are with their People and with Zion* and *A Group of Young People from Eretz Israel.*

Vocalisation The indication of vowel sounds in Hebrew script by means of marks or points placed above or below consonants. Originally Hebrew was written only with consonants, which were 'vocalised' to show where vowel sounds occurred and what vowels should be sounded. Eventually the letter yod came to represent the long i and e sounds, and the letter vav the long u and o sounds. At the end of the Talmudic period a system of distinctive signs to indicate vowels began to develop and eventually three so-called 'punctuation' systems evolved: Babylonian, Palestinian and Tiberian. The Tiberian system became fixed in two different forms associated with the masoretic schools of Ben Asher and Ben Naphtali. The Ben Asher system passed into common use and is found in printed Bibles.

Vogel, David (1891–1944) Russian Hebrew poet and writer. He was born in Satanov, Russia, and settled in Vienna in 1912. He suffered periods of imprisonment during World War II (in French detention camps, to 1941), before being arrested by the Nazis in 1944. He wrote novels as well as poetry and is regarded as an important forerunner of Hebrew modernism.

Volterra, Meshullam [Meshullam ben Menaḥem of Volterra] (fl. 15th cent.) Italian financier. He inherited his father's loan bank in Florence. In 1481 he travelled to Palestine. After a month's stay he returned to Florence via Venice. His *Massa Meshullam mi-Volterra ha-Eretz Yisrael* is an account of his voyage.

Vow A solemn pledge binding on the person making it. In Jewish tradition it was common to make religious vows undertaken voluntarily to perform a specific act or behave in a certain way. In talmudic law there are two types of vow: a promise to provide Temple sacrifices or to make gifts of property to the Temple or to charity; and the commitment to abstain from eating specified food or from the financial exploitation of specified property. Vows are binding even if no special formal or invocation of the divine name is used in making them.

Vulgate The principal Latin translation of the Bible. It was made in Palestine at the end of the 4th century by Jerome.

W

In a kindergarten class, the teacher asks her five year olds to name the most famous man who every lived and offers ten dollars to the child who gives the correct answer. A little Irish boy puts up his hand and says: 'St Patrick.' The teacher says, 'I'm sorry, Sean. That's not correct.'

Then a little Scottish boy raises his hand and says, 'St Andrew.' 'I'm sorry, Hamish,' the teacher says, 'that isn't correct either.'

Then a little Jewish boy raises his hand and says, 'Jesus Christ.'

The teacher says, 'That's correct, Max. Come up here and collect the ten dollars.'

As the teacher is giving Max the money, she says to him, 'Since you are Jewish, what made you say Jesus Christ?'

Max says to her, 'In my heart I knew it was Moses, but business is business.'

* * * * *

Jewish jokes often satirise Jewish attitudes toward money. Here a kindergarten class is asked who is the most important person who ever lived. A five-year-old Jewish boy names Jesus even though he thinks it was Moses because he is intent on getting a ten-dollar prize for the right answer. The joke amusingly cautions against dishonest business practice.

Wages According to the Bible, the employer is enjoined to pay wages without delay (Leviticus 19:13). The *Talmud* explains that a person hired for the day is to be paid not later than the next morning; one hired for the night by the following evening. Whoever withholds such payment violates several biblical prohibitions.

Waal, Meir (fl. 17th cent.) Lithuanian talmudist, son of Saul Wahl. He was rabbi of Brest and a founder in 1623 of the Council of Lithuania, an autonomous governing body for Lithuanian Jewry.

Wahl, Saul (1541–1617) Lithuanian financier. He was the son of Samuel Judah ben Abraham, who was rabbi at Venice and Padua. Wahl became court agent to Sigismund III, and used his influence on behalf of Jews in Poland and Lithuania. According to legend, he was chosen to be King of Poland for a day.

Wald, Herman (1906–1970) South African sculptor. He was born in Cluj, Hungary. He went to Paris in 1933 and later to London. In 1937 he settled in South Africa. Some of his art is influenced by Jewish subjects.

Waldman, Morris David (1879–1963) Amercian communal worker. He was born in Barfa, Hungary, and was taken to the US as a child. From

1908 to 1917 he was Managing Director of the United Hebrew Charities of New York. In 1921 he organised relief for central European Jewish communities, and from 1928 he served as Executive Secretary of the American Jewish Joint Distribution Committee. His writings include an autobiography, *Not by Power,* a study of Hitler's treatment of the Jews.

Waley, Jacob (1818–1873) English lawyer and communal leader. He served as Professor of Political Economy at University College, London. He was a founder of the United Synagogue, President of the Anglo-Jewish Association, and President of the Jews Hospital and Orphan Asylum.

Walkowitz, Abraham (1878–1965) American painter. He was born in Siberia, and went to the US in 1889. His works include *Faces of the Ghetto.*

Wallace [Wallenchinsky], Irving (1916–90) American novelist. Born in Chicago, he grew up in Kenosha, Wisconsin. He studied at the Williams Institute, Berkeley and Los Angeles City College. His novels include *The Chapman Report, The Prize, The Word, The Fan Club, Ther Second Lady* and *The Miracle.*

Wallant, Edward (1926–1962) American novelist. He was born in New Haven, Connecticut, and worked in a New York advertising agency. His novels deal with Jewish characters.

Wallenstein, Meir (1903–1996) British orientalist. He was born in Jerusalem. He taught in Palestine and Manchester, then from 1946 was Reader in Medieval and Modern History at Manchester University. He settled in Jerusalem in 1970. His publications include studies of Moses Judah Abbas and his contemporaries, hymns from the Judean scrolls, and piyyutim from the Cairo Genizah.

Walter, Bruno (1876–1962) German conductor. Born in Berlin, he was opera coach at the Municipal Opera of Cologne. Later he became Assistant Conductor of the Hamburg Stadt Theatre, and then served as Second Conductor in Pressburg. Eventually he became Conductor at the Berlin Opera. He eventually served as assistant at the Vienna Opera; in 1923 he went to Munich where he conducted performances of Mozart operas. When the Nazis came to power, he conducted in Amsterdam, Salzburg and Vienna. He then went to France, and later to the US.

Wandering Jew [Ahasuerus] Figure from a medieval Christian legend. The story concerns a Jewish cobbler called Ahasuerus, condemned to wander eternally for taunting Jesus on his way to the crucifixion. Among many literary treatments of the legend are David Pinski's Yiddish play *The Eternal Jew,* Rudyard Kipling's short story *The Wandering Jew* and a novel by Stefan Heym, also called *The Wandering Jew.*

Warburg, Edward (1908–1992) American communal leader, son of Felix Warburg. He was involved in a variety of cultural, communal and philanthropic activities. He served as Chairman of the American Jewish Joint Distribution Committee, and of the United Jewish Appeal. In 1967 he became President of the United Jewish Appeal of Greater New York.

Warburg, Felix (1871–1937) American banker and communal leader, brother of Max Warburg. He was born in Hamburg, and in 1894 went to the US where he became a partner in the banking firm of Kuhn, Loeb and Co. in New York. He served as Chairman of the American Jewish Joint Distribution Committee and supported Jewish educational institutions, including the Hebrew Union College, the Jewish Theological Seminary, and the Graduate School for Jewish Social Work.

Warburg, Max (1867–1946) German banker, brother of Felix Warburg. He served as a German delegate to the Paris Peace Conference at the end of World War I and was active in Jewish affairs. He settled in the US in 1939.

Warburg, Otto (1859–1938) German botanist, cousin of Max and Felix Warburg. He was born in Hamburg. He became professor at the University of Berlin in 1892. An active Zionist, he was instrumental in founding the Palestine office at Jaffa in 1908, and served as President of the World Zionist Organisation from 1911 to 1920. From 1921 he was head of the Jewish Agency's experimental station at Tel Aviv, and he also taught at the Hebrew University.

War of Independence War for Israeli independence fought in Palestine in 1947–49. After the UN resolution was passed on 29 November 1947 to partition Palestine into Jewish and Arab states, Palestinian Arabs initiated hostilities against the Jewish popuation. They were soon joined by volunteers from Arab states. Jewish forces were largely organised in the Haganah. In May 1948 the forces of the Arab League invaded the country. Eventually, between February and July 1949, armistice agreements were signed between Israel and Egypt, Jordan, Lebanon and Syria. These permitted Israel to maintain a defensive force in the Negev desert.

War Scroll One of the Dead Sea Scrolls. It describes the war at the end of time between the Sons of Light and the Sons of Darkness.

Wassermann, Jakob (1873–1934) German novelist. He was born in Fürth, and from 1898 lived in Vienna. His works include *My Life as a German and Jew, The Jews of Zirndorf, Caspar Hauser, The Goose Man,* and *The Maurizius Case.*

Wasserman, Oscar (1869–1934) German banker and communal leader. He was born in Bamberg. He became a director of the Berlin branch of his family bank, and in 1912 joined the board of directors of the Deutsche Bank, which later merged with the Disconto-Gesellschaft. Later he was appointed a member of the Council of the Reichsbank. In 1933 he was dismissed from these posts. An active Zionist, he held various positions in the Jewish community including the presidency of the Karen ha-Yesod in Germany.

Waten, Judah (1911–1985) Australian novelist, critic and essayist. He was born in Odessa. In 1914 he emigrated with his family to Perth, where later he worked as a literary critic. In the 1940s he served as a member of the Jewish Council to Combat Facism and Anti-Semitism. Some of his work deals with Jewish themes.

Water (Hebrew 'mayim') Biblical and rabbinic law prescribe ablutions and immersion in water for various reasons. In the aggadah water is regarded as a symbol of the Torah.

Waxman, Meyer (1887–1969) American scholar. He was born in Slutsk in Belorussia. In 1905 he emigrated to the US where he became Principal of the Mizraḥi Teachers Seminary, and later Director of the Mizraḥi Zionist Organisation. In 1924 he joined the faculty of the Hebrew Theological College in Chicago. He was later appointed Professor of Hebrew Literature and Philosophy there. His writings include *A Handbook of Judaism, Judaism: Religion and Ethics,* and *A History of Jewish Literature.*

Weidman, Jerome (1913–1998) American writer. He wrote 200 short stories as well as plays and novels. In much of his work he draws on the conflict between Jewish and American culture. Among his better-known works are the novels *The Centre of the Action* and *Fourth Street East.*

Weights and measures In biblical times the unit of weight for silver was the shekel; there were various standard weights based on this unit. Hollow measures included the ephah, the seah, the hin, the ḥomer, the omer, and kav and the log. For ritual purposes the measures 'olive-sized' and 'egg-sized' were used. There were two systems of measuring length, the ordinary ammah ('cubit'), about 46 cm, and the large ammah, 52 cm. The cubit was divided into two units of a zeret ('span'), six units of a tephaḥ ('hand's breadth'), or 24 units of an etzba ('finger').

Weil, Gotthold (1882–1960) Israeli orientalist and librarian, of German origin. He was born in Berlin. He became Director of the oriental department at the Berlin State Library in 1906, and in 1920 Professor at Berlin University. He was appointed professor of Semitic Languages at the University of Frankfurt in 1934. After moving to Palestine he served as head of the National and University Library in Jerusalem and was Professor of Turkish Studies at the Hebrew University. He published works on Arabic and Turkish subjects.

Weil, Gustav (1808–1889) German orientalist. He was born in Salzburg, Baden. He worked as a French instructor at a medical school in Cairo, then, after returning to Germany, as a librarian and teacher in Heidelberg. He wrote studies of Jewish influences on the Koran, Muslim history and Arabic literature. He also translated the *Arabian Nights* into German.

Weil, Simone (1909–1943) French religious writer. She was born in Paris. She gave up teaching philosophy to become a factory worker. In 1936 she joined the Republicans in the Spanish Civil War. After the Nazi invasion of France she worked as a farm labourer in the south. She spent a period in the US, but returned to France to join the Resistance. She was fiercely critical of Judaism.

Weiler, Moses Cyrus (1907–2000) South African rabbi. He was born in Riga, Latvia, and was educated in Pales-

tine and later in the US. In 1933 he settled in South Africa where he founded the non-Orthodox progressive movement and served as a rabbi. He moved to Israel in 1958 to teach at the Hebrew Union College in Jerusalem.

Weill, Alexandre (1811–1899) French philosopher. After a talmudic education he abandoned traditional Judaism. A friend of Hugo, Balzac and Baudelaire, he was prominent in the literary world. In later life he returned to a study of the Bible.

Weill, Kurt (1900–1950) German composer. Born in Dessau, he studied at the Hochschule für Music in Berlin and became conductor of the municipal opera in Ludenscheid. His early compositions include *Concerto for Violin and Wind Orchestra*, *Der Protagonist* and *Der Zar läst such photograhieren*. Later he collaborated with Bertholdt Brecht. In 1933 he went to Paris, and later settled in the US.

Weinberg, Elbert (1928–1991) American sculptor. He was born in Hartford, Connecticut. Some of his works deal with biblical subjects and others with the Holocaust.

Weinberger, Jacob (1879–1956) American composer. He was born in Odessa, and taught there from 1915 to 1921. He emigrated to Palestine in 1922, and later settled in the US.

Weinberger, Jaromir (1896–1967) American composer. He was born in Prague, and taught there and in various other cities. In 1937 he emigrated to the US, and settled in St Petersburg, Florida. His compositions include works based on biblical themes.

Weiner, Lazar (1897–1982) American composer, of Russian origin. He settled in the US in 1914. His compositions include a setting of the Friday evening service and other liturgical works.

Weingreen, Jacob (1908–1995) English Hebrew grammarian and biblical scholar. He was born in Manchester. He became Professor of Hebrew at the University of Dublin. His works include *A Practical Grammar for Classical Hebrew*, *Themes of Old Testament Stories*, *English Versions of the Old Testament*, and *The Concepts of Retaliation and Compensation in Biblical Law*.

Weinreich, Max (1894–1969) American scholar. He was born in Kuldiga, Latvia. He served as research director of YIVO in Vilnius from 1923, and later at the institute's new Center in New York. From 1947 he was professor at City College, New York. He published studies of Yiddish linguistics, folklore, literary history, psychology, pedagogy and sociology.

Weinreich, Uriel (1925–1967) American scholar of linguistics, editor and educator. He was the son of Max Weinreich. He was born in Vilnius, and emigrated to the US in 1940. He became Professor of Yiddish Language, Literature and Culture at Columbia University in 1939. His writings include *College Yiddish: an Introduction to the Yiddish Language and to Jewish Life and Culture*, *Language and Culture Atlas of Ashkenazic Jewry*, and *Modern English-Yiddish, Yiddish-English Dictionary*.

Weinryb, Bernard Dov (1900–1982) American economic and social historian. He was born in Turobin, Poland. He worked as the librarian of the Breslau Rabbinic Seminary before emigrating in 1934 to Palestine, where he lectured at the School of Social Work and School of Economics. Later he settled in New York and held a succession of teaching posts: at the Herzliah Teacher's Seminary, Brooklyn College, and Yeshiva University. From 1949 he was Professor of Jewish History and Economics at Dropsie College. He wrote studies of Jewish life and history.

Weisgal, Meyer Wolf (1894–1977) Israeli Zionist. He was born in Kikol, Poland, and moved to the US in 1905.

He served as National Secretary of the Zionist Organisation of America, and as Chaim Weizmann's political representative in the US. Later he became Secretary-General of the Jewish Agency for Palestine. He subsequently settled in Israel and became President and chancellor of the Weizmann Institute of Science at Rehovot.

Weisgall, Hugo (1912–1997) Amercian composer and educator. He was born in Ivančice (now in Czechoslovakia), and settled in the US in 1920. He taught at Queen's College, New York, and served as Chairman of Faculty at the Cantor's Institute of the Jewish Theological Seminary. He lectured extensively on the subject of Jewish music.

Weiss, Isaac Hirsch (1815–1905) Moravian talmudic scholar. He lectured at the Vienna bet midrash from 1861. His *Dor Dor be-Doreshav* is a history of the development of the Oral Law down to the Middle Ages.

Weizmann, Chaim (1874–1952) Israeli Zionist leader and statesman. He was born in Motel near Pinsk, in Belorussia. He settled in England and in 1904 became a lecturer in biological chemistry at Manchester University. In 1916 he was appointed Director of the British Admiralty Chemical Laboratories. His Zionist activities began when he became associated with the Democratic Fraction in 1901; the following year he and Berthold Feiwel proposed the creation of the Hebrew University. In 1903 Weizmann opposed the plan for the establishment of a Jewish homeland in Uganda and became a supporter of synthetic Zionism. He was the prime mover behind the Balfour Declaration of British support for Zionism in 1917. At the Paris Peace Conference of 1919 Weizmann (together with Menaḥem Mendel Ussishkin and Nahum Sokolow) represented the Zionist movement, and in the same year he became President of the World Zionist Organisation. He later retired to Rehovot to work at the Weizmann Institute, which he had helped to found. In 1948 he became the first President of the State of Israel.

Weizmann, Ezer (1924–2005) Israeli military commander, nephew of Chaim Weizmann. He served as a pilot in the British Air Force during World War II, then in 1958 became commander of the Israeli air force He was appointed chief of operations of the Israeli general staff in 1966, and played an important role in the Six-Day War in 1967.

Wengeroff, Pauline W. (1833–1916) Russian writer. She was born in Bobruisk, Belorussia, and became the wife of Hanan Wengeroff, a banker and communal worker in Minsk. Her memoirs depict the life of a rich Jewish family in the period before and after the Haskalah.

Werblowsky, Raphael Juda Zwi (1924–2015) Israeli scholar. He was born in Frankfurt am Main. He taught first in England at the universities of Leeds and Manchester, and then at the Hebrew University. He wrote extensively on areas of Jewish studies and served as co-editor of the *Encyclopedia of the Jewish Religion.*

Werfel, Franz (1890–1945) Austrian novelist, playwright and poet. He was born in Prague, and served in the Austrian army. From 1940 he lived in the US. Some of his writing deals with Jewish themes.

Werner, Eric (1901–1988) American musicologist. He was born in Vienna. He lectured at the rabbinical seminary in Breslau before moving to the US in 1938. He became Professor of Liturgical Music at the Hebrew Union College in Cincinnati, and in 1948 founded the college's School of Sacred Music. From 1967 to 1971 he served as head of the department of musicology at Tel Aviv University. He wrote studies of early Christian, medieval and Renaissance music, and of the relationship between Ancient Greek and Hebrew hymnology and musical theories.

Wertheimer, Joseph von (1800–1887) Austrian educator and author. He was born in Vienna, where he later was active as a merchant. He founded the city's first kindergarten in 1830, and in 1843 set up a Jewish kindergarten. His other acts of philanthropy included the establishing of a society to assist released criminals and provide guidance for juvenile delinquents, and the founding of the Society for the Care of Needy Orphans of the Israelite Community. He also played a leading role in the struggle to achieve equal social and political status for Jews.

Wertheimer, Samson (1658–1724) German court Jew. He was born in Worms. In 1684 he went to Vienna to join the bank of Samuel Oppenheimer, and he eventually became a court banker. In 1719 Carl VI appointed him Chief Rabbi of Hungary. Wertheimer was active on behalf of Jewish communities, and in 1700 obtained an order from the Emperor Leopold which resulted in the withdrawal from circulation of Johann Eisenmenger's anti-Jewish book, *Endecktes Judentum.* He also created a fund to help paupers in Palestine.

Wesker, Arnold (1932–2016) English playwright. He was born in London. He held various jobs, including kitchen porter and pastry cook, before becoming a full-time writer. His plays include *Chicken Soup and Barley, Roots, I'm Talking about Jerusalem,* and *Chips with Everything.*

Wessley [Weizel], Naphtali Herz (1725–1805) German Hebrew writer and leader of the early Haskalah movement. He was born in Hamburg, and lived in Copenhagen. His business affairs also took him to Amsterdam and Berlin. His first work was a study of the origins of Hebrew words and synonyms in the Hebrew language. Later he published a commentary on Avot and an annotated Hebrew translation (from the original Greek) of the Wisdom of Solomon. He also participated in the writing of Moses Mendelssohn's commentary on the Pentateuch. Wessley's *Words of Peace and Truth*, written under the influence of Joseph II's Edict of Toleration, advocated an educational programme for Jewish youth in the spirit of the Haskalah. Subsequently he published the epic story *Shire Tipheret*, which relates biblical events from the Exodus to the revelation on Mount Sinai.

Western Wall (Hebrew: 'Kotel Maaravi', Wailing Wall) Name given to the surviving part of the outer wall of the Temple, dating from c.35 BCE. Owing to its proximity to the Holy of Holies at the west end of the Temple, the wall is regarded as sacred. Regular services have been held there since the 10th century.

Whitman, Ruth (1922–1999) American translator and poet. She was born in New York. She lectured on poetry at Harvard University and Radcliffe College. She edited and translated *An Anthology of Modern Yiddish Poetry* and published several volumes of her own poetry.

Whole offering (Hebrew 'kalil') Term used in the context of the Temple sacrifice to denote any offering that was consumed entirely when it was burnt. Specifically it is used of the meal offering consumed in this way (Leviticus 6:15–16). In this more limited sense 'whole offering' is parallel to 'burnt offering' (olah), the one referring to a sacrifice of meal and the other to an animal sacrifice.

Wicked Priest In the Dead Sea Scrolls, the figure portrayed as the opponent of the Teacher of Righteousness. Initially he was on the side of truth, but later betrayed the law for gain and persecuted the Teacher of Righteousness.

Widow According to the Bible, a widow is a privileged person, who is to be protected and maintained (Exodus 22:21; Deuteronomy 27:19). She is entitled to payment of the sum stipulated by her husband in the marriage contract, or alternatively to support by her husband's descendants.

Wiener, Norbert (1894–1964) Amercian mathematician. Born in Columbia, Missouri, he was the son of Leo Wiener, a professor of Slavic studies at Harvard. He studied at Tufts and later at Harvard. He taught at Massachusetts Institute of Technology. His works include *Ex-Prodigy: My Childhood, The Human Use of Human Beings, Cybernetics* and *The Tempest.*

Wiernik, Peter (1865–1936) American Yiddish writer, of Lithuanian origin. He went to the US in 1885. He served as editor of the Yiddish daily *Morgen-Journal* from its foundation in 1901, and also of the weekly *Der Amerikaner.* His writings include *History of the Jews of America.*

Wiesel, Elie (1928–2016) American author. He was born in Sighet, Romania. A survivor of the concentration camps, he later lived in Paris and New York. He became a foreign correspondent for an Israeli daily newspaper, and from 1957 he worked for the *Jewish Daily Forward.* In 1976 he was appointed Professor of Humanities at Boston University. His works include *Night, The Gates of the Forest, Legends of our Time, The Jews of Silence, A Beggar in Jerusalem,* and *The Trial of God.* In 1986 he was awarded the Nobel Peace Prize.

Wig From talmudic times it was common practice for women to wear wigs. According to Jewish law, married women must cover their hair, and from the 15th century it became customary to fulfil this prescription by wearing a wig (known as a 'sheitel').

Wilensky, Mosheh (1910–1997) Israeli composer. He was born in Warsaw, and settled in Palestine in 1932. He wrote many popular Israeli songs.

Will The declaration (usually written) of a person's wishes regarding the disposal of property after the individual's death. According to Jewish law, the property owned by a person at the time of death passes (after all debts have been paid) to the next of kin (Numbers 27:8–11). Nevertheless it is possible for an estate to be distributed differently. This may be ensured by the making of a will (embodying the correct legal formulae) while a person is sound in body and mind. If no will exists an individual may, during a final illness, dispose of all or any part of his property by issuing verbal instructions before witnesses. If the person recovers, however, these instructions are regarded as void.

Willow One of the four species of plant, branches of which are used ceremonially on the feast of Sukkot. Willows growing near Jerusalem supplied adornment for the altar during the festival and branches were carried during the hakkaphot circuits. The shaking of willow twigs and leaves on Hoshanah Rabbah symbolically expresses the desire for rain.

Willstätter, Richard (1872–1942) German organic chemist. He was born in Karlsruhe. From 1902 he taught at the University of Munich, but in 1924 he resigned his chair in protest against the university's anti-Semitic policy. He received the Nobel Prize for chemistry in 1915.

Winchell, Walter (1897–1972) Amercian journalist. He was a vaudeville performer and later contributed gossip material to *Billboard* and *Vaudeville News*. Later he worked for the *New York Evening Graphic* and New York *Daily Mirror*. He also had a weekly radio programme.

Winchevsky, Morris (1856–1933) Lithuanian Yiddish poet and essayist.

His activities as a socialist agitator led to his being imprisoned and banished from Germany and Denmark. He moved to London in 1879, and later lived in New York. He wrote poetry for Yiddish periodicals. He is regarded as the founder of Yiddish socialist literature.

Winder, Ludwig (1889–1946) Moravian novelist. He was born in Schaffa. He worked as a journalist on the *Deutsche Zeigtung Bohemia* in Prague until 1938. A number of his works deal with Jewish topics.

Wine In Ancient Israel wine was drunk at meals (though ascetics such as the Nazirites and Rechabites abstained from it). In the Temple it was poured on the altar with the sacrifices. Wine has also played an important role in later rituals, such as Kiddush, Havdalah and the Passover seder. A special benediction is recited before and after drinking it. At the festival of Purim and on Simhat Torah overindulgence in wine is encouraged as part of the celebration. Vine leaves and grapes were used on Jewish coins during the Second Temple period, and in synagogue art during the talmudic period. The wine of the gentiles is forbidden according to Jewish law.

Wischnitzer, Mark (1882–1995) Russian historian, sociologist and communal worker. He lived in Galicia, Vienna and Berlin. After returning to Russia, he lectured at the institute of Baron David Günzburg in St Petersburg. From 1914 to 1916 he was editor of the periodical *History of the Jewish People* in Moscow. He lived in London for a time, then moved to Germany and served as secretary to the Hilfsverein Der Deutschen Juden. In the period 1933–37 he helped to organise the emigration of Jews from Germany. Subsequently he became Professor of Jewish History at Yeshiva University in New York. His writings include studies of Eastern-European Jewish history.

Wischnitzer, Rachel (1882–1989)
Polish art historian. she was born in
Minsk in Belorussia. A pioneer of the
study of Jewish art, she edited some
of the first periodicals on this subject.
From 1934 to 1938 she served as Director of the Jewish museum in Berlin. In
1940 she went with her husband to
New York, where she published studies
of synagogue art.

Wisdom (Hebrew 'hokhmah') According to the Bible wisdom results
from education and experience, and is
conferred by God. It is not spoken of
as existing only in Israel, but is found
among other nations as well. The Book
of Proverbs emphasises its significance.
In the post-explicit period wisdom was
identified with knowledge of the Torah
and law.

Wisdom literature Term used of a
body of biblical and apocryphal literature in which wisdom is portrayed as
being based on fear of God and knowledge of the commandments. The works
concerned are the books of Proverbs,
Job, and Ecclesiastes, and Psalms 37,
49 and 73, and the apocryphal books
of Ecclesiasticus, Wisdom of Solomon,
and IV Maccabees.

Wise, George S. (1906–1987) Israeli
administrator. He was born in Pinsk,
Belorussia, and emigrated to the US
in 1926. He was Associate Director of
the Bureau of Applied Social Research
from 1949 to 1952. After moving to
Israel he served as Chairman of the
Hebrew University's board of governors. From 1963 he was President of
Tel Aviv University.

Wise, Isaac Mayer (1819–1900) American Reform leader. He was born in
Steingrub, Bohemia, and emigrated to
the US in 1846. He served as rabbi of
Congregation Beth El in Albany, then
in 1854 became minister of a congregation in Cincinnati, where his most
important work was carried out. He
founded an English-language weekly,

The Israelite, and a German language
weekly, *Die Deborah.* He also published
an American Reform prayer book,
Minhag America. In 1855 he attempted
to found a rabbinical seminary, Zion
College. Though he was unsuccessful
at the time, he was later a prime mover
in the establishment of the Hebrew
Union College in 1875. He summoned
rabbinic conferences in 1869 and 1871,
helped to form the Union of American
Hebrew Congregations in 1873, and in
1889 organised the Central Conference
of American Rabbis.

Wise, James Waterman (1901–1983)
American editor and author, son of
Stephen S. Wise. He served as Director of the Stuyvesant Neighbourhood
House in New York, and national secretary of Avukah, the American students' Zionist Federation. He also was
editor of *Opinion.* His writings include
*Liberalising Liberal Judaism, Jews are like
that, Legend of Louise,* and *A Jew Revisits
Germany.*

Wise, Stephen Samuel (1874–1949)
American rabbi and Zionist leader. He
was born in Budapest, and emigrated to
the US as a child. He served as rabbi
of Congregation B'nai Jeshurun in New
York, and later in Portland, Oregon. In
1907 he established the Free Synagogue
of New York, and in 1922 founded the
Jewish Institute of Religion. He was
Secretary to the Federation of American
Zionists, which subsequently became
the Zionist Organisation of America,
and Chairman of the Provision Committee for Zionist Affairs. For many
years he was President of the American
Jewish Congress.

**Wissenschaft des Judentums [Jüdi-
sche Wissenschaft] (German 'Science of Judaism')** Term applied to
the scientific study of Jewish history,
literature and religion. The methodology developed in Europe in the 19th
century as a result of the Haskalah and
the rise of Reform Judaism. Its first
exponents are generally considered to

be Leopold Zunz and Abraham Geiger. Despite its connection with the Jewish Enlightenment and liberal religious views, Orthodox scholars also adopted this approach.

Wissotzky, Kalonymos Ze'ev (1824–1904) Russian merchant, philanthropist and Zionist. He was born in Zhagare. In 1858 he moved to Moscow and established a tea firm. An active supporter of Ḥibbat Zion, he visited Palestine where he supported religious settlers, and contributed to the foundation of the Haifa Technion.

Witness (Hebrew 'eid') According to Jewish law, a person who is in possession of evidence concerning an event is obliged to testify before a court. In civil cases the testimony of a single witness obligates the accused to take an oath that he is not liable for the claim made against him. Similarly, in matters of religious law regarding things permitted or prohibited, the testimony of one witness is valid. In all other cases the evidence of two witnesses is needed to prove a charge.

Wittels, Fritz (1880–1950) Austrian psychoanalyst. He was born in Vienna. He was the first biographer of Sigmund Freud. In 1904 he wrote *Der Tauffjude* (The Convert Jew), which argued that Jews should resist the temptation to join the majority culture and should stand up for their own interests.

Wittgenstein, Ludwig (1889–1951) British philosopher of Austrian origin. His father was a Protestant and his mother a Roman Catholic of Jewish origin. Born in Austria, he studied at Linz, Berlin, Manchester and Cambridge where he became professor. His works include *Tractatus Logico-Philosophicus* and *Philosophical Investigations.*

Wolf, Johann Christoph (1683–1730) German Hebraist. He was born in Wernigerode, Prussia, and became Professor of Oriental Languages and Literature at the Hamburg gymnasium. His *Bibliotheca hebraea* is a list of Hebrew books based on the collection of David Oppenheimer.

Wolf, Lucien (1857–1930) English historian, journalist and communal worker. He was born in London. He was foreign editor of the *Daily Graphic* and editor of the *Jewish World,* and also edited the periodical *Darkest Russia.* In 1917 he became Secretary of the Deputies of British Jews and the Anglo-Jewish Association. After World War I he attended the Paris Peace Conference in 1919. He published articles and works dealing with the period between the expulsion and resettlement of English Jewry (c.1290–1650) and with the mission of Manasseh Ben Israel to Oliver Cromwell.

Wolf, Simon (1836–1923) American communal leader. He was born in Hinzweiler, Germany, and emigrated to the US in 1848. Living in Washington, he intervened with presidents and other government officials to obtain equity for Jews in America and abroad. From 1878 to 1911 he was Chairman of the standing committee of the Board of Delegates of Civil and Religious Rights. He also served as Consul-General to Egypt, and as President of B'nai B'rith.

Wolffsohn, David (1856–1914) German Zionist leader. He was born in Dorbiany, Lithuania, and lived in Cologne, where he was a timber merchant. An active Zionist, he was a co-founder of a society to promote Jewish agricultural work and handicrafts in Palestine. Later he became an assistant to Theodor Herzl, who entrusted him with the preparations for the founding of the Jewish Colonial Trust. In 1898 he went with Herzl to Palestine to meet Kaiser William II. Wolffsohn was elected to succeed Herzl as President of the World Zionst Organisation in 1905.

Wolfskehl, Karl (1869–1948)   German poet. He was born in Darmstadt. In 1934 he left Germany and lived successively in Italy, Switzerland, and New Zealand. He was influenced by the poet Stefan George. His series of poems, *Die Stimme spricht* gives expression to the German Jewish tragedy.

Wolfson, Harry Austryn (1887–1974)   American historian of philosophy He was born in Belorussia, and emigrated to the US in 1903. In 1925 he became Professor of Hebrew Literature and Philosophy at Harvard University. His publications include studies of Ḥasdai ben Abraham Crescas, Spinoza and Philo.

Wolfson, Sir Isaac (1897–1991)   Scottish businessman and philanthropist. He was born in Glasgow. He became chairman of Great Universal Stores in 1946. After World War II he devoted himself to philanthropic activities. The Edith and Isaac Wolfson trust provided funds for building the Supreme Rabbinical Centre in Jerusalem, 50 synagogues throughout Israel, and the Kiryat Wolfson housing project for new immigrants. Wolfson also served as Chairman of the Joint Palestinian Appeal of Great Britain and Ireland, and President of the United Synagogue.

Woman   According to the Bible, woman was created as a helpmate for man. Under rabbinic law, women are granted various rights, such as the right to own property, but they are restricted in certain spheres: they may not, for example, give evidence in a court of law. Rabbinic Judaism focuses on the woman's role in the home. Women are exempt from observing the numerous religious obligations enjoined on men by the positive commandments. The position of women in Jewish society changed significantly with the effective abolition among Ashkenazi Jews of polygamy around 1000. Nevertheless women continued to occupy an inferior position in terms of education, especially in Eastern Europe. In the modern period women have played a central role in Jewish life, in the Zionist movement, and in religious education. Among non-Orthodox congregations girls receive the same religious instruction as boys and celebrate an equivalent to the bar mitzvah. Recently women have been trained as rabbis and cantors in non-Orthodox movements, though in Orthodoxy Jewry they continue to taken no active part in the worship of the synagogue.

Wouk, Herman (b.1915)   American novelist and playwright. He was born in New York. Initially he worked as a radio scriptwriter, but later served in the US Navy as a line officer. His writing includes *The Cain Mutiny, Marjorie Morningstar,* and *This is my God.*

Writing   In ancient times writing was done with a pen and ink on potsherds or on leather scrolls. It was common in the upper classes to dictate to a scribe. During the tannaitic period (c.100 BCE–200 CE) there were elaborate rules for writing holy books. The parchment was ruled with a stylus and the letters were written suspended from the line. There was also a fixed orthography. Until the modern period Jews used Hebrew script for writing both Hebrew and other languages. Although Hebrew presses have existed for centuries, Jewish law dictates that certain books and documents must be handwritten: the Scrolls of the Law and the Scrolls of Esther for use in the synagogue; the parchments enclosed in phylacteries and mezuzah, and divorce documents and marriage certificates are also often written by hand.

Written Law   The law given by God to Moses on Mt Sinai; according to tradition, the Written Law is the

Pentateuch. By extension the term is also used for the prophetic books and the Hagiographa. The Written Law is complemented by the Oral Law, which is traditionally believed to originate in God's revelation to Moses of the interpretation of the law.

Wyner, Yehudi (b.1929) American composer and educator. He was born in Calgary, Canada, and went to the US at an early age. He taught at Yale University, and at SUNY at Purchase. He wrote a number of compositions for the synagogue.

Y

A Jew who claims to have a talking parrot brags about the bird to his friends. But no one believes him. They ridicule him until he takes bets that the parrot will join in prayers at the next Friday night service. The following Friday the man brings his parrot to synagogue. But despite much prodding, the parrot doesn't talk. The man is enraged, and tells off the parrot on the way home. 'Now I'll have to pay off all those bets because you didn't say anything,' he complains.

'Yes,' says the parrot. 'But think how much you will make if you take bets on Yom Kippur.'

* * * * *

Many Jewish jokes satirise Jewish attitudes to making money. Here a Jewish man has a talking parrot. He makes a bet with his friends that the parrot will join in Sabbath prayers. But when the parrot lets him down, he is incensed. But, the parrot tells him he will now make a killing taking bets on Yom Kippur.

Yaaleh ('May it arise') Opening word (and hence title) of a hymn sung in the synagogue during the evening services on the Day of Atonement. It occurs in the Italian, Ashkenazi and (in an altered form) Polish rites, and introduces the seliḥot. It is based on the prayer *Yaaleh ve-yavo.*

Yaaleh ve-yavo ('May it arise and come') Opening words of a paragraph added to the Amidah and Grace after Meals at New Year and festivals. In the Spanish and Yemenite rites it is also added to the Amidah in the additional service for the New Year and the Day of Atonement.

Yaari, Avraham (1899–1966) Israeli scholar, of Galician origin, brother of Yehudah Yaari. He settled in Palestine in 1920. After teaching at a school in Tel Aviv, he worked in the Hebrew National Library and Tel Aviv University Library. He published studies dealing with Hebrew bibliography and the history of Jewish settlement in Palestine.

Yaari, Yehudah (1900–1982) Israeli writer and diplomat, of Galician origin, brother of Avraham Yaari. He emigrated to Palestine in 1920 and served in the head office of Keren ha-Yesod. He held a number of diplomatic posts: as Cultural Attaché to the Israeli Legation in Scandinavia, Director of the Department for Cultural Relations of the Israeli foreign ministry, and as Consul-General in Amsterdam. He wrote stories and romances dealing with Eastern-European life during the 20th century and with pioneer youth in Israel.

Yadayim ('Hands') Eleventh tractate in the Mishnah order of Tohorot. It sets down rabbinic decrees concerning ritual impurity of hands, and the means of their ablution. It also deals with the canonicity of the Song of Songs and Ecclesiastes, the Aramaic language in Ezra and Daniel, the Ancient Hebrew script, and disagreements between Pharisees and Sadducees.

Yadin, Yigael (1917–1984) Israeli archaeologist and soldier. He was born in Jerusalem. He became a member of the Haganah and served in various official positions. He was chief of operations during the Israeli War of Independence, and chief of staff of the Israeli army from 1949 to 1952. He then taught archeology at the Hebrew University, where he became professor. He published studies of the Dead Sea Scrolls and directed excavations at Hazor and Masada.

Yaḥad ('unity') Term used in the Dead Sea Scrolls to describe the unifying spirit of the sect that produced the scrolls.

Yah Ribbon Olam ('God, master of the universe') Opening words (and hence title) of an Aramaic hymn. Composed by Israel ben Moses Najara, it is generally sung at the table during the Sabbath meal.

Yahrzeit (Yiddish) Term used by Ashkenazi Jews for the anniversary of the death of a relative. It is observed by kindling a light and reciting the kaddish. In some communities it is also marked by fasting.

Yahuda, Abraham Shalom (1877–1951) Palestinian orientalist. He was born in Jerusalem. He taught at the Hochschule für die Wissenschaft des Judentums in Berlin and at the Uni-

versity of Madrid. In 1942 he became professor at the New School for Social Research in New York. He published biblical and philological studies, attempted to establish correspondence between Egyptian texts and the Pentateuch, and edited the Arabic text of Baḥya ibn Pakuda's *Duties of the Heart.*

Yaknehaz (i) Mnemonic for the order of the blessings in the kiddush recited on a festival that begins on Saturday night. The letters stand for 'yayin' (wine), 'kiddush' (sanctification), 'ner' (light), 'havdalah' (blessing for the end of the Sabbath), and 'zeman' (the benediction She-heḥeyanu). The term has been associated with the German phrase 'jag den Has' (chase the hare); for this reason manuscripts of the Passover Haggadah were often illustrated with hunting scenes.

Yaknehaz (ii) Pseudonym of Isaiah N. Goldberg (1858–1927). Lithuanian and Yiddish author. He was a teacher in Lithuania from 1880, and served as permanent assistant on the Hebrew newspaper *Ha-Melitz.* He wrote stories and sketches for the Hebrew and Yiddish press.

Yalkut ('compilation') Title of several midrashic compilations including the *Yalkut Shimoni, Yalkut ha-Meiri,* and *Yalkut Reuveni.*

Yalkut Reuveni ('Compilation of Reuben') Anthology of homiletical writings on the Pentateuch. Composed in the 17th century by Reuben Kahana of Prague, it is arranged in order of the weekly positions assigned to be read in the synagogue.

Yalkut Shimoni ('Compilation of Simeon') Anthology of midrashic writings on all the books of the Bible. It was compiled by Simeon Kayyara.

Yamin Noraim ('Days of Awe') Term used of the New Year (Rosh ha-Shanah) and Day of Atonement (Yom Kippur), and also of the period between them – the Ten Days of Penitence. According to Jewish tradition all people stand before the divine throne of judgement at the New Year, and judgement is pronounced upon them on the Day of Atonement.

Yannai (i) (fl. 3rd cent.) Palestinian amora. He was a pupil of Judah ha-Nasi and Ḥiyya. He established an academy at Akhbara in Upper Galilee, the teachings of which are cited in the Palestinian and Babylonian Talmuds as 'de-ve Rabbi Yannai' (school of Rabbi Yannai).

Yannai (ii) (fl.? 6th cent.) Hebrew liturgical poet. He probably lived in Palestine. He introduced rhyme into religious poetry, wrote piyyutim related to the weekly portion of the Torah, and determined the final form of the Kerovah. His piyyutim (with the exception of *Av Tov Nissim* in the Ashkenazi rite for the Passover Haggadah) were forgotten until the 19th century, when scholars discovered others of his poems. Further examples were found in the Cairo Geniza.

Yaoz-Kest, Itamar (b.1934) Israeli poet and fiction writer. He was born in Szarvas, Hungary. He survived incarceration at the concentration camp at Bergen-Belsen in 1944–45. In 1952 he went to Israel where he became an editor in the publishing house Eked. Some of his work deals with modern Jewish history.

Yarmulke Skull cap, worn by male Jews. It is worn by observant Jews at all time, and for prayers even by the less Orthodox. The derivation of the word is unknown.

Yehoshua, Avraham B. (b.1936) Israeli writer. He was born in Jerusalem. He served in the Israeli army. After living in Paris for a time, he settled in Haifa. He published stories about heroes haunted by indecision.

Yehudai (fl. 8th cent.) Babylonian gaon. He was born in Pumbedita. He succeeded Solomon bar Ḥasdai as head of the Sura academy in 757 and served until 761. He entered into relations with Jewish communities in North Africa, and attempted to enforce Babylonian usages in Palestine. His code of the law, *Halakhot Pesukot*, was written down for him by his pupils, since he was blind.

Yehudi ben Sheset (fl. 10th cent.) Spanish grammarian. A pupil of Dunash ben Labrat, he wrote a reply (consisting of 150 verses of introduction and a prose section) to the polemic directed against Dunash by the pupils of Menaḥem ben Saruk.

Yekke (Yiddish) A German.

Yekum purkan (Aramaic: 'May redemption come') Opening words of two Aramaic prayers. The first is for the welfare of the communal and scholastic heads of Palestine and Babylonia; the other is for the general community. Composed during the gaonic period, they are recited in Ashkenazi communities after the reading of the law on the Sabbath.

Yellin, David (1864–1941) Palestinian scholar. He was one of the organisers of the founding conference of the Teachers' Association at Zikhron Ya'akov in 1903. Later he served as Deputy Director of the teachers' seminary founded by the Hilfsverein der Deutschen Juden in Jerusalem, and also lectured on Hebrew poetry of the Spanish period at the Hebrew University. He published studies of medieval Jewish poetry and Hebrew philology, a Hebrew dictionary and grammar, and an edition of the poems of Todros Abulafia. Besides his scholarly work, he was Deputy Mayor of Jerusalem and head of the Vaad Leumi.

Yenta (Yiddish) A shrew, a gossipy woman, or a woman of vulgar manners.

Yeshivah ('academy') Jewish school devoted to the study of the *Talmud* and rabbinic literature. The institution of the yeshivah is a continuation of the academies in Babylonia and Palestine during the talmudic and gaonic periods. Many modern yeshivot teach a programme of secular studies to complement the traditional talmudic studies.

Yeshivah bucher (Yiddish) A young man who studies at a yeshivah, or a scholarly person. By extension an inexperienced individual.

Yetzer ha-ra Evil inclination.

Yetzer ha-tov Good inclination.

Yevamot ('Levirates') First tractate in the Mishnah order of Nashim. It deals with the status of the widow of a man who has died childless. His brother must contract a Levirate marriage with her or carry out the ceremony known as Ḥalitzah.

Yevin, Shemuel (1896–1982) Israeli archaeologist of Russian origin. He went to Palestine before World War I, participating in various archeological explorations. He was Secretary of the Vaad ha-Lashon, and from 1948 to 1959 was Director of the Israeli government's Department of antiquities His publications include studies of the Bar Kokhba revolt.

Yevesektzia Jewish branch of the Russian Communist Party, formed in 1918 and active until 1930. It was responsible for the elimination of Jewish communal organisations and institutions, the boycotting of synagogues, and activities against Judaism and the Hebrew language. It initiated plans for Jewish territories in Crimea in 1926, and later in Birobidan. It published the daily paper *Emes*.

Yezierska, Anzia (1885–1970) American novelist, of Russian origin. She went to New York at the age of 16, and worked in a tailor's shop. Later she found better-paid work and ran away from home. Her short stories and novels deal with the adjustment of the Jewish immigrant to American life.

Yid A disparaging and offensive term for a Jew.

Yiddish Language spoken by Ashkenazi Jews from the Middle Ages. It derives from Hebrew, Loez, German and Slavic. Since its formation in c.1000–1250, Yiddish has undergone constant development. It can be classified chronologically into Old Yiddish (1250–1500), Middle Yiddish (1500–1750), and modern Yiddish (1750–21st century). Different Yiddish dialects were spoken in Lithuania (the northern dialect) and in the area extending from Romania and Poland across Ukraine (the southern dialect). The standard pronunciation of modern Yiddish is based on the northern dialect. The language is written in Hebrew letters. Its spelling was standardised in 1937 by YIVO.

Yiddishkeit (Yiddish) Jewish culture.

Yiddish literature The first important works of Yiddish literature date from the 16th century. The most popular romance was the *Bovo-buch* (or *Bovo-maase*). The *Shmuel-buch* is a heroic epic of Old Yiddish, and the *Maase-buch*, a prose collection of talmudic legends and folktales. The *Tz'emah u-re'enah* is a combination of stories and teachings based on the Bible; and other sacred works in Yiddish include devotional prayers ('tekhines') composed for women. During the 19th century Yiddish was used as a medium of enlightenment by writers of the Haskalah. They were followed by a group of classic Yiddish writers: Mendele Mocher Sephorim, Isaac Leib Peretz and Sholem Aleichem; in fiction contemporaries of the classicists were Jacob Dinesohn, Mordecai Spector, S. An-Ski and Shomer. Abraham Goldfaden is traditionally regarded as the father of the Yiddish theatre. In the 20th century playwrights wrote for the Yiddish theatre in the US, and in both Europe and the US Yiddish writers continue to produce lyrics, short stories and novels. Prominent among modern Yiddish writers are Sholem Asch and Isaac Bashevis Singer. YIVO, founded in Vilnius in 1925, and later transferred to New York, is the principal institution for the study of Yiddish literature.

Yideneh (Yiddish) Derogatory term for an older Jewish woman; also a gossipy shallow person.

Yigdal ('May he be magnified') Opening word (and hence title) of a liturgical hymn. Based on Maimonides' 13 principles of faith, it originated in Italy in c.1300. Its author may have been Daniel bar Judah, who was a dayyan in Rome at that time. It is recited on the Sabbath eve in the Sephardi and Italian rites. Among the Ashkenazim it is used as an opening hymn for the daily morning service. On high holy days it is chanted to a special melody.

Yiḥus Distinguished ancestral decent.

Yimaḥ shemo ('May his name be blotted out') Phrase uttered when mentioning the name of an enemy of the Jewish people.

Yishar koaḥ ('May your strength increase') Phrase of congratulation spoken to a person who has read or spoken in public. It has been shortened to 'Shekoaḥ'.

Yishtabbaḥ ('May his name be praised') Opening word (and hence title) of the concluding blessing of the Pesuke de-Zimrah. It contains 15 terms of praise and adoration and in some rites is recited standing.

Yishuv Settlement or population group. In the modern period it refers specifically to the Jewish community of Israel.

Yizkor ('He shall remember') Opening word (and hence title) of the prayer in commemoration of the dead, recited in Ashkenazi communities on the last days of Passover, Shavuot and Sukkot, and on the Day of Atonement. The term is also applied to the memorial service held on each of those days, at which the members of the congregation remember their relatives who have died.

Yod Tenth letter of the Hebrew alphabet. Its numerical value is 10.

Yoma ('The Day') Fifth tractate in the Mishnah order of Moed. It describes the Temple service of the high priest on the Day of Atonement. It also contains discussions of the regulations regarding the fast, and the significance of atonement and repentance.

Yom Atzmaut [Independence Day] Anniversary of Israel's Declaration of Independence made on 14 May 1948 (5 Iyyar 5708). It is observed as a public holiday in Israel.

Yom Kippur [Day of Atonement] Solemn fast day observed on 10 Tishri (Leviticus 23:32). To keep it one must refrain from work and cleanse oneself from sin (Leviticus 16:30). It ends the Ten Days of Penitence. In biblical times on the Day of Atonement the high priest entered the Holy of Holies dressed in white linen. The Synagogue service contains prayers for forgiveness.

Yom Kippur Katan ('Minor Day of Atonement') Fast observed on the day before the New Moon. The practice of fasting on this day existed in Palestine in the 16th century. It was brought from there to Italy by Moses Cordovero and it eventually spread to Germany. The day is marked by a special order of prayer, consisting of psalms and seliḥot, added to the usual afternoon prayer service.

Yom Tov ('A good day') A term applied to all festivals, which connotes joy and festivity.

Yomtov ben Abraham Ishbili [Ritba] (c.1250–1330) Spanish talmudist. A student of Aaron ha-Levi of Barcelona and Solomon ben Adret, he became a ḥakham and dayyan in Zaragoza.

His talmudic commentaries contain summaries of the views of previous authorities. He also wrote a defence of Maimonides and a commentary on the Passover Haggadah.

Yomtov ben Isaac of Joigny (d.1190) Liturgical poet, of Spanish origin. He settled in York in c.1180. He wrote commentaries on the Bible and engaged in anti-Christian polemics. He composed an elegy on the Blois martyrs of 1171 and the hymn *Omnam Ken* for the eve of the Day of Atonement. According to tradition, he inspired the heroic mass suicide of the Jews of York in 1190.

Yose ben Halaphta (fl. 2nd cent.) Palestinian tanna. A pupil of Akiva, he became the head of the academy in Sepphoris, and one of the leaders of the assemblies at Usha and Jabneh after the abolition of the Hadrianic decrees against the practice of Judaism. According to tradition, he was the author of the chronological work *Seder Olam Rabbah*. In the *Talmud* he is referred to as 'Rabbi Yose'.

Yose ben Joezer (fl. 2nd cent.) Palestinian rabbi and nasi. He and Yose ben Johanan of Jerusalem were the first of the scholars known as the 'zugot'. A disciple of Antigonus of Sokho, he served as nasi (head of the Sanhedrin).

Yose ben Yose (fl.? 5th cent.) Palestinian liturgical poet (the first paytan known by name). He lived in Palestine. His poems were highly regarded by the Babylonian geonim, and some were incorporated into the high holy day liturgy (notably the Avodah of the Sephardi rite for the Day of Atonement).

Yose ha-Gelili (fl. 2nd cent) Palestinian tanna. At an early age he went to Jabneh, where he engaged in discussion with Tarphon and Akiva. His halakhot are found throughout the Mishnah, especially in the order Kodashim. He was known for the efficacy of his prayers for rain.

Yoseph, Dov (1889–1980) Israeli public figure. He was born in Canada, and settled in Palestine in 1921. From 1945 to 1948 he was a member of the executive of the Jewish Agency, and later he served as its treasurer. During the War of Independence he served as Military Governor of Jerusalem. He was elected to the Knesset in 1949 as a member for Mapai, and led several cabinet positions, as Minister of Commerce and Industry, of Development, and of Justice.

Yotzer ('He createth') Name derived from the opening word of the first of the blessings that frame the Shema and applied to various elements of the liturgy. In some rites it is used of the service of morning prayer (Shaḥarit). It also applied to a hymn preceding the Shema. More generally it denotes all the special hymns added to the blessings of the Shema on Sabbaths and festivals. The term is misleadingly used in the plural ('yotzerot') to mean the entire group of liturgical hymns added at various points in the morning service.

Yudghan (fl. 8th cent.) Persian religious leader. A disciple of Abu Issa al-Isfahani, he lived in Hamadan. He was influenced by the doctrines of Islamic Sufism: he maintained that he was a prophet, advocated a mystical interpretation of the Torah, and argued that all religious symbols are allegories; he also supported the prohibition on wine and animal food introduced by the Israelites. A group of disciples grew up around him, which became known as Yudghanites.

Yushkevich, Semyon (1868–1927) Russian novelist and playwright. He was a physician in Odessa. In his plays and narrative works he contrasted poor and virtuous Jews with their vulgar, rich co-religionists. After the 1917 Bolshevik Revolution he settled in the US.

Z

Rabbi Glickstein has always been sad that he's never been able to eat pork. So one day he flies to a remote tropical island and books into a fancy hotel. 'No one will find me here,' he tells himself. On the first evening he goes to the best restaurant on the island and orders the roast pork special. While he's waiting, he hears someone call his name. He looks up and sees a member of his congregation walking towards his table. What bad luck they both had to visit the same restaurant on the same island on the same day. Just at that moment, the waiter puts a whole roasted pig on the table with an apple in its mouth, and says, 'Your special, sir.'

Rabbi Glickstein looks up sheepishly at his congregant and says, 'Would you believe it. You order an apple in this restaurant, and look how they serve it.'

* * * * *

Many Jewish jokes satirise rabbis. Here the rabbi sneaks away from his congregation to treat himself to a pork meal. But he is caught in the act by one of his congregants. Amusingly the joke points out the dangers of religious hypocrisy.

Zach, Nathan (b.1930) Israeli poet. He was born in Berlin, and went to Palestine in 1935. He published poetry, translated Arabic folk songs, and edited the selected works of Ya'akov Steinberg.

Zacuto, Abraham [Abraham ben Samuel Zacut] (1452–c.1515) Spanish astronomer and historian. His ancestors were French Jewish exiles who went to Castile in 1306. He studied and taught in Salamanca. His *Ha-Ḥibbur ha-Gadol*, a Hebrew work on astronomy, was translated into Spanish and Latin. He was the first to make a metal astrolabe, and he also drew up astronomical tables which were used by Christopher Columbus. When Jews were expelled from Spain in 1492, he became astronomer and astrologer at the court of John II of Portugal. He was consulted by Vasco da Gama before his journey to India. Eventually he settled in Tunis, where he completed his *Sepher Yuḥasin* on the history of rabbinic scholarship.

Zacuto, Moses ben Mordedai (c.1620–1697) Italian Kabbalist and poet. He was born in Amsterdam. During a pilgrimage to Palestine, he was persuaded to go to Italy, where he served as a rabbi in Venice and Manuta. He composed mystical and devotional poetry, some of which was used in the Italian liturgy. He wrote responsa, a poetical vision of the afterlife, and a drama about Abraham.

Zadok (fl. 11th cent. BCE) Israelite priest. He was a descendant of Aaron. He went to David at Hebron after Saul's death, and, with Abiathar, became David's chief priest. He was loyal to David during Absalom's rebellion, and at David's behest he anointed Solomon as the next king. Solomon subsequently appointed Zadok's son high priest in the Temple. From that time onward the high priesthood remained in the Zadokite family until the beginning of the Hasmonean dynasty (2nd cent. BCE).

Zaftig (Yiddish) Plump buxom, by extension provocative; used figuratively it means juicy.

Zakhur la-tov ('May he be remembered for good') Expression of respect and blessing uttered in connection with the name of a person who has died. It has now largely been replaced by the expression 'Zikhrno li-verakah' (May his memory be for a blessing).

Zamenhof, Ludwig Lazarus (1859–1917) Polish philologist. He was born in Bialystok, and lived in Warsaw. In 1887 he published a pamphlet that set out the fundamentals of Esperanto. In 1905 he convened the first international Congress of Esperantists. He translated the Bible as well as German, Russian and English literature into this new language.

Zangwill, Israel (1864–1926) English author. He was born in London, where he later taught at the Jewish Free School. His writings include *Children of the Ghetto, Ghetto Tragedies, Ghetto Comedies,* and *The King of the Shnorrers.* He also produced essays on Jewish themes, and translations of Jewish liturgical poetry and the poems of Solomon ibn Gabirol. Initially an enthusiastic Zionist, he helped to found the Jewish Territorial Organisation in 1903.

Zaragoza, Purim of Festival celebrated by oriental Jews to commemorate the deliverance in 1380 (or 1420) of the community in Zaragoza from a false accusation of plotting against the King. It is celebrated on 17–18 Shevat with the reading of a special megillah.

Zaritsky, Yosef [Zarfutti, Yossef] (1891–1985) Israeli painter. He was born in Ukraine, and went to Palestine in 1923. He painted watercolours of Safed, Tiberius and Jerusalem, and his later works chiefly depict the Israeli landscape.

Zavim ('Sufferers from flux') Ninth tractate in the Mishnah order of Tohorot. It deals with ritual uncleanliness caused by a flux in both men and women (Leviticus 15). It also describes how a person or thing can become unclean through contact with a person suffering from a discharge.

Zayde (Yiddish) Old man, grandfather.

Zayin Seventh letter of the Hebrew alphabet. Its numerical value is 7.

Zealots Jewish political party active during the Second Temple period. Founded by Judah the Galilean and Zadok the priest, the Zealots' first purpose was to oppose the Roman demand for a census under Quirinius, the governor of Judea. They developed their own religious outlook and proclaimed God the sovereign ruler of the nation. Suppressed by the procurators, they continued to struggle against Roman rule. After the conflict with Rome began (66 CE), Menaḥem (the son of Judah the Galilean) claimed messianic status, and was slain by Eleazar ben Hananiah, the captain of the Temple. Menaḥem's comrades (the Sicarii), led by Eleazar ben Jair, fled to Masada. After a Zealot uprising in Jerusalem, the Zealots under Eleazar ben Simeon were driven into the inner court of the Temple, but they eventually regained control of the city. At the time of the destruction of Jerusalem in 70, many of the Zealots were killed, others committed suicide or fled the country.

Zebulun (fl.? 19th–16th cent. BCE) Israelite, sixth son of Jacob and Leah. His descendants, the tribe of Zebulun, received territory in central Palestine.

Zechariah (i) (fl. 8th cent. BCE) King of Israel (743 BCE), son of Jeroboam II. He was assassinated by Shallum of Jabesh, who seized the throne (II Kings 15:8–13).

Zechariah (ii) Biblical book, one of the books of the 12 Minor Prophets. It records the prophecies of the Israelite prophet Zechariah (fl. 6th cent. BCE), who predicted material prosperity, the ingathering of the exiles, liberation from foreign dominations, and the expansion of Jerusalem. He also encouraged the people to rebuild the Temple.

Zedekiah (i) [Mattaniah] (fl. 6th cent. BCE) King of Judah (597–586 BCE), son of Josiah. He was originally called Mattaniah, but took the name Zedekiah when he was appointed king by Nebuchadnezzar in succession to Jehoiachin. Initially he refused to join an anti-Babylonian coalition, but later conspired with Egypt against Babylonia; as a result, the Babylonians invaded Judah and captured Jerusalem. Zedekiah was subsequently imprisoned in Babylon (II Kings 25; Jeremiah 52).

Zedekiah (ii) (fl. 9th cent. BCE) Israelite false prophet. He incorrectly predicted that Ahab would be successful in his invasion of Ramoth Gilead. He made iron horns to symbolise Ahab's victory (I Kings 22).

Zederbaum, Alexander [Tsederboym, Aleksander] (1816–1893) Polish editor and author. He was born in Zamość, and lived in Lubin and Odessa. He founded the Hebrew newspaper *Ha-Melitz* in 1860, and in 1862 began to issue *Kol mevaser* in Yiddish. Later he settled in St Petersburg where he established the city's first Russian Jewish periodical (*Vyestnik russkikh yevreyev*) and first modern Yiddish periodical (*Yidishes folks-blat*).

Zeira (fl. 4th cent) Babylonian amora. He was a pupil of Huna and after moving to Palestine became an important teacher himself.

Zeira, Mordechai (1905–1968) Israeli composer. He was born in Ukraine and went to Palestine after having been arrested as a member of a Zionist youth organisation. He initially found employment as a construction worker and fisherman, but in 1927 he moved to Tel Aviv and joined the Ohel Theatre. Later he worked for the Palestine Electric Corporation. He wrote numerous songs, which were in part influenced by Eastern-European cantorial and Hasidic idioms.

Zeitlin, Hillel [Cejtlin, Hillel] (1871–1942) Russian philosopher. He was born in Korma, Belorussia, and in the 1890s lived in Homel. Initially he was a Zionist, but in reaction to the Kishinev pogrom, he became a supporter of Territorialism. After settling in Vilnus, he published works in Yiddish opposing assimilation and secularism. In the 1920s he returned to Zionism. He is an important representative of Hasidic thought in Yiddish literature.

Zeitlin, Solomon (1892–1977) American scholar, of Russian origin. He emigrated to the US in 1915 and taught at Yeshiva College. In 1921 he became Professor of Rabbinics at Dropsie College. He wrote studies on rabbinics, Josephus, the Apocrypha, Christianity and the Dead Sea Scrolls. He also served as editor of the *Jewish Quarterly Review*.

Zekhor Berit ('Remember the Covenant') Penitential hymn composed by Gershon ben Judah. It is recited on the eve of Rosh ha-Shanah in the Ashkenazi rite. The day before New Year is therefore called Zekhor Berit. The hymn is also recited during the concluding service on the Day of Atonement.

Zekhut Avot ('Merit of the Fathers') In Jewish tradition, the idea that the pious deeds of the fathers help to protect and gain salvation for their descendants. The concept is applied particularly to the patriarchs, Abraham, Isaac, and Jacob.

Zelophehad, daughters of (fl. 13th cent. BCE) Name given to the five daughters of the Manassite Zelophehad

(Numbers 26:33). When Zelophehad died, they asked Moses for a ruling upon their title to their father's prospective property in the Promised Land. They received an affirmative reply, and their claim was put into effect when Joshua conquered Canaan (Joshua 17:3–6). The case served as a precedent for later generations and led to the decree that, in the absence of sons, a man's property might pass to a daughter, provided she were married to a member of her father's tribe (Numbers 27:11; 36:6–8).

Zemirot ('songs', 'hymns') Among the Ashkenazim the term refers to hymns and songs sung during Sabbath meals and at the end of the Sabbath. Although the zemirot were composed largely during the 16th and 17th centuries, some are the works of earlier poets. Printed prayer books include zemirot for the Sabbath eve, the Sabbath day and the end of the Sabbath. In the Sephardi and Yemenite rites the term designates the part of the morning prayer service known as the Pesuke de-Zimrah.

Zephaniah (i) (fl. 7th cent. BCE) Judean prophet. He was a member of a noble Judean family, and his prophecies were uttered during the early part of Josiah's reign. He described the Day of the Lord, when the wicked will be punished, the poor will inherit the land, and the Lord will be universally acknowledged.

Zephaniah (ii) Biblical book, one of the books of the 12 Minor Prophets. It contains the account of Zephaniah's prophecies.

Zerahiah Levi [Ferrer Saldin] (fl. 15th cent.) Spanish scholar and poet. A disciple of Ḥasdai Crescas, he served as rabbi of Zaragoza and all the communities of Aragon. He was a talmudist, preacher, physician and translator, and also participated in the Disputation of Tortosa.

Zeraim ('Seeds') First order of the Mishnah. It deals with agricultural laws, and also with the laws of prayer.

Zerubbabel (fl. 6th cent. BCE) Israelite leader, grandson of Jehoiachin. With the consent of Cyrus II of Persia, he returned to Judah from Babylon to help rebuild Jerusalem. Together with Joshua the priest, he set up an altar, re-established the festivals, and began the rebuilding of the Temple.

Zevaḥim ('Animal sacrifices') First tractate in the Mishnah order of Kodashim. It deals with the laws governing the offering of sacrificial animals and birds.

Zhitlovski, Chaim (1863–1943) Russian philosopher and essaysit. He was born in a small town near Vitebsk, Belorussia. He initially was involved in the revolutionary activities of the Narodniki. Later he founded the Jewish section of the Socialist Revolutionary Party, which advocated Jewish national emancipation and Yiddish as the language of national rebirth. In 1888 he left Russia and settled in Switzerland, where he edited the *Russian Worker*. He returned to Russia after the revolution of 1905 and helped to found the Semyist party. In 1908 he went to New York, where he edited *Das neie leben*.

Zikhrono li-verakhah ('May his memory be for a blessing') Expression of respect and blessing, uttered when mentioning someone who has died.

Zikhronot ('Remembrances') The name of the second of the three sections in the additional Amidah service on Rosh ha-Shanah (the others are Malkhuyyot and Shopharot). It contains ten biblical verses with an introductory paragraph and a concluding blessing. The shophar is sounded after its recital.

Zilpah (fl.? 19th–16th cent. BCE) Israelite woman, handmaid of Leah. Leah gave Zilpah to Jacob as a wife. She bore Gad and Asher (Genesis 30:9–13).

Zimra, David ben Solomon ibn Avi [David ben Solomon ibn Zimra; Radbaz] (fl. 16th cent.) Spanish talmudist and Kabbalist. He was born in Spain, and studied in Safed, Fez and Cairo, where he became Chief Rabbi. He later returned to Spain and served as a dayyan. He composed responsa, a commentary on Maimonides' *Mishneh Torah*, Kabbalistic works, and talmudic novellae.

Zimri (i) (fl.? 13th cent. BCE) Israelite, head of a clan of the tribe of Simeon. He consorted with a Midianite woman, and with her was stabbed by Phinehas, the grandson of Aaron. This act ended a plague which had been visited on the Israelites for committing harlotry with Midianite women and worshipping Baal Peor (Numbers 25).

Zimri (ii) (fl. 9th cent. BCE) King of Israel (855 BCE). As captain of half the chariots of the Israelites, he killed Elah, son of Baasha, when he had reigned for only a short time. After Zimri assumed power he executed all the male relatives and admirers of Baasha (I Kings 16:11). However, he reigned for only seven days. Omri was proclaimed king by his own men and besieged Tirza the capital city. Zimri set his own palace on fire and died in the blaze, thus evading capture.

Zinberg, Israel (1873–1939) Ukrainian historian of Hebrew and kiddish literature. He was born near Kremenets, Volhynia, and worked as a chemical engineer. He wrote eight volumes of a history of Jewish literature from the Spanish period (c.10th century) to the end of the Russian Haskalah.

Zion Jebusite stronghold in Jerusalem. It was captured by David and became part of the City of David (II Samuel 5:6–7). Its location is uncertain. During the Maccabean period, Mount Zion was identified with the Temple Mount and the City of David to the south-east, but Josephus identified Zion with the Upper City on the western ridge. The name is used in poetic and prophetic language to refer to Jerusalem as a whole. In religious terms Zion symbolises the spiritual capital of the world, the messianic city of God. In this sense it also became a symbol of Jewish restoration.

Zionism International political and ideological movement devoted to securing the return of the Jewish people to the Land of Israel. Modern political Zionism was conceived by Theodor Herzl and launched at the First Zionist Congress in 1897. His vision drew on a long religious tradition of messianic hope in the restoration of Zion, and at the same time aimed to solve the problem of the Jewish community in the diaspora by meeting the need and desire for a Jewish homeland As an ideology Zionism was opposed by large numbers of Orthodox Jews, who claimed that divine intervention in history should not be usurped by human action. In addition many Reform Jews were opposed to Zionism as a political policy After the death of Herzl in 1904, Russian Zionists demanded the immediate beginning of practical colonisation work ('practical Zionism') in Palestine. Other Zioinists advocated diplomatic activity ('diplomatic Zionism'), pursuing Herzl's attempt to win support from Turkey and the European powers for a Jewish homeland. In 1911 a compromise between practical and diplomatic Zionism ('synthetic Zionism') was adopted as a general policy following Herzl's death. After the establishment of a Jewish State in 1948 the Zionist movement continued its activities, raising money to support settlement in Israel and encouraging immigration.

Zipporah (fl.? 13th cent. BCE) Israelite woman, wife of Moses. She was the daughter of Jethro, priest of Midian. She travelled to Egypt with Moses to plead with Pharaoh for the release of the Israelites. On the journey she saved the life of her son Gershon by circumcising him (Exodus 4:24–26). She returned alone to her father, with her sons Gershon and Eliezer. Jethro later took them to rejoin Moses on Mt Sinai (Exodus 18:1).

Zirelsohn, Judah Lob (1860–1941) Romanian rabbi and communal leader. He was born in Kozelets in Ukraine, and served as rabbi of Priluski and Kishinev. He initially was a supporter of Zionism, but later dissociated himself from the movement. In 1912 he was one of the founders of Agudat Israel. When Bessarabia was incorporated into Romania in 1920, he became Chief Rabbi of Bessarabia and the leader of Orthodox Jewry there. In 1922 he was elected a deputy in the Romanian parliament, and in 1926 a senator. His writings include responsa, homilies, eulogies, essays and poems.

Zitron, Samuel Lob (1860–1930) Russian writer. He was born in Minsk, Belorussia. He studied at Lithuanian yeshivah and became interested in the ideas of the Haskalah. In 1876 he went to Vienna, and later studied in Germany. He contributed to the Yiddish press and to Hebrew periodicals in the diaspora. His writings include studies of the Zionist movement and its precursors, and Hebrew literature.

Zodiac Imaginary zone in the sky divided into 12 equal areas, called 'signs of the zodiac', each named after the constellation in which it once lay; the paths of the planets and the sun appear to move across the zodiac. The signs of the zodiac are discussed in midrashic literature where the 12 constellations are correlated with the 12 tribes of Israel. They also play a role in Jewish art.

Zogerin [sagerin] (Yiddish: 'sayer') Title given to the woman who recites in the synagogue the prayers in the vernacular for those women unable to read Hebrew. This was a common practice in Russia and Poland.

Zohar Mystical commentary on the Pentateuch and parts of the Hagiographa. According to tradition, it was composed in the 2nd century by Simeon ben Yohai, his colleagues and disciples. It was first published in Spain by Moses de Leon in the 13th century. The work is written partly in Hebrew and partly in Aramaic. Lengthy homiletic passages alternate with short discourses and parables. The *Zohar* is one of the principal kabbalistic works, and all subsequent mystical writing is based on it. The most important commentaries on the *Zohar* are *Ketem Paz* by Simeon ben Lavi, *Or ha-Ḥammah* by Abraham Azulai, and *Mikdash Melekh* by Shalom Buzaglo.

Zorach, William (1887–1966) American sculptor. He was born in Eurburg, Lithuania, and emigrated to the US in 1891. He studied art in Cleveland, New York and Paris. In his later works he utilised Jewish subject matter.

Zuckermandel, Moses Samuel (1836–1917) Moravian talmudist. He served as a rabbi in Moravia and Germany. He compiled what became the standard edition of the Tosephta, published in 1880.

Zugot ('pairs') Term designating the pairs of Palestinian sages who for five generations led the rabbinic tradition of Judaism (2nd century BCE to 1st century CE). They are listed in Avot. According to tradition, one was the president of the Sanhedrin (nasi) and the other head judge (av bet din) of the court (bet din). The zygot were: Yose ben Joezer and Yose ben Johanan; Joshua ben Peraḥ yah and Nittai the Arbelite; Judah ben Tabbai and Simeon ben Shetah; Shemaiah and Avtalyon; and Hillel and Shammai.

Zulay, Menahem (1901–1954) Israeli scholar. He was born in Oschcianci, Galicia, and settled in Palestine in 1920. He worked at the Schocken Institute for the study of Hebrew Poetry. He was an expert on early Palestinian piyyutim and edited the collection of such poems discovered in the Cairo Genizah, among which the most notable were those of Alexander Yannai.

Zunser, Eliakum (1836–1913) Lithuanian Yiddish poet. He was born in Vilnius. He was conscripted into the military, and later worked in Rovno as a braider of gold lace for uniforms. He became Russia's foremost wedding bard. In 1889 he moved to New York. Many booklets of his poems were published.

Zunz, Leopold (1794–1886) German historian. He was born in Detmold. He helped found the Verein für Kultur und Wissenschaft der Juden in Berlin in 1819, and his work is regarded as having laid the foundations for the scientific study of Jewish history. From 1840 to 1850 he served as Principal of the Berlin Teachers' Seminary. His early writings include a biography of Rashi, a history of Jewish homiletics, and a survey of Jewish names from biblical times. Among his later publications are a history of Jewish geographical literature, a history of Jewish liturgy, studies of medieval piyyutim and their authors, and Bible studies. He also edited the works of Nahman Krochmal.

Zutra, Mar I (d.c.414) Babylonian exilarch (401–409). He was the successor of Mar Kahana and a contemporary of Ashi.

Zutra, Mar, II (c.496–520) Babylonian exilarch (512–20). Son of Huna, he defeated the Persians and set up a Jewish State, which lasted for seven years. During this time he made Mahoza his residence.

Zutra, Mar III (fl. 6th cent.) Babylonian exilarch. Although he served as exilrch he left Babylonia and settled in Palestine.

Zweifel, Eliezer Trevi (1815–1888) Russian Hebrew author and essayist. He was born in Mohilev, Belorussia. He wandered through Russia stopping in various towns, and worked as a preacher and teacher. In 1853 he was appointed lecturer in Mishnah and Tamud at the government rabbinical seminary in Zhitomir. Later he lived in Russia and Poland and finally settled in Glukhov in Ukraine. In his *Shalom al-Yisrael* he defended Hasidism, and demonstrated the movement's Kabbalistic roots.

Zweig, Arnold (1887–1968) German novelist and playwright. He was born in Gross-Glogau, Silesia. He worked as a freelance writer in Bavaria and Berlin where he edited the Zionist journal *Jüdische Rundschau.* After moving to Haifa, he co-edited the weekly *Orient.* In 1948 he settled in East Berlin. A number of his works deal with Jewish themes.

Zweig, Stefan (1881–1941) Austrian author. He was born in Vienna and became a member of the young Vienna group of Jewish intellectuals. In 1918 he wrote the pacifist play *Jeremiah.* His works include a number of biographies, short stories and novels.